Russian-English Dictionary of Proverbs and Sayings

Русско-Английский Словарь Пословиц и Поговорок

Русско-Английский Словарь Пословиц и Поговорок

Александр Маргулис

Ася Холодная

McFarland & Company, Inc., Publishers

Jefferson, North Carolina, and London

Russian-English Dictionary of Proverbs and Sayings

ALEXANDER MARGULIS
ASYA KHOLODNAYA

McFarland & Company, Inc., Publishers
Jefferson, North Carolina, and London

To the memory of
MARK MARGULIS

Памяти
МАРКА МАРГУЛИСА

The present work is a reprint of the library bound edition of Russian-English Dictionary of Proverbs and Sayings, *first published in 2000 by McFarland.*

LIBRARY OF CONGRESS CATALOGUING-IN-PUBLICATION DATA

Margulis, Alexander, 1974–
Russian-English dictionary of proverbs and sayings / Alexander Margulis, Asya Kholodnaya.
p. cm.
Added t.p. title: Russko-angliiskii slovar' poslovits i pogovorok.
Includes bibliographical references and index.

ISBN 978-0-7864-3748-1
softcover : 50# alkaline paper ∞

1. Proverbs, Russian—Dictionaries—English. I. Title: Russko-angliiskii slovar' poslovits i pogovorok. II. Kholodnaya, Asya, 1928– III. Title.

PN6505.S5 M34 2008
398.9'9171'03—dc21 99-58987

British Library cataloguing data are available

Manufactured in the United States of America

McFarland & Company, Inc., Publishers
Box 611, Jefferson, North Carolina 28640
www.mcfarlandpub.com

This collection of Russian and English proverbs and sayings is the product of many years' gathering. The material was drawn not only from centuries-old collections; contemporary collections of both Russian and English proverbs and sayings were used as the main source of the material for this book. We feel obliged to acknowledge our special indebtedness to Wolfgang Mieder, S. A. Kingsbury and K. B. Harder, compilers of *A Dictionary of American Proverbs*, William G. Smith, compiler of *The Oxford Dictionary of English Proverbs,* W. McMordie, compiler of the book *English Idioms and How to Use Them,* В. П. Жуков, compiler of *Словарь русских пословиц и поговорок,* В. П. Аникин, editor of *Русские пословицы и поговорки.*

We wish to express our heart-felt gratitude to Professor Donald Fanger of Harvard University, Robert Digiovanni, former professor at Bunker Hill Community College, Massachusetts, Anne Bertran, compiler of *NTC's Dictionary of Proverbs and Clichés*, William Rubin, administrator of Congregation *Beth Israel*, Massachusetts, Ruth McDonald, retired executive editor of Simon and Schuster, Sterling Giles, professor of English at Roxbury Community College, Massachusetts, Roberta Cole, an English teacher, Christine Dow, director of Alumni Affairs, Bunker Hill Community College, William Grealish, curator of Boston Public Library, Daniel R. Liporto, M.A., and many other people for their help.

Our greatest indebtedness is to the late Mark Margulis, journalist, for his substantial assistance in defining the meaning of Russian proverbs and sayings.

Table of Contents

Содержание

The Dictionary

Bibliography

Библиография

Ammer, Christine. *A Dictionary of Clichés: Have a Nice Day; No Problem.* New York, 1992.

Apperson, G. L. *English Proverbs and Proverbial Phrases: A Historical Dictionary.* London, New York, 1929.

Bertran, Anne. *NTC's Dictionary of Proverbs and Clichés.* Lincolnwood, Ill., 1993.

Beale, Paul. *A Dictionary of Slang and Unconventional English.* New York, 1984.

Boatner, Maxime Tull, John Edward Gates and Adam Makkai. *A Dictionary of American Idioms.* New York, 1977.

Borkovski, P. *The Great Russian-English Dictionary of Idioms and Set Expressions.* London, 1973.

Brewer, E. C. *A Dictionary of Phrase and Fable.* London, 1971.

Brown, Raymond Lamont. *A Book of Proverbs.* Newton Abbot, 1983.

Browning, D. C. *Everyman's Dictionary of Quotations and Proverbs.* London, New York, 1962.

Chapman, Robert L. *New Dictionary of American Slang.* New York, 1986.

_____. *American Slang.* New York, 1987.

Christy, Robert. *Proverbs, Maxims and Phrases.* New York, London, 1888.

Collins, Harry. *101 American English Proverbs.* Lincolnwood, Ill., 1993.

Collins, V. H. *A Book of English Proverbs with Origins and Explanations.* London, 1974.

Cordry, Harold V. *The Multicultural Dictionary of Proverbs.* Jefferson, N.C., 1997.

Cowie, A. P., R. Mackin and J. R. McGaig. *The Oxford Dictionary of Current Idiomatic English. Vol. 2. Phrase, Clause and Sentence Idioms.* Oxford, 1984.

Fergusson, Rosalind. *The Penguin Dictionary of Proverbs.* New York, 1983.

Flexner, Stuart, and Doris Flexner. *Wise Words and Wives' Tales.* New York, 1993.

Fowler, W. S. *A Dictionary of Idioms.* London, 1976.

Freeman, W. A. *A Concise Dictionary of English Idioms.* London, 1975.

Gluski, Jerzy. *Proverbs Proverbes Sprichwörter Proverbi Proverbios Пословицы.* Amsterdam, London, New York, 1971.

Green, Jonathan. *The Dictionary of Contemporary Slang.* New York, 1985.

Henderson, J. A. *A Dictionary of English Idioms. Part II. Colloquial Phrases.* London, 1964.

Houghton, Patricia. *A World of Proverbs.* Poole, Dorset, 1981.

Johnson, A. *Common English Proverbs.* London, 1965.

_____. *Common English Quotations.* London, 1963.

The Kenkyusha Dictionary of Current English Idioms. Tokyo, 1969.

Kin, D. *Dictionary of American Proverbs.* New York, 1955.

Knowles, Elizabeth. *The Oxford Dictionary of Phrase, Saying and Quotation.* Oxford, New York, 1997.

Krylov, C. A. *Russian Proverbs and Sayings in Russian and English.* New York, 1973.

Kuskovskaya, S. *English Proverbs and Sayings.* Minsk, 1987.

Longman Dictionary of English Idioms. London, 1986.

Makkai, Adam. *A Dictionary of American Idioms.* New York, 1987.

McMordie, W. *English Idioms and How to Use Them.* London, 1972.

Mertvago, Peter. *The Comparative Russian-English Dictionary of Russian Proverbs and Sayings.* New York, 1995.

Mieder, W., S. A. Kingsbury, K. B. Harder. *A Dictionary of American Proverbs.* New York, Oxford, 1992.

Morris, William, and Mary Morris. *Dictionary of Word and Phrase Origins.* Vol. 3. New York, London, 1971.

Ong, Y. E., and Y. L. Yang. *A Complete Dictionary of English Phrases with Bilingual Explanations.* Shanghai, 1926.

The Oxford English-Russian Dictionary. New York, Oxford, 1984.

Packham, Jo. *Wedding Toasts and Speeches.* New York, 1993.

Partridge, Eric. *A Dictionary of Catch Phrases.* London, 1977.

_____. _____. New York, 1992.

_____. *A Dictionary of Clichés.* New York, 1940.

_____. _____. London, 1941.

_____. *A Dictionary of Slang and Unconventional English.* New York, 1984.

_____. *A Dictionary of the Underworld.* New York, 1950.

Plotkin, David. *Dictionary of American Proverbs.* New York, 1955.

Ridout, R., and C. Witting. *English Proverbs Explained.* London, 1967.

Rogers, James. *The Dictionary of Clichés.* New York, 1987.

Savvy Sayin's. Tuscon, 1986.
Simpson, J. A. *The Concise Oxford Dictionary of Proverbs.* Oxford, New York, 1982.
Smith, William G. *The Oxford Dictionary of English Proverbs.* Oxford, 1970.
Spears, Richard A. *NTC's American Idioms Dictionary.* Lincolnwood, Ill., 1994.
_____. *NTC's Dictionary of American English Phrases.* Lincolnwood, Ill., 1995.
_____. *NTC's Dictionary of American Slang and Colloquial Expressions.* Lincolnwood, Ill., 1990.
Stevenson, Burton. *The Macmillan Home Book of Proverbs, Maxims and Familiar Phrases.* New York, 1948.
Tallman, M. *Dictionary of American Folklore.* New York, 1959.
Taylor, Archer, and Bartlet Jere Whiting. *American Proverbs and Proverbial Sayings.* Cambridge, Mass., and London, 1958.
Titelman, Gregory. *Random House Dictionary of Popular Proverbs and Sayings.* New York, London, 1996.
Valentine, Joseph W. *A Book of Clichés.* New York, 1963.
Vitek, A. J. *Russian-English Idiom Dictionary.* Detroit, 1973.
Vizetelly, F. H., L. J. De Bekker. *A Desk Book of Idioms and Idiomatic Phrases in English Speech and Literature.* New York, London, 1926.
Whiting, Bartlet Jere. *Early American Proverbs and Proverbial Phrases.* Cambridge, Mass., and London, 1977.
_____. *Modern Proverbs and Proverbial Sayings.* Cambridge, Mass., and London, 1989.
Wilson, F.P. *The Oxford Dictionary of English Proverbs.* Oxford, 1970.
Wood, J. *The Nuttel Dictionary of Quotations from Ancient and Modern English and Foreign Sources Including Phrases, Mottoes, Maxims and Proverbs.* London, New York, 1965.
Woods, Henry F. *American Sayings, Famous Phrases, Slogans and Aphorisms.* New York, 1945.

Баранцев, К. Т. *Англо-украинский фразеологический словарь.* Киев, 1969.
Буковская, М. В., С. И. Вяльцева, З. И. Дубянская, Л. П. Зайцев, Я. Г. Биренбаум. *Словарь употребительных английских пословиц.* Москва, 1985.
Гальперин, И. Р. *Большой англо-русский словарь.* Москва, 1977.
Даль, В. *Пословицы русского народа.* Москва, 1987.
_____. *Толковый словарь живого великорусского языка.* Москва, 1955.
Дубровин, М. И. *Английские и русские пословицы и поговорки.* Москва, 1993.

Жуков, В. П. *Словарь русских пословиц и поговорок.* Москва, 1966.

Кудрявцев, А. Ю. *Англо-русский словарь-справочник табуизированной лексики и эвфемизмов.* Москва, 1993.

Кузьмин, С. С., Н. Л. Шадрин. *Русско-английский словарь пословиц и поговорок.* Москва, 1989.

Кунин, А. В. *Англо-русский фразеологический словарь.* Москва, 1967.

_____. *Англо-русский фразеологический словарь.* Москва, 1984.

Селиванов, Ф. М., Б. П. Кирдан, и В. П. Аникин. *Русские пословицы и поговорки.* Под редакцией В. П. Аникина. Москва, 1988.

Соболев, А. И. *Русские пословицы и поговорки.* Москва, 1983.

Уолш, И. А., В. П. Берков. *Русско-английский словарь крылатых слов.* Москва, 1984.

Фелицина, В. П., *Прохоров Ю. Е. Русские пословицы, поговорки и крылатые слова. Лингво-страноведческий словарь.* Москва, 1979.

To the Reader

The Russian-English Dictionary of Proverbs and Sayings comprises 2,375 entries of Russian proverbs and sayings and their English equivalents and analogues. The dictionary also contains some variants of Russian and English proverbs and sayings which are recorded in the same entry with the main unit.

This is the first Russian-English dictionary of proverbs and sayings that includes English equivalents and analogues of Russian proverbs and sayings current in the United States of America, in England, or in both countries, which is correspondingly marked. The interpretation of the Russian proverbs and sayings, which eliminates the likelihood of misunderstanding their meaning and, in turn, a possible wrong choice of an English proverb or saying, seems to be an important distinguishing feature of the dictionary.

Both the Russian and the English languages have a considerable number of synonymous proverbs and sayings. Cross-references to Russian synonyms in the entries as well as synonymous English proverbs and sayings recorded in the entries make the utility of this work greater than that of a mere bilingual dictionary. The reader can also use it both as a Russian and an English dictionary of synonymous proverbs and sayings.

The English Proverb and Saying Key Word Index, in which the proverbs and sayings are cross-referred to the entries, makes it possible to use the dictionary as an English-to-Russian one, by picking out one of the key words of an English proverb or saying, when the reader needs to find a Russian equivalent.

The Russian Proverb and Saying Key Word Index will help the reader find a Russian proverb or saying, in case he does not know its exact form, by picking out one of its most significant words.

When selecting the material for the dictionary, we proceeded from the criterion according to which proverbs and sayings are units of language that have the syntactical structure of a completed simple, compound or complex sentence.

The dictionary contains only those Russian proverbs and sayings that have English equivalents or analogues. In five cases, English proverbs with opposite meanings were resorted to, which is often practiced in translation ("Не вижу, так и не верю"—"Seeing is believing," "Одному ехать и дорога долга"—"Good company upon the road is the shortest cut" and others.)

Proverbs and sayings current both in spoken Russian and English and in works of literature are included in the dictionary. Which proverbs and sayings are more or less widely used is a matter of personal judgment. Some of them are current in the cities or in rural areas, others may be in use only in certain parts of the country, which is vividly reflected in Mieder, et al., *A Dictionary of American Proverbs*.

We believe that both English and Russian readers of the dictionary will find it helpful when dealing with proverbs and sayings, that it will meet their needs in extending their knowledge of Russian and English as well as when teaching these languages. It is hoped that the book will also serve as a reliable guide to translators, journalists and many other people speaking these two languages.

К ЧИТАТЕЛЮ

Предлагаемый читателю *РУССКО-АНГЛИЙСКИЙ СЛОВАРЬ ПОСЛОВИЦ И ПОГОВОРОК* содержит 2375 русских пословиц и поговорок, их английские соответствия, а также некоторые варианты этих русских и английских пословиц и поговорок.

В настоящее издание в качестве английских аналогов и эквивалентов, впервые в практике составления русско-английских словарей пословиц и поговорок, включены соответственно помсчснныс пословицы и поговорки, употребляемые в Соединённых Штатах Америки, в Великобритании или в обеих странах. Важной особенностью словаря представляется толкование значения русских пословиц и поговорок, что исключает возможность их неправильного понимания и неадекватного подбора английских соответствий.

Русский и английский языки содержат значительное количество синонимичных пословиц и поговорок. Перекрёстные ссылки на русские синонимы, а также синонимические ряды английских пословиц и поговорок, представленные в словарных статьях, расширяют область применения данного издания, предоставляя читателю возможность пользоваться им дополнительно как словарём русских и английских синонимичных пословиц.

УКАЗАТЕЛЬ КЛЮЧЕВЫХ СЛОВ РУССКИХ ПОСЛОВИЦ И ПОГОВОРОК, снабженный перекрестными ссылками на словарные статьи, поможет читателю отыскать нужную русскую пословицу или поговорку по одному из ключевых слов, если он не уверен в её точной словарной форме.

УКАЗАТЕЛЬ КЛЮЧЕВЫХ СЛОВ АНГЛИЙСКИХ ПОСЛОВИЦ И ПОГОВОРОК, имеющий перекрёстные ссылки на словарные статьи, окажется полезным при поиске русских соответствий английским по одному из ключевых слов английских пословиц и поговорок.

При отборе материала за основу был принят критерий, согласно которому пословицами и поговорками являются единицы языка, имеющие синтаксическую структуру законченного простого, сложносочинённого и сложноподчинённого предложения.

Словарь содержит русские и английские пословицы и поговорки, употребляющиеся в разговорном языке и в художественной литературе. Какие из них более или менее употребимы—вопрос личного суждения. Некоторые пословицы и поговорки можно услышать в городе, другие—в сельской местности; они могут иметь хождение в разных частях страны, что ярко отражено в словаре *A Dictionary of American Proverbs*, составителями которого являются Wolfgang Mieder, S. A. Kingsbury и K. B. Harder.

В словарь вошли только те русские пословицы и поговорки, к которым оказалось возможным подобрать английские зквиваленты или аналоги.

Словарь адресован всем лицам, интересующимся обоими языками—русским и английским. Он поможет не только читателю, изучающему русский или английский язык, углубить свои знания и найти ответ на свои вопросы в области пословиц и поговорок, но и преподавателям русского или английского языка, переводчикам, журналистам и людям многих других профессий, говорящим на этих двух языках.

The Structure of the Dictionary

The Russian-English Dictionary of Proverbs and Sayings consists of three parts: (1) the main body of the dictionary—Russian proverbs and sayings with their variants and their English equivalents and analogues; (2) a Russian Proverb and Saying Key Word Index of the Russian proverbs and sayings supplied with cross-references to the entries in which they appear; (3) an English Proverb and Saying Key Word Index in which English proverbs and sayings are cross-referred to the entries in which they appear.

The Russian proverbs and sayings are alphabetized under the first word regardless of whether it is a syntactic or a notional word. Russian synonymous proverbs and sayings are registered in their own separate entries.

Each entry consists of five sections.

(1) A boldface entry head—a Russian proverb or saying.

(2) A definition or an explanation of the meaning of a Russian proverb or saying that follows the boldface entry. The dictionary contains a great number of Russian synonymous proverbs and sayings. But only the entry representing, in our opinion, the most widely used one (the dominant) is supplied with a definition. If a proverb has two meanings, two definitions marked by the letters "*(a)*" and "*(b)*" are given in the entry.

(3) A cross-reference to Russian synonymous proverbs and sayings, if any, that follows the indication "*See.*" The most widely used Russian proverb or saying (the dominant) has cross-references to all its synonyms which, in their turn, are cross-referred to the dominant. For example,

Б

103. Брань на вороту не виснет. *See 1929 (С), 1931 (С), 2203 (Х)*

С

1929. Словом человека не убьёшь. *See 103 (Б)*

1931. Слово не обух—в лоб не бьёт. *See 103 (Б)*

Х

2203. Хоть горшком назови, только в печку не ставь. *See 103 (Б)*

(4) Alphabetized alternate forms—variants of a Russian proverb or saying, if any, that follow the indication "*Var.:*". Variants of proverbs, in turn, can have alternate components, which are shown in parentheses. Two or more alternate components in parentheses are separated by a comma. For example, "Кума с воза—возу (кобыле, куму) легче." In many cases variants of proverbs have components that can either be used or omitted. In such instances they are in slashes. For example, "Знай /всяк/ сверчок свой шесток";

(5) Alphabetized English equivalents or analogues of Russian proverbs and sayings that are marked with the abbreviations "(Am.)," "(Br.)" or "(Am., Br.)" depending on whether they are current in the United States, Britain, or in both countries. In the English proverbs and sayings, like in the Russian ones, alternate components are shown in parentheses and separated by a comma if there are two or more of them—"There's a Jack for every Jane (Jean, Jenny, Jill)." The component that can be either used or omitted is enclosed in slashes—"Better /be/ safe than sorry."

The reader can find additional English equivalents and analogues of Russian proverbs and sayings in the cross-referred entries.

The **English Proverb and Saying Key Word Index** is arranged alphabetically. To make it easier to use the Index, homonymous key words are introduced by one word (**ORDER**—"command" and **ORDER**—"a state of neatness," **LIE**—"a false statement" and **LIE**—"to be in a prostrate position"). Under each key word, proverbs and sayings are alphabetized as well. The article preceding an English proverb or saying is placed at the end of it in parentheses—"(A)" or "(The)." If the usage of the indefinite or the definite article is alternate, both are placed in parentheses and separated by a slash—"(A/The)." In cases when a proverb or a saying is current both with and without an article, the latter is taken into parentheses and slashes—"(/A/)" or "(/The/)."

The **English Proverb and Saying Key Word Index**, which follows the **Russian Proverb and Saying Key Word Index**, is arranged in alphabetical order. Nouns are registered in nominative case, singular; adjectives—

in nominative case, singular, the positive degree of comparison, masculine (with the exception of the adjectives which change their root form in the comparative degree—"больше," "меньше," etc.); adverbs—in the positive degree of comparison; possessive pronouns—in nominative case, singular, masculine.

Структура словаря

Словарь состоит из трёх частей: (1) корпус словаря—русские пословицы и поговорки, их варианты и английские эквиваленты и аналоги русских единиц; (2) Указатель ключевых слов русских пословиц и поговорок с отсылкой на соответствующую словарную статью; (3) Указатель ключевых слов английских пословиц и поговорок также с отсылкой на словарную статью.

Русские пословицы и поговорки пронумерованы и расположены в алфавитном порядке вне зависимости от того, является ли первое слово служебным или знаменательным. Русские синонимичные пословицы и поговорки приведены в отдельных словарных статьях.

Словарная статья состоит из пяти разделов.

1) Русская пословица или поговорка под своим порядковым номером.

2) Толкование значения русской пословицы или поговорки на английском языке. В словарь включено большое количество синонимичных русских пословиц и поговорок, однако толкование приводится только в словарной статье, содержащей наиболее употребимую, на наш взгляд, пословицу или поговорку синонимического ряда—доминанту. Пословицы с двумя значениями имеют два толкования, помеченные буквами *“a)”* и *“b)”*.

3) Отсылка на русские синонимичные пословицы и поговорки—“*See.*” наиболее употребимая пословица или поговорка (доминанта) имеет отсылки на все члены синонимического ряда, а те, в свою очередь,—на доминанту. например:

Б

103. Брань на вороту не виснет. *See 1929 (С), 1931 (С), 2203 (Х)*

С

1929. Словом человека не убьёшь. *See 103 (Б)*

1931. Слово не обух—в лоб не бьёт. *See 103 (Б)*

Х

2203. Хоть горшком назови, только в печку не ставь. *See 103 (Б)*

4) Варианты русской пословицы или поговорки, расположенные в алфавитном порядке—"*Var.:*". В тех случаях, когда они содержат варьирующиеся компоненты, последние заключены в круглые скобки и отделены друг от друга запятой—"Кума с воза—возу (кобыле, куму) легче." Компоненты, которые могут быть опущены, заключены в косые скобки—"Кошки /дома/ нет, мышам раздолье."

5) Английские соответствия к русской пословице или поговорке, расположенные в алфавитном порядке и помеченные аббревиатурой "(Am.)," "(Br.)" или "(Am., Br.)" в зависимости от того, где они употребляюся—в Соединённых Штатах, в Великобритании или же в обеих странах. В английских пословицах и поговорках, как и в русских, варьирующиеся компоненты заключены в круглые скобки—"There's a Jack for every Jane (Jean, Jenny, Jill)," а в косые скобки—компоненты, которые могут быть опущены—"Better /be/ safe than sorry."

В пяти случаях в качестве английских соответствий приводятся антонимичные единицы, что широко применяется в практике перевода ("Не вижу, так и не верю"—"Seeing is believing," "Одному ехать и дорога долга"—"Good company upon the road is shortest cut" и другие).

При необходимости читатель может найти дополнительные английские эквиваленты и аналоги русским пословицам и поговоркам в тех словарных статьях, на которые даны перекрёстные ссылки.

Указатель ключевых слов английских пословиц и поговорок составлен в алфавитном порядке. Для того, чтобы облегчить пользование **Указателем**, ключевые слова-омонимы представлены в нем под одним словом (**ORDER**—"порядок" и **ORDER**—"приказ," **LIE**—"ложь" и **LIE**—"лежать"): существительные—в единственном числе, глаголы—в неопределенной форме, прилагательные и наречия—в положительной степени.

Под каждым ключевым словом пословицы и поговорки также расположены в алфавитном порядке. Артикль, стоящий в начале пословицы или поговорки, вынесен в конец и взят в круглые скобки—

"(A)" или "(The)." В тех случаях, когда возможно взаимозаменяемое употребление определённого и неопределённого артикля, оба заключены в круглые скобки и разделены косой скобкой—"(A/The)." Если же пословица функционирует в языке как с артиклем, так и без него, артикль взят в круглые и в косые скобки—"(/A/)" или "(/The/)."

Указатель ключевых слов русских пословиц и поговорок организован в алфавитном порядке. Существительные представлены в именительном падеже единственного числа; глаголы—в неопределенной форме; прилагательные—в именительном падеже единственного числа, мужского рода, положительной степени (за исключением таких форм как "больше," "меньше" и других, в которых наблюдается изменение корня); наречия—в положительной степени; количественные числительные—в именительном падеже; порядковые числительные—в именительном падеже единственного числа, мужского рода; притяжательные местоимения—в именительном падеже единственного числа, мужского рода.

Пословицы и поговорки под каждым ключевым словом также расположены в алфавитном порядке.

The Dictionary

А

1. Авось да небось—хоть вовсе брось. *If you do some job, do it properly; if not, do not do it*

Cf.: /Be the labor great or small,/ do it well or not at all (Am.). Do it right or not at all (Br.). If a thing is worth doing, it is worth doing well (Am., Br.)

2. Аз да буки, а там и науки. *Master the first stages of a skill before you can do more complex things*

Var.: Сперва аз да буки, а потом науки

Cf.: A child must learn to crawl before it can walk (Am.). Children learn to creep ere they can go (Br.). Learn to creep before you leap (walk) (Am., Br.). Learn to say before you sing (Am., Br.). Learn to walk before you run (Br.). You have to learn to walk before you can run (Am.)

3. А ларчик просто открывался. *The problem has a simple solution. See 198 a (В)*

Cf.: That accounts for the milk in the coconut (Am., Br.)

4. Алмаз алмазом режется. *Craft and obstinacy can be overcome or outwitted by similar actions. See 1205 (Н)*

Cf.: Diamond cuts diamond (Am., Br.). Iron cuts iron (Am.)

5. Алмаз и в грязи виден. *See 683 (З)*

Cf.: A diamond is valuable though it lie on a midden (Br.). A diamond on a dunghill is a precious diamond still (Am.). A good name keeps its lustre in the dark (Br.)

6. Алтынного вора вешают, полтинного чествуют. *See 2286 (Ч)*

Cf.: We hang little thieves and take off our hats to great ones (Am., Br.)

7. Аппетит приходит во время еды. *The more you are interested in doing or having something, the greater your desire for it is. See 2255 (Ч)*

Cf.: The appetite comes while (with) eating (Am., Br.). Eating and scratching, it's all in the beginning (Am.). Eating and scratching wants but a beginning (Br.). The more you eat (get), the more you want (Am.). The more you have, the more you want (Am., Br.)

8. Апрель с водою, а май с травою. *Adversity is followed by good times. See 1727 (П)*

Cf.: /March wind and/ April showers bring forth May flowers (Br.). /March winds and/ April showers bring /forth/ May flowers (Am.)

9. Апрель тёплый, май холодный—год плодородный. *The crop will be rich if it is warm in April and cold in May. See 165 (В), 1108 (М)*

Var.: Май холодный—не будешь голодный

Cf.: A cold April and a wet May fill the barn with grain and hay (Am.). A cold May and a windy makes a full barn and findy (Br.). A dry March, wet April and cool May fill barn and cellar and bring much hay (Br.). A fall of snow in May is worth a ton of hay (Am.)

10. Аптека и лечит, так калечит. *When taking medicines for some disease, you often do harm to other organs of your body*

Var.: Аптека не прибавит века. Одно лечит, а другое калечит

Cf.: The cure is worse than the disease (Am., Br.). Cure the disease and kill the patient (Am., Br.). Good for the liver may be bad for the spleen (Am.). Physicians kill more than they cure (Am., Br.). The remedy is worse than the disease (Am., Br.). That which is good for the back, is bad for the head (Am.). That which is good for the head, is evil for the neck and the shoulders (Am.)

11. Артель атаманом крепка. *If you have a good leader, you are strong, otherwise you are weak. See 1519 (О), 1948 (С)*

Cf.: An army of hogs led by a lion is more formidable than an army of lions led by a hog (Br.). An army of stags led by a lion would be more formidable than one of lions led by a stag (Br.). Every plane has its pilot (Am.). Every ship needs a captain (Am.). A headless army fights badly (Am.). When the chief fails, the host quails (Br.). When the head aches, all the body is the worse (Am.)

12. Артель воюет, а один горюет. *See 139 (В)*

Var.: Один и дома горюет, а двое в поле воюют

Cf.: Let us all hang together or hang separately (Am.). One man does not make a team (Am.). One man is no man (Br.). United we stand, divided we fall (Am., Br.)

13. Артельный котёл гуще кипит. *Many people get a job done easier and quicker than one man working alone. See 61 (Б), 849 (К), 1135 (М), 1523 (О)*

Cf.: Many hands make light work (Am. Br.). Many hands make quick work (Br.)

14. Артелью хорошо и недруга бить. *See 130 (В)*

Cf.: There is safety (strength) in crowds (multitude, numbers) (Am., Br.). There's security in numbers (Am.)

15. Ахал бы дядя, на себя глядя. *See 2334 (Ч)*

Cf.: The kettle should not call the pot black (Am.). Look who's talking! (Am.). The pot calling (calls) the kettle black (Am., Br.). The skillet can't call the pot black (Am.)

Б

16. Баба—бабе, баба—борову, а потом по всему городу. *See 232 (В)*

Var.: Свинья /скажет/ борову, а боров всему городу

Cf.: It is no secret that is known to three (Am.). A secret between more than two is no secret (Br.). A secret shared is no secret (Am., Br.)

17. Баба с воза—кобыле легче. *Thanks Gog I have got rid of the person unwanted or disliked*

Var.: Кума с возу—возу (кобыле, куму) легче

Cf.: /A/ good riddance /to (of) bad rubbish/ (Am., Br.)

18. Бабушка ещё надвое сказала. *You never know if the desired will be fulfilled. See 1018 (Л), 1897 (С), 1922 (С), 2351 (Э)*

Var.: Бабка надвое сказала. Бабушка ещё надвое гадала

Cf.: Between the cup and the lip a morsel may slip (Br.). There is many a slip twixt /the/ cup and /the/ lip (Am.). There's many a slip between ('twixt) the cup and the lip (Br.). You never can tell (Am., Br.)

19. Беда—глупости сосед. *It is our own foolish actions that are often the cause of the troubles that strike us*

Cf.: In every fault there is a folly (Am., Br.)

20. Беда к нам приходит верхом, а от нас уходит пешком. *See 23 (Б)*

Cf.: Agues come on horseback but go away on foot (Br.). It is easier to raise the devil than to lay him (Br.). Misfortune arrives on horseback but departs on foot (Am.). Misfortunes come on wings and depart on foot (Am.)

21. Беда, коли сапожник начнёт печь пироги, а кузнец тачать сапоги. *See 1295 а (Н)*

Cf.: A cobbler must not go beyond his last (Br.). Shoemaker, stick to your last (shoes) (Am.)

22. Беда не ходит одна. *See 1778 (П)*

Var.: Беда никогда не приходит одна: сама идёт и другую ведёт. Лиха беда не живёт одна

Cf.: Bad luck comes in threes (Am.). An evil chance seldom comes alone (Br.). If it's not one thing, it's another (Am.). Misery never comes singly (Am.). Misfortune comes in bunches (Am.). Misfortunes never come alone (singly) (Br.). One woe doth tread upon another's heels (Br.). Sorrow never comes singly (Am.). Troubles never come alone (Br.). Troubles never come singly (Am., Br.)

23. Беда приходит пудами, а уходит золотниками. *Consequences of great troubles are very long in passing. See 20 (Б), 90 (Б)*

Cf.: Evil (Ill) comes in by ells and goes away (out) by inches (Br.). It is easier to raise the devil than to lay him (Br.). Mischief comes by the pound and goes away by the ounce (Br.). Mischief comes by the pound and goes by the ounce (Am.). Misfortune comes by the yard and goes by the inch (Br.)

24. Беднее всех бед, как денег нет. *Lack of means of livelihood makes a person extremely unhappy*

Var.: Хуже всех бед, когда денег нет

Cf.: A light purse, a heavy heart (Am.). A light purse is a heavy curse (makes a heavy heart) (Am., Br.). No woe to want (Br.)

25. Бедному все сапоги по ноге. *A poor man should accept any help he is offered. See 76 (Б), 1331 (Н)*

Cf.: Beggars cannot (can't) be choosers (Am., Br.). Nothing comes amiss to a hungry man (stomach) (Br.). When in great need, everything will do (Am.)

26. Бедному жениться и ночь коротка. *Circumstances are against an unfortunate man even when he is about to get something*

Cf.: When it is raining gold (soup), I am caught with a leaky teaspoon (Am.). When it rains porridge, the beggar has no spoon (Br.). Why is it when it rains good things we've left our slickers at the wagon? (Am.)

27. Бедному зятю и тесть не рад. *A poor man is welcome by nobody, even by his own people. See 37 (Б), 1769 (П)*

Cf.: No one claims kindred (is akin) to the poor (Br.). The poor is hated even of his own neighbors (Am.). The poor is hated even of his own neighbour (Br.). A poor man has no friends (Am.). Poverty has no kin (Am.). Poverty parts fellowship (friends) (Am.)

28. Бедному нужно многое, жадному—всё. *Unlike a poor man, there is no satisfying a greedy person. See 1377 (Н)*

Cf.: Avarice is never satisfied (Am.). A poor man wants some things, a covetous man all things (Br.). Poverty is in want of much, avarice of everything (Br.). Poverty wants many things and avarice (covetousness) all (Br.). Poverty wants many things, but covetousness all (Am.). Poverty wants some things, luxury many things, avarice all (Am.)

29. Бедному с богатым судиться—лучше в ложке утопиться. *The law is never on the side of the poor*

Cf.: One law for the rich and another for the poor (Br.). There is one law for the rich and another for the poor (Am.)

30. Бедность не грех, а до греха доводит. *Poverty often leads to crime. See 1796 (П)*

Cf.: The Devil dances in an empty pocket (Br.). It is hard to be poor and honest (Br.). The lack of money is the root of all evil (Am.). Poverty is the mother of crime (Am.). Poverty is the worst guard to chastity (obstructs the road to virtue) (Br.). There is no virtue that poverty destroys not (Br.). There is no virtue that poverty does not destroy (Am.). Want of money is the root of all evil (Am.)

31. Бедность не порок. *Said to excuse one's own or someone else's poverty, or to console a man who is poor*

Cf.: Poverty is no crime (no disgrace) (Am.). Poverty is no sin (not a crime) (Am., Br.). Poverty is no vice (Br.)

32. Бедность не порок, а большое свинство. *It is not a vice to be poor, but there is nothing good in it*

Cf.: It's hell to be poor (Am.). It's no disgrace to be poor, but a terrible inconvenience (but it may as well be) (Am.). Poverty is no disgrace /, but it is a great inconvenience/ (Br.). Poverty is no sin /, but it is terribly inconvenient/ (Am.). Poverty is not a sin but something much worse (Br.)

33. Беды мучат, уму учат. *The ordeals that you go through make you understand how to avoid them. See 170 (В), 388 (Г), 1250 (Н), 1595 (О)*

Var.: Беда мучит, да беда и выучит. Что мучит, то и учит.

Cf.: Adversity is a good discipline (a good teacher, a great schoolmaster) (Br.). Adversity makes men wise (Am., Br.). After crosses and losses, men grow humbler and wiser (Am.). Misfortunes make us wise (Am.). There is no education like adversity (Am.). The things which hurt, instruct (Am.). Trouble brings experience, and experience brings wisdom (Br.). The wind in a man's face makes him wise (Br.)

34. Без горести нет радости. *See 1453 (Н), 1481 (Н)*

Var.: Горесть не принять, радость (сладость) не видать

Cf.: The bitter must come before the sweet (Am.). Every day has its night, every weal its /own/ woe (Am.). No joy without alloy (Br.). There is no pleasure without pain (Am., Br.)

35. Безделье—мать пороков. *People who do not work learn to do wrong. See 1006 (Л), 1926 (Л), 2074 (Т)*

Cf.: By doing nothing we learn to do ill (Am., Br.). The devil finds work for idle hands (Am., Br.). The devil some mischief finds for idle hands to do (Am.). Idle hands are the devil's tools (Am.). An idle mind is the devil's workshop (Am., Br.). Idleness is the devil's workshop (the mother of all evil, the mother of sin, the mother of vice) (Br.). Idleness is the mother of evil (of mischief) (Am.). Idleness is the parent of many vices (Am.). Idleness is the parent of vice (Br.). Idleness is the root of all evil (Am., Br.). Satan finds mischief (work) for idle hands (Br.). Satan has some mischief /still/ for idle hands to do (Am.). Sloth is the mother of vice (Am.)

36. Безделье ум притупляет. *By doing nothing you become stupid. See 1007 (Л)*

Cf.: Idleness dulls the wit (Am.). Idleness makes the wit rust (rusts the mind) (Br.). Idleness turns the edge of wit (Am.). Too much bed makes a dull head (Am.)

37. Без денег—везде худенек. *See 27 (Б), 1769 (П)*

Cf.: The poor is hated even of his own neighbors (Am.). The poor is hated even of his own neighbour (Br.). A poor man has no friends (Am.)

38. Без денег сон крепче. *The less rich a man is, the less worries he has. See 1123 (М), 1141 (М)*

Cf.: Little goods, little care (Am.). Little wealth, little care (sorrow) (Br.). Small riches hath most rest (Br.)

39. Бездна бездну призывает. *One temptation, vice, etc. begets another one which is much worse*

Cf.: Deep calls unto deep (Am.). The deep calls unto the deep (Br.)

40. Бездонную бочки водой не наполнишь. *See 2018 (С)*

Cf.: The beggar's bag has no bottom (Br.). The beggar's wallet has no bottom (is a mile to the bottom) (Am.)

41. Без кота мышам раздолье. *People misbehave in the absence of a person in authority*

Var.: Без кота мышам масленица. Кошки дома нет—мышам воля /раздолье/. Мыши танцуют, когда кота не чуют

Cf.: The cat is absent, the mice dance (Am.). The mouse lordships where a cat is not (Br.). Rats will play while the cat's away (Am.). Well kens the mouse when the cat's out of the house (Br.). When (While) the cat is away, the mice will play (Am., Br.)

42. Без крыльев не улетишь. *See 48 (Б)*

Cf.: The fiddle cannot play without the bow (Am.). No flying without wings (Br.). You cannot play a fiddle without a fiddle-stick (Am.). You can't go far in a rowboat without oars (Am.)

43. Без муки нет науки. *One cannot acquire good knowledge without studying hard*

Cf.: If you want knowledge, you must toil for it (Am.). Knowledge has bitter roots but sweet fruits (Br.). Learn weeping, and you shall gain laughing (Br.). There is no royal road to learning (Am., Br.)

44. Без начала нет конца. *You have to start doing something in order to finish it*

Cf.: Everything has a beginning (Am.). Everything must have a beginning (Am., Br.)

45. Без охоты неспоро у работы. *If you are reluctant to do your work, you will always find it difficult*

Cf.: Nothing is easy to the unwilling (Am.)

46. Без пары не живут и гагары. *Everyone gets a mate in the end. See 260 (В), 2102 (У)*

Cf.: Every Jack has his Gill (Am., Br.). Every pot has its cover (Am.). Every rag meets its mate (Am.). For every Jack there is a Jill (Am.). No matter how black the kettle, there is always a lid to fit it (Am.). There is no goose so grey in the lake, that cannot find a gander for her make (Br.). There's a Jack for every Jill (Jane, Jean, Jenny) (Am.). There's a lid for every pot (a pot for every lid) (Am.). There's never a goose so old and gray but what a gander would wander her way (Am.). There's never a Jennie but there's a Johnny (Am.). There was never a shoe but had its mate (Am.)

47. Без причины нет кручины. *Any sorrow has its cause. See 231 (В)*

Cf.: Every why has a wherefore (Am., Br.)

48. Без топора—не плотник, без иглы—не портной. *Nothing can be done without proper tools. See 42 (Б), 49 (Б)*

Var.: Без топора—не плотник, без лопаты—не огородник

Cf.: Neither wise men nor fools can work without tools (Br.). No flying without wings (Br.). What is a workman without his tools? (Am., Br.). You cannot play a fiddle without a fiddle-stick (Am.). You can't go far in a rowboat without oars (Am.)

49. Без топора по дрова не ходят. *See 48 (Б)*

Cf.: Don't try to fly without wings (Br.). You cannot play a fiddle without a fiddle-stick (Am.)

50. Без труда не вытащишь и рыбку из пруда. *You cannot achieve anything without working hard. See 347 (Г), 1116 (М), 1220 (Н), 1343 (Н), 1376 (Н), 1391 (Н), 1400 (Н), 1412 (Н), 1502 (Н), 1632 (П), 1644 (П), 2178 (Х), 2282 (Ч)*

Var.: Без труда /и в саду/ нет плода. Без труда ничего не даётся

Cf.: A cat in gloves catches no mice (Br.). The cat in gloves catches no mice (Am.). He that will eat the kernel must crack the nut (Am., Br.). He that would eat the fruit must climb the tree (Br.).

He that would have the fruit must climb the tree (Am.). He who would search for pearls must dive below (Am., Br.). Muffled cats are not good mousers (Am.). Muffled cats catch no mice (Br.). No pains, no gains (Am., Br.). No pains, no gains; no sweat, no sweet (Am.). No sweet without /some/ sweat (Br.). Roasted ducks don't fly into your mouth (Am.). While honey lies in every flower, no doubt, it takes a bee to get the honey out (Am.). You can't catch trout with dry trousers (Am.)

51. Безумье и на мудрого бывает. *See 738 (И)*
Cf.: Every man has a fool in (up) his sleeve (Am., Br.)

52. Без хвоста и ворона не красна. *See 1517 (О)*
Cf.: Fine feathers make fine birds (Am., Br.). Fine feathers make fine fowl (Am.)

53. Без хлеба не обойдёшься. *See 2177 (Х)*
Cf.: Bread is the staff of life (Am., Br.). No such thing as brown bread (Br.)

54. Без худа добра не бывает. *Every thing has its defects. See 173 (В), 737 (И), 1008 (Л), 1452 (Н), 1453 (Н)*
Cf.: Every advantage has its disadvantage (Am.). Every light has its shadow (Am., Br.). Every white has its black (Br.). He is a gentle horse that never cast his rider (Br.). No corn without chaff (Br.). No land without stones, or meat without bones (Br.). No summer but has its winter (Br.). There is nothing perfect in the world (Br.). There's good and bad in everything (Am.). There was never a good town but had a mire at one end of it (Br.)

55. Бей сороку и ворону—добьёшься до ясного сокола. *Begin doing little things, with practice and time greater things will be accomplished by you*
Var.: Бей галку и ворону: руку набьёшь, сокола убьёшь
Cf.: He who has carried the calf will be able by and by to carry the ox (Br.). He who shoots may hit at last (Am.)

56. Бело, да не серебро. *See 1301 (Н)*
Cf.: All is not gold that glitters (Am., Br.). All that shines is not silver (Br.)

57. Береги бровь, глаз цел будет. *Extra measures of precaution will do no harm, they will save you from trouble. See 59 (Б)*
Cf.: It is better to be safe than sorry (Am., Br.). Precaution is better than repentance (Br.). You cannot be too careful (Am., Br.)

58. Берегись тихой собаки да тихой воды. *See 294 (В)*
Cf.: Beware of a silent dog and silent water (Am.). Beware of a silent dog and still water (Br.)

59. Бережёного Бог бережёт. *To avoid danger one should take a safe course of action. See 57 (Б), 1571 (О), 1572 (О)*
Cf.: Although it rain, throw not away your watering-pot (Br.). Although the sun shine, leave not thy (your) cloak at home (Br.). Caution is the parent of safety (Am., Br.). The cautious seldom cry (Am.). Discretion is the better part of valo(u)r (Am., Br.). Don't throw caution to the wind (Am.). It is best to be on the safe side (Br.). It is better to be on the safe side (Am.). It is good to have a cloak for a rainy day (Br.). Safety first (Am., Br.). Though the sun shine, leave not your cloak at home (Am.)

60. Бери ношу по себе, чтоб не падать при ходьбе. *Do not undertake more than it is within your power to do. See 1838 a (Р)*
Cf.: An ass endures his burden, but no more than his burden (Br.). Catch no more fish than you can salt (Am.).

Don't bite off more than you can chew (Am., Br.). It is not the burden but the overburden that kills the beast (Br.). Take no more on you than you're able to bear (Br.)

61. Берись дружно, не будет грузно. *See 13 (А)*

Cf.: Many hands make light work (Am., Br.)

62. Берись за то, к чему ты годен. *See 1295 а (Н)*

Cf.: Every man to his business (craft, trade) (Am., Br.). The gunner to the linstock, and the steersman to the helm (Br.). If you are a cock, crow; if a hen, lay eggs (Am.). Let every tailor stick to his goose (Br.). Shoemaker, stick to your last (shoes) (Am.)

63. Беседа дорогу коротает. *When you go somewhere, time passes quickly if you have nice fellow-travelers. See 256 (В), 1546 (О), 2132 (У)*

Cf.: Cheerful company shortens the miles (Am.). Good company on the road is the shortest cut (Br.). Good company upon the road is shortest cut (Am.). Make short miles with talk and smiles (Br.). A merry companion is a waggon in the way (Br.). Pleasant company shortens the miles (Am.)

64. Бесчестье хуже смерти. *See 1067 (Л)*

Cf.: It's better to die with honor than to live in infamy (Am.). Shame is worse than death (Br.)

65. Бил дед жабу, грозясь на бабу. *The innocent is punished, not the guilty. See 1392 (Н), 1841 (Р)*

Var.: Бил дед жабу, сердясь на бабу

Cf.: The dog bites the stone, not him that throws it (Am.). Many beat the sack and mean the miller (Br.). You kick the dog (Am.)

66. Битая посуда два века живёт. *People, who keep complaining of weak health, often live long. See 1915 (С)*

Cf.: A cracked plate always lasts longer than a new one (Am.). The cracked pot lasts the longest (Am.). Cracked pots last longer (Br.). The cracked saucer lasts longest (Am.). The ill stake stands long (longest) (Br.). An ill stake stands the longest (Am). The loose stake stands long (longest) (Br.). The sickest is not the nearest to the grave (Am.)

67. Битого, пролитого да прожитого не воротишь. *One cannot have back what is lost. See 1127 (М), 2281 а (Ч), 2295 а (Ч)*

Var.: Вчерашнего дня не воротишь. Прожито, что пролито—не воротишь. Прошлого не воротишь

Cf.: A (The) mill cannot grind with the water that is passed (Br.). The mill cannot grind with the water that is past (Am.). No grist is ground with the water that is passed (Am.). No man can call again yesterday (Am., Br.). One cannot put back the clock (Br.). On Monday morning don't be looking for Saturday night (Br.). There are no birds in the last year's nest (Am.). The water that is past doesn't turn the wheel (Am.)

68. Битому псу только плеть покажи. *See 1788 (П)*

Var.: Битому коню лишь лозу покажи

Cf.: A beaten dog is afraid of the stick's shadow (Am.). A burnt child dreads the fire (Am., Br.)

69. Ближняя—ворона, а дальняя—соколёна. *See 1917 (С)*

Cf.: Blue are the hills that are far from us (Br.). Distant fields look greener (greenest) (Am.). Distant pastures are greener (Br.). Faraway fields look greenest (Am.). Faraway fowls have fair feathers (Br.). Faraway hills are green (Am.). Far-off cows have long horns (Br.). The greenest pasture is just over the fence (Am.)

70. Ближняя копеечка дороже дальнего рубля. *See 1421 (Н)*

Var.: Ближняя соломка лучше дальнего сенца

Cf.: A bird in the hand is worth two in the bush (Am., Br.). One dollar in your hand beats the promise of two in somebody else's (Am.). A pound in the purse is worth two in the book (Br.)

71. Близкий сосед лучше дальней родни. *Kind people that live near are preferable to estranged kindred*

Var.: Лучше добрые соседи, чем далёкая родня. Не меняй ближнего соседа на дальнюю родню

Cf.: Better a neighbor near than a brother far (Am.). Better is a neighbour that is near than a brother far off (Br.). A close neighbor is better than a faraway relative (Am.). A near neighbour is better than a far-dwelling kinsman (Br.)

72. Близ норы лиса на промысел не ходит. *Never do any mischief in the area you live or in the place where you work. See 1653 (П)*

Cf.: Dogs don't kill sheep at home (Am.). The fox (wolf) preys farthest from his home (Br.). Jaybirds don't rob their own nest (Am.). No man fouls his hands in his own business (Br.). A wise fox will never rob his neighbour's henroost (Br.)

73. Близок локоть, да не укусишь. *The desired seems easy to be obtained, but still we are unable to get it. See 152 (В), 153 (В)*

Cf.: The elbow is near, but try and bite it (Am.). So near and yet so far (Am., Br.)

74. Близ царя—близ смерти. *High social position or post is fraught with danger. See 302 (В)*

Cf.: He sits not sure that sits high (Am.). The highest branch is not the safest roost (Am., Br.). Highest in court, nearest the widdie (Br.). High places have their precipies (Am., Br.). Near the death he stands that stands near the crown (Br.). Near the king, near the gallows (Br.)

75. Блины, и те надоедают. *See 2187 (Х)*

Cf.: Too good is stark nought (Br.). Too much of a good thing is good for nothing (Br.). Too much of a good thing is worse than none at all (Am.)

76. Богатому как хочется, а бедному как можется. *See 25 (Б)*

Cf.: Beggars cannot (can't) be choosers (Am., Br.)

77. Богатому телята, а бедному ребята. *Rich people enlarge their wealth, whereas the poor enlarge their families*

Var.: Богатому деньги, а бедному дети

Cf.: Children are poor men's riches (Am., Br.). Men with the smallest income have the largest families (Am.). The rich get richer, and the poor have children (get babies) (Am.). A rich man for dogs and a poor man for babies (Am.)

78. Богатством ума не купишь. *Wisdom is a gift of nature, you cannot get it for money*

Var.: Ума на (Ум за) деньги не купишь. Чего Бог не дал, того за деньги не купишь

Cf.: The price of wisdom is above rubies (Br.). Wisdom is a pearl of great price (Am.)

79. Богатство родителей—порча детям. *Children growing up in rich families are often spoiled*

Var.: Богатство родителей—кара детям

Cf.: Abundance of money ruins youth (Am.). The abundance of money ruins youth (Br.). On fat land grow foulest weeds (Br.)

80. Богатую взять—станет попрекать. *A poor man who marries a rich woman*

is doomed to humiliation. See 1059 (Л), 1838b (P)

Cf.: A great dowry is a bed full of brambles (Br.). He that marries for wealth, sells his liberty (Br.). He who marries for wealth, loses his liberty (Am.). If you marry for money, you sell your freedom (Am.). Marry above your match and you get a master (Am.)

81. Богатый бедному не брат. *See 2032 (C)*

Var.: Богатый бедному не товарищ

Cf.: The fat ox in the stall gives no thought to the hungry as they pass by (Am.). The full do not believe the hungry (Am.). He that is warm thinks all are so (Am.). He whose belly is full believes not him who is fasting (Br.)

82. Бог дал, Бог и взял. *Man is born and he must die. (This is an expression used to console someone on the occasion of a loss of a loved one)*

Cf.: The Lord gives and the Lord takes away (Am., Br.). The Lord who gave can take away (Am.)

83. Бог даст день, Бог даст и пищу. *There is always another day tomorrow and the hope that we will have means of sustenance*

Var.: Дал Бог денёчек, даст и кусочек

Cf.: Another day, another dollar (Am.). Every day brings bread with it (Am., Br.). Every tomorrow supplies its loaf (Br.). Let the morn come, and the meat with it (Br.). The Lord will provide (Am.). A new day, a new dollar (Am.). Tomorrow is another day (Am., Br.)

84. Бог даст роток, так даст и кусок. *When a baby is born, food is always found for it*

Var.: Будет роток, будет и кусок

Cf.: God never sends a mouth but he feeds it (Am.). God never sends a mouth but he sends meat (Br.). God never sends mouths but he sends meat (Am.)

85. Бог-то Бог, да и сам не будь плох. *See 1176 (H)*

Cf.: God helps those who help themselves (Am., Br.). God reaches us good things by our own hands (Br.). Heaven helps those that help themselves (Am.). Heaven (Lord) helps those who help themselves (Br.). Help yourself and heaven will help you (Am.). The Lord helps those who help themselves (Am.)

86. Бог троицу любит. *Let us do it for a third time*

Cf.: All good things come in threes (Am., Br.). All things thrive at thrice (Br.). The third time is a charm (Am., Br.). Third time is lucky (Br.)

87. Бог шельму метит. *See 1183 a (H)*

Var.: Бог плута метит

Cf.: Every man's faults are written on their foreheads (Am.). Every one's faults are written in (on) their foreheads (Br.)

88. Бодливой корове Бог рог не даёт. *Wicked people who would like to abuse their power are not given the opportunity to do it*

Var.: Не дал Бог свинье рогов, а бодуща была б

Cf.: A cursed cow has short horns (Am.). Curst cows have curt horns (Br.). Cussed cows have short horns (Am.). God gives the vicious ox short horns (Br.). God sends a curst cow short horns (Br.)

89. Бойся гостя стоячего. *We say so of a guest who, when leaving, starts a conversation anew*

Cf.: Everyone who says goodbye is not gone (Am.). Speed the parting guest (Am.)

90. Болезнь приходит пудами, а уходит золотниками. *See 23 (Б)*

Cf.: Agues come on horseback but go away on foot (Br.). A man is not so soon healed as hurt (Br.). One is not so soon healed as hurt (Am.). Sickness comes in haste and goes at leisure (Am.)

91. Болтун—находка для врага. *People who talk much will say what should better be left unsaid because it can cause harm*

Cf.: Loose lips sink ships (Am.). Loose talk costs lives (Am.). A slip of the lip will sink a ship (Am.)

92. Большая беда молчит, а малая кричит. *People plunged in great grief keep silent about it. See 994 (Л)*

Cf.: The deeper the sorrow, the less the tongue hath it (Br.). Great griefs are mute (Am.). Light sorrows speak; great ones are dumb (Am., Br.). Little griefs are loud, great griefs (sorrows) are silent (Br.). One who complains the most suffers less (Am.). Small sorrows speak; great ones are silent (Br.). Secret griefs are the sharpest (Am.). Sorrow is /always/ dry (Br.). They complain most who suffer least (Am.)

93. Большая река течёт спокойно. *See 2051 (Т)*

Cf.: Waters that are deep don't babble as they flow (Br.). Where the river is deepest it makes least noise (Am., Br.)

94. Большая рыба маленькую целиком глотает. *The mighty destroy the weak. See 925 (К)*

Cf.: The big fish eat the little ones (Am.). The great fish eat up the small (Br.). Great trees keep down little ones (keep little ones down) (Am.)

95. Больше думай, меньше говори. *See 1977 (С)*

Cf.: First think, then speak (Br.). Think more and talk less (Am.)

96. Больше слушай, меньше говори. *It is wiser to keep silent and let other people speak*

Cf.: Be swift to hear, slow to speak (Br.). Give every man thine ear, but few thy voice (Br.). Give every man your ear but few your voice (Am.). Have a long (a wide) ear and a short tongue (Am.). Hear all and say nothing (Am.). Hear all, say nothing (Br.). Hear much, speak little (Am., Br.). It is better to play with the ears than with the tongue (Br.). Keep your mouth shut and your ears open (Br.). Listen much and speak little (Am.). Talk less; listen more (Am.)

97. Большой, да дурной. *Said of a grown up but silly person. See 138 (В), 366 (Г), 1031 (Л), 1836 (Р)*

Var.: Большой вырос, а ума не вынёс

Cf.: Better fed than taught (Br.). A big head and little wit (Br.). Big head and little wit (Am.). Big head, little sense (Am.). Mickle head, little wit (Br.). Muckle head, little wit (Am.)

98. Большой секрет—знает весь свет. *What you are telling me is supposed to be a secret, but it is not*

Cf.: The dogs are barking in the street (Br.). Every barber knows that (Am., Br.). It's an open secret (Am.). The lid is off (Br.)

99. Большому кораблю—большое и плаванье. *A man of outstanding abilities should be given a large sphere of activity. See 1893 (С)*

Cf.: Big ships require deep waters (Am.). A great ship asks (requires) deep waters (Br.). A great ship asks for deeper (deep) water (Am.)

100. Борода не в честь, а усы и у кошки есть. *Man is respected for his intellect but not for the growth of hair on his face which comes with age. See 2124 (У)*

Var.: Не в бороде честь—борода и у козла есть

Cf.: Beard creates lice, not brains (Br.). The brains don't lie in the beard (Br.). An old goat is never the more revered for his beard (Am.). Wisdom goes not always by years (Am.)

101. Боюсь данайцев и дары приносящих. *You should not trust people you are not on friendly terms with* *who offer you benefits or presents. See 1338 (Н)*

Cf.: Beware of the Greeks bearing gifts (of the gift-bearing Greeks) (Am.). I fear the Greeks, even when bringing gifts (Br.)

102. Браки заключаются на небесах. *You cannot foresee who will become your husband or wife, it is predestinated. See 2017 (С)*

Cf.: Hanging and wedding go by destinies (Br.). Marriage and hanging go by destiny (Am.). Marriage comes by (is) destiny (Br.). Marriages are made in heaven (Am., Br.)

103. Брань на вороту не виснет. *Abuse can be tolerated, insulting as it may be. See 1929 (С), 1931 (С), 2203 (Х)*

Var.: Брань—не дым, глаза не ест

Cf.: Hard words break no bones (Am., Br.). Names break no bones (Am.). Sticks and stones may break my bones, but names will never hurt me (Am., Br.). Sticks and stones may break my bones, but words can never hurt (touch) me (Am.). Sticks and stones may break my bones, but words will never hurt me (Br.). A tongue-lashing leaves no scars (Br.). Words may pass, but blows fall heavy (Br.)

104. Брюхо сыто, да глаза голодны. *A person has quite enough of something but still desires more of it. See 342 (Г)*

Var.: Зоб полон, а глаза голодны

Cf.: The eye is bigger than the belly (Am., Br.). The eye is bigger than the mouth (Am.). The eyes are bigger than the stomach (are larger than the belly) (Am., Br.)

105. Будет дождь, будет и вёдро. *See 1725 (П)*

Cf.: After black clouds, a clear sun (Am.). After black clouds, clear weather (Br.). After clouds, a clear sun (clear weather) (Am., Br.). After clouds comes (there is) sunshine (Br.). After rain comes sunshine (Am., Br.). After rain, fair weather (Am., Br.). After rain, sunshine (Br.). After the rain, the sun (Am.)

106. Будет и на нашей улице праздник. *We will eventually achieve success; our hopes will come true. See 489 (Д), 1770 (П), 1772 (П), 2101 (У)*

Cf.: Better luck next time (Am., Br.). Every dog has his day (Am., Br.). Every dog has his day and every man his hour (Am.). There's always /a/ next time (Am.). We shall have our day too (Br.). The worse luck now, the better another time (Br.)

107. Будешь трудиться, будешь кормиться. *You must work to have your means of livelihood*

Cf.: Let him that earns eat (Br.). Let him that earns the bread eat it (Am.)

108. Будь друг, да не вдруг. *It takes time to know a man so well as to become real friends. See 509 (Д), 1312 (Н). 1377 (Н)*

Var.: Вдруг не станешь друг. Сердечный друг не родится вдруг

Cf.: Before you choose (make) a friend, eat a bushel of salt with him (Br.). Before you make a friend, eat a peck of salt with him (Am.). Friendship made in a moment is of no moment (Br.). Of chance acqaintance beware (Am.). Sudden friendship, sure repentance (Am., Br.). True friendship is a plant of slow growth (Am.)

109. Будь лишь мёд, много мух нальнёт. *See 899 (К)*

Cf.: Cover yourself with honey and the flies will fasten on you (Br.). Make yourself all honey and the flies will devour you (Br.). Make yourself honey and flies will devour you (Am.)

110. Будь, что будет. *Things will happen as they will. Said when you rely only on good luck or take a risk. See 323 (Г), 727 (И)*

Var.: Что будет, то и будет

Cf.: Be /that/ as it may (Am., Br.). Come hell or high water (Am.). Come high, come low (Br.). Come what may (might) (Br.). Let chance decide (Br.). What will be, will be (Am., Br.)

111. Бумага всё терпит. *You can write whatever lie or tendentious statement you like*

Var.: Бумага от стыда не краснеет. Бумага терпит, перо пишет

Cf.: A document does not blush (Br.). Letters blush not (Am.). Paper bleeds little (Am., Br.). Paper does not blush (Am.). Paper is patience; you can put anything on it (Am.). Pens may blot, but they cannot blush (Br.)

112. Буря только рощу валит, а кусты к земле гнёт. *In hard times, it is only adaptable and flexible people that can survive*

Cf.: High cedars fall when low shrubs remain (Br.). Oaks may fall when reeds stand the storm (Br.). A reed before the wind lives on, while mighty oaks do fall (Am., Br.)

113. Бывает, что и корова летает. *I do not believe your improbable and extraordinary statement. See 1210 (Н), 1373 (Н)*

Var.: Бывает, что и вошь кашляет (что и курица петухом поёт)

Cf.: If a pig had wings, he might fly (Am.). Pigs might fly /if they had wings/ (, but they are very unlikely birds) (Br.). A sow may whistle, though it has an ill mouth for it (Br.)

114. Была бы голова здорова, а на голове шапка будет. *A clever man will always find a way to earn his livelihood*

Var.: Была бы голова на плечах, а хлеб будет

Cf.: A good head does not want for hats (Am.). A hat will never be worn without a head (Am.). Who has a head will not want a hat (Br.)

115. Была бы краса, кабы не дождь да осенняя роса. *See 560 (Е)*

Cf.: If "ifs" and "ands" were pots and pans, there would be no need for tinkers (Am.). If ifs and ands were pots and pans (Br.). If wishes were butter cakes, beggars might bite (Br.). If wishes were horses, beggars could ride (Am.). If wishes were horses, beggars might (would) ride (Am., Br.)

116. Была бы охота—заладится всякая работа. *See 339 (Г)*

Cf.: If you will, you can (Am.). It is easy to do what one's own self wills (Br.). Nothing is impossible to a willing heart (Am., Br.). Nothing is impossible to a willing mind (Am.). What we do willingly is easy (Br.)

117. Была бы собака, а палка найдётся. *If you feel like punishing anyone, you will always find a weapon to do it with*

Var.: Коли быть собаке битой, найдётся и палка. Кому надо собаку ударить, тот и палку сыщет. Сердитому палка найдётся

Cf.: Any stick /will do/ to beat the dog (Br.). He who has a mind to beat a dog will easily find a stick (Am.). He who has a mind to beat his dog will easily find a stick (Br.). It's an easy thing to find a stick to beat a dog with (Am., Br.). A man that will fight may find a cudgel in every hedge (Br.). A staff (A stick) is quickly (soon) found to beat a dog with (Br.)

118. Была бы спина, найдётся и вина. *A pretext can always be found to lay a blame on someone or to punish him*

Cf.: If you want a pretence to whip a dog, say that he ate the frying pan (Br.). If you want a pretense to whip a dog, it is enough to say he ate up a frying pan (Am.). Malice seldom wants a mark to shoot at (Am.). Who would do ill, ne'er wants occasion (Am.)

119. Была бы шея, а хомут найдётся. *Work is always found for a hard working man to do it*

Cf.: The back is shaped to the load (Ам., Br.). God fits the back to the burden (Am.). God shapes the back for the burden (Br.)

120. Был конь, да изъездился. *One is no longer in the prime of life or is no longer in the swim and is of no account. See 2107 (У)*

Var.: Был конь, да заезжен, был молодец, да подержан

Cf.: The days of our pride are gone (Br.). I have had my day (Br.). An old ass is never good (Br.). The old gray mare ain't what she used to be (Am.). We have known (seen) better days (Br.)

121. Быль молодцу не укор. *Do not reproach a man with his old sins or faults. See 970 (К)*

Cf.: Forgive and forget (Am., Br.). Let bygones be bygones (Am., Br.)

122. Быть бычку на верёвочке. *One will not escape penalty and will have to pay for his ill deeds. See 1907 (С)*

Cf.: The end of the thief is the gallows (Am.). Every fox must pay with his skin to the flayer (furrier) (Br.). The pitcher goes often to the well /but is broken at last/ (Br.). The pitcher went once too often to the well (Am., Br.). The smartest fox is caught at last (Am.)

В

123. Вашими бы устами да мёд пить. *I would like it to be as you are saying. (It is used to express doubt in response to a prediction of success.) See 716 (И)*

Cf.: From your lips to God's ears (Am.). If only it were true (Am., Br.). It is too good to be true (Am., Br.). May your words come true (Br.). Out of thy mouth into God's ears (Br.)

124. В глаза не льсти, а за глаза не брани. *It is not fair to slander a man in his absence and extol him in his presence*

Var.: Не хвали меня в очи, не брани за глаза

Cf.: Admonish your friends in private, praise them in public (Am., Br.). He is a good friend who speaks well of us behind our back (Br.). He is my friend who speaks well behind my back (Am.). Praise publicly; blame privately (Am.). Reprove your friend privately; commend him publicly (Am.)

125. В гости ходить, к себе водить. *To maintain friendly relations with people and be invited to their place you also have to be friendly and hospitable. See 1074 (Л), 2211 (Х), 2328 (Ч)*

Cf.: Be friendly and you will never want friends (Am). Friendship cannot stand all on one side (Am.). Friendship cannot stand on one side (Br.). One complimentary letter asks another (Br.). The best way to gain a friend is to be one (Am.). The way to have a friend is to be one (Br.)

126. В гостях хорошо, а дома лучше. *However poor your home may be, it is the place where you feel happiest. See 282 (В), 497 (Д)*

Var.: В гостях хорошо, а дома лучше того

Cf.: Be it ever so humble there's no place like home (Am.). East or West home is best (Am., Br.). The fire burns brightest on one's own hearth (Am.). Home is home, be it ever so homely (Am.). Home is home though it be ever so homely (Am., Br.). The smoke of a man's house is better than the fire of another's (Br.). The tar of my country is better than the honey of others (Am.). There is no place like home (Am., Br.)

127. В добрый час молвить, в худой промолчать. *Considering the situation, sometimes it is wiser to say nothing*

Cf.: He cannot speak well that cannot hold his tongue (Am., Br.). Hold your tongue in an ill time (Am.). There is a time to speak and a time to be silent (Br.)

128. В долг давать—дружбу терять. *Lending money to a friend can ruin the friendship. See 634 (З), 888 (К)*

Cf.: Credit makes enemies (Am.). Lend a dollar, lose a friend (Am.). Lend and lose the loan, or gain an enemy (Br.). Lend money and you get an enemy (Am.). Lend your money and lose your friend (Am., Br.). A loan oft loses both itself and a friend (Am.). When I lent I had a friend, when I asked he was unkind (Br.)

129. В доме повешенного не говорят о верёвке. *In his presence you must not mention such things that remind the man of his weak points, drawbacks, etc. See 1322 (Н)*

Cf.: It's ill halting before a cripple (Am.). Name not a halter (a rope) in his house that hanged himself (that was hanged) (Br.). Never talk of rope in the house of a man who has been hanged (Am.)

130. В единении—сила. *Union gives strength, even to weak men. See 14 (А), 139 (В), 518 (Д), 1532 (О), 1962 (С)*

Var.: В единстве—сила

Cf.: Even weak men when united are powerful (Br.). In union there is strength (Am.). Union is strength (Am., Br.). Unity is strength (Br.). Weak things united become strong (Am.)

131. Везёт в картах—не везёт в любви. *He who wins when playing cards is a loser in love affairs. See 1282 (Н)*

Var.: Кому везёт в картах, тому не везёт в любви

Cf.: Lucky at cards, unlucky in love (Am., Br.). Lucky at play, unlucky in love (Am.). Lucky in cards, unlucky in love (Br.)

132. Везёт как утопленнику. *One is utterly unlucky. See 565 (Е)*

Cf.: As good luck as had the cow that struck herself with her own horn (Br.). Bread always falls buttered side down (Am.). The bread (The cake) never falls but on its buttered side (Br.). I must have killed a Chinaman (Br.). Just bad luck (Am.). No butter will stick to my bread (Br.). What is worse than ill luck? (Br.)

133. Век долог, всем полон. *See 603 (Ж)*

Cf.: It's all in a lifetime (Am., Br.). You must take the rough with the smooth (Am., Br.)

134. Век живи, век надейся. *Never give way to dispair. See 1195 (Н)*

Cf.: Don't give up hope till hope is dead (Am.). Never say die (Am., Br.)

135. Век живи, век учись. *We will profit from our mistakes; we are made wiser by age. See 1465 (Н)*

Cf.: As long as you live you must learn how to live (Am.). Live and learn (Am., Br.)

136. Век живучи, споткнёшься идучи. *Life is long, and in its course one cannot always act properly. See 2251 (Ч)*

Cf.: He is dead that is faultless (Am.). A man's walking is a succession of falls (Br.)

137. Век изжить—не рукой махнуть. *There is no man who, in his lifetime, has not been through some trouble, trial, vexation, humiliation, etc. See 387 (Г), 603 (Ж)*

Var.: Век изжить—не рукавицей тряхнуть

Cf.: Every man must eat a peck of dirt before he dies (Am., Br.). Every man must eat a peck of salt before he dies (Br.). Into each (every) life some rain must fall (Am.). Life is a long lesson of humility (Am.). There is a crook in the lot of every one (Br.). We must all eat a peck of dirt before we die (Am.)

138. Велика Федора, да дура. *See 97 (Б)*

Var.: Велика фигура, да дура

Cf.: Better fed than taught (Br.). A big head and little wit (Br.). Big head and little wit (Am.)

139. Веника не переломишь, а по пруту весь веник переломаешь. *As long as we stick together, we are safe; if we keep apart, we can be easily defeated. See 12 (А), 130 (В), 517 (Д), 1520 (О)*

Var.: По прутику всю метлу переломить можно

Cf.: A house (kingdom) divided against itself cannot stand (Am., Br.). Let us all hang together or hang separately (Am.). One stick is easier broken than a bunch (Am.). Stick together or get stuck separately (Am.). United we stand, divided we fall (Am., Br.)

140. Весенний день целый год кормит. *To reap good harvest you have to work hard in spring*

Var.: Вешний день весь год кормит

Cf.: April and May are the keys of the year (Br.). When April blows its horn, it's good for hay and corn (Am.)

141. Ветра в рукавицу не поймаешь. *It is mere waste of time doing what is futile. See 160 (В), 688 (И), 1038 (Л), 1130 (М) 2242 (Ч), 2339 (Ш)*

Var.: Руками ветра не поймаешь

Cf.: A fog cannot be dispelled with a fan (Br.). The wind cannot be caught in (with) a net (Br.). You cannot catch the wind in the palm of your hand (Am.)

142. Вещь вещи рознь. *Each thing has its own peculiarities*

Cf.: All bread is not baked in one oven (Am., Br.). Not everything is alike (Br.). There are no two alike (Am.). There may be blue and better blue (Br.)

143. Вещь вещи рознь, человек человеку рознь. *People vary very much in character, habits, manners and inclinations. See 270 (В), 749 (И), 1089 (Л)*

Cf.: All bread is not baked in one oven (Am., Br.). Every fish is not a sturgeon (Am.). Every man in his own way (Am.). Every man in his way (Am., Br.). Every man is exceptional (Br.). It takes all kinds of people to make the world (Am.). It takes all sorts to make a world (Br.). There are no two alike (Am.). There may be blue and better blue (Br.). You can't put the same shoe on every foot (Am.)

144. Вещь хороша, пока новая, а друг—когда старый. *See 2011 (С)*

Cf.: New things are the best things, but old friends are the best friends (Am.). No friend is like an old friend (Am.). Old fish, old oil and an old friend are best (Br.). Old friends and old wine and old gold are best (Am.). Old friends and old wine are best (Br.). Old friends are best (Am.). Old tunes are sweetest; old friends are surest (Am.)

145. В зависти нет ни проку, ни радости. *There is no point envying anybody because you gain neither satisfaction nor profit by it. See 585 (Ж)*

Cf.: The envious man grows lean (shall never want woe) (Br.). Envy never enriched any man (Am.)

146. В закрытый рот муха не залетит. *There are times when it is better to keep silent not to get harmed or get into trouble*

Cf.: A closed mouth catches no flies (Am.). A close mouth catches no flies (Br.). A fish who keeps his mouth shut will never get caught (Am.). Into a mouth shut (a shut mouth) flies fly not (Br.)

147. В запас воздухом не надышишься. *There are things you have to keep doing all the time, so make good use of the time you have*

Cf.: The only way to save an hour is spend it wisely (Am.). You cannot eat for tomorrow (Am., Br.)

148. В здоровом теле—здоровый дух. *Physical health contributes to man's morale*

Cf.: A sound mind (spirit) in a sound body (Br.). A strong body makes the mind strong (Am.)

149. Взял корову—возьми и подойник. *When you are fulfilling some task, do not neglect anything, do it to the end*

Var.: Взял топор—возьми и топорище

Cf.: Do not swallow the cow and worry with the tail (Am.). If you buy the cow, take the tail into the bargain (Br.). Let the horns go with the hide (Br.). Let the tail follow the skin (Br.). The tail goes with the hide (Am.)

150. Взялся за гуж, не говори, что не дюж. *Once we have committed ourselves to doing something, we must go through it whatever difficulties may arise and give it as much of our time and efforts as it requires. See 609 (З)*

Cf.: He that takes the devil into his boat must carry him over the sound (Am., Br.). In for a dime, in for a dollar (Am.). In for a mill, in for a million (Am.). In for a penny, in for a pound (Am., Br.). Once you pledge, don't hedge (Am.). You can't back out (Am., Br.)

151. Видать птицу по полёту. *A person can be judged by his manners*

Var.: Видать сову по полёту. Знать сокола по полёту, а доброго молодца по походке

Cf.: A bird is known by its flight (Br.). Manners make the man (Am., Br.). The style is the man (Am., Br.)

152. Видит кот молоко, да в кувшине глубоко. *See 73 (Б)*

Var.: Видит кот молоко, да рыло коротко

Cf.: The elbow is near, but try and bite it (Am.). So near and yet so far (Am., Br.)

153. Видит око, да зуб неймёт. *See 73 (Б)*

Cf.: The elbow is near, but try and bite it (Am.). So near and yet so far (Am., Br.)

154. Видно мастера по работе. *It is by the quality of the work done that you can appreciate the skill of a workman*

Var.: По работе и мастера знать. Работа мастера хвалит

Cf.: As is the garden, such is the gardener (Am.). A carpenter is known by his chips (Am.). A good workman is known by his chips (Br.). A workman is known by his chips (Am.). A workman is known by his work (Am., Br.). The work praises the artist (Br.). The work praises the workman (Am.). The work shows the workman (Br.). You can tell a woodsman by his chips (Am.)

155. Виноватому всё кажется, что про него говорят. *A guilty person thinks that everybody knows about his guilt*

Cf.: Conscience does make cowards of us all (Br.). Conscience makes cowards of us all (Am.). The faulty stands on his guard (Br.). Guilt makes the bravest man a coward (Am.). A guilty conscience feels continuous fear (Am.). The guilty flee when no man pursues (Am.). He that commits a fault thinks everybody is speaking of it (Br.). He that has a great nose thinks everybody is speaking of it (Am., Br.). Suspicion always haunts the guilty party (Am.). The truest jester sounds worst in guilty ears (Am.). The truest jests sound worst in guilty ears (Br.)

156. Вино уму не товарищ. *Mental degradation is the result of hard drinking. See 960 (К)*

Cf.: Drinking and thinking don't mix (Am.). When ale (drink) is in, wit is out (Br.). When the ale (the rum, the whiskey, the wine) is in, wit is out (Am.). When wine is in, wit is out (Am., Br.). Where drink goes in, wit goes out (Br.)

157. В каждой шутке есть доля правды. *A joke is often a hint at unpleasant facts the listener may not like to hear. See 299 (В)*

Cf.: Half in jest, whole in earnest (Am.). Many a true word is spoken in jest (Am., Br.). Many a truth is spoken in jest (Am.). A truth is often told in a joke (Am.)

158. В каждом посаде в своём наряде. *See 2300 (Ч)*

Var.: Во всяком посаде в своём наряде

Cf.: Every country has its /own/ custom (customs) (Am., Br.)

159. В каком народе живёшь, того обычая и держись. *See 297 (В)*

Var.: В чужой стране жить—чужой обычай любить

Cf.: When in Rome, do as the Romans do (Am., Br.)

160. В камень стрелять—только стрелы терять. *See 141 (В)*

Cf.: The wind cannot be caught in (with) the net (Br.). You cannot catch the wind in the palm of your hand (Am.)

161. В кривом глазу всё криво. *A sinful man always suspects others of some knavish intention. See 1591 (О), 2108 (У)*

Cf.: Bad eyes never see any good (Am.). A crook thinks every man is a crook (Am.). Evil will never said well (Br.). Guilty men see guilt written on the faces of saints (Am.). He who does evil suspects evil on the part of his fellow man (Am.). Ill-doers are ill thinkers (Am., Br.). Ill will never said well (Br.). Ill will never speaks well or does well (Am.). The thief thinks that everyone else is a thief (Am.)

162. Владеет городом, а помирает голодом. *See 1916 (С)*

Cf.: The ass loaded with gold still eats thistles (Br.). Even if the ass is laden with gold, he will seek his food among the thorns (Am.). Moles and misers live in their graves (Br.). A rich miser is poorer than a poor man (Am.)

163. В лес дров не возят, в колодец воду не льют. *You should never take anything to a place where there is already plenty of it*

Cf.: Don't carry coals to Newcastle (Am., Br.). Don't send owls to Athens (Br.)

164. В людях ангел, а дома чёрт. *The person is very nice when in public, but is unbearable at home*

Var.: В людях—ангел, не жена, дома с мужем—сатана

Cf.: An angel on the street, a devil at home (Am.). A saint abroad, a devil at home (Br.). Saint abroad and devil at home (Am)

165. В мае дождь—родится рожь. *See 9 (А)*

Cf.: A cold April and a wet May will fill the barn with grain and hay (Am.). A cold May and a windy makes a full barn and a findy (Br.). A fall of snow in May is worth a ton of hay (Am.). May makes or mars the wheat (Br.)

166. В могилу глядит, а над копейкой дрожит. *Old people are often reluctant to spend their money or to give it to anybody*

Cf.: Avarice is the old man's sin (Am., Br.). Old birds are hard to pluck (Br.). The older the bird, the more unwillingly it parts with its feathers (Br.). The older the crab, the tougher his claws (Am.). The older the goose, the harder to pluck (Br.)

167. В мутной воде хорошо рыбу ловить. *It is easy to benefit from disturbances*

Cf.: It's good fishing in troubled waters (Am., Br.)

168. Внешность обманчива. *Things and men are not always what they seem to be, do not judge them by the way* *they look. See 723 (И), 1300 (Н), 1301 (Н), 1304 (Н), 1305 (Н), 1314 (Н), 1417 (Н)*

Var.: Наружность обманчива

Cf.: Appearances are deceiving (Am.). Appearances are deceptive (Am., Br.). Judge not according to appearances (Am.). Looks are deceiving (Am.). Never judge by (from) appearances (Am., Br.). None can guess the jewel by the casket (Br.). Things are not always what they seem (Am.). You cannot judge a book by its binding (a sausage by its shin, /of/ a tree by its bark, the horse by the harness) (Br.). You cannot (can't) know the wine by the barrel (Br.). You can't tell a book by its cover (Am.)

169. В ногах правды нет. *Do not keep standing, do sit down*

Cf.: It's as cheap sitting as standing (Am., Br.). Take the load off your feet (Am.). Take the weight off your feet (Br.)

170. В нужде и кулик соловьём свищет. *See 33 (Б)*

Cf.: Adversity is a good discipline (a good teacher, a great schoolmaster) (Br.). There is no education like adversity (Am.)

171. В нужде с кем ни поведёшься. *Adversity often compels men to associate with uncongenial people*

Cf.: Adversity (Misery) makes strange bedfellows (Am., Br.). Misfortunes cause queer bedfellows (Am.). Poverty makes strange bedfellows (Am., Br.). Want makes us acquainted with strange bedfellows (Br.)

172. Во всяком подворье своё поверье. *See 2300 (Ч)*

Cf.: Every country has its own custom (customs) (Am., Br.)

173. Во всяком хлебе мякина есть. *See 54 (Б)*

Cf.: In much corn is some cockle (Br.). No corn without chaff (Br.). Nothing is perfect (Am., Br.). There is no wheat without chaff (Br.). There's no corn without chaff (Am.)

174. В огороде бузина, а в Киеве дядька. *What you are saying has nothing to do with the matter under discussion. See 2358 (Я)*

Cf.: I talk to you of cheese, you talk to me of chalk (Br.). What's that got to do with the price of apples (eggs, horses)? (Am.)

175. Вода не мутит ума. *If you drink water but never strong drinks, you will always be mentally sound*

Cf.: Drink only with the duck (Br.). It is all right to drink like a fish if you drink what a fish drinks (Am.). Water is the only drink for a wise man (Am.)

176. В одной шерсти и собака не проживёт. *You need to eat in order to live*

Cf.: The belly carries the feet (the legs) (Br.). The stomach carries the feet (Am.)

177. В одно ухо входит, а в другое выходит. *One does not listen to, pays no attention to or forgets what he is told*

Var.: В одно ухо влетает, а в другое вылетает

Cf.: In at one ear and out of the other (Am., Br.)

178. В одну ловушку два раза зверя не заманишь. *See 2005 (С)*

Cf.: A fox is not caught twice in the same place (trap) (Am.). A fox is not taken twice in the same snare (trap) (Br.). It is a silly fish that is caught twice with the same bait (Am., Br.). An old fox does not run into the same snare a second time (Am.)

179. В озере два чёрта не живут. *See 420 (Д)*

Cf.: Two wives in a house never agree in one (Br.). Two women in the same house can never agree (Am.)

180. Возьмётся болтун болтать—ничем не унять. *Idle or foolish men babble without stopping*

Cf.: Foolish tongues talk by the dozen (Am.). Fools cannot hold their tongues (Am.). Many speak much who cannot speak well (Am.). The shallowest persons are the most loquacious (Am.). They talk most who have least to say (Am.). The tongue of idle persons is never idle (Br.)

181. Война кровь любит. *Wars result in heavy casualties. See 1479 (Н)*

Var.: Война не лечит, а калечит

Cf.: Wars bring scars (Am., Br.). War is death's feast (Am.). War is the death's feast (Br.)

182. Волка ноги кормят. *To earn one's living one has to search for it but not stay in one place. See 397 (Г)*

Cf.: The bee that gets the honey doesn't hang around the hive (Am.). Change of pasture makes fat calves (Am., Br.). The dog that trots about finds a bone (Br.). The dog that trots about finds the bone (Am.). A going foot always gets something, if it is only a thorn (Am.)

183. Волк волка не съест. *See 196 (В)*

Cf.: Dog does not eat dog (Am., Br.). The ravens don't peck one another's eyes out (Am.). Wolf never wars against wolf (Br.). Wolves never prey upon wolves (Am.)

184. Волк каждый год линяет, да обычая не меняет. *See 383 (Г)*

Var.: Волк каждый год линяет, а всё сер бывает

Cf.: The fox changes his skin but keeps his knavery (Br.). The fox changes his skin but not his habits (Am.). The fox may grow gray (grey), but never good (Am., Br.). A leopard cannot change (never changes) his spots (Am., Br.). The wolf can lose his teeth, but never his nature (Br.). The wolf changes his coat (skin), but not his disposition (nature) (Br.). Wolves may lose their teeth, but they never lose their nature (Am.)

185. Волк не пастух, свинья не огородник. *Do not give a man access to a place or position where he can do much harm, or which he intends to benefit by. See 702 (И), 1023 (Л), 1284 (Н), 1792 (П)*

Cf.: Don't put the fox to guard the henhouse (Am.). Don't set a wolf to watch the sheep (Am.). Never trust a wolf with the care of lambs (Br.). Send not a cat for lard (Br.). Set not the wolf to keep the sheep (Br.)

186. Волков бояться—в лес не ходить. *A man who is afraid of the danger he may encounter when doing some job should not undertake it. See 1633 (П), 1824 (Р), 2072 (Т)*

Cf.: He that fears every bush must never go a-birding (Br.). He that fears leaves, let him not go into the wood (Br.). He that fears leaves must not come into the wood (Am.). He that is afraid of wounds must not come near (nigh) a battle (Br.). He that will not sail till all dangers are over must not put to sea (Am., Br.). He who is afraid of every nettle must not walk through the tall grass (Am.)

187. Волос долог, да ум короток. *The person wears the hair long but is stupid*

Var.: У бабы волос долог, а (да) ум короток

Cf.: Hair long, wisdom little (Am.). Long hair and short sense (Am.). Long hair, little brains (Am.). Long hair, short wit (Br.). Women have long hair and short brains (Br.). You can't grow hair and brains in the same head (Am.)

188. Вольному воля. *It is up to you or someone else. (Said to or of a man who will not take any advice and acts in his own way)*

Var.: Вольному воля, спасённому рай

Cf.: Be my guest (Am.). A wilful man must (will) have his way (Br.). A willful beast must have his own way (Am.)

189. Вольно псу и на владыку брехать. *Common people have their own rights too*

Cf.: A cat may look at a king (Am., Br.). The cat may look at the queen (Am.)

190. Вора миловать—доброго губить. *If you acquit a dishonest man, you will do harm to honest people*

Cf.: He does injury to the good who spares the bad (Br.). He injures the good who spares the bad (Am.). If you help the evil, you hurt the good (Am.). If you pity rogues, you are no great friend of honest men (Am., Br.). Mercy to the criminal may be cruelty to the people (Am., Br.). Pardoning the bad is injuring the good (Am., Br.)

191. Вор вора не обидит. *See 196 (В)*

Cf.: Dog does not eat dog (Am., Br.). One thief will not rob another (Br.). There is honor (honour) among thieves (Am., Br.)

192. Вор вора скорее поймает. *An evil person knows best how to deal with other evil men*

Cf.: It takes a rogue to catch a rogue (a thief to catch a thief) (Am.). An old poacher makes the best game keeper (Am., Br.). An old thief makes a good sheriff (Am.). Rats know the way of rats (Am.). Set a thief to catch a thief (Am., Br.)

193. Вор вором губится. *Ruthless competition takes no account of loyalty or fellowship*

Cf.: Dog eat dog (Am., Br.). Life is a matter of dog eat dog (Am.). One thief robs another (Am., Br.)

194. Вор крадёт деньги, а друг время. *Friendship takes much of our time*

Cf.: Friends are thieves of time (Br.)

195. Ворона за море летала, а умнее не стала. *A stupid person never becomes any wiser wherever he may go. See 816 (К), 1567 (О), 1696 (П)*

Var.: Ворона за море летала, да вороной и вернулась

Cf.: If an ass goes a-traveling, he'll not come back a horse (Am.). If an ass goes a-travelling, he'll not come home a horse (Br.). Lead a pig to Rhine, it remains a pig (Br.). An ox remains an ox, even if driven to Vienna (Br.). Send a donkey to Paris, he'll return no wiser than he went (Br.). Send a fool to France and he'll come a fool back (Br.). Send a fool to the market, and a fool he'll return (Am., Br). Who goes a beast to Rome, a beast returns (Br.)

196. Ворон ворону глаз не выклюет. *People bound by common, most often mercenary, interests will never act against one another. See 183 (В), 191 (В), 671 (З), 1840 (Р), 1951 (С), 2271 (Ч)*

Cf.: A crow does not pull out the eye of another crow (Am.). Dog does not eat dog (Am., Br.). Hawks will not pick hawks' eyes out (Br.). One raven will not pluck another's eyes (Br.). The ravens don't peck one another's eyes out (Am.). There is honor (honour) among thieves (Am., Br.)

197. Вору потакать, что самому воровать. *He who assists a criminal is a dishonest man himself. See 1441 (Н), 2112 (У)*

Var.: Что самому воровать, что вору стремянку держать

Cf.: The accomplice is as bad as the thief (Am., Br.). He is as guilty who holds the bag as he who puts in (Br.). He that hinders not a mischief is guilty of it (Br.). He who holds the ladder is as bad as the thief (Am.). The receiver is as bad as the thief (Am., Br.)

198. Вот где собака зарыта. *a) That is where the reason lies. See 3 (А); b) That is where the difficulty or the problem is*

Cf.: a) That accounts for the milk in the coconut (Am., Br.); *b)* That's where the shoe pinches (Am., Br.). There lies the rub (Br.). There's the rub (Am., Br.)

199. Вот такие пироги. *That is how bad or complicated the state of things is. See 2035 (T)*

Cf.: It's a fine (nice, pretty) kettle of fish (Am., Br.). That's the way it is (Am., Br.). That's the way the cookie crumbles (Am., Br.)

200. Вот тебе, бабушка, и Юрьев день. *I am very disappointed, or surprised that my hopes or expectations have not come true*

Cf.: Here's (That's) a fine (nice, pretty) how-de-do (how-d-ye-do) (Am., Br.)

201. Вот Бог, а вот порог. *You can leave, no one insists that you stay. See 1902 (C)*

Cf.: Beat it! (Am.). Be off with you (Br.). Cut your capers (timber) (Br.). Here's the door, and there's the way (Br.). Never darken my door again (Am.). Shut the door on your way out (Am.). There is the door the carpenter made (Am., Br.). There's the door, use it (Am.). Walk your chalk (Br.). You may hoist your sail (Br.)

202. В поле и жук мясо. *See 1174 (H)*

Var.: Как нет мяса, и жук мясо

Cf.: All is good in a famine (Am., Br.)

203. В постылом всё немило. *If you do not like a person, whatever he does seems wrong to you. See 2143 (У)*

Cf.: Faults are thick when love is thin (Am.). Faults are thick where love is thin (Br.). When love cools all faults are seen (Br.). Where love fails, we espy all faults (Br.). Where there is no love, all are faults (Br.). Where there is no love, all faults are seen (Am.)

204. В радости сыщут, в горе забудут. *Many people seek your company when you are happy, but when in grief, you are left alone to bear the hardships. See 251 (B), 1901 (C)*

Cf.: Adversity has no friends (Br.). Feast and your halls are crowded (Am.). In time of prosperity, friends will be plenty; in time of adversity, not one amongst twenty (Br.). In time of prosperity, friends will be plenty; in time of adversity not one in twenty (Am.). Laugh and the world laughs with you; cry and you cry alone (Am.). Laugh and the world laughs with you; weep and you weep alone (Am., Br.). Smile and the world smiles with you /; weep and you weep alone/ (Am.). When good cheer is lacking, our friends will be packing (Br.). When we laugh, everyone sees; when we cry, no one sees (Am.). When we sing everybody hears us, when we sigh nobody hears us (Br.)

205. Вранью короткий век. *A lie is soon found out. See 2114 (У)*

Cf.: A liar is sooner caught than a cripple (Am., Br.). A lie has no legs (Am.). A lie runs until it is overtaken by truth (Am.). Lies have short legs (Br.). Nothing is lasting that is feigned (Br.). You can get far with a lie, but not come back (Am.)

206. Временем в горку, а временем в норку. *See 1879 (C)*

Cf.: Fortune is changeable (Br.). Fortune is fickle (Am.). Our lives have ups and downs (Br.). We all have our ups and downs (Am.)

207. Время бежит, как вода. *Time passes quickly*

Cf.: Life is short, and time is swift (Am., Br.). Time flies (Am., Br.). Time flies like the wind (Am.). Time has wings (Br.). Time marches on (Am., Br.)

208. Время всему научит. *Long life experience gives a man wisdom and skill*

Cf.: The grand instructor is time (Am.). There is no better counsellor than time (Br.). Time is a great (the best) teacher (Am.)

209. Время—деньги. *Time is very valuable, do not waste it*
Var.: Время дороже золота
Cf.: An inch of time is an inch of gold (Am.). Time has a wallet (Am.). Time is money (Am., Br.)

210. Время красит, безвременье старит. *See 1323 (Н)*
Var.: Время красит, а безвременье сушит
Cf.: Adversity flatters no man (Am., Br.). Care brings grey hair (Br.)

211. Время—лучший лекарь. *Time passes and we forget our grief. See 216 (В), 2040 (Т)*
Var.: Время всё излечит. Время—лучший врач (исцелитель)
Cf.: There is no grief that time will not soften (Br.). There is no pain so great that time will not soften (Am.). Time cures all griefs (Br.). Time cures all ills (Am.). Time dresses the greatest wounds (Am.). Time erases all sorrows (Am.). Time heals all /wounds/ (Am., Br.). Time is a great healer (Am., Br.). Time is an herb that cures all diseases (Am.). Time is a true friend to sorrow (Am.). Time is the best doctor (Am.). Time is the best healer (Br.). Time tames the strongest grief (Br.)

212. Время не ждёт. *Do not linger, we have not got much time*
Var.: Время не терпит
Cf.: The sands are running out (Br.). Time is running out (Am.). Time is short (Am., Br.). Time presses (Am., Br.)

213. Время никого не ждёт. *Time goes on without regard to man, so you should take advantage of the chances offered*
Cf.: Time and tide stay for (tarry) no man (Br.). Time and tide wait for no man (Am., Br.). Time waits for no man (Am.)

214. Время подойдёт, так и лёд пойдёт. *See 233 (В)*
Cf.: All in good time (Br.). There's a season for all things (Am.)

215. Время покажет. *I don't know; future will show how things will turn out. See 1678 (П)*
Cf.: Time /alone/ will show (tell) (Am., Br.). Wait till we see how the cat jumps (Am.). We'll wait and see (Am., Br.)

216. Время пройдёт—слёзы утрёт. *See 211 (В)*
Cf.: Nothing dries sooner than tears (Am.). Time cures all griefs (Br.). Time erases all sorrows (Am.)

217. Время работает на нас. *In the nearest future things will turn out to our advantage*
Cf.: Time is on our side (Am., Br.)

218. Время рассудит. *It is only after some period of time passes that you can rightly estimate an event or someone's action*
Var.: Время—судья
Cf.: Time is the father of truth (Br.). Time tries truth (Am., Br.). Truth is the daughter of time (Am.). Truth is time's daughter (Br.)

219. Ври, да знай меру. *That is enough, stop telling incredible stories*
Var.: Ври, да не завирайся
Cf.: Cut the crap (the story)! (Am.). Draw it mild! (Br.)

220. Ври, да помни. *A man who tells lies must keep in mind what he says not to find himself in a predicament*
Cf.: A liar needs a good memory (Am.). Liars have need of good memories (Br.). No man has a good enough memory to be a successful liar (Am.). Tell the truth all the time and you won't have to remember what you said (Am.)

221. В своей семье и сам большой. *See 275 (B)*

Cf.: Every man is a king (a master) in his own house (Br.). A man is king in his home (Am.)

222. Всё возвращается на круги своя. *What we witness now occurred in the past, and what is now will happen again in the future. See 751 (И)*

Cf.: It will be all the same a hundred years hence (in a hundred years) (Am.)

223. Все девушки хороши, но откуда злые жёны берутся? *A woman's character often changes for the worse after marriage*

Var.: Все невесты хороши, но откуда злые жёны берутся?

Cf.: All are good girls, but where do the bad wives come from? (Am.). All are good lasses, but whence come bad wives? (Br.). A good maid sometimes makes a bad wife (Am.)

224. Все дороги ведут в Рим. *Whatever ways, means, or methods one chooses, all of them will eventually converge*

Cf.: All roads lead to Rome (Am., Br.)

225. Всё едино, что хлеб, что мякина. *It is all the same; it is a matter of no difference. See 2034 (T), 2049 (T), 2215 (X), 2285 (Ч)*

Var.: Всё одно, что дерево, что бревно

Cf.: Another yet the same (Br.). It is all one (Br.). It is as broad as it's long (as long as it's broad) (Br.). It is six of one and half a dozen of the other (Br.). It's six of one, half a dozen of the other (Am.). The same stew only the name is new (Br.)

226. Всё идёт как по маслу. *Everything is going fine. See 426 (Д), 1340 (H)*

Cf.: All is gas and gaiters (Am., Br.). /All is well and/ the goose hangs high (Am.). Everything in the garden is lovely (Am., Br.). Everything in the garden is rosy (Br.). Everything is George (Br.). Everything is lovely and the goose hangs high (Br.). God's in the heaven; all's right with the world (Am.). That's real George (Am.). The world is my oyster (Am.)

227. Всё к лучшему в этом лучшем из миров. *What is happening around us is intended for the best. See 2279 (Ч)*

Cf.: All is for the best in the best of /all/ possible worlds (Am., Br.)

228. Все люди смертны. *See 240 (B)*

Cf.: All men are mortal (Am., Br.). All men must die (Am., Br.)

229. Всё может случиться—и богатый к бедному стучится. *The rich and powerful may sometimes need the help of the poor and weak*

Cf.: A lion may come to be beholden to a mouse (Br.)

230. Всем угодлив, так никому не пригодлив. *He who wants to be good to everybody will do no good to anybody*

Var.: Всем брат—никому не брат

Cf.: A friend to all is a friend to none (Am., Br.). A friend to everybody is a friend to nobody (Am., Br.).He who tries to please everybody pleases nobody (Am.). If you try to please all, you will please none (Br.)

231. Всему есть своя причина. *There is no effect that is not caused by something. See 47 (Б), 1971 (C)*

Cf.: Everything has its seed (Br.). Every why has a wherefore (Am., Br.). Never a rip without a tear (Am.). No reek without heat (Br.). Nothing ever comes to pass without a cause (Am.). Nothing happens for nothing (Am.)

232. Всему свету по секрету. *Once a secret is imparted to someone, he reveals it to other people. See 16 (Б), 676 (З), 1529 (О), 1642 (П), 1825 (Р), 1895 (С), 2171 (Ф), 2291 (Ч)*

Var.: Говоришь по секрету, а пойдёт по всему свету. Я ему по секрету, а он по всему свету

Cf.: Confide in an aunt and the whole world knows it (Br.). A secret shared is no secret (Am., Br.). Three may keep counsel if two be away (Am.). Two can keep a secret is one is dead (Am.). Two may keep counsel if one be away (if one of them's dead) (Br.). When three know it, all know it (Br.)

233. Всему своё время. *Things should be done at appropriate time; particular events take place when their time comes. See 214 (В), 279 (В), 284 (В), 1093 (Л), 1717 (П), 1771 (П)*

Var.: Всему свой час (черёд)

Cf.: Everything has its time (Am., Br.). Everything in its season (Am.). The morning to the mountain, the evening to the fountain (Br.). Shake the tree when the fruit is ripe (Br.). There is a time for all things (Am., Br.). There is a time to fish and a time to dry nets (Am.)

234. Всему своё время и место. *Things should be done in proper places and at appropriate time*

Cf.: There is a time and a place for everything (Br.). There is a time and place for everything (Am.)

235. Все мы люди, все мы человеки. *We all have our failings, so we must be excused for the imperfection of our human nature. See 236 (В), 737 (И), 907 (К), 1487 (Н)*

Cf.: The best of men are but men afterward (Am.). Every man has his faults (his weak side) (Am., Br.). Every man has the defects of his / own/ virtues (of his qualities) (Br.). He is dead (lifeless) that is faultless (Am.). He is lifeless who is faultless (Br.). Men are not angels (Am., Br.). None of us are perfect (Am.). We are all human beings (Br.). We are only human (Am.)

236. Все мы не без греха. *See 235 (В)*

Cf.: Every man has his besetting sin (Am.). He is dead (lifeless) that is faultless (Am.). He is lifeless who is faultless (Br.). You can find faults in an angel if you look hard enough (Am.)

237. В семье не без урода. *In every community there is sure to be at least one disreputable person*

Var.: И в хорошей семье выродок бывает

Cf.: Every family has a black sheep (Br.). An idiot—they happen in the best of families (Am.). It is a strange wood that never has a withered bough in it (Br.). There is a black sheep in every flock (Am., Br.). There is at least one rotten apple in every barrel (Am., Br.). There's a bad apple in every box (Am.). There's a black sheep in every family (Am.). There's always a bad egg in every crowd (Am.)

238. Все одного отца дети. *See 242 (В)*

Cf.: Human blood is all one color (Am.). We are all Adam's children (Am., Br.)

239. Всё перемелется, мука будет. *Ultimately all will be fine. See 665 (З), 1509 (О), 1782 (П), 2048 (Т)*

Cf.: Everything will turn out (work out) for the best (Am.). Hard luck can't last one hundred years (Am.). In the end, all will mend (Am.). In the end things will mend (Br.). It'll all come right in the end (Br.). It's a bad wind that never changes (Am.). It will all come out (come right) in the wash (Am., Br.). It will all work out in the end (Am.). It will soon blow over (Am.). The man shall have his mare again (Br.). There is always a tomorrow (Am.). This, too, shall (will) pass (Am.). Tomorrow is another day (Am.)

240. Все под Богом ходим. *No man lives eternally. See 228 (В), 244 (В), 1607 (О), 1938 (С)*

Cf.: All men are mortal (must die) (Am., Br.). Charon waits for all (Br.). Grass and hay, we are all mortal (Br.). Kings and queens must die, as well as you and I (Am.). Man is mortal (Am., Br.). Once born, once must die (Br.)

241. Всё познаётся в сравнении. *It is only when we compare things, people, situations or our feelings that we can appraise them*

Cf.: Bad is called good when worse happens (Am.). Bad is never good until worse happens (Am.). It is /the/ comparison that makes men happy or miserable (Br.). Nothing is good or bad but by comparison (Am.)

242. Все равны под солнцем. *All people have equal rights and are entitled to equal opportunities. See 238 (В)*

Cf.: /All/ men are created equal (Am., Br.)

243. Всё тайное становится явным. *Anything that you would like to be concealed will be revealed. See 2336 (Ш), 2337 (Ш)*

Var.: Нет ничего тайного, что не стало бы явным

Cf.: Secrets are never long-lived (Am.). There is nothing hidden that is not shown (Am.). There is nothing so secret but it comes to light (Br.). What goes on in the dark must come out in the light (Am.). What is done in the night appears in the day (Am.)

244. Все там будем. *We all will end up in the grave. (It is a remark made apropos of the death of some person). See 240 (В)*

Cf.: All men must die (Am., Br.). Death comes to us all (Br.). Graves are of all sizes (Am.). The grave will receive us all (Am.)

245. Всё течёт, всё изменяется. *Time works great changes. See 604 (Ж)*

Cf.: All things are in the flux (Br.). Time changes all things (everything) (Am.)

246. Всё хорошо в меру. *See 2187 (Х)*

Var.: Во всём надо знать меру

Cf.: Enough is as good as a feast (Am., Br.). Measure is a treasure (Am.). Moderation in all things (Am., Br.). Safety lies in the middle course (Br.). There is a measure in all things (Am., Br.). There is enough where there is not too much (Br.). Without measure medicine will become poison (Am.)

247. Всё хорошо в своё время. *See 503 (Д)*

Cf.: Everything is good in its season (Br.). There's a season for all things (Am.)

248. Всё хорошо, что хорошо кончается. *Despite all the difficulties everything turned out successfully*

Cf.: All's well that ends well (Am., Br.). Nothing is ill that ends well (Br.)

249. Вскачь не напашешься. *See 1741 (П)*

Cf.: Haste makes waste (Am., Br.)

250. Вскорми ворона—он тебе глаза выклюет. *If you are kind to an ungrateful man, he will return evil for good. See 300 (В), 631 (З), 1307 (Н), 2159 (У)*

Var.: Вскорми ворона—он тебе очи выклюет

Cf.: Breed up a crow and he will peck out your eyes (Br.). Bring up a raven, he will pick out your eyes (Br.). No good deed goes unpunished (Am.). Save a stranger from the sea, and he'll turn your enemy (Br.). Save a thief from the gallows, and he'll be the first to cut your throat (Am.). Save a thief from the gallows, and he'll cut your throat (and he will hate you) (Br.)

251. В слезах никто не видит, а в песне всяк слышит. *See 204 (В)*

Cf.: When we laugh, everyone sees; when we cry, no one sees (Am.). When we sing everybody hears us, when we sigh nobody hears us (Br.)

252. Встать пораньше, шагнуть подальше. *If you get up early, you will succeed in doing much work. See 954 (К), 961 (К), 1822 (Р)*

Var.: Кто встал пораньше, шагнул подальше

Cf.: Early start makes easy stages (Br.). He that would thrive must rise at five (Am.)

253. В ступе воду толочь—вода и будет. *See 708 (И)*

Var.: Воду варить (толочь)—вода и будет

Cf.: From nothing, nothing is made (Am.). Whether you boil snow or pound it, you can have but water of it (Br.)

254. В суд ногой, в карман рукой. *When you start a lawsuit, you should be prepared to bear great expenses*

Cf.: Law is a bottomless pit /; keep far from it/ (Br.). Lawyers are thieves (Am.)

255. Всяк Аксён про себя умён. *See 775 (К)*

Cf.: Everyone is witty for his own purpose (Br.). Everyone speaks for his own interest (Am.)

256. Всякая дорога вдвоём веселей. *See 63 (Б)*

Cf.: Good company on the road is the shortest cut (Br.). Good company upon the road is shortest cut (Am.)

257. Всякая козявка лезет в букашки. *See 974 (К)*

Var.: Всякая свинка лезет в скотинки

Cf.: Every ass thinks himself worthy to stand with the king's horses (Am., Br.). Every sprat now-a-days calls itself a herring (Br.)

258. Всякая курица своим голосом поёт. *See 270 (В)*

Var.: Всякая птица своим голосом (свои песни) поёт

Cf.: Every cock sings in his own manner (Br.). Every man after his own heart (Am.). Every man in his own way (Am., Br.)

259. Всякая лисица свой хвост хвалит. *See 269 (В)*

Cf.: Every cook praises his own broth (Am., Br.)

260. Всякая невеста для своего жениха родится. *Every female gets a husband in the end. See 46 (Б)*

Cf.: All meat is to be eaten and all maids to be wed (Am.). All meats to be eaten, all maids to be wed (Br.). Every girl has her day (Am.). If one will not, another will (Br.). If one will not, another will, so are all maidens wed (Am.). There is never a pot too crooked but what there's a lid to fit it (Am.). There is no goose so grey in the lake, that cannot find a gander for her make (Br.). There's a Jack for every Jane (Jenny, Jill, Joan) (Am.). There's never a goose so old and gray but what a gander would wander her way (Am.)

261. Всякая птица своё гнездо любит. *See 276 (В)*

Cf.: Each bird likes his own nest best (Am.). Every bird thinks his nest best (Br.)

262. Всякая пуля грозит, но не всякая разит. *Not all threats are brought into effect. See 1309 (Н), 1310 (Н)*

Cf.: All clouds bring not rain (Am.). Every cloud is not a sign of storm (Am.). Every shot does not bring down a bird (Br.). Every wind blows not down the corn (Br.)

263. Всякая рука к себе загребает. *See 771 (К)*

Cf.: Every man drags water to his own mill (Am.). Every miller draws water to his own mill (Br.)

264. Всякая рыба хороша, коли на удочку пошла. *See 479 (Д)*

Cf.: All is fish that comes to the net

(Br.). All is grist that comes to the mill (Br.). All is grist /that goes/ to the mill (Am.). All's fish that comes to his net (Am.)

265. Всякая сосна своему бору шумит. *Every person acts in his own interests or in those of his relatives or friends. See 1868 (C)*

Cf.: All thoughts of a turtle are of turtle, of a rabbit, rabbit (Am.). Charity begins at home (Am., Br.). Close sits my shirt, but closer my skin (Am., Br.). Every man is nearest himself (Br.). Every man will have his own turn served (Br.). The parson always christens his own children first (Br.). Self comes first (Br.). Self loves itself best (Am., Br.)

266. Всякая тряпица в три года пригодится. *Lay things by, they may be useful some day*

Cf.: Everything is of use to a housekeeper (Br.). Keep a thing for seven years and it will come in handy (Am.). Keep a thing long enough (Br.). Keep a thing seven years and you will find a use for it (Am., Br.). Nothing but is good for something (Am., Br.). A stone that may fit in a wall is never left by the way (Am.)

267. Всяк за себя. *Every man must be self-reliant and take care of his own interests. See 591 (Ж), 1975 (C)*

Var.: Сова о сове, а всяк о себе

Cf.: Every kettle has to sit on its own bottom (Am.). Every man must pay his Scot (must skin his own skunk) (Am.). Every man must stand on his own two legs (Am., Br.). Everyone for himself (Am., Br.). Every person should row his own boat (Am.). Every tub must stand on its own bottom (Am., Br.). Let every man skin his own eel (Am.). Let every peddler carry his own pack (Am.). Let every pedlar carry his own burden (pack) (Br.). Let every pig dig for himself (Br.). Stand on your own two feet (Am.)

268. Всякий Демид для себя норовит. *See 771 (К)*

Cf.: Every man drags water to his own mill (Am.). Every miller draws water to his own mill (Br.)

269. Всякий купец свой товар хвалит. *Every man praises himself, his relatives, friends, doings or things that belong to him. See 259 (В), 276 (В), 289 (В)*

Var.: Всякий цыган свою кобылу хвалит. Всяк своё хвалит

Cf.: A dealer in rubbish sounds the praise of rubbish (Am.). Each priest praises his own relics (Br.). Every cook praises his own broth (Am., Br.). Every pedlar praises his needles (Br.)

270. Всякий молодец на свой образец. *Every man has his own habits, manners, inclinations, etc. See 143 (В), 258 (В), 271 (В), 273 (В), 274 (В), 288 (В), 1494 (Н), 2089 (У), 2093 (У), 2106 (У)*

Cf.: All bread is not baked in one oven (Am., Br.). Every cock sings in his own manner (Br.). Every man after his fashion (Br.). Every man after his own heart (Am.). Every man in his own way (Am., Br.)

271. Всякий поп по-своему поёт. *See 270 (В)*

Cf.: Every man in his own way (Am., Br.)

272. Всякий трус о храбрости беседует. *Cowardly men are brave only when there is no danger*

Cf.: The cat is mighty dignified until the dog comes by (Am.). The greatest braggarts are generally the greatest cowards (Br.). Lions in peace, hares in war (Br.)

273. Всякий Филат на свой лад. *See 270 (В)*

Cf.: Every man in his /own/ way (Am., Br.)

274. Всяк канонер на свой манер. *See 270 (В)*

Cp.: Every man in his own way (Am., Br.)

275. Всяк кулик на своём болоте велик. *It is in his own place, his business or family that a man is influential. See 221 (В), 269 (В), 287 (В)*

Cf.: The cock is master of (on) his own dunghill (Br.). A cock is mighty in his own backyard (Am.). A dog is a lion at home (Am., Br.). Every cock crows the loudest upon his own dunghill (Am.). Every cock is proud on his own dunghill (Br.). Every groom is a king at home (Br.). Every man is a king (a master) in his own house (Br.). A man is a lion in his own house (Am.). A man is king in his home (Am.)

276. Всяк кулик своё болото хвалит. *Every man is of a high opinion of what belongs to him. See 261 (В), 269 (В), 462 (Д)*

Var.: Каждая курица свой насест хвалит. Каждая сорока своё гнездо хвалит

Cf.: Each bird likes his own nest best (Am.). Every bird likes its own nest (Br.). Every bird thinks her /own/ nest beautiful (thinks his nest best) (Br.). Every man likes his own thing best (Br.)

277. Всякое дело до мастера. *See 431 (Д)*

Cf.: Few things are impossible to diligence and skill (Am.). He works best who knows his work (Br.). In every art it is good to have a master (Br.). Work is afraid of a resolute man (Am.)

278. Всякое начало трудно. *See 1025 (Л)*

Cf.: The hardest step is that over the threshold (Am., Br.)

279. Всякое семя знает своё время. *See 233 (В)*

Var.: Яблочное семя знает своё время

Cf.: Everything has its time (Am., Br.). There's a season for all things (Am.)

280. Всякое умение трудом даётся. *It is only by hard work that we become competent. See 430 (Д), 1190 (Н), 2044 (Т)*

Cf.: Diligent working makes an expert workman (Br.). He that shoots oft at last will hit the mark (Br.). He who shoots may hit at last (Am.). In doing we learn (Br.). Practice makes perfect (Am., Br.). Use makes the craftsman (Am., Br.)

281. Всякой вещи своё место. *There are certain places for certain things to be done. See 234 (В)*

Cf.: Everything is good in its place (Am.). /There is/ a place for everything, and everything in its place (Am., Br.)

282. Всякому мила своя сторона. *See 126 (В)*

Cf.: East or West, home is best (Am., Br.)

283. Всякому мужу своя жена мила. *Most men believe their wife to be the best one*

Cf.: There is one good wife in the country, and every man thinks he has her (Br.)

284. Всякому овощу своё время. *See 233 (В)*

Cf.: All in good time (Br.). There's a season for all things (Am.)

285. Всякому своя слеза солона. *See 768 (К)*

Cf.: Everyone thinks his own cross the hardest to bear (Br.). To everyone his own cross is heaviest (Am.)

286. Всякому терпению приходит конец. *There comes a point when even the meekest man would not endure ill-treatment any longer. See 1727 (П), 2047 (Т), 2244 (Ч)*

Cf.: A bow long bent at last waxes weak (Br.). A bow too much bent will break (Am.). Even a worm will turn (Am., Br.). A man may bear till his back break (Br.). A man may provoke his own dog to bite him (Am., Br.). Patience is a stout horse, but it will tire at last (Br.). Rub a galled horse and he will kick (Am.). There's a limit to everything (Am., Br.). Tramp on a snail, and she'll shoot out her horns (Br.). Tread on a worm and it will turn (Am., Br.). Tread on a worm's tail and it will turn (Br.). When the well is full, it will run over (Br.). The worm will turn (Am.)

287. Всяк петух на своём пепелище хозяин. *The head of the family or of a business gives the orders. See 275 (В), 1237 (Н)*

Var.: В своём курятнике петух хозяин

Cf.: The cock is master of (on) his own dunghill (Br.). A cock is mighty in his own backyard (Am.). Every cock crows the loudest upon his own dunghill (Am.). Every man is a king (a master) in his own house (Br.). Everyone is master in his own shop (Br.)

288. Всяк портной на свой покрой. *See 270 (В)*

Cf.: Every man in his own way (Am., Br.)

289. Всяк сам себе загляденье. *Every man is of a very high opinion of himself. See 269 (В)*

Var.: Всяк сам себе хорош

Cf.: Each bird loves to hear himself sing (Br.). Every bird likes to hear himself sing (Am.)

290. Всяк сверчок знай свой шесток. *See 1295 b (Н)*

Cf.: The bear wants a tail and cannot be lion (Br.). Everyone to his equal (Am.). Every sheep with its like (Am.). Geese with geese, and women with women (Br.). Keep to your own kind (Am.)

291. В темноте и гнилушка светит. *See 1174 (Н)*

Cf.: All is good in a famine (Am., Br.). Among the blind the one-eyed man is king (Br.)

292. В ту пору будет досуг, как вон понесут. *See 1691 (П)*

Cf.: Only in the grave is there rest (Am.). Peace is found only in the graveyard (Am.)

293. В тесноте, да не в обиде. *Come and stay with us though the place is already full of people or not very spacious. See 1133 (М)*

Cf.: More sacks to the mill (Br.). The more, the merrier (Am., Br.). /There is/ always room for one more (Am.)

294. В тихом омуте черти водятся. *You never know the way a silent or a reticent man may conduct himself. See 58 (Б), 355 (Г), 1273 (Н), 2050 (Т)*

Var.: В тихой воде омуты глубоки. Тиха вода, да омуты глубоки

Cf.: Dumb dogs /and still waters/ are dangerous (Br.). Serpents engender in still waters (Br.). The silent dog is first to bite (Am.). The smoothest waters are not always the safest (Br.). Still waters have deep bottoms (Am., Br.)

295. В хорошем житье кудри вьются, а в плохом секутся. *Prosperity and happiness make people look attractive, whereas troubles and poverty tell on them*

Var.: В хорошем житье лицо белится

Cf.: An empty purse fills the face with wrinkles (Am., Br.). A good life keeps away wrinkles (Am.). The joy of the heart makes the face fair (Br.). Wrinkled purses make wrinkled faces (Am.)

296. В чужих руках пирог велик. *What belongs to others seems to be better than what we have. See 2185 (Х)*

Var.: В чужих руках кусок больше кажется. В чужих руках ломоть велик (ноготок с локоток). В чужой лодке всегда больше рыбки. На чужой улице и щепка велика. Пирог в чужом рту всегда слаще

Cf.: The grass is always greener on the other side of the fence (Am., Br.). A morsel always looks big in other people's hands (Br.). The next man's cows have the longest horns (Am.). The other man's pasture always looks the greenest (Am.). The other side of the road always looks cleanest (Br.). Your pot broken seems better than my whole one (Br.)

297. В чужой монастырь со своим уставом не ходят. *Adapt yourself to the customs and manners of those you live among or are closely associated with. See 159 (В), 1864 (С), 1866 (С)*

Cf.: Follow the customs, or fly the country (Br.). When at Rome, live as the Romans live (Br.). When in Rome, do as the Romans /do/ (Am., Br.). When you are at Rome, do as Rome /does/ (Am., Br.)

298. В чужом глазу сучок велик. *We notice other men's insignificant imperfections but are unaware of our own great ones. See 1288 (Н)*

Var.: В чужом глазу и соринка видна, а в своём и бревна не видно

Cf.: We see a mote in other men's eyes when there's a beam in our own (Br.). We see a mote in our brother's eyes and don't see a (the) beam in our own (Am.). We see the failings of others but are blind to our own (Am.). We see the faults of others but not our own (Am.). We see the splinter in others' faults, but never the spike in our own (Am.)

299. В шутку сказано, да всерьёз задумано. *See 157 (В)*

Cf.: There's many a true word said in jest (Am., Br.). The worst jests are the true ones (Am.)

300. Выкормил змейку на свою шейку. *See 250 (В)*

Cf.: Breed up a crow and he will peck out your eyes (Br.). No good deed goes unpunished (Am.). Save a thief from the gallows, and he'll be the first to cut your throat (Am.). Save a thief from the gallows, and he'll cut your throat (Br.)

301. Высоко голову несёшь—споткнёшься да упадёшь. *See 556 (Д)*

Cf.: Pride goes before a fall (before destruction) (Am., Br.)

302. Высоко летаешь, да низко садишься. *He risks disgrace, failure or disappointment whose ambition or position is high. See 74 (Б), 309 (Г)*

Var.: Высоко летишь—где-то сядешь. Кто высоко летает, тот низко падает. Летала пташка высоко, а села недалеко

Cf.: The bigger they are, the harder they fall (Br.). The bigger they come, the harder they fall (Am.). Climb not too high lest the chips fall in thine eye (Br.). A great tree has a great fall (Am.). He sits not sure that sits too high (Am., Br.). He who climbs too high is near a fall (Br.). He who climbs too high is near to fall (Am.). The higher standing, the lower fall (Br.). The higher the mountain, the greater descent (Br.). The higher the place, the harder the fall (Am.). The higher they go, the lower they fall (Am.). The higher you climb, the harder you fall (Am., Br.). The highest tree has the greatest fall (Br.). Look high and fall in the dirt (Br.). Look high and fall low (Am.)

303. Выстрелив, пулю не схватишь, а слово, сказав, не поймаешь. *See 1930 (С)*

Cf.: Time and words can never be recalled (Am.). Words once spoken you can never recall (Am.). A word spoken is past recalling (Am., Br.)

304. Выше головы не прыгнешь. *One cannot do what is beyond his abilities. See 305 (В), 306 (В), 748 (И), 1366 (Н)*

Var.: Выше головы носа не поднимешь. Выше себя не вырастешь

Cf.: A man can do no more than he can (Am., Br.). A nail can go no farther than its head will let it (Am.). No man can see over his height (Br.). The stream can never rise above the fountain (the spring-head) (Br.). The stream cannot rise above its source (Am., Br.). A stream never rises higher than its source (Am.)

305. Выше лба уши не растут. *There is a limit to everything. (It is applied to what is not realizable.) See 304 (В)*

Var.: Выше головы волосы не растут. Выше лба глаза не растут

Cf.: It is impossible to hoist oneself by one's own boots' straps (Br.). One cannot see through a brick wall (Br.). One can't shoe a runaway horse (Br.). One can't shoe a running horse (Am.). A stream never rises higher than its source (Am.). There is no building a bridge across the ocean (Br.)

306. Выше меры и конь не скачет. *See 304 (В)*

Var.: Через силу и конь не скачет

Cf.: A man can do no more than he can (Am., Br.). No man can see over his height (Br.). A stream never rises higher than its source (Am.)

307. Выше нос! *Do not despair, make the best of a difficult or painful situation. See 1484 (Н)*

Var.: Выше голову!

Cf.: Brazen it out! (Am.). Grin and bear it! (Am.). Keep a stiff upper lip! (Am.). Keep your chin (head) up! (Am., Br.). Keep your pecker up! (Br.). Make the best of a bad bargain (Am., Br.). Make the best of a bad market (Br.)

308. Вяжись лычко с лычком, ремешок с ремешком. *Associate with people of your own standing. See 402 (Г), 675 (З), 1838 b (Р), 1853 (С)*

Cf.: Everyone to his equal (Am.). Every sheep with its like (Am.). Geese with geese, and women with women (Br.). Keep to your own kind (Am.). Let beggar match with beggar (Br.)

Г

309. Гарцевал пан, да с коня упал. *See 302 (В)*

Cf.: He who climbs too high is near a fall (Br.). He who climbs too high is near to fall (Am.). The higher standing, the lower fall (Br.). The higher they go, the lower they fall (Am.). High places have their precipices (Am., Br.). One who climbs high falls low (Am.)

310. Где волчьи зубы, а где лисий хвост. *In certain circumstances slyness is more effective than brutal force. See 334 (Г), 1024 (Л), 1375 (Н)*

Var.: Не волчьи зубы, так лисий хвост

Cf.: Cunning is more than strength (Am.). Cunning surpasses strength (Br.). Either by might or by slight (Br.). He that is not strong should be cunning (Am.). If the lion's skin cannot, the fox's shall (Br.)

311. Где горе, там и радость. *See 1725 (П)*

Cf.: After rain comes sunshine (Am., Br.). Behind bad luck comes good luck (Am.). It's a long lane (road) that has no turning (Am., Br.). When the worst comes, the worst is going (Am.)

312. Где двое, там третий лишний. *The third person should leave two people who are having a romantical affair alone*

Var.: Двум любо, третий не суйся

Cf.: Two is a couple, three is a crowd (Am.). Two is company and three is none (Br.). Two is company; three is a crowd (Am., Br.). Two's company, three's trumpery (Br.)

313. Где дрова, там и щепа. *See 1011 (Л)*

Cf.: You cannot make an omelet(te) (pancakes) without breaking eggs (Am., Br.)

314. Где едят, там крошки падают. *See 2160 a (У)*

Cf.: Every honest miller has a thumb of gold (a golden thumb). (Br.). He is an ill cook that cannot lick his own fingers (Am., Br.)

315. Где кража, там и вор. *When a crime is committed, there is always someone guilty of it*

Cf.: It didn't happen by itself (Am.). Nothing is stolen without hands (Br.)

316. Где мёд, там и мухи. *For an attractive and good thing there are always people ready to avail themselves of it. See 1223 (Н)*

Cf.: Everyone fastens where there is gain (Br.). A fly follows the honey (Am.)

317. Где мёд, там и пчёлы. *You cannot make money without being industrious. See 50 (Б), 329 (Г)*

Cf.: By labor comes wealth (Am.). Look for the honey where you see the bee (Am.). Things turn out for the man who digs (Am.). Where there are bees, there is honey (Am., Br.). Where there is honey to be found, there will be bees (Br.). While honey lies in every flower, no doubt, it takes a bee to get the honey out (Am.)

318. Где мило, семь вёрст не криво. *To see the person you love you cover a great distance with ease. See 464 (Д)*

Cf.: For a good friend the journey is never too long (Am., Br.). He who has love in his heart has spurs in his heels (Br.). A spur in the head is worth two in the feet (Am.). A spur in the head is worth two in the heel (Br.). To a friend's house the trail is never long (Am.). Where the will is ready, the feet are light (Am.). A willing heart carries a weary pair of feet a long way (Am.). A willing mind makes a light foot (Am.)

319. Где много воды, там больше будет; где много денег — ещё прибудет. *See 441 (Д)*

Var.: Где вода была, там и будет; куда деньга пошла, там и скопится

Cf.: He that has a goose will get a goose (Br.). Money begets (draws) money (Am., Br.). Money breeds money (Br.). Money comes to (gets, makes) money (Am.). To him who has shall be given (Am.)

320. Где много пастухов, там овцы дохнут. *See 2145 (У)*

Cf.: The common horse is worst shod (Am., Br.). Everybody's business is nobody's business (Am., Br.). A pot that belongs to many is ill stirred and worse boiled (Br.). A public hall is never swept (Br.). Two captains will sink the (will wreck a) ship (Am.)

321. Где много слов, там мало дела. *See 932 (К)*

Var.: Где много толков, там мало толку

Cf.: Big talker, little doer (Am.). Great talkers are little doers (Br.). Great talkers, little doers (Am.). Much talk, little work (Am.)

322. Где нас нет, там по две милостыни дают. *See 1917 (С)*

Cf.: Blue are the hills that are far from us (Br.). Hills look green far away (Am.)

323. Где наше не пропадало. *I am determined, or I advise you, to run the risk. See 110 (Б), 423 a (Д), 727 (И), 1527 (О), 1884 (С), 2265 b (Ч)*

Cf.: I'll stick my head out (Br.). I'll stick my neck out (Am.). Over shoes, over boots (Br.)

324. Где несчастье, там зависти нет. *Nobody is envious of him that is poor or is in trouble*

Cf.: Envy does not enter an empty house (Am., Br.)

325. Где огонь, там и дым. *See 1453 (Н)*
Var.: Огонь без дыма не живёт
Cf.: No fire without smoke (Br.). There is no fire without some smoke (Am.). Where there is fire there is smoke (Am.)

326. Где отвага, там и победа. *See 1937 (С)*
Var.: Где смелость, там и победа
Cf.: Fortune favo(u)rs the bold (the brave) (Am., Br.)

327. Где пиры да чаи, там и немочи. *Eating too much will ruin your health. See 615 (З)*
Cf.: Feasting is the physician's harvest (Am.). Gluttony kills more than the sword (Am., Br.). Greedy eaters dig their graves with their teeth (Am.). Many dishes make many diseases (Am.). Many dishes, many diseases (Br.). More die of food than famine (Am.). Much meat, much malady (Br.). The platter kills more than the sword (Am.). Surfeit has killed more than hunger (Br.). You dig your grave with your fork (Am.). You dig your grave with your own teeth (Am., Br.)

328. Где плохо лежит, туда и вор глядит. *People steal where you do not take precautions against robbery. See 1427 (Н), 1655 (П)*
Cf.: At open doors dogs come in (Am., Br.). A bad padlock invites a picklock (Am., Br.). The hole calls (invites) the thief (Am.). An open door may tempt a saint (Am., Br.). Opportunity makes a thief (Am.). Opportunity makes the thief (Br.). The righteous man sins before an open chest (Br.). When the house is open, the honest man sins (Am.)

329. Где работают, там густо, а в ленивом доме—пусто. *Where you have industrious people there is wealth, whereas idlers are poor. See 317 (Г)*
Cf.: He becomes poor that deals with a slack hand, but the hand of diligence makes rich (Am.). He who works with a slack hand becomes poor (Am.). No bees, no honey; no work, no money (Am., Br.)

330. Где радость, там и горе. *See 2024 (С)*
Cf.: After joy comes sorrow (Am.). After laughter, tears (Am.). After sunshine come showers; after pleasure comes sorrow (Am.). Grief often treads upon the heels of pleasure (Am.). Sorrow treads upon the heels of mirth (Am., Br.)

331. Где река глубже, там она меньше шумит. *See 2051 (Т)*
Cf.: The shallow brook warbles, while the still water is deep (Am.). Smooth waters run deep (Br.). Still waters run deep (Am., Br.)

332. Где река мельче, там она больше шумит. *See 1791 (П)*
Cf.: Deep rivers move with silent majesty; shallow brooks are noisy (Am.). Shallow streams make most din (Br.). Shallow streams make the most noise (Am.). Shallow waters make most din (Br.)

333. Где сила, там и власть. *See 965 (К)*
Cf.: Might beats right (Am.). Might goes before (is) right (Br.). Might makes (overcomes) right (Am., Br.). Where force prevails, right perishes (Am.)

334. Где силой не возьмёшь, там хитрость на подмогу. *See 310 (Г)*
Var.: Хитростью силу берут
Cf.: Cunning is more than strength (Am.). Cunning surpasses strength (Br.). Either by might or by slight (Br.). He that is not strong should be cunning (Am.)

335. Где счастье поведётся, там и петух несётся. *See 1538 (О)*
Var.: У кого счастье поведётся, у того и петух несётся

Cf.: If luck is with you, even your ox will give birth to a calf (Am.). If you are lucky, even your rooster will lay eggs (Am.). When a man has luck, even his ox calves (Br.). Whom God loves, his bitch brings forth pigs (Br.)

336. Где тонко, там и рвётся. *If men or things are in a miserable state, something else happens to make it still worse*

Cf.: The chain bursts at its weakest link (Am., Br.). The thread breaks where it is weakest (Br.). The weakest fruit drops earliest to the ground (Am.). Where it is weakest, there the thread breaks (Am.). The worst spoke in a cart breaks first (Br.)

337. Где труд, там и счастье. *See 1839 (P)*

Cf.: Business is the salt of life (Br.). Labor is the law of happiness (Am.). Labor makes life sweet (Am.). Man was never so happy as when he was doing something (Am.). Work makes life pleasant (Am.)

338. Где хозяин ходит, там земля родит. *See 1614 (O)*

Cf.: The master's footsteps fatten the soil (Br.). No eye like the master's eye (Am.)

339. Где хотенье, там и уменье. *When a person is determined to do some job, however difficult it may be, he will learn how to. See 116 (Б)*

Cf.: All things are easy, that are done willingly (Am.). It is easy to do what one's own self wills (Br.). Nothing is impossible to a willing heart (Am., Br.). To him that wills, ways are not wanting (Am.). Where there's a will, there's a way (Am., Br.). You can do anything you want to if you want to bad enough (Am.)

340. Гладко было на бумаге, да забыли про овраги. *Despite careful planning, things often go wrong in their final accomplishment. See 2246 (Ч)*

Cf.: The best-laid plans of mice and men often go astray (Am.). The best-laid schemes of mice and men gang aft agley (Am., Br.). It sounded (sounds) right on paper (Br.)

341. Глаза—бирюза, а душа—сажа. *See 1859 (C)*

Cf.: An angel on top but a devil underneath (Am.). A fair face, a false heart (Br.). A fair face may hide a foul heart (Am., Br.)

342. Глаза завидущие, руки загребущие. *A covetous man is never satisfied with what he has and always wants more. See 104 (Б)*

Cf.: Greedy folk have long arms (Br.). Greedy folks have long arms (Am.). The greedy never know when they have had enough (Am.)

343. Глаза—зеркало души. *Your eyes do not lie. See 1026 (Л)*

Cf.: The eye is the mirror of the soul (the window of the heart, the window of the mind) (Br.). The eyes are the mirror of the mind (Am.). The eyes are the mirrors (the windows) of the soul (Am.). The heart's letter is read in the eyes (Br.). In the forehead and the eye the lecture of the mind doth lie (Br.)

344. Глаза не видят—сердце не болит. *If you are not together with the people who are in trouble, you cannot fell unhappy about them. See 1871 (C)*

Cf.: Unseen, unrued (Am.). What the eye does not see, the heart cannot grieve (does not grieve over) (Br.). What the eye doesn't see, the heart doesn't feel (grieve for) (Am.). What the eye sees not the heart rues not (Am., Br.)

345. Глаза страшатся, а руки делают. *Do not be a faint heart, have a go and you will be surprised at your own ability*

Var.: Глаза боятся, а руки делают

Cf.: You can never tell till you've tried (Am.). You never know what you can do till you try (Br.)

346. Глас народа—глас Божий. *People's opinion is always right and indisputable, you must take it into consideration*

Cf.: The voice of the people is the voice of God (Am., Br.)

347. Глину не мять—горшков не видать. *See 50 (Б)*

Cf.: Nothing can be got without pains (Br.). Nothing is gained without work (Am.)

348. Глупа та птица, которой гнездо своё не мило. *One should not speak bad of the people he lives or works with*

Cf.: It is a foolish bird that defiles (fouls) its own nest (Br.). It is an ill bird that fouls its own nest (Am., Br.). It's a poor bird that will dirty its own nest (Am.)

349. Глупость заразительна. *Association with stupid people makes others stupid too*

Cf.: Fools multiply folly (Am.). One fool makes a hundred (Br.). One fool makes many (Am., Br.)

350. Глупый болтает, а умный думает. *A clever man thinks before giving his opinion, whereas a fool just babbles. See 536 (Д)*

Cf.: A fool talks while a wise man thinks (Am.). Knowledge talks lowly; ignorance talks loudly (Am.). The less people think, the more they talk (Br.). People who know little talk much; people who know much talk little (Am.). The wise man has long ears and a short tongue (Br.). Wise men have their mouth in their heart, fools their heart in their mouth (Br.). Wise men silent, fools talk (Br.)

351. Глупый да малый всегда правду говорят. *It is only foolish and naïve people that always tell what they really think*

Cf.: Children and fools cannot lie (Br.). Children and fools speak the truth (Am., Br.). Children and fools tell the truth (Am.). If you want the truth, go to a child or a fool (Am.)

352. Глупый ищет большого места. *A foolish man always seeks to be in the focus of everybody's attention*

Cf.: A fool always rushes to the fore (Br.). A fool's name appears everywhere (is seen in many places) (Am.). Fools' names and fools' faces are always seen in public places (Am., Br.)

353. Глупый поп свенчает, умному не развенчать. *See 535 (Д)*

Cf.: A fool may throw a stone into a well which a hundred wise men cannot pull out (Br.). Fools set stools for wise folks to stumble at (Br.). Fools set stools for wise men to fall over (to stumble) (Am.). Fools tie knots, and wise men loosen them (Am.). Fools tie knots, and wise men loose them (Br.)

354. Глухому поп по две обедни не служит. *You had to listen, I will not say it again. See 1935 (С)*

Cf.: He who has ears let him hear (Am.). Must I tell you a tale and find your ears too ? (Br.). Wake up and smell the coffee (Am.)

355. Глядит овцой, а пахнет волком. *The man only looks friendly or harmless, but he is really an ill-doer. See 294 (В)*

Cf.: The cross on the breast, and the devil in the heart (Br.). The devil lurks (sits) behind the cross (Br.). Outwardly a lamb, inwardly a wolf (Am.). Vice is often clothed in virtue's habit (Br.). Vice knows she's ugly, so she puts on her mask (Am.)

356. Гнев—плохой советчик. *A man, when he is angry, cannot judge things in a sensible way. See 848 (К)*

Cf.: Anger and haste hinder a good

counsel (Br.). Anger and haste hinder good counsel (Am.). Anger and love give bad counsel (Am.). Fire in the heart sends smoke into the head (Am., Br.). A man in passion rides a mad (wild) horse (Am.). Sleep with your anger (Am.)

357. Гни дерево, пока гнётся; учи дитятко, пока слушается. *It is when children are very little that they should be brought up properly. See 1463 (Н)*

Var.: Гни дерево, пока молодо; учи ребёнка, пока мал

Cf.: Bend the twig while it is still green (Am.). Bend the willow (the tree) while it's young (Am.). Best to bend while it is a twig (Br.). A tree must be bent while it is young (Br.). You may bend a sapling, but never a tree (Am.)

358. Говорил горшку котелок: уж больно ты чёрен, дружок! *See 2334 (Ч)*

Cf.: It's the shovel that laughs at the poker (Am.). The kettle called the pot smutty (Am.). The kettle calls the pot black (Br.). The kettle should not call the pot black (Am.). The pot calling (calls) the kettle black (Am., Br.)

359. Говори меньше, умнее будешь. *You will learn more by listening to others than by talking yourself. See 936 (К)*

Cf.: From hearing comes wisdom (Br.). He is a wise man (wise) who speaks little (Am.). He knows most who speaks least (Am., Br.). He knows much who knows how to hold his tongue (Br.). A still mouth makes a wise head (Am.). A still tongue makes a wise head (Am., Br.)

360. Говорит бело, а делает черно. *See 1170 (М)*

Cf.: Fine words dress ill deeds (Br.). A saint's words and a cat's claws (Br.). There are daggers behind men's smiles (Am.). Too much courtesy, too much craft (Am.)

361. Говорить, так договаривать. *If you start telling something, you have to finish. See 652 (З)*

Cf.: Let him that begins the song make an end (Br.). Never say A without saying B (Am.)

362. Говорят, что за морем кур доят. *I do not believe the wonders you or someone else is telling about*

Var.: Говорят, что в Москве кур доят, а коровы яйца несут

Cf.: The biggest liar in the world is they say (Am.). "They say" is a /tough old/ liar (Am.). "They say so" is half a liar (Br.). "They say so" is half a lie (Am., Br.)

363. Год на год не приходится. *Things are going worse now than before. See 1817 (Р)*

Var.: Год году не равен

Cf.: Some days are darker than others (Am.). There are no two years alike (Br.)

364. Годы хребет горбят. *When a man gets old, he suffers from the infirmities of his age, he becomes weak. See 1248 (Н), 2003 (С), 2107 (У)*

Cf.: Age breeds aches (Am.). The feet are slow when the head wears snow (Am., Br.). An old ass is never good (Br.)

365. Голова не колышек, не шапку на неё вешать. *Our head is given to us to think*

Var.: Не для шапки только голова на плечах

Cf.: Use your head for something besides a hat rack (Am.)

366. Голова что чан, а ума ни на капустный кочан. *See 97 (Б)*

Var.: Голова с короб, а ум с орех. Голова с лукошко, а мозгу ни крошки. Голова-то есть, да в голове-то нет

Cf.: A big head and little wit (Br.). Big head and little wit (Am.). Big head, little sense (Am.). Mickle head, little wit (Br.). Muckle head, little wit (Am.)

367. Голод и волка из лесу гонит. *When a man is hungry, he will leave his home to search for food. See 1496 (Н)*

Var.: Гонит голод и волка из колка

Cf.: Hunger causes the wolf to sally from the wood (Am.). Hunger drives the wolf out of the wood (Br.). Hunger fetches the wolf out of the wood (Am., Br.)

368. Голод—лучший повар. *Those really hungry are not particular about what they eat. See 373 (Г), 374 (Г)*

Cf.: Appetite furnishes the best sauce (Am.). For a good appetite there is no hard bread (Am.). Hunger finds no fault with cookery (is a good cook) (Br.). Hunger is a good kitchen (the best sauce) (Am., Br.). Hunger is good meat (the best relish) (Br.). Hunger is the best cook (pickle) (Am.). Hunger makes hard beans sweet (Am., Br.). Hunger never saw bad bread (Am.). Hunger sweetens what is bitter (Am.). Hungry dogs will eat dirty puddings (Am., Br.). A hungry horse makes a clean manger (Br.)

369. Голод не тётка, калачика не подложит. *Strained circumstances will force a man to yield to necessity or to act against his will. See 1498 (Н), 1499 (Н), 1992 (С)*

Var.: Голод не тётка, пирожка не подсунет. Голод не тёща, блины не поднесёт

Cf.: Need makes a naked man run (Am.). Need makes the naked man run (Br.). Need makes the old wife trot (Am., Br.). Need must when necessity drives (Am.)

370. Голодное брюхо ко всему глухо. *A hungry man will listen to no reasoning. See 371 (Г)*

Var.: У голодного брюха нет уха

Cf.: The belly has no (wants) ears (Br.). Hungry bellies have no ears (Am., Br.). A hungry stomach has no ears (Am.). It is no use preaching to a hungry man (Br.)

371. Голодное брюхо к учению глухо. *A hungry person is reluctant to study. See 370 (Г)*

Cf.: The belly has no ears (Br.). Lean belly never feeds a fat brain (Am.)

372. Голодной курице просо снится. *A man in need of something keeps thinking about it. See 878 (К), 1022 (Л), 1409 (Н), 1957 (С)*

Var.: Голодной куме хлеб на уме

Cf.: The ass dreams of thistles (Br.). The hungry man often talks of bread (Am.)

373. Голодному Федоту и репа в охоту. *See 368 (Г)*

Cf.: Hunger never saw bad bread (Am.). Hunger sweetens what is bitter (Am.). A hungry horse makes a clean manger (Br.). Monkeys in hard times eat red peppers (Am.). To the hungry soul, every bitter thing is sweet (Am., Br.)

374. Голодный волк и завёртки рвёт. *See 368 (Г)*

Cf.: Hunger is a good kitchen (the best sauce) (Am., Br.). Hunger makes hard beans sweet (Am., Br.). Hunger never saw bad bread (Am.)

375. Голой овцы не стригут. *You can take nothing from a man who has not got anything*

Cf.: It is very hard to shave an egg (Am., Br.). No man can flay a stone (Am., Br.). No one can give what he hasn't got (Am.). Sue a beggar and get a louse (Br.). Sue a beggar, and you'll get a louse (Am.). You can't draw water from a dry well (Am.). You can't get (pick, take) feathers off a toad (Am.). You can't take the shirt off a naked man (Am.). You go to a goat (an ass) for wool (Br.)

376. Голос крови не заглушить. *See 896 (К)*

Cf.: Blood is thicker than water (Am., Br.)

377. Голый разбоя не боится. *A pauper is not afraid of being robbed or of any loss. See 950 (К)*

Var.: Голому разбой не страшен. Голый—что святой, не боится беды. Мокрый дождя, а нагой разбоя не боится

Cf.: A beggar can never be bankrupt (Am., Br.). The beggar may sing before a footpad (a pickpocket) (Br.). The beggar may sing before the thief (Am., Br.). He that has nothing need fear to lose nothing (Br.). He who has nothing fears nothing (Am.). If you have nothing, you've nothing to lose (Am.). Naked men never lose anything (Am.)

378. Голь на выдумки хитра. *Lack or need of something makes men resourceful and contriving. See 1498 (Н), 1781 (П)*

Var.: Голь хитра, голь мудра, голь на выдумки пошла

Cf.: Poverty and hunger have many learned disciples (Br.). Poverty is crafty; it outwits even a fox (Br.). Poverty is the mother of all arts (Am.). Poverty is the mother of art (Br.). Poverty is the mother of invention (Am.). Poverty is the sixth sense (Am., Br.). Want makes wit (Br.)

379. Гони любовь хоть в дверь, она влетит в окно. *See 1083 (Л)*

Cf.: Love will creep where it cannot go (Am., Br.)

380. Гони природу в дверь, она влетит в окно. *See 383 (Г), 779 (К)*

Cf.: Drive nature out of the door and it will return by the window (Am.). Though you cast out nature with a fork, it will still return (Br.). Throw nature out of the door, it will come back /again/ (it will return) through the window (Br.). What is bred in the bone will not /come/ out of the flesh (Am., Br.)

381. Гора родила мышь. *Little was achieved after a great deal of efforts. (This is said ironically)*

Cf.: A mountain in labor (labored and) brought forth a mouse (Am.). The mountain /in labour/ has brought forth a mouse (Br.)

382. Гора с горой не сходится, а человек с человеком сойдётся. *People encounter at last. (You say so when coming across people unexpectedly and expressing the hope to see them again some day)*

Cf.: Friends (Men) may meet but mountains never /greet/ (Br.). Men may meet, though mountains cannot (Am.). Two men may meet, but never two mountains (Am., Br.)

383. Горбатого могила исправит. *Once a person's basic character has been formed, it cannot be changed. See 184 (В), 380 (Г), 672 (З), 715 (И), 796 (К), 892 (К), 1235 (Н), 1776 (П), 1955 (С), 2268 (Ч), 2269 (Ч), 2304 (Ч)*

Cf.: Can the Ethiopian change his colour (his skin)? (Br.). Can the leopard change his spots? (Br.). A (The) leopard cannot (does not) change his spots (Am., Br.). What is bred in the bone will not /come/ out of the flesh (Am., Br.). What's in the bone is in the marrow (Am.). You can never scare a dog from a greasy hide (Br.). You cannot make a crab walk straight (Br.). You can't take the grunt out of a pig (Am.)

384. Гордись не ростом, а умом. *It is not that a man is tall or not that matters, but whether he is clever or stupid*

Cf.: A man is (Men are) not measured by inches (Br.). Men are not to be measured by inches (Am.)

385. Гордыня до добра не доведёт. *See 556 (Д)*

Cf.: Pride goes before a fall (before destruction) (Am., Br.)

386. Горе ваше, что без масла каша. *See 2324 (Ч)*

Cf.: Another's cares will not rob you of sleep (Am.). It is easy to bear the misfortunes of others (Br.). We can always bear our neighbors' misfortunes (Am.)

387. Горе да беда с кем не была. *There is no man who has not been through some trouble in his lifetime. See 137 (В), 603 (Ж)*

Cf.: Into each (every) life some rain must fall (Am.). Tears and trouble are the lot of all (Am.). There is a crook in the lot of everyone (Br.)

388. Горе заставит—бык соловьём запоёт. *See 33 (Б)*

Cf.: Adversity is a good teacher (Br.). Need makes the naked man run and sorrow makes websters spin (Br.). There is no education like adversity (Am.)

389. Горе на двоих—полгоря. *See 390 (Г), 1209 (Н)*

Cf.: Grief divided is made lighter (Br.). Grief is lessened when imparted to others (Br.). Our sorrows are less if in our anguish we find a partner in distress (Am.). A trouble shared is a trouble halved (Br.). Trouble shared is trouble halved (Am.). Two in distress make sorrow (trouble) less (Am.). Two in distress makes sorrow less (Br.)

390. Горе на двоих—полгоря, радость на двоих—две радости. *It is easier to bear trouble if someone shares it with you, and you feel happier if someone shares your joy. See 389 (Г), 1814 (Р)*

Cf.: Happiness is not perfect until it is shared (Am.). Shared joys are doubled; shared sorrows are halved (Am.). Shared pleasures are doubled; shared griefs are halved (Am.). A sorrow shared is half a trouble, /but/ a joy that is shared is a joy made double (Br.)

391. Горе не молодит, а голову белит. *See 1323 (Н)*

Cf.: Adversity flatters no man (Am., Br.). Sorrow and an evil (an ill) life make soon an old wife (Br.)

392. Горе только одного рака красит. *See 1323 (Н)*

Cf.: Adversity flatters no man (Am., Br.)

393. Горяч блин, да скоро остыл. *The stronger a feeling or action is, the less time it lasts. See 722 (И)*

Cf.: The harder the storm, the sooner it's over (Am.). A heavy shower is soon over (Am.). The sharper the storm, the sooner 'tis over (Br.). Soon hot, soon cold (Br.)

394. Готовь летом сани, а зимой телегу. *You should have all you need ready not at the last moment, but beforehand. See 398 (Г)*

Var.: Готовь сани с весны, а колёса с осени

Cf.: Clothe thee in war, arm thee in peace (Br.). Dig the well before it rains (before you get thirsty) (Am.). In fair weather prepare for foul (Am., Br.)

395. Гречневая каша сама себя хвалит. *See 269 (В), 1849 (С)*

Cf.: Each priest praises his own relics (Br.). Every cook praises his own broth (Am., Br.). Every cook praises his own stew (Am.). /There is/ nothing like leather (Br.)

396. Грешить легко, трудно каяться. *It is much easier to commit a fault than to confess it*

Cf.: It is difficult to admit your faults (to own up to your own mistakes) (Am.). It is easy to make a mistake, hard to ask forgiveness (Am.). Repentance costs very dear (Br.)

397. Грибы ищут—по лесу рыщут. *See 182 (В)*

Cf.: The dog that trots about finds a bone (Br.). The dog that trots about finds the bone (Am.)

398. Гром не грянет—мужик не перекрестится. *You have to get ready with all you need in time but not at the last moment when you are compelled to do it. See 394 (Г), 785 (К)*

Cf.: Don't have thy cloak to make when it begins to rain (Br.). A fool wants his cloak on a rainy day (Br.). Have not the cloak to be made when it begins to rain (Am.). Thatch your roof before rainy weather; dig your well before you are thirsty (Am.). Thatch your roof before the rain begins (Am.)

399. Грязное к чистому не пристанет. *Pure and virtuous people are not easily corrupted. See 1773 (П)*

Var.: К доброму плохое не пристанет

Cf.: The sun is never the worse for shining on a dunghill (Br.). The sun is not less bright for sitting on a dunghill (Am.)

400. Грязью играть—руки марать. *When you get involved in crime, vice, or other mean business, you become dishonest. See 1451 (Н)*

Cf.: He that has to do with what is foul never comes away clean (Br.). He who scrubs every pig he sees will not long be clean himself (Br.). He who touches pitch will get black (Am.). If you play with sand, you'll get dirty (Am.). Touch pitch and you'll be defiled (Am., Br.). Who deals in dirt has foul fingers (Am.)

401. Гулять так гулять, работать так работать. *See 696 (И)*

Cf.: Play while you play, work while you work (Am.). Work is work, and play is play (Br.)

402. Гусь свинье не товарищ. *People of different social standings or nature have nothing in common. See 308 (В), 1295 b (Н), 1852 (С), 2270 (Ч)*

Var.: Волк коню не товарищ. Пеший конному не товарищ

Cf.: Everyone to his equal (Am.). Every sheep with its like (Am.). Geese with geese, women with women (Br.). Keep to your own kind (Am.). Tigers and deer do not stroll together (Am.)

Д

403. Дадут дураку честь, так не знает, где и сесть. *There is no one so arrogant and demanding as an unprincipled person. See 406 (Д)*

Cf.: Give him an inch and he'll take a mile (an ell, a yard) (Am., Br.) Give knaves an inch and they will take a yard (Br.)

404. Дадут ломоть, да заставят неделю молоть. *See 2329 (Ч)*

Cf.: Another's bread costs dear (Br.). Bitter is the bread of charity (Am). Who receives a gift sells his liberty (Br.)

405. Дай Бог тому честь, кто умеет её несть. *Hono(u)r should be given to a man who is worthy of it. See 1679 (П)*

Cf.: Give credit to whom credit is due (Am., Br.). Hono(u)r to whom hono(u)r is due (Am., Br.). Let him who deserves the palm carry it (Am.)

406. Дай волю на ноготок—он возьмёт на весь локоток. *If you grant some men a small favo(u)r, little freedom of action, they will want to get more. See 403 (Д), 408 (Д), 409 (Д), 1665 (П), 1793 (П)*

Var.: Дай с ноготок, попросят с локоток

Cf.: Give him a finger and he will take a hand (Am.). Give him an inch and he'll take a mile (an ell, a yard) (Am., Br.). Give him a ring, and he'll want your whole arm (Br.). Give knaves an inch and they will take a yard (Br.). Give the devil an inch and he will take an ell (Am.)

407. Дай глупому лошадь, он на ней и к чёрту уедет. *Some men given enough freedom of action will eventually overreach themselves, cause their* *own downfall, or cause trouble. See 650 (З)*

Cf.: Action without thought is like shooting without aim (Am.). Beggars mounted run their horse to death (Br.). Give a beggar a horse and he'll ride it to death (Am.). Give a calf rope enough and it will hang itself (Am.). Give a fool (a thief, him) enough rope /and he'll hang himself/ (Am., Br.). Give a man rope enough and he'll hang himself (Am., Br.). Set a beggar (a rogue) on horseback, and he'll ride to the devil (Br.)

408. Дай курице гряду—изроет весь огород. *See 406 (Д)*

Var.: Пусти курицу на грядку—исклюёт весь огород

Cf.: Give him an inch and he'll take a mile (an ell, a yard) (Am., Br.). Give knaves an inch and they will take a yard (Br.). Give the devil an inch and he will take an ell (Am.)

409. Дай чёрту волос, а он и за всю голову. *See 406 (Д)*

Cf.: Give him an inch and he'll take a mile (an ell, a yard) (Am., Br.). Give knaves an inch and they will take a yard (Br.). Give the devil an inch and he will take an ell (Am.)

410. Далёкая вода жажды не утолит. *That which is inaccessible is of no use or help*

Cf.: Out of reach is not worth having (Am.). Water afar won't quench a fire at hand (Br.)

411. Дали орехи белке, когда зубов не стало. *Sometimes we get what we need too late when we are unable to use it. See 1676 (П)*

Var.: Когда зубов не стало, тогда и орехи принесли

Cf.: The gods send nuts to those who have no teeth (Am., Br.). Good that comes too late is good as nothing (Am.). When a dog is drowning everyone offers him drink (Am.). When a dog is drowning every one offers him drink (Br.). When the horse is starved, you bring him oats (Br.). The wished for comes too late (Br.). Youth is wasted on the young (Am.)

412. Дал слово, держись, а не дал—крепись. *You must keep your word if you cannot refrain from promising something. See 2095 (У), 2365 (Я)*

Var.: Давши слово, держись, а не давши, крепись

Cf.: Be slow to make a promise, but swift to keep it (Am.). Be slow to promise and quick to perform (Am., Br.). An honest man's word is as good as his bond (Am., Br.). Perform whatever you promise (Am.). A promise is a debt (a promise) (Am., Br.). A promise made is a debt unpaid (Am.). Words bind men (Br.)

413. Да минует меня чаша сия. *Let this trouble or affliction be taken away that I may not be compelled to undergo it*

Cf.: Let this cup pass from me (Am., Br.)

414. Дарёному коню в зубы не смотрят. *Do not try to find, or point out defects in something freely offered to you. See 416 (Д)*

Cf.: Do not look a gift horse in the mouth (Am., Br.). Do not look a given horse in the mouth (Br.)

415. Даю голову на отсечение. *I am convinced my information is completely trustworthy*

Cf.: I'll bet my boots (my life) (Br.). I'll bet my bottom dollar (Am.). I'll eat my boots (my hat, my head) (Br.). I'll give my head for it (Br.). You bet (Am., Br.). You bet your boots (your /sweet/ life) (Am.). You can bet your shirt (Br.)

416. Дают—бери, а бьют—беги. *Do not hesitate to take what you are offered. See 414 (Д)*

Cf.: Do not look a gift horse in the mouth (Am., Br.). Never refuse a good offer (Br.). Take while the taking is good (Am.). Throw no gift again at the giver's head (Br.). When a pig is proffered, hold up the poke (Br.)

417. Дающего рука не оскудеет. *Helping others will never impoverish you*

Cf.: Alms never make poor (Br.). Giving alms never lessens the stock (Br.). No one becomes poor through giving alms (Am.). No one ever impoverished himself by almsgiving (Br.). One never loses by doing a good turn (Am.)

418. Два вора дерутся—честному польза. *When the dishonest quarrel or fight, honest men gain by it*

Cf.: The death of the wolves is the safety of the sheep (Br.). When knaves (rogues) fall out, honest men come by their own (Am., Br.). When thieves fall out, honest men come by their own (Br.). When thieves fall out, honest men get their due (Am.)

419. Дважды даёт, кто скоро даёт. *Promptness in giving, helping or doing someone a favo(u)r increases the value of the good turn. See 1422 (Н)*

Var.: Кто скоро помог, тот дважды помог

Cf.: He gives twice who gives in a trice (Br.). He gives twice who gives promptly (Am.). He gives twice who gives quickly (Am., Br.). Soon enough is well enough (Br.)

420. Два медведя в одной берлоге не живут. *Two rivals cannot get along in one place. See 179 (В), 424 (Д), 425 (Д)*

Var.: Два вора в одном лесу не уживутся. Два чёрта в одном болоте не живут

Cf.: Masters two will not do (Br.). No house was ever big enough for two women (Am.). One house cannot keep two dogs (Br.). Two cats and a mouse, two wives in a house, two dogs and a bone never agree in one (Br.). Two kings in one kingdom cannot reign (Br.). Two kitchen fires burn not on one hearth (Br.). Two sparrows on one ear of corn make an ill agreement (Br.). Two women in the same house can never agree (Am.)

421. Два сапога—пара. *One person is as bad as the other*

Var.: Гусь да гагара—два сапога пара

Cf.: All tarred with the same brush (Am., Br.). /There's/ not a pin to choose between them (Br.). They make a pair (Br.)

422. Двум господам не служат. *You cannot render your assistance to two people at the same time. See 1119 (М)*

Cf.: Between two stools one falls (goes) to the ground (Br.). Between two stools we come to the ground (Am.). Don't embark on two boats, for you'll be split and thrown on your back (Am.). Don't run with the hound and hold on to the hare (Am.). If you try to sit on two chairs, you'll sit on the floor (Am.). No man can serve two masters (Am., Br.). You cannot run with the hare and hunt with the hounds (Br.)

423. Двум смертям не бывать, а одной не миновать. *See a) 323 (Г); b) 1527 (О)*

Cf.: a) A man can die but once, go ahead and give it a try (Br.). What will be, will be (Am., Br.)

b) A man can die but once (Am.). A man can only die once (Am., Br.)

424. Двум собакам одной кости не поделить. *Two rivals will not share one thing. See 420 (Д)*

Cf.: Two dogs over one bone seldom agree (Am., Br.)

425. Двум шпагам в одних ножнах не ужиться. *See 420 (Д)*

Cf.: Two wives in a house never agree in one (Br.). Two women in the same house can never agree (Am.)

426. Дела идут—контора пишет. *Things are in progress. See 226 (В)*
Cf.: All is gas and gaiters (Am., Br.). All is well and the goose hangs high (Am.). Everything is lovely and the goose hangs high (Br.). The goose hangs high (Am.)

427. Дела, как сажа бела. *The state of things is rotten. See 435 (Д)*
Cf.: It's all up (Am., Br.). It's SNAFU (Am.). It's the pits (Am.). Life is hell (Am., Br.). None too bright, could be better (Br.). The same old seven and six (Am.). Things couldn't be worse (Am., Br.). This is a day (a week) from hell (Am.)

428. Делами славен человек. *See 1621 (О)*
Var.: Славен человек не словами, а делами
Cf.: Actions speak louder than words (Am., Br.). Judge a man by his deeds, not by his words (Am.). Man is known by his deeds (Br.)

429. Дело в шляпе. *Things proceed as planned*
Cf.: All systems are go (Am.). The devil is dead (Am.). It's all over but the shouting (Am., Br.). It's a wrap (Am.). It's in the bag (Am., Br.)

430. Дело делу учит. *See 280 (В)*
Cf.: In doing we learn (Br.). Practice makes perfect (Am., Br.). We learn to do by doing (Am.)

431. Дело мастера боится. *The job is perfect because it is done by a competent person. See 277 (В), 802 (К)*
Cf.: As is the workman, so is his work (Am.). As is the workman, so is the work (Br.). Few things are impossible to diligence and skill (Am.). He works best who knows his work (Br.). In every art it is good to have a master (Br.). Work is afraid of a resolute man (Am.)

432. Дело не медведь—в лес не уйдёт. *Work can wait. (You say this when you put off doing some work, or as a piece of advice to someone to do the same.) See 1196 (Н)*
Var.: Дело—не сено, пять лет не сгниёт. Дело не сокол, не улетит. Работа—не волк, в лес не убежит
Cf.: Business tomorrow (Br.). Don't burden today's strength with tomorrow's load (Am.). It will be here tomorrow (Am.). It will keep (Am.). Tomorrow is a new day (Am., Br.). Why do today what you can do tomorrow? (Am.)

433. Дело с бездельем не смешивай. *See 696 (И)*
Ср.: Work is work, and play is play (Br.). Work while you work, and play while you play (Am.). You can't mix business and pleasure (Am.)

434. Дело сделано. *The harm is done, it is too late to prevent the undesirable*
Cf.: The damage is done (Am., Br.). The fat is in the fire (Am., Br.). The game is lost (Am.). The game is up (Br.). It's all up! (Am.). The milk is spilled (Br.)

435. Дело—табак. *The situation is hopeless, we have completely failed. See 427 (Д)*
Cf.: All fouled up (Am.). All hope is gone (Am., Br.). All's lost (Am., Br.). It's all Betty (Am.). It's all up! (Am., Br.). It's SNAFU (Am.). It's the pits (Am.)

436. Делу—время, потехе—час. *One must first do his work, and it is spare time that should be given to fun. See 696 (И), 864 (К)*
Cf.: Business before pleasure (Am., Br.). Business first, pleasure afterwards (Br.). Duty before pleasure (Am.). Work before play (Am.). Work is done, time for fun (Br.)

437. Денег ни гроша, да слава хороша. *See 470 (Д)*

Cf.: A good name is a golden girdle (Am., Br.). A good name is better than gold (Am.). A good name is better than riches (Br.). A good reputation is more valuable than money (Am.)

438. Денежки труд любят. *You have to work hard to earn money. See 444 (Д)*
Cf.: Gold grows not on trees (Am.). Money doesn't grow on trees (Am., Br.)

439. Деньги все двери открывают. *Money is powerful and influential, and you can achieve much with it. See 684 (З), 685 (З), 687 (З)*
Cf.: An ass laden with gold climbs to the top of the castle (Br.). The golden key opens every door (Am.). A gold key opens every door (Br.). Gold rules the world (Am.). If money go before, all ways do lie open (Br.). Money is a universal language speaking any tongue (Am.). Money is power (Am., Br.). Money makes the wheels (the world) go round (Am.). Money masters all things (Am., Br.). Money runs the world (speaks) (Am.). Money talks (Am., Br.). No lock will hold against the power of gold (Br.). A rich man has the world by the tail (Am.). A silver key can open an iron lock (Am., Br.)

440. Деньги глаза слепят. *Lust for money makes men neglect morality*
Cf.: Gold dust blinds all eyes (Am.). The love of money is the root of all evil (Am., Br.)

441. Деньги к деньгам идут. *A rich man gets richer. See 319 (Г)*
Var.: Деньги к деньгам льнут
Cf.: He that has a goose will get a goose (Br.). Money begets (draws) money (Am., Br.). Money breeds money (Br.). Money comes to (gets, makes) money (Am.). Much will have more (Br.). The standing sack fills quicker (Am.). To him that has shall be given (Am.). Two pennies will creep together (Am.)

442. Деньги—крылья. *Money is spent or lost quickly. See 446 (Д)*
Var.: Денежки—крылышки
Cf.: Money calls but does not stay; it is round and rolls away (Br.). Money has wings (Am.). Money is round and rolls away (Am.). Money is round—it truckles (Br.). Riches have wings (Am., Br.)

443. Деньги не пахнут. *Money is valuable whether it was got by right or by wrong*
Cf.: Money doesn't get dirty (Am.). Money has no smell (Am., Br.)

444. Деньги не щепки, на полу не подымешь. *See 438 (Д)*
Cf.: Money doesn't grow on trees (Am., Br.)

445. Деньги пропали—ещё наживёшь, время пропало—его не вернёшь. *Time is very precious, do not waste it. See 1746 (П), 1847 (С)*
Var.: Время—не деньги, потеряешь—не найдёшь
Cf.: The greatest expense we can be at is that of our time (Am., Br.). An hour wasted can never be regained (Am.). Lost time is never found again (Am., Br.). Time lost cannot be recalled (Br.). Time wasted is time lost (Am.). What greater crime than loss of time? (Am., Br.)

446. Деньги, что вода. *See 442 (Д)*
Var.: Богатство—вода: пришла и ушла. Деньги приходят и уходят, как вода
Cf.: Money calls but does not stay; it is round and rolls away (Br.). Money is round and rolls away (Am.). Riches have wings (Am., Br.)

447. День да ночь и сутки прочь. *I live a dull life, nothing special happens*
Var.: День да ночь и сутки прочь—так и отваливаем
Cf.: Come day, go day /, God send Sunday/ (Br.). Go day, come day, God send Sunday (Am.)

448. День долог, а век короток. *One day seems to last long, but our lifetime passes quickly*

Cf.: Life is but a dream (Am.). Life is but a span (Br.). Life is short (Am., Br.)

449. День мой—век мой. *See 1526 (О)*

Var.: День наш—век наш

Cf.: Be gay today, for tomorrow you may die (Am.). Enjoy yourself: it's later than you think (Am.). Gather ye rosebuds while ye may (Am., Br.). Have fun in this life: you'll never get out of it alive (Am.). Live today, for tomorrow may not come (for tomorrow you may die) (Am.). Live today; tomorrow may be too late (Am.)

450. День придёт и заботу принесёт. *Every day has its cares*

Cf.: No day passes without grief (Br.). No day passes without some grief (Am.)

451. Дерево ценят по плодам, а человека по делам. *See 1621 (О)*

Var.: Дерево славится плодами, а человек делами. Дерево смотри в плодах, а человека в делах

Cf.: By their fruits you shall know them (Am., Br.). Judge a tree by its fruit (Am.). Man is known by his deeds (Br.). A tree is known by its fruit (Am., Br.)

452. Держи голову в холоде, живот в голоде, а ноги в тепле. *To be in good health one should not eat much, have warm shoes and not a very warm hat on in cold weather*

Cf.: A cool mouth and warm feet live long (Br.). Feed a cold and starve a fever (Am.). Keep the bowels open, the head cool, and the feet warm and a fig for the doctors (Br.)

453. Держи карман шире! *Do not hope that you will get it from me or from someone else. See 847 (К)*

Cf.: Coming, and so is Christmas (Br.). Don't hold your breath (Am.). If the sky falls, we shall catch larks (Am., Br.). If you cut down the woods, you'll catch the wolf (Br.). I've got a bit of string with a hole in it (Am., Br.). Lots of luck, Charlie! (Am.). When it rains pottage you must hold up your dish (Br.)

454. Держи порох сухим. *Keep prepared for action*

Cf.: Keep the rake near the scythe, and the cart near the rake (Am.). Keep your powder dry (Am., Br.). Keep your sails trimmed (Am.)

455. Держи рот на замке, а гляди в оба. *Keep silent but watch what is going on*

Cf.: Keep your mouth shut and your eyes open (Am., Br.)

456. Дети есть дети. *Children behave in a childish way, and they cannot be expected to act like grown up people*

Cf.: Boys will be boys (Am., Br.). Children will be children (Am.). Girls will be girls (Am.). God's lambs will play (Br.). Young colts will canter (Br.)

457. Дети не в тягость, а в радость. *To bring up a child is not a burden, it is delight*

Cf.: A babe in the house is a well-spring of pleasure (Am.). A babe in the house is a well-spring of pleasure (Br.). It takes children to make a happy family (Am.)

458. Дёшево, да гнило; дорого, да мило. *Things that cost little money are never quality things, it is better to pay a high price and buy something fine. See 459 (Д), 2197 (Х)*

Cf.: A bargain is a pinch-purse (Am.). Best is best cheap (Br.). The best is cheapest /in the end/ (Am.). Cheap goods are not good, good things are not cheap (Am.). Dear is cheap, and cheap is dear (Am., Br.). Dirt is cheap; it takes money to buy wool (Am.). A good bargain is a pick-purse (Am., Br.). What costs nothing is worth nothing (Br.). You get what you pay for (Am.)

459. Дешёвому товару—дешёвая цена. *It is only things of poor quality that are not expensive. See 458 (Д)*

Cf.: Cheap goods are not good, good things are not cheap (Am.). What costs nothing is worth nothing (Br.). You get what you pay for (Am.)

460. Дитя не плачет—мать не разумеет. *You can count on help if you complain*

Cf.: He who bewails himself has the cure in his hands (Br.). It's the crying baby that gets the milk (Am.). The squeaking wheel gets the oil (Am.). The squeaky axe (gate) gets the oil (Br.). The wheel that does the squeaking is the one that gets the grease (Am.)

461. Дитятко, что тесто: как замесил, так и выросло. *A person's personality is shaped the way he was brought up when a child*

Cf.: As the twig is bent, so grows the tree (Am.). As the twig is bent, so the tree is inclined (Am., Br.)

462. Дитя хоть и криво, да отцу-матери мило. *Parents are partial to their children. See 276 (В)*

Var.: Всякому своё дитя милее. Своё дитя и горбато, да мило

Cf.: All one's geese are swans (Am., Br.). The crow thinks her own bird fairest (Br.). The crow thinks her own bird the fairest (Am.). Each old crow thinks her young are the blackest (Am.). Every mother's duck is a swan (Am.). Every mother thinks her own gosling a swan (Br.). The owl thinks all her young ones beauties (Am.). The owl thinks her own young fairest (Br.). There's only one pretty child in the world and every mother has it (Br.)

463. Длинная нитка—ленивая швея. *It is an indolent person who uses a long thread not to thread the needle twice*

Cf.: A bad seamstress uses a long thread (Am., Br.). A long thread, a lazy tailor (Am.)

464. Для друга и семь вёрст не околица. *See 318 (Г)*

Var.: Для друга нет круга. Если мил друг, и десять вёрст—не круг. К милому и семь вёрст не околица

Cf.: For a good friend, the journey is never too long (Am.). He that has love in his breast, has spurs in his side (Br.). He who has love in his heart has spurs in his heels (Br.). To a friend's house the trail is never long (Am.)

465. Для ленивой лошади и дуга в тягость. *Any effort is hard for a lazy person to make*

Var.: Ленивой лошади и хвост в тяжесть

Cf.: It's a sorry ass that will not bear his own burden (Am.). A lazy sheep thinks its wool heavy (Am., Br.)

466. Для милого дружка и серёжка из ушка. *There is nothing you will grudge your best friend. See 508 (Д)*

Var.: Ради милого дружка и серёжка из ушка

Cf.: Anything for a friend (Am.). Friends tie their purses with a spider's web (Am.). Friends tie their purse with a cobweb thread (Br.). Love locks no cupboard (Br.)

467. Добра соль, а переложишь—рот воротит. *See 2187 (Х)*

Cf.: Even sugar itself may spoil a good dish (Am., Br.)

468. Добрая жена да жирные щи—другого добра не ищи. *A good wife and healthy food are most essential for a husband*

Cf.: A good wife and health are a man's best wealth (Am., Br.)

469. Добрая жена дом сбережёт. *A wife who is a good homekeeper is a guarantee of a family's prosperity and happiness. See 2182 (Х)*

Cf.: Where there is no wife there is no home (Am.). The wife is the key of the house (Br.). Wife make your own candle, spare penny to handle (Am.)

470. Добрая слава дороже богатства. *It is most significant what people think and say about you. See 437 (Д)*

Var.: Добрая слава лучше мягкого пирога

Cf.: Fame is better than fortune (Am.). A good name is a golden girdle (a rich heritage, better than riches) (Br.). A good name is better than gold (Am.). A good reputation is more valuable than money (Am.)

471. Добрая слава лежит, а худая бежит. *The good deeds a man does are not known of, while his mean actions become widely known. See 482 (Д), 1648 (П)*

Var.: Добрая слава в углу (за печкой) сидит, а худая по дорожке (свету) бежит. Добрая слава до порога, а худая за порог. Хорошая слава шагом плетётся, а худая вскачь несётся

Cf.: A bad deed never dies (Am.). Bad deeds follow you; the good ones flee (Am.). Good fame sleeps, bad fame creeps (Br.). A good reputation stands still; a bad one runs (Am.). Injuries are written in brass (Br.). Ten good turns lie dead, and one ill deed report abroad does spread (Br.)

472. Добро век не забудется. *See 622 (З)*

Cf.: An act of kindness is well repaid (Am.). Cast thy bread upon the waters, for thou shalt find it after many days (Br.). Cast your bread upon the water; it will return to you a hundredfold (Am.). The good that men do lives after them (Am.). A good turn goes a long way (Am.)

473. Добродетель—сама себе награда. *Satisfaction you gain from being righteous is sufficient to feel happy*

Cf.: Virtue is its own reward (Am., Br.)

474. Добро добро покрывает. *See 622 (З)*

Cf.: An act of kindness is well repaid (Am.). The good you do to others will always come back to you (Am.). The hand that gives gathers (Am., Br.)

475. Доброе дело—правду говорить смело. *See 2179 (X)*

Cp.: It pays to tell the truth (Am.). Speak the truth and shame the devil (Am., Br.). Speak the truth bravely, cost as it may; hiding the wrong act is not the way (Am.). Tell the truth and shame the devil (Am., Br.). The truth always pays (Am.)

476. Доброе дело само себя хвалит. *People will appreciate all your good deeds, you do not need to talk about them*

Cf.: The deed will praise itself (Am.). Good actions speak for themselves, they need no tin horn (Am.)

477. Доброе начало полдела откачало. *A piece of work started in a proper way is not likely to go wrong. See 656 (З), 1799 (П)*

Var.: Доброе начало—половина дела. Хорошее начало полдела откачало

Cf.: A good beginning is half the battle (Am., Br.). A good beginning is half the business (the task) (Am.). A good lather is half a shave (Br.). A good outset is half the voyage (the way) (Br.). A good start is half the race (Am.). A job started right is a job half done (Am.). Well begun is half done (Am., Br.). Well lathered, half shaved (Am.). Work well begun is half ended (Am.)

478. Доброе семя—добрый и всход. *See 1615 (О)*

Cf.: The fruit of a good tree is also good (Am.). A good seed makes a good crop (Am.). He that sows good seed, shall reap good corn (Br.)

479. Доброму вору всё впору. *Anything is welcome that comes your way and can be made use of. See 264 (В)*

Cf.: All is fish that comes to the net (Br.). All is grist that comes to the mill (Br.). All is grist /that goes/ to his mill (Am.). All's fish that comes to his net (Am.)

480. Доброму добрая память. *An honest man will be ever remembered with respect*

Cf.: A good name will shine forever (Am.). He that sows virtue, reaps fame (Br.)

481. Добро помни, а зло забывай. *Never forget good turns, but forgive the evil done to you*

Cf.: Neglect will kill an injury sooner than revenge (Br.). Remedy for injuries is not to remember them (Br.). Write injuries in dust, but kindness in marble (Am.)

482. Добро скоро забывается. *Men tend to forget good turns done to them but remember the evil ones. See 471 (Д)*

Var.: Лихо помнится, а добро забывается. Худое долго помнится, а хорошее скоро забудется

Cf.: Acts of kindness are soon forgotten, but the memory of an offence remains (Br.). Bad deeds follow you; the good ones flee (Am.). Eaten bread is soon forgotten (Am., Br.)

483. Добрые вести не лежат на месте. *It does not take long for good news to become known*

Cf.: Good news travels fast (Am.)

484. Добрые слова лучше мягкого пирога. *See 985 (Л)*

Var.: Добрые слова лучше сладкого пирога

Cf.: All doors /are/ open to courtesy (Br.). Fair and soft (softly) goes far / in a day/ (Br.). Fair and softly go far in a day (Am.). Fair words make the pot boil (Am.). A kind word goes a long way (Am.). A kind word is never lost (Br.). Mouth civility is no great pains but may turn to a good account (Br.)

485. Добрый друг лучше ста родственников. *Friends are more reliable and compassionate than relatives*

Cf.: Father is a treasure, brother is a comfort but a friend is both (Br.). Friends are to be preferred to relatives (Am.). A good friend is better than a hundred relatives (Am.). A good friend is my nearest relation (Am., Br.). A good friend is worth more than a hundred relatives (Br.)

486. Добрый повар стоит доктора. *To enjoy good health you should eat wholesome food*

Cf.: Diet cures more than the doctor (Am., Br.). Diet cures more than the knife (the lancet) (Br.). Kitchen physic is the best physic (Br.)

487. Добрый совет ко времени хорош. *Good counsel is of use if it is given when neded, but not after that. See 503 (Д)*

Var.: Совет хорош вовремя

Cf.: Advice after mischief is taken like medicine after death (Am.). Advice comes too late when a thing is done (Am.). Advice is handy only before trouble comes (Am.). Advice should precede the act (Am., Br.). When a thing is done, advice comes too late (Br.). A word before is worth two after (Am., Br.). A word before is worth two behind (Am.)

488. Добрый совет на примету бери. *Good advice should be taken into consideration*

Cf.: Counsel must be followed not praised (Am., Br.). If the counsel is good, take it, even from a fool (Am.)

489. Доведётся и нам свою песенку спеть. *See 106 (Б)*

Cf.: Every dog has his day (Am., Br.). We shall have our day too (Br.)

490. Доверяй, да проверяй. *You should not place confidence in a man before you are sure he is honest and reliable. See 1978 (C)*

Cf.: First try and then trust (Br.). If you trust before you try, you may repent before you die (Br.). Test before trusting (Am.). Trust, but not too much (Br.). Try before you trust (Am., Br.)

491. Довольствуйся тем, что имеешь. *If you are satisfied with what you have and do not envy others, you will be happy. See 1433 (H)*

Cf.: Be content with what you have (Am.). A contented mind is a continual feast (Am., Br.). Contentment is better than riches (Am.). Enough is great riches (Am., Br.). The greatest wealth is contentment with a little (Br.). He is rich enough that wants nothing (who is contented with little) (Br.). He is rich who does not desire more (Am.). Richest is he who wants least (Am.). Since we cannot get what we like, let us like what we can get (Am.). To be content with little is true happiness (Am.)

492. Догадался, как проигрался. *You realize what should have been done or said when it is too late. See 620 (З), 1730 (П)*

Cf.: After the danger everyone is wise (Am.). Wise after the event (Br.)

493. Долги помнит не тот, кто берёт, а кто даёт. *The man who lends remembers it, but he who borrows forgets about it*

Cf.: Creditors have better memories than debtors (Am., Br.)

494. Долг не ревёт, а спать не даёт. *When you owe something, you feel depressed*

Cf.: Debt is a heavy burden to an honest man (Am.). Debts make the cheek black (Br.). A man in a debt is caught in a net (Am.)

495. Долго выбирать—замужем не бывать. *A too fastidious person will never find a spouse*

Var.: Много выбирать—женатым не бывать

Cf.: The girl that thinks no man is good enough for her is right, but she's left (Am.). If you always say "No", you will never be married (Br.). If you want to stay single, look for a perfect woman (Am.)

496. Долг платежом красен. *Help received ought to be repaid. See 2117 (У), 2148 (У)*

Cf.: One good turn deserves another (Am., Br.)

497. Дома и солома едома. *See 126 (B)*

Var.: Дома и солома съедобна

Cf.: Dry bread at home is better than roast meat abroad (Am., Br.). Home is home though it be never so homely (Am., Br.). There is no place like home (Am., Br.)

498. Дома и стены помогают. *When at home, you know better how to overcome your difficulties*

Var.: В своей хате и углы помогают. Хозяину и стены помогают

Cf.: At home everything is easy (Am.). There is no place like home (Am., Br.)

499. Домашняя копейка лучше заезжего рубля. *One's own possession, be it very modest, is more valuable than another man's riches. See 500 (Д), 1862 (C)*

Cf.: Dry bread at home is better than roast meat abroad (Am., Br.)

500. Домашний телёнок лучше заморской коровы. *See 499 (Д), 1862 (C)*

Cf.: Dry bread at home is better than roast meat abroad (Am., Br.)

501. Дом с детьми—базар, без детей—могила. *Without children you live a quiet but miserable life*

Cf.: He that has no children knows not what is love (Br.). The house without children is a cemetery (Am.)

502. Дорога в ад вымощена благими намерениями. *Good motives may have harmful results*

Cf.: /The road to / hell is paved with good intentions (Am., Br.). The way to hell is paved with good intentions (Am.)

503. Дорога ложка к обеду. *That is valuable which you get or is done for you when you need it. See 247 (В), 487 (Д), 504 (Д), 506 (Д)*

Cf.: Everything is good in its season (Br.). Fast enough is well enough (Am., Br.). Good that comes too late is good as nothing (Am.). A word before is worth two after (Am., Br.)

504. Дорога помощь в пору. *See 503 (Д), 1542 (О)*

Cf.: Fast enough is well enough (Am., Br.). Good that comes too late is good as nothing (Am.). Slow help is no help (Br.). A word before is worth two after (Am., Br.)

505. Дороги не ищут, а спрашивают. *When trying to find a way to solve a problem, you should not be self-reliant only; not to fail you must ask experienced people for advice*

Cf.: Better ask than lose your way (Br.). Better ask twice than lose yourself once (Am.). Better to ask than go astray (Br.). It is better to ask twice than to go wrong once (Am.)

506. Дорого яичко к Христову дню. *See 503 (Д)*

Var.: Дорого яичко к великому (светлому) дню

Cf.: Everything is good in its season (Br.). Good that comes too late is good as nothing (Am.). A word before is worth two after (Am., Br.). A word before is worth two behind (Am.)

507. Дорогу осилит идущий. *Success comes with tenacity. See 906 (К)*

Cf.: It is dogged as (that) does it (Am., Br.). One can only do by doing (Am.). Plodding wins the race (Am.). The race is got by running (Br.). To do, one must be doing (Br.). We learn by doing, achieve by pursuing (Am.). You must run to win the race (Am.)

508. Друга иметь—себя не жалеть. *When a friend needs your help, you must do for him what you can without any delay. See 466 (Д)*

Cf.: Anything for a friend (Am.). When a friend asks, there is no tomorrow (Am., Br.)

509. Друга узнать—вместе пуд соли съесть. *See 108 (Б)*

Var.: Друга узнать—куль соли съесть

Cf.: Before you choose (make) a friend, eat a bushel of salt with him (Br.). Before you make a friend eat a peck of salt with him (Am.)

510. Друг до поры—тот же недруг. *When a friendship is broken, a person who was not your real friend gets hostile to you*

Var.: Друг до поры хуже недруга. Раздружится друг—хуже недруга

Cf.: False friends are worse than bitter enemies (Br.). False friends are worse than open enemies (Am., Br.). He that ceases to be a friend, never was one (Am.). Never trust a broken staff (Am.). A treacherous friend is the most dangerous enemy (Br.)

511. Других не суди, на себя погляди. *People whose own conduct is open to criticism should not criticize others. See 1087 (Л), 1128 (М), 1247 (Н), 1288 (Н), 1405 (Н), 1459 (Н), 1798 (П), 2334 (Ч)*

Var.: Не кивай на соседа, а гляди (погляди) на себя

Cf.: Before healing others, heal yourself (Am.). He that mocks a cripple, ought to be whole (Br.). People living in glass houses should not throw stones (Am., Br.). People who live in glass houses shouldn't throw stones

(Am.). Physician, heal thyself (Am., Br.). Point not at others' spots with a foul finger (Am.)

512. Друг не испытанный—что орех не сколотый. *You can never be sure if you have a true friend until he is tried in adversity*

Var.: Друг не испытанный—что орех не расколотый

Cf.: A friend is never known till a man has need (until needed) (Am.). A friend is never known till a man have need (till needed) (Br.)

513. Друг спорит, а недруг поддакивает. *A true friend is not a yes-man, whereas a false friend will never tell you when you are wrong*

Cf.: All are not friends that speak us fair (Am., Br.). I cannot be your friend and your flatterer (Am., Br.). If he is your flatterer, he can't be your friend (Am.). They love us truly who correct us freely (Br.)

514. Дружба—дружбой, а денежкам счёт. *In spite of close relations people should be accurate when it concerns money*

Var.: Дружба—дружбой, а денежки врозь

Cf.: Brotherly love for brotherly love, but cheese for money (Am.)

515. Дружба—дружбой, а служба—службой. *Sentiment or friendship should not influence business relations. See 1738 (П)*

Cf.: Business is business (Am., Br.). Business is business, and love is love (Am.)

516. Дружба что стекло: сломаешь—не починишь. *See 1718 (П)*

Var.: Дружба как стекло: разобьёшь—не сложишь

Cf.: A broken friendship may be soldered but will never be sound (Am.). Broken friendships may be soldered, but never sound (Br.)

517. Дружно—не грузно, а врозь—хоть брось. *See 139 (В), 1520 (О)*

Cf.: Let us all hang together or hang separately (Am.). One man is no man (Br.). Stick together or get stuck separately (Am.). Two hands are better than one (Am.). United we stand, divided we fall (Am., Br.)

518. Дружные сороки и гуся утащут. *See 130 (В)*

Var.: Дружные сороки и гуся съедят. Дружные чайки и ястреба забьют

Cf.: Union is strength (Am., Br.)

519. Дружный табун волков не боится. *There is protection afforded by co-operative efforts. See 130 (В)*

Cf.: In unity there is strength (Am.). Union is strength (Am., Br.)

520. Друзей-то много, да друга нет. *You can be on friendly terms with many people and still without a single true friend*

Cf.: He who has many friends has no friends (Am.). Many acquaintances, but few friends (Am., Br.)

521. Друзья познаются в беде. *A friend who remains loyal to you in adversity is a true friend. See 867 (К), 1446 (Н), 1353 (Н)*

Var.: Друг познаётся в беде. Друзья познаются в несчастье

Cf.: Adversity is the test of friendship (Am.). A friend in need is a friend indeed (Am., Br.). A friend is best found in adversity (Am.). A friend is never known till a man has need (until needed) (Am.). A friend is never known till a man have need (till needed) (Br.). Friends are made in wine and proved in tears (Br.). Prosperity makes friends, and adversity tries them (Br.). Prosperity makes friends; adversity tries them (Am.)

522. Дуракам везёт. *The stupid that least deserve it are fortunate. See 543 (Д)*

Var.: Дуракам всё счастье. Счастье дураков любит

Cf.: Fools are lucky (Am., Br.). Fools for luck (Br.). Fortune favo(u)rs fools (Am., Br.). God sends fortune to fools (Br.). The worse knave, the better luck (Br.). You don't need brains if you have luck (Am.)

523. Дуракам закон не писан. *Foolish or reckless men act contrary to common sense*

Cf.: Fools rush in where angels fear to tread (Am., Br.)

524. Дуракам полработы не показывают. *Incompetent people ought not to be shown an unfinished piece of work because they are unable to envision what it will be like when completed*

Cf.: Fools and bairns should not see half-done work (things half-done) (Br.). Never show a fool a half-done job (Am.)

525. Дуракам счёту нет. *Fools are numerous. See 1211 (Н)*

Cf.: A fool is born every minute (Am.). Fools go in crowds (Am., Br.). If all fools wore feathers (white caps), we should seem a flock of geese (Br.). If all fools wore white caps, we'd all look like geese (Am.). If every fool held a bauble, fuel would be dear (Br.). There is one born every minute (Br.). There's a sucker born every minute (Am., Br.). The world is full of fools (Am., Br.)

526. Дурака учить, что мёртвого лечить. *See 541 (Д)*

Var.: Мёртвого не вылечишь, а дурака не выучишь

Cf.: Fools will be fools (Br.). Fools will be fools still (Am.)

527. Дурак времени не знает. *Fools do not wait for the appropriate time to act or to speak*

Cf.: A fool always rushes to the fore (Br.). A fool talks when he should be listening (Am.)

528. Дурак врёт, врёт, да и правду скажет. *See 739 (И)*

Var.: Дурак врёт, врёт, да и правду соврёт

Cf.: A fool may give a wise man counsel (Am.). A fool may sometimes speak to the purpose (Br.). A fool's bolt may sometimes hit the mark (Br.)

529. Дурак дом построил, а умный купил. *Work is done by one person, but someone else enjoys the benefit. See 1114 (М)*

Cf.: Asses fetch the oats and the horses eat them (Br.). Fools build houses and wise men buy them (Br.). Fools build houses for wise men to live in (Am.). Fools lade the water, and wise men catch the fish (Br.). Fools make feasts and wise men eat them (Am., Br.). One beats the bush, and another catches the birds (has the hare) (Br.). One man makes the chair, and another man sits in it (Br.). One /man/ sows and another reaps (Br.). One man works, and another reaps the benefits (Am.). What one man sows another man reaps (Am.)

530. Дурак дурака хвалит. *One fool flatters another*

Cf.: A fool always finds a bigger fool to praise him (Am.). One fool praises another (Am., Br.)

531. Дурак-дурак, а себе на уме. *You think the man is a simpleton, but he knows very well what is beneficial for him. See 775 (К)*

Var.: Дурак-дурак, а хитрый

Cf.: Everyone is witty for his own purpose (Br.). Everyone speaks for his own interest (Am.). Half a fool, half a knave (Br.)

532. Дурак дураком останется. *See 541 (Д)*

Cf.: Fools will be fools (Br.). Fools will be fools still (Am.).

533. Дурак завяжет узел—умный не скоро развяжет. *See 535 (Д)*

Var.: Умный не всегда развяжет /то/, что глупый завяжет

Cf.: Fools tie knots, and wise men loosen them (Am.). Fools tie knots, and wise men loose them (Br.)

534. Дураки о добыче спорят, а умные её делят. *While some men are disputing their right to something, others get hold of it*

Cf.: Two dogs fight (strive) for a bone, and a third runs away with it (Br.). Two dogs fight over a bone, while the third always runs away with the bone (Am.)

535. Дурак кинет в воду камень, а десять умных не вынут. *One fool creates problems which many wise men have to solve. See 353 (Г), 533 (Д)*

Var.: Дурак в воду камень закинет, десятеро умных не вытащат. Один глупый камень в море бросит, а сто умных не вынут

Cf.: A fool may throw a stone into a well which a hundred wise men cannot pull out (Br.). Fools set stools for wise folks to stumble at (Br.). Fools set stools for wise men to fall over (to stumble) (Am.). Fools tie knots, and wise men loosen them (Am.). Fools tie knots, and wise men loose them (Br.)

536. Дурак кричит, умный молчит. *See 350 (Г)*

Cf.: Full vessels give the least sound (Br.). He who knows does not speak; he who speaks does not know (Am.). Knowledge talks lowly; ignorance talks loudly (Am.). People who know little talk much; people who know much talk little (Am.). A wise head makes a close mouth (Br.). The wise man keeps his own counsel (Am., Br.). Wise men have their mouths in their heart, fools their heart in their mouth (Br.). Wise men silent, fools talk (Br.)

537. Дурак, кто с дураком свяжется. *Never have anything to do with a fool*

Var.: Свяжись с дураком, сам дурак будешь. С дураком связаться — не развязаться

Cf.: Arguing with a fool shows there are two (Am., Br.). Fool is he who deals with a fool (Br.). A fool is he who deals with other fools (Am.). He is an ass that brays against another ass (Br.). He is not the fool that the fool is but he that with the fool deals (Br.). If an ass (a donkey) bray at you, don't bray at him (Br.). If you argue with a fool, that makes two fools arguing (Am.)

538. Дурак не дурак, а от роду так. *See 539 (Д)*

Cf.: Foolishness grows by itself — no need to sow it (Am.). Fools are born, not made (Br.). Once a fool, always a fool (Am.)

539. Дураков не сеют, не жнут — сами родятся. *If one is a fool, he is a fool from the cradle. See 538 (Д)*

Var.: Дураков не орут, не сеют — сами родятся

Cf.: Foolishness grows by itself — no need to sow it (Am.). Fools are born, not made (Br.). Fools grow of themselves without sowing or planting (Br.). Fools grow without watering (Am., Br.). Weeds need no sowing (Am.). Weeds want no sowing (Am., Br.)

540. Дураком на свете жить — ни о чём не тужить. *Fools never feel miserable*

Cf,: Children and fools have merry lives (Am., Br.). A fool's head never grows white (Am.)

541. Дураком родился — дураком и помрёшь. *A fool will never grow wise. See 526 (Д), 532 (Д), 1803 (П), 2236 (Ч)*

Cf.: Folly is an incurable disease (Am.). Folly is the most incurable of maladies (Br.). Fools will be fools (Br.). Fools will be fools still (Am.). He who is born a fool is never cured (Am., Br.). Live a fool, die a fool (Am.). Once a fool, always a fool (Am.). There is no cure for folly (Br.)

542. Дурак сам скажется. *Folly betrays itself. See 1566 (О)*

Cf.: A fool is known by his conversation (Am.). A fool is known by his laughing (Br.). A fool is known by his speech (Am.). A fool's bolt is soon shot (Am., Br.). Fools need no passport (Br.)

543. Дурак спит, а счастье в головах лежит. *See 522 (Д)*

Var.: Дурак спит, а счастье /у него/ в головах сидит (стоит)

Cf.: Fools have fortune (Br.). Fortune favo(u)rs fools (Am., Br.). Good comes to some while they are sleeping (Am.)

544. Дураку всегда компания найдётся. *There are enough fools, and they easily make one another's company*

Cf.: A fool always finds another fool (Am.). Fools go in crowds (Am., Br.)

545. Дураку всё смех на уме. *Fools are always laughing, they are never serious. See 1941 (С)*

Cf.: It's a trifle that makes fools laugh (Am.). Too much laughter discovers folly (Br.)

546. Дураку семь вёрст не крюк. *See 624 (З)*

Cf.: Little wit in the head makes much work for the feet (Am., Br.)

547. Дурная слава накрепко пристаёт. *It is difficult to get rid of an ill reputation. See 549 (Д), 996 (Л), 1819 (Р)*

Var.: Дурная кличка накрепко пристаёт

Cf.: Give a dog a bad name and hang him (Am., Br.). Give a dog a bad name /, and his work is done/ (Br.). Give a dog a bad name, and it will stay with him (Am.). Glass, china, and reputation are easily cracked and never well mended (Am.). He that has an ill name is half hanged (Br.). He who has a bad name is half hanged (Am.). A wounded reputation is seldom cured (Am.)

548. Дурни думкой богатеют. *Stupid people dream of, or believe in the realization of their groundless hopes or projects*

Var.: Дурак думой богатеет

Cf.: As the fool thinks, so the bell clinks (Br.). Dreams give wings to fools (Am.). Fools are fain of nothing (Br.). Show him an egg and instantly the whole air is full of feathers (Br.)

549. Дурное слово, что смола: пристанет—не отлепится. *See 547 (Д)*

Cf.: Give a dog a bad name and hang him (Am., Br.)

550. Дурные вести не лежат на месте. *Reports of misfortunes always reach us quickly. See 2189 (Х)*

Var.: Дурная весть имеет крылья. Худые вести не лежат на месте

Cf.: Bad news has wings (Br.). Bad news travels fast (Am., Br.). Ill news comes apace (Am., Br.). Ill news flies (travels apace) (Br.). Ill news travels fast (Am., Br.)

551. Дурные примеры заразительны. *See 1904 (С)*

Var.: Плохие примеры заразительны

Cf.: Evil communications corrupt good manners (Am., Br.). An evil lesson is soon learnt (Am.). Nothing is so infectious as example (Am.). That which is evil is soon learned (Am., Br.)

552. Дух бодр, да плоть немощна. *Man would do much, but he is not always strong enough to fulfil it. See 754 (И)*

Cf.: The spirit is willing, but the flesh is weak (Am., Br.)

553. Дым столбом, а огня не видно. *See 1143 (М)*

Cf.: Great cry but little wool (Am.). Much smoke, little fire (Br.). Much talk, little work (Am.)

554. Дым с чадом сошёлся. *See 1267 (Н)*

Cf.: Diamond cuts diamond (Am., Br.). Iron cuts iron (Am.). When Greek meets Greek, then comes the tug of war (Am., Br.)

555. Дышите глубже. *Do not take it close to heart. See 610 (З)*

Var.: Дышите глубоко

Cf.: Breathe easy (Am.). Relax and enjoy it (Am.). Take a deep breath (Am.). Take it easy (Am., Br.)

556. Дьявол гордился, да с неба свалился. *Sooner or later, a man's pride has a rebuff. See 301 (В), 385 (Г), 1341 (Н)*

Var.: Сатана гордился—и с неба свалился.

Cf.: Pride goes before a fall (Am., Br.). Pride goes before, and shame follows after (Am., Br.). Pride goes before destruction (Am., Br.). Pride goes forth on horseback grand and gay, and comes back on foot and begs its way (Am.). Pride must suffer pain (Br.)

557. Дядя, достань воробышка. *You are so tall. (This is said as a joke to a tall man)*

Var.: Дядя, поймай воробышка

Cf.: How is it up there? (Am.). How's the weather up there? (Am.). Is it cold up there? (Br.)

558. Дятел и дуб продалбливает. *See 830 (К)*

Cf.: Little strokes fell big oaks (Br.). Little strokes fell great oaks (Am., Br.). Small strokes cut down the oaks (fell big oaks) (Am.). With many strokes is an oak overthrown (Br.)

Е

559. Едешь на день, хлеба бери на неделю. *Take extra food when you go to some place where you can get none, because you may stay there longer than you are planning*

Cf.: Who goes for a day into the forest should take bread for a week (Am.)

560. Если бы, да кабы, да во рту росли грибы, тогда бы был не рот, а целый огород. *(Said ironocally.) You would be or would have been successful if nothing impeded or had impeded. See 115 (Б), 562 (Е), 759 (К), 761 (К), 762 (К), 763 (К), 764 (К), 765 (К)*

Var.: Если бы, да кабы /, во рту росли б грибы (бобы)/

Cf.: If "ifs" and "ands" were pots and pans /there would be no need for tinkers (tinkers' hands)/ (Am.). If ifs and ans were pots and pans /there'd be no trade for tinkers/ (Br.). If my aunt had been a man, she'd have been my uncle (Am., Br.). If pigs had wings, they would be angels (Br.). "Ifs" and "buts" butter no bread (Am.). If wishes were horses, beggars might (would) ride (Am., Br.). Were it not for the bone in the leg, all would be carpenters (Br.)

561. Если бы молодость знала, если бы старость могла. *Young people are unexperienced; old people have experience, but they are too weak to make use of it*

Var: Если бы молодость умела, а старость могла

Cf.: If the young knew, if the old could, there's nothing but would be done (Br.). If the young man would and the old man could, there would be nothing undone (Am.). If youth but knew and age but could do (Am.). If youth but knew, if age but could (Br.)

562. Если бы на горох не мороз, он давно бы через тын перерос. *See 560 (Е)*

Var.: Если б не мороз, то овёс бы до неба дорос

Cf.: If "ifs" and "ands" were pots and pans /, there would be no need for tinkers (tinkers' hands)/ (Am.). If ifs and ans were pots and pans /, there'd be no trade for tinkers/ (Br.). If the sky falls (fall), we shall catch larks (Am., Br.)

563. Если вода не течёт за тобою, иди ты за водою. *See 564 (Е)*

Cf.: If the mountain will not come (won't go) to Mahomet (Mohammed), Mahomet (Mohammed) must go to the mountain (Am., Br.). Mohammed has to go to the mountain—the mountain will not come to him (Am.)

564. Если гора не идёт к Магомету, то Магомет идёт к горе. *If the man you need does not come to see you, you must put aside your pride and go and see him. See 563 (Е)*

Cf.: If the mountain will not come (won't go) to Mahomet (Mohammed), Mahomet (Mohammed) must go to the mountain (Am., Br.). Mohammed has to go to the mountain—the mountain will not come to him (Am.)

565. Если не везёт, так не везёт. *See 132 (В), 857 (К)*

Cf.: Bread always falls buttered side down (Am.). The bread always falls on the buttered side (Am.). The bread (The cake) never falls but on its buttered side (Br.). A man born to misfortune will fall on his back and fracture his nose (Am.)

566. Если танцевать не умеешь, не говори, что каблуки кривые. *See 1111 (М)*

Cf.: A bad worker finds fault with his tools (Br.). A bad workman quarrels with his tools (Am., Br.). If you don't know how to dance, you say that the drum is bad (Am.)

567. Ест тихо и работает не лихо. *See 820 (К)*

Cf.: A man eats so he works (Am.). Slow at meat, slow at work (Br.)

568. Есть болезнь, есть и лекарство. *In any difficult situation a way out can be found*

Var.: На всякую хворь найдётся лекарство

Cf.: Every sore has its salve (Am.). There's a salve for every sore (Am., Br.)

569. Есть в мошне, так будет и в квашне. *He who has money will have food to eat*

Cf.: Money makes the pot boil (Am., Br.)

570. Есть—горько, бросить—жалко. *I am already full, but I cannot help eating up all the food that is served. See 1047 (Л), 1369 (Н), 2027 (С), 2204 (Х)*

Var.: Горько есть, да жалко покинуть

Cf.: Better belly burst than good victuals wasted (Br.). Better the belly burst than good drink (meat) lost (Br.). It's better a belly burst than good food wasted (Am.)

571. Есть ещё порох в пороховницах. *One is still strong, energetic, and enthusiastic enough to go on working, struggling, trying to achieve success, etc. See 596 (Ж)*

Cf.: Alive and kicking (Am., Br.). Live and well (Am.). There is life in the old dog yet (Am., Br.). There is life in the old horse yet (Br.). There is plenty of shot in the locker (Br.)

572. Есть пирожки—есть и дружки; нет пирожков—нет и дружков. *See 1901 (С)*

Cf.: As long as the pot boils, friendship lasts (Am., Br.). The dinner over, away go the guests (Am.). Feast and your halls are crowded (Am.)

573. Есть чем звякнуть, так можно и крякнуть. *When you have money, you feel confident to give your opinion, and everything you say is accepted as being clever or witty*

Cf.: A full purse makes a mouth speak (Am.). He that has money in his purse cannot want a head for his shoulders (Br.). Money makes the man (Am., Br.). A rich man's joke is always funny (Am., Br.). Success makes a fool seem wise (Am., Br.). Wealth makes worship (Am., Br.)

574. Ешь вволю, пей в меру. *You can eat as much as you like, but do not indulge in drinking*

Cf.: Bread at pleasure, drink by measure (Br.). Eat at pleasure; drink by measure (Am.). Eat at pleasure, drink in (with) measure (Am., Br.)

575. Ехал прямо, да попал в яму. *See 2128 (У)*

Cf.: Better go about (around) than fall into the ditch (Am.). Better to go about than fall into the ditch (Br.)

576. Ешь мёд, да берегись жала. *See 1075 (Л)*

Cf.: Honey is sweet, but bees sting (Am.). Honey is sweet, but the bee stings (Br.)

577. Ешь пирог с грибами, да держи язык за зубами. *Do not bother to speak, give advice, object, etc.*

Var.: Держи язык за зубами (на привязи). Ешь калачи, да поменьше лепечи. Ешь капусту, да не мели попусту

Cf.: Hold your tongue (Am., Br.). Hold your tongue with your teeth (Am.). Keep your breath to cool your porridge (Br.). Keep your breath to cool your soup (Am.). Keep your tongue in your mouth (within your teeth) (Am., Br.). Save your breath to cool your broth (Am.). Save your breath to cool your porridge (Am., Br.)

578. Ешь хлеб, коли пирогов нет. *If you cannot have something which is very good, be content with that which is worse. See 579 (Е)*

Cf.: They that have no other meat bread and butter are glad to eat (Br.). They that have no other meat gladly bread and butter eat (Am.)

579. Ешь щи с мясом, а нет, так и хлеб с квасом. *Take delight in it when you have much, but when in strained circumstances be content with little. See 578 (Е), 1174 (Н)*

Cf.: If thou hast not a capon, feed on an onion (Br.). They that have no other meat, bread and butter are glad to eat (Br.). They that have no other meat gladly bread and butter eat (Am.)

Ж

580. Жадность фраера сгубила. *Covetousness often results in trouble or great inconvenience. See 1030 (Л), 2081 (Т)*

Cf.: Avarice loses all in seeking to gain all (Am.). Covetousness brings nothing home (Br.). Greed killed the wolf (Am.). Too much covetousness breaks (bursts) the bag (Br.)

581. Жалеет—значит любит. *Love implies the feeling of compassion for the person you love*

Cf.: Pity is akin to love (Am., Br.). Sympathy is akin to love (Am.)

582. Жало остро, а язык острей того. *See 1932 (С)*

Cf.: There is no venom like that of the tongue (Br.). A word hurts more than a wound (Am.)

583. Ждать да гадать—только время терять. *Deferring the work you have to do is mere waste of time which usually results in nothing being done at all. See 1784 (П)*

Var.: Оттягивать да откладывать—только время терять

Cf.: Procrastination brings loss (Br.). Procrastination is the thief of time (Am., Br.). "Time enough" lost the ducks (Br.)

584. Желающего судьба ведёт, нежелающего—тащит. *It is easier for him that does some work readily than for him who acts under compulsion*

Cf.: Fate leads the willing and drags the unwilling (Br.). The fate leads the willing but drives the stubborn (Br.). The fates lead the willing man; the unwilling they drag (Am.)

585. Железо ржа съедает, а завистливый от зависти сохнет. *Envy is a destructive feeling, it harms the envier himself, it rusts his heart and soul. See 145 (B)*

Var.: Завистливого /и/ сон неймёт. Завистливый от зависти по чужому счастью сохнет

Cf.: The envious man grows lean (shall never want woe) (Br.). Envy eats nothing but its own heart (Br.). Envy envies itself (Am., Br.). Envy is a two-edged sword (Am.). Envy shoots at others and wounds itself (Br.)

586. Жена—в доме глава. *The wife plays the decisive role in solving all the family problems. See 1161 (M)*

Cf.: The grey mare is the better horse (Br.). The husband is the head of the house, but the wife is the neck—and the neck moves the head (Am.). Man is the head, but the woman turns it (Am.)

587. Жена Цезаря должна быть выше подозрений. *A person closely related to, or connected with those in power must have an immaculate reputation not to become an object of criticism*

Cf.: Caesar's wife must be above suspicion (Am., Br.)

588. Женился на скорую руку, да на долгую муку. *If you marry rashly before you get to know your partner well, you may regret your marriage later. See 939 (K), 1442 (H), 1857 (C)*

Var.: Женился скоро, да на долгое горе

Cf.: Hasty love is soon hot and soon cold (Br.). Marry in haste and repent at leisure (Am., Br.). Quick choice, long repentance (Br.)

589. Женщине столько лет, на сколько она выглядит. *A woman's age is of no importance; what matters is how old or young she looks*

Cf.: A man is as old as he feels, and a woman as old as she looks (Am., Br.). A woman is no older than she looks /, and a man than he feels/ (Am.)

590. Живая собака лучше мёртвого льва. *It is more desirable to be alive, even if one is an insignificant man, than to be once powerful but dead*

Cf.: Better a live coward than a dead hero (Br.). It is better to be a live rabbit than a dead tiger (Am.). A live coward is better than a dead hero (Am.). A live (living) dog is better than a dead lion (Am., Br.). A live soldier is better than a dead hero (Am.). A live trout is better than a dead whale (Am.). A living ass (donkey) is better than a dead lion (Br.)

591. Живи всяк своим умом да своим горбом. *Rely on yourself and make your own decisions in your life and work. See 267 (B), 1975 (C)*

Cf.: Every herring must hang by its own gill (Br.). Everyone for himself (Am., Br). Every man must skin his own skunk (Am.). Every person should row his own boat (Am.). Let each tailor mend his own coat (Br.). Let every fox take care of his own brush (Br.). Let every herring hang by its own tail (sheep hang by its own shank) (Br.). Let every peddler carry his own pack (Am.). Let every tub stand on its own bottom (Am., Br.)

592. Живи для людей, поживут и люди для тебя. *See 622 (З)*

Cf.: The hand that gives gathers (Am., Br.)

593. Живи и жить давай другим. *Tolerate others and refrain from trying to direct the way they run their lives*

Cf.: Live and let live (Am., Br.). Pull devil, pull baker (Br.)

594. Живи не скупись, с друзьями веселись. *See 1526 (O)*

Cf.: Eat, drink and be merry /,for tomorrow we (you) die/ (Br.). Eat, drink, and be merry, for tomorrow we may die (Am.)

595. Живи не так, как хочется, а так, как можется. *See 1708 (П)*

Cf.: Cut the coat according to the cloth (Am.). Do as you may if you cannot as you would (Br.)

596. Жив курилка. *See 571 (E)*

Cf.: Alive and kicking (Am., Br.). Live and well (Am.). The man (Richard) is himself again (Br.). There is life in the old dog yet (Am., Br.)

597. Живой о живом и думает. *While you are alive, you should be interested in all earthly matters and enjoy life. See 599 (Ж)*

Cf.: Live your own life, for you die your own death (Am.). There is always life for a living one (for the living) (Br.). There is aye life for a living man (Am.). We must live by the living, not by the dead (Br.)

598. Живой смерти не ищет. *No one wants to die*

Var.: Живой смерти боится

Cf.: Men fear death as children do going in the dark (Am.). No church is so handsome that a man would desire straight to be buried (Br.). No man is so old but thinks he may live another day (Am.). No man is so old, but he thinks he may yet live another year (Br.)

599. Живому именины, мёртвому помины. *You should not grieve for the dead all your life, you have to find strength to enjoy life. See 597 (Ж)*

Var.: Мёртвому помины, живому именины

Cf.: There is always life for the living (Br.). There is aye life for a living man (Am.). We must live by the living, not by the dead (Br.)

600. Живот крепче, на сердце легче. *Any trouble is easier to bear when one has food to eat. See 1683 (П), 1745 (П)*

Cf.: All sorrows are less with bread (Br.). Fat sorrow is better than lean sorrow (Am., Br.). A full belly makes a brave heart (Am.). Full stomach, contented heart (Am.). Griefs with bread are less (Br.). When the belly is full, the bones are at rest (Am.). When the belly is full, the bones would be at rest (Br.). When the stomach is full the heart is glad (Am.)

601. Жизнь бьёт ключом. *People in the community or place live an interesting and intensive life*

Cf.: The joint is jumping (Am.). Life brims over the edge (Br.). Never a dull moment (Am.)

602. Жизнь прожить—не поле перейти. *Life is complicated, and the way through it is not easy. See 603 (Ж), 1180 (Н)*

Var.: Век не поле: вдруг не перескочишь. Век прожить—не поле перейти

Cf.: It is a great journey to life's end (Br.). The road of life is lined with many milestones (Am.)

603. Жизнь протянется—всего достанется. *Don't expect your life to be always easy; accept bad times philosophically. See 133 (В), 602 (Ж), 1179 (Н), 1879 (С)*

Var.: Век протянется—всего достанется

Cf.: It's all in a lifetime (Am., Br.). Life and misery begin together (Am.). Life has its ups and downs (Br.). Life is just one damned thing after another (Am.). Life is no bed of roses (not wholly beer and skittles) (Am.). Life is not a bed of roses (all beer and skittles, all clear sailing in calm water, all honey) (Br.). No life without pain (Am.). Take things as they are (Br.). We all have our ups and downs (Am.). You have to take the bitter with the sweet (the fat with the lean, the good with the bad) (Am.). You must take the bad with the good (the fat with the lean) (Br.). You must take the rough with the smooth (the sour with the sweet) (Am., Br.)

604. Жизнь—это движение. *Life is constantly changing. See 245 (В)*

Cf.: In this world nothing is permanent except change (Am.). Life is movement (Br.). Nothing is permanent except changes (Am., Br.). There is nothing constant but inconstancy (Am.)

605. Жил—полковник, помер—покойник. *See 2149 (У)*

Cf.: Death is a great leveler (Am.). Death is the grand leveler (Br.)

606. Жнут поле в пору. *See 977 (К)*

Cf.: Make haste while the sun shines (Am.). Make hay while the sun shines (Am., Br.)

607. Жребий брошен. *A decision is made, a step is taken and cannot be revoked*

Cf.: The die is cast (Am., Br.). The die is thrown (Br.)

З

608. За бездельника язык работает. *Those who do little talk much. See 932 (К)*

Cf.: A cackling hen doesn't always lay (Am.). Great talkers are little doers (Br.). Great talkers, little doers (Am.). 'Tis not the hen that cackles most that lays the most eggs (Am.)

609. Заварил кашу—не жалей масла. *Once you started doing some work, go on and do not spare your time, efforts or money. See 150 (В)*

Cf.: In for a dime, in for a dollar (Am.). In for a mill, in for a million (Am.). In for a penny, in for a pound (Am., Br.)

610. Завивай горе верёвочкой. *Take your troubles easy. See 555 (Д)*

Var.: Завяжи горе верёвочкой

Cf.: Hang care (sorrow) (Br.). Laugh your troubles away (Am.). Leave your cares to the wind (Am.). Never lay sorrow to your heart (Br.). Take it easy (Am., Br.)

611. Завистливые глаза всегда не сыты. *An envious man is never content with what he has*

Var.: Завидливые глаза всегда не сыты

Cf.: Envy and covetousness are never satisfied (Br.). Envy has no holiday (Br.). Envy never has a holiday (Am.)

612. За всё браться—ничего не сделать. *See 617 (З)*

Var.: Кто /сразу/ за всё берётся, тому ничего не удаётся

Cf.: Doing everything is doing nothing (Am.). He who undertakes too much seldom succeeds (Br.). Who undertakes too much seldom succeeds (Am.)

613 За всё браться—ничего не уметь. *A person who follows many diverse occupations is never competent in any*

Cf.: He teaches ill, who teaches all (Am.). He that sips many arts drinks none (Am.). Jack of all trades is master of none (Am., Br.). A man of many trades begs his bread on Sunday (Am.)

614. Завтраками сыт не будешь. *Mere promises will not help the needy. See 1360 (Н), 1968 (С)*

Cf.: The belly is not filled with fair words (Br.). Promises don't fill the belly (Am.). Talk does not cook rice (Am.)

615. Завтрак съешь сам, обедом поделись с другом, а ужин отдай врагу. *If you wish to stay healthy, do not eat much. See 327 (Г)*

Var.: Ужин отдай врагу

Cf.: By suppers more have been killed than Galen ever cured (Br.). Eat few suppers and you'll need few medicines (Am.). Lightest (Little) suppers make long lives (Am.). Suppers kill more than the greatest doctors can cure

(Am.). To lengthen your life, lessen your meals (Am.)

616. За глаза и царя ругают. *When you fear a person, you dare to abuse him only in his absence. See 923 (К)*

Cf.: He that (who) fears you present, will hate you absent (Br.). When a man's away, abuse him you may (Am.)

617. За двумя зайцами погонишься, ни одного не поймаешь. *If you undertake many things to do at the same time, none will be accomplished. See 612 (З), 1886 (С)*

Cf.: Dogs that put up many hares kill none (Br.). He who chases two hares catches neither (Am.). He who hunts two hares leaves one and loves the other (Br.). If you run after two hares, you will catch neither (Am., Br.)

618. За деньги и поп пляшет. *Men will do anything if they are paid*

Var.: За деньги и кляча поскачет

Cf.: Money makes the mare go (Am., Br.). No ear is deaf to the song that gold sings (Am.)

619. Задний ум хорош, да никуда не гож. *It is of no help saying what should have been done to prevent some trouble after it took place. See 621 (З), 1730 (П)*

Cf.: After-wit is dear bought (Br.). Hindsight is better than foresight (Am.). If a man's foresight were as good as his hindsight, we would all get somewhere (Am.)

620. Задним умом всяк крепок. *It is easy to say what should have been done after some trouble has taken place. See 492 (Д), 619 (З), 1749 (П)*

Var.: Русский мужик задним умом крепок

Cf.: After the danger everyone is wise (Am.). After-wit is everybody's wit (Br.). Everybody is wise after the event (Br.). If things were to be done twice, all would be wise (Am., Br.). It is easy to be wise after the event (Am., Br.). It is easy to prophesy after the event (Br.). We are all wise after the event (Br.)

621. Задним умом дела не поправишь. *See 619 (З)*

Cf.: After-wit is dear bought (Br.). Hindsight is better than foresight (Am.)

622. За добро добром и платят. *If you help people, they will repay in the same way; if somebody does you a favo(u)r, repay in the same way. See 472 (Д), 474 (Д), 592 (Ж), 836 (К), 1197 (Н), 2148 (У), 2188 (Х)*

Cf.: An act of kindness is well repaid (Am.). Do well and have well (Br.). Do well, have well (Am). Give and take (Br.). Give and you shall receive (Am.). A good deed is never forgotten (Am.). A good deed is never lost (Br.). The good you do to others will always come back to you (Am.). The hand that gives, gathers (Am., Br.). Kindness always begets kindness (Am.). A kindness is never lost (wasted) (Am.). One good deed deserves another (Am.). One good turn deserves another (Am., Br.). One kindness deserves another (is the price of another) (Am.). One never loses by doing a good turn (Am., Br.). Repay kindness with kindness (Am.). Scatter with one hand, gather with two (Am., Br.)

623. За дружбу дружбой платят. *See 2211 (Х)*

Cf.: Friendship cannot always stand on one side (Br.). Friendship stands not on one side (Am.). To have a friend, be one (Am.)

624. За дурной головой и ногам непокой. *A stupid man does much of unnecessary walking. See 546 (Д)*

Var.: Дурная голова ногам покоя не даёт. За глупой головою и ногам нет покою. С дурною головою и ногам нет покою

Cf.: Brains in the head saves blisters on the feet (Am.). A forgetful head makes a weary pair of heels (Br.). If you don't use your head, you must use your legs (Am.). Little wit in the head makes much work for the feet (Am., Br.). My silly head will never save my feet (Br.). Use your head and save your heels (Am.). What you haven't got in your head, you have in your feet (Am.). What your head forgets, your heels must remember (Am.). A witless head makes weary feet (Br.)

625. Зажила рана, а всё рубцы есть. *Your grief or sorrow may ease, but it will never be completely forgotten*

Cf.: Though the wound be healed, the scar (yet a scar) remains (Am.). A wound never heals so well that the scar cannot be seen (Br.)

626. Закон, что дышло: куда повернёшь, туда и вышло. *The law can be used arbitrarily, as a rule it is in favo(u)r of those who are powerful or have money*

Var.: Закон—дышло: куда хочешь, туда и воротишь

Cf.: Every law has a loophole (Br.). Every loop has a hole (Br.). The law is like an axle: you can turn it whichever way you please if you give it plenty of grease (Am.). Laws are made to be broken (evaded) (Am.)

627. Залезают на дерево не с вершины. *You cannot gain a high post without going through all the positions, beginning at the lowest one*

Cf.: He that climbs a ladder must begin at the first round (Am.). He who would climb the ladder must begin at the bottom (Br.). Nobody starts at the top (Am.). One begins to climb the ladder from the bottom (Am.)

628. Залез в богатство, забыл и братство. *When a man becomes rich, famous or powerful, he breaks up with his former friends*

Cf.: A beggar ennobled does not know his own kinsmen (Am.). A dog in the kitchen desires no company (Am.). A dog with a bone knows no friend (Am.). A friend in power is a friend lost (Am.). Hono(u)rs change manners (Am., Br.). There is no pride like that of a beggar grown rich (Am.). When a knave is in a plum-tree, he hath neither friend nor kin (Br.). While the dog (the hound) gnaws a bone companions would be none (Br.)

629. За малым погонишься, большое потеряешь. *By trying to gain a trifling, you will miss getting much. See 1339 (H), 1510 (O)*

Var.: За краюшкой погонишься, каравай потеряешь. Малое пожалеешь, большое потеряешь

Cf.: Don't spoil the ship for half a penny's worth of tar (Am.). Don't waste ten dollars looking for a dime (Am.). It is no use losing a sheep (spoiling a ship) for a halfpenny worth of tar (Br.). A penny soul never came to twopence (Br.). A penny soul never 'came twopence (Am.). Penny-wise and pound foolish (Am., Br.). Penny-wise, pound foolish (Am.). Save at the spigot and waste at the bung (Am.). We spare at the spigot and spill at the bung (Br.)

630. Замиренный друг ненадёжен. *See 1718 (П)*

Cf.: A broken friendship may be soldered but will never be sound (Am.). Broken friendships may be soldered, but never sound (Br.). An injured friend is the bitterest of foes (Am.). Once a torn friendship, a patch can't be sewn (Am.). A reconciled friend is a double enemy (Am., Br.)

631. За моё же добро да мне же поломали ребро. *See 250 (B)*

Var.: Твоим же добром тебя же челом

Cf.: Breed up a crow and he will peck out your eyes (Br.). No good deed goes unpunished (Am.). Save a thief from the gallows, and he'll be the first to cut your throat (Am.)

632. За мухой не с обухом, за комаром не с топором. *See 713 (И)*

Var.: За комаром не с топором

Cf.: Don't take a hatchet to break eggs (Am.). Take not a musket to kill a butterfly (Br.)

633. За неимением гербовой пишут на простой. *See 1174 (Н)*

Cf.: If you cannot have the best, make the best of what you have (Br.). If you can't get a horse, ride a cow (Am.). A man must plough with such oxen as he has (Br.). They that have no other meat, bread and butter are glad to eat (Br.). They that have no other meat gladly bread and butter eat (Am.)

634. Занимает, кланяется; а отдаёт, так чванится. *When borrowing, people are polite, but when they have to pay their debt, they become rude. See 128 (В)*

Cf.: He borrows like an angel and pays back like the devil himself (Am.). He who likes borrowing dislikes paying (Br.). Lend money and you get an enemy (Am.). Quick to borrow are always slow to pay (Am., Br.). When I lent I had a friend, when I asked he was unkind (Br.)

635. За ничто ничего не купишь. *To obtain something you must pay for it*

Cf.: Everything that is worth having must be paid for (Am.). No pay, no play (Br.). No penny, no paternoster (Am., Br.). No such thing as a free lunch (Am.). Nothing for nothing /, and very little for halfpenny/ (Br.). There is no good that does not cost a price (Am.). There's no /such thing as a/ free lunch (Am.). Touch pot, touch penny (Br.). You get nothing for nothing (Am., Br.)

636. За один раз дерева не срубишь. *See 730 (И)*

Var.: За один взмах дерева не срубишь

Cf.: An oak is not felled at one stroke (Am.) An oak is not felled with one stroke (Br.). One stroke fells not an oak (Am.)

637. Запас кармана не дерёт. *What is put away for future use does no harm*

Var.: Запас кармана не дерёт и каши не просит. Запас кармана не трёт (места не пролежит, мешка не дерёт, плеч не тянет). Запас не ноша, рук не оттянет. Запас ни пить, ни есть не просит

Cf.: Save up for a rainy day (Am., Br.). Spare and have is better than spend and crave (Am.). Store is no sore (Br.)

638. Запасливый нужды не терпит. *See 1856 (С)*

Var.: Запасливый нужды не знает

Cf.: A dollar saved is a dollar earned (Am.). A penny saved is a penny earned (Am., Br.). A penny saved is a penny gained (Br.). Save today, safe tomorrow (Am.)

639. Заплатишь долг скорее, так будет веселее. *Pay all your debts as soon as you can, it will make you feel happy*

Cf.: He who pays his debts enriches himself (Am.). Once paid and never craved (Br.). Out of debt, out of danger (Am., Br.). Pay what you owe (Am.). Without debt, without care (Am.)

640. Запретный плод сладок. *We enjoy doing or desire to obtain what is not allowed or disapproved of. See 1200 (Н)*

Cf.: Everything forbidden is sweet (Am.). Forbidden fruit is sweet (sweetest) (Br.). Forbidden fruit is the sweetest (Am.). Stolen apples (kisses, pleasures, waters) are sweetest (Br.). Stolen cherries are the sweetest (Am.). Stolen fruit is always sweeter (Am.). Stolen fruit is sweet (Br.). Stolen kisses are sweet (the best) (Am.). Stolen sweets are /always/ sweeter (Br.). Stolen waters are sweet (Am.)

641. За признание—половина наказания. *See 1661 (П)*

Cf.: A fault confessed is half forgiven (half redressed) (Am., Br.). A sin confessed is half forgiven (Am., Br.)

642. Запрос в карман не лезет. *See 649 (З)*

Cf.: Nothing is lost for asking (Br.). There is no harm in asking (Am.)

643. Зарекался козёл в огород ходить. *Men cannot get rid of their evil inclinations. See 1877 (С)*

Cf.: Once a thief, always a thief (Am., Br.)

644. Заруби себе это на носу. *Remember what I am telling you and never do it again or act the way you intend to*

Cf.: Bite on that (Br.). Put it into your pipe and smoke it! (Am.). Put it (that, this) in your pipe and smoke it! (Am., Br.). You mark my words (Am.)

645. Заря деньгу даёт. *See 961 (К)*

Var.: Заря денежку берёт (куёт, родит). Заря золотом осыпает

Cf: He that will thrive must rise at five (Br.). He that would thrive must rise at five (Am.). An hour in the morning is worth two in the afternoon (in the evening) (Am.)

646. За семь вёрст комара искали, а комар на носу. *See 1355 (Н), 2120 (У)*

Cf.: The butcher looked for his knife and it was (while he had it) in his mouth (Br.). If it had been a bear (a dog, a snake), it would have bitten you (Am.). If it were a bear, it would bite you (Am., Br.). People don't see things on their own doorsteps (Am.)

647. Засиженное яйцо всегда болтун, занянченный сынок—всегда шалун. *Too much care and tenderness spoils the child*

Var.: Засиженное яйцо всегда болтун, занянченный сын всегда шалун (занянченное дитя всегда дурак)

Cf.: Bring up your beloved child with a stick (Am.). A child may have too much of his mother's blessing (Br.). Mothers' darlings make but milksop heroes (Br.). Spare the rod and spoil the child (Am., Br.)

648. За спасибо шубу не сошьют. *See 1976 (С)*

Var.: Из спасиба шапки не сошьёшь

Cf.: Keep your thanks to feed your cat (chicken) (Br.). Thanks is a poor payment (Br.). Thanks is poor pay /on which to keep a family/ (Am.). Thanks killed the cat (Am.). Thanks would starve a cat to death (Br.). You can't put thanks into your pocket (Am.)

649. За спрос денег не берут. *You do not risk anything when asking a question, but you get a chance to learn what you need. See 642 (З), 1985 (С)*

Var.: За спрос не бьют в нос

Cf.: It costs nothing to ask (Am.). It never hurts to ask (Am.). Lose nothing for asking (Am., Br.). Nothing is lost for asking (Br.). There is no harm in asking (Am.)

650. Заставь дурака Богу молиться, он и лоб расшибёт. *Unexperienced people, who are too enthusiastic in doing some job, get harmed as the consequence of their actions. See 407 (Д), 2146 (У)*

Cf.: Action without thought is like shooting without aim (Am.). Give a calf rope enough and it will hang itself (Am.). Give a fool rope enough and he'll hang himself (Br.). Give a man rope enough and he'll hang himself (Am., Br.). Zeal without knowledge is a fire without light (Am., Br.). Zeal without knowledge is a runaway horse (sister of folly) (Br.). Zeal without knowledge is the sister of folly (Am.)

651. За то собаку кормят, что она лает. *You employ a man to do the work he is paid for*

Cf.: Don't keep a dog and bark yourself (Br.). I will not keep a dog and bark myself (Am.). No sense in keeping a dog when doing your own barking (Am.)

652. Затянул песню, так веди до конца. *Complete once you started doing something, make a good job of it. See 150 (В), 361 (Г), 1257 (Н)*

Var.: Наладил песню—пой, хоть тресни

Cf.: Always finish a task begun (Am.). Do nothing by halves (Am.). Do what you do with all your might: things done half are never done right (Am.). If a task is once begun, never leave it till it's done (Am.). Let him that begins the song make an end (Br.). Never do things by halves (Br.). Never give up once you have started (Br.). Never leave a task until it is done (Am.). Never say A without saying B (Am.). Things done half are never done right (Am.)

653. За хорошей женой и муж пригож. *A man becomes better under the influence of a good wife*

Var.: У хорошей жены и мужу нет цены (и плохой муж будет молодцом)

Cf.: Behind every good man there is a good woman (Am.). A good wife makes a good husband (Am., Br.). Jack is as good as Jill (Br.)

654. Захотел молочка от бычка. *This man will not help you or give it to you because he cannot; where nothing is nothing can be obtained. See 826 (К)*

Cf.: It is very hard to shave an egg (Br.). Look not for musk in a dog's kennel (Br.). No man can flay a stone (Am., Br.). 'Tis very hard to shave an egg (Am.). You cannot get blood from a turnip (Am.). You cannot get blood out of a stone (Am., Br.). You can't draw water from a dry well (squeeze water from a stone) (Am.). You seek cold water under cold ice (Am.)

655. Зачем и клад, коли в семье лад. *Harmony in family life is the most precious thing*

Var.: Где лад, там и клад. На что и клад, коли в семье лад

Cf.: He is happy who finds peace in his own home (Am.)

656. Зачин дело красит. *See 477 (Д)*

Cf.: A beard well lathered is half a shave (Br.). Getting started is half of the fight (Am.). A task well begun is half done (Am.). Well begun is half done (Am., Br.)

657. За что купил, за то и продаю. *I say just what I have heard and cannot guarantee that the information is correct. See 1088 (Л)*

Cf.: I give it for what it is worth (Br.). I will tell you for what it's worth (Am.)

658. За чужим погонишься, своё потеряешь. *See 2221 (Х)*

Var.: Кто чужого желает, скоро своё потеряет

Cf.: Ill-gotten gains are soon lost (Am.). Ill-gotten goods seldom prosper (Br.)

659. За чужой щекой зуб не болит. *See 2325 (Ч)*

Cf.: Another's cares will not rob you of sleep (Am.). It is easy to bear the misfortunes of others (Br.). We can always bear our neighbors' misfortunes (Am.)

660. Здоровье всего дороже. *Health is above all. See 1398 (Н)*

Var.: Здоровье дороже богатства (золота). Здоровью цены нет

Cf.: Find health better than gold (Am.). The first wealth is health (Am., Br.). Good health is above wealth (Br.). Good health is priceless (Am.). Health is better than wealth (is great riches) (Br.). Health is /the best/ wealth (Am.). He that wants health wants all (Br.). Wealth is nothing without health (Br.). Without health no one is rich (Am.)

661. Здоровья за деньги не купишь. *Very often money cannot help you when you are in very bad health*

Cf.: Wealth can buy no health (Am.)

662. Зелен виноград. *To belittle the worth of a thing desired one says this just because he cannot have it*

Cf.: Foxes, when they cannot reach the grapes, say they are not ripe (Am.). The grapes are sour (Am., Br.). It is easy to despise what you cannot get (Am.). "Sour grapes," said the fox when he could not reach them (Am.)

663. Земля на трёх китах стоит. *You are talking nonsense. (You say this to someone to show his foolish ignorance)*

Cf.: The moon is made of green cheese (Am., Br.)

664. Зёрнышко к зёрнышку—будет мешок. *See 979 (К)*

Cf.: A bushel of wheat is made up of single grains (Br.). Little and often makes a heap in time (Am.). Many a little (a pickle) makes a mickle (Br.). Many a mickle makes a muckle (Am.). One grain fills not the sack but it helps his fellow (Br.). Though one grain fills not the sack, it helps (Am.)

665. Зима—не лето, пройдёт и это. *These troubles are temporary, be patient and things will work out. See 239 (В)*

Cf.: In the end things will mend (Br.). This, too, shall (will) pass (Am.)

666. Злой человек не проживёт в добре век. *A villainous man will suffer himself in the end. See 921 (К)*

Cf.: Evil be to him who evil thinks (Br.). The evil doer weeps (Am.). Evil to him who evil does (thinks) (Am.). A wicked man is his own hell (Am., Br.)

667. Злой язык убивает. *See 1932 (С)*

Cf.: An evil tongue may do much (Br.). The hard words cut the heart (Am.). The tongue is not steel but (yet) it cuts (Am., Br.)

668. Злом зла не поправишь. *Acting wickedly to retaliate for the injury done to you will not improve matters. See 706 (И), 1516 (О), 2326 (Ч)*

Cf.: Can two wrongs make a right? (Br.). Evil does not cure evil (Br.). Never do evil for evil (Am.). Never do evil hoping that good will come of it (Am.). Two blacks do not make a white (Am., Br.). Two wrongs do not make a right (Am., Br.). You cannot fight evil with evil (Am.)

669. Злые языки страшнее пистолета. *See 1932 (С)*

Var.: Злые языки—острый меч

Cf.: Slander is sharper than the sword (Am.). Slander's sting is sharper than the sword (Am.). The tongue is not steel but (yet) it cuts (Am., Br.). The tongue stings (Am., Br.). A word hurts more than a wound (Am.). Words cut (hurt) more than swords (Br.)

670. Змею обойдёшь, а от клеветы не уйдёшь. *No man can go through life without having been falsely accused of something harmful to his reputation. See 828 (К)*

Var.: От молвы не уйдёшь

Cf.: The best things (Everything) may be abused (Br.). Nothing is safe from fault-finders (Br.). Not one escapes unscathed (Am.). No wool is so white that a dyer cannot blacken it (Br.). No wool is so white that the dye can't make it black (Am.). There's no one so clean that somebody doesn't think they're dirty (Am.)

671. Змея змее на хвост не наползёт. *See 196 (В)*

Cf.: Dog does not eat dog (Am., Br.). There is honor /even/ among thieves (Am.). There is honour among thieves (Br.)

672. Змея, меняя шкуру, не меняет натуру. *See 383 (Г)*

Cf.: The wolf changes his coat (skin), but not his disposition (nature)

(Br.). Wolves may lose their teeth, but they never lose their nature (Am.)

673. Знает кошка, чьё мясо съела. *The person realizes that he is guilty and that he may be punished for his wrongdoings. See 1183 b (H)*

Var.: Чует кошка, чьё мясо съела

Cf.: The cat knows whose butter he has eaten (Br.). If the cap fits, put it on (Am.). If the cap fits, wear it (Am., Br.). If the shoe fits, put it on (wear it) (Am.)

674. Знай, кошка, своё лукошко. *See 1295 b (H)*

Cf.: The bear wants a tail and cannot be lion (Br.). Everyone to his equal (Am.). Every sheep with its like (Am.). Geese with geese, and women with women (Br.)

675. Знай сорока сороку, ворона ворону. *See 308 (B)*

Cf.: Everyone to his equal (Am.). Every sheep with its like (Am.). Geese with geese, and women with women (Br.). Keep to your own kind (Am.). Tigers and deer do not stroll together (Am.)

676. Знала бы наседка, узнает и соседка. *See 232 (B)*

Cf.: Confide in an aunt and the world will know (Br.). A secret shared is no secret (Br.). Secret shared is no secret (Am.). Two can keep a secret if one is dead (Am.). Two may keep counsel if one be away (if one of them's dead) (Br.)

677. Знание лучше богатства. *You may lose your money but not your knowledge which will always provide for you*

Cf.: Better an empty purse than an empty head (Am.). Education is a gift that none can take away (Am.). If a man empties his purse into his head, no one can take it from him (Am.). An investment in knowledge pays the best interest (Am.). Knowledge is better than riches (wealth) (Am., Br.). Knowledge is the treasure of the mind (Am.). Money spent on the brain is never spent in vain (Br.). Silver and gold tarnish away, but a good education will never decay (Am.)

678. Знание—сила. *An educated person is powerful*

Cf.: He who has knowledge has force (Am.). Knowing is power (Am.). Knowledge is power (Am., Br.)

679. Знания на плечи не давят. *Knowledge you gain will never be a hindrance to you, it will always be to your advantage*

Var.: Знания никому не в тягость

Cf.: Knowledge is no burden (Br.). The weight of knowledge is never measured (Am.)

680. Знать не знаешь, так и вины нет. *See 2237 (Ч)*

Cf.: What one doesn't know won't hurt him (Am.). What you don't know won't hurt you (Br.). What you don't see you won't get hung for (Am.). Without knowledge there is no sin or sinner (Am.)

681. Знать птицу по перьям, а молодца по речам. *A person is judged rather by his conversation than by his looks. See 1504 (O), 1566 (O)*

Cf.: A bird is known by his note and a man by his talk (Am., Br.). The bird is known by its note, and the man by his words (Br.). A bird is known by its song (Br.). Conversation makes the man (Br.). Speech is the index of the mind (Am., Br.). Speech is the picture of the mind (Br.). Tell an ox by his horns, but a man by his word (Am.). Your tongue is your ambassador (Am., Br.)

682. Золотая клетка соловью не потеха. *Freedom is above all*

Var.: Воля птичке лучше золотой клетки. Не нужна соловью золотая клетка, а нужна зелёная ветка. Птичке ветка дороже золотой клетки

Cf.: A golden cage is still a cage (Am.). Nightingales will not sing in a cage (Br.). A nightingale won't sing in a cage (Am.). No man loves /his/ fetters, be they made of gold (Br.)

683. Золото и в грязи блестит. *A really virtuous person is not degraded in any surroundings. See 5 (А), 871 (К)*

Var.: Золото и в болоте видно (светится)

Cf.: A diamond is valuable though it lie on a midden (Br.). A diamond on a dunghill is a precious diamond still (Am.). A good name keeps its lustre in the dark (Br.)

684. Золотой ключик все двери открывает. *See 439 (Д)*

Cf.: The golden key opens every door (Am.). A gold key opens every door (Br.). No ear is deaf to the song that gold sings (Am.)

685. Золото железо переедает. *See 439 (Д)*

Cf.: Money is power (Am., Br.). Money masters all things (Am., Br.)

686. Золото не в золото, не побывав под молотом. *The true value of a person is tested by hardships*

Cf.: Adversity is the touchstone of virtue (Am.). Adversity tries virtue (Am.). Fire is the test of (proves the) gold (Am.). Gold is tried in the fire (Br.). Gold must be tried by fire (Am.)

687. Золото не говорит, да много творит. *See 439 (Д)*

Cf.: Gold rules the world (Am.). Money is power (Am., Br.). Money masters all things (Am., Br.). Money runs the world (Br.)

И

688. И большой бадьёй реки не вычерпать. *See 141 (В)*

Cf.: A fog cannot be dispelled with a fan (Br.). You cannot catch the wind in the palm of your hand (Am.)

689. И в мякине зёрна находятся. *In a mass of unworthy people or useless things there is always a worthy one to be found*

Cf.: Much corn lies under the straw that is not seen (Br.). There is a diamond in the rough (Am.)

690. И в пепле искра бывает. *See 1293 (Н)*

Cf.: In the coldest flint there is hot fire (Br.). Strike a flint and you get fire (Am.)

691. И всё-таки она вертится! *I insist that I am right*

Cf.: And /yet/ it does move! (Am., Br.). But it does move! (Am.)

692. И в сосне дупло есть. *See 737 (И)*

Cf.: Many a rosy apple is rotten to the core (Am.). A prize apple can have a worm inside (Br.). The reddest apple may have a worm in it (Am.)

693. Игла в стог сена попала—пиши пропало. *It is impossible to find it in a mass of things*

Var.: Игла в стог сена упала—считай пропала

Cf.: Gone for a holiday (Br.). Gone with the wind (Am.). It's like looking for a needle in a haystack (Am.). Lost like a needle in a bundle of hay (Br.). Lost like a needle in a haystack (Am., Br.)

694. И гладок, да гадок. *See 1859 (С)*

Var.: Личиком гладок, а делами гадок

Cf.: An angel on top but a devil underneath (Am.). A fair face and a foul heart (Br.). A fair face may hide a foul heart (Am., Br.). A fair thing full false (Br.)

695. Иглой дороги не меряют. *There is no point in doing something with improper tools as it is mere waste of time*

Cf.: You cannot chop wood with a penknife (cut blocks with a razor) (Br.). You can't fill pails with a spoon (Br.). You can't saw wood with a hammer (Am.)

696. Игра игрою, а дело делом. *Work does not go with amusement. See 401 (Г), 433 (Д), 436 (Д), 1635 (П)*

Cf.: Play while you play; work while you work (Am.). There is a time for all things (Am., Br.). Work is work, and play is play (Br.). You can't mix business and pleasure (Am.).

697. Игра не доводит до добра. *Gambling, as a rule, results in loss of money or getting into trouble*

Var.: Игра не доведёт до добра

Cf.: Cards are the devil's books (Br.). Cards are the devil's tools (Am.). Gambling is the son of avarice and the father of despair (Am.). Gambling is the son of avarice, the brother of iniquity and the father of mischief (Am.)

698. Игра не стоит свеч. *Profits, pleasures or results gained are not worth the trouble, the time or the expenses involved*

Cf.: The game is not worth the candle (Am., Br.). The game is not worth the money (Am.). It is not worth powder and shot (Br.). It's not worth the effort (Br.)

699. И за рекой люди живут. *There are nice people to be found elsewhere. See 1860 (С)*

Var.: И за горами люди

Cf.: All the keys are not at one man's girdle (Br.). All the keys hang not at one's girdle (Am.). Behind the mountains there are people to be found (Br.). There are as good fish in the sea as ever came out of it (Am., Br.). There are always other people and other places (Am.). There is always the next train coming (Am.)

700. Избави меня, Боже, от друзей, а с врагами я сам справлюсь. *A tactless or stupid friend can often cause more mischief than an enemy*

Cf.: God defend (deliver) me from my friends; from my enemies I can (will) defend myself (Am., Br.). God protect me from my friends /; my enemies I know enough to watch/ (Am.). God save me from my friends (Br.). Save me from my friends (Am.)

701. Из большой тучи, да малый дождь. *See 1140 (М)*

Var.: Большая туча, да малый дождь

Cf.: More bark than bite (Br.). When the thunder is very loud, there's very little rain (Am.)

702. Из волка пастух не выйдет. *See 185 (В)*

Cf.: Don't set a wolf to watch the sheep (Am.). Give never the wolf the wether to keep (Br.)

703. Из грязи да в князи. *The man came from a very mean or poor family. (This is a catch phrase applied to a parvenu)*

Cf.: From rags to riches (Am., Br.). How we apples swim! (Am., Br.). Risen from the dunghill (from the ranks) (Br.)

704. Из двух зол выбирают меньшее. *If you are in a situation that necessitates a choice between two unpleasant alternatives, give preference to that one which is less harmful to you. See 1056 (Л), 1070 (Л)*

Cf.: Better cut the shoe than pinch the foot (Am., Br.). Better one-eyed than stone-blind (Br.). Better eye sore than all blind (Br.). Choose the lesser of two evils (Am.). Of two evils choose the least (the lesser) (Am., Br.). Of two evils choose the prettier (Am.). Of two harms (mischiefs) choose the least (Br.). Of two ills choose the least (Am.)

705. Из-за деревьев леса не видать. *A multitude of details prevents one from forming a general idea of some fact*

Cf.: Sometimes one can't see the wood for the trees (Am.). You can't see the forest for the trees (Am.). You can't see the wood for the trees (Br.)

706. Из зла добро не родится. *Mischief can never bring good results*

Var.: Зло на зло—добра не будет

Cf.: Good can never grow out of bad (evil) (Br.). Never do evil hoping that good will come of it (Am.). Of evil grain no good seed can come (Am., Br.)

707. Из молодых, да ранний. *He is very young, but he already shows his inclinations*

Cf.: It early pricks that will be a thorn (Am., Br.). It will be a forward cock that crows in the shell (Br.). That which will become a thorn grows sharp early (Am.)

708. Из ничего ничего не сделаешь. *Not a single thing comes into existence out of nought. See 253 (B), 1581 (O)*

Cf.: From nothing, nothing is made (Am.). Nothing comes from (produces) nothing (Br.). Nothing comes of nothing (Am., Br.). You can't make something out of nothing (Am.)

709. Из огня да в полымя. *When trying to escape one difficulty or trouble, you find yourself in as bad a situation as before, or even in a worse one. See 1582 (O)*

Cf.: /Don't jump/ from the frying pan into the fire (Am.). From smoke into smother (Br.). Out of the frying-pan (frying pan) into the fire (Am., Br.)

710. Из одних слов шубы не сошьёшь. *See 1968 (C)*

Cf.: Promises don't fill the belly (Am.). Talking well will not make the pot boil (Am.). Talk is but talk, but it's the money that buys the house (Am.). Talk is cheap /, but it takes money to buy land (liquor, whiskey)/ (Am.). Words pay no debts (Am., Br.)

711. Из песка верёвки не вьют. *Nothing strong or durable can be made if you use worthless material*

Cf.: Walls of sand are sure to crumble (Am.). You cannot make ropes of sand (Br.)

712. Из песни слова не выкинешь. *I have to tell the whole story without omitting any unpleasant part of it*

Cf.: Excuse my French (my language) (Am.). If you'll pardon the expression (Am.). Pardon my French (Am.). Varnished tale can't be round (Br.)

713. Из пушки по воробьям не стреляют. *Do not take extreme measures to get rid of something quite trivial. See 632 (З), 1561 (O)*

Cf.: Don't take a hatchet to break eggs (Am.). Never take a stone to break an egg, when you can do it with the back of your knife (Br.). Send not for a hatchet to break open an egg with (Br.). Take not a musket to kill a butterfly (Br.)

714. Из рогожи не сделаешь кожи. *You cannot make anything fine or refined out of material that is of poor quality. See 718 (И), 805 (K)*

Var.: Из ежовой кожи шубы не сошьёшь

Cf.: No man can make a good coat with bad cloth (Br.). One cannot make a horn of a pig's tail (Br.). Sour grapes can never make sweet wine (Am.). There never was a good knife made of bad steel (Am.). You cannot make a silk purse out of a sow's ear (Am., Br.). You can't make a silk purse out a pig's ear (Am.)

715. Из собаки блох не выбьешь. *See 383 (Г)*

Var.: Из собаки блох не выколотишь

Cf.: It is hard to break a hog of an ill custom (Br.). Wash a dog, comb a dog, still a dog (Am.). You can't take a grunt out of a pig (Am.)

716. Из твоих уст да Богу в уши. *See 123 (В)*
Var.: Твои бы речи да Богу в уши
Cf : From your lips to God's ears (Am.). Out of thy mouth into God's ears (Br)

717. Из хама не сделаешь пана. *It is impossible to turn a boor into a refined man. See 1567 (О)*
Cf.: You can get the man out of the country, but you can't get the country out of the man (Am.). You cannot make a silk purse out of a sow's ear (Am., Br.)

718. Из худого не сделаешь хорошее. *See 714 (И)*
Cf.: Sour grapes can never make sweet wine (Am.). You cannot make a silk purse out of a sow's ear (Am., Br.)

719. Из чужого кармана платить легко. *See 2324 (Ч)*
Cf.: It is easy to be generous with what is another's (Br.). It is easy to spend someone else's money (Am.)

720. И калачи приедаются. *See 2187 (Х)*
Cf.: Too much of a good thing is good for nothing (Br.). Too much of a good thing is worse than none at all (Am.)

721. И комар лошадь свалит, коли волк подсобит. *You can do any work if you get help. See 2199 (Х)*
Cf.: He may well swim that is held up by the chin (Br.). He that is carried down the stream need not row (Am., Br.)

722. И комары кусают до поры. *That which is evil does not last for ever, it has an end. See 1570 (О)*
Cf.: The harder the storm, the sooner it's over (Am.). A heavy shower is soon over (Am.). The sharper the storm, the sooner 'tis over (Br.). That which is sharp is not long (Br.). Violent fires soon burn out (Br.)

723. И космато, да не медведь. *See 168 (В)*
Cf.: Appearances are deceiving (Am.). Appearances are deceptive (Am., Br.). Don't mistake an old goat for a preacher because of his beard (Am.)

724. И красное солнышко на всех не угождает. *See 1184 (Н)*
Cf.: One cannot please all the world and his wife (Br.). You cannot please everybody (everyone) (Am., Br.). You can't please the whole world and his wife (Am.)

725. Или всё, или ничего. *See 727 (И)*
Cf.: All or nothing /at all/ (Am.). Eat whole hog or die (Am.). Either win the mare or lose the halter (Br.). The whole tree or not a cherry on it (Br.)

726. Или грудь в крестах, или голова в кустах. *See 727 (И)*
Var.: Либо грудь в крестах, либо голова в кустах
Cf. Do or die (Am., Br.). Eat whole hog or die (Am.). /I will/ either lose the horse or win the saddle (win the saddle or lose the horse) (Br.). Kill or cure (Br.). Make a spoon or spoil a horn (Am., Br.)

727. Или пан, или пропал. *Perish or survive, fail or succeed, but I am determined to try and do it in spite of all the danger or risk involved. See 110 (Б), 323 (Г), 725 (И), 726 (И), 1017 (Л), 1019 (Л), 1020 (Л), 1021 (Л)*
Var.: Или полковник, или покойник. Либо пан, либо пропал
Cf.: Do or die (Am., Br.). Double or quits (Br.). Make a spoon or spoil a horn (Am., Br.). Make /it/, or break /it/ (Am., Br.). Make or mar (Br.). Neck or nothing (Br.). Root, hog, or die (Am.). Rule or ruin (Am.). Sink or swim (Am., Br.). Sink, swim, or die (Am.). Win or lose (Br.)

728. Или пень об сову, или сову об пень—всё рано ей больно. *See 2215 (Х), 2285 (Ч)*

Var.: Что совою об печь, что печью о сову—всё больно

Cf.: Between two evils 'tis not worth choosing (Br.). Whether the pitcher strikes the stone, or the stone the pitcher it is bad for the pitcher (Am.)

729. И ложь правдой статься может. *Sometimes when lying, you do not know that you are telling the truth*

Cf.: Tell a lie and find a truth (Am.)

730. И Москва не вдруг строилась. *It takes time and efforts to do something great. See 636 (З), 1107 (М), 1281 (Н), 1965 (С)*

Var.: Не сразу Москва строилась

Cf.: Little by little the bird builds its nest (Br.). An oak is not felled at one stroke (Am.). An oak is not felled with one stroke (Br.). One by one spindles are made (Br.). One step at a time (Am.). One stroke fells not an oak (Am.). Paris was not built in a day (Am.). Rome was not built in a day (Am., Br.). Step after step the ladder is ascended (Br.). Step by step one goes a long way (Am.). Step by step the ladder is ascended (Am.)

731. И мы не лыком шиты. *In a certain respect, I am not worse than some other person. See 1168 (М)*

Var.: И мы не лыком шиты, не лаптем щи хлебаем. И мы не на руку лапоть обуваем

Cf.: I am as good as the next person (Am.)

732. И мы пахали. *You are of little significance, and you overrate your participation in the action or event*

Cf.: The fly sat upon the axle-tree of the chariot-wheel and said, What a dust do I raise! (Br.). How we apples swim! (Am.). We got the coach (Am.). We got the coach up the hill (Br.). "We hounds killed the hare," quoth the lap dog (Br.). We killed the bear (Am.)

733. И мышь в свою норку тащит корку. *See 771 (К)*

Cf..: Every man drags water to his own mill (Am.). Every miller draws water to his own mill (Br.)

734. Имя им легион. *They are extremely numerous*

Cf.: Their name is legion (Am., Br.)

735. И на жемчуге бывает царапина. *See 737 (И)*

Cf.: The best cloth may have a moth in it (Br.). Every bean (white) has its black (Br.). He who wants a mule without fault, must walk on foot (Br.). Nothing is perfect (Am., Br.)

736. И на Машку бывает промашка. *See 738 (И)*

Var.: Живёт и на Машку промашка

Cf.: Every man has a fool in (up) his sleeve (Am., Br.)

737. И на солнце есть пятна. *The best people or things have some defect. See 54 (Б), 235 (В), 692 (И), 735 (И), 1171 b (М), 1430 (Н), 1452 (Н)*

Cf.: Every light has its shadow (Am., Br.). Every man has his faults (Am., Br.). Every man has his weak side (Br.). Every man has the defects of his /own/ virtues (his qualities) (Br.). Every sky has its cloud (Am.). No gold (silver) without his dross (Br.). None of us are perfect (Am.). None's so good that's good at all (Br.). No sun without a shadow (Br.). Nothing is perfect (Am., Br.). A prize apple can have a worm inside (Br.). The reddest apple may have a worm in it (Am.). There are spots /even/ on (in) the sun (Br.). There is nothing perfect in the world (Am.)

738. И на старуху бывает проруха. *Even most experienced and clever people sometimes err. (This is said to excuse one's own or someone else's fault, blunder, etc.) See 51 (Б), 736 (И), 866 (К), 1187 (Н), 2251 (Ч)*

Var.: У всякой старушки свои прорушки

Cf.: Every man has a fool in (up) his sleeve (Am., Br.). A good marksman may miss (Br.). Great men are not always wise (Am.). Homer sometimes nods (sleeps) (Br.). No man is always a fool, but every man is sometimes (Am.). No man is wise at all times (Am., Br.). No one is infallible (Am.). The wisest man may fall (Br.)

739. Иной раз и дурак молвит слово в лад. *Even an unexperienced or silly person can sometimes express a sensible opinion, give a good piece of advice. See 528 (Д)*

Var.: И глупый иногда молвит слово в лад

Cf.: A fool may give a wise man counsel (Am.). A fool may sometimes speak to the purpose (Br.). A fool's bolt may sometimes hit the mark (Br.)

740. Иные времена, иные нравы. *Each succeeding generation has its own way of life and standard of conduct*

Cf.: As times are, so are the customs (Am.). Different times, different manners (Br.). Other days, other ways (Am., Br.). Other times, other customs (Am.). Other times, other fashions (Br.). Other times, other manners (Am., Br.). Times change, and we change with them (and men change with them, and people change, and people change their ideas) (Am.)

741. И от доброго отца родится бешеная овца. *It may happen that a mean son or daughter is brought up in a respectable family*

Cf.: A good cow may have a bad (a black, an evil, an ill) calf (Br.). Many a good cow has a bad calf (Am., Br.). Many a good father has a bad son (Am., Br.)

742. И под дырявой шапкой живёт голова. *See 1488 (Н)*

Cf.: A brave and gentle character is often found under the humblest clothes (Am.). Under a ragged (threadbare) coat lies wisdom (Br.). You can't always tell what is under a worn coat (Am.)

743. И поджарый живот без еды не живёт. *Any living being needs food to stay alive and be strong. See 2155 (У)*

Cf.: The belly carries the feet (the legs) (Br.). Even rosy lips must be fed (Am.). A full belly makes a strong back (Am.). A man cannot live on air (Am.). The stomach carries the feet (Am.). When the belly is full, the bones are at rest (Am.). When the belly is full the bones would be at rest (Br.)

744. И пономарь, и владыка в земле равны. *See 2149 (У)*

Cf.: Death is a great leveler (Am.). Death is the grand leveler (Br.)

745. И сам не ам, и другому не дам. *See 1950 (С)*

Cf.: The dog in the manger won't eat the oats or let anyone else eat them (Am.). Do not grudge others what you cannot enjoy yourself (Am.). Like the dog in the manger he will neither eat himself nor let the horse eat (Br.). You will neither dance nor hold the candle (Br.)

746. Исключение подтверждает правило. *An example, that is contrary to a certain rule, accepted way of conduct, etc., shows that they are still valuable and necessary in most cases*

Cf.: The exception proves the rule (Am., Br.)

747. Искру туши до пожара, беду отводи до удара. *Any trouble should be nipped in the bud before the situation is precarious. See 1555 (О)*

Cf.: Better early than late (Am., Br.). A danger foreseen is half avoided (Am., Br.). A little fire is quickly trodden out (Br.). Prevention is better than cure (Am., Br.). Prevent rather than repent (Am.)

748. И сокол выше солнца не летает. *See 304 (В)*

Cf.: A man can do no more than he can (Am., Br.)

749. И сорока в одно перо не родится. *See 143 (В)*

Var.: В одно перо и птица не родится

Cf.: It takes all kinds of people to make the world (Am.). It takes all sorts to make a world (Br.)

750. Истина в вине. *Wine loosens a man's tongue and he tells what should be concealed. See 2312 (Ч)*

Cf.: Ale in, truth out (Br.). In wine there is truth (Am., Br.). Wine /is/ in, truth /is/ out (Br.). Wine is the discoverer of secrets (Am.)

751. История повторяется. *In the course of time all events take place again in one or another way. See 222 (В), 1486 (Н)*

Cf.: History repeats itself (Am., Br.)

752. И ты, Брут! *And you betray me, or are against me, too! (You say this to a friend or a supporter who betrays or accuses you when others do, it being unexpected to you)*

Cf.: And you too! (Am., Br.). You too, Brutus! (Am., Br.)

753. И у самого длинного дня есть конец. *See 1725 (П)*

Cf.: Be the day never so long, at length comes evensong (Am.). It is a long road that does not end (has no ending) (Am.). It's a long lane (road) that has no turning (Am., Br.). It's a long line that has no turning (Am.). Long as the day may be, the night comes at last (Am.). The longest day has an end (Am., Br.). 'Tis a long run that never turns (Br.)

754. И хочется, да не можется. *I would like to do it but I cannot for some reason or other. See 552 (Д)*

Cf.: The spirit is willing, but the flesh is weak (Am., Br.). The strength is weak, but the desire is great (Br.)

755. И хочется, и колется. *See 2209 (Х)*

Var.: И хочется, и колется, и мама (матушка) не велит

Cf.: All cats love fish but fear to wet their paws (Br.). The cat would eat fish, but she will not wet her feet (Am.)

756. И через золото слёзы текут. *You can be rich but very unhappy. See 2023 (С)*

Cf.: A man may buy gold too dear (Br.). Money can't buy happiness (Am.). Some swim in wealth but sink in tears (Am.)

757. Ищи ветра в поле. *Somebody or something that is being looked for or pursued has gone away or has disappeared*

Cf.: The bird has flown (Br.). The bird (chicken) has flown the coop (Am.). Gone for a holiday (Br.). Gone with the wind (Am.). Look where the partridge were last year (Br.)

758. Ищи да обрящешь. *See 922 (К)*

Cf.: Look and you shall find (Am.). Seek, and you shall find (Am., Br.)

К

759. Кабы бабушка не бабушка, так была б она дедушкой. *See 560 (Е)*

Cf.: If "ifs" and "ands" were pots and pans /, there would be no need for tinkers (tinkers' hands)/ (Am.). If my aunt had been a man, she'd have been my uncle (Br.)

760. Кабы знал, где упасть, так соломки б подостлал. *If I had known of the grave consequences of my actions, I would have taken precautions*

Вар.: Кабы знал, где упасть, так соломки бы постлал (припасть)

Cf.: Danger foreseen is half avoided (Am., Br.). Forewarned is forearmed (Am., Br.)

761. Кабы на коня не спотычка, ему бы и цены не было. *See 560 (Е)*

Cf.: If wishes were horses, beggars would ride (Am., Br.)

762. Кабы на хмель не мороз, так он бы и тын перерос. *See 560 (Е)*

Var.: Если бы на горох не мороз, он бы давно через тын перерос. Если бы не мороз, так овёс бы до неба дорос

Cf.: If "ifs" and "ands" were pots and pans, /, there would be no need for tinkers (tinkers' hands)/ (Am.). If ifs and ans were pots and pans (Br.). If turnips were watches, I would wear one by my side (Br.)

763. Кабы не кабы да не но, был бы генералом давно. *See 560 (Е)*

Var.: Кабы не кабы да не но, были бы мы богаты давно. Кабы не кабы, так и было бы море, а не пруды

Cf.: If "ifs" and "ands" were pots and pans /, there would be no need for tinkers (tinkers' hands)/ (Am.). If ifs and ans were pots and pans (Br.)

764. Кабы не плешь, так бы не голо. *See 560 (Е)*

Cf.: If "ifs" and "ands" were pots and pans /there would be no need for tinkers/ (Am.). If my aunt had been a man, she'd have been my uncle (Br.)

765. Кабы сивому коню чёрную гриву, был бы буланый. *See 560 (Е)*

Var.: Кабы хвост да грива, так бы цела кобыла

Cf.: If "ifs" and "ands" were pots and pans /, there would be no need for tinkers (tinkers' hands)/ (Am.). If ifs and ans were pots and pans (Br.). If wishes were horses, beggars would ride (Am., Br.)

766. Каждая река к морю течёт. *Every man makes his contribution to some common cause*

Cf.: All rivers run into the sea (Br.). All rivers run to the sea (Am.)

767. Каждому своё. *a) Each person has his own taste. See 599 (Ж); b) See 1182 (Н)*

Cf.: a) To each his own (Am., Br.)

b) Give every man his due (Am., Br.). Give every man the credit that he deserves (Am.). Render unto Caesar the things that are Caesar's (Br.). Render unto Caesar the things which are Caesar's (Am.)

768. Каждому своя болезнь тяжела. *Every man considers his troubles are most grievous. See 285 (В), 770 (К)*

Var.: Всякому своя болячка больна

Cf.: Everyone thinks his own cross the hardest to bear (Br.). To everyone his own cross is heaviest (Am.)

769. Каждому своя милая—самая красивая. *There is no such thing as beauty in itself; people or things look beautiful to you when you like them. See 1361 (Н), 1395 (Н)*

Cf.: Beauty is in the beholder's eyes (Br.). Beauty is in the eye of the beholder (Am., Br.). Beauty lies in the lover's eyes (Am., Br.). Fair is not fair, but that which pleases (Br.)

770. Каждому своя ноша тяжела. *Everyone thinks he works hardest or has to put up with more difficulties than anyone else*

Cf.: Every horse thinks his pack heaviest (Am., Br.). Every horse thinks its /own/ sack heaviest (Br.). Every man thinks his own burden the heaviest (Am.). Every one thinks his own burden heavy (his own cross the hardest to bear, his pack heaviest) (Br.). Everyone thinks his sack heaviest (Am., Br.). To everyone his own cross is heaviest (Am.)

771. Каждый в свою нору тянет. *Every man seizes any advantage of what he can. See 263 (В), 268 (В), 733 (И), 876 (К)*

Cf.: Every man drags water to his own mill (Am.). Every miller (one) draws water to his own mill (Br.)

772. Каждый для себя мудрый. *See 775 (К)*

Cf.: Everyone is witty for his own purpose (Br.). Everyone speaks for his own interest (Am.)

773. Каждый дом имеет свой содом. *See 1670 (П)*

Cf.: No house without mouse (Br.). There is a skeleton in every house (Am., Br.). There's a skeleton in everybody's closet (every family /closet/) (Am.)

774. Каждый по-своему с ума сходит. *Every man has his own oddities and whims. See 2086 (У), 2088 (У)*

Cf.: Every man has his foible (Br.). Every man is mad on some point (Br.). Everyone enjoys himself in his own way (Am.)

775. Каждый свой интерес знает. *In the first place, everyone thinks of his own advantage. See 255 (В), 531 (Д), 772 (К)*

Cf.: Every one is witty for his own purpose (Br.). Everyone speaks for his own interest (Am.). It is in his own interest that the cat purrs (Am.)

776. Каждый смотрит со своей колокольни. *Different people judge things differently, according to their perception or interests*

Cf.: The donkey means one thing and the driver another (Br.). Everything is according to the color of the glass with which one views it (Am.). It's all in the way you look at it (Am.). We all see the world through different lenses (Am.). What we see depends mainly on what we look for (Am.)

777. Каждый человек свою цену имеет. *No man is so honest that he cannot be bribed for a smaller or larger amount of money*

Cf.: Every man has his price (Am., Br.)

778. Как аукнется, так и откликнется. *See 824 (К)*

Cf.: As the call, so the echo (Br.). Do unto others as they do unto you (Am.). What goes around comes around (Am.)

779. Как волка ни корми, он всё в лес глядит. *However hard you can try to improve a man's mean nature, it will manifest itself sooner or later. See 380 (Г), 853 (К)*

Var.: Сколько волка ни корми, /а/ он всё в лес смотрит

Cf.: Bring a cow into the hall and she'll run to the byre (Br.). Drive nature out of the door and it will return by the window (Am.). The frog cannot out of her bog (Br.). Nature is deeper than nurture (Am.). Throw nature out of the door, it will come back /again/ (it will return) through the window (Br.). What is bred in the bone will not /come (go)/ out of the flesh (Am., Br.)

780. Как вор ни ворует, а тюрьмы не минует. *In the end, one will be punished for the crimes committed. See 1033 (Л), 1042 (Л), 1907 (С)*

Var.: Сколько вору ни воровать, а кнута (петли) не миновать

Cf.: The end of the thief is the gallows (Am.). Every fox must pay with his skin to the flayer (furrier) (Br.). Long runs the fox, but at last is caught (Am.)

781. Как живёшь, так и слывёшь. *See 818 (К)*

Cf.: A crooked stick throws a crooked shadow (Br.). A crooked stick will cast (will have) a crooked shadow (Am.)

782. Как жил, так и умер. *The man died as he deserved by the way of life he had lived. See 1953 (С)*

Cf.: As a man lives, so shall he die; as a tree falls, so shall it lie (Am., Br.). A good life makes a good death (Br.). An ill life, an ill end (Am., Br.). Such a life, such a death (Br.). They die well that live well (Am.). We die as we live (Am.)

783. Какие корешки, такие и ветки, какие родители, такие и детки. *See 2357 (Я)*

Cf.: As mother and father, so is daughter and son (Am.). The fruit of a good tree is also good (Am.). If the parents are good, the children follow in their footsteps (Am.). Like parents, like children (Br.). Parents are patterns (Am.). The young ravens are beaked like the old (Am.)

784. Как месяц ни светит, а всё не солнышко. *An ordinary man cannot be equaled to a bright talented person*

Var.: Как месяц ни свети, а всё не солнца свет

Cf.: Every light is not the sun (Br.). Stars are not seen by sunshine (Am.). The stars are not seen where the sun shines (Br.)

785. Как на охоту ехать, так собак кормить. *See 398 (Г)*

Var.: Не тогда собак кормить, как на охоту идти

Cf.: Don't have thy cloak to make when it begins to rain (Br.). Have not the cloak to be made when it begins to rain (Am.)

786. Как ни ликовать, а беды не миновать. *There is no way to avoid misfortune in one's lifetime. See 1611 (О)*

Cf.: No fence against ill fortune (Am., Br.). No man shall pass his whole life free from misfortune (Am.)

787. Каков Ананий, такова у него и Маланья. *The wife is just as bad or good as the husband. See 1162 (М), 2162 (У)*

Cf.: As is the gander, so is the goose (Am.). A bad Jack may have a bad Jill (Am.). A good husband makes a good wife (Am.). A good Jack makes a good Jill (Am., Br.). A good yeoman makes a good wife (Br.). Like pot, like pot-lid (Am.). Such pot, such pot-lid (Am.). There is always a Jill as bad as a Jack (Am.). There's no so bad a Jill, but there's as bad a Jack (a Will) (Br.)

788. Какова Маланья, таковы у ней и оладьи. *See 802 (К)*

Cf.: As is the workman, so is his work (Am.). As is the workman, so is the work (Br.)

789. Какова матка, таковы и детки. *See 2357 (Я)*

Var.: Какова матка, таково и ягнятко

Cf.: Children are what their mothers are (Am.). Like hen, like chicken (Am.). Like hen, like children (Br.)

790. Какова мать, такова и дочь. *See 2357 (Я)*

Cf.: As is the mother, so is the daughter (Am.). Like mother, like child (Br.). Like mother, like daughter (Am., Br.)

791. Какова от пса ловля, такова ему и кормля. *See 794 (К)*

Cf.: As the work, so the pay (Br.). A good servant must have good wages (Am.). The labo(u)rer is worthy of his hire (Am., Br.). A workman is worthy of his hire (Am.)

792. Какова постель, таков и сон. *See 2303 (Ч)*

Cf.: As you make your bed, so you must lie in it (Am., Br.)

793. Какова пряха, такова на ней и рубаха. *See 802 (К)*

Cf.: As is the gardener, so is the garden (Am.). As is the workman, so is his work (Am.). As is the workman, so is the work (Br.). Such a bird, such a nest (Am.)

794. Какова работа, такова и плата. *The reward depends on whether the job done was good or bad. See 791 (К), 1714 (П)*

Var.: Каков молебен, такова и плата

Cf.: As the work, so the pay (Br.).

A good servant must have good wages (Am.). The labo(u)rer is worthy of his hire (Am., Br.). Pay the piper his due (Am.). A workman is worthy of his hire (Am.)

795. Какова устинья, такова у ней и ботвинья. *See 802 (К)*

Var.: Какова Аксинья, такова и ботвинья

Cf.: As is the workman, so is his work (Am.). As is the workman, so is the work (Br.)

796. Каков в колыбельку, таков и в могилку. *See 383 (Г)*

Cf.: What is bred in the bone will not out of the flesh (Am., Br.)

797. Каков Дёма, таково у него и дома. *The order maintained in the household depends on the master. See 802 (К)*

Cf.: As is the gardener, so is the garden (Br.). Like master, like land (Br.). Such a bird, such a nest (Am.). Such bird, such nest (Br.)

798. Каков дядя до людей, таково дяде от людей. *See 824 (К)*

Cf.: As we do unto others, so it is done unto us (Br.). As you do to others, expect others to do to you (Br.). Do unto others as they do unto you (Am.). What goes around comes around (Am.)

799. Каков есть, такова и честь. *See 1679 (П), 1723 (П)*

Cf.: A bad cat deserves a bad rat (Am.). A good dog deserves a good bone (Am., Br.). Sweets to the sweet and sour to the sour (Am.)

800. Каков корень, таков и плод. *See 2357 (Я)*

Var.: Каков корень, таков и отпрыск (таково и семя)

Cf : As mother and father, so is daughter and son (Am.). Like father, like child (Br.). Like father, like son (Am., Br.)

801. Каков лён, такова и пряжа. *See 805 (К)*

Cf.: As the tree, so the wood (Br.). There never was a good knife made of bad steel (Am.)

802. Каков мастер, такова и работа. *The quality of the job done depends on the skill of the workman. See 431 (Д), 788 (К), 793 (К), 795 (К), 797 (К), 819 (К), 1649 (П), 1702 (П)*

Cf.: As is the gardener, so is the garden (Am.). As is the workman, so is his work (Am.). As is the workman, so is the work (Br.). Like author, like book (Br.). Like carpenter, like chips (Am.). Such a bird, such a nest (Am.). Such bird, such nest (Br.). Such carpenter, such chips (Br.)

803. Каков мех, такова и шуба. *See 805 (К)*

Cf.: As the tree, so the wood (Br.). There never was a good knife made of bad steel (Am.)

804. Каков ни будь грозен день, а вечер настанет. *See 1725 (П)*

Cf.: After a storm comes a calm (Br.). After the storm comes the calm (Am.). Be the day never so long, at length comes evensong (Br.). There's always a quiet after a storm (Am.)

805. Каково волокно, таково и полотно. *The quality of a thing is conditioned by the quality of the stuff it is made of. See 714 (И), 801 (К), 803 (К), 2284 (Ч)*

Cf.: As the tree, so the wood (Br.). Like wood, like arrows (Br.). There never was a good knife made of bad steel (Am.).

806. Каково дерево, таков и клин, каков батька, таков и сын. *See 2357 (Я)*

Var.: /Какова хата, таков и тын,/ каков отец, таков и сын

Cf.: As father, as son (so the son) (Am.). Like father, like son (Am., Br.). Such a father, such a son (Br.).

Such is the father, such is the son (Am.)

807. Каково дерево, таковы и сучья. *See 2357 (Я)*

Cf.: Bad bird, bad eggs (Am.). Like parents, like children (Br.). Such as the tree is, so (such) is the fruit (Am.)

808. Каково лукошко, такова и покрышка. *See 1723 (П)*

Cf.: A bad cat deserves a bad rat (Am.). A good dog deserves a good bone (Am., Br.). Such cup, such cover (Br.)

809. Каково начало, таков и конец. *It is the first steps that the result of some undertaking depends on. See 1652 (П), 1799 (П)*

Cf.: A bad beginning has a bad ending (Br.). A bad day never has a good night (Am.). A good beginning makes a good ending (Am., Br.). If you miss the first buttonhole, you will not succeed in buttoning up your coat (Am.). So goes Monday, so goes all the week (Am.). Such beginning, such end (Br.). You can tell the day by the morning (Am.)

810. Каково семя, таково и племя. *See 2357 (Я)*

Var.: Каково семя, таков и плод

Cf.: As mother and father, so is daughter and son (Am.). As the tree, so the fruit (Am., Br.). Like parents, like children (Br.)

811. Каково сошьёшь, таково и износишь. *See 2303 (Ч)*

Var.: Каково испечёшь, таково и съешь

Cf.: As you sow so you shall reap (Am., Br.)

812. Каков отец, таков и молодец. *See 2357 (Я)*

Cf.: As father, as (so the) son (Am.). Like father, like child (Br.). Like father, like son (Am., Br.). Such a father, such a son (Br.). Such is the father, such is the son (Am.)

813. Каков пастырь, таковы и овцы. *See 817 (К)*

Cf.: As the man, so his cattle (Br.). Like king (priest), like people (Am., Br.)

814. Каков Пахом, такова и шапка на нём. *See 1723 (П)*

Cf.: A bad cat deserves a bad rat (Am.). A good dog deserves a good bone (Am., Br.). Such cup, such cover (Br.)

815. Каков плод, таков и приплод. *See 2357 (Я)*

Var.: Каков род, таков и приплод

Cf.: Like begets like (Am., Br.). Like breeds like (Br.). The like breeds the like (Am.)

816. Каков поехал, таков и приехал. *See 195 (В)*

Cf.: Send a fool to the market, and a fool he'll return (Am., Br.)

817. Каков поп, таков и приход. *The subordinates are as good or bad as their leader. See 813 (К), 822 (К)*

Cf.: As the man, so his cattle (Br.). Like king, like people (Am., Br.). Like priest, like people (Am., Br.). Like prince, like people (Br.). Like teacher, like pupil (Br.). Such captain, such retinue (Br.)

818. Каков Савва, такова ему и слава. *A mean person has a bad reputation. See 781 (К), 1709 (П)*

Var.: Какова пава, такова ей и слава

Cf.: A crooked stick throws a crooked shadow (Br.). A crooked stick will cast (have) a crooked shadow (Am.). A crooked tree throws only a crooked shadow (Am.). If the staff be crooked, the shadow cannot be straight (Br.)

819. Каков строитель, таков и дом. *See 802 (К)*

Cf.: As is the workman, so is his work (Am.). As is the workman, so is the work (Br.). Such a bird, such a nest (Am.). Such bird, such nest (Br.)

820. Каков у дела, таков и у хлеба. *There exists interdependence between how quickly or slowly a man eats and works. See 567 (Е), 919 (К)*

Cf.: A man eats so he works (Am.). Quick at meat, quick at work (Am., Br.). Slow at meat, slow at work (Br.). A swift eater, a swift worker (Am.). Who eats with heart is a worker smart (Br.)

821. Каков усол, таков и вкус. *The quality of food depends on the stuff it is made of. See 2284 (Ч)*

Cf.: Fat hens make rich soup (Am.). Such beef, such broth (Br.)

822. Каков хозяин, таков и слуга. *The servant takes after his boss. See 817 (К)*

Cf: As the master is, so is his dog (Am.). A bad master makes a bad servant (Am., Br.). Good masters make good servants (Br.). Jack is as good as his master (Am., Br.). Like lord, like chaplain (Br.). Like master, like dog (Br.). Like master, like man (Am., Br.). Like mistress, like maid (Br.). Such as the priest, such is the clerk (Br.)

823. Каковы сами, таковы и сани. *See 1723 (П)*

Cf.: A bad cat deserves a bad rat (Am.). A good dog deserves a good bone (Am., Br.). Like cup, like cover (Br.)

824. Какой привет, такой и ответ. *People treat you like you treat them, and vice versa. See 778 (К), 798 (К), 1197 (Н)*

Var.: По привету и ответ

Cf.: As the call, so the echo (Br.). As we do unto others, so it is done unto us (Br.). As you salute, you will be saluted (Am.). Such answer as a man gives, such will he get (Br.). Such welcome, such farewell (Br.). What bread men break is broke to them again (Br.). What goes around comes around (Am.). What we gave we have (Br.). You get what you give (Am.)

825. Как постелешь, так и поспишь. *See 2303 (Ч)*

Cf.: As you make your bed, so you will lie in it (Am., Br.). You shall reap what you sow (Am.)

826. Как с быком ни биться, а молока от него не добиться. *You will not get from a man that of which he has none. See 654 (З)*

Var.: Сколько с быком ни биться, а молока от него не добиться

Cf.: A dry well pumps no water (Am.). It is very hard to shave an egg (Am., Br.). No man can flay a stone (Am., Br.). You cannot get (wring) blood (milk, water) from a flint (Br.). You cannot get blood from a stone (Am., Br.). You can't draw water from a dry well (Am.). You can't get (pick, take) feathers off a toad (Am.)

827. Как свинью в кафтан ни ряди, она свиньёй останется. *Refining a man's appearance does not make him nobler or wiser. See 839 (К), 1235 (Н), 1236 (Н), 1563 (О), 1636 (П), 1743 (П)*

Cf.: An ape is an ape, a varlet is a varlet, though they be clad in silk and scarlet (Am.). An ape's an ape, a varlet's a varlet, though they be clad in silk or scarlet (Br.). An ass is an ass, though laden with gold (Am.). An ass is but an ass, though laden with gold (Br.). A boor remains a boor though he sleeps on a silken bolster (Br.). Dress a monkey as you will, it remains a monkey still (Am.). A golden bit does not make a horse any better (Br.). A golden bit does not make the horse any better (Am.)

828. Как себя ни поведёшь, от напраслин не уйдёшь. *See 670 (З)*

Cf.: The best things (Everything) may be abused (Br.). There's no one so clean that somebody doesn't think they're dirty (Am.)

829. Как хочу, так и ворочу. *Nobody can order me how I should act. See 1869 (С)*

Cf.: As I will so I command (Br.). I do as I please (Am.)

830. Капля и камень долбит. *Persistently repeated efforts, however negligible, can yield great results. See 558 (Д), 1107 (М), 1662 (П)*

Var.: Капля и камень точит. Капля по капле и камень долбит

Cf.: Constant dripping wears away a stone (Am.). Constant dropping wears away a stone (Br.). Constant dropping wears away the stone (Am.). Drop by drop the lake is drained (Br.). The falling drops at last will wear the stone (Am.). It's a steady stream that wears a stone (Am.). Many drops of water will sink a ship (Am.). Spit on a (the) stone, /and/ it will be wet at last (Br.). A steady drop makes a hole in a rock (Am.)

831. Карман сух, так и судья глух. *See 1387 (Н)*

Var.: Карман сух—и поп глух

Cf.: An empty hand is no lure for the hawk (Br.). Empty hands allure no hawks (Am.)

832. Кашу маслом не испортишь. *Abundance of what you need, of what is useful or healthy will do you no harm*

Cf.: Never too much of a good thing (Br.). Plenty is no plague (Br.). You can never have too much of a good thing (Am.). You can't be too rich or too thin (Am.). You can't have too much of a good thing (Am., Br.)

833. К большому терпению придёт и умение. *See 2044 (Т)*

Var.: Без терпения нет и умения

Cf.: Always at it wins the day (Br.). Diligent working makes an expert workman (Br.). If at first you don't succeed, try, try again (Am.). If at first you don't succeed, try, try, try again (Br.). Perseverance conquers all things (Am.). Perseverance wins (Br.). Time and patience change the mulberry leaf to satin (Am.)

834. К воронам попал, по-вороньи каркай. *See 1866 (С)*

Var.: С воронами летать—по-вороньи каркать

Cf.: He who kennels with wolves must howl (Br.). When you are with wolves, you must howl with them (Am.)

835. Кесарю кесарево. *Treat people as they deserve. See 1679 (П)*

Cf.: Give every man his due (Am., Br.). Give every man the credit that he deserves (has earned) (Am.). Render to (unto) Caesar the things that are Caesar's (Br.). Render unto Caesar the things which are Caesar's (Am.)

836. Кинь в окошко крошки, в дверь придёт лепёшка. *See 622 (З)*

Cf.: Cast thy bread upon the waters, for thou shalt find it after many days (Br.). Cast your bread upon the water; it will return to you a hundredfold (Am.). A good deed comes back a thousandfold (Am.). Scatter with one hand, gather with two (Am., Br.)

837. Клевета что уголь: не обожжёт, так замарает. *Slander always leaves a trail behind and some of it finds belief*

Cf.: Fling dirt enough and some will stick (Am., Br.). If coals do not burn, they blacken (Br.). If the ball does not stick to the wall, it will at least leave a mark (Br.). If you throw enough pitch, some of it is sure to stick (Am.). If you throw mud enough, some of it will stick (Br.). Plaster thick, and some will stick (Br.). Slander leaves a scar behind (Am., Br.). Slander that is raised is ill to fell (Am.). Throw mud enough, and some will stick (Am.)

838. Клин клином вышибают. *Consequences of some action or condition should be eliminated by means similar to those that caused them. See 2264 (Ч)*

Cf.: Dangers are conquered by dangers (Am.). Dangers are overcome by dangers (Br.). Desperate cures to desperate ills apply (Am.). Desperate diseases must have desperate cures (Am.). Desperate diseases require desperate cures (Br.). Desperate evils require desperate remedies (Am.). Fight fire with fire (Am., Br.). Fight the devil with his own tools, or fight the devil with fire (Am.). Habit cures (is overcome by) habit (Br.). The hair of the dog is good for the bite (is the cure of his bite) (Am.). Like cures like (Am., Br.). One nail drives out another (Am., Br.). A peg is driven out by a peg, a nail by a nail (Am.). Take a hair of the dog that bit you (Br.). Take the hair of the same dog that bit you, and it will heal the wound (Am.)

839. Кляча и в золотой узде не конь. *See 827 (К)*

Cf.: A golden bit does not make a horse any better (Br.). A golden bit does not make the horse any better (Am.)

840. К мокрому телёнку все мухи льнут. *See 1172 (Н)*

Cf.: Flies go to (hunt) the lean horse (Br.). The lean dog is all fleas (Am.). An unhappy man's cart is easy to overthrow (Am.)

841. Ко всему привыкаешь. *See 2309 (Ч)*

Cf.: It is nothing when you are used to it (Br.). Once a use and ever a custom (Br.). Once a use, ever a custom (Br.). One can get used to everything—even hanging (Am.)

842. Когда деньги говорят, тогда правда молчит. *With money you can do anything, be it even unjust*

Cf.: When gold speaks, everyone is silent (other tongues are dumb) (Am.). When money speaks, truth keeps its mouth shut (keeps silent) (Am.). You may speak with your gold and make other tongues dumb (Br.). You may speak with your gold and make other tongues silent (Am.)

843. Когда дрова горят, тогда и кашу варят. *See 977 (К)*

Var.: Обед тогда варят, когда дрова горят

Cf.: Strike while the iron is hot (Am., Br.)

844. Когда лошадь бежит, не надобно шпор. *A good worker needs no driving on. See 1228 (Н)*

Cf.: The beast that goes always never wants blows (Br.). Don't spur a willing horse (Am., Br.). Don't whip the horse that is pulling (Am.). A good horse should be seldom spurred (Am., Br.). A running horse needs no spur (Br.)

845. Когда не везёт, утонешь и в ложке воды. *See 857 (К)*

Cf.: A man born to misfortune will fall on his back and fracture his nose (Am.). An unfortunate (unlucky) man would be drowned in a tea-cup (Br.). An unhappy man's cart is easy to overthrow (Am.)

846. Когда не можешь кончить, не начинай. *Never undertake a job if you are not sure that you will be able to accomplish it*

Cf.: Better never begin than never make an end (Am.). Better never to begin than never to make an end (Br.). Don't start anything /what/ you can't finish (Am.)

847. Когда рак свистнет и рыба запоёт. *It will never happen; you will never get it. See 453 (Д), 1729 (П)*

Cf.: If you cut down the woods, you'll catch the wolf (Br.). If the sky falls, we shall catch larks (Am., Br.). Lots of luck, Charlie! (Am.). When pigs fly (Am., Br.). When the cows come home (Br.)

848. Когда рассердишься, сосчитай до ста. *If you are enraged, wait a little till you calm down. See 356 (Г)*

Cf.: A good remedy for anger is delay (Am.). If you are angry, count to ten /, if very angry count to ten again/ (Am.). If you are angry, you may turn the buckle of your girdle behind you (Br.). Sleep with your anger (Am.). When angry count a hundred (recite the alphabet) (Br.). When in anger, count to ten before you speak (Am.). When in anger, say the alphabet (Am.)

849. Когда рук много, работа спорится. *See 13 (А)*

Cf.: Many hands make light work (Am., Br.). Many hands make quick work (Br.)

850. Когда хата сгорит, сажи не трусят. *See 1730 (П)*

Cf.: It is too late to cast anchor when the ship's on the rocks (Br.). It is too late to cover the well when the child is drowned (Am.). It is too late to lock the stable door when the steed is stolen (Am., Br.). It is too late to throw water on the cinders when the house is burned down (Am.). When the calf is drowned, we cover the well (Br.). When the house is burned down you bring water (Br.)

851. Кого Бог захочет погубить, у того сначала отнимет разум. *He whom fortune will ruin she robs of his wits*

Var.: Если Бог хочет наказать, он разума лишает

Cf.: Whom God would destroy He first makes mad (Br.). Whom God would ruin He first deprives of reason (Br.). Whom the gods would destroy they first make mad (Am.)

852. Коготок увяз—всей птичке пропасть. *One blameworthy action leads to many more which results in grave consequences*

Cf.: Of one ill come many (Am.). One evil breeds (brings) another (Am.). Submitting to one wrong brings on another (Br.)

853. Козла сколько ни корми, а он всё в огород лезет. *See 383 (Г), 779 (К)*

Cf.: Bring a cow into the hall and she'll run to the byre (Br.). What is bred in the bone will not /come (go)/ out of the flesh (Am., Br.)

854. Коли повезёт, так и бык телёнка принесёт. *When circumstances are favo(u)rable, you can be successful. See 335 (Г), 1538 (О)*

Cf.: If luck is with you, even your ox will give birth to a calf (Am.). If you are lucky, even your rooster will lay eggs (Am.). When man has luck, even his ox calves (Br.). Whom God loves, his bitch brings forth pigs (Br.)

855 Кому много дано, с того много и взыщется. *Greater demands are made of a gifted or skillful man than of a mediocre one*

Var.: Кому многое дано, с того много и спросится

Cf.: For all those to whom much is given, much is required (Am.). Much is expected where much is given (Br.). Whomsoever much is given, of him shall be much required (Am.)

856. Кому на месте не сидится, тот добра не наживёт. *A man that keeps changing his job and moving from one place to another will never accomplish much*

Cf.: A plant often removed cannot thrive (Br.). A rolling stone gathers no moss (Am., Br.). A tree often transplanted bears no fruit (Am., Br.). A tree often transplanted neither grows nor thrives (Am.). Trees often transplanted seldom prosper (Am.)

857. Кому не повезёт, тот и на ровном месте упадёт. *When luck is not with you, you will, without any apparent cause, get into trouble. See 565 (Е), 845 (К), 1172 (Н)*

Cf.: A man born to misfortune will fall on his back and fracture his nose (Am.). An unfortunate (unlucky) man would be drowned in a tea-cup (Br.). An unhappy man's cart is easy to overthrow (Am.)

858. Кому служу, тому и пляшу. *See 1264 (Н)*

Cf.: Every man bows to the bush he gets bield of (Br.). Whose bread I eat, his song I sing (Am.)

859. Кому суждено быть повешенным, тот не утонет. *See 1610 (О)*

Cf.: He that is born to be hanged shall never be drowned (Br.). He whose destiny is to be hanged will never be drowned (Am.). If you're born to be hanged, then you'll never be drowned (Am.)

860. Кому счастье служит, тому и люди. *People prefer to be on good terms with those who are successful or rich*

Cf.: All the world loves a winner (Am.). Everyone is akin to the rich (Br.). A full purse has many (never lacks) friends (Am.). He that has a full purse never wanted a friend (Br.). Rich folk have many friends (Br.). The rich has many friends (Br.). A rich man never lacks relatives (Am.). Success has many friends (is befriended by many people) (Br.). Wealth makes many friends (Am.)

861. Кому счастье служит, тот ни о чём не тужит. *Fortunate people live a carefree life and are always lucky. See 2199 (Х)*

Cf.: Give a man fortune and cast him into the sea (Br.). Give a man luck enough and throw him into the sea (Br.). He dances well to whom fortune pipes (Am., Br.)

862. Кому что, а курице просо. *See 1182 (Н)*

Cf.: A barley-corn is better than a diamond to a cock (a rooster) (Br.). Each to his own taste (Am.). A pig used to dirt turns up its nose at rice boiled in milk (Am.). The sow loves bran better than roses (Br.). To each his own (Am., Br.)

863. Конец—делу венец. *A successful completion of your work is its triumphant conclusion*

Var.: Конец венчает дело

Cf.: The end crowns all (the work) (Am., Br.)

864. Кончил дело, гуляй смело. *After you have completed your work, you can enjoy yourself without remorse. See 436 (Д)*

Var.: Сделал дело, гуляй смело

Cf.: Business before pleasure (Am., Br.). Business comes before pleasure (Br.). Business first, pleasure afterwards (Br.). Duty before pleasure (Am.). When the job is well done, you can hang up the hammer (Am.). Work before play (Am.). Work is done, time for fun (Br.)

865. Конь вырвется—догонишь, а слова сказанного не воротишь. *See 1930 (С)*

Var.: Коня на вожжах удержишь, а слово с языка не воротишь

Cf.: Time and words can never be recalled (Am.). Words once spoken you can never recall (Am.). A word spoken is past recalling (Am., Br.)

866. Конь о четырёх ногах, да и тот спотыкается. *See 738 (И)*

Var.: Без спотычки и конь не пробежит. И на доброго коня бывает спотычка

Cf.: The best cart may overthrow (Am., Br.). A horse stumbles that has four legs (Br.). It is a good horse that never stumbles (Br.). It is a good horse who never stumbles (Am.)

867. Конь узнаётся при горе, а друг при беде. *See 521 (Д)*

Cf.: A friend in need is a friend indeed (Am., Br.). A friend is never known till needed (Br.). A friend is never known until needed (Am.)

868. Копейка к копейке—проживёт и семейка. *Small amounts, when added up, make a lot. See 869 (К), 979 (К)*

Cf.: Every (Many a) little makes a mickle (Br.). Every little makes a nickel (Am.). Light gains make a heavy purse (heavy profits) (Am.). Light gains (winnings) make heavy purses (Br.). Little and often fills the purse (Am., Br.). Many a little makes a nickel (Am.). Pennies make dollars (Am.). Penny and penny laid up will be many (Am., Br.)

869. Копейка рубль бережёт. *If you are thrifty when handling small amounts of money, you will have much. See 868 (К)*

Var.: Без копейки рубль не живёт (рубля не бывает). Копейками рубль держится

Cf.: Of saving comes having (Am.). Look after the pennies and the pounds will take care of themselves (Am.). Sparing is the first gaining (Br.). Take care of the dimes (of the nickels, of your pennies) and the dollars will take care of themselves (Am.). Take care of the pence and the pounds will take care of themselves (Am., Br.). Take care of the pennies and the pounds will take care of themselves (Br.). Who will not keep a penny never shall have many (Br.). Who will not keep a penny shall never have many (Am.)

870. Корова черна, да молоко у неё бело. *A person may have a plain appearance but be very good at work. See 891 (К), 894 (К), 1169 (М), 1358 (Н), 2267 (Ч)*

Var.: Некрасива коровка, да молочко даёт. От чёрной коровки (коровы), да белое молочко

Cf.: Black fowl can lay white eggs (Am.). A black hen always lays a white egg (Am.). A black hen lays a white egg (Br.). Spice is black but has sweet smack (Br.)

871. Король и в рубище король. *A really worthy man is not affected by poor clothes or surroundings. See 683 (З), 1488 (Н)*

Cf.: A diamond on a dunghill is a precious diamond still (Am.). A pearl is often hidden in an ugly shell (Am.). Right coral needs no colouring (Br.). True coral needs no painter's brush (Br.)

872. Коротко да ясно, от того и прекрасно. *A concisely expressed idea is easy to understand and is worth much. See 887 (К)*

Cf.: Brevity is the soul of wit (Am., Br.). Few words are best (Am.)

873. Коси коса, пока роса. *See 977 (К)*

Cf.: Make hay while the sun shines (Am., Br.)

874. Кота в мешке не покупают. *Never buy anything before you make sure of the quality of the thing you are going to purchase*

Var.: Кота в мешке покупать нельзя

Cf.: Do not buy a pig in a poke (Am., Br.). Never buy anything before you see it (Am.). Try it before you buy it (Am.)

875. Которая корова пала, та по два удоя давала. *Men are inclined to exaggerate the worth of a thing that is lost*

Var.: Который конь пал, тот рысак был

Cf.:: Blessings brighten as they take their flight (Am.). The fish that escapes is the biggest fish of all (Am.)

876. Кот скребёт на свой хребет. *See 771 (К)*

Var.: Кошка скребёт на свой хребет

Cf.: Every man drags water to his own mill (Am.). Every miller (one) draws water to his own mill (Br.)

877. Кошачья лапка мягка, да коготок востёр. *A man conceals his cruel nature under outward kindness. See 988 (Л), 1170 (М), 2201 (Х)*

Var.: Гладка шёрстка, да коготок (ноготок) остёр

Cf.: Cats hide their claws (Am., Br.). Velvet paws hide sharp claws (Br.)

878. Кошка спит, а мышку видит. *See 372 (Г)*

Var.: Кошка спит, а всё мышей видит. Сова спит, а кур видит

Cf.: The ass dreams of thistles (Br.). The hungry man often talks of bread (Am.)

879. Кошке игрушки, а мышке слёзки. *Amusement for the powerful is sorrow for the weak. See 1548 (О), 2039 (Т)*

Var.: Кошке смех, а мышке слёзы

Cf.: The dainties of the great are tears of the poor (Br.). It may be fun for you, but it is death to the frog (Br.). One man's fancy is another man's poison (Am.). One man's laugh is another man's groan (Br.). One man's pleasure is another man's poison (Am.). The pleasures of the mighty are the tears of the poor (Br.). This may be play to you, 'tis death to us (Br.)

880. Кошку бьют, а невестке наветки дают. *You scold or punish an innocent man meaning someone else you won't dare to. See 65 (Б), 1392 (Н)*

Var.: Кошку бьют, невестке знак подают. Одного бьют, а другому наветки дают. Свекровь дочку бранит—невестке науку даёт. Свекровь кошку бьёт, а невестке наветки даёт

Cf.: He that cannot beat the ass (the horse), beats the saddle (Br.). Many beat the sack and mean the miller (Br.). You kick the dog (Am.)

881. Кошку девятая смерть донимает. *The man is of great vitality*

Cf. A cat has nine lives (Am., Br.)

882. Краденый поросёнок в ушах визжит. *See 1476 (Н)*

Cf.: A guilty conscience is a self-accuser (Br.). A guilty conscience is its own accuser (needs no accuser) (Am., Br.). A guilty conscience needs no condemner (Am.)

883. Крайности сходятся. *People, theories, beliefs, etc., as different from each other as they can be, draw together*

Cf.: Extremes meet (Am., Br.). Opposites attract /each other/ (meet) (Am.). Too far East is West (Br.)

884. Красота до венца, а ум до конца. *Marry an intelligent rather than a beautiful man or woman. See 885 (К), 886 (К), 1356 (Н), 1925 (С)*

Cf.: Beauty is but skin-deep; common sense is thicker than water (Am.). Beauty is no inheritance (Am., Br.). Beauty is only skin-deep (Am., Br.). Looks aren't everything (Am.)

885. Красота до вечера, а доброта навек. *Marry a kind person rather than a beautiful one. See 884 (К), 886 (К)*

Cf.: Beauty is only skin-deep (Am., Br.). Beauty is only skin-deep; goodness goes to the bone (Am.). Beauty is skin-deep; it is the size of the heart that counts (Am.). Looks aren't everything (Am.)

886. Красотой сыт не будешь. *An attractive appearance alone does not provide livelihood. See 884 (К), 885 (К)*

Cf.: Beauty doesn't make the pot boil (Am.). Beauty is a fine thing, but you can't live on it (Am.). Beauty is no inheritance (Am., Br.). Beauty will buy no beef (Br.). Beauty won't buy groceries (Am.). Looks aren't everything (Am.). One cannot live on beauty alone (Am.). Prettiness makes no pottage (Br.)

887. Краткость—сестра таланта. *See 872 (К)*

Cf.: Brevity is the soul of wit (Am., Br.)

888. Кредит портит отношения. *See 128 (В)*

Cf.: Credit makes enemies (Am.). If

you want to keep a friend, never borrow, never lend (Am.). Lend money, lose a friend (Am.). Lend your money and lose your friend (Br.)

889. Кремень на кремень—искра. *When two men or parties matching in power do not yield each other, a great struggle starts. See 1267 (Н)*

Cf.: When Greek meets Greek, then comes the tug of war (Am., Br.)

890. Крепче запрёшь—вернее найдёшь. *Safeguard your property, and it will be there for your use when you want it. See 1666 (П)*

Cf.: Fast bind, fast find (Br.). He that hides can find (Br.). Hiders are good (make the best) finders (Am., Br.). Safe bind, safe find (Br.). Sure bind, sure find (Br.). Them that hides can find (Am.). Those who hide know how to find (Am.)

891. Криво дерево, да яблоки сладки. *See 870 (К)*

Cf.: A black hen always lays (will lay) a white egg (Am.). A black hen lays a white egg (Br.). Crooked furrows grow straight grain (Am.). Spice is black but has (hath) sweet smack (Br.)

892. Кривое дерево не разогнётся прямо. *See 383 (Г)*

Cf.: A crooked tree will never straighten its branches (Am.). That which is crooked cannot be made straight (Br.). What is bred in the bone will not /come (go)/ out of the flesh (Am., Br.). Wood that grows warped can never be straightened (Br.). You can't make a crooked stick lay straight (Am.)

893. Кривой среди слепых—король. *Even a limited ability makes one be hono(u)red by those who have none at all. See 1174 (Н)*

Var.: В царстве слепых и кривому честь. Меж слепых и кривой в чести (зрячий). Среди слепых и одноглазый король

Cf.: Among the blind the one-eyed man is king (Br.). Blessed are the one-eyed among those who are blind (Br.). In the country (kingdom) of the blind the one-eyed man is king (Am., Br.). In the land of the blind the one-eyed are kings (Am.)

894. Кривы дрова, да прямо горят. *See 870 (К)*

Cf.: A crooked log makes a good fire (Br.). Crooked logs make a straight fire (Br.). Crooked logs make straight fires (Am.). A crooked stick makes a straight fire (Am.). Crooked wood makes an even fire (Am.)

895. Кровь за кровь. *See 1550 (О)*

Var.: Кровь за кровь, смерть за смерть

Cf.: Blood asks blood, and death must death requite (Am.). Blood asks blood and death will death requite (Br.). Blood will have blood (Am., Br.)

896. Кровь не вода. *Relatives share strong ties and help each another. See 376 (Г), 1865 (С)*

Cf.: Blood is blood (Am.). Blood is thicker than water (Am., Br.)

897. Кроёного не перекроить. *See 1872 (С)*

Cf.: Things done cannot be undone (Am.). What is done cannot be undone (Am., Br.)

898. Кроме смерти от всего вылечишься. *See 1606 (О)*

Cf.: There is a remedy for all dolours but death (Br.). There is a medicine for all things except death and taxes (Am.). There is a remedy for all things but death (Am., Br.)

899. Кроткая овца всегда волку по зубам. *If you are too bashful, people will dominate or ruin you. See 109 (Б), 1944 (С), 1945 (С), 2142 (У)*

Var.: Не будь овцой, так и волк не съест. Смирная овца волку по зубам

Cf.: Cover yourself with honey and

the flies will fasten on you (Br.). Daub yourself with honey and you will have plenty of flies (Am.). Don't make yourself a mouse, or the cat will eat you (Br.). He that makes himself a sheep shall be eaten by the wolves (Am.). He that maketh himself a sheep shall be eaten by the wolf (Br.). Make yourself all honey and the flies will devour you (Br.). Make yourself honey and flies will devour you (Am.)

900. Кручина иссушит в лучину. *See 1323 (Н)*

Cf.: Adversity flatters no man (Am., Br.). Care brings grey hair (Br.). Care killed the cat (Am., Br.)

901. Крысы бегут с тонущего корабля. *The weaklings, the cowards and the scoundrels are the first to desert or betray a cause in a dangerous situation or in times of trouble*

Cf.: Rats abandon (always leave) a sinking ship (Am.). Rats desert a sinking ship (Am., Br.). Rats forsake (leave) a falling house (a sinking ship) (Br.)

902. Кряхти, да гнись, а упрёшься — переломишься. *See 1048 (Л)*

Cf.: Better bend than break (Br.). Better bow than break (Am., Br.). It is better to bend than break (Am.)

903. К своему рту ложка ближе. *See 1868 (С)*

Cf.: Charity begins at home (Am., Br.)

904. К своим и чёрт хорошо относится. *Success and good fortune come to mean people who do not deserve it*

Cf.: The devil is ever kind to (is fond of) his own (Am.). The devil is good to his own (Am., Br.). The devil is kind to (looks after) his own (Br.). The devil protects (takes care of) his own (Am., Br.)

905. Кстати промолчать, что большое слово сказать. *See 1933 (С)*

Cf.: No wisdom like silence (Am., Br.). Silence is the best policy (Am.)

906. Кто бежит, тот и догоняет. *See 507 (Д)*

Cf.: The race is got by running (Br.). You must run to win the race (Am.)

907. Кто Богу не грешен, царю не виноват? *See 235 (В)*

Cf.: He is dead that is faultless (Am.). He is lifeless that is faultless (Am., Br.)

908. Кто боится, у того в глазах двоится. *See 2154 (У)*

Cf.: Fear has a hundred eyes (Br.). Fear has many eyes (Am.)

909. Кто бы говорил, а ты бы помалкивал. *See 2334 (Ч)*

Cf.: Look who's talking! (Am.). The pot calling (calls) the kettle black (Am., Br.)

910. Кто везёт, на того и накладывают. *Everyone takes advantage of an industrious man. See 1199 (Н)*

Cf.: All lay load (loads) on a willing horse (Br.). All lay the load on the willing horse (Am.). Everyone lays a burden on the willing horse (Am.). If you agree to carry the calf, they'll make you carry the cow (Br.). Make yourself an ass and everyone will lay a sack on you (Am.). The willing horse carries the load (Am.)

911. Кто везёт, того и погоняют. *It is a hard-working man that is always driven on*

Cf.: The horse that draws best is most whipped (Am.). The willing horse gets the whip (Am.)

912. Кто в лес, кто по дрова. *There is no co-ordination in actions or opinions within a group of people*

Cf.: All at sixes and sevens (Br.). Everything is at sixes and sevens (Am.)

913. Кто в кони пошёл, тот и воду вози. *See 1201 (Н)*

Cf.: If you pledge, don't hedge (Br.). Once you pledge, don't hedge (Am.)

914. Кто вчера солгал, тому и завтра не поверят. *A man once caught at a lie will never be trusted. See 1961 (С)*

Var.: Раз соврал, в другой раз не поверят. Раз солгал, а навек лгуном стал. Солжёшь сегодня, не поверят и завтра

Cf.: He that once deceives is ever suspected (Br.). He who lies once is never believed again (Am.). A liar is not believed when he speaks (tells) the truth (Am., Br.). No one believes a liar when he tells the truth (Am.)

915. Кто говорит без умолку, в том мало толку. *See 932 (К)*

Cf.: The greatest talkers are the least doers (Am., Br.). 'Tis not the hen that cackles most that lays the most eggs (Am.)

916. Кто гостю рад, тот и собачку его накормит. *See 1076 (Л)*

Cf.: Love me, love my dog (Am., Br.)

917. Кто другому яму копает, тот сам в неё попадает. *Evil wished or done to others, as a rule, recoils on the perpetrator. See 921 (К), 1598 (О), 2294 (Ч)*

Var.: Не копай (рой) другому яму, сам в неё попадёшь

Cf.: Curses like chickens come home to roost (Br.). Curses, like chickens, come home to roost (Am.). The curse sticks to the tongue of the curser (Am.). The evil that comes out of (goeth out of, issues from) thy mouth flieth into thy bosom (Br.). He that diggeth a pit for another should look that he fall not into it himself (Br.). He who digs a grave for another falls in himself (Am.). He who hurts gets hurt (Am., Br.). He who lays a snare for another, himself falls into it (Am.). If you dig a ditch for your neighbor, you will fall into it yourself (Am.). If you dig a pit for someone else, you will fall into it yourself (Am.). Ill be to him that ill thinks (Br.). When you plot mischief for others, you're preparing trouble for yourself (Am.). Whoso digs a pit, he shall fall therein (Am., Br.)

918. Кто едет, тот и правит. *See 965 (К)*

Cf.: Might makes right (Am., Br.)

919. Кто ест скоро, тот и работает споро. *See 820 (К)*

Cf.: Quick at meat, quick at work (Am., Br.). A swift eater, a swift worker (Am.). Who eats with heart is a worker smart (Br.)

920. Кто ждёт, тот дождётся. *He who can wait patiently for his hopes to come true will be rewarded in the end. See 1188 (Н), 2046 (Т)*

Cf.: All good things come to those who wait (Am.). All things come to him who waits (Am., Br.). Everything comes to him who waits (Am., Br.). Patient waiters are no losers (Br.). Time brings everything to those who can wait (Am.). Wait and you will be rewarded (Am.)

921. Кто за худым пойдёт, тот добра не найдёт. *See 666 (З), 917 (К), 964 (К)*

Var.: За худым пойдёшь—худое найдёшь

Cf.: The biter is /often/ bit (Br.). The biter is sometimes bit (Am.). Evil be to him who evil thinks (Br.). Evil to him who evil does (thinks) (Am.). Gather thistles, expect prickles (Am.). Harm watch, harm catch (Am., Br.). He that mischief hatches, mischief catches (Am., Br.). Ill be to him that thinks ill (Br.). Injure others, injure yourself (Am.). Match-makers often burn their fingers (Br.). A wicked man is his own hell (Am., Br.)

922. Кто ищет, тот всегда найдёт. *An initiative person will always achieve success. See 758 (И)*

Cf.: Fortune comes to him who seeks her (Am.). He that seeketh findeth (Br.). Long looked for comes at last (Am., Br.). Look and you shall find (Am.). Seek, and you shall find (Am., Br.)

923. Кто кого за глаза бранит, тот того боится. *Expressing your low opinion of a man only in his absence means that you fear him. See 616 (З)*

Cf.: He that (who) fears you present, will hate you absent (Br.). When a man's away, abuse him you may (Am.)

924. Кто кого обидит, тот того и ненавидит. *One has a feeling of hostility towards the man he has done harm to*

Cf.: Folks often injure all they fear and hate all they injure (Am.). He that does you an ill turn will never forgive you (Br.). The injured often forgive but those who injure neither forgive nor forget (Am.). Men hate where they hurt (Am.). The offender never pardons (Am.). Offenders never pardon (Am., Br.). They never pardon who have done the wrong (Am.). We hate those whom we have wronged (Am.)

925. Кто кого смог, тот того и с ног. *The strong and powerful ruin the weak. See 94 (Б)*

Var.: Кто кого сможет, тот того и гложет. Кто кого согнёт, тот того и бьёт

Cf.: The big fish eat the little ones (Am.). The great fish eat up the small (Br.). Great trees keep down little ones (keep little ones down) (Am.)

926. Кто легко верит, тот легко и погибает. *A trustful man is often betrayed*

Cf.: He who believes easily is easily deceived (Am.). Sudden trust brings sudden repentance (Am.). Trust is the mother of deceit (Br.)

927. Кто любит арбуз, а кто свиной хрящик, никто никому не указчик. *See 1182 (Н)*

Var.: У кого какой вкус: кто любит дыню, а кто—арбуз. У кого какой вкус, один другому не указчик: кто любит арбуз, а кто свиной хрящик

Cf.: A barley-corn is better than a diamond to a cock (a rooster) (Br.). Every one to his own liking (Br.). The sow loves bran better than roses (Br.). Tastes differ (Am., Br.). A thistle is a fat salad to an ass's mouth (Br.). To each his own (Am., Br.)

928. Кто любит занимать, тому не сдобровать. *If you often get into debts, you will pay for it*

Cf.: Borrow and borrow adds up to sorrow (Am.). The borrower runs in his own debt (Am., Br.). Borrowing brings sorrowing (Am.). He that borrows must pay again with shame and loss (Br.). He that goes a-borrowing, goes a-sorrowing (Am., Br.)

929. Кто любит попа, кто попадью, кто попову дочку. *See 1182 (Н)*

Var.: Кому попадья, а кому попова дочка

Cf.: Every man to his taste (Am., Br.)

930. Кто меч поднимет, от меча и погибнет. *If you commit violence, you must expect violence to be paid back in full*

Var.: Меч поднявший от меча и погибнет

Cf.: All they that take the sword shall perish by (with) the sword (Br.). He who lives by the sword shall perish by the sword (Am.). They that live by the sword will die (will perish) by the sword (Br.)

931. Кто много болтает, тот много врёт. *A chatterer often makes false statements or talks nonsense. See 2366 (Я)*

Cf.: Great talkers are great liars (Br.). He cannot speak well that cannot hold his tongue (Am., Br.). He that talks much lies much (Br.). He who talks much says many foolish things (Am.)

932. Кто много говорит, тот мало делает. *Those who boast of doing much do little. See 321 (Г), 608 (З), 913 (К), 915 (К), 1143 (М)*

Cf.: The cow that moos the most gives the least milk (Am.). A dog that barks much is never a good hunter (Br.). Great boaster, little doer (Am.). Great braggarts are little doers (Am.). The greatest talkers are the least doers (Am., Br.). Great talkers are little doers (Br.). Great talkers, little doers (Am., Br.). Much talk, little work (Am.). Never was a mewing cat a good mouser (Br.). They brag most that can do least (Am., Br.). 'Tis not the hen that cackles most that lays the most eggs (Am.)

933. Кто много обещает, тот ничего не сделает. *See 934 (К)*

Cf.: Expect nothing from him who promises a great deal (Am.). Great promises and small performances (Br.). Long on promises, short on performance (Am., Br.)

934. Кто много сулит, тот мало делает. *People who pledge to do much never keep their word. See 933 (К)*

Var.: Кто много сулит, тот мало даёт

Cf.: Big words seldom go with good deeds (Am.). Expect nothing from him who promises a great deal (Am.). Great promises and small performances (Br.). He that promises much means nothing (Am., Br.). Long on promises, short on performance (Am., Br.). A long tongue has a short hand (Am.). A long tongue is a sign of a short hand (Am., Br.). No greater promisers than those who have nothing to give (Am., Br.)

935. Кто может украсть телёнка, украдёт и корову. *Once a person commits a little theft, he may well become a real thief*

Var.: Кто украдёт яйцо, тот украдёт и лошадь. Кто украл яйцо, украдёт и курицу

Cf.: He that steals an egg will steal a chicken (an ox) (Am.). He that will steal an egg, will steal an ox (Br.). He that will steal an ounce will steal a pound (Am.). He that will steal a pin will steal a better thing (Am.). He that will steal a pin will steal a pound (Br.). Little rogues easily become great ones (Am.)

936. Кто молчит, тот двух научит. *See 359 (Г)*

Cf.: He is a wise man (wise) who speaks little (Am.). He knows most who speaks least (Am., Br.). He who knows does not speak; he who speaks does not know (Am.). Still tongue, wise head (Am.)

937. Кто молчит, тот соглашается. *See 1154 (М)*

Cf.: Silence gives consent (Am., Br.). Silence implies (is, means) consent (Br.)

938. Кто мотает, в том пути не бывает. *If you squander money, you will have none when you need it*

Cf.: He who spends more than he should shall not have to spend when he would (Am.). Who spends more than he should, shall not have to spend when he would (Br.). Wilful waste makes woeful want (Br.). Willful waste makes wasteful (woeful) want (Am.). Willful ways make woeful want (Am.)

939. Кто на борзом коне жениться поскачет, тот скоро поплачет. *See 588 (Ж)*

Var.: На коне резвом жениться не езди

Cf.: Marry in haste and repent at leisure (Am., Br.)

940. Кто над людьми шутки пошучивает, тот на себя плеть накручивает. *Mockers suffer the consequences of their own mockeries. See 1194 (Н), 2345 (Ш)*

Cf.: He makes a foe who makes a jest (Am.). If you give (make) a jest, you must take a jest (Br.). Jesting lies bring serious sorrows (Am.). People who are sharp cut their own fingers (Br.). To laugh at someone is to be laughed back at (Am.). True jests breed bad blood (Am.)

941. Кто не бежит, тот не спотыкается. *See 1384 (H)*

Cf.: He that never climbed (rode), never fell (Br.). Who never climbed never fell (Am.). You will not stumble while on your knees (Am.)

942. Кто не в своё дело суётся, тому достаётся. *See 1086 (Л)*

Cf.: He who meddles smarts (will smart) for it (Br.). Never be breaking your shin on a stool that is not in your way (Am.). That fish is soon caught who nibbles at every bait (Am.)

943. Кто не любит шуток, над тем не шути. *A man devoid of sense of humo(u)r may get offended if you play a joke on him. See 1674 (П)*

Cf.: Better lose a jest than a friend (Am., Br.)

944. Кто не работает, тот не ест. *No man should live by another's labo(u)r*

Cf.: He who does not work, neither should he eat (Br.). A horse that will not carry a saddle must have no oats (Br.). No mill, no meal (Am., Br.). No paternoster, no penny (Br.). No song, no supper (Br.). No work, no recompense (Br.). Those who will not work shall not eat (Am.)

945. Кто не рискует, тот не пьёт шампанского. *See 1834 (P)*

Cf.: No risk, no gain (Am.). Nothing risk, nothing gain (Br.)

946. Кто не с нами, тот против нас. *Anyone who does not support us in our cause is our enemy*

Cf.: He that is not with me is against me (Am., Br.)

947. Кто не умеет рисовать, должен краски растирать. *Those who cannot excel in doing subtle work should be content to do simple one. See 1460 (H)*

Cf.: If you cannot drive the engine, you can clear the road (Br.). If you can't be the sun, be a star (Am.). Who cannot sing, may whistle (Am.)

948. Кто ничего не делает, тому всегда некогда. *Idlers are always short of time*

Var.: Ленивому всегда некогда

Cf.: Idle folk have the least leisure (Am.). Idle folks have the least leisure (Br.). Idle people have the least leisure (Am.). Who is more busy than he who has least to do? (Br.)

949. Кто ничего не знает, тот ни в чём не сомневается. *Ignorant people are sure that they know everything. See 2256 (Ч)*

Cf.: He that knows nothing, doubts nothing (Br.). He who knows nothing never doubts (Am.)

950. Кто ничего не имеет, тот ничего не боится. *See 377 (Г)*

Cf.: The beggar may sing before a footpad (a pick-pocket) (Br.). The beggar may sing before the thief (Am., Br.). He that is down need fear no fall (Am.)

951. Кто нужды не видал, тот и счастья не знает. *See 1291 (H)*

Cf.: He knows best what good is that has endured evil (ill) (Br.). Those who have not tasted the bitterest of life's bitters can never appreciate the sweetest of life's sweets (Am.). We know the sweet when we have tasted the bitter (Am.). Who has never tasted bitter knows not what is sweet (Br.)

952. Кто опоздает, тот воду хлебает. *See 956 (K)*

Var.: Опоздаешь — воду хлебаешь

Cf.: First winner, last loser (Am.). To those who come late the bones

(Br.). Who doesn't come at the right time must take what is left (Am.)

953. Кто от кого, тот и в того. *See 2357 (Я)*

Cf.: An apple does not fall far from the tree (Am.). As the tree, so the fruit (Am., Br.). The fruit doesn't fall far from the tree (Am.). Like cow, like calf (Br.)

954. Кто первый пришёл, первый муку смолол. *The man who is prompt to do his job has the best chances. See 252 (В), 963 (К), 1638 (П), 1822 (Р)*

Var.: Кто первый пришёл, первый молол

Cf.: The cow that's first up, gets the first of the dew (Br.). First come, first served (Am., Br.). First there, first served (Am.). The foremost dog catches the hare (Am., Br.). He who comes first grinds first (Am.)

955. Кто платит музыканту, тот и заказывает музыку. *He who stands the expenses has the right to decide what is to be done*

Cf.: He who pays the piper calls (may call) the tune (Am., Br.). You pay your money and you take your choice (Br.)

956. Кто поздно приходит, тот ничего не находит. *A man who is late always loses. See 952 (К), 1680 (П)*

Var.: Кто поздно пришёл, тому обглоданный мосол. Поздно пришёл, одни кости нашёл

Cf.: First winner, last loser (Am.). For the last the bones (Br.). To those who come late the bones (Br.). Who comes late lodges ill (Br.). Who doesn't come at the right time must take what is left (Am.)

957. Кто привык лгать, тому трудно отвыкать. *See 1039 (Л)*

Cf.: Deceit breeds deceit (Br.). A false tongue will hardly speak the truth (Br.). A lie begets a lie (Br.). A lie begets a lie until they become a generation (Am.). One lie leads to another (Am., Br.)

958. Кто пришёл без приглашения, тот уйдёт без угощения. *See 1345 (Н)*

Var.: Пришёл без приглашения, не жди угощения

Cf.: He who comes uncalled sits unserved (Br.). An unbidden guest knows not where to sit (Am., Br.)

959. Кто прямо ездит, дома не ночует. *See 1231 (Н)*

Var.: Кто прямо ездит, в поле ночует. Напрямки ездить—дома не ночевать. Прямо ворона летает, да дома не ночует

Cf.: The nearest way is commonly the foulest (Br.). A short cut is not always the fastest way (is often a wrong cut) (Br.). A short cut is often the wrong cut (Am.). Short cuts are roundabout ways (Br.)

960. Кто пьёт хмельное, тот говорит дурное. *See 156 (В)*

Cf.: Drinking and thinking don't mix (Am.). When ale (drink) is in, wit is out (Br.). When the ale (the whiskey) is in, wit is out (Am.). When wine is in, wit is out (Am., Br.)

961. Кто рано встаёт, тому Бог даёт. *The man who takes the earliest opportunity of doing his job will get the reward. See 252 (В), 645 (З)*

Var.: Кто рано встаёт, тому Бог подаёт

Cf.: The early bird catches (gets) the worm (Am.). He that will thrive, must rise at five (Br.). He that would thrive must rise at five (Am.). He who gets up early has gold in his mouth (Am.). An hour in the morning is worth two in the evening (Am., Br.). It is the early bird that catches the worm (Br.). The morning has gold in its mouth (Am.). The morning hour has gold in its mouth (Am., Br.). Plow deep while sluggards sleep /, and you shall have corn to sell and to keep/ (Am.)

962. Кто рано ложится и рано встаёт, здоровье, богатство и ум наживёт. *If you keep good hours, you will benefit physically, financially and intellectually. See 1036 (Л)*

Cf.: Early to bed, early to rise makes a man healthy, wealthy and wise (Am., Br.)

963. Кто раньше на мельницу придёт, раньше смелет. *See 954 (К)*

Cf.: First come, first served (Am., Br.). First there, first served (Am.). He that comes first to the mill may sit where he will (Br.). He who comes first grinds first (Am.)

964. Кто сеет ветер, пожнёт бурю. *Those who start an evil action will end up suffering much worse evils. See 917 (К), 921 (К), 1598 (О)*

Var.: Посеешь ветер—пожнёшь бурю

Cf.: Gather thistles, expect prickles (Am.). He that blows dust fills his own eyes (Am.). He that blows in the dust fills his eyes with it (Br.). He that sows iniquity shall reap sorrows (Br.). He who sows the wind, reaps (shall reap) whirlwind (Br.). Sow the wind and reap the whirlwind (Am.)

965. Кто сильнее, тот и правее. *He who is powerful can prove that he is right. See 333 (Г), 918 (К)*

Var.: Чья сторона сильнее, та и правее

Cf.: Accusation is proof when malice and power sit in judge (Am.). Accusing is proving where malice and force sit judges (Br.). Might beats (knows no) right (Am.). Might goes before (is) right (Br.). Might makes (overcomes) right (Am., Br.). The right is with the strongest (Br.). When the foxes pack the jury box, the chicken is always found guilty as accused (Am.). Where force prevails, right perishes (Am.). The wolf finds a reason for taking the lamb (Br.)

966. Кто смел, тот и съел. *See 1937 (С)*

Var: Кто смел, тот два съел (и на коня сел, наперёд поспел)

Cf.: Cheek brings success (Br.). Fortune favo(u)rs the bold (the brave) (Am., Br.). None but the brave deserves the fair (Am., Br.)

967. Кто с нетерпением ждёт, тот долго ждёт. *Waiting anxiously for something makes it seem to take too much time*

Cf.: A watched fire never burns (Am.). A watched kettle (pot) never boils (Am., Br.). A watched pan (pot) is long in boiling (Am., Br.). A watched pan never boils (Br.). Watched rosebuds open slowly (Am.)

968. Кто собою не управит, тот и другого на разум не наставит. *To instruct others you should be able to control yourself*

Var.: Не управишь собою, не управишь и другими

Cf.: He is not fit to command others that cannot command himself (Br.). If you can't command yourself, you can't command others (Am.)

969. Кто спит весною, плачет зимою. *He who is lazy to do his work in proper time will have nothing when in need. См. 1013 (Л), 1014 (Л)*

Cf.: He who sings in summer will weep in winter (Am.). They must hunger in frost that will not work in heat (Am., Br.). They must hunger in winter that will not work in summer (Br.)

970. Кто старое помянёт, тому глаз вон. *Let old wrongdoings be forgotten. See 2281 b (Ч), 2295 b (Ч), 2305 (Ч)*

Var.: Кто прошлое вспомянёт, тому глаз вон

Cf.: Bury the past (Br.). Do not rip up old sores (Am.). Don't rip up old sores and cast up old scores (Am.). Forgive and forget (Am., Br.). Let bygones be bygones (Am., Br.). Let the dead bury the dead (Am., Br.). Never rip up old grievances (sores) (Br.). Reopen not a wound once healed (Am.)

971. Кто чесноку поел—сам скажется. *See 1183 a (Н)*

Cf.: Every man's faults are written on their foreheads (Am.). Every one's faults are written in (on) their foreheads (Br.). Guilty conscience gives itself away (Br.)

972. Куда дерево клонилось, туда и повалилось. *Evil predispositions result in bad consequences*

Var.: Куда дерево клонится, туда и повалится

Cf.: As the tree is bent, so the tree is inclined (Am.). A tree falls the way it leans (Br.)

973. Куда иголка, туда и нитка. *One person acts like the other. (This is said of two closely related people, especially of a husband and a wife)*

Var.: Куда грива, туда и хвост. Куда лошадь, туда и телега. Куда пастушок, туда и посошок

Cf.: The thread follows the needle (Am.). The wagon must go wither the horses draw it (Br.). Where the needle goes, the thread follows (Am.)

974. Куда конь с копытом, туда и рак с клешнёй. *Insignificant men try to equal people of a higher class, incompetent and weak men want to equal qualified and strong people, etc. See 257 (В), 1002 (Л), 1295 b (Н), 1991 (С)*

Cf.: Attempt not to fly like an eagle with the wings of a wren (Am.). The bear wants a tail and cannot be lion (Br.). Every ass thinks himself worthy to stand with the king's horses (Am., Br.). Every duck thinks it is a swan (Am.)

975. Куда ни кинь, всё клин. *The situation is hopeless and there are no means by which it may be solved. See 2202 (Х)*

Var.: Как ни кинь, /а/ всё клин. Куда ни кинь, везде клин

Cf.: Damned if you do, damned if you don't (Am.). One is too few, three /is/ too many (Br.). There is no way out (Am., Br.)

976. Куда один баран, туда и всё стадо. *It takes one person to do something, and the crowd follows him blindfold*

Var.: Куда одна овца, туда и всё стадо

Cf.: The flock follow the bell-wether (Br.). If a sheep loops the dyke, all the rest will follow (Br.). If one sheep has left the fold, the rest will follow (Am.). If one sheep leaps over the ditch, all the rest will follow (Br.). One sheep follows another (Am., Br.). When one sheep leads the way, the rest follow (Am.). Where one man goes, the mob will follow (Am.)

977. Куй железо, пока горячо. *While circumstances are favo(u)rable, seize the right moment to do what you have to. See 606 (Ж), 843 (К), 873 (К), 1198 (Н), 2057 (Т)*

Cf.: Enjoy your ice cream while it's on your plate (Am.). Hoist up the sail while the gale does last (Am.). Hoist your sail while the wind is fair (Br.). Make hay while the sun shines (Am., Br.). Strike while the iron is hot (Am., Br.). While it is fine weather mend your sails (Br.)

978. Курица соседа всегда выглядит гусыней. *See 296 (В)*

Cf.: The grass is always greener on the other side of the fence (Am., Br.). The grass is always greener on the other side of the street (Am.). The hen of our neighbour appears to us as a goose (Br.). The next man's cows have the longest horns (Am.). Our neighbour's cow yields more milk than ours (Br.)

979. Курочка по зёрнышку клюёт, да сыта бывает. *Be content with little,* *as many little things or amounts accumulate to form a big thing or a large amount. See 664 (З), 868 (К), 1686 (П), 1694 (П), 1740 (П), 1801 (П), 1956 (С)*

Var.: По крупице и птица собирает, а сыта бывает

Cf.: Drop by drop and the pitcher is full (Am.). Grain by grain and the hen fills her belly (Br.). Little and often fills the purse (Am., Br.). Little and often makes a heap in time (Am.). A little makes a lot (Am.). Many a little (a pickle) makes a mickle (Br.). Many a mickle makes a muckle (Am.). One grain fills not the sack, but it helps his fellow (Br.). A pin a day is a groat a year (Am., Br.)

980. Куст тот, да не та ягода. *See 2170 (Ф)*

Cf.: Every like is not the same (Am., Br.). No like is the same (Br.)

Л

981. Ладно уселся, так и сиди. *See 1584 (О)*

Cf.: If you have a good seat, keep it (Br.). Leave (Let) well /enough/ alone (Am., Br.)

982. Лакома нажива, да востёр крючок. *See 2201 (Х)*

Cf.: The bait hides the hook (Am., Br.)

983. Ласка вернее таски. *Better results can be achieved by treating a man gently rather than by force. See 986 (Л), 1118 (М), 1692 (П)*

Cf.: Flies are easier caught with honey than with vinegar (Br.). Honey catches more flies than vinegar (Am.). An iron anvil should have a hammer of feathers (Am., Br.). Kindness is the noblest weapon to conquer with (Am.). The rough net is not the best catcher of birds (Am., Br.). A spoonful of oil on the troubled waters goes farther than a quart of vinegar (Am.). Tart words make no friends: a spoonful of honey will catch more flies than a gallon of vinegar (Am.). There is a great force hidden in sweet command (Br.). You can catch more flies with molasses than vinegar (Am.)

984. Ласковое слово и буйную голову смиряет. *See 1692 (П)*

Var.: Ласковое слово и бурю укрощает (и кость ломит)

Cf.: A soft answer turns away wrath (Am.). Soft words win hard hearts (Br.). A spoonful of oil on the troubled waters goes farther than a quart of vinegar (Am.)

985. Ласковое слово не трудно, да споро. *You never lose anything by courteous behavio(u)r, but you win much. See 484 (Д)*

Cf.: Civility costs nothing (Am., Br.). Courtesy costs nothing (Am., Br.). A good word for a bad one is worth much and costs little (Am.). Good words are good cheap (cost nothing and are worth much, cost nought) (Br.). Kind words are worth much and they cost little (Br.). Lip-honour costs little, yet may bring in much (Br.). Nothing costs less than civility (Am.). Politeness costs nothing and gains everything (Am.). Politeness costs nothing but gains everything (Br.)

986. Ласковое слово пуще дубины. *See 983 (Л)*

Cf.: Honey attracts (catches, gathers) more flies than vinegar (Am.). An iron anvil should have a hammer of feathers (Am., Br.). Kindness is the noblest weapon to conquer with (Am.). A smile goes a long way (Am.). There is a great force hidden in sweet command (Br.)

987. Ласковое теля двух маток сосёт. *He who is demure and kind gets everybody's help, protection and favo(u)r*

Cf.: The silent sow gets all the swill (Am.). The stillest hog gets the most swill (Am.). The still pig gets all the slop (Am.). The still sow drinks all the slop (Am.). The still sow eats up all the draff (Br.). Still swine eat all the draff (Br.)

988. Ласковый взгляд, да на сердце яд. *See 877 (К)*

Cf.: The fox is all courtesy and all craft (Am.). Full of courtesy, full of craft (Br.). Too much courtesy, too much craft (Am.)

989. Ласточка лепит гнёзда, пчёлка—соты. *See 1295 a (Н)*

Cf.: Every man to his trade (Am., Br.). The gunner to the linstock, and the steersman to the helm (Br.). If you are a cock, crow; if a hen, lay eggs (Am.)

990. Лбом стены не прошибёшь. *a) See 1786 a (П); b) See 1786 b (П)*

Cf.: a) There is no arguing with a large fist (Am.). What may the mouse do against the cat? (Am., Br.). You cannot fight City Hall (Am., Br.). You can't fight guns with sticks (Br.)

b) Do not kick against the pricks (Br.). Don't kick against pricks (Am.). It is ill striving against the stream (Br.). Strive not against the stream (Am.)

991. Легко в долг брать, отдавать трудно. *It is always easier to borrow than to pay the debts*

Var.: В долг брать легко, да отдавать тяжело. Легко взять, да трудно отдать

Cf.: Laugh when you borrow and you'll cry when you pay (Am.). You can run into debt, but you have to crawl out (Am.)

992. Легко дитятко нажить, нелегко вырастить. *It takes much more pains to bring up a child than to give birth to him. See 2118 (У)*

Cf.: The best colt needs breeding (Br.). Birth is much, but breeding is more (Am., Br.)

993. Легко добыто, легко и прожито. *Profits gained without effort are not lasting. See 1779 (П), 2221 (Х)*

Var.: Легко нажито, легко и прожито. Что без труда (легко) наживается, легко и проживается

Cf.: Come easy (light), go easy (light) (Am.). Come with the wind, go with water (Br.). Easy (lightly) come, easy (lightly) go (Am., Br.). Light come, light go (Br.). Lightly won, lightly gone (Br.). A thing easy to get is easy to lose (Am.)

994. Лёгкое горе болтливо, тяжёлое—молчаливо. *See 92 (Б)*

Cf.: Light sorrows speak; great ones are dumb (Am., Br.). Little griefs are loud, great griefs (sorrows) are silent (Br.). Secret griefs are the sharpest (Am.). They complain most who suffer least (Am.)

995. Легко начать, да нелегко кончить. *It is not when you begin, but when you have to complete some work that the difficulty comes. See 1272 (Н), 1374 (Н)*

Cf.: The beginning is not everything (Am.). Good to begin well, better to end well (Am., Br.)

996. Легко очернить, нелегко обелить. *When you besmirch a person's reputation, it is very hard for him to recover it. See 547 (Д)*

Cf.: A bad wound is cured, /but/ not a bad name (Br.). An evil wound is cured, not an evil name (Br.). Give a dog a bad name and hang him (Am., Br.). Give a dog a bad name and his work is done (Br.). Give a dog an ill name, and hang him (Br.). Glass, china, and reputations are easily cracked and never well mended (Am.). A good name is sooner lost than won (Am.). An ill wound, but not an ill name, may be healed (Am.). An ill wound is cured, /but/ not an ill name (Am., Br.). A wounded reputation is seldom cured (Am.)

997. Легко сказать, да тяжело сделать. *See 1913 (С)*

Var.: Легко сказать, да нелегко

орла поймать. Легче сказать, чем сделать

Cf.: Easier said than done (Am., Br.). Saying goes good cheap (Br.). Sayings go cheap (Am.). Saying is one thing, and doing is another (Br.)

998. Легче друга потерять, чем найти. *Real friendship should be cherished*

Cf.: A friend is easier lost than found (Am.). A friend is not so soon gotten as lost (Am., Br.). It takes years to make a friend, but minutes to lose one (but you can lose one in an hour) (Am.)

999. Легче счастье найти, чем удержать. *Luck can come by chance, but to make it lasting great efforts are required*

Var.: Легче счастье найти, нежели удержать

Cf.: Fortune is easily found, but hard to be kept (Br.). Fortune is easy to find, but hard to keep (Am.)

1000. Лёжа хлеба не добудешь. *See 1005 (Л), 1145 (М), 1671 (П)*

Var.: Лёжа пищи не добудешь

Cf.: A lazy dog catches no meat (finds no bone) (Am.). A setting hen gathers no feathers (Am., Br.). The sleeping fox catches no poultry (Am., Br.)

1001. Лежачего не бьют. *You should spare a man in trouble and not do him additional harm*

Cf.: Don't hit a man when he is down (Am., Br.). Don't kick a dog (a fellow) when he is down (Am.). Don't kick (strike) a man when he is down (Br.). Don't throw water on a drowned rat (Am.). Never hit a man when he is down (Am.). Pour not water on a drowned mouse (Br.). Press not a falling man too hard (Am.). When a man is down, don't kick him lower (Am.)

1002. Лезет в волки, а хвост собачий. *See 974 (К)*

Var.: Не суйся в волки с пёсьим (собачьим, телячьим) хвостом

Cf.: The bear wants a tail and cannot be lion (Br.). Every ass thinks himself worthy to stand with the king's horses (Am., Br.)

1003. Ленивому всегда праздник. *See 2113 (У)*

Var.: Ленивому и в будни праздник

Cf.: Every day is holiday with sluggards (Br.). A lazy man always finds excuses (Am.)

1004. Ленивый к работе—ретивый к обеду. *People who do not like to work indulge in eating*

Cf.: Lazy folks' stomachs don't get tired (Am.)

1005. Леность наводит на бедность. *From laziness comes poverty. See 1000 (Л), 1993 (С), 1994 (С)*

Cf.: Idleness goes in rags (Am.). Idleness is the key of beggary (the mother of want) (Am.). Idleness is the key to beggary (Br.). Laziness travels so slow that poverty overtakes him (Am.). Sloth is the key to poverty (Am., Br.). The sluggard must be clad in rags (Br.). There is no luck in laziness (Am.)

1006. Лень до добра не доводит. *Lazy men get into trouble or make it*

Var.: Лень добра не делает. Лень—мать всех пороков

Cf.: Doing nothing is doing ill (Am., Br.). An idle brain is the devil's workshop (Am., Br.). Idleness breeds trouble (Am.). Idleness is the mother of evil (mischief, sin) (Am.). Idleness is the parent of many vices (Am.). Idleness is the parent of vice (Br.). No good comes of idleness (Br.). Of idleness comes no goodness (Am.). Sloth is the mother of vice (Am.). Trouble springs from idleness (Am.)

1007. Лень человека портит. *People, who are not kept busy, get degraded. See 36 (Б), 1833 (Р)*

Cf.: Idleness dulls the wit (Am.). Idleness is the Dead Sea that swallows all virtues (Am.). Idleness makes the wit rust (Br.). Idleness rusts the mind (Br.). Too much bed makes a dull head (Am.). Too much rest is rust (Am.)

1008. Лес без лешего не стоит. *See 54 (Б)*

Var.: Лес не без шакала

Cf.: Nothing is perfect (Am., Br.)

1009. Лес видит, а поле слышит. *See 2153 (У)*

Cf.: Hedges have eyes, and walls have ears (Am., Br.). Hedges have eyes and woods have ears (Br.). The wall has ears and the plain has eyes (Am.). Walls have ears (Am., Br.)

1010. Лес по дереву не плачет, море по рыбе не тужит. *See 1860 (С)*

Cf.: There are as good fish in the sea as ever came out of it (Am., Br.). There are better fish in the sea than have ever been caught (Am.)

1011. Лес рубят—щепки летят. *When doing a great job, it is not without sacrificing, hurting someone or damaging something. See 313 (Г), 2160 b (У)*

Var.: Дрова рубят—щепки летят

Cf.: You cannot make an omelet(te) (pancakes) without breaking eggs (Am., Br.). You can't have an omelette unless you break the eggs (Am.)

1012. Лесть без зубов, а с костьми ест. *Flattery does much injury to people*

Cf.: The flatterer's bite is poisonous (Am.). Flattery is sweet poison (Am.)

1013. Летом дома сидеть—зимой хлеба не иметь. *See 969 (К)*

Cf.: They must hunger in frost that will not work in heat (Am., Br.). They must hunger in winter that will not work in summer (Br.)

1014. Лето пролежишь, зимой с сумой побежишь. *See 969 (К)*

Var.: Летом с удочкой, зимой с сумочкой

Cf.: They must hunger in frost that will not work in heat (Am., Br.). They must hunger in winter that will not work in summer (Br.)

1015. Лето собирает, а зима подбирает. *Crop is grown and stored when it is warm and consumed when it is cold. See 2293 (Ч)*

Var.: Лето—припасиха, а зима—подбериха

Cf.: The bee works in the summer and eats honey all winter (Am.). Winter discovers what summer conceals (Am.). Winter eats what summer gets (Am.). Winter eats what summer lays up (Br.). Winter finds out what summer lays up (Am., Br.)

1016. Лживый человек правды боится. *A liar suffers for it when truth is discovered*

Cf.: Those who live on lies choke on the truth (Am., Br.)

1017. Либо в стремя ногой, либо в пень головой. *See 727 (И)*

Cf.: Do or die (Am., Br.). Either win the saddle or lose the horse (Br.)

1018. Либо дождик, либо снег, либо будет, либо нет. *You never know if it will happen or not, if you will obtain it or not, etc. See 18 (Б), 1897 (С), 2351 (Э)*

Var.: Либо дождь, либо снег, либо будет, либо нет

Cf.: May be yes, may be no, may be rain, may be snow (Am., Br.). There is many a slip twixt /the/ cup and /the/ lip (Am.). There's many a slip between ('twixt) the cup and the lip (Br.)

1019. Либо мёд пить, либо биту быть. *See 727 (И)*

Cf.: Eat whole hog or die (Am.). Win or lose (Br.)

1020. Либо рыбку съесть, либо на мель сесть. *See 727 (И)*

Cf.: Eat whole hog or die (Am.). Win or lose (Br.)

1021. Либо сена клок, либо вилы в бок. *See 727 (И)*
Cf.: Do or die (Am., Br.)

1022. Лиса и во сне кур считает. *See 372 (Г)*
Var.: Спит лиса, а во сне кур щиплет
Cf.: The hungry man often talks of bread (Am.). When the ass dreams it is of thistles (Br.)

1023. Лиса кур не сбережёт. *See 185 (В)*
Cf.: Don't put the fox to guard the henhouse (Am.). Put not the cat near the goldfish bowl (Br.)

1024. Лиса семерых волков проведёт. *See 310 (Г)*
Cf.: Cunning is more than strength (Am.). Cunning surpasses strength (Br.). 'Tis sleight, not strength, that gives the greatest lift (Am.)

1025. Лиха беда начало. *The most difficult part of doing something is getting started, it will be easier to go on. See 278 (В), 2071 (Т)*
Var.: Лиха беда начать
Cf.: All things are difficult before they are easy (Am., Br.). The beginning is the hardest (Am.). Beware beginnings (Br.). Every beginning is hard (Br.). The first step is always the hardest (Am.). The first step is the hardest (Br.). The first step is the only difficulty (Br.). The hardest step is over the threshold (Am.). The hardest step is that over the threshold (Br.). It is the first step which is troublesome (Br.). It's the first step that costs (Am., Br.)

1026. Лицо—зеркало души. *You can judge a person by his face. See 343 (Г), 2287 (Ч)*
Cf.: The countenance is the index of the mind (Am.). The face is the index of the heart (Br.). The face is the index of the mind (Am., Br.)

1027. Личиком бел, да душою чёрен. *See 1859 (С)*
Var.: Личиком белёнок, да душой чернёнок
Cf.: A fair face, a false heart (Br.). Fair face, foul heart (Am.). A fair face may hide a foul heart (Am., Br.)

1028. Лишнее говорить—себе вредить. *See 2364 (Я)*
Cf.: Nothing ruins a duck but (like) his bill (Am.). An ox is taken by the horns, and a man by the tongue (Am., Br.)

1029. Лишнее говорить—только делу вредить. *The more one talks, the more harm will be done; the less one talks, the less harm will be done. See 2258 (Ч)*
Cf.: Least said is soonest mended (Am., Br.). Least said, soonest mended (Am.). Little said is soonest mended (Am., Br.). Nothing said is soonest mended (Am., Br.)

1030. Лишнее пожелаешь—последнее потеряешь. *Avarice often results in a loss in the end. See 580 (Ж), 1142 (М), 2081 (Т)*
Cf.: All covet, all lose (Am., Br.). Covetousness (Greediness) bursts the bag (Br.). Grasp a little, and you may secure it; grasp too much, and you will lose everything (Am.). If you wish for too much, you will end up with nothing (Am.)

1031. Лоб что лопата, а ума небогато. *See 97 (Б)*
Cf.: A big head and little wit (Br.). Big head and little wit (Am.)

1032. Лови момент! *When you have a chance to do or to obtain something, use it*
Cf.: Enjoy your ice cream while it's on your plate (Am.). If opportunity knocks, let her in (Am.). It's catch as

catch can (Am.). Opportunity knocks but once (Am., Br.). Put out your tubs when it is raining (Br.). Take time by the forelock (Am., Br.). Take time when time is, for time will away (Am.). The tide must be taken when it comes (Br.). When fortune knocks, open the door (Am.). When fortune smiles, embrace her (Am.). When fortune smiles, embrace it (Br.). When the shoulder of mutton is going, 'tis good to take a slice (Br.)

1033. Ловит волк, да ловят и волка. *See 780 (К)*

Cf.: Every fox must pay /with/ his skin to the flayer (furrier) (Br.). Long runs the fox, but at last is caught (Am.)

1034. Лодырь всегда найдёт причину, лишь бы не работать. *See 2091 (У)*

Cf.: Idle folks lack no excuses (Br.). A lazy man always finds excuses (Am.)

1035. Лодырь и бездельник празднуют и в понедельник. *See 2113 (У)*

Cf.: Every day is holiday with sluggards (Br.). A lazy man always finds excuses (Am.)

1036. Ложись с курами, а вставай с петухами. *See 962 (К)*

Cf.: Early to bed, early to rise makes a man healthy, wealthy and wise (Am., Br.). Go to bed with the lamb and rise with the lark (Br.)

1037. Ложка дёгтя испортит бочку мёда. *A little of a bad thing can harm all that is good. See 1536 (О)*

Var.: Одна ложка дёгтя испортит бочку мёда

Cf.: One drop of poison can affect the whole (Am.). One drop of poison infects the whole tun of wine (Br.). One spoonful of tar spoils a barrel of honey (Br.). A rotten egg spoils the pudding (Am.)

1038. Ложкой моря не исчерпаешь. *See 141 (В)*

Var.: Море ложкой не наполнишь. Песком моря не засыплешь

Cf.: A fog cannot be dispelled with a fan (Br.). The sea cannot be scooped up in a tumbler (Am.). The wind cannot be caught in (with) a net (Br.). You cannot catch the wind in the palm of your hand (Am.). You cannot empty the sea with a nutshell (with a spoon) (Br.)

1039. Ложь ложью погоняет. *When you start lying, you cannot stop. See 957 (К), 1100 (М), 1535 (О)*

Cf.: He that tells a lie must invent twenty more to maintain it (Am.). A lie begets a lie (Br.). A lie begets a lie until they become a generation (Am.). Lies hunt in packs (Br.). Nothing stands in need of lying but a lie (Br.). One falsehood leads to another (Am.). One lie calls for (makes) many (Br.). One lie leads to another (Am., Br.)

1040. Ломать—не строить. *It is easier to ruin something than to create*

Var.: Ломать—не делать

Cf.: It is easier to pull down than to build (Br.). It is easier to pull down (to tear down) than to build up (Am.)

1041. Лошадей на переправе не меняют. *When you are in the middle of fulfilling some task, you should not make drastic changes*

Cf.: Don't change horses in the middle of the stream (Am., Br.). Don't swap horses crossing a stream (in midstream, in the middle of the road, in the middle of the stream) (Am.). Don't swap horses while crossing the stream (Br.). Never change horses in midstream (Br.)

1042. Лукава лисица, да в капкан попадает. *See 780 (К), 1033 (Л), 2037 (Т)*

Var.: И лиса хитра, да шкуру её продают. Уж на что лиса хитра, да и её ловят. Хитра лиса, а в силки попадает

Cf.: The end of the thief is the gallows (Am.). Even foxes are outwitted and caught (Br.). The fox knows much, but more he that catches him (Br.). Long runs the fox, but at last is caught (Am.). The old fox is caught at last (Br.). The smartest fox is caught at last (Am.)

1043. Лучше беднее, да честнее. *Poverty and honesty is better than wealth got in a dishonest way. See 1044 (Л), 1052 (Л), 2208 (Х)*

Var.: Беден, да честен

Cf.: Better go to heaven in rags than to hell in embroidery (Br.) Better poor with honor than rich with shame (Am.). A clean fast is better than a dirty breakfast (Br.). A penny by right is better than a thousand by wrong (Br.)

1044. Лучше бедность да честность, нежели прибыль да стыд. *See 1043 (Л)*

Cf.: Better poor with honor than rich with shame (Am.). A clean fast is better than a dirty breakfast (Br.)

1045. Лучше быть головой собаки, чем хвостом льва. *See 1046 (Л)*

Var.: Лучше быть головой кошки, чем хвостом льва. Лучше быть головой осла, чем хвостом лошади

Cf.: Better be the head of a dog than the tail of a lion (Am., Br.). Better be the head of a fox (a lizard, a mouse) than the tail of a lion (Br.). Better be the head of an ass than the tail of a horse (Am., Br.). It is better to be the biggest fish in a small puddle than the smallest fish in a big puddle (Am.). It's better to be the beak of a hen than the tail of an ox (Am.)

1046. Лучше быть первым в деревне, чем последним в городе. *It is better to be foremost among commoners than the lowest of the aristocracy. See 1045 (Л)*

Cf.: Better a big fish in a little pond (puddle) than a little fish in a big pond (puddle) (Am.). Better be a big toad in a small puddle than a small toad in a big puddle (Am.). Better be first in a village than second at Rome (Br.). Better be the head of the yeomanry than the tail of the gentry (Br.). Better to be a big frog in a little pool than a little frog in a big pool (Am.). I'd rather be king among dogs than a dog among kings (Am.). It's better to be a big duck in a little puddle than be a little duck in a big puddle (Am.)

1047. Лучше в нас, чем в таз. *See 570 (Е)*

Cf.: Better the belly burst than good drink (meat) lost (Br.). It's better a belly burst than good food wasted (Am.)

1048. Лучше гнуться, чем переломиться. *It is better to yield than to be harmed by resistance. See 902 (К)*

Cf.: Better bend than break (Br.). Better bend the neck than bruise the forehead (Am.). Better bent than broken (Am.). Better bow than break (Am., Br.). It is better to bend than break (Am.)

1049. Лучше горькая правда, чем красивая ложь. *Truth, unpleasant as it may be, is preferable to any lie. See 2179 (Х)*

Var.: Худая правда лучше хорошей лжи

Cf.: Better speak truth rudely, than lie correctly (Br.). Truth is (pays) best (Am.). The truth is better than a lie (Am.)

1050. Лучше дать, чем взять. *It is better to be helpful to somebody than to be helped*

Cf.: Better give than receive (take) (Br.). Better to give than to take (Am.). It is better to give than to receive (Am.). /It is/ more blessed to give than to receive (Am., Br.). Not so good to borrow as to be able to lend (Am., Br.)

1051. Лучшее—часто враг хорошего. *In trying to reach perfection we often spoil what is or might be good enough. See 1584 (О)*

Cf.: The best is the enemy of the good (Am., Br.). Leave (Let) well alone (Br.). Leave (Let) well enough alone (Am., Br.)

1052. Лучше жить бедняком, чем разбогатеть с грехом. *See 1043 (Л)*

Var.: Лучше быть бедняком, чем разбогатеть с грехом

Cf.: Better poor with honor than rich with shame (Am.). A penny by right is better than a thousand by wrong (Br.)

1053. Лучше жить в зависти, чем в жалости. *It is better when people are jealous of your success than sorry for you*

Var.: Лучше быть у других в зависти, нежели самому в кручине

Cf.: Better be envied than pitied (Am., Br.)

1054. Лучше лишиться жизни, чем доброго имени. *There is nothing worse than to have one's reputation blemished*

Var.: Лучше глаза лишиться, чем доброго имени

Cf.: Better death than dishono(u)r (Am., Br.). It's better to die with honor than to live in infamy (Am.)

1055. Лучше лишиться яйца, чем курицы. *See 704 (И)*

Cf.: Better lose the saddle than the horse (Br.). Better the fruit lost than the tree (Am.). Of two evils choose the lesser (Am., Br.)

1056. Лучше мало, чем совсем ничего. *To have a little of what you need is better than to have nothing at all. See 1070 (Л), 1974 (С)*

Cf.: Better a small fish than an empty dish (Am., Br.). A bit in the morning is better than nothing all day (Am., Br.). Half a loaf is better than no bread (none) (Am., Br.). Half an egg is better than an empty shell (Br.). Half an egg is better than the shell (Am.). A little is better than none (Br.). One penny is better than none (Am.)

1057. Лучше меньше, да лучше. *To say little to the point, or to produce little of good quality is better than much that is bad*

Cf.: The half is better than the whole (Am.). Half is more than the whole (Am.). The half is more than the whole (Br.). It is quality rather than quantity which counts (Am.). A little and good fills the trencher (Am.). Quality is better than quantity (Am., Br.)

1058. Лучше молчать, чем пустое врать. *See 1501 (Н)*

Cf.: Better say nothing than not to the purpose (Br.). If it isn't worth saying, don't say it at all (Am.). Speak not rather than speak ill (Am.)

1059. Лучше на убогой жениться, чем с богатой браниться. *If you have to choose between a kind poor girl and a rich masterful one, you should better marry the poor girl. See 80 (Б)*

Cf.: A great dowry is a bed full of brambles (Br.). Marry above your match and you get a master (Am.)

1060. Лучше низом, нежели горою. *Find an easy and safe way when doing something. See 2128 (У)*

Cf.: Better go about (around) than fall into the ditch (Am.). Better to go about than to fall into a ditch (Br.). Cross the stream where it is shallowest (Am., Br.). A low hedge is easily leaped over (Am.). Men leap over where the hedge is lowest (Br.)

1061. Лучше нужду неси, а взаймы не проси. *It is better to be poor than to be in debt*

Cf.: Better go to bed supperless than rise in debt (Am.). Better to go to bed supperless than rise in debt (Br.). Rather go to bed supperless than rise in debt for a breakfast (Am.). Rather than run into debt, wear your old coat (Am.). Sleep without supping, and wake without owing (Am., Br.)

1062. Лучше один раз увидеть, чем сто раз услышать. *To get a real idea of*

some thing or event, one has to see or watch it rather than rely on someone else's opinion. See 1286 (H), 1289 (H)

Cf.: I'll believe it (that) when I see it (Am., Br.). It is better to trust the eye than the ear (Am., Br.). Never judge before you see (Am.). One eye has more faith than two ears (Am.). One eye-witness is better than ten hearsays (Am., Br.). One eyewitness is better than two hear-so's (Br.). Seeing is believing (Am., Br.). What we see we believe (Am.)

1063. Лучше оступиться, чем оговориться. *See 1930 (C)*

Cf.: Better /a/ slip with the foot than with the tongue (Am.). Better the foot slip than the tongue (Am., Br.). Better the foot slip than the tongue trip (Br.). A slip of the foot and you may soon recover, but a slip of the tongue you may never get over (Am.)

1064. Лучше поздно, чем никогда. *One had done what he had to or came extremely late. (This is an apology for one's own being late in coming or doing something, or an excuse for someone else's similar conduct.)*

Cf.: All behind—like a fat woman (Am.). Better come late to church than never (Am.). Better late than never (Am., Br.). Better late than not at all (Am.). It is not lost that comes at last (Br.)

1065. Лучше сегодня яичко, чем курица завтра. *See 1421 (H)*

Cf.: Better an egg today than a hen tomorrow (Am., Br.). A bird in the hand is worth two in the bush (Am., Br.). Bread today is better than cake tomorrow (Am.). An egg today is worth a hen tomorrow (Am.). One today is worth two tomorrows (Am., Br.)

1066. Лучше синица в руках, чем журавль в небе. *See 1421 (H)*

Var.: Лучше воробей в руке, чем петух на кровле. Лучше голубь в тарелке, чем глухарь на току. Лучше рябчик в руках, чем два на ветке

Cf.: A bird in the hand is worth two in the bush (Am., Br.). One dollar in your hand beats the promise of two in somebody else's (Am.). A pullet in the pen is worth a hundred in the fen (Br.). A sparrow in the hand is better than a pigeon in the roof (is worth a pheasant that flies by) (Br.)

1067. Лучше смерть славная, чем жизнь позорная. *There is nothing worse than a shameful life. See 64 (Б)*

Var.: Лучше смерть, нежели позор. Смерть лучше бесчестья

Cf.: Better a glorious death than a shameful life (Br.). Better death than dishonor (Am.). Better die standing than live kneeling (Br.). Better die with honour than live in shame (Br.). Better to die on one's feet than to live on one's knee (Br.). It's better to die with honor than to live in infamy (Am.). Shame is worse than death (Br.)

1068. Лучше сносить, чем сгноить. *Use what you have and enjoy it rather than keep it until it becomes worthless*

Cf.: Better wear out than rust out (Br.). /It is/ better to wear out than to rust out (Am.)

1069. Лучше с умным потерять, чем с глупым найти. *Though you may bear some losses with a clever person, spiritual communication with him outweighs what you gain with a silly man*

Cf.: It is better to sit with a wise man in prison than with a fool is paradise (Am.). 'Tis better to lose with a wise man than to win with a fool (Am.)

1070. Лучше хоть что-нибудь, чем ничего. *If you cannot have what you want, try to be content with what you have. See 1056 (Л), 1974 (C)*

Var.: Всё лучше того, как нет ничего

Cf.: Anything is better than nothing (Am.). Better a bare foot than none at all (Am.). Better a lean jade than an empty halter (a mouse in the pot than no flesh at all, my hog dirty than no hog at all, one-eyed than stone-blind) (Br.). Better some of the pudding than none of the pie (Am., Br.). Better some than none (something than nothing) (Am.). Better something than nothing at all (Am., Br.). A crust is better than no bread (Br.). Half a loaf is better than none (Am., Br.). One foot is better than two crutches (Am., Br.). A second-rate something is better than a first-rate nothing (Am.)

1071. Любви, огня да кашля от людей не утаишь. *Things come out to light however hard you may try to conceal them. See 2336 (Ш)*

Cf.: Love and a cough cannot be hidden (Am.). Love and cough cannot be hidden (Br.). Love and smoke cannot be hidden (Am., Br.)

1072. Любит и кошка мышку. *See 1677 (П)*

Cf.: The crow bewails the sheep, and then eats it (Br.). Crows weep for the dead lamb and then devour him (Am.)

1073. Любить тепло—и дым терпеть. *There is no advantage without some disadvantage. See 1077 (Л)*

Var.: Любишь тепло—терпи и дым

Cf.: Conveniences have their inconveniences and comforts their crosses (Am.). Every commodity has its discommodity (Br.). He that would have eggs must endure the cackling of hens (Am., Br.). If you want to gather honey, you must bear the stings of bees (Am.). If you would enjoy the fire, you must put up with the smoke (Br.). No convenience without inconvenience (Br.)

1074. Любишь гостить, люби и к себе звать. *See 125 (В)*

Cf.: The best way to gain a friend is to be one (Am.). Friendship cannot stand all on one side (Am.). Frienship cannot stand on one side (Br.). Friendship stands not on one side (Am.). A man, to have friends, must show himself friendly (Am.). One complimentary letter asks another (Br.). The way to have a friend is to be one (Br.)

1075. Любишь кататься, люби и саночки возить. *You must pay the price of every pleasure, joy, convenience, etc. See 576 (Е), 1073 (Л), 1918 (С)*

Cf.: After dinner comes the reckoning (Br.). After the feast comes the reckoning (Am., Br.). After your fling, watch for the sting (Am., Br.). He who calls the tune must pay the piper (Am.). If you dance, you must pay the fiddler (Br.). If you want to dance, you must pay the fiddler (Am.). Sweet is the wine, but sour is the payment (Am.)

1076. Любишь меня, так люби и собачку мою. *True affection for some person should be extended to everyone closely connected with him. See 916 (К)*

Var.: Любишь меня, так люби и мою родню

Cf.: He that loves the tree, loves the branch (Br.). He who loves the tree loves the branch (Am.). If you like the sow, you like her litter (Am.). If you love the boll, you cannot hate the branches (Br.). Love me, love my dog (Am., Br.)

1077. Любишь смородину, люби и оскомину. *See 1073 (Л)*

Cf.: He that would have eggs must endure the cackling of hens (Am., Br.)

1078. Любовь всё побеждает. *Love will overcome all difficulties and obstacles. See 1083 (Л)*

Cf.: Love conquers all (Am., Br.). Love triumphs over all (Am.)

1079. Любовь за деньги не купишь. *You cannot make a person love you for money*

Cf.: Love can neither be bought, nor sold (Br.). Love can neither be bought, nor sold; its only price is love (Am.).

Love is neither bought nor sold (Br.). Love is not found in the market (Br.). Money cannot buy love (Am.). You can't buy love (Am.)

1080. Любовь зла—полюбишь и козла. *See 1085 (Л)*

Cf.: Fancy passes (surpasses) beauty (Br.). Love covers many faults (Am., Br.). Love covers many infirmities (Br.). Love is blind (Am., Br.). Love is deaf as well as blind (Am.). Love is without reason (Br.)

1081. Любовь—кольцо, а у кольца нет конца. *True love never dies*

Cf.: Love is a thirst that is never slaked (Am.). Love without end has no end (Br.)

1082. Любовь лечит или калечит. *Love may bring not only happiness, joy, consolation, etc., but sorrow and destruction as well*

Cf.: Fancy kills and fancy cures (Br.). Fancy may kill or cure (Br.). Love can be a blessing or a curse (Am.)

1083. Любовь на замок не закроешь. *Love has such power that it will overcome all obstacles. See 379 (Г), 1078 (Л)*

Var.: Любовь на замок не запрёшь

Cf.: Love conquers all (Am., Br.). Love laughs at locksmiths (Am., Br.). Love will creep where it cannot go (Am., Br.). Love will find a way (Am., Br.). Love will go through stone walls (Br.)

1084. Любовь не картошка, не выбросишь в окошко. *You cannot make yourself get rid of your love for a person. See 1594 (О)*

Cf.: No herb will cure love (Am., Br.)

1085. Любовь слепа. *When you are in love, you do not see any faults in the person you love. See 1080 (Л), 1684 (П), 1701 (П)*

Cf.: Affection blinds reason (Br.). Blind love makes a harelip for a dimple (Am.). Fancy may bolt bran and think it flour (Am., Br.). Fire in the heart sends smoke into the head (Am., Br.). If Jack's in love, he's no judge of Jill's beauty (Br.). In the eye of the lover, pockmarks are dimples (Am.). In the eyes of the lover, pockmarks (pock-marks) are dimples (Br.). Love covers many faults (Am., Br.). Love is blind (Am., Br.). Love sees no faults (Am.)

1086. Любопытной Варваре нос оторвали. *It will not do any good to be too curious or inquisitive. See 942 (К), 1138 (М), 1419 (Н)*

Var.: Любопытному на базаре нос прищемили

Cf.: Curiosity has a spiteful way of turning back on the curious (Am.). Curiosity killed the cat (Am., Br.). The fish will soon be caught that nibbles at every bait (Br.). He that pries into every cloud, may be stricken by a thunderbolt (with a thunder) (Br.). He that pries into the clouds may be struck with a thunderbolt (Am.). He who meddles smarts (will smart) for it (Br.). That fish is soon caught who nibbles at every bait (Am.). Too much curiosity lost Paradise (Br.)

1087. Людей не осуждай, а за собою примечай. *See 511 (Д)*

Var.: На соседа не кивай—за собой примечай

Cf.: Blame not others for the faults that are in you (Am.). He that mocks a cripple, ought to be whole (Br.). He that scoffed at the crooked had need to go very upright himself (Br.). He that scoffs at the crooked had need go very upright himself (Am.). He whose windows are of glass should never throw stones (Am.). Know your own faults before blaming others for theirs (Br.). People living in glass houses should not throw stones (Am., Br.)

1088. Люди ложь, и мы то ж. *See 657 (З)*

Var.: Люди врут, так и мы врём

Cf.: I give it for what it is worth (Br.). I will tell you for what it's worth (Am.)

1089. Люди разные бывают. *See 143 (В)*

Cf.: All bread is not baked in one oven (Am., Br.). One shoe does not fit every foot (Br.). There may be blue and better blue (Br.). You can't put the same shoe on every foot (Am.)

1090. Людская молва что морская волна. *What people talk about gets around. See 1261 (Н)*

Var.: Мирская молва что морская волна

Cf.: Anyone can start a rumor, but none can stop one (Am.). Gossip needs no carriage (Am.). Gossips are frogs, they drink and talk (Br.). Gossips drink and talk; frogs drink and squawk (Am.). Rumour grows as it goes (Br.). Rumour is a bubble that soon bursts (Br.)

1091. Людским речам вполовину верь. *See 1303 (Н)*

Cf.: Believe not all that you see nor half what you hear (Br.). Believe only half of what you see and nothing you hear (Am.). Half is false of what you hear (Am.). Season all you hear with salt (Am.)

1092. Людской стыд—смех, а свой—смерть. *You may laugh at the disgrace of other people, but you suffer when it concerns you or some of your close relative. See 2327 (Ч)*

Cf.: Everything is funny as long as it happens to someone else (Am.)

1093. Лягушка квакает в своё время. *See 233 (В)*

Cf.: Everything has its time (Am., Br.). There's a season for all things (Am.)

1094. Ляжешь подле огня, не хотя, обожжёшься. *Some good things or people get harmful when you come into close contact with them*

Cf.: The fire which warms us at a distance will burn us when near (Br.). The nearer the fire, the hotter it is (Am.)

М

1095. Мавр сделал своё дело, мавр может уходить. *One has completed his work and his help is no longer needed, so he may be free*

Cf.: The Moor has done his duty, let him go (Br.). When you are done, you can go (Am.)

1096. Мала искра, да великий пламень родит. *See 1156 (М)*

Var.: От малой искры, да большой пожар

Cf.: From a spark a conflagration (Br.). A little spark kindles a great fire (Am., Br.). Of a small spark a great fire (Br.). Sparks become flame (Am.)

1097. Мала метёлка, да чисто метёт. *See 1099 (М)*

Cf.: A little rain stills a great wind (Am.). Small rain allays a great wind (Br.). A small rain lays a great dust (Am.). Small rain lays (will lay) great dust (Br.)

1098. Мала птичка, да ноготок востёр. *A short or insignificant man a) excites admiration by his abilities, b) fills you with apprehension. See a) 1099 (М), 1165 (М); b) 2375 (Я)*

Var.: Мал ноготок, да остёр. Невелика мышка, да зубок остёр. Невелика птичка, да ноготок остёр

Cf.: a) A little rain stills a great wind (Am.). The smallest axe may fell the hugest oak (Br.). Small rain allays a great wind (Br.). A small rain lays a great dust (may allay a great storm) (Am.). Small rain lays (will lay) great dust (Br.)

b) A little wind kindles a big flame (Am.). No viper so little, but has its venom (Br.). A thorn is small, but he who has felt it doesn't forget it (Am.)

1099. Мал, да удал. *A young or a short man has many merits or is capable of doing great things. See 1097 (M), 1098 a (M), 1105 (M), 1165 (M), 1320 (H), 1843 (P)*

Cf.: An inch is as good as an ell (Br.). A little axe cuts down big trees (Am..). Little bodies have great souls (Am.). Little bodies may have great souls (Br.). Little chips light great fires (Br.). A little key will open a large door (Am.). A little man may have a large heart (Am.). Little pigeons can carry great messages (Br.). A little rain stills a great wind (Am.). Small head, big ideas (Am.)

1100. Маленькая ложь за собой большую ведёт. *See 1039 (Л)*

Cf.: A lie begets a lie until they become a generation (Am.). One lie calls for (makes) many (Br.). One lie leads to another (Am., Br.)

1101. Маленькая собачка лает—большой подражает. *Children usually behave like their parents do. See 2347 (Щ), 2357 (Я)*

Var.: Маленькая собачка лает—от большой слышит

Cf.: As the dogs bark, the young ones learn (Am.). As the old cock crows, so crows the young (Br.). As the old cock crows, the young cock learns (so the young bird chirrups) (Am.). The old one crows, the young one learns (Am.). The young cock crows as he hears the old one (Am., Br.). The young pig grunts as the old sow (Br.)

1102. Маленькие дети спать не дают, большие жить не дают. *As the children grow, they give you more trouble. See 1103 (M), 1106 (M)*

Var.: Малое дитя спать не даёт, а при большом и сама не уснёшь. Малые дети заснуть не дают, большие вырастут—сама не спишь. Малые дети тяжелы на коленях, а большие—на сердце

Cf.: Little children, little sorrows; big children, great sorrows (Br.). Little children, little troubles, big children, big troubles (Am.). Little children step on your toes, big children step on your heart (Am.). When a child is little, it pulls at your apron strings; when it gets older, it pulls at your heart strings (Am.)

1103. Маленькие детки—маленькие бедки, а вырастут велики—большие будут. *See 1102 (M)*

Var.: Малые дети—малая печаль, большие дети—большая печаль. Малые детки—малые бедки, а большие детки—большие и бедки. С малыми детками горе, а с большими—вдвое

Cf.: Little children, little sorrows; big children, great sorrows (Br.). Little children, little troubles, big children, big troubles (Am.)

1104. Маленькое дело лучше большого безделья. *It is better to do something than nothing at all*

Cf.: A little along is better than a long none (Am.)

1105. Мал золотник, да дорог. *See 1099 (M)*

Var.: Мал соловей, да голос (голосом) велик

Cf.: Little bodies have great souls (Am.). Little bodies may have great souls (Br.). A little man may have a large heart (Am.). Small head, big ideas (Am.)

1106. Малое дитя грудь сосёт, а большое—сердце. *See 1102 (M)*

Cf.: Little children, little sorrows; big children, great sorrows (Br.). Little children, little troubles, big children, big troubles (Am.). Little children step on your toes, big children step on your heart (Am.)

1107. Мало-помалу птичка гнездо свивает. *See 730 (И), 830 (К)*

Cf.: Little by little and bit by bit (Br.). Little by little one goes (travels) far (Am.). Little by little the bird builds his nest (Am.). Little by little the bird builds its nest (Br.). One by one the spindles are made (Br.). Step by step one goes a long way (Am.). Step by step one goes far (Br.). Step by step the ladder is ascended (Am., Br.)

1108. Март сухой да мокрый май, будет каша и каравай. *See 9 (A)*

Var.: Сухой март, а май мокрый делают хлеб добрый

Cf.: A cold April and a wet May fill the barn with grain and hay (Am.). A dry March, wet April and cool May fill barn and cellar and bring much hay (Br.). A fall of snow in May is worth a ton of hay (Am.)

1109. Маслом огонь не заливают. *Never do anything that can start a conflict or make someone's anger worse*

Var.: Огонь маслом заливать— лишь огня прибавлять

Cf.: Add not fuel to flames (Am., Br.). Add not fuel to the fire (Am.). Add not oil to the fire (Br.). Butter is good for anything but to stop an oven (Br.). Pour not oil on flame (on the fire) (Br.). To pour oil on the fire is not the way to quench it (Am., Br.)

1110. Масло по маслу не приправа. *See 2187 (X)*

Cf.: Butter to butter is no relish (Br.). Too good is stark nought (Br.). Too much of a good thing is worse than none at all (Am.). Too much of one thing is good for nothing (Br.)

1111. Мастер глуп—нож туп. *An unskilled man will blame his tools for bad work done rather than admit his own incompetence. See 566 (E), 1654 (П), 2063 (T), 2139 (У)*

Cf.: A bad gardener quarrels with his rake (Br.). A bad shearer never had a good sickle (Br.). A bad worker finds faults with his tools (Br.). A bad workman /always/ blames his tools (Br.). A bad workman quarrels with his tools (Am., Br.). If you don't know how to dance, you say that the drum is bad (Am.). The losing horse blames the saddle (Am.)

1112. Мастерские руки от доброй науки. *See 1190 (H)*

Cf.: Practice makes perfect (Am., Br.)

1113. Масть к масти подбирается. *See 1842 (P)*

Cf.: Birds of a feather flock together (Am., Br.). Each kind attracts its own (Am.). They that know one another salute afar off (Br.). Water finds its own level (Am., Br.). Water seeks its own level (Am.)

1114. Медведь пляшет, а поводырь деньги берёт. *One man works and another benefits by it. See 529 (Д), 2200 (X)*

Cf.: Asses fetch the oats and the horses eat them (Br.). Fools make feasts and wise men eat them (Am., Br.). I kill the boars, another enjoys their flesh (Br.). One beats the bush, and (while) another catches the birds (has the hare, takes the bird) (Br.). One /man/ sows and another reaps (Br.). One man works, and another reaps the benefits (Am.). What one man sows another man reaps (Am.)

1115. Медведя не убив, шкуры не продавай. *See 2228 (Ц)*

Var.: Медведь в лесу, а шкура продана. Не дели шкуру неубитого медведя. Не продавай шкуры, не убив медведя

Cf.: Catch before hanging (Am.). Catch the bear before you cook him (sell his skin) (Br.). First catch your hare (Br.). First catch your hare before you skin it (Am., Br.). First catch your rabbit and then make your stew (Am.). Make not your sauce till you have caught the fish (Am., Br.). Never fry a fish till it's caught (Br.)

1116. Мёд есть—в улей лезть. *See 50 (Б)*

Cf.: If you want roasted bananas,

you must burn your fingers first (Am.). If you want to gather honey, you must bear the stings of bees (Am.). No pains, no gains (Am., Br.). No pains, no gains; no sweat, no sweet (Am.)

1117. Медленно, да верно. *You do it slowly, and it is certain to be a success. See 2054 (Т)*

Cf.: Slow but sure (Am., Br.). Slowly but surely (Br.). Slow things are sure things (Am.). Slow wind also brings the ship to harbor (Am.)

1118. Мёдом больше мух наловишь, чем уксусом. *See 983 (Л)*

Cf.: A drop of honey catches more flies than a hogshead of vinegar (Am., Br.). Flies are easier caught with honey than vinegar (Br.). Honey attracts (catches) more flies than vinegar (Am.). Molasses catches more flies than vinegar (Am.). More flies are caught with honey than vinegar (Br.). More wasps are caught by honey than by vinegar (Am.). An ounce of honey draws more flies than a gallon of gall (Am.). A teaspoon of sugar will catch more flies than a gallon of vinegar (Am.)

1119. Между двумя стульями не усидишь. *Do not try to adhere to two opposite opinions, you will lose your opportunity. See 422 (Д)*

Cf.: Between two stools one falls (goes) to the ground (Br.). Between two stools we come to the ground (Am.)

1120. Мельница мелет—мука будет, язык мелет—беда будет. *A man who talks much cannot but say things that can do harm. See 2364 (Я)*

Cf.: The mill that is always going grinds coarse and fine (Br.). An ox is taken by the horns, and a man by his tongue (Am., Br.). Tongue double brings trouble (Am.)

1121. Мена—не грабёж. *Do not be angry that the swap was good only for me*

Cf.: Exchange is no robbery (Am., Br.)

1122. Меньше говори, да больше делай. *See 1503 (Н)*

Cf.: The best of the sport is to do the deed and say nothing (Br.). Deeds, not words (Am., Br.). Few words and many deeds (Br.). Few words, many deeds (Am.). Speak little; do much (Am.)

1123. Меньше денег, меньше хлопот. *See 38 (Б)*

Cf.: Little gain, little pain (Am.). Little gear, less care (Am., Br.). Little goods, little care (Am.). Little wealth, little care (sorrow) (Br.). Small riches hath most rest (Br.)

1124. Мёртвого льва и собаки лижут. *See 1650 (П)*

Cf.: Hares may pluck (pull) dead lions by the beard (Br.). The timid hare dares to pluck the dead lion by the beard (Am.). When the eagle is dead, the crows pick out his eyes (Am.)

1125. Мёртвые не вредят. *Dead people cannot hurt. See 1551 (О)*

Cf.: A dead dog never bites (Am.). Dead dogs bite not (don't bite) (Br.). Dead men do no harm (Am.). Dead men don't bite (Am., Br.). Dead men never bite (Am.)

1126. Мёртвый не выдаст. *Dead men do not give away incriminating evidence*

Var.: Мёртвый не расскажет

Cf.: Dead dogs bark not (Br.). A dead dog tells no tales (Am.). Dead men don't talk (Am.). Dead men tell no tales (Am., Br.)

1127. Мёртвых с погоста не носят. *We cannot call back the past. See 67 (Б)*

Cf.: Dead men don't walk again (Am.). From the cemetery no one is brought back (Am.). No man can call again yesterday (Am., Br.). Things past cannot be recalled (Br.)

1128. Мети всяк перед своими воротами. *Do not critcize others for faults committed or mistakes made by yourself. See 511 (Д)*

Cf.: Keep your own doorstep clean (Am.). Start housecleaning in your own house (Am.). Sweep before (the path to) your own door (Br.). Sweep in front of your own door first (Am.). Sweep your own porch clean first (Br.). Weed your own garden first (Am.)

1129. Мешай дело с бездельем, проживёшь век с весельем. *Changes in our activity make life enjoyable. See 2116 (У)*

Cf.: All work and no play isn't much fun (Am.). All work and no play makes Jack a dull boy (Am., Br.). All work and no play makes Jack a dull boy; all work and no spree makes Jill a dull she (Am.). All work and no play makes Johnny a dull boy (Am.). Variety is the spice of life (Am.)

1130. Мешком солнышко не поймаешь. *See 141 (В)*

Cf.: The wind cannot be caught in (with) a net (Br.). You cannot catch the wind in the palm of your hand (Am.)

1131. Мил гость, что недолго гостит. *People do not like when their guests stay too long. See 1827 (Р)*

Var.: Мил гость, что недолго сидит

Cf.: /The/ best fish smell when they are three days old (Br.). Don't wear out your welcome (Am., Br.). Fish and callers smell in three days (Am.). Fish and company smell in three days (Br.). Fish and visitors smell in three days (Am., Br.). Fresh fish and new-come guests smell in three days (Br.). A short visit is best (Am.). Short visits make long friends (Am.). Visits should be short, like a winter's day (Am.)

1132. Милиционер родился. *See 2052 (Т)*

Var.: Дурак родился

Cf.: An angel is passing overhead (Am., Br.). It must be the ten minute lull (Am.). It must be twenty past the hour (Am.)

1133. Милости прошу к нашему шалашу. *Come in and share the meal with us. (This is an informal invitation) See 293 (В), 2254 (Ч)*

Cf.: Come and eat your mutton with me (Br.). Come and have a pickle (Br). Come and have (take) potluck with us (Am.). Come and have (take) pot-luck with us (Br.). Welcome to my humble abode (Am.)

1134. Милые бранятся—только тешатся. *Lovers' tiffs are harmless*

Cf. The falling out of lovers is the renewal of love (Br.). The falling out of lovers is the renewing of love (Am.). A lover's anger is short-lived (Am.). Lovers' quarrels are soon mended (Br.). Love's anger is fuel to love (Am.)

1135. Миром и горы сдвинем. *See 13 (А)*

Cf.: By the hands of many a great work is made light (Am.). Many hands make light work (Am., Br.)

1136. Мир не без добрых людей. *If you do not help me, some other people will. See 699 (И), 1860 (С)*

Var.: Свет не без добрых людей

Cf.: All the keys are not at one man's girdle (Br.). All the keys hang not at one's girdle (Am.). The sea is full of other fish (Am.). There are more pebbles on the beach (Br.). There is always the next train coming (Am.)

1137. Мир тесен. *I did not expect to meet you here or that we have mutual acquaintances*

Cf.: It's a small world (Am., Br.). The world is a small place (Am., Bare.). The world is but a little place, after all (Br.)

1138. Много будешь знать, скоро состаришься. *You are too prying, I* *will not tell you anything about it. See 1086 (Л)*

Var.: Всё будешь знать, скоро состаришься

Cf.: Curiosity killed the cat (Am., Br.). The old brown cow laid an egg (Br.). Too much curiosity killed the cat (Am.). Too much knowledge makes the head bold (Br.)

1139. Много говорено—мало сказано. *There is little information in this lengthy talking. See 1885 (С)*

Cf.: Big talking, but little saying (Am.)

1140. Много грозит, да мало вредит. *One threatens but does not do much harm. See 701 (И), 1325 (Н)*

Cf.: A dog's bark is worse than his bite (Am.). His bite isn't as bad as his bark (Am.). More bark than bite (Br.). When the thunder is very loud, there's very little rain (Am.)

1141. Много денег—много и хлопот. *A rich person is never at ease. See 38 (Б)*

Var.: Много денег—много забот

Cf.: A great fortune is a great slavery (Am., Br.). A great fortune is a great servitude (Am.). Great possessions are great cares (Am.). Much coin (gold), much care (Br.). Riches and cares are inseparable (Am.). Riches bring care /and fears/ (Br.). Those who have money have trouble about it (Am.)

1142. Много желать, добра не видать. *An unreasonable desire may result in getting nothing. See 1030 (Л)*

Var.: Много желать, ничего не видать

Cf.: All covet, all lose (Am., Br.). Grasp a little, and you may secure it; grasp too much, and you will lose everything (Am.). He that (who) grasps at too much holds nothing fast (Br.). If you wish for too much, you will end up with nothing (Am.). Too much covetousness breaks (bursts) the bag (the sack) (Br.)

1143. Много слов, а мало дела. *One talks much about work but does little. See 553 (Д), 932 (К), 1244 (Н), 2173 (Х), 2338 (Ш)*

Var.: Звону много, /да/ дела (толку) мало. Много дыму, да мало пылу. Много крику (шуму), мало толку

Cf.: All gong and no action (Br.). All talk and no cider (no do) (Br.). Great (Much) cry and little wool (Br.). Great cry but little wool (Am.). Great talkers are little doers (Am., Br.). Much smoke, little fire (Br.). Much talk, little work (Am.). 'Tis not the hen that cackles most that lays the most eggs (Am.)

1144. Много снега—много хлеба. *A snowy winter guarantees a rich crop*

Cf.: A snow year, a rich year (Am., Br.). Snowy winter, plentiful harvest (Am.)

1145. Много спать—добра не видать. *A lazy man will never earn his living. See 1000 (Л), 1227 (Н), 1993 (С), 2212 (Х)*

Var.: Долго спать—добра не видать (с долгом встать)

Cf.: Drowsiness shall clothe (dresses) a man in rags (Am.). He that sleeps catches no fish (Am.). He who sleeps all the morning, may go a-begging all the day after (Br.). He who sleeps catches no fish (Br.). A lazy dog finds no bone (Am.). Sleeping cats catch no mice (Am.). A (The) sleeping dog catches no poultry (Br.). The sleeping fox catches no chickens (Am.). The sleeping fox catches no poultry (Am., Br.). When the fox sleeps no grapes fall in his mouth (Br.)

1146. Много шуму из ничего. *An insignificant cause called forth much groundless commotion*

Cf.: The devil rides on a fiddlestick (Br.). Great fuss about nothing (Br.). Much ado about nothing (Am., Br.)

1147. Могло быть и хуже. *We do not have to despair, things are not so*

terrible. (One says so to console himself or someone else). See 2349 (Э)

Cf.: It's never so bad that it can't be worse (Am.). It's not the end of the world (Am., Br.). Nothing so bad but it might have been worse (Am., Br.). Nothing so bad that it couldn't be worse (Am.). Worse things happen at sea (Br.)

1148. Моё—моё и твоё—моё. *I will have both, what belongs to you and to me*

Cf.: Heads I win, tails you lose (Br.). What's yours is mine, and what's mine I am keeping (is my own) (Br.). What's yours is mine, and what's mine is mine (Am.)

1149. Мой дом—моя крепость. *A man is safest in his own house*

Cf.: The house is a castle which the king cannot enter (Am.). A man's home is his castle (Am.). A man's house is his castle (Am., Br.). My house is my castle (Br.)

1150. Молодец против овец, а против молодца и сам овца. *A coward or a weak man makes a brave show of valo(u)r only before those who are weaker or less powerful than he is, but is afraid of strong and powerful people*

Var.: Молодец на овец, а на молодца и сам овца

Cf.: The cat is mighty dignified until the dog came along (comes by) (Am.). Who takes a lion when he is absent, fears a mouse present (Br.)

1151. Молодо—зелено, погулять велено. *Let the young enjoy life while they can*

Cf.: Every man must sow his wild oats (Am.). Gather rosebuds while ye may (Am., Br.). Have fun while you are young (Am.). The young will sow their wild oats (Br.). You're only young once (Am., Br.). Youth comes but once in a lifetime (Am.). Youth will be served (Am., Br.). Youth will have its course (Br.). Youth will have its fling (swing) (Am., Br.)

1152. Молодость—пташкой, а старость—черепашкой. *A young man is strong and full of energy, an old man is weak and sluggish*

Cf.: Youth is full of vitamins, age is full of germs (Am.). Youth is nimble, age is lame (Am., Br.)

1153. Молод—перебесится, а стар—не переменится. *The young are flexible while the old cannot change their character or way of life. See 2002 (C)*

Cf.: An old dog cannot alter his way of barking (Br.). You can't teach an old dog new tricks (Am., Br.)

1154. Молчание—знак согласия. *Refraining from making any comments suggests that you approve of the matter on hand. See 937 (K)*

Cf.: No answer is also an answer (Am., Br.). Silence gives consent (Am., Br.). Silence implies (is, means) consent (Br.)

1155. Молчи—за умного сойдёшь. *You should better keep silent not to betray your folly or ignorance*

Cf.: Even a fool, when he holds his peace, is counted wise (Am., Br.). A fool when he is silent is counted wise (Am., Br.). Let a fool hold his tongue, and he can pass for a sage (Am.)

1156. Москва от копеечной свечки сгорела. *Insignificant causes may result in grave consequences. See 1096 (M), 1283 (H)*

Var.: Москва от искры загорелась. От копеечной свечи Москва сгорела

Cf.: From a spark a conflagration (Br.). Great events from little causes spring (Br.). A little fire burns up a great deal of corn (Br.). A little hole will sink a ship (Am.). A little spark kindles a great fire (Am., Br.). Little sticks kindle large fires (Am.). A little stone may upset a large cart (Am.). A little wind kindles a big flame (Am.).

A small leak will sink a great ship (Am., Br.)

1157. Москва слезам не верит. *Tears and complaints are of no help, to find a way out of a grave situation we must act. See 1604 (О), 1920 b (С)*

Cf.: Crying does not pay (will not mend matters) (Br.). The only cure for grief is action (Am.). Pick yourself up and dust yourself off (Am.). Sorrow will pay no debt (Br.). We must not lie down and die (Am.)

1158. Мошна туга—всяк ей слуга. *If you are rich, people are ready to serve you*

Cf: All things are obedient to money (Br.). Money is power (Am., Br.). No silver, no servant (Am., Br.)

1159. Моя хата с краю. *I have nothing to do with it. See 1372 (Н), 2372 (Я)*

Cf.: Am I my brother's keeper? (Am., Br.). I am not my brother's keeper (Am.). I'm a stranger here (Br.). It's no dirt down my neck (no hair off my head) (Br.). It's no skin off my back (Am., Br.). It's no skin off my butt (nose, tail) (Am.). It's no sweat off my back (Am.). That's no business of mine (Am., Br.). That's no skin off my teeth (Am.). That's not my street (Br.). What have I to do with Brawshaw's windmill? (Br.)

1160. Муж без жены—что гусь без воды. *Men cannot do without a wife*

Var.: Муж без жены—что конь без узды

Cf.: He that has not got a wife is not yet a complete man (Am.). Life isn't life without a wife (Am.). A man is only half a man without a wife (Am.). A man without a woman is like a ship without a sale (Am.)

1161. Муж—голова, жена—шея, куда захочет, туда и повернёт. *It is the wife who virtually makes all the decisions though the husband seems to play the main role. See 586 (Ж)*

Cf.: The grey mare is the better horse (Br.). The husband is the head of the house, but the wife is the neck—and the neck moves the head (Am.)

1162. Муж и жена—одна сатана. *A husband and a wife are alike, they share similar interests and opinions. See 787 (К)*

Cf.: As is the gander, so is the goose (Am.). As is the goose so is the gander (Am.). One bone, one flesh (Br.)

1163. Мужик тонул—топор обещал, вытащили—топорища жаль. *When in danger, people may have good intentions, but once out of it, they forget about them*

Var.: Когда тонул—топор сулил, а когда вытащили—топорища не дал

Cf.: Danger makes men devout (Br.). Danger past and God forgotten (Br.). Danger past, God is forgotten (Am.). The devil was sick, the devil a monk (a saint) would be; the devil was well, the devil of a monk (a saint) was he (Br.). Once on the shore, we pray no more (Am., Br.). The river past, and God forgotten (Am.). A vow made in the storm is forgotten in the calm (Am.). Vows made in storms are forgotten in the calms (Br.). When it thunders, the thief becomes honest (Am., Br.). When the devil was sick, a monk was he; when the devil was well, the devil of a monk was he (Am.). When the sea is crossed, the saint is generally forgotten (Am.). When the voyage is over, the saint is forgotten (Am.)

1164. Муж с женой бранятся, чужой не вяжись. *See 1861 (С)*

Cf.: Never interfere with family quarrels (Am.). Put not your finger (hand) between the bark and the tree (Br.)

1165. Муравей невелик, а горы копает. *See 1098 a (М), 1099 (М)*

Var.: Мал муравей, да горы копает

Cf.: A little rain stills a great wind

(Am.). The smallest axe may fell the hugest oak (Br.)

1166. Мутная вода течёт не из чистого озера. *Ill phenomena have their ill causes*

Cf.: Muddy spring, muddy stream (Br.). Muddy springs will have muddy streams (Am.)

1167. Мы едим, чтобы жить, а не живём, чтобы есть. *The sense of our life is enjoying and contributing to it, not mere consumption of food*

Cf.: Eat to live (Br.). Eat to live; do not live to eat (Am.). Live not to eat, but eat to live (Br.). We must eat to live and not live to eat (Am.)

1168. Мы и сами с усами. *I am not stupid and I know myself what to do. See 731 (И)*

Cf.: I am as good as the next person (Am.)

1169. Мыло серо, да моет бело. *See 870 (К)*

Cf.: A black hen always lays (will lay) a white egg (Am.). A black hen lays a white egg (Br.)

1170. Мягко стелет, да жёстко спать. *The person conceals his ill intentions beneath outward politeness. See 360 (Г), 877 (К), 1269 (Н), 1927 (С)*

Cf.: Bees that have honey in their mouths have stings in their tails (Br.). Fine words dress ill deeds (Br.). Full of courtesy, full of craft (Br.). Many a one says well that thinks ill (Br.). Many kiss the hand they wish to cut off (Am., Br.). Many kiss the hand they wish to see cut off (Am.). There are daggers behind men's smiles (Am.). Too much courtesy, too much craft (Am.)

1171. Мяса без костей не бывает. *a) There is no meat without bones. (This is an answer to a customer who complains that the meat has too many bones); b) See 737 (И)*

Cf.: a) The bones bear the beef home (Br.). Bones bring meat to town (Br.)

b) No land without stones, or meat without bones (Br.). Nothing is perfect (Am., Br.)

Н

1172. На бедного Макара все шишки валятся. *Troubles always befall an unlucky and miserable person. See 840 (К), 857 (К), 1253 (Н), 1658 (П)*

Var.: На бедного Макара все шишки валятся—и с сосен, и с ёлок

Cf.: All the Tracys have always the wind in their faces (Br.). Flies go to (hunt) the lean horse (Br.). The lean dog is all fleas (Am.). A man born to misfortune will fall on his back and fracture his nose (Am.). No butter will stick to his bread (Br.). An unfortunate (unlucky) man would be drowned in a tea-cup (Br.). An unhappy man's cart is easy to overthrow (Am.). An unhappy man's cart is easy to tumble (Br.). What is worse than ill luck? (Br.)

1173. На безлюдье и сидни в чести. *See 1174 (Н)*

Var.: На безлюдье и Фома дворянин

Cf.: All is good in a famine (Am., Br.). Among the blind the one-eyed man is king (Br.). In the land of the blind the one-eyed are kings (Am.)

1174. На безрыбье и рак рыба. *We must do with the thing or man we have at our disposal for want of a better one. See 202 (В), 291 (В), 579 (Е), 633 (З), 893 (К), 1173 (Н), 1175 (Н), 2028 (С)*

Cf.: All is good in a famine (Am., Br.). Among the blind the one-eyed man is king (Br.). A bad bush is better than the open field (Am., Br.). Make the most of what you have (Am.). There is little choice in a barrel of rotten apples (Am.). There is small choice in rotten apples (Am., Br.). There's no choice among stinking fish (Am.). They that have no other meat, bread and butter are glad to eat (Br.). They that have no other meat, gladly bread and butter eat (Am.). When /all/ fruit fails, welcome haws (Br.). When the fruit fails, welcome haws (Am.)

1175. На бесптичье и ворона соловей. *See 1174 (Н)*

Cf.: All is good in a famine (Am., Br.). Among the blind the one-eyed man is king (Br.). In the land of the blind the one-eyed are kings (Am.)

1176. На Бога надейся, а сам не плошай. *People that want to get something done must rely on themselves and do it. See 85 (Б)*

Var.: На Бога уповай, а сам не плошай

Cf.: Fortune helps them that help themselves (Am., Br.). God helps those who help themselves (Am., Br.). God reaches us good things by our own hands (Br.). Help yourself and heaven will help you (Am.). Lie not in the mire and say "God help" (Br.). Lord helps those who help themselves (Br.). The Lord helps those who help themselves (Am.). Pray to God, but keep hammering (Am.). Pray to God, but keep the hammer going (Br.). Pray to God, sailor, but pull for the shore (Br.). Put your trust in God, but keep your powder dry (Am., Br.). Self-help is the best help (Am.). Self is the best servant (Am.)

1177. На большом пути и малая ноша тяжела. *Even a slight effort one keeps making for a long time makes him weary. See 2151 (У)*

Var.: На сто вёрст и иголка тяжела

Cf.: On a long journey even a straw is heavy (wieghs) (Br.). Too long burden makes weary bones (Br.)

1178. На брюхе шёлк, а в брюхе-то щёлк. *The man tries to look smart and rich, but he does not have a single penny to his name. See 1214 (Н), 1789 (П), 1854 (С), 2335 (Ш)*

Cf.: Great boast and small roast (Am., Br.)

1179. На веку—не на боку, всего будет. *See 603 (Ж)*

Cf.: Take the evil with the good (Am.). Take the fat with the lean (Br.). You have to take the bitter with the sweet (the good with the bad) (Am.). You must take the bad with the good (Br.). You must take the rough with the smooth (the sour with the sweet) (Am., Br.)

1180. На веку, что на долгом волоку. *See 602 (Ж)*

Var.: На веку, что на долгой ниве

Cf.: It's a great journey to life's end (Br.). Life is no bed of roses (Am.). Life is not a bed of roses (all bear and skittles, all cake and ale, all honey) (Br.). Life is not wholly bear and skittles (Am.)

1181. На вид пригож, а внутри на чёрта похож. *See 1859 (С)*

Cf.: An angel on top but a devil underneath (Am.). A fair face may hide a foul heart (Am., Br.). Fair without and false within (Br.)

1182. На вкус, на цвет товарища нет. *What one likes another does not; you must tolerate people's individual likings strange as they may be. See 767 a (К), 862 (К), 927 (К), 929 (К), 1512 (О), 2087 (У)*

Cf.: All meat pleases not all mouths (Br.). A black grape (plum, raisin) is as sweet as a white (Br.). Different strokes for different folks (Am.). Each to his own taste (Am.). Every man to his /own/ taste (Am., Br.). No dish pleases all palates alike (Br.). One man's sweet is another man's sour (Am.). Tastes differ (Am., Br.). To each his own (Am., Br.)

1183. На воре шапка горит. *a) The conduct and the appearance of a man guilty of something gives him away. See 87 (Б), 971 (К), 1508 (О); b) If you take* *it as referring to yourself, there must be some reason for it. See 673 (З)*

Cf.: a) Every man's faults are written on their foreheads (Am.). Every one's faults are written in (on) their foreheads (Br.). Guilty conscience gives itself away (Br.)

b) The cat knows whose butter he has eaten (Br.). If the cap fits, put it on (Am.). If the cap fits, wear it (Am., Br.). If the the shoe fits, put it on (wear it) (Am.)

1184. На всех не угодишь. *Do not worry that somebody is displeased with you, you cannot make everybody happy. See 724 (И), 1185 (Н), 1189 (Н), 1669 (П)*

Var.: На весь мир не угодишь (мягко не постелешь, не будешь мил). На всякий нрав не угодишь

Cf.: He labors in vain who tries to please everybody (Am.). He that would please all and himself too, takes more in hand than he is like to do (Am.). He who pleased everybody died before he was born (Br.). It is hard to please all parties (Br.). No gale can equally serve all passengers (Br.). Not even Jupiter can please everybody (Br.). One cannot please all the world and his wife (Br.). You cannot please everybody (Am., Br.). You can't please the whole world and his wife (Am.)

1185. На всех угодить—себя истомить. *It is very difficult to act to the satisfaction of all people. See 1184 (Н)*

Cf.: He labors in vain who tries to please everybody (Am.). He that all men will please shall never find ease (Br.)

1186. На всякого дурака ума не напасёшься. *Sometimes it is hard for a wise man to manage with a fool or an incompetent man*

Cf.: A fool can ask more questions in a minute than a wise man can answer in an hour (Am.). A fool can ask more questions in an hour than a wise man can answer in seven years (Am.). A fool can ask questions that wise men cannot answer (Am.). A fool may ask more questions /in an hour/ than a wise man can answer /in seven years/ (Br.)

1187. На всякого мудреца довольно простоты. *See 738 (И)*

Cf.: Even a wise man stumbles (Br.). Every man has a fool in his sleeve (Am.). Every man has a fool up his sleeve (Am., Br.). A good sailor may mistake in a dark night (Br.). No man is always wise (Am.). None are so well shod but they may slip (Br.)

1188. На всякое хотение есть терпение. *All you desire cannot be realized immediately, do not complain for it takes time. See 920 (К)*

Cf.: Everything comes to him who knows how to wait (Br.). Everything comes to him who waits (Am., Br.). He that can have patience can have what he will (Am.). Patience conquers (Am.). Wait and you will be rewarded (Am.)

1189. На всякое чиханье не наздравствуешься. *See 1184 (Н)*

Var.: На всякий чих не наздравствуешься

Cf.: One cannot please all the world and his wife (Br.). You cannot please everybody (everyone) (Am., Br.). You can't please the whole world and his wife (Am.)

1190. Навык мастера ставит. *It is only by doing a thing again and again that you can attain skill. See 280 (В), 1112 (М), 1557 (О)*

Cf.: A barber learns to shave by shaving (Am.). By writing we learn to write (Br.). Custom makes the thing easy (Br.). It is working that makes a workman (Am.). Dexterity comes with experience (Am.). Practice is the best master (Am., Br.). Practice makes perfect (Am., Br.). Use makes perfect (perfection, the craftsman) (Br.). We learn to do by doing (Am.)

1191. На глупый вопрос—шальной ответ. *You cannot expect a smart answer when you ask a senseless question*

Cf.: Answer a fool according to his folly (Am., Br.). Ask a silly question and you'll get a silly answer (Am., Br.). Like question, like answer (Br.). Silly question, silly answer (Am.)

1192. На голове густо, да в голове пусто. *He has thick hair but an empty head*

Cf.: Bush natural; more hair than wit (Am., Br.)

1193. На двух свадьбах сразу не танцуют. *When a person is engaged in doing something, you cannot expect him to do another job simultaneously*

Cf.: A horse can't pull while kicking (Am.). A man cannot reel and spin together (whistle and drink at the same time) (Br.). A man cannot whistle and eat a meal at the same time (Am.). No man can do two things at once (sup and blow together) (Br.). One cannot be in two places at once (Am., Br.). When a mule is kicking, he is not pulling; and when he is pulling, he is not kicking (Am.). You can't dance at two weddings with one pair of feet (Am.) You can't follow two paths (Am.). You can't ride two horses at the same time (Am.)

1194. Над другими посмеёшься, над собой поплачешь. *See 940 (К)*

Cf.: He makes a foe who makes a jest (Am.). Jesting lies bring serious sorrows (Am.). People who are sharp cut their fingers (Br.)

1195. Надеждой жив человек. *Though one's situation or condition may be discouraging at present, there is still hope for a change for the better. See 134 (В), 1682 (П)*

Var.: Сердце надеждой живо

Cf.: Don't give up hope till hope is dead (Am.). Hope keeps a man from hanging and drowning himself (Am.). Hope keeps man alive (Br.). Hope keeps the heart from breaking (Am.). Hope springs eternal /in the human heart/ (Am., Br.). If it were not for (without) hope, the heart would break (Br.). To hope is to live (Am.). While there's life there's hope (Am., Br.)

1196. Над нами не каплет. *See 432 (Д)*

Cf.: Business tomorrow (Br.). It will be here tomorrow (Am.). It will keep (Am.). Tomorrow is a new day (Am., Br.)

1197. На добрый привет и добрый ответ. *If you treat people kindly, they will treat you in the same way. See 824 (К)*

Cf.: Do well and have well (Am.). Do well, have well (Am.). The good we confer on others recoils on ourselves (Am.). The good you do to others will always come back to you (Am.). Kindness always begets kindness (Am.). One good deed deserves (brings forth) another (Am.). One good turn deserves another (Am., Br.). One kindness deserves another (Am.). Repay kindness with kindness (Am.). Speak kind words and you will hear kind answers (Am.)

1198. Надо веять, пока ветер веет. *See 977 (К)*

Cf.: Hoist up the sail while the gale does last (Am.). Hoist your sail while the wind is fair (Br.). Strike while the iron is hot (Am., Br.)

1199. На дураках воду возят. *People take advantage of those who do the work others do not want to. See 910 (К), 1601 (О), 1808 (Р)*

Cf.: All lay load (loads) on a willing horse (Br.). All lay the load on the willing horse (Am.). Everyone lays a burden on the willing horse (Am.). He that makes himself an ass must not complain if men ride him (Am.). The willing horse carries the load (Am.)

1200. На запретный товар весь базар. *See 640 (З)*
Var.: На опальный товар много купцов
Cf.: Forbidden fruit is sweet (sweetest) (Br.). Forbidden fruit is the sweetest (Am.). Stolen fruit is always sweeter (Am.). Stolen fruit is sweet (Br.)

1201. Назвался груздем—полезай в кузов. *If you committed yourself to do something, there is no going back. See 913 (К), 1751 (П)*
Cf.: If you pledge, don't hedge (Br.). Once you pledge, don't hedge (Am.). You can't back out (Am., Br.)

1202. На злое дело всякого станет. *It is not hard to incite a man to some ill deed*
Cf.: An evil lesson is soon learnt (Am.). That which is evil is soon learned (Am., Br.)

1203. Назло мужу сяду в лужу. *Do not do anything in a fit of temper that will offend somebody but will also harm you. See 1287 (Н)*
Cf.: Don't bite off your nose to spite your face (Br.). Don't cut off your nose to spite your face (Am., Br.)

1204. На кого Бог, на того и добрые люди. *People hurt a man that is already in trouble*
Cf.: All dogs bite the bitten dog (Am.). When a man is down, everyone runs over him (steps on him) (Am.). When a man is going downhill, everyone gives him a push (Am.)

1205. На крепкий сук—острый топор. *Somebody or something is found to subdue a man's obstinacy, arrogance or cunning. See 4 (А)*
Cf.: Diamond cuts diamond (Am., Br.). Iron cuts iron (Am.). Iron whets iron (Br.). A stubborn driver to a stubborn ass (Br.). To a good rat a good cat (Br.)

1206. Налетел топор на сук. *See 1267 (Н)*
Var.: Налетел острый топор, да на острый сук
Cf.: Diamond cut diamond (Br.). Diamond cuts diamond (Am., Br.). Iron cuts iron (Am.)

1207. На ловца и зверь бежит. *I wanted to see you and here you are. See 1513 (О)*
Cf.: The ball comes to the player (Br.). The game walks into the bag (Br.). /Here's/ just the person I need (Am., Br.). Speak of the devil and he'll appear (Am., Br.)

1208. На лошадь не плеть покупай, а овёс. *See 2155 (У)*
Cf.: The belly carries the feet (the legs) (Br.). The stomach carries the feet (Am.)

1209. На миру и смерть красна. *It is easier to bear pain, danger or trouble if other people share it with us. See 389 (Г), 1946 (С)*
Var.: На людях горе вполгоря (и смерть красна, умирать легче)
Cf.: Company in distress makes trouble less (Am., Br.). Company in misery makes it light (Am., Br.). Grief is lessened when imparted to others (Br.). Two in distress makes sorrow less (Br.). Two in distress make trouble less (Am.). Woes invite friends (Br.)

1210. На море овин горит, по небу медведь летит. *See 113 (Б)*
Cf.: If a pig had wings, he might fly (Am.). Pigs might fly /if they had wings/ (, but they are very unlikely birds) (Br.)

1211. На наш век дураков хватит. *See 525 (Д)*
Cf.: A fool is born every minute (Am.). If all fools wore white caps, we'd all look like geese (Am.). There is one born every minute (Br.). There's a sucker born every minute (Am., Br.). The world is full of fools (Am., Br.)

1212. На незваного гостя не припасена и ложка. *See 1345 (Н)*

Var.: Незваного гостя с пира долой

Cf.: An unbidden guest knows not where to sit (Am., Br.). An unbidden guest must bring his stool with him (Br.). Unbidden guests are most welcome when they are gone (Am.)

1213. На нет и суда нет. *If you cannot do or give it, nothing can be done*

Cf.: If there isn't any, one (we) must do without /it/ (Br.). No one can ask for more than your best (Am.)

1214. На ногах сапоги скрипят, а в горшке мухи кипят. *See 1178 (Н)*

Cf.: Great boast, small roast (Am., Br.)

1215. На обеде—все соседи, кончился обед—соседа нет. *See 1901 (С)*

Var.: На обеде—все соседи, а пришла беда—они прочь, как вода

Cf.: As long as the pot boils, friendship lasts (Am., Br.). The bread eaten, the company dispersed (Br.). The dinner over, away go the guests (Am.). Feast and your halls are crowded (Am.). Having finished the meal, the company leaves (Am.)

1216. На одних словах далеко не уедешь. *See 1513 (Н)*

Cf.: Fine words without deeds go not far (Br.). Good words fill not a sack (Br.). Talk does not cook rice (Am.). Talking well will not make the pot boil (Am.). Talk is cheap (Am.). Words never filled a belly (Am.)

1217. На одном гвозде всего не повесишь. *See 1414 (Н)*

Var.: На однин гвоздь всего не вешают

Cf.: Do not hang all on one nail (Am.). Don't carry (put) all your eggs in one basket (Am.). Don't put all your eggs into one basket (Br.). Never venture all in one bottom (Br.)

1218. На одном месте и камень мохом обрастает. *People get used to the routine of life and lose their interest in striving for some change of its monotony. See 2014 (С)*

Var.: И камень лёжа обомшится

Cf.: If you rest, you rust (Am.). Standing pools gather filth (Am., Br.). Still water breeds vermin (Br.)

1219. На одном потеряешь, на другом найдёшь. *Failure in some enterprise is followed by success in another one. See 1389 (Н)*

Cf.: Every ebb has its flow (Br.). No great loss but some small profit (Am.). No great loss without some small gain (Br.). One cannot win them all (Am.). What the ebb takes out, the flood brings in (Am.). What we lose in hake, we shall have in herring (Br.). What we lose on the roundabouts we will make up on the swings (Am.). What you lose on the swings you gain (make up, win) on the roundabouts (Br.). When one door closes, another one opens (Am.). When one door shuts, another opens (Am., Br.)

1220. На окошке грибы не растут. *See 50 (Б)*

Cf.: Apples don't grow on monkey-trees (Br.). God gives (sends) every bird its food, but he does not throw it into the nest (Am.). No pains, no gains (Am., Br.). Potatoes don't grow by the side of the pot (Br.)

1221. На ошибках других учимся. *The experience of others should be a good lesson to us not to repeat their mistakes. See 2315 (Ч)*

Cf.: By others' faults wise men correct their own (Am., Br.). The folly of one man is the fortune of another (Am., Br.). From errors of others a wise man corrects his own (Am.). Learn from the mistakes of others (Am., Br.). Learn wisdom by the follies of others (Am., Br.). One man's fault is another man's lesson (Br.). Profit by the experience of others

(Br.). Profit by the folly of others (Am.)

1222. На ошибках учатся. *It is our own bad experience that is a lesson to us not to repeat our mistakes. See 1352 (Н), 1385 (Н), 1639 (П)*

Cf.: By falling we learn to go safely (Am.). Failure is the only highroad to success (Br.). Failures are the stepping-stones to success (Am.). Failure teaches success (Am., Br.). Mistakes are often the best teachers (Am.). We learn by our mistakes (Am.). We profit by mistakes (Am.). Where ever an ass falls there will he never fall again (Br.)

1223. На падаль и собака бежит. *Men take advantage of someone else's bankruptcy, death, grave condition, etc. See 316 (Г), 1627 (П)*

Cf.: Wheresoever the carcass is, there will eagles (ravens) be gathered (Br.). Where the carcass is, there the buzzards gather (there the ravens will collect together, there will the eagles be gathered) (Am.)

1224. Наперёд не знаешь, где найдёшь, где потеряешь. *See 1478 (Н)*

Cf.: Nothing is certain but the unforeseen (Am., Br.). You never know what you'll lose and what you'll gain (Am.)

1225. Наплюй в глаза, скажет: божья роса. *You abuse an unscrupulous person, and he pretends it is not an abuse*

Var.: Бесстыжему хоть плюй в глаза—всё божья роса

Cf.: Spit in a whore's face and she'll say it's raining (Am.)

1226. На погосте жить, всех не оплачешь. *When you see too much grief, you cannot take it all to your heart. (One says so to excuse himself for being indifferent to someone's sorrow)*

Cf.: He who weeps for everybody soon loses his eyesight (Am.)

1227. На полатях лежать, так и ломтя не видать. *See 1145 (М)*

Var.: На полатях лежать—ломтя не достать. На полатях лежать, так и хлеба не видать

Cf.: A lazy dog finds no bone (Am.). A sleeping fox catches no geese (Am.). The sleeping fox catches no poultry (Am., Br.). When the fox sleeps no grapes fall in his mouth (Br.)

1228. На послушного коня кнута не надо. *See 844 (К)*

Var.: На ретивого коня (ретивую лошадь) не кнут, а вожжи.

Cf.: A boisterous horse must have a rough bridle (Am., Br.). Don't spur a willing horse (Am., Br.). A good horse should be seldom spurred (Am., Br.)

1229. На посуле, как на стуле: посидишь и встанешь. *See 1506 (О)*

Cf.: Fair words fill not the belly (Br.). Promises don't fill the belly (Am.)

1230. На правду суда нет. *See 1759 (П)*

Var.: Правда суда не боится

Cf.: Truth fears nothing but concealment (Am.). Truth fears no trial (Br.). Truth seeks no corners (Am., Br.)

1231. Напрямик—ближе, кругом—скорее. *The main road that may be long and roundabout is often a safer and quicker way to your destination than a short one. See 959 (К), 1357 (Н)*

Cf.: The farther way about is the nearest way home (Am.). The farthest (longest) way about is the nearest way home (Br.). He that leaves the highway to cut short, commonly goes about (Br.). The highway is never about (Am., Br.). The longest way around is the shortest way home (Am.). The longest way round is the nearest (the shortest) way home (Am., Br.)

1232. На резвом коне жениться не езди. *Think twice before you take the decision to marry*

Cf.: Before you marry 'tis well to tarry (Am.). A young trooper should have an old horse (Br.)

1233. Нарочно не придумаешь. *See 2235 (Ч)*

Cf.: Facts are stranger than fiction (Am.). There are stranger things in reality than can be found in romances (Am.). Truth is stranger than fiction (Am., Br.)

1234. Наряди пенёк в вешний денёк, так и пенёк будет паренёк. *See 1517 a (О)*

Var.: Наряди пень /в вешний день/, и пень будет хорош

Cf.: Dress up a stick and it does not appear to be a stick (Br.). Fine feathers make fine birds (Am., Br.). Fine feathers make fine fowl (Am.)

1235. Наряди свинью хоть в серьги, а она всё в навоз пойдёт. *See 315 (Г), 827 (К)*

Cf.: A golden bit does not make a horse any better (Br.). A golden bit does not make the horse any better (Am.). Pigs are pigs (Am.)

1236. На свинью хоть седло надень— всё конём не будет. *See 827 (К)*

Cf.: An ass is an ass, though laden with gold (Am.). An ass is but an ass, though laden with gold (Br.)

1237. На своей печи сам себе голова. *See 287 (В)*

Cf.: A cock is mighty in his own backyard (Am.). Every man is a king (a master) in his own house (Br.). A man is king in his home (Am.)

1238. На своей улочке храбра и курочка. *Every man is brave when he is in his own place, among his friends and supporters. See 1239 (Н), 2144 (У)*

Cf.: A cock is /always/ bold on his own dunghill (Br.). A cock is mighty in his backyard (Am.). A cock is valiant on his own dunghill (Br.). A dog is bold on his own dunghill (Br.). A dog is brave in his own yard (Am.). Every dog is a lion at home (Am., Br.). Every dog is brave in his own yard (Am.). Every dog is valiant at his own door (Am., Br.). A man is a lion in his own house (Am.)

1239. На своём пепелище и курица бьёт. *See 1238 (Н)*

Cf.: A cock is /always/ bold on his own dunghill (Br.). A cock is mighty in his own backyard (Am.)

1240. На сердитых воду возят. *An angry or irritated man will endure most of all. (This is said to a man whose bad temper does not stir up your sympathy and seems groundless)*

Cf.: Anger is a sworn enemy (Am., Br.). Anger profits nobody (Am.). Anger punishes itself (Am., Br.). The angry beggar gets a stone instead of a hand (Am.). An angry man never wants woe (Br.). Two to one in all things against the angry man (Br.)

1241. Насильно мил не будешь. *Nothing but love breeds mutual love. See 1890 (С)*

Var.: Силой милому не быть. Силою не будешь милою

Cf.: Fanned fire and forced love never did well yet (Br.). Forced love does not last (Br.). Love can neither be bought nor sold; its only price is love (Am.). Love cannot be forced (compelled, ordered) (Br.). Love is neither bought nor sold (Br.)

1242. Наскоро заучишь—скоро забудешь. *Superficial knowledge is not kept in memory. See 2310 (Ч)*

Cf.: Quickly learned, soon forgotten (Br.). Soon learnt, soon forgotten (Br.). What is quickly done is quickly undone (Am.)

1243. Наскочила кость на кость. *See 1267 (Н)*

Cf.: Diamond cuts diamond (Am., Br.)

1244. На словах и так и сяк, а на деле никак. *See 1143 (М)*

Cf.: Good words and no deeds (Br.). Much talk, little work (Am.)

1245. На смелого собака лает, а трусливого рвёт. *A brave man is not afraid of danger and can deal with it, but it hurts a coward*

Cf.: He who handles a nettle tenderly is soonest stung (Br.). Stroke a nettle and it will sting you; grasp it and it is as soft as silk (Am.)

1246. На смерть поруки нет. *See 1607 (О)*

Cf.: Death takes no denial (Br.). They that live longest must die at last (Am.)

1247. На соседа не кивай—за собой примечай. *See 511 (Д)*

Var.: Не кивай на соседа, а погляди на себя

Cf.: Everybody ought to sweep before his own door (Br.). Point not at others' spots with a foul finger (Am.)

1248. На старого и немочи валятся. *See 364 (Г)*

Cf.: Age breeds aches (Am.). An old ass is never good (Br.)

1249. Наступление—лучший вид обороны. *When having an argument or competing with someone, it is better to be active*

Var.: Нападение—лучший вид защиты

Cf.: Attack is the best /form (method) of/ defence (Br.). A good offense is the best defense (Am.). Offence is the best defence (Br.)

1250. Натерпишься горя—научишься жить. *See 33 (Б)*

Var.: Натерпишься горя—узнаешь, как жить

Cf.: Adversity makes men wise (Am., Br.)

1251. На торной дороге трава не растёт. *Much used ways of doing something do not give new fruitful results*

Var.: На битой (прохожей) дороге и трава не растёт

Cf.: Grass doesn't grow on a busy street (Am.). Grass grows not at the market cross (br.). Grass grows not upon the highway (Am., Br.). A trodden path bears no grass (Am.)

1252. На троих готовили—и четвёртый сыт. *If you have enough, you can share it with one person more*

Cf.: There'll always be enough (Am.). What's enough for one is enough for two (Br.)

1253. На убогого всюду каплет. *See 1172 (Н)*

Cf.: All the Tracys have always the wind in their faces (Br.). Flies go to (hunt) the lean horse (Br.). The lean dog is all fleas (Am.). An unhappy man's cart is easy to overthrow (Am.)

1254. Науке учиться—старости нет. *See 2168 (У)*

Cf.: /It is/ never too late to learn (Am., Br.). Never too old to learn (Am., Br.)

1255. На хороший товар и купцов много. *See 2194 (Х)*

Cf.: Good things soon find a purchaser (Am.). Good ware makes a quick market (Br.). Pleasing ware is half sold (Am.)

1256. Начал смехами, кончил слезами. *If you are prematurely happy, you will pay for it later. See 1820 (Р)*

Cf.: He who laughs on Friday will weep on Sunday (Br.). Laugh before breakfast and you'll cry before supper (Br). Laugh before breakfast, you'll cry before sunset (night, supper) (Am.). Laugh before seven, cry before eleven (Br.). Rejoice today and repent tomorrow (Am.). Sing before breakfast, and you'll cry before night (supper) (Am.)

1257. Начатого дела не бросай. *See 652 (З)*

Var.: Начатое дело доводи до конца

Cf.: Do nothing by halves (Am.). If a task is once begun, never leave it till it's done (Am.). Never do things by halves (Br.). Never give up once you have started (Br.). Never leave a task until it is done (Am.). Never say A without saying B (Am.)

1258. Начиная дело, о конце думай. *When you start doing something, think of how to complete the job*

Cf.: Begin nothing until you have considered how it is to be finished (Am.). In every beginning think of the end (Br.). Look to (Mark) the end (Br.). Think of the end before you begin (Br.)

1259. На что и клад, когда дети идут в лад. *Children are the riches of parents. See 1697 (П)*

Cf.: Happy is he who is happy in his children (Br.). It takes children to make a happy family (home) (Am.)

1260. На чужой каравай рот не разевай. *Do not desire to obtain that which is not yours*

Var.: В чужой прудок не кидай неводок. На чужой ломоток не разевай роток. На чужую кучу нечего глаза пучить

Cf.: Covet not which belongs to others (Am.). Pluck not where you never planted (Br.). Scald not your lips in another man's porridge (Br.). Wish not to taste what does not to you fall (Am.)

1261. На чужой роток не накинешь платок. *You cannot make people keep silent and not spread rumo(u)rs defaming you or another person. See 1090 (Л)*

Var.: В чужой рот не поставишь ворот. На чужой рот пуговицы не нашьёшь. Рот не огород, не затворишь ворот. Чужой роток не свой хлевок, не затворишь

Cf.: Gossip needs no carriage (Am.). Gossips are frogs, they drink and talk (Br.). Gossips drink and talk; frogs drink and squawk (Am.). He that will stop every man's mouth must have a great deal of meal (Br.). Pigs grunt about everything and nothing (Br.)

1262. На чужой совет без зову не ходи. *Never thrust your opinion on, or give advice to people if you are not asked to*

Cf.: Come not to counsel uncalled (Br.). Give neither counsel nor salt till you are asked for /it/ (Br.). Give neither salt nor advice till asked for it (Am.)

1263. На чужую одежду плохая надежда. *It is not reliable to count on someone's goods*

Cf.: Borrowed clothes (garments) never fit (Am.). Borrowed garments fit not (never fit well) (Br.). He goes long barefoot that waits for dead men's shoes (Br.). He that waits for a dead man's shoes may long go barefoot (Am.). He that waits for dead men's shoes may go a long time barefoot (Am.). You can't get warm on another's fur coat (Am.)

1264. На чьём возу сижу, того и песенку пою. *Every man pays respect to him that he gains by. See 858 (К), 1589 (О), 1693 (П), 2109 (У), 2241 (Ч), 2333 (Ч)*

Cf.: Every man bows to the bush he gets bield of (Br.). Whose bread I eat, his song I sing (Am.)

1265. Наше дело телячье. *I obey someone else's orders and nothing depends on me. See 2181 (Х)*

Var.: Наше дело—сторона /, поел да в закут/

Cf.: Orders must not be challenged (Am.). Ours is not to question why, ours is to do or die (Br.). Yours is not to question why; yours is but to do or die (Am.)

1266. На Шипке всё спокойно. *The state of affairs is favo(u)rable. (The implication is that there may be trouble or danger later)*
Cf.: All is quiet along (on) the Potomac (Br.). All quiet on the Western front (Am.). All's quiet in the Shipka Pass (Am.). It's all serene (Br.). So far, so good (Am., Br.)

1267. Нашла коса на камень. *Unyielding men will not give in to one another. See 554 (Д), 889 (К), 1206 (Н), 1243 (Н), 1569 (О)*
Cf.: Diamond cuts diamond (Am., Br.). Iron cuts iron (Am.). When Greek meets Greek, then comes the tug of war (Am., Br.)

1268. Наш пострел везде поспел. *He is an intrusive and pushing man*
Cf.: He has a finger in every pie (Am.). The scamp has a finger in every pie (Br.)

1269. На языке медок, а на сердце ледок. *The man speaks nicely but thinks evil. See 1170 (М)*
Var.: На словах медок, а на сердце ледок. На устах мёд, а на сердце лёд. На языке мёд, а в сердце (на уме, под языком) лёд
Cf.: He has honey in the mouth and razor at the girdle (Br.). A honey tongue, a heart of gall (Br.). Sweet as honey, bitter as gall (Br.). There are daggers behind men's smiles (Am.). Too much courtesy, too much craft (Am.)

1270. На язык пошлин нет: что хочет, то и лопочет. *See 2360 (Я)*
Var.: Язык мягок: что хочет, то и лопочет
Cf.: Lying pays no tax (Br.). Talking pays no toll (Am.). The tongue is an unruly member (Am.)

1271. Не боги горшки обжигают. *Man can do a most difficult job and make most sophisticated things. See 339 (Г)*
Var.: Не боги города строят
Cf.: Whatever man has done man may do (Br.). What man has done man can do (Am.)

1272. Не бойся начала, а бойся конца. *See 995 (Л)*
Cf.: The beginning is not everything (Am.). Good to begin well, better to end well (Am., Br.)

1273. Не бойся собаки, что лает, а бойся той, что молчит да хвостом виляет. *You should be afraid of secretive men but not of those who threaten you openly. See 294 (В), 1952 (С)*
Var.: Не бойся собаки брехливой, а бойся молчаливой. Не та собака кусает, что лает, а та, что молчит да хвостом виляет
Cf.: Beware of a silent dog and silent water (Am.). Beware of a silent dog and still water (of a silent man and a dog that does not bark) (Br.). Dumb dogs /and still waters/ are dangerous (Br.). Look out for the man that does not talk and the dog that does not bark (Am.). The silent dog is first to bite (Am.). The slowest barker is the surest biter (Br.)

1274. Не буди лихо, пока оно тихо. *Do not disturb a man or a state of affairs that causes no trouble at present but can do some. See 1337 (Н), 1354 (Н)*
Cf.: Avoid evil and it will avoid you (Am.). Avoid the evil and it will avoid thee (Br.). Do not trouble trouble until trouble troubles you (Am., Br.). Don't wake a sleeping lion (Am., Br.). Don't wake a sleeping wolf (Br.). Don't wake it up (Am.). Let sleeping dogs (the sleeping dog) lie (Am., Br.). When sorrow is asleep, wake it not (Am.. Br.)

1275. Не было б везения, кабы не было умения. *Success in doing some work depends on one's competence*
Cf.: Ability, not luck, conquers (Am.). Skill and luck go together (Br.)

1276. Не было бы счастья, да несчастье помогло. *See 1456 (Н)*

Cf.: Afflictions are best blessings (Am.). Afflictions are blessings in disguise (Br.). After a typhoon there are pears to gather up (Br.). Behind bad luck comes good luck (Am.). Sweet are the uses of adversity (Br.)

1277. Не было у бабы хлопот, купила баба порося. *People, of their own accord, assume responsibilities which give them concern or trouble later. See 1620 (О), 2248 (Ч)*

Var.: Не знала баба горя (хлопот), так купила баба порося

Cf.: He who has no worries makes himself some (Br.). People create their own problems (Am.). Will is the cause of woe (Br.)

1278. Не валяй дурака. *Do not make a ridiculous fool of yourself*

Var.: Не валяй Ваньку

Cf.: Cut the comedy (the funny stuff)! (Am.). Don't make a Judy of yourself (Br.). Don't play the giddy goat (Br.). Go along with you (Br.). Stop fooling around (Am.)

1279. Не в бровь, а в глаз. *The critical remark is neat and correct*

Cf.: The cap fits (Br.). A good shot (Am., Br.). It's right on the mark (Am.). Well-aimed (Br.). You don't pull any punches (Am.). You hit the nail on the head (Am.)

1280. Не в деньгах счастье. *There are more important considerations than how much or little money one has*

Cf.: Gold is but muck (Br.). Money is not everything (Am., Br.). Money isn't everything in life (Am.)

1281. Не вдруг всё делается. *See 730 (И)*

Cf.: Paris was not built in a day (Am.). Rome was not built in a day (Am., Br.)

1282. Не везёт в картах, повезёт в любви. *Do not take to heart that you are a losing card-player. See 131 (В)*

Cf.: Unlucky at cards, lucky in love (Am., Br.). Unlucky gambler, lucky lover (Br.)

1283. Невелика болячка, а на тот свет гонит. *See 1156 (М)*

Cf.: A little leak will sink a big ship (Am.). A little leak will sink a great ship (Br.). Small leaks sink big ships (Am.). A small leak will sink a great ship (Am., Br.)

1284. Не верь козлу в капусте, а волку в овчарне. *See 185 (В)*

Cf.: Don't set a wolf to watch the sheep (Am.). Give never the wolf the wether to keep (Br.)

1285. Не верь словам, а верь делам. *See 1503 (Н)*

Cf.: Actions speak louder than words (Am., Br.). The act proves the intention (Br.). Deeds speak louder than words (Am., Br.). Words don't mean a thing; it's the action that counts (Am.)

1286. Не верь чужим речам, верь своим очам. *See 1062 (Л)*

Var.: Не верь ушам, а верь /своим/ глазам

Cf.: It is better to trust the eye than the ear (Am.). Men's ears are less reliable than their eyes (Br.). Seeing is believing (Am., Br.). What we see we believe (Am.)

1287. Невестке в отместку. *See 1203 (Н)*

Cf.: Don't bite off your nose to spite your face (Br.). Don't cut off your nose to spite your face (Am., Br.)

1288. Не видит сова, какова сама. *See 139 b (В), 511 (Д)*

Cf.: The eye that sees all things else sees not itself (Br.). The eye that sees all things sees not itself (Am.). A hunchback cannot see his hunch (Am.). The hunchback does not see his own hump, but sees his companion's (Br.). The hunchback only sees the hump of his neighbor (Am.)

1289. Не вижу, так и не верю. *See 1062 (Л)*

Cf.: Seeing is believing (Am., Br.). What we see we believe (Am.)

1290. Не в коня корм. *This man cannot appreciate or is unworthy of what is done for him. See 1368 (Н)*

Cf.: Don't cast pearls before swine (Am., Br.). Honey is not for the ass's mouth (Br.). It is caviar (caviare) to the general (Br.). That's money down the drain (Am., Br.)

1291. Не вкусив горького, не узнаешь и сладкого. *It is only a man who has been through trouble that can comprehend what joy and happiness are. See 951 (К), 1458 (Н)*

Var.: Не отведав горького, не узнаешь и сладкого

Cf.: He deserves not sweet that will not taste of sour (Am.). He deserves not the sweet that will not taste the sour (Br.). He is worth no weal that can bide no woe (Br.). He knows best what good is that has endured evil (ill) (Br.). Misfortunes tell us what fortune is (Br.). One does not appreciate happiness unless one has known sorrow (Am.). We know the sweet when we have tasted the bitter (Am.). Who has never tasted bitter knows not what is sweet (Br.)

1292. Не в обиду будь сказано. *Do not get offended at what I am going to say*

Cf.: God bless (save) the mark (Br.). Heaven bless the mark (Br.). No offence (Br.). No offense meant (Am.)

1293. Неворошенный жар под пеплом лежит. *Some active and live energy is often hidden under a thick veil of inertness or restraint. See 690 (И)*

Cf.: The fire in the flint shows not till it's struck (Br.). The fire in the flint shows not until it is struck (Am.). Hidden fires are always the hottest (Am.). In the coldest flint there is hot fire (Br.). Strike a flint and you get fire (Am.)

1294. Не время волос белит, а кручина. *See 1323 (Н)*

Cf.: Adversity flatters no man (Am., Br.). Care brings grey hair (Br.). Care is beauty's thief (Am.)

1295. Не в свои сани не садись. *a) People should not undertake a task they do not know how to do, and they should not speak about matters they are ignorant of. See 21 (Б), 62 (Б), 989 (Л), 1344 (Н), 1420 (Н); b) You must know your place and should not try to equal people superior to you. See 290 (В), 402 (Г), 674 (З), 974 (К), 1002 (Л), 1853 (С), 1991 (С)*

Cf.: a) The cobbler must stick to his last (Br.). Every man as his business lies (to his business, to his craft) (Br.). Every man to his trade (Am., Br.). If you are a cock, crow; if a hen, lay eggs (Am.). Let every man do what he was made for (Br.). Let not the cobbler go beyond his last (Br.). Let the cobbler stick to his last (Am., Br.). A shoemaker should stick to his last (Br.). Shoemaker, stick to your last (to your shoes) (Am.)

b) As a bear has no tail, for a lion he will fail (Br.). Everyone to his equal (Am.). Every sheep with its like (Am.). Geese with geese, and women with women (Br.). Keep to your own kind (Am.). Tigers and deer do not stroll together (Am.)

1296. Не всегда ненастье, не всегда и несчастье. *See 1725 (П)*

Var.: Не всё ненастье—проглянет и красное солнышко

Cf.: After rain comes sunshine (Am., Br.). After the rain, the sun (Am.). Even the weariest river winds somewhere safe to the sea (Br.). Rain before seven, clear before eleven (Br.). Rain before seven, fine before eleven

(Am., Br.). The sun will shine through the darkest clouds (Am.). The tide never goes so far, but it always comes in again (Br.)

1297. Не всё коту масленица. *You cannot always enjoy your time; your easy and carefree life has come to an end. See 1766 (П)*

Var.: Не всё коту масленица, будет (бывает) и великий пост

Cf.: After a Christmas comes a Lent (Br.). All good things come to an end (Am., Br.). All good things must come to an end (Am.). Every day is not a holiday (Am.). Every day is not Sunday (Br.). Good things do not last for ever (Br.). We don't kill a pig every day (Br.)

1298. Не всем казакам в атаманах быть. *Not every man can be a boss or a leader*

Cf.: All men can't be first (masters) (Br.). Be content in your lot; one cannot be first in everything (Am.). Every man cannot be a lord (a master) (Br.). Everyone can't be first (Am.). Not every man can be vicar of Bowden (Br.). We can't all be masters (Am.).

1299. Не всё ровно—есть и горы и овраги. *The way through life is not always easy. See 603 (Ж)*

Cf.: Every path has a puddle (Am., Br.). Every path has its puddle (Am.). Every road has hills to be climbed (Am.). You must take the rough with the smooth (the sour with the sweet) (Am., Br.)

1300. Не все те повара, у кого ножи долгие. *See 168 (В)*

Cf.: All are not cooks who sport white caps and carry long knives (Am.). All are not hunters who blow the horn (Am., Br.). Appearances are deceptive (Am., Br.)

1301. Не всё то золото, что блестит. *Things or a men may not be so as they look. See 56 (Б), 168 (В), 1859 (С)*

Var.: Не всякая блёстка—золото

Cf.: All is not gold that glitters (Am., Br.). All that glistens is not gold (Am., Br). Beauty may have fair leaves but (yet) bitter fruit (Br.). The handsomest flower is not the sweetest (Am.). Many a fine dish has nothing on it (Br.)

1302. Не всё то падает, что шатается. *See 1308 (Н)*

Cf.: All that shakes falls not (Br.). Every slip is not a fall (Am.). Everything does not fall that totters (Am.)

1303. Не всё то правда, что люди говорят. *You cannot rely on the trustworthiness of all that is told. See 1091 (Л), 1316 (Н)*

Cf.: Believe not all that you see nor half what you hear (Br.). Believe only half of what you hear (Br.). Believe only half of what you see and nothing you hear (Am.). Put no faith in tale bearers (Am.). Season all you hear with salt (Am.)

1304. Не всё, что бело, снег. *See 168 (В)*

Cf.: Appearances are deceptive (Am., Br.)

1305. Не всё, что серо, волк. *A man may be not so bad or evil as he looks. See 168 (В)*

Cf.: All are not thieves that dogs bark at (Am., Br.). Appearances are deceiving (Am.). Appearances are deceptive (Am., Br.). I am black, but I am not the devil (Br.)

1306. Не в службу, а в дружбу. *Do it as kindness or courtesy but not because of duty*

Cf.: Do it as a personal favo(u)r (Am., Br.)

1307. Не вспоя, не вскормя, ворога не наживёшь. *See 250 (В)*

Var.: Не поя, не кормя, ворога не наживёшь

Cf.: Breed up a crow and he will

peck out your eyes (Br.). Do no good and you shall find no evil (Am.). No good deed goes unpunished (Am.). Save a thief from the gallows, and he'll be the first to cut your throat (Am.)

1308. Не всякая болезнь к смерти. *A grave state of things does not always result in complete failure, crash or ruination; things may improve. See 1302 (Н), 1317 (Н), 2138 (У)*

Cf.: All is not lost that is in danger (Am.). All is not lost that is in peril (Br.). All that shakes falls not (Br.). Everything does not fall that totters (Am.). Near dead never filled the kirkyard (Am.). No man is dead till he's dead (Am.)

1309. Не всякая пуля по кости, иная и по кусту. *See 262 (В)*

Var.: Не всякая пуля в кость да в мясо, иная и в поле

Cf.: Every cloud engenders not a storm (Br.). Every cloud is not a sign of storm (Am.). Every shot does not bring down a bird (Br.)

1310. Не всякая туча грозовая. *See 262 (В)*

Cf.: All clouds bring not rain (Am., Br.). Every cloud engenders not a storm (Br.). Every cloud is not a sign of a storm (Am.). Every wind blows not down the corn (Br.)

1311. Не всяк весел, кто поёт. *Gaiety can be just a pretence which conceals sadness, sorrow or despair*

Cf.: All are not merry that dance lightly (Br.). Every man is not merry that dances (Am.). Just because a man sings, it's no sign he's happy (Am.). Not everyone who dances is happy (Br.)

1312. Не всякий встречный—друг сердечный. *Do not trust all the people you meet by chance. See 108 (Б)*

Cf.: Of chance acquaintance beware (Am.). Short acquaintance brings repentance (Br.). Sudden friendship, sure repentance (Am, Br.). Sudden short acquaintances bring repentance (Am.)

1313. Не всякий умён, кто богато наряжён. *Folly is often found beneath rich clothes. See 1381 (Н)*

Var.: Не всякий умён, кто хорошо наряжён

Cf.: A broad hat does not always cover a venerable head (Am., Br.). Clothes do not make the man (Am., Br.)

1314. Не всяк монах, на ком клобук. *The clothes a man wears do not always indicate his occupation. See 168 (В), 1417 (Н)*

Var.: Не всяк игумен, на ком клобук

Cf.: All are not cooks who sport white caps and carry long knives (Am.). Appearances are deceptive (Am., Br.). The cowl (hood) does not make the monk (Br.)

1315. Не всякое лыко в строку. *One should not be blamed for every inadvertence; negligible slips should be pardoned*

Var.: Не каждое лыко в строку

Cf.: An inch breaks no square (Br.). Wink at small faults (Am., Br.)

1316. Не всякому слуху верь. *See 1303 (Н)*

Cf.: Believe not all that you see nor half what you hear (Br.). Believe only half of what you see and nothing you hear (Am.). Season all you hear with salt (Am.)

1317. Не всяк умирает, кто хворает. *See 1308 (Н)*

Cf.: All that shakes falls not (Br.). Near dead never filled the kirkyard (Am.)

1318. Не всякую правду сказывай. *In some cases you have an excuse to disguise the truth not to hurt someone or do harm to yourself*

Cf.: All truth is not to be told at all

times (Am., Br.). Always tell the truth, but don't always be telling the truth (Am.)

1319. Не выливай помоев, не приготовив чистой воды. *Do not get rid of a thing that is not very good before you get a better one*

Cf.: Cast not out /the/ foul water till you bring /in the/ clean (Br.). Cast not out the foul water till you have clean (Am.). Don't throw away old shoes till you've got new ones (Br.). Don't throw away your dirty water until you get clean (Am.). Don't throw away your old shoes before you get new ones (Am.). Don't throw out your dirty water before you get in fresh (Br.)

1320. Не высок водоспуск, а реку держит. *See 1099 (M)*

Cf.: An inch is as good as an ell (Br.). A little rain stills a great wind (Am.)

1321. Не говори "гоп", пока не перескочишь. *Do not be prematurely elated at having escaped a danger, solved a difficult problem or completed some work. See 1468 (H), 1469 (H), 1821 (P), 2172 (X), 2174 (X), 2228 (Ц)*

Var.: Не говори "гоп", пока не перепрыгнешь

Cf: Do not shout until you are out of the woods (Am.). Do not triumph before the victory (Br.). Don't cackle till your egg is laid (Br.). Don't celebrate victories before you have conquered (Br.). Don't count your corpses before they are cold (Am.). Don't halloo (shout, whistle) till you are out of the wood (Br.). Don't halloo till you're out of the woods (Am.). Don't say "hop" until you've jumped over (Am.). Don't sing your triumph before you have conquered (Am.). Don't whistle before you leap (Br.). Don't whistle your triumph before you have conquered (Am.). It is not good praising a ford till a man be over (Br.)

1322. Не говори с косым о кривом. *See 129 (B)*

Var.: С кривым о косом не беседуют

Cf.: It's ill halting before a cripple (Am.). Name not a halter (a rope) in his house that hanged himself (that was hanged) (Br.). Never talk of rope in the house of a man who has been hanged (Am.)

1323. Не годы старят, а горе. *Troubles affect one greatly. See 210 (B), 391 (Г), 392 (Г), 900 (К), 1294 (H), 1397 (H)*

Var.: Не старость калечит, а горе

Cf.: Adversity flatters no man (Am., Br.). Care brings grey hair (Br.). Care is beauty's thief (Am.). Sorrow and an ill life make soon an old wife (Am.)

1324. Не гоняй лошадь к воде, если ей пить не хочется. *You cannot make a man follow your advice if he is unwilling*

Cf.: A man can be led but he can't be driven (Am.). One man can lead a horse to water, but ten men can't make him drink (Am.). One man may lead a horse to the river (the water), but twenty cannot make him drink (Br.). You can lead a horse to water, but you can't make him drink (Am.). You can take (may lead) a horse to the water, but you cannot make him drink (Br.). You may lead a mule to water, but you can't make him drink (Am.)

1325. Не горазд биться, а горазд грозиться. *The man can just make threats but he never dares to bring them about. See 1472 (H), 1140 (M), 1952 (C)*

Cf.: Bullies are always (generally) cowards (Br.). A bully is always a coward (Am., Br.). The dog without teeth barks the most (Am.). He threatens who is afraid (Am.). It is one thing to flourish and another to fight (Br.). To flourish is one thing, to fight another (Am.). Those who threaten don't fight (Br.)

1326. Не грози попу кадилом. *Do not threaten a person with what he lives by, with what is beneficial to him*

Cf.: A dog will not cry if you beat him with a bone (Am., Br.). A dog will not howl if you beat him with a bone (Br.)

1327. Не давай коню тощать—в дороге не станет. *See 2155 (У)*

Cf.: The belly carries the feet (the legs) (Br.). The stomach carries the feet (Am.)

1328. Не делай другим того, чего себе не желаешь. *Treat others like you would have them treat you*

Var.: Чего сам не любишь, того и другому не желай (не делай)

Cf.: Do as you would be done by (Am., Br.). Don't do to others what you would not have done to you (Am.). Do unto others as you would have them do unto you (Am., Br.)

1329. Не держи посулом, одолжи отказом. *Do not comply with people's requests if you are unable to keep your word*

Cf.: A bad promise is better broken than kept (Am.). Better deny at once than promise long (Br.)

1330. Не до Бога, когда беда у порога. *Those in despair often forget about God*

Cf.: God is too good for a desperate mood (Br.)

1331. Не до жиру, быть бы живу. *The circumstances are so strained that I have to make do with little and not think of much. See 25 (Б)*

Cf.: Poor folks are glad of porridge (Am.). Small change is riches to a beggar (Br.)

1332. Не дом хозяина красит, а хозяин дом. *It is a hospitable and nice host that makes his place likeable. See 1363 (Н)*

Var.: Не место человека красит, а человек место

Cf.: Grace your house, and not let that grace you (Am.). The house is a fine house when good folks are within (Br.). It is not the place that honours the man, but the man that honours the place (Br.). The owner should bring honor to the house, not the house to the owner (Am.)

1333. Не до пляски, не до шутки, когда пусто в желудке. *When a man is hungry, he is in bad humo(u)r*

Cf.: A hungry man, an angry man (Am.). A hungry man is an angry man (Am., Br.)

1334. Не дорог подарок, дорога любовь. *The good will or affection, that lies behind an act or a present, is more important than the act or the present itself*

Var.: Не дорог обед, дорог привет

Cf.: It is the thought that counts (Am., Br.). It's not the gift that counts, but the thought behind it (Am., Br.)

1335. Недосол на столе, пересол на спине. *When doing any work, you should know the right measure because too much zeal may result in spoiling the work*

Var.: Пересол хуже недосола

Cf.: Better underdone than overdone (Br.). Overdone is worse than underdone (Am., Br.). Salt cooks bear blame, but fresh bear shame (Br.)

1336. Недоученный хуже неученого. *A man with poor knowledge of what should be done will spoil the job. See 1699 (П)*

Cf.: Amateur tactics cause grave wounds (Br.). Better untaught than ill taught (Am.). Better untaught than ill-taught (Br.). A little knowledge (learning) is a dangerous thing (Am., Br.)

1337. Не дразни собаку, так не укусит. *See 1274 (Н)*

Cf.: Let the sleeping dog lie (Am., Br.). It is ill to waken sleeping dogs (Br.)

1338. Недруг дарит, зло мыслит. *See 101 (Б)*

Cf.: Beware the Greeks bearing gifts (Am.). An enemy's gifts are no gifts (Br.). Gifts from enemies are dangerous (Br.)

1339. Не жалей алтына—отдашь полтину. *See 629 (З)*

Cf.: Don't be penny-wise and dollar-foolish (Am.). Don't spoil the ship for half a penny's worth of tar (Am.). It is no use losing a sheep for a halfpenny worth of tar (Br.). A penny soul never came to twopence (Br.). A penny soul never 'came twopence (Am.)

1340 Не житьё, а масленица. *Life is pleasant and easy. See 226 (В)*

Cf.: Life is a bed of roses (Am., Br.). Life is but a bowl of cherries (Am.)

1341. Не задирай нос кверху, а то упадёшь. *See 556 (Д)*

Cf.: Pride goes before a fall (Am., Br.)

1342. Незаменимых людей нет. *However competent a man may be, an adequate specialist can be found to take his place. See 1870 (С)*

Cf.: No man is indispensable (Br.). No man is necessary (Am.). No one is indispensable (Am.)

1343. Не замочив рук, не умоешься. *See 50 (Б)*

Cf.: He who would catch fish must not mind getting wet (Am., Br.)

1344. Не за своё дело не берись. *See 1295 a (Н)*

Cf.: Every man must labour in his own trade (must walk in his own calling) (Br.). Every man to his trade (Am.). Let the cobbler stick to his last (Am., Br.)

1345. Незваный гость хуже татарина. *Never pay a visit if you are not invited. See 958 (К), 1212 (Н)*

Var.: Не вовремя гость хуже недруга (татарина)

Cf.: The unbidden guest is a bore and a pest (Am.). Unbidden guests are most welcome when they are gone (Am.). Unbidden guests are welcome when they are gone (Br.). Unbidden guests quickly outstay their welcome (Am.)

1346. Незнание закона не есть оправдание. *Not knowing something that you must know is not an argument*

Cf.: Ignorance of the law excuses no man (Br.). Ignorance of the law is no excuse (Am., Br.)

1347. Не зная броду, не суйся в воду. *Never start doing anything if you have not carefully considered possible difficulties and dangers*

Var.: Не спросясь броду, не суйся в воду

Cf.: Before you go into a canyon, know how you'll get out (Am.). Do not wade in unknown waters (Am.). If you cannot see the bottom, do not cross the river (Br.). /It's/ no safe wading in unknown water (Br.). Look before you leap (Am., Br.). Try the ice before you venture upon it (Am.)

1348. Не зная дела, не суди. *If you are incompetent in some matter, do not give your opinion on it. See 1921 (С)*

Cf.: A blind man is no judge of colors (Am.). A blind man should not judge colo(u)rs (Am., Br.)

1349. Не изведаешь, пока не отведаешь. *The true value of anything can be judged only from practical experience. See 1401 (Н)*

Cf.: The proof of the pudding is in the eating (Am., Br.). The test of the pudding is in the eating (Am.)

1350. Не имей сто рублей, а имей сто друзей. *Friends who help you out of trouble or make your life pleasant are worth more than money*

Var.: Не держи сто рублей, /а/ держи сто друзей

Cf.: A faithful friend is better than gold (Am.). They are rich who have true friends (Am.)

1351. Неисповедимы пути господни. *We cannot foresee what may happen*

Cf.: God moves in a mysterious way /, his wonders to perform/ (Br.). God moves in mysterious ways (Am.). The ways of God are inscrutable (Br.)

1352. Не испортив дела, мастером не будешь. *See 1222 (Н)*

Cf.: Failure teaches success (Am., Br.). You must spoil before you spin well (Br.)

1353. Неиспытанный друг ненадёжен. *You cannot rely on a man if you do not know how he behaves in adversity. See 521 (Д)*

Cf.: A friend is never known till a man has need (until needed) (Am.). A friend is never known till a man have need (till needed) (Br.)

1354. Не ищи беды, беда сама тебя сыщет. *See 1274 (Н)*

Cf.: Do not trouble trouble until trouble troubles you (Am., Br.). Don't borrow (look for) trouble (Am.). It is ill to waken sleeping dogs (Br.). Never trouble yourself with trouble till trouble troubles you (Br.)

1355. Не ищи зайца в бору—на опушке сидит. *Do not make a close search after what is under your nose. See 646 (З)*

Cf.: The butcher looked for his knife and it was (while he had it) in his mouth (Br.). If it had been a bear (a dog, a snake), it would have bitten you (Am.). If it were a bear, it would bite you (Am., Br.). People don't see things on their own doorsteps (Am.)

1356. Не ищи красоты, ищи доброты. *The beautiful appearance of a person is not so valuable as the inner good qualities. See 884 (К), 1925 (С)*

Cf.: Beauty is only skin deep (Am., Br.). Beauty is only skin-deep /; goodness goes to the bone/ (Am.). Beauty is skin-deep; it is the size of the heart that counts (Am.). Choose not a wife by the eye only (Br.). Don't look upon the vessel but upon that which it contains (Am., Br.)

1357. Не ищи просёлочной, когда есть столбовая. *Do not neglect the experience of others, profit from it*

Cf.: A beaten path is a safe one (Am.). The beaten road is the safest (Am., Br.). Don't leave a travelled road to follow a trail (Am.). Don't quit the highway for a short cut (Br.). Don't take unnecessary risks (Br.). The highway is never about (Am.). Keep the common road and you are safe (Am.)

1358. Неказиста кляча, да в беге хороша. *See 870 (К)*

Var.: Неказисто дерево, да вкусен плод

Cf.: A black hen always lays (will lay) a white egg (Am.). A black hen lays a white egg (Br.)

1359. Не кони везут, а овёс. *See 2155 (У)*

Cf.: The belly carries the feet (the legs) (Br.). The stomach carries the feet (Am.)

1360. Не корми завтраками, а сделай сегодня. *See 614 (З)*

Cf.: The belly is not filled with fair words (Br.). One today is worth two tomorrows (Am., Br.). Promises don't fill the belly (Am.)

1361. Не красивая красива, а любимая. *See 769 (К)*

Cf.: Beauty is in the eye of the beholder (Am., Br.). Fair is not fair but that which pleases (Br.)

1362. Некрасив лицом, да хорош умом. *The person is not beautiful but he is kind and clever*

Cf.: A deformed body may have a beautiful soul (Am.). A pearl is often hidden in an ugly shell (Am.). Under the coarsest rind, the sweetest meat (Am.)

1363. Не красна изба углами, а красна пирогами. *It is the hospitality of the hosts that makes the house attractive, but not its decor. See 1332 (H)*

Cf.: A fine cage does not fill a bird's belly (Br.). A fine cage won't feed the /hungry/ bird (Am.). The house is a fine house when good folks are within (Br.)

1364. Не кричи о себе—пусть другие о тебе хоть тихо скажут. *See 1467 (H)*

Cf.: Let another man praise you /, and not your own mouth (not yourself)/ (Am.). Self-praise is no praise (Am.). Self-praise is no recommendation (Am., Br.)

1365. Не купи двора, а купи соседа. *When you come to live in a new place, it is very important to have nice neighbo(u)rs*

Var.: Не купи дом (места), купи соседа

Cf.: A good neighbor is a precious thing (Am.). A good neighbour, a good morrow (Br.). We can live without our friends, but not without our neighbours (Br.). When you buy a house you buy a neighbour too (Br.)

1366. Нельзя объять необъятное. *See 304 (B)*

Cf.: A man can do no more than he can (Am., Br.)

1367. Не мерь всех на свой аршин. *Do not make yourself the standard of right or wrong when judging other people*

Cf.: Don't judge others by yourself (Am.). Don't judge others according to your measures (Br.). Don't measure another man's foot by your own last (Br.). Don't measure other men by your own yardstick (Br.). Don't measure other people's corn by your own bushel (Br.). Don't square other men by your rule (Br.). Never judge others' corn by your own bushel (half-bushel) (Am.)

1368. Не мечи бисер перед свиньями. *Avoid doing favo(u)r to people who are incapable of appreciating it or are ungrateful. See 1290 (H)*

Cf.: Don't cast pearls before swine (Am., Br.). Kindness is lost upon an ungrateful man (Am.). To do good to the ungrateful is like throwing water into the see (Am.)

1369. Не могу, а ем по пирогу. *See 570 (E)*

Cf.: Better the belly burst than good drink (meat) lost (Br.). It's better a belly burst than good food wasted (Am.)

1370. Не можешь, как хочешь, делай, как можешь. *See 1708 (П)*

Cf.: Cut the coat according to the cloth (Am.). Cut your coat according to your cloth (Br.). Do as you may if you cannot as you would (Br.). He who can't do what he wants must want what he can do (Am.). If you cannot have the best, make the best of what you have (Br.). Man must plough with such oxen as he has (Br.)

1371. Не можно исцелить, так лучше отрубить. *It is better to put an end to troublesome things at once than to be vexed with them*

Cf.: Better a finger off than aye wagging (Br.). Better a tooth out than always aching (Am.). Better eye out than always ache (Br.). Better face danger than be always in fear (Am.). Better pass danger once than always be in fear (Br.)

1372. Не мой воз, не мне его и везти. *That is not my concern. See 1159 (M)*

Cf.: Am I my brother's keeper? (Am., Br.). It's not my pigeon (Br.). That's no business of mine (Am., Br.)

1373. Немой караул закричал, безногий на пожар побежал. *See 113 (Б)*

Cf.: If a pig had wings it might fly (Am.). Pigs might fly if they had wings (Br.)

1374. Не мудрено начать, мудрено кончать. *A good beginning is of no value unless one is persistent to the end. See 995 (Л), 1416 (Н)*

Cf.: The beginning is not everything (Am.). Better is the end of a thing than the beginning thereof (Br.). Good to begin well, better to end well (Am., Br.)

1375. Не мытьём, так катаньем. *There are more metods than one to get something done; if it cannot be done smoothly, do it roughly or vice versa. See 310 (Г)*

Cf.: Forsaken by the wind, you must use the oars (Br.). If one cannot bite, he scratches (Br.). If you can't beat (lick) them, join them (Am.). Kiss the hand you cannot bite (Am.). There are more ways than one to kill (to skin) a cat (Am., Br.). There are more ways to kill a dog than by choking him (/to death/ on hot butter) (Am.). There are more ways to kill a dog than by hanging (Br.). There are more ways to the wood than one (Am., Br.). There is more than one way to cook a goose (Am.). There's more than one way to skin a cat without tearing her hide (Am.)

1376. Не мявши, не тёрши, не будет калач. *See 50 (Б)*

Cf.: Nothing is gained without work (Am.). Nothing to be got without pains (Br.)

1377. Ненасытному всё мало. *There is no satisfying a covetous man. See 135 (В)*

Cf.: Avarice is never satisfied (Am.). Covetousness is always filling a bottomless vessel (Br.). Envy and covetousness are never satisfied (Br.). The greedy never know when they have had enough (Am.). They need much whom nothing will content (Br.)

1378. Не начавши—думай, а начавши—делай. *Do not act rashly, but once having started, you should act resolutely*

Cf.: Look before you leap (Am., Br.). Look before you leap, but having leapt never look back (Br.)

1379. Не ноги кормят брюхо, а брюхо ноги. *See 2155 (У)*

Cf.: The belly carries the feet (the legs) (Br.). The stomach carries the feet (Am.)

1380. Не ножа бойся, а языка. *See 1932 (С)*

Cf.: The hard words cut the heart (Am.). /Many/ words cut (hurt) more than swords (Br.). The tongue is not steel but it cuts (Am., Br.). A word hurts more than a wound (Am.)

1381. Не одежда красит человека. *It is not a man's appearance that makes him attractive but his inmost self. See 1313 (Н), 1707 (П)*

Var.: Человека красит голова, а не шляпа

Cf.: Clothes do not make the man (Am., Br.). Fine feathers do not make fine birds (Am.). It is not the gay coat that makes the gentleman (Am., Br.). Looks are not enough (Br.). Looks are not everything (Am.). Pants don't make the man (Am.). What counts most is what you've got under your hat (Am.)

1382. Не откладывай на завтра то, что можно сделать сегодня. *If a thing has to be done, do it as soon as you can*

Cf.: Best time is present time (Br.). Never leave for tomorrow what you can do today (Am.). Never leave till tomorrow what can be done today

(Br.). Never put off until tomorrow what you can do today (Am., Br.). Now is the /best/ time (Am.). There is no future like the present (Am.). /There is/ no time like the present (Am., Br.)

1383. Не от хлеба ходят, а к хлебу. *Do not give up a job or take an action that can deprive you of your living. See 1584 (O)*

Var.: От хлеба хлеба не ищут

Cf.: Beware lest you lose the substance by grasping the shadow (Am.). Catch not at the shadow and lose the substance (Br.). Don't quarrel with your bread and butter (Br.). If you have bread, don't look for cake (Am.). Never leave certainty for hope (Br.). Never quarrel with your bread and butter (Am.). Never quit certainty for hope (Am., Br.)

1384. Не ошибается тот, кто ничего не делает. *When doing some work, you cannot but err sometimes. See 941 (K)*

Var.: Ничего не портит тот, кто ничего не делает

Cf.: He that never climbed, never fell (Br.). He who makes no mistakes makes nothing (Br.). He who never made a mistake never made anything (Am.). Show me the man that does not make a mistake, and I will show you the man that does not do anything (Am.). Who never climbed never fell (Am.). You will not stumble while on your knees (Am.)

1385. Не ошибёшься—не поумнеешь. *See 1222 (H)*

Cf.: Failure teaches success (Am., Br.)

1386. Не плюй в колодезь, пригодится напиться. *Never do harm to, or break friendly relations with people whose support you may need in future. See 1404 (H)*

Var.: Не плюй в водицу: сгодится (случится) напиться. Не плюй в колодезь (колодец), пригодится воды напиться

Cf.: Cast no dirt in the well that gives you water (Am.). Cast no dirt into the well that gives you water (Br.). Don't muddy the water, you may have to drink it (Br.). Don't throw dirt into the well that gives you water (Am., Br.). Let every man praise the bridge he goes over (Br.). Let every man speak well of the bridge that carries him over (Br.). Never cast dirt in the fountain that has given you refreshing drink (Am.). Never cast dirt into that fountain of which thou hast sometime drunk (Br.). Praise the bridge that carries you over (Am.)

1387. Не подмажешь—не поедешь. *You will achieve nothing if you do not bribe. See 2019 (C)*

Cf.: An empty hand is no lure for the hawk (Br.). Empty hands allure no hawks (Am.). Every palm likes to be greased (Br.). He who greases well drives well (Am.). Mills will not grind if we give them no water (Am.). Mills will not grind if you give them not water (Br.). Money greases the axle (Am.). Nothing enters into a closed hand (Am.). Nothing enters into a close hand (Br.). Oil not, neither will you spin (Am.). Without bait you can't catch fish (Am.)

1388. Не поймав, не щиплют. *See 2228 (Ц)*

Cf.: Catch before hanging (Am.). Don't clean your fish before you catch it (Am.). Don't sell the bear's skin before you have caught the bear (you've caught him) (Br.). Gut no fish till you get them (Br.). Make not your sauce till you have caught your fish (Am.)

1389. Не поймал карася, поймаешь щуку. *See 1219 (H)*

Var.: Карась сорвётся, щука навернётся

Cf.: What we lose on the roundabouts we will make up on the swings (Am.). What you lose on the swings you gain (make up, win) on the roundabouts (Br.). Win some, lose some (Am.)

1390. Не пойман—не вор. *When there is no direct evidence of guilt against a person, he is regarded innocent. See 1443 (Н)*

Cf.: All are presumed good till found at (until they are found in a) fault (Am.). All are presumed good till they are found in a fault (Br.). A blot is no blot till (unless) it be hit (Br.). Every one is held to be innocent until he is proved guilty (Br.). He is not a thief until he is caught (Am.). One is innocent until proven guilty (Am.)

1391. Не поклонясь до земли, и грибка не подымешь. *See 50 (Б)*

Cf.: No pains, no gains (Am., Br.)

1392. Не по коню, так по оглобле. *See 65 (Б), 880 (К), 1841 (Р)*

Cf.: The dog bites the stone, not him that throws it (Am.). He that cannot beat the ass (the horse), beats the saddle (Br.). You kick the dog (Am.)

1393. Не по словам судят, а по делам. *See 1503 (Н)*

Cf.: Actions speak louder than words (Am., Br.). Deeds not words are the test (Br.). Deeds speak louder than words (Am.). It is not words that count but deeds (Br.). Johnny is as Johnny does (Am.). Well is that well does (Br.)

1394. Не потопаешь, не полопаешь. *See 182 (В), 1671 (П)*

Cf.: The dog that trots about finds a bone (Br.). The dog that trots about finds the bone (Am.). A setting goose has no feathers on her breast (Am.). A setting hen never gets fat (Am., Br.)

1395. Не по хорошему мил, а по милу хорош. *It is not the person that is really nice that you like, but one you like that seems nice to you. See 769 (К), 1701 (П)*

Var.: Не то мило, что хорошо, а то хорошо, что мило

Cf.: Beauty is in the eye of the beholder (Am., Br.). Fair is not fair but that which pleases (Br.). Nobody's sweetheart is ugly (Am.)

1396. Не просит ремесло хлеба, а само кормит. *A man who has learned some trade can always earn his living. See 1830 (Р), 1988 (С), 2121 (У), 2141 (У)*

Var.: Ремесло пить-есть не просит, а само кормит

Cf.: He that has a trade has a share everywhere (Am.). He who has an art has a place everywhere (Am.). He who has an art, has everywhere a part (Br.). Learn a trade and earn a living (Am.). They that can cobble and clout shall have work when others go without (Br.). Trade is the mother of money (Br.). A useful trade is a mine of gold (Br.)

1397. Не работа крушит, а забота сушит. *Cares and troubles ruin your health and make you look older than you really are. See 1323 (Н)*

Var.: Не работа старит (сушит,) а забота. Сушит человека не работа, а забота

Cf.: Adversity flatters no man (Am., Br.). Care brings grey hair (Br.). Care is beauty's thief (Am.). Care is no cure (Br.). Care killed the cat (Am., Br.). It is not work that kills but worry (Am., Br.). Many cares make the head white (Am.). Sorrow and an ill life make soon an old wife (Am.)

1398. Не рад больной и золотой кровати. *See 660 (З)*

Cf.: Find health better than gold (Am.). Health is /the best/ wealth (Am.). Wealth is nothing without health (Br.)

1399. Не радуйся нашедши, не плачь потерявши. *Do not despair when things go wrong nor rejoice exceedingly when fortunate*

Cf.: If rich, be not elated; if poor, be not dejected (Am.). Meet success like a gentleman and disaster like a man (Am.). Of thy sorrow be not too sad, of thy joy be not too glad (Br.)

1400. Не разгрызёшь ореха—не съешь ядра. *See 50 (Б)*

Var.: Не разгрызёшь ореха—не съешь и зерна

Cf.: He that will eat the kernel must crack the nut (Am., Br.). He that will have the kernel must crack the shell (Am.). He who would eat the nut must first crack the shell (Br.)

1401. Не разжевав, вкуса не узнаешь. *See 1349 (Н)*

Cf.: The proof of the pudding is in the eating (Am., Br.). The test of the pudding is in the eating (Am.)

1402. Не реви раньше смерти. *Do not worry about a problem ahead of time*

Cf.: Call not a surgeon before you are wounded (Am.). Don't bid the devil good morning until you have met him (Am.). Don't climb the hill before you get to it (Br.). Don't climb the hill until you get to it (Am.). Don't cross the bridge before you get (till you come) to it (Am., Br.). Don't cross your rivers before you get to them (Am.). Don't cry before you are hurt (Br.). Don't cry till you are hurt (Am.). Enjoy the present moment and don't grieve for tomorrow (Am.). Never cross the stream before you come to it (Am.). Never howl till you are bit (Br.). Never howl till you are hit (Am.). Never meet trouble halfway (Am., Br.). Sufficient for (to, unto) the day /is the devil thereof/ (Am., Br.). Tomorrow can look after (can take care of) itself (Br.)

1403. Не родись красивым, а родись счастливым. *People who have luck on their side always succed. See 2022 (С)*

Var.: Не родись богатым, а родись кудрявым. Не родись ни умён, ни красив (ни хорош, ни пригож), а родись счастлив

Cf.: Better be happy than wise (Br.). Better to be born lucky than rich (Am., Br.). 'Tis better to be born fortunate than wise (Br.). You don't need brains if you have luck (Am.)

1404. Не руби сук, на котором сидишь. *Make sure you can do without the man or position you depend on before you harm or break up with them. See 1386 (Н)*

Cf.: Don't bite the hand that feeds you (Am., Br.). Don't bite the hand that butters your bread (Am.). Don't cut the bow you are standing on (Br.). Don't cut the limb which bears your weight (Am.). Don't saw off the branch you are sitting on (Am.)

1405. Не смейся, братец, чужой сестрице: своя в девицах. *See 511 (Д)*

Cf.: He that mocks a cripple, ought to be whole (Br.). He who laughs at crooked men should need walk very straight (Br.). People living in glass houses should not throw stones (Am., Br.). Point not at others' spots with a foul finger (Am.)

1406. Не смейся, горох, не лучше бобов. *See 2334 (Ч)*

Var.: Не смейся, квас, не лучше нас. Не смейся, хрен, не слаще редьки

Cf.: Look who's talking! (Am.). Jeerers must be content to taste of their own broth (Br.). One ass calls another long ears (Am.). The pot calling (calls) the kettle black (Am., Br.)

1407. Не смотри на кличку—смотри на птичку. *What really counts is if people and things are worthy and good or not, but not what they are called*

Cf.: A polecat is a polecat, no matter what you call it (Am.). A rose by any other name would smell as sweet (Am., Br.). What good can it do to an ass to be called a lion? (Br.). What's in a name? (Am., Br.)

1408. Не спеши, куманёк, не вздут огонёк. *Do not act prematurely*

Cf.: Don't fire until you see the white of his eye (Am.). Don't fly till your wings are fledged (Br.). Don't shoot till you see the whites of their eyes (Am.). Draw not your bow till your arrow is fixed (Br.). Set not your loaf in till the oven's hot (Br.). Set not your loaf till the oven's hot (Am.)

1409. Не спится—хлеб снится. *See 372 (Г)*

Cf.: The ass dreams of thistles (Br.). The hungry man often talks of bread (Am.)

1410. Не спрашивай старого, спрашивай бывалого. *It is a competent man that can give you good advice*

Var.: Не спрашивай умного, а спрашивай бывалого

Cf.: Ask the judge (Am.). Believe one who has had experience (Br.). He who wishes to know the road through the mountains must ask those who have already trodden it (Am.)

1411. Не сробеешь, так врага одолеешь. *See 1937 (С)*

Cf.: Courage wins (Br.). Fortune favo(u)rs the bold (the brave) (Am., Br.)

1412. Не срубишь дуба, не отдув губы. *See 50 (Б)*

Cf.: No pains, no gains (Am., Br.)

1413. Не ставь врага овцою, ставь волком. *Do not underestimate your enemy, antagonist or opponent not to face a defeat. See 1480 (Н)*

Cf.: Despise not your enemy (Am.). Little enemies and little wounds must not be despised (Br.). There is no little enemy (Am.)

1414. Не ставь всё на одну карту. *Do not risk losing all you have in one undertaking. See 1217 (Н)*

Cf.: Don't carry all your eggs in one basket (Am.). Don't put all your eggs in one basket (Am.). Don't put all your eggs into one basket (Br.). Never venture all in one bottom (Br.). Put not all your crocks on one shelf (Br.). Venture not all in one boat (Am.)

1415. Не стоит гроша, да походка хороша. *Though beautiful, the person is worth nothing. See 1859 (С)*

Cf.: Beauty and folly are old companions (Am.). Beauty and folly go often together (Br.). Fair face, foul heart (Am.). Fair without and false within (Br.)

1416. Не стращай началом, покажи конец. *See 1374 (Н)*

Cf.: The beginning is not everything (Am.). Good to begin well, better to end well (Am., Br.)

1417. Не суди об арбузе по корке, а о человеке—по платью. *Do not form an opinion about a person or thing based on appearance alone. See 168 (В), 1314 (Н)*

Cf.: Don't judge a horse by its harness (Br.). Don't judge a man by the coat he wears (Am.). Judge not according to appearances (Am.). Never judge from appearances (Am., Br.). You cannot know the wine by the barrel (Br.). You can't judge a book by its cover (binding) (Am.). You can't judge a horse by its harness, nor people by their clothing (Am.). You can't tell how far a frog will jump or a horse will run by the color of his hide (Am.)

1418. Не судите, да не судимы будете. *Do not censure other people, and they will not censure you*

Var.: Не суди, да не судим будешь

Cf.: Judge not and you shall not (won't) be judged (Am.). Judge not lest you be judged (Am., Br.). Judge not that ye be not judged (Br.). Judge not that you be not judged (Am.)

1419. Не суй свой нос в чужой вопрос. *Carry on your own affairs and* *do not become concerned with those of other people. See 1086 (Л)*

Var.: Не суй (тычь) носа в чужое просо

Cf.: Curiosity killed the cat (Am., Br.). Don't thrust your sickle into another's corn (Am.). Enquire not what boils in another's pot (Br.). Every person should row his own boat (Am.). Go home and say your prayers (Br.). Hoe your own row (Am.). It that lies not in your gate breaks not your shin (Br.). Keep your nose out of other people's business (Am.). A man should not stick his nose in his neighbor's pot (Am.). Meddle not with another man's matter (Br.). Mind your own business (Am., Br.). Never be breaking your shin on a stool that is not in your way (Am.). Paddle your own canoe (Am., Br.). Skeer your own fire (Br.). The stone that lies not in your gate breaks not your toe (Br.)

1420. Не суйся в ризы, коль не поп. *See 1295 a (Н)*

Cf.: Every man as his business lies (Br.). Let the cobbler stick to his last (Am., Br.). Shoemaker, stick to your last (Am.)

1421. Не сули журавля в небе, дай синицу в руки. *It is better to have a little at present than to live on hope of getting much in future. See 70 (Б), 1065 (Л), 1423 (Н), 1549 (О), 1787 (П)*

Var.: Не сули бычка, а дай стакан (чашку) молочка

Cf.: An acre of performance is worth the whole world of promise (Am.). A bird in the hand is worth two in the bush (Am., Br.). A bird in the sack is worth two on the wing (Am.). A feather in the hand is better than a bird in the air (Am., Br.). A gift in the hand is better than two promises (Am., Br.). A gift is better than a promise (Am.). One acre of performance is worth twenty of the Land of Promise (Br.). One bird in the cage is worth two in the bush (Am.). One bird in the net is better than a hundred flying (Br.). One dollar in your hand beats the promise of two in somebody else's (Am.)

1422. Не сули с гору, а подай в пору. *Help given when it is needed is better than promising mountains. See 419 (Д)*

Cf.: He gives twice who gives promptly (Am.). He gives twice who gives quickly (Am., Br.). Soon enough is well enough (Br.)

1423. Не сули собаке пирога, а кинь краюху. *Little help given to a man who needs it is better than promising much. See 1421 (Н)*

Cf.: An acre of performance is worth the whole world of promise (Am.). Bread today is better than cake tomorrow (Am.). A gift in the hand is better than two promises (Am., Br.). One acre of performance is worth twenty of the Land of Promise (Br.)

1424. Несчастья бояться—счастья не видать. *See 2266 (Ч)*

Cf.: He deserves not sweet that will not taste of sour (Am.). He deserves not the sweet that will not taste the sour (Br.)

1425. Не считай утят, пока не вылупились. *See 2228 (Ц)*

Cf.: Don't count your chickens before they are hatched (Am., Br.)

1426. Не так страшен чёрт, как его малюют. *In reality the man or the thing is not so fearful as you believe it*

Cf.: The devil is not as black as he is painted (Am.). The devil is not so black as he is painted (Br.). The lion is not so fierce as he is painted (Br.)

1427. Не там вор крадёт, где много, а там, где лежит плохо. *See 328 (Г)*

Var.: Не там вор ворует, где много, а там, где лежит плохо (где оплошно)

Cf.: At open doors dogs come in (Am., Br.). Opportunity makes a thief

(Am.). Opportunity makes the thief (Br.)

1428. Нет в голове, нет и в мошне. *See 2096 (У)*

Cf.: A fool and his money are soon parted (Am., Br.). Fools never prosper (Am.). Without wisdom wealth is worthless (Br.)

1429. Нет вестей—добрые вести. *When in trouble, it is comforting to think that getting no news means there is no bad news*

Cf.: No news, good news (Br.). No news is good news (Am., Br.)

1430. Нет дороги без изъяна. *See 737 (И)*

Cf.: Every path has a puddle (Am., Br.). Every path has its puddle (Am.)

1431. Нет друга, так ищи, а нашёл, так береги. *When you have a real friend, you should value his friendship and try not to lose it*

Cf.: Be slow in choosing a friend, but slower in changing him (Am., Br.)

1432. Нет дыма без огня. *There is really reason for the rumo(u)r*

Var.: Где дым, там и огонь

Cf.: The flame is not far from the smoke (Am.). It never thunders but it rains (Am.). /There is/ no mud without a puddle (Am.). /There is/ no smoke without fire (Am., Br.). Where there are reeds there is water (Br.). Where there is smoke, there is fire (Am., Br.). Where there's reek, there's heat (Br.)

1433. Не тем богат, что есть, а тем богат, что рад. *See 491 (Д)*

Cf.: Content is all (is better than riches) (Br.). Content is happiness (is more than a kingdom) (Am., Br.). Happy is he who is content (Am.). He is not rich that possesses much, but he that is content with what he has (Br.). He is rich who does not desire more (Am.). He who is content has enough (Am., Br.). Where content is there is a feast (Br.)

1434. Нет жены—нет заботы. *A single man is carefree, a married man has many worries*

Cf.: He that has a wife, has a strife (Br.). He that takes a wife takes care (Am.)

1435. Нет лучше шутки, как над собою. *If you can laugh at your own shortcomings, nobody will laugh at you*

Cf.: He is not laughed at that laughs at himself first (Br.)

1436. Нет людей без недостатков. *We all have our shortcomings. See 1449 (Н)*

Cf.: Every man has the defects of his /own/ qualities (his virtues) (Br.). He is dead that is faultless (Am.). He is lifeless that is faultless (Am., Br.). None of us are perfect (Am., Br.). None's so good that's good at all (Br.). No one is infallible (Am.). No one is without his own faults (Br.)

1437. Нет ничего такого, чего бы не поглотило время. *With time both the good and the bad passes and is forgotten eventually*

Cf.: Time devours all things (Am., Br.)

1438. Не то зерно, что в поле, а то, что в амбаре. *See 2228 (Ц)*

Var.: Не то хлеб, что в поле, а то, что в амбаре

Cf.: Don't count your chickens before they are hatched (Am., Br.)

1439. Не только людей что Фома да Фаддей. *See 1860 (С)*

Cf.: There are as good fish in the sea as ever came out of it (Am., Br.). There are better fish in the sea than have ever been caught (Am.). There are more pebbles on the beach (shore) (Br.). There are plenty of pebbles on the shore (Br.). There is more than one grain of sand on the seashore (Am.)

1440. Не только света, что в окошке. *See 1860 (С)*

Cf.: There are as good fish in the sea as ever came out of it (Am., Br.). There are better fish in the sea than have ever been caught (Am.). There is as good fish in the sea as ever came out of it (Br.)

1441. Не только тот вор, что крадёт, а и тот, кто лестницу подаёт. *See 197 (В)*

Var.: Не только тот вор, кто ворует, но и тот, кто ворам потакает

Cf.: He sins as much who holds the bag as he who puts into it (Br.). He who holds the ladder is as bad as the thief (Am.). The receiver is as bad as the thief (Am., Br.)

1442. Не торопись жениться, чтобы потом на себя не сердиться. *See 588 (Ж)*

Cf.: Marry in haste and repent at leisure (Am., Br.)

1443. Не тот вор, кто украл, а тот, кто попался. *See 1390 (Н)*

Cf.: A blot is no blot till (unless) it be hit (Br.). He is not a thief until he is caught (Am.)

1444. Не тот глухой, кто глух, а тот, кто не желает слышать. *People will not listen to what they are stubbornly determined not to. See 2224 (Х)*

Var.: Хуже всякого глухого, кто не хочет слышать

Cf.: No ear is so deaf as one which wishes not to hear (Am.). None so deaf as he who won't hear (Am.). None so deaf as those who won't hear (Am., Br.). There's none so deaf as they (those) who won't listen (Br.)

1445. Не тот живёт больше, кто живёт дольше. *The essential thing is how you enjoy your life, but not how long it lasts*

Var.: Не тот живёт больше, чей век дольше

Cf.: He lives longest who lives best (Am.). He lives long that lives well (Br.). He lives twice who lives well (Am.). It matters not how long we live, but how (Am.). It's not how long but how well you live (Br.)

1446. Не тот друг, кто на пиру гуляет, а тот, кто в беде помогает. *See 521 (Д)*

Cf.: Feasting makes no friendship (Br.). A friend in need is a friend indeed (Am., Br.). Friends are made in wine and proved in tears (Br.). Prosperity makes friends, and adversity tries them (Br.). Prosperity makes friends; adversity tries them (Am.)

1447. Не тот хорош, кто лицом пригож, а кто на дело гож. *A man is judged by his skills, not by his appearance. See 1621 (О)*

Var.: Не тот хорош, кто лицом пригож, а тот хорош, кто для дела гож

Cf.: Beauty is as beauty does (Am.). Handsome is as (that) handsome does (Am., Br.). Handsome is who handsome does (Br.). Pretty is as pretty does (Am.)

1448. Нет правил без исключения. *There always exists something that diverges from, or contradicts any established theory, belief, behavio(u)r, etc.*

Cf.: There is an exception to every rule (Am.). There is no general rule without exception (Am., Br.). There's no rule without an exception (Am., Br.)

1449. Нет пророка без порока. *See 1436 (Н)*

Cf.: Every man has the defects of his /own/ virtues (Br.). None of us are perfect (Am.)

1450. Нет пророка в своём отечестве. *A man is recognized as a great*

personality except by his family, close friends, colleagues, etc. See 2253 (Ч)

Var.: Не славен пророк в своём отечестве

Cf.: Familiarity breeds contempt (Am., Br.). Intimacy breeds contempt (Am.). Intimacy lessens fame (Br.). No man is a hero in his hometown (to his wife or his butler) (Am.). No man is a hero to his valet (Am., Br.). No prophet is accepted in his own country (Br.). A prophet is not without hono(u)r, save in his own country /and his own house/ (Am., Br.). A prophet is without honor in his own country (Am.). Respect is greater from a distance (Br.)

1451. Не трись возле сажи—сам замараешься. *See 400 (Г)*

Cf.: He that has to do with what is foul never comes away clean (Br.). Touch pitch and you'll be defiled (Am., Br.). You can't rub on a black pot without getting black (Am.)

1452. Нет розы без шипов. *There is nothing good or attractive that does not have some kind of imperfection. See 54 (Б), 737 (И)*

Cf.: Always a thorn among roses (Am.). Every rose has its thorn (Am., Br.). A good garden always has weeds (Am.). No garden without its weeds (Am., Br.). No house without mouse /; no throne without thorn/ (Br.). No rose without prickles (Br.). No rose without thorns (Am.). The rose has its thorn, the peach its worm (Am.)

1453. Нет сладкого без горького. *Pleasure or joy is never entirely free from sorrow or sadness. See 34 (Б), 54 (Б), 325 (Г), 1698 (П)*

Cf.: Every day has its night, every weal its woe (Am.). Every sweet has its bitter (sour) (Am.). Every white will have its black, /and/ every sweet its sour (Br.). No joy without annoy (Am., Br.). No weal without woe (Br.). Sweet meat will have its sour sauce (Br.). There is no joy without alloy (Am.). There is no pleasure without pain (Am., Br.)

1454. Нет таких трав, чтоб знать чужой нрав. *See 2319 (Ч)*

Cf.: The human heart is a mystery (Br.). You can look in the eyes but not in the heart (Am.)

1455. Нет тяжелее бремени, чем безделье. *You get very tired when you have nothing to do*

Cf.: The hardest job is no job (Am.). The hardest work is to do nothing (Br.). He has hard work indeed who has nothing to do (Am.). He has hard work (works hard) who has nothing to do (Br.). It is more painful (pain) to do nothing than /to do/ something (Br.). The lazy man takes the most pain (Am.). A lazy man works the hardest (Am.)

1456. Нет худа без добра. *There is always some comforting or bright side to a sad situation you may not be aware of. See 1276 (Н)*

Cf.: Bad luck often brings good luck (Br.). Behind bad luck comes good luck (Am.). Every bitter has its sweet (Am.). Every black has its white (Br.). Every cloud has a silver lining (Am., Br.). Ill luck is good for something (Br.). The inner side of every cloud is bright and shining (Am.). It is an ill wind that blows nobody any good (Am., Br.). Never an ill wind blows but that it doesn't do someone some good (Am.). Nothing so bad in which there is not something good (Am., Br.). There is nothing so bad in which there is not something good (Am.)

1457. Не узнавай друга в три дня, узнавай в три года. *See 108 (Б)*

Cf.: Before you make a friend eat a bushel of salt with him (Br.). Before you make a friend, eat a peck of salt with him (Am.). True friendship is a plant of slow growth (Am.)

1458. Не узнав горя, не узнаешь и радости. *See 1291 (Н)*

Var.: Не узнав горя, не узнаешь и счастья

Cf.: He knows best what good is that has endured evil (ill) (Br.). One does not appreciate happiness unless one has known sorrow (Am.). Those who have not tasted the bitterest of life's bitters can never appreciate the sweetest of life's sweets (Am.). Who has never tasted bitter knows not what is sweet (Br.)

1459. Не указывай на людей пальцем, не указали б на тебя и всей рукой. *See 511 (Д)*

Cf.: Cast the beam out of your own eye before you try to cast the mole from the eyes of your neighbor (Am.). People living in glass houses should not throw stones (Am., Br.). Point not at others' spots with a foul finger (Am.)

1460. Не умеешь шить золотом, так бей молотом. *See 947 (К)*

Cf.: If you cannot drive the engine, you can clear the road (Br.). If you can't be the sun, be a star (Am.). Some tasks require a strong back and a weak mind (Am.). Who cannot sing may whistle (Am.)

1461. Не умер Данило—болячка задавила. *See 2285 (Ч)*

Cf.: It is six of one and half a dozen of the other (Br.). It's six of one, half a dozen of the other (Am.)

1462. Не учи плавать щуку, щука знает свою науку. *See 1466 (Н)*

Cf.: Never offer to teach fish to swim (Br.). Old foxes want no tutors (Am., Br.). An old fox needs not to be taught tricks (Am., Br.)

1463. Не учили, покуда поперёк лавки укладывался, а во всю вытянулся—не научишь. *See 357 (Г)*

Var.: Не учила сына, когда кормила, а тебя кормить станет—не научишь. Учи дитя, пока поперёк лавки ложится (укладывается)

Cf.: Best to bend while it is a twig (Br.). An old tree is hard to straighten (Am.). A tree must be bent while it is young (Br.). You may bend a sapling, but never a tree (Am.). A young twig is easier twisted than an old tree (Am.)

1464. Не учи рыбу плавать, а собаку—лаять. *See 1466 (Н)*

Cf.: Don't teach a dog to bark (Br.). Never offer to teach fish to swim (Br.). An old fox needs not to be taught tricks (Am.)

1465. Не учись до старости, а учись до смерти. *See 135 (В)*

Cf.: Live and learn (Am., Br.)

1466. Не учи учёного. *Do not tell a man how to do something which he himself can do perfectly well. See 1462 (Н), 1464 (Н), 2006 (С), 2164 (У), 2368 (Я)*

Var.: Не учи учёного есть хлеба печёные (хлеба есть печёного)

Cf.: Cooks are not to be taught in their own kitchen (Br.). Never offer to teach fish to swim (Br.). Old foxes want no tutors (Am., Br.). An old fox needs learn no craft (Br.). An old fox needs not to be taught tricks (Am., Br.)

1467. Не хвали себя сам, пусть тебя люди похвалят. *It is the praise of other people that we have to regard, not that of your own. See 1364 (Н)*

Var.: Не хвали себя сам, пусть тебя другие похвалят. Собой не хвастай, дай наперёд похвалить тебя людям

Cf.: He that praises himself spatters himself (Br.). Let another man praise you /, and not your own mouth (not yourself)/ (Am.). Man's praise in his own mouth stinks (Br.). Self-praise is no praise (stinks) (Am.). Self-praise is no recommendation (Am., Br.)

1468. Не хвались идучи на рать, а хвались идучи с рати. *See 1321 (Н)*

Var.: Не хвались в поле едучи, хвались с поля. Не хвались едучи на рать, а хвались едучи с рати

Cf.: Do not boast until you see the enemy dead (Br.). Do not shout until you are out of the woods (Am.). Do not triumph before victory (Br.). Don't count your corpses before they are cold (Am.). Don't sing your triumph before you have conquered (Am.). Never say adieu to the devil until you have met him (Am.)

1469. Не хвались отъездом, а хвались приездом. *See 1321 (Н)*

Cf.: Do not shout until you are out of the woods (Am.). Don't halloo (shout) till you are out of the wood (Br.). Don't halloo till you're out of the woods (Am.). Don't whistle before you leap (until you are out of the wood) (Br.)

1470. Не хитро говорить, хитро дело творить. *See 1913 (С)*

Cf.: Easier said than done (Am., Br.)

1471. Не хлебом единым жив человек. *Spiritual needs of a person are no less important than those of his body*

Var.: Не хлебом единым сыт человек

Cf.: Man cannot (does not) live by bread alone (Am.). Man shall not live by bread alone (Br.). Not by bread alone (Br.)

1472. Не храбрись на медведя, а храбрись при медведе. *It is easy to make a brave show when there is no danger, but it is difficult to prove one's courage in the face of danger. See 1325 (Н)*

Cf.: It's one thing to flourish and another to fight (Br.). Many soldiers are brave at the table who are cowards in the field (Am.). To flourish is one thing, to fight another (Am.)

1473. Нечего на зеркало пенять, коли рожа крива. *Do not accuse other people of your own failures, mistakes and defects*

Cf.: Blame not others for the faults that are in you (Am.). Don't blame your own faults on others (Br.). Don't lay your own faults at another person's (at other persons') door (Br.)

1474. Нечего тому бояться, у кого совесть чиста. *An innocent man should not be afraid of any slander or charge of a wrongdoing. See 2110 (У), 2275 (Ч)*

Cf.: A clear conscience fears no accuser (Am.). A clear conscience fears not (laughs at) false accusations (Br.). A clear conscience is a coat of mail (a sure card) (Am., Br.). A clear conscience is a wall of brass (Am.)

1475. Нечестно живёшь—себя подведёшь. *To succeed in business one should be honest. See 2085 (У)*

Cf.: Cheaters never prosper (win) (Am.). Cheating play never thrives (Am.). Cheats never prosper (Br.)

1476. Нечистая совесть спать не даёт. *When you have done something wrong you have no peace of mind. See 882 (К), 1958 (С)*

Cf.: Conscience is the avenging angel in the mind (Am.). A guilty conscience feels continual fear (Br.). A guilty conscience is a self-accuser (Br.). A guilty conscience is its own accuser (needs no accuser) (Am., Br.). A guilty conscience needs no condemner (Am.). No whip cuts so sharply as the lash of conscience (Am., Br.). There is no hell like a bad conscience (Am.). You cannot hide from your conscience (Am.)

1477. Не шути с огнём—обожжёшься. *Do not trifle with danger, you can become a victim of it. See 1963 (С), 2043 (Т)*

Cf.: Do not play with edged tools (Am., Br.). Don't play with fire (Am., Br.). Don't skate on thin ice (Br.). Fire is a good servant but a bad master (Am., Br.). He that handles thorns shall prick the fingers (Br.). He who plays with a cat must expect to be scratched (Am.). If you play with matches, you will get burned (Am., Br.). There is no jesting with fire (Br.). The thin edge of the wedge is dangerous (Br.). You may play with the bull till you get his horn in your eye (Br.)

1478. Никто не знает, что его ожидает. *Good or evil, which one least anticipates, often occurs. See 1224 (Н), 2239 (Ч)*

Cf.: The future is a sealed book (Am.). It's always the unexpected that happens (Am.). Many things happen unlooked for (Br.). Nothing is certain but the unforeseen (Am., Br.). Nothing is so certain as the unexpected (Br.). One never knows what a day may bring forth (Am.). You never know what you'll lose and what you'll gain (Am.)

1479. Ни моря без волны, ни войны без крови. *See 181 (В)*

Cf.: War is death's feast (Am.). War is the death's feast (Br.)

1480. Ни одна блоха не плоха. *See 1413 (Н)*

Cf.: Even a flea can bite (Am.). Little enemies and little wounds must not be despised (Br.). There is no little enemy (Am.)

1481. Ни печали без радости, ни радости без печали. *Happiness and grief follow one another. See 34 (Б), 2024 (С)*

Cf.: Every day has its night, every weal its woe (Am.). Joy and sorrow are next-door neighbors (Am.). Sadness a gladness succeeds (Am.). Sadness and gladness succeed each other (Br.)

1482. Ни пуха, ни пера! *We wish you success in your work*

Cf.: God speed! (Am., Br.). Good luck! (Am., Br.)

1483. Ни рыба, ни мясо. *Someone is a mediocre man with no strong will or intelligence*

Var.: Ни рыба, ни мясо, ни кафтан, ни ряса

Cf.: Neither fish, flesh, nor fowl (Am.). Neither fish, nor flesh, nor good red herring (Br.)

1484. Ничего не попишешь. *We are powerless to change things for the better, so make the best of the bad situation. See 307 (В)*

Cf.: Grin and bear it (Am.). Nothing doing (Am., Br.). You must grin and bear it (Am., Br.)

1485. Ничто не вечно под луной. *See 2262 (Ч)*

Cf.: Everything has an end (Am., Br.). The morning sun never lasts a day (Am., Br.). Nothing can last forever (Am.). There is nothing permanent under the moon (the sun) (Br.). Time ends all things (Am.)

1486. Ничто не ново под луной. *There is nothing in the world that did not happen before; the nature of things does not change. See 751 (И)*

Cf.: All the future exists in the past (Br.). History repeats itself (Am., Br.). The more it changes, the more it remains the same (Am.). Nothing is said now that has not been said before (Am.). That which hath been is now; and that which is to be hath already been (Br.). /There is/ nothing new under the sun (Am., Br.). What used to be will be again (Am.)

1487. Ничто человеческое нам не чуждо. *It is in human nature to be imperfect. See 235 (В)*

Cf.: Every man has his besetting sin (Am.). /I am a man and/ nothing human is alien to me (Am.). Not one is perfect (Am.). We are all human beings (Br.)

1488. Нищета не отнимает ни чести, ни ума. *Though being poor a man can possess rare virtues. See 742 (И), 871 (К)*

Cf.: A brave and gentle character is

often found under the humblest clothes (Am.). A pearl is often hidden in an ugly shell (Am.). Pride and poverty are ill met, yet often seen together (Br.). Pride may lurk under a threadbare coat (Br.). A ragged coat may cover an honest man (Br.). Wisdom sometimes walks in clouted shoes (Br.)

1489. Новая ложка в чести, а отхлебается—и под лавкой валяется. *Anything new stops being sensational very soon*

Cf.: Everything new is fine (Br.). The novelty of noon is out of date by night (Am.). No wonder lasts over three days (Br.). A wonder lasts but nine days (Br.)

1490. Новая метла чисто метёт. *A newly appointed manager starts with radical changes*

Cf.: A new broom sweeps clean (Am., Br.). New brooms sweep clean (Am., Br.). New lairds make new laws (Am., Br.). New lords, new laws (Am., Br.)

1491. Новое—это хорошо забытое старое. *What was in fashion long ago will be in fashion again*

Cf.: Everything old is new again (Am.). Keep a dress long enough and it will come back in style (Am.). Keep a dress seven years and it will come back into style (Am.). The new is what has been forgotten (Am., Br.)

1492. Новых друзей наживай, а старых не теряй. *There is no one so devoted as an old friend, do not make new friends at the expense of old ones*

Cf.: Don't trade /in/ old friends for new (Am.). Forsake not old friends for new (Am.). Keep old friends with the new (Am.). Make new friends but keep the old /, for one is silver and the other is gold/ (Am.). To keep a new friend, never break with the old (Br.)

1493. Ночью все кошки серы. *In obscure circumstances the difference between people or things is indistinguishable*

Var.: Ночью все кони (лошади) вороные

Cf.: All cats are alike at night (Br.). All cats are black at night (look alike in the dark) (Am.). All cats are gray (grey) in the dark (Am., Br.). All colors will agree in the dark (Am.). The fair and the foul, by dark are like store (Am.). Joan's as good as my lady in the dark (Br.). When candles are out all cats are gray (grey) (Am., Br.)

1494. Нрав на нрав не приходится. *See 270 (В)*

Cf.: All bread is not baked in one oven (Am., Br.). Every man after his fashion (Br.). Every man in his own way (Am., Br.)

1495. Нужда горюет, нужда воюет. *See 1873 (С)*

Cf.: Poverty breeds strife (Br.). Want makes strife (Br.). Want makes strife between man and wife (Am.)

1496. Нужда да голод выгоняют на холод. *See 367 (Г)*

Var.: Голод гонит на холод. Нужда да голод прогонят на холод

Cf.: Hunger causes the wolf to sally from the wood (Am.). Hunger drives the wolf out of the wood (Br.). Hunger fetches the wolf out of the wood (Am., Br.)

1497. Нужда закона не знает, а через шагает. *Want of something or poverty drives a man to unlawful actions*

Var.: Для нужды нет закона. Нужда свой закон пишет

Cf.: Necessity has (knows) no law (Am., Br.). Need has no law (Br.)

1498. Нужда научит ворожить, когда нечего в рот положить. *See 369 (Г), 1499 (Н)*

Var.: Нужда всему научит. Нужда научит горшки обжигать (калачи есть, решетом воду носить)

Cf.: The belly teaches all arts (Br.).

Necessity is a good teacher (Am.). Necessity is the mother of invention (Am., Br.). Necessity is the mistress of all arts (Br.). Poverty and hunger have many learned disciples (Br.). Poverty is the mother of all arts (Am.). Want makes wit (Br.)

1499. Нужда скачет, нужда пляшет, нужда песенки поёт. *Hard times make it necessary or unavoidable for one to do anything, no matter how unpleasant. See 369 (Г), 1498 (Н)*

Cf.: He must needs go whom the devil drives (Am., Br.). Hunger breaks stone walls (Br.). Hunger will break through stone walls (Am.). Need makes a naked man run (Am.). Need makes the naked man run (Br.). Need makes the old wife trot (Am., Br.). Needs must when necessity drives (Am.). Needs must when the devil drives (Am., Br.). Scornful dogs will eat dirty puddings (Br.)

1500. Нужда цены не знает. *When you need something badly, you pay any price for it, be it too high*

Cf.: Necessity never made a good bargain (Am.)

1501. Нужно молчать, коли нечего сказать. *It is better not to speak up if you cannot give a reasonable opinion. See 1058 (Л)*

Var.: Не стыдно молчать, коли нечего сказать

Cf.: Be silent, or say something better than silence (Br.). Be silent or speak something worth hearing (Am.). Better say nothing than not to the purpose (Br.). If it isn't worth saying, don't say it at all (Am.). Say well or be still (Br.). Silence is wisdom when speaking is folly (Am., Br.). Speak fitly or be silent wisely (Am., Br.). When you have nothing to say, say nothing (Br.)

1502. Нужно наклониться, чтоб из ручья воды напиться. *See 50 (Б)*

Var.: Надо наклониться, чтобы из пруда (ручья) напиться

Cf.: No pains, no gains (Am., Br.)

1503. Нужны дела, а не слова. *Words are of no value, it is actions that are needed. See 1122 (М), 1216 (Н), 1285 (Н), 1393 (Н), 1596 (О), 1928 (С)*

Cf.: Actions are mightier than words (Br.). Actions, not words (Am.). Actions speak louder than words (Am., Br.). Brag is a good dog, but Holdfast is better (Br.). Deeds are fruits, words are /but/ leaves (Am.). Deeds, not words (Am., Br.). Deeds will show themselves, and words will pass away (Br.). Doing is better than saying (Am., Br.). Fine words without deeds go not far (Br.). Good acts are better than good intentions (Br.). /It is/ better to do well than to say well (Br.). Old brag is a good dog, but hold fast is a better one (Am.). Promise little but do much (Am., Br.). Say well and do well end with one letter; say well is good, but do well is better (Br.). "Say well" is good, but "do well" is better (Am.)

О

1504. Обед узнают по кушанью, а ум по слушанью. *The folly or wit of a man becomes apparent when he begins talking. See 681 (З), 1566 (О)*

Cf.: Conversation makes one (the man) what he is (Br.). Speech is the index of the mind (Am., Br.)

1505. Обещанная шапка на уши не лезет. *See 1968 (С)*

Cf.: Fair words butter no cabbage (Am.). Fair words fill not the belly (Br.). Fine words butter no parsnips (Br.). Promises don't fill the belly (fill no sack) (Am.). You can't live on promises (Am.)

1506. Обещанного три года ждут. *I do not believe what you, or someone else, promised will be done soon, if at all. See 1229 (Н), 2301 (Ч)*

Cf.: Between promising and performing a man may marry his daughter (Br.). Between saying and doing there is a long road (Am.). It's one thing to promise, another to perform (Am., Br.)

1507. Обжёгшись на горячем, дуешь на холодное. *See 1788 (П)*
Var.: Обжёгшись на молоке (ухе), дуют на воду
Cf.: A burnt child dreads the fire (Am., Br.). He complains wrongly on the sea that twice suffers a shipwreck (Br.). He who has suffered shipwreck fears sail upon the seas (Am.). Once burned, twice shy (Am.). Once burnt, twice cautious (Am.). A (The) scalded cat (dog) fears cold water (Am., Br.). Scalded cats fear even cold water (Am.). A scalded dog thinks cold water hot (Am.). A singed cat dreads the fire (Am.)

1508. Обличье—уличье. *See 1183a (H)*
Cf.: Every man's faults are written on their foreheads (Am.). Every one's faults are written in (on) their foreheads (Br.)

1509. Обойдётся, оботрётся—всё по-старому пойдёт. *See 239 (B)*
Cf.: In the end, all will mend (Am.). In the end things will mend (Br.)

1510. Обрадовался крохе, да ломоть потерял. *See 629 (З)*
Var.: Погнался за крохою, потерял ломоть. Погнался за ломтем, да хлеб потерял
Cf.: Penny-wise and pound-foolish (Am., Br.). Penny-wise, pound-foolish (Am.)

1511. Обычай крепче закона. *The long-standing ways people act or behave are not subject to new laws and can hardly be changed*
Var.: Обычай сильнее закона
Cf.: Customs are stronger than laws (Am.). Customs rule the law (Br.). Manners are stronger than law (Br.)

1512. О вкусах не спорят. *You must accept the fact that different people cannot like or dislike the same things. See 1182 (H)*
Cf.: /There is/ no accounting for tastes (Am., Br.). There is no disputing about tastes (Br.). There is no disputing concerning tastes (Am.)

1513. О волке толк, а тут и волк. *The man shows up unexpectedly just after he was talked about. See 1207 (H), 1892 (C)*
Var.: Помяни волка, а волк тут. Про волка речь, а он навстречь
Cf.: Speak of angels and you'll hear the rustling of their wings (Am.). Speak of Satan and you'll see his horns (Am.). Speak of the devil /, and he'll appear/ (Am., Br.). Talk about the devil and his imps will appear (Am.). Talk of the angel and you'll hear the fluttering of his wings (Br.). Talk of the devil and his imp appears (Am., Br.). Talk of the devil and you'll see his horns (Br.). Talk of the Dule and he'll put out his horns (Br.)

1514. Овчинка выделки не стоит. *See 698 (И)*
Var.: Вся свадьба песни не стоит
Cf.: The game is not worth the candle (Am., Br.)

1515. Огня без дыма, человека без ошибок не бывает. *See 2251 (Ч)*
Cf.: He is dead that is faultless (Am.). He is lifeless that is faultless (Am., Br.)

1516. Огонь огнём не погасишь. *By retaliating you only aggravate the situation. See 668 (З)*
Cf.: Add not fire to fire (Br.). Two wrongs do not make a right (Am., Br.)

1517. Одежда красит человека. *People will judge you by the way you are dressed. See 52 (Б), 1234 (H)*
Cf.: Apparel makes the man (Am., Br.). Clothes make the man (Am., Br.). Fair feathers make fair fowls (Am., Br.). Fine clothes make the man (Br.). Fine feathers make fine birds (Am.,

Br.). Fine feathers make fine fowl (Am.). The garment (tailor) makes the man (Br.). Nine tailors make the man (Am.)

1518. Один Бог знает. *I do not have the slightest idea*

Var.: Бог его знает

Cf.: Beats me (Am.). Christ (Goodness, Heaven, Hell, Lord) knows (Br.). Don't ask me (Am.). God knows and he won't tell (Am.). God knows, but he won't tell (Br.). God /only/ knows (Am., Br.). I haven't the clue (Am.). Search me (Am.). Who knows (Am., Br.). You can (may) search me (Am., Br.). Your guess is as good as mine (Am.)

1519. Один воин тысячу водит. *One strong and determined man can head a great number of people. See 11 (A)*

Cf.: Every plane has a pilot (Am.). Every ship needs a captain (Am.). One dog can drive a flock of sheep (Br.)

1520. Один в поле не воин. *You cannot cope with a difficult problem alone, without supporters. See 61 (Б), 139 (В), 517 (Д), 1524 (О), 1537 (О), 1544 (О), 1547 (О)*

Cf.: The lower millstone (millstone) grinds as well as the upper (Am., Br.). One is no number (Br.). One man does not make a team (Am.). One man is no man (Br.). One stone alone cannot grind corn (Am.). The voice of one man is the voice of none (Br.)

1521. Один женился—свет увидал; другой женился—с головой пропал. *For some people marriage is a happy choice, for others it is not*

Cf.: The day you marry, it is either kill or cure (Am., Br.). A man's best fortune or his worst is his wife (Br.). A man's wife is his blessing or his bane (Br.). Marriage is a lottery (Am., Br.). Marriage is heaven or hell (Am). Marriage makes or mars a man (Br.)

1522. Один за всех, все за одного. *Every man supports all the other partners, and all of them support each other*

Cf.: All for one, /and/ one for all (Am.). One for all, and all for one (Br.)

1523. Один и камень не поднимешь, а миром и город передвинешь. *See 13 (A)*

Var.: Один—камень не сдвинешь, артелью—гору подвинешь

Cf.: By the hands of many a great work is made light (Am.). Many hands make light work (Am., Br.). Many hands make work light (Br.)

1524. Один палец не кулак. *See 1520 (O)*

Cf.: One hand will not clasp (Br.). One man is no man (Br.). One stone alone cannot grind corn (Am.)

1525. Один пирог два раза не съешь. *You cannot enjoy the advantage of two incompatible activities*

Cf.: If you sell the cow, you sell her milk (Br.). If you sell the cow, you sell the milk too (Am.). The sun doesn't shine on both sides of the hedge at once (Am., Br.). You cannot burn the candle at two ends (Am., Br.). You cannot have it both ways (Am., Br.). You cannot sell the cow and drink (sup) the milk (Br.). You cannot sell the cow and have the milk (Am.). You can't eat the same bread twice (Am.). You can't eat your cake and have it (Br.). You can't eat your cake and have it too (Am.)

1526. Один раз живём. *Enjoy life while you can. See 449 (Д), 594 (Ж), 1646 (П)*

Cf.: Be gay today, for tomorrow you may die (Am.). Eat, drink and be merry /for tomorrow we (you) die/ (Br.). Eat, drink, and be merry, for tomorrow we may die (Am.). Enjoy yourself: it's later than you think (Am.). Gather ye rosebuds while ye may (Am., Br.). Have fun in this life: you'll never get out of it alive (Am.). Life is short (Am., Br.). Live today; tomorrow may be too late (Am.). Take thine ease, eat, drink and be merry (Br.). We only live once (Am., Br.). Yesterday is past; tomorrow may never come; this day is ours (Am.)

1527. Один раз мать родила, один раз и умирать. *Let us face the danger bravely. See 323 (Г), 423 b (Д), 1823 (Р)*
Var.: Два раза не умирать
Cf.: A man can die but once (Am.). A man can die only once (Br.)

1528. Один раз не в счёт. *The fact that you managed to do something one single time does not mean that you will be successful when repeating the attempt*
Cf.: First game is kid's game (Am.). Once is no custom (rule) (Br.). Once is not enough (Am.). One day does not a summer make (Am.). That's the beginner's luck (Am.)

1529. Один—тайна, два—полтайны, три—нет тайны. *See 232 (В)*
Cf.: A secret shared is no secret (Br.). Secret shared is no secret (Am.). Three may keep counsel if two be away (Am.). Two can keep a secret if one is dead (Am.). Two may keep counsel if one be away (if one of them's dead) (Br.). When three know it, all know it (Br.)

1530. Одна беда не беда. *One trouble can be dealt with. (We say so to console a person in trouble)*
Cf.: Blessed is the misfortune that comes alone (Br.). 'Tis a good ill that comes alone (Br.)

1531. Одна голова хорошо, а две лучше. *Two people co-operating are more efficient than one. See 2135 (У)*
Var.: Один ум хорошо, а два—лучше
Cf.: Four eyes are better (see more) than two (Am., Br.). Many heads are better than one (Br.). Many wits are better than one (Br.). Two heads are better than one (Am., Br.). Two minds are better than one (Am.)

1532. Одна головня и в печи гаснет, а две и в поле курятся. *See 130 (В)*
Cf.: Two are stronger than one (Am.). Union is strength (Am., Br.). Unity is strength (Br.)

1533 Одна ласточка весны не делает. *One single sign of a phenomenon is not enough to prove its existance. See 1541 (О)*
Var.: Первая ласточка весны не делает (лета не приносит)
Cf.: It takes more than a robin to make a spring (Am.). One day does not a summer make (Am.). One flower makes no garland (Am., Br.). One robin doesn't make a spring (Am.). One swallow does not make a spring (a summer) (Am., Br.). One swallow makes not a spring, nor a woodcock a winter (Br.). One swallow makes not a spring, nor one woodchuck a winter (Am.)

1534. Одна лающая собака всполошила всю улицу. *It takes one man to start a rumo(u)r, and all the people around will talk*
Cf.: One barking dog sets all the street a-barking (Br.). One dog barks at nothing; the rest bark at him (Am.). When one dog barks, another at once barks too (Br.)

1535. Одна ложь тянет за собой другую. *See 1039 (Л)*
Cf.: He that tells a lie must invent twenty more to maintain it (Am.). A lie begets a lie until they become a generation (Am.). One lie makes many (Br.). One lie needs seven lies to wait upon it (Br.). One seldom meets a lonely lie (Am.)

1536. Одна паршивая овца всё стадо портит. *One mean man spoils the whole community or family, or their reputation. See 1037 (Л), 1597 (О)*
Var.: Паршивая (Шелудивая) овца всё стадо портит
Cf.: One black sheep will mar a whole flock (Br.). One ill weed will

mar a whole pot of porridge (Br.). One scabbed sheep infects the whole flock (Br.). One scabbed sheep will mar a flock (Am.). One sickly sheep infects the flock (Am., Br.). A rotten egg spoils the pudding (Am.). The rotten tooth injures its neighbours (Br.)

1537. Одна пчела не много мёду натаскает. *See 1520 (O)*

Cf.: The lower millstone grinds as well as the upper (Am.). The lower mill-stone grinds as well as the upper (Br.). One man is no man (Br.). One stone alone cannot grind corn (Am.)

1538. Одна удача идёт, другую ведёт. *Success in some undertaking is followed by success in another one. See 335 (Г), 854 (K)*

Cf.: Luck goes in cycles (Br.). Nothing succeeds like success (Am., Br.). Success breeds success (Am.). Success makes success as money makes money (Am.)

1539. Одни плачут, а другие скачут. *Some people are successful and lucky, others are miserable*

Cf.: Some have the hap, others stick in the gap (Br.). Some of us have the hap; some stick in the gap (Am.). There's no great banquet but some fare ill (Br.). The world is a ladder for some to go up and some down (Am., Br.)

1540. Одно дело говорить, другое дело—делать. *See 1913 (C)*

Cf.: Between saying and doing there is a long road (Am., Br.). It is one thing to say and another to do (Br.). Saying and doing are two different things (Am.). Saying and doing are two things (Am., Br.). Saying is one thing, and doing is another (Br.). There is a big difference between word and deed (Br.). There is a difference between saying and doing (Am., Br.)

1541. Одно дерево ещё не сад. *See 1533 (O)*

Cf.: One flower makes no garland (Am., Br.)

1542. Одно и то же, что отказать, что поздно дать. *Help given too late is of no use. See 504 (Д)*

Cf.: A gift long waited for is sold, not given (Am., Br.). Help which is long on the road is no help (Br.). Slow help is no help (Am., Br.)

1543. Одной надеждой не проживёшь. *What you expect to have in future cannot satisfy you if you need it at present. See 1966 (C)*

Cf.: Don't feed yourself on false hopes (Am.). He that lives upon hope will die fasting (Am.). Hope is a good breakfast, but a bad supper (Am.). Hope is a good breakfast, but it is a bad supper (Am., Br.). Hope is a slender reed for a stout man to lean on (Am.). Hope is the poor man's bread (Am.). Who lives by hope will die by hunger (Br.)

1544. Одной рукой и узла не завяжешь. *See 1520 (O)*

Cf.: The lower millstone grinds as well as the upper (Am.). The lower mill-stone grinds as well as the upper (Br.). One man is no man (Br.). One stone alone cannot grind corn (Am.). You cannot fly with one wing (Am.)

1545. Одному глазом мигни, а другого дубиной толкни. *See 2127 (У)*

Cf.: A hint is as good as a kick (Am.). A nod for a wise man, and a rod for a fool (Br.)

1546. Одному ехать и дорога долга. *Time passes slowly if you travel alone. See 63 (Б)*

Cf.: Good company on the road is the shortest cut (Br.). Good company upon the road is shortest cut (Am.)

1547. Одному и у каши не споро. *See 1520 (O)*

Cf.: One man is no man (Br.). One stone alone cannot grind corn (Am.)

1548. Одному потеха, а другому не до смеха. *See 879 (K)*

Cf.: This may be play to you, 'tis death to us (Br.). What is good for one man, may not be good for another (Am.)

1549. Одно нынче лучше двух завтра. *See 1421 (H)*

Cf.: One today is worth two tomorrows (Am., Br.). A penny today is worth two tomorrow (Am.)

1550. Око за око, зуб за зуб. *An evil deed will be retaliated. See 895 (K)*

Cf.: An eye for an eye /, a tooth for a tooth/ (Am., Br.). /A/ life for /a/ life (Br.). Measure for measure (Am.). One bad turn deserves another (Am.). /A/ Roland for /an/ Oliver (Br.). Tit for tat (Am., Br.). Tit for tat's fair play (Am.)

1551. Околевший пёс не укусит. *See 1125 (M)*

Cf.: Dead dogs don't bite (Br.). Dead dogs (men) never bite (Am.). Dead men don't bite (Am., Br.)

1552. Около кости мясо слаще. *See 1568 (O)*

Cf.: The closer to the bone, the sweeter the meat (Am.). The nearer the bone, the sweeter the flesh (the meat) (Am., Br.). The sweetest meat is closest the bone (Am.)

1553. Около святых черти водятся. *Good and evil exist side by side*

Cf.: Where God has a church, the devil has a chapel (Am.). Where God has his church (temple), the devil will have his chapel (Br.)

1554. О мёртвых или хорошо, или ничего. *If you cannot speak well of the dead, keep silent about them, for they cannot speak for themselves*

Var.: О мёртвых (покойнике) плохо не говорят

Cf.: Never speak ill of the dead (Am.). Say nothing but good of the dead (Br.). Slander not the dead (Am.). Speak well of the dead (Am., Br.)

1555. Опасайся бед, пока их нет. *Take precautions against trouble before you get into it. See 747 (И)*

Var.: Берегись бед, пока их нет

Cf.: A danger foreseen is half avoided (Am., Br.). An ounce of prevention is worth a pound of cure (Am.). Prevention is better than cure (Am., Br.). Study sickness while you are well (Br.)

1556. О присутствующих не говорят. *Do not get offended at what I am going to say, it does not concern those who are here*

Cf.: Present company excepted (Am., Br.)

1557. Опыт—лучший учитель. *See 1190 (H)*

Cf.: Experience is a hard master but a good teacher (Am.). Experience is the best teacher (Am., Br.). Experience is the father of wisdom (the mother of knowledge) (Am., Br.). Experience is the mother of wisdom (Br.). Experience teaches (Br.). With experience comes knowledge (Am.)

1558. Опыт полезнее тысячи советов. *Knowledge gained from one's own practice is most reliable*

Cf.: Bought wit is best (Am.). An ounce of practice is worth a pound of preaching (Br.). An ounce of wit that is bought is worth a pound that is taught (Am.). A thorn of experience is worth a wilderness of advice (Am.). Wit once bought is worth twice taught (Br.)

1559. Орёл мух не ловит. *Insignificant things are beneath a great man's contempt*

Var.: Лев мышей не ловит

Cf.: An (The) eagle does not hawk at flies (Br.). Eagles don't catch flies (Am.). The elephant does not catch mice (Br.)

1560. Орёл орла плодит, а сова сову родит. *See 2357 (Я)*

Cf.: Like begets like (Am., Br.). Like breeds like (Br.). The like breeds the like (Am.)

1561. Орлом комара не травят. *See 713 (И)*

Cf.: Don't take a hatchet to break eggs (Am.). Take not a musket to kill a butterfly (Br.)

1562. Осёл осла длинноухим обзывает. *See 2334 (Ч)*

Cf.: The pot calling (calls) the kettle black (Am., Br.)

1563. Осёл ослом остаётся и в орденах, и в лентах. *See 827 (К)*

Var.: Осёл ослом остаётся, хоть осыпь его звёздами

Cf.: An ass is an ass, though laden with gold (Am.). An ass is but an ass, though laden with gold (Br.)

1564. Осердясь на блох, да и шубу в печь. *Do not ever take extreme measures to get rid of something trivial. See 1565 (О)*

Var.: Рассердясь на блох, да и одеяло (шубу) в печь

Cf.: Burn not your house to frighten (to rid of) the mouse (Br.). Burn not your house to frighten the mouse away (to scare away the mice) (Am.)

1565. Осерчав на корову, да подойник оземь. *See 1564 (О)*

Cf.: Burn not your house to frighten (to rid of) the mouse (Br.). Burn not your house to frighten the mouse away (to scare away the mice) (Am.)

1566. Осла знать по ушам, медведя—по когтям, а дурака—по речам. *Folly and ignorance are betrayed by talking. See 542 (Д), 681 (З), 1504 (О)*

Var.: Осла узнают по ушам, а глупца по речам

Cf.: An ass is known by his ears (Br.). Cracked pipkins are discovered by their sound (Br.). A fool is known by his conversation (speech) (Am.). You can tell a bad penny by its ring (Am.)

1567. Осла хоть в Париж, а он всё будет рыж. *A stupid, unmannerly or rude man cannot become clever and refine. See 717 (И)*

Cf.: Send a donkey to Paris, he'll return no wiser than he went (Br.). Send a fool to the market, and a fool he'll return (Am., Br.). You can get the man out of the country, but you can't get the country out of the man (Am.)

1568. Остатки—сладки. *That which you get towards the end, when not much of it is left, is the best. See 1552 (О)*

Cf.: The nearer the bone, the sweeter the flesh (Br.). The rest is the best (Br.). The sweetest meat is closest the bone (Am.). That which is last is best (Am.)

1569. Остёр топор, да и сук зубаст. *See 1267 (Н)*

Cf.: Diamond cuts diamond (Am., Br.). Iron cuts iron (Am.)

1570. Остёр шип на подкове, да скоро сбивается. *See 722 (И)*

Cf.: A heavy shower is soon over (Am.). No extreme will hold long (Br.). That which is sharp is not long (Br.)

1571. Осторожного коня и зверь не берёт. *See 59 (Б)*

Var.: Бережливого коня и зверь в поле не берёт

Cf.: Caution is the parent of safety (Am., Br.). The cautious seldom cry (Am.). It is better to be on the safe side (Am., Br.)

1572. Осторожность и зверя бережёт. *See 59 (Б)*

Cf.: Caution is the parent of safety (Am., Br.). It is better to be on the safe side (Am., Br.)

1573. Осторожность—мать мудрости. *He is wise who is cautious*

Cf.: Caution is the eldest child of wisdom (Am.). Discretion is the mother of other virtues (Br.). An ounce of discretion is worth a pound of knowledge (Am.). An ounce of discretion is worth a pound of learning (Br.). An ounce of discretion is worth a pound of wit (Am., Br.)

1574. Острое словечко колет сердечко. *See 1932 (С)*

Cf.: The tongue is not steel, but /yet/ it cuts (Am., Br.)

1575. Острый язык, что бритва. *See 1932 (С)*

Cf.: /Many/ words cut (hurt) more than swords (Br.). A word hurts more than a wound (Am.)

1576. От бобра—бобрёнок, от свиньи—поросёнок. *See 2357 (Я)*

Var.: От лося—лосята, от свиньи—поросята

Cf.: Like begets like (Am., Br.). Like breeds like (Br.). The like breeds the like (Am.)

1577. От больного места рука не отходит. *See 2111 (У)*

Cf.: A man in suffering finds relief in rehearsing his ills (Am.). A man lays his hand where he feels the pain (Br.). The tongue returns to the aching tooth (Am.). Where the pain is, the finger will be (Br.)

1578. Отвага—половина спасения. *See 1937 (С)*

Var.: Отвага мёд пьёт

Cf.: Fortune favo(u)rs the bold (the brave) (Am., Br.). Grasp the nettle and it won't sting you (Br.). Success is the child of audacity (Am.)

1579. От вежливых слов язык не отсохнет. *You must be polite, it will never do you any harm. See 1689 (П)*

Var.: От доброго слова (ласковых слов) язык не отсохнет

Cf.: Cool words scald not a tongue (Am.). Courtesy never broke one's crown (Br.). Fair words break no bones (Am., Br.). Fair words hurt not the mouth (the tongue) (Br.). A kind word never hurt anyone (Am.). No one has ever been killed by kindness (Am.). One never loses anything by politeness (Br.). Soft words break no bones (Am., Br.). You can't hurt a tongue by speaking softly (Am.)

1580. От великого до смешного один шаг. *You have but slightly to get immoderate in your ambitions and you become a laughing-stock*

Cf.: A descent from the sublime to the ridiculous is quick (Br.). From the sublime to the ridiculous is only a step (Am.). One step above the sublime makes the ridiculous (Br.)

1581. От воды навару не будет. *See 708 (И)*

Cf.: From nothing, nothing is made (Am.). Nothing comes of nothing (Am., Br.). Whether you boil snow or pound it, you can have but water of it (Br.). You can't make something out of nothing (Am.)

1582. От волка бежал, да на медведя напал. *See 709 (И)*

Var.: От волка ушёл—на медведя набрёл. От горя бежал, да в беду попал

Cf.: Don't jump from the frying pan into the fire (Am.). Out of the frying-pan (frying pan) into the fire (Am., Br.)

1583. От греха подальше. *One should be cautious not to get involved into imminent trouble*

Cf.: Keep out of harm's way (Am.). Keep your nose clean (Am.). Stay out of harm's way (of trouble) (Am., Br.)

1584. От добра добра не ищут. *There is no need to make drastic changes in the existing state of things or way of life because you can never be sure that the changes will be for the better. See 981 (Л), 1051 (Л), 1383 (Н)*

Cf.: Don't budge if you are at ease

where you are (Br.). Don't quarrel with your bread and butter (Br.). If you have a good seat, keep it (Br.). If you have bread, don't look for cake (Am.). Leave (Let) well alone (Br.). Leave (Let) well enough alone (Am., Br.). Never quit certainty for hope (Am., Br.)

1585. От доброго обеда и к ужину останется. *When there is much, not everything is consumed*

Cf.: Cook enough to feed an army (Am.). Of enough men leave (Br.). There was never enough where nothing was left (Br.)

1586. Отец накопил, а сын раструсил. *Children squander money their parents made and saved*

Cf.: A miserly father makes a prodigal son (Am., Br.). A miser's son is a spendthrift (Am.). A thrifty father rarely has a thrifty son (thrifty sons) (Am.)

1587. Отец—рыбак, и дети в воду смотрят. *The children earn their living like their parents do*

Cf.: He that comes of a hen, must scrape (Br.). He that is born by a hen must scrape for a living (Br.). The son of the cat pursues the rat (Am.). That that comes of a cat will catch mice (Am.). The young ox learns to plough from the older (Br.)

1588. Отзвонил, да и с колокольни долой. *When you finish your job, you are carefree*

Cf.: I have done my duty to God and country (Am.)

1589. От кого чают, того и величают. *See 1264 (Н)*

Cf.: Every man bows to the bush he gets bield of (Br.). Whose bread I eat, his song I sing (Am.)

1590. Открыл Америку! *It is stale news, I know it*

Cf.: The ark rested on Mt. Ararat (Br.). Don't give me the old abdabs! (Am.). The Dutch are in (have taken) Holland (Br.). My Lord, Baldwin's dead (Br.). Queen Ann (Queen Anne, Queen Bess, Queen Elizabeth) is dead! (Br.). Tell me news! (Am., Br.). Tell me something I don't know (something new) (Am., Br.). Tell me the old, old story (Br.). Tell that for a tale (Am., Br.). You are telling me! (Am., Br.). You kid me! (Am.)

1591. От лихого не услышишь доброго слова. *A base or rude man will never say a kind word. See 161 (В)*

Cf.: Evil (Ill) will never said well (Br.). If you talk with a hog, don't expect anything but a grunt (Am.). What can you expect from a hog but a grunt? (Am., Br.). What can you expect from a pig but a grunt? (Br.)

1592. Отложил на осень, а там и вовсе бросил. *Procrastination ends up in nothing being done at all. See 2099 (У)*

Cf.: Anytime is no time (Br.). Anytime means no time (Am., Br.). By the street of "by and by" one arrives at the house of never (Am., Br.). Hard by the road called "by and by" there stands a house called "never" (Am.). One of these days is none of these days (Br.). One of these days is no time (Am., Br.). To delay may mean to forget (Am.). Tomorrow never comes (Am., Br.)

1593. От любви до ненависти один шаг. *Disillusionment in a person can easily turn your fondness for him into hatred*

Cf.: The greatest hate comes from the greatest love (Am.). The greatest hate springs from the greatest love (Br.). Love and hate are the two closest emotions (Am.). The thinnest line is between love and hate (Am.)

1594. От любви нет лекарства. *See 1084 (Л)*

Cf.: No herb will cure love (Am., Br.)

1595. От нужды волк лисой запел. *See 33 (Б)*

Cf.: Adversity is a good teacher (Br.). Poverty is the mother of all arts (Am.)

1596. От одних слов толку мало. *See 710 (И), 1503 (Н)*

Cf.: Fair words butter no cabbage (Am.). Good words fill not the sack (Br.). Good words without deeds are rushes and weeds (Br.). It is not with saying "honey, honey" that sweetness comes into the mouth (Am.). It is not with saying "honey, honey" that sweetnes will come into the mouth (Br.). Sweet words butter no parsnips (Am.). Talk is but talk (Br.). Talk is but talk, but it's the money that buys the house (Am.). Talk is cheap (Am.). Words and feathers the wind carries away (Br.). Words are but wind (Br.). Words, like feathers, are carried away by the wind (Am.)

1597. От одного порченого яблока целый воз загнивает. *See 1536 (О)*

Cf.: One bad apple spoils the lot (Am.). One rotten apple can spoil a lot of good ones (a whole barrel full, the whole bunch) (Am.). One rotten apple decays the bushel (Br.). One rotten apple will spoil a bushel (Am.). The rotten apple injures its companion (Am.). The rotten apple injures its neighbours (Br.)

1598. Отольются кошке мышкины слёзки. *Evil done to others generally recoils on the doer's head. See 917 (К), 964 (К), 1602 (О), 2294 (Ч)*

Var.: Отольются волку овечьи (медведю коровьи) слёзы

Cf.: The biter is /often/ bit (Br.). The biter is sometimes bit (Am.). He that mischief hatches, mischief catches (Am., Br.). He that sows thistles shall reap prickles (Br.). He who sows brambles reaps brambles (Am.)

1599. От правды не уйдёшь. *See 1755 (П)*

Var.: От правды никуда не денешься

Cf.: Truth will come to light (Br.). The truth will out (Am.)

1600. От пули не уйдёшь. *One cannot avoid being harmed if that is his predestination. See 1610 (О)*

Cf.: Every bullet finds its billet (Br.). Every bullet has its billet (Am., Br.). If the bullet has your name on it, you'll get it (Am.)

1601. От работы кони дохнут. *I cannot understand why you are working; I refuse to work*

Cf.: Only fools and horses work (Am.)

1602. От расплаты не уйдёшь. *Retribution may take a long time, but it will unavoidably be inflicted on you. See 1598 (О), 1790 (П)*

Cf.: Every sin brings its punishment with it (Br.). Every sin carries its own punishment (Am.). God's mills grind slowly, but sure (Br.). The mills of God grind slowly (Am., Br.). The mills of the gods grind slowly /, but they grind exceedingly fine (small)/ (Am.). Punishment follows hard upon the crime (Br.). Punishment is lame, but it comes (Br.). The wheels of the gods grind slowly (Am.). Your sins will find you out (Am.)

1603. Отсеки собаке хвост — не будет овца. *You can change a man's appearance but not the man himself*

Cf.: Cut off a dog's tail and he will be a dog still (Br.). Cut off a dog's tail and he will still be a dog (Am.)

1604. От слёз ничего не прибудет. *When in trouble, crying is of no avail, it will not help. See 1157 (М)*

Cf.: Crying will not mend matters (Br.). Sorrow will pay no debt (Br.). Worrying doesn't mend nor pay (Am.). Worry never crossed a bridge (Am.)

1605. От слова до дела — сто перегонов. *See 2115 (У)*

Var.: От слова до дела—бабушкина (целая) верста

Cf.: Between saying and doing there is a long road (Am., Br.). From saying to doing is a long stride (Br.). From word to deed is a great space (Br.)

1606. От смерти зелья нет. *There is no cure when a man is going to die. See 898 (К)*

Var.: На одну смерть лекарства нет. От смерти лекарства нет

Cf.: Death defies the doctor (Am., Br.). There is a medicine for all things except death and taxes (Am.). There is a remedy for all dolours but death (Br.). There is a remedy for all things but death (Am., Br.)

1607. От смерти не уйдёшь. *It is inevitable for all men to die. See 240 (В), 1246 (Н), 1939 (С)*

Var.: От смерти бегством не избавишься (не откупишься, не отмолишься)

Cf.: Death comes to us all (Br.). Death is a black camel which kneels at every man's gate (Am.). Death is but death, and all in time shall die (Am., Br.). Death is deaf and will hear no denial (Am.). Death takes all (Br.). Death takes no denial (Br.). Every door may be shut but death's door (Am., Br.). Nothing is so sure as death (Am., Br.). When death knocks at your door, you must answer it (Am.)

1608. От совы не родятся соколы. *Nothing bad can produce anything good*

Var.: Не родит верба груши. От ивы (осины) яблочко не родится

Cf.: Eagles do not breed doves (Br.). Figs do not grow on thistles (Am.). One cannot gather grapes of thorns or figs of thistles (Br.). Of a thorn springs not a fig (grape) (Br.). You can't grow figs from thorns (Am.)

1609. От спеху чуть не наделал смеху. *See 1741 (П)*

Cf.: Haste makes waste (Am., Br.)

1610. От судьбы не уйдёшь. *One cannot avoid anything that awaits him in his life. See 859 (К), 1600 (О), 2261 (Ч)*

Cf.: Each cross has its inscription (Br.). The fated will happen (Am., Br.). For whom ill is fated, him it will strike (Br.). A man who was born to drown will drown on a desert (Am.). No flying from fate (Br.). There is no fence against ill fortune (Am.). There's no flying from fate (Am.). What must be, must be (Am., Br.)

1611. От сумы да от тюрьмы не отказывайся. *None of us is safe from misfortune or trouble. See 786 (К)*

Var.: От сумы да от тюрьмы не зарекайся (не отрекайся)

Cf.: Man is born into trouble (Am.). No fence against ill fortune (Am., Br.). There is no fence against ill fortune (Am.)

1612. От такого же слышу. *You are as bad as the person you are criticizing. (You say this in response to someone's insulting words)*

Cf.: Look who's talking (Am.). The same to you (Am.). The same to you with brass knobs on! (Br.). So's your aunt Susie (Br.). So's your old man (Am., Br.). So's your sister's cat (Am.). So's your sister's cat's grandmother (Br.). You are another (Am., Br.). You're no better than I am (Am., Br.)

1613. От трудов праведных не наживёшь палат каменных. *One cannot get very rich without dirtying his hands*

Var.: Правдою жить, палат каменных не нажить

Cf.: Ever busy, ever bare (Br.). Honour and profit lie not in one sack (Br.). Muck and money go together (Br.). Riches and virtue do not often keep each other company (Am.). Virtue and riches seldom settle on the man (Am.)

1614. От хозяйского глаза скотина жиреет. *If you supervise the work*

yourself, you will get best results. See 338 (Г), 1863 (С)

Cf.: The eye of the master fattens his herd (Am.). The eye of the master will do more work than both his hands (Am., Br.). If the owner keeps his eye on the horse, it will fatten (Am.). The master's eye makes the horse fat (Am., Br.). No eye like the eye of the master (Br.). No eye like the master's eye (Am.). One eye of the master sees more than ten of the servants (Br.)

1615. От хорошего дерева—хороший плод. *Good parents bring up good children. See 2357 (Я)*

Var.: От доброго дерева добрый и плод

Cf.: The fruit of a good tree is also good (Am.). A good tree cannot bring forth evil fruit (Br.)

1616. От худого семени не жди доброго племени. *Bad parents do not bring up, as a rule, good children. See 1617 (О), 2357 (Я)*

Cf.: Bad bird, bad eggs (Am.). Good can never grow out of bad (evil) (Br.). Good fruit never comes from a bad tree (Am., Br.). No good apple on a sour stock (Br.). Of an evil crow an evil egg (Br.). Of evil grain no good seed can come (Am., Br.). We may not expect a good whelp from an ill dog (Br.). A wild goose never laid a tame egg (Am., Br.)

1617. От худой курицы худые яйца. *See 1616 (О), 2357 (Я)*

Cf.: Bad bird, bad eggs (Am.). Bad hen, bad eggs (Br.). An evil crow, an evil egg (Br.). A wild goose never laid a tame egg (Am., Br.)

1618. Отцы тёрпкое поели, а у деток оскомина. *The wrongs done by the previous generation are paid for by the next one*

Cf.: Adam ate the apple and our teeth still ache (Am.). The sins of fathers are visited on their children (Am., Br.)

1619. От яблони яблоко родится, от ели—шишка. *See 2357 (Я)*

Cf.: Like begets like (Am., Br.). Like breeds like (Br.). The like breeds the like (Am.)

1620. Охота пуще неволи. *One undertook a hard job at his own will, but not because he had to. (Said as a sensure.) See 1277 (Н)*

Var.: Своя воля страшней неволи

Cf.: He who has no worries makes himself some (Br.). People create their own problems (Am.)

1621. О человеке судят не по словам, а по его делам. *Men are judged by what they do rather than by what they say they will do. See 428 (Д), 451 (Д), 1447 (Н)*

Cf.: Handsome is that handsome does (Am., Br.). Handsome is who handsome does (Br.). Johnny is as Johnny does (Am.). Judge a man by his deeds, not by his words (Am.). Judge a man by what he does, not by what he says (Am.). Judge a tree by its fruit (Am.). Man is known by his deeds (Br.)

1622. О чём тому тужить, кому есть чем жить. *A man that is well off can live a carefree life*

Cf.: A heavy purse makes a light heart (Am., Br.)

1623. Ошибайся, да сознавайся. *You should not be afraid to confess that you were wrong or made a mistake*

Cf.: Admitting error clears the score and proves you wiser than before (Am.). It is no disgrace to acknowledge an error (Br.)

1624. Ошибка в фальшь не ставится. *A mistake made by a person is not to be regarded as a deliberate fraud*

Var.: Ошибка не обман

Cf.: Erring is not cheating (Am., Br.)

1625. Ошибка красна поправкой. *See 2119 (У)*

Cf.: It is never too late to mend (Am., Br.)

1626. Ошпаренный кот боится холодной воды. *See 1788 (П)*

Cf.: A burnt child dreads the fire (Am., Br.). A (The) scalded cat (dog) fears cold water (Br.). Scalded cats fear even cold water (Am.). A scalded dog thinks cold water hot (Am.). A singed cat dreads the fire (Am.)

П

1627. Павшее дерево рубят на дрова. *Men are apt to turn misfortunes of other people to their own advantage. See 1223 (Н)*

Var.: Упавшее дерево рубят на дрова

Cf.: Every hand fleeces where the sheep goes naked (Br.). The tree is no sooner down than every one runs for his hatchet (Br.). When a man is down, everyone picks on him (Am., Br.). When an oak falls every one gathers wood (Br.). When the ox is down, many are the butchers (Am.). When the tree is fallen everyone goes to it with his hatchet (Am.). When the tree is fallen, every one runs to it with his axe (Br.). When the tree is thrown down any one who likes may gather the wood (Br.)

1628. Палка о двух концах. *The result of an action can have both good and bad consequences*

Cf.: It cuts both ways (Am., Br.). The same heat that melts the wax will harden the clay (Br.). The same knife cuts both bread and fingers (Br.). The same sunshine that will melt butter will harden the clay (Br.). The same sun that will melt butter will harden clay (Am.). When you pick up a stick at one end, you also pick up the other end (Am.)

1629. Палка по мясу бьёт, а слово до костей достаёт. *See 1932 (С)*

Cf.: /Many/ words cut (hurt) more than swords (Br.). The tongue breaketh bone, though itself hath none (Am.). The tongue breaks the bone, and herself has none (Am., Br.). The tongue is sharper than the sword (Am.). A word hurts more than a wound (Am.)

1630. Паны дерутся, а у холопов чубы трещат. *When those in power are in disagreement, it is the common people that endure the bad consequences of it*

Var.: Паны дерутся, а у хлопцев чубы летят (а у холопов чубы трясутся)

Cf.: The humble suffer from the folly of the great (Am.). Kings go mad, and the people suffer for it (Br.). The poor always pay (Am.). The poor do penance for the sins of the rich (Br.). The poor man pays for all (Am., Br.). The poor suffer all the wrong (Br.)

1631. Пар костей не ломит. *I do not feel uneasy because of it being hot, or because I am too warmly dressed*

Cf.: Heat breaks no bones (Br.)

1632. Пар любить—баню топить. *See 50 (Б)*

Cf.: No sweat, no sweet (Am.). No sweet without /some/ sweat (Br.)

1633. Пару бояться—в баню не ходить. *Do not undertake a job if you are afraid of the difficulties it involves. See 186 (В)*

Cf.: If you can't stand the heat, get out of the kitchen (Am.). If you can't stand the heat, stay out of the kitchen (Am., Br.)

1634. Пастуху дремать, так стада не видать. *When a man neglects his duties, he finds himself in trouble*

Cf.: Careless shepherds make many a feast for the wolf (Am., Br.). A careless watch invites the vigilant foe (Am.). Wolves rend sheep when the shepherds fail (Br.)

1635. Пахать, так в дуду не играть. *See 696 (И)*

Cf.: Work is work, and play is play (Br.). Work while you work, and play while you play (Am.)

1636. Пень—так пень, хоть золотое платье надень. *See 827 (К)*

Cf.: A golden bit does not make a horse any better (Br.). A golden bit does not make the horse any better (Am.)

1637. Первое впечатление обманчиво. *At the first glimpse, you cannot get the right idea of what men or things are like*

Cf.: First impressions are untrustworthy (Br.). Judge not of men and things at first sight (Br.). Judge not of men or things at first sight (Am.). Never judge by first impressions (Am.)

1638. Первому гостю—первое место. *Those who come first profit most. See 954 (К)*

Cf.: First come, first served (Am., Br.). First there, first served (Am.). First winner, last loser (Am.). He that comes first to the mill may sit where he will (Br.)

1639. Первый блин комом. *When you do something for the first time, you cannot succeed from the start. (You say this to encourage a man who failed in his first attempt, or to excuse your own unsuccessful first attempt). See 1222 (Н)*

Cf.: A bad (poor) beginning makes a good ending (Am.). It's the new hand who always gets the short-handed rake (Am.). No man is his craft's master the first day (Br.). There's always /a/ next time (Am., Br.). /You must/ spoil before you spin /well/ (Br.)

1640. Перед смертью не надышишься. *At the last moment, you cannot manage to do what you had to do beforehand*

Cf.: It's an eleventh hour try (Am.)

1641. Перестань о том тужить, чему нельзя пособить. *If you have some trouble for which no cure can be found, stop worrying*

Cf.: What can't be cured must be endured (Am., Br.). What can't be helped must be endured (Am.)

1642. Петух скажет курице, а она—всей улице. *See 16 (Б), 232 (В)*

Var.: Скажешь курице, а она—всей улице

Cf.: A secret shared is no secret (Am., Br.). Two can keep a secret if one is dead (Am.). Two may keep counsel if one be away (if one of them's dead) (Br.)

1643. Пироги да блины, а там сиди да гляди. *See 1880 (С)*

Cf.: Chickens today, feathers tomorrow (Am.). Cookie today, crumb tomorrow (Am.). Fasting comes after feasting (Br.). Feast today makes fast tomorrow (Am.). Who dainties love shall beggars prove (Br.)

1644. Пироги на кустах не растут. *See 50 (Б)*

Cf.: Apples don't grow on monkey trees (Br.). God gives (sends) every bird its food, but he does not throw it into the nest (Am.). Potatoes don't grow by the side of the pot (Br.)

1645. Пироги со стола, друзья со двора. *See 1901 (С)*

Cf.: As long as the pot boils, friendship lasts (Am., Br.). The bread eaten, the company dispersed (Br.). The dinner over, away go the guests (Am.). Having finished the meal, the company leaves (Am.). In time of prosperity, friends will be plenty; in time of adversity, not one amongst twenty (Br.). In time of prosperity, friends will be plenty; in time of adversity, no one in twenty (Am.)

1646. Пить будем, гулять будем, а смерть придёт—помирать будем. *See 1526 (О)*

Cf.: Eat, drink and be merry /, for tomorrow you (we) die/ (Br.). Eat, drink, and be merry, for tomorrow we may die (Am.)

1647. Плетью обуха не перешибёшь. *See 1786 a (П), 1786 b (П)*

Cf.: a) There is no arguing with a large fist (Am.). What may the mouse do against the cat? (Am.). You cannot fight City Hall (Am., Br.)

b) Do not kick against the pricks (Br.). Don't kick against pricks (Am.). It is ill striving against the stream (Br.). Strive not against the stream (Am.). You can't fight guns with sticks (Br.)

1648. Плохая молва на крыльях летит. *See 471 (Д)*

Var.: Худая молва на крыльях летит

Cf.: Good fame sleeps, bad fame creeps (Br.). A good reputation stands still; a bad one runs (Am.). Old sins cast (have) long shadows (Am.)

1649. Плохие пчёлы—плохой и мёд. *See 802 (К)*

Cf.: As is the workman, so is his work (Am.). As is the workman, so is the work (Br.). Like carpenter, like chips (Am.). Such carpenter, such chips (Br.)

1650. Плохого волка и телята лижут. *When a powerful man loses his stregth, even weak people can do him harm. See 1124 (М), 1673 (П)*

Cf.: Even hares insult a dead lion (Br.). Hares can gambol over the body of a dead lion (Br.). Hares may pluck (pull) dead lions by the beard (Br.). The timid hare dares to pluck the dead lion by the beard (Am.). When the eagle is dead, the crows pick out his eyes (Am.)

1651. Плохое колесо больше хорошего скрипит. *An inefficient or lazy worker is the one who does all the complaining*

Var.: Худое колесо больше (громче) скрипит

Cf.: The bad wheel creaks the most (Am.). The weakest wheel creaks loudest (Am.). The worst wheel of the cart creaks most (Am., Br.). The worst wheel of the cart (on the wagon) makes the most noise (Am.)

1652. Плохое начало не к доброму концу. *A piece of work started not in the proper way is likely to go wrong. See 809 (К), 2222 (Х)*

Var.: Плохое начало—плохой и конец

Cf.: A bad beginning has a bad (makes a worse) ending (Br.). A bad day never has a good night (Am.). If you miss the first buttonhole, you will not succeed in buttoning up your coat (Am.). An ill beginning, (has) an ill ending (Br.). Ill begun, ill done (Br.). So goes Monday, so goes all the week (Am.)

1653. Плохой тот вор, что около себя грабит. *See 72 (Б)*

Var.: Худой вор, который в своей деревне ворует

Cf.: Dogs don't kill sheep at home (Am.). The fox (wolf) preys farthest from his den (home) (Br.). Jaybirds don't rob their own nest (Am.). A wise fox will never rob his neighbour's henroost (Br.)

1654. Плохому танцору одежда мешает. *See 1111 (М)*

Var.: Плохому танцору и штаны мешают

Cf.: A bad workman quarrels with his tools (Am., Br.). If you don't know how to dance, you say that the drum is bad (Am.). The losing horse blames the saddle (Am.)

1655. Плохо не клади, вора в грех не вводи. *See 328 (Г)*

Var.: На дороге не клади, вора в грех не вводи

Cf.: An open door may tempt a saint (Am., Br.). Opportunity makes a thief

(Br.). Opportunity makes the thief (Am.). When the house is open, the honest man sins (Am.)

1656. Плох тот солдат, который не надеется быть генералом. *You should strive for a greater success*
Cf.: Aim for the star (Am.). Every French soldier carries a marshal's baton in his knapsack (Br.). Hitch your wagon to a star (Am., Br.)

1657. Победителей не судят. *The victory was won, and it does not matter by what means*
Cf.: Success is never blamed (Am., Br.)

1658. По бедному Захару всякая щепа бьёт. *See 1172 (Н)*
Cf.: All the Tracys have always the wind in their faces (Br.). An unfortunate (unlucky) man would be drowned in a tea-cup (Br.). An unhappy man's cart is easy to overthrow (Am.)

1659. Повадился кувшин по воду ходить, там ему и голову сложить. *One will be punished for constant wrongdoings. See 1907 (С)*
Var.: До поры кувшин воду носит: оторвётся—разобьётся
Cf.: The end of the thief is the gallows (Am.). The jug goes to the well until it breaks (Am.). The pitcher goes often to the well but is broken at last (Br.). A pitcher that goes to the well too often is broken at last (Am.). The pitcher went once too often to the well (Am., Br.). The pot goes so long to the water that it is broken at last (Br.)

1660. По ватаге атаман, по овцам пастух. *The chief is like his men*
Cf.: A mad parish must have a mad priest (Am., Br.)

1661. Повинную голову и меч не сечёт. *He is not punished that will repent. See 641 (З)*
Cf.: Confessed faults are half mended (Br.). Confession of a fault makes half amends for it (Am.). A fault confessed is half forgiven (half redressed) (Am., Br.). A sin confessed is half forgiven (Am., Br.)

1662. По волоску всю бороду выщиплешь. *See 830 (К)*
Cf.: Feather by feather a goose is plucked (Am.). Feather by feather the goose is plucked (Br.). Hair by hair you pull out the horse's tail (Br.)

1663. Повторение—мать учения. *To know or to do something properly you have to learn or do it more than once*
Cf.: Repetition is the mother of learning (Am., Br.). Repetition is the mother of skill (Am.)

1664. По горшку и покрышка. *See 1723 (П)*
Var.: Каково лукошко, такова ему и покрышка. По кубышке и покрышка
Cf.: A bad cat deserves a bad rat (Am.). A good dog deserves a good bone (Am., Br.). Like cup, like cover (Br.). Such cup, such cover (Br.)

1665. Подай палец, а за руку сам возьму. *See 406 (Д)*
Cf.: Give a dog a finger and he will want a whole hand (Am.). Give him a finger and he will take a hand (Am.). Give him an inch and he'll take a mile (an ell, a yard) (Am.). Give him a ring, and he'll want your whole arm (Br.). Give knaves an inch and they will take a yard (Br.)

1666. Подальше положишь—поближе возьмёшь. *See 890 (К)*
Cf.: Hiders are good (make the best) finders (Am., Br.). Safe bind, safe find (Br.). Sure bind, sure find (Br.). Them that hides can find (Am.)

1667. Подальше—роднее, пореже—милее. *See 1828 (Р)*
Cf.: Absence makes the heart grow fonder (Am., Br.). Short visits and seldom are best (Am.)

1668. По две пошлины с одного товара не берут. *See 1964 (С)*

Var.: С одного тягла по две дани не берут

Cf.: Double charge will rive a cannon (Br.). You can't charge the same man twice (Am.)

1669. Под всякую песню не подпляшешь, под всякие нравы не подладишь. *See 1184 (Н)*

Cf.: One cannot please all the world and his wife (Br.). You cannot please everybody (Am., Br.). You can't please the whole world and his wife (Am.)

1670. Под каждой крышей свои мыши. *There is no community or family that does not have any troubles or shameful secrets. See 773 (К), 2104 (У)*

Cf.: Accidents /will/ happen in the best of families (Am.). Accidents will happen in the best regulated families (Am., Br.). No house without mouse (Br.). No larder but has its mice (Br.). There is a skeleton in every house (Am., Br.). There's a skeleton in every family /closet/ (Am.)

1671. Под лежачий камень вода не течёт. *If you undertake no action, you will achieve nothing. See 1000 (Л)*

Cf.: The foot at rest meets nothing (Am.). He that stays in the valley shall (will) never get over the hill (Am., Br.). If you don't touch the rope, you won't ring the bell (Br.). Nothing seek, nothing find (Br.). Nothing ventured, nothing gained (Am., Br.). Nothing venture, nothing gain (win) (Am., Br.). A setting hen gathers no feathers (never gets fat) (Am., Br.)

1672. Подобный подобного любит. *See 1842 (Р)*

Cf.: An ass is beautiful to an ass, and a pig to a pig (Br.). An ass to an ass is beautiful (Am.). A donkey looks beautiful to a donkey (Am.). Each kind attracts its own (Am.). Like attracts like (Am., Br.). Like draws to (likes) like (Br.). Likeness causes liking (Br.)

1673. Подстреленного сокола и ворона носом долбит. *See 1650 (П)*

Cf.: Even hares insult a dead lion (Br.). The timid hare dares to pluck the dead lion by the beard (Am.)

1674. Подшучивать над другом — нажить врага. *Do not ridicule your friends because they will get offended. See 943 (К)*

Cf.: Better lose a jest than a friend (Am., Br.). A joke never gains over an enemy, but often loses a friend (Am.)

1675. По дыму над баней пару не угадаешь. *Outer signs which are characteristic of some phenomenon can sometimes be misleading*

Cf.: Just because there's snow on the roof, that doesn't mean the fire's out inside (Am.). You cannot tell the depth of the well by the length of the handle of the pump (Am.)

1676. Поезд ушёл. *We are offered what we wanted or needed too late when we cannot avail ourselves of it. See 411 (Д)*

Cf.: The gods send nuts to those who have no teeth (Am., Br.). The wished for comes too late (Br.). Youth is wasted on the young (Am.)

1677. Пожалел волк кобылу, оставил хвост да гриву. *One just says that he is sorry for some person, but actually he did harm to the man. See 1072 (Л), 2225 (Ц)*

Var.: Сжалился волк над ягнёнком — оставил кости да кожу

Cf.: Carrion crows bewail the dead sheep, and then eat them (Br.). The crow bewails the sheep, and then eats it (Br). Crows weep for the dead lamb and then devour him (Am.)

1678. Поживём — увидим. *I do not know, we must wait to find out what will happen or what should be done. See 215 (В), 2280 (Ч)*

Cf.: Time /alone/ will show (Br.).

Time /alone/ will tell (Am., Br.). We'll wait and see (Am., Br.). We shall see what we shall see (Br.)

1679. По заслугам и честь. *Every person gets what he deserves. See 405 (Д), 799 (К), 835 (К), 1723 (П)*

Var.: По заслугам и почёт. По заслугам молодца и жалуют

Cf.: A bad cat deserves a bad rat (Am.). Give every man his due (Am., Br.). A good dog deserves a good bone (Am., Br.). A good rat to match a good cat (Br.). Honor to whom honor is due (Am.). Honour to whom honour is due (Br.). Like cup, like cover (Br.). Such cup, such cover (Br.). To a good cat a good rat (Am.). Sweets to the sweet and sour to the sour (Am.)

1680. Позднему гостю—кости. *See 956 (К)*

Var.: Поздние гости глодают кости. Поздно пришёл, одни кости нашёл

Cf.: To those who come late the bones (Br.). Who doesn't come at the right time must take what is left (Am.)

1681. По Ивашке и рубашка. *See 1723 (П)*

Cf.: A bad cat deserves a bad rat (Am.). A good dog deserves a good bone (Am., Br.). Like cup, like cover (Br.). Such cup, such cover (Br.)

1682. Пока дышу, надеюсь. *While we are alive, we believe that all will turn out for the best. See 1195 (Н)*

Var.: Пока живу, надеюсь

Cf.: As long as (While) I breathe I hope (Br.). Where (While) there's life there's hope (Am., Br.). While the sick man has life, there is hope (Am.)

1683. Пока есть хлеб да вода, всё не беда. *It is easier to bear any trouble if you are not hungry. See 600 (Ж)*

Cf.: All griefs (sorrows) are less with bread (Br.). Fat sorrow is better than lean sorrow (Am., Br.). Full stomach, contented heart (Am.)

1684. Покажется сатана лучше ясного сокола. *See 1085 (Л)*

Var.: Полюбится сатана лучше ясного сокола

Cf.: Fancy flees before the wind (Br.). Love is blind (Am., Br.). Love sees no faults (Am.)

1685. Пока зацветут камыши, у нас не будет души. *See 1687 (П)*

Cf.: While the grass grows the horse starves (Am., Br.)

1686. По капельке—море, по зёрнышку—ворох. *See 979 (К)*

Var.: Из крошек—кучка, из капель—море. По капельке—море, по зёрнышку—ворох, по былинке (травинке)—стог. По капле—дождь, по росинке—роса

Cf.: Add little to little and there will be a great heap (Am.). A bushel of wheat is made up of single grains (Br.). Little drops of water, little grains of sand, make a (the) mighty ocean and a (the) pleasant land (Am.). Little drops produce a shower (Am.). Many drops make a flood (a shower) (Br.). Many drops of water make an ocean (Am.). Many small make a great (Br.). Many small makes a great (Am.)

1687. Пока солнце взойдёт, роса очи выест. *Something longed for can take so much time to be realized that when you get it at last, you will be unable to use it. See 411 (Д), 1685 (П), 1688 (П)*

Cf.: While men go after a leech, the body is buried (Br.). While the grass grows the horse starves (Am., Br.). While the grass grows the steed starves (Br.)

1688. Пока трава вырастет, кобыла сдохнет. *See 1687 (П)*

Cf.: While the grass grows the horse starves (Am., Br.)

1689. Поклониться—голова не отвалится. *It will do you no harm if*

you are respectful. See 1579 (О), 1690 (П)

Cf.: Cap in hand never harmed anyone (Br.). No one has ever been killed by kindness (Am.). One never loses anything by politeness (Br.)

1690. Поклоном шеи не свихнёшь. *See 1689 (П)*

Var.: Поклоном поясницы не переломишь (спины не надсадишь)

Cf.: Cap in hand never harmed anyone (Br.). No one has ever been killed by kindness (Am.). Courtesy never broke one's crown (Br.)

1691. Покой нам только снится. *Man is never free from troubles, cares or worries. See 292 (В)*

Cf.: No rest for the weary (Am.). Only in the grave is there rest (Am.). Peace is found only in the graveyard (Am.)

1692. Покорное слово гнев укрощает. *A mild reply can alleviate anger or hostility. See 983 (Л), 984 (Л)*

Var.: Кроткое слово гнев побеждает

Cf.: Kindness is the noblest weapon to conquer with (Am.). A soft answer turns away wrath (Am., Br.). Soft words win a hard heart (Am.). Soft words win hard hearts (Br.)

1693. По которой реке плыть, той и песенки петь. *See 1264 (Н)*

Cf.: Every man bows to the bush he gets bield of (Br.). Whose bread I eat, his song I sing (Am.)

1694. Полено к полену—костёр. *See 979 (К)*

Cf.: Many a little (a pickle) makes a mickle (Br.). Many a mickle makes a muckle (Am.). Many small makes a great (Am.)

1695. По лесу ходит, дров не найдёт. *People fail to find things which are in abundance*

Cf.: Don't go through the woods and pick up a crooked stick (Am.). Some men go through a forest and see no firewood (Br.)

1696. Полетели гуси за море, а прилетели тоже не лебеди. *See 195 (В)*

Cf.: If an ass goes a-traveling, he'll not come back a horse (Am.). If an ass goes a-travelling, he'll not come home a horse (Br.)

1697. Полна хата детей, так и счастливо в ней. *It is a happy family in which there are many children. See 1259 (Н)*

Cf.: Children are the parents' riches (Br.). It takes children to make a happy family (home) (Am.)

1698. Полного счастья не бывает. *See 1453 (Н)*

Cf.: Every inch of joy has an ell of annoy (Br.). No joy without alloy (Br.). No joy without annoy (Am., Br.). There is no joy without affliction (Am.). There is no joy without alloy (Am.)

1699. Полузнание хуже незнания. *See 1336 (Н)*

Cf.: Amateur tactics cause grave wounds (Br.). A little knowledge (learning) is a dangerous thing (Am., Br.)

1700. Полюбите нас чёрненькими, а беленькими всякий полюбит. *Be friendly with us whether we are poor or prosperous*

Var.: Полюбите нас чёрненькими, а красненькими всяк полюбит

Cf.: Accept us as we are (Am., Br.). Take us as you find us (Am., Br.)

1701. Полюбится сова—не надо райской птички. *See 1085 (Л), 1395 (Н)*

Cf.: Beauty is in the eye of the beholder (Am., Br.). Fair is not fair but that which pleases (Br). Nobody's sweetheart is ugly (Am.)

1702. По мастеру и закрой. *See 802 (K)*

Cf.: As is the workman, so is his work (Am.). As is the workman so is the work (Br.)

1703. Помирать, так с музыкой. *If you are losing, do it with dignity*

Cf.: If you are going down, go down in a blaze of glory (Am.). If you are going out, go out in style (Am.). If you are going to go, go all the way (go in style) (Am.). If you must go down, go down in flames (Am.)

1704. Помрёшь—ничего с собой не возьмёшь. *See 2133 (У)*

Cf.: A shroud has no pockets (Am., Br.). When you die, you can't take it with you (Am.)

1705. По образчику узнают и сукно. *We can judge of the quality of a whole thing by a little piece*

Cf.: By a small sample we may judge the whole piece (Am.). The sack is known by the sample (Br.). You don't have to eat a whole tub of butter to get the taste (Am.). You may know by a handful the whole sack (Br.). You may know by the handful the whole sack (Am.)

1706. По одежде встречают. *It is the person's looks that you pay your attention to when meeting him for the first time*

Cf.: Appearances go a great ways (Am.). Good clothes open all doors (Am., Br.). A smart coat is a good letter of introduction (Am., Br.)

1707. По одёжке встречают, по уму провожают. *It is only when you first meet a man that you pay your attention to his looks, but later you judge him by his intellect. See 1381 (H)*

Var.: По платью встречают, по уму провожают

Cf.: Clothes do not make the man (Am., Br.). It is not the gay coat that makes the gentleman (Am., Br.)

1708. По одёжке протягивай ножки. *Spend no more than your budget allows you. See 595 (Ж), 1370 (H), 1712 (П)*

Cf.: Ask your purse what you should buy (Am.). Cut the coat according to the cloth (Am.). Cut your coat according to your cloth (Br.). Limit your wants by your wealth (Br.). Make your pudding according to your plums (Am.). Put your hand no farther than your sleeve will reach (Am., Br.). Stretch your arm no farther than your sleeve will reach (Am., Br.). Stretch your legs according to the length of your blanket (Am.). Stretch your legs according to your coverlet (Br.). You must cut your garment according to the cloth (Am.)

1709. По Павушке и славушка. *See 818 (K)*

Cf.: A crooked stick will cast (will have) a crooked shadow (Am.). If the staff be crooked, the shadow cannot be straight (Br.)

1710. Попал в стаю, лай не лай, а хвостом виляй. *See 1866 (C)*

Cf.: One must howl with the wolves (Br.). When you are with wolves, you must howl with them (Am.)

1711. Попался, который кусался. *One is caught and will be punished for his wrongdoings. See 1598 (O)*

Cf.: The biter is bit (Br.). The biter is sometimes bit (Am.). The jig is up (Br.)

1712. По приходу и расход держи. *See 1708 (П)*

Cf.: Ask your purse what you should buy (Am.). Cut the coat according to the cloth (Am.). Cut your coat according to your cloth (Br.)

1713. Попытка не пытка. *It is worth making an attempt as you risk nothing*

Cf.: /There is/ no harm in trying (Am., Br.)

1714. По работе и деньги. *See 794 (К)*
Cf.: As the work, so the pay (Br.). A good servant must have good wages (Am.). The labo(u)rer is worthy of his hire (Am., Br.). A workman is worth of his hire (Am.)

1715. Пора гостям и честь знать. *It is time to leave not to tire the hosts*
Var.: Пора гостям по своим дворам
Cf.: Don't wear out your welcome (Am., Br.). Don't wear your visit out (Am.). Let's go before we wear out our visit (Am., Br.)

1716. Пора на пору не приходится. *See 1817 (Р)*
Var.: Время на время не приходится. День на день не приходится
Cf.: Every day is not yesterday (Br.). Some days are darker than others (Am.). There are no two days (years) alike (Am.). Things are not always the same (Br.)

1717. Пора придёт и вода пойдёт. *See 233 (В)*
Cf.: All in good time (Br.). There's a season for all things (Am.)

1718. Порванную верёвку как ни вяжи, а всё узел будет. *Once love or friendship is destroyed, it is next to impossible to restore them. See 516 (Д), 630 (З), 1812 (Р), 1906 (С), 2070 (Т)*
Cf.: A broken egg cannot be put back together (Am.). A broken friendship may be soldered but will never be sound (Am.). Broken friendships may be soldered, but never sound (Br.). A cracked bell can never sound well (Am., Br.). A cracked bell is never sound (Br.). When one reknots a broken cord, it holds, but one feels the knot (Am.)

1719. Порядок—душа всякого дела. *In any enterprise order ensures success*
Cf.: Order and method render things easily (Am.). Order is heaven's first law (Am.)

1720. Посади свинью за стол, она и ноги на стол. *Give hono(u)r to an ill-bred or impudent person and he will demonstrate his ill breeding or impudence*
Cf.: A pig in the parlo(u)r is still a pig (Am., Br.). Pigs are pigs (Am.)

1721. По своей воле лучше неволи. *See 1867 (С)*
Cf.: A burden of one's choice is not felt (Br.). The burden of one's own choice is not felt (Am.)

1722. По семени и плод. *See 2357 (Я)*
Cf.: As the tree, so the fruit (Am., Br.). A good seed makes a good crop (Am.)

1723. По Сеньке и шапка. *Every person gets what he is worthy of. See 799 (К), 814 (К), 823 (К), 1664 (П), 1679 (П), 1681 (П)*
Var.: По барину и говядина. По пташке и клетка. По Савке и свитка. По Сеньке—шапка, по Ерёме—кафтан (колпак)
Cf.: A bad cat deserves a bad rat (Am.). A good dog deserves a good bone (Am., Br.). A good rat to match a good cat (Br.). Let a good pot have a good lid (Br.). Like cup, like cover (Br.). Such cup, such cover (Br.)

1724. После бури наступает затишье. *See 1725 (П)*
Cf.: After a storm comes a calm (Am., Br.). After a storm, the sun always shines (Am.). After the storm comes the calm (Am.). There's always a quiet (quietness) after a storm (Am.)

1725. После грозы—вёдро. *Adversity is followed by good fortune. See 8 (А), 105 (Б), 311 (Г), 753 (И), 804 (К), 1296 (Н), 1724 (П), 1728 (П), 1891 (С), 2042 (Т)*
Cf.: After a storm comes a calm (Br.). After the storm comes the calm

(Am.). April showers bring May flowers (Am.). Behind bad luck comes good luck (Am.). A blustering night, a fair day (Am., Br.). Rain one day, shine the next (Am.). There's always a quiet (quietness) after a storm (Am.). When things are at their worst, they will mend (Am., Br.)

1726. Последнего и собаки рвут. *Weak or incompetent people who fail and lag behind must expect the worst fate*

Cf.: The devil takes the hindmost (Am.). The devil take the hindmost (Am., Br.). Each (Every man) for himself, and the devil take the hindmost (Br.). Every fellow for himself, and the devil take the hindmost (Am.)

1727. Последняя капля переполняет чашу. *Any endurance has a limit. See 286 (В)*

Cf.: The cord breaks at the last but the weakest pull (Br.). It is the last feather that breaks the camel's back (Br.). The last drop makes the cup run over (Am., Br.). The last drop makes the cup turn over (Am.). The last drop wobbles; the cup flows over (Am.). The last ounce (straw) breaks the camel's back (Br.). The last straw will break the camel's back (Am.). When the pot's full, it runs over (Am.). When the pot's full it will boil over (Br.). When the well is full, it will run over (Br.)

1728. После дождичка будет солнышко. *See 1725 (П)*

Var.: После дождичка солнце выглянет

Cf.: After rain comes fair weather (Br.). After the rain, the sun (Am.). Behind the clouds the sun is shining (Am.). A blustering night, a fair day (Am., Br.). Rain one day, shine the next (Am.)

1729. После дождичка в четверг. *See 847 (К)*

Cf.: When pigs fly (Am., Br.)

1730. После драки кулаками не машут. *After trouble, there is no use taking precautions or being indignant if you cannot help it. See 492 (Д), 619 (З), 621 (З), 850 (К), 1732 (П), 1983 (С), 2175 (Х)*

Cf.: It is no time to stoop when the head is off (Br.). It is too late to close the barn door after the horse has bolted (Br.). It is too late to lock the stable door when the steed is stolen (Am., Br.). It is too late to spare when the bottom is bare (Am., Br.). It is too late to throw water on the cinder when the house is burned down (Am.). When the devil comes, it is too late to pray (Am.). When the house is burned down, you bring water (Br.)

1731. После нас хоть потоп. *I do not care about the consequences of my actions, be they disastrous*

Var.: После нас хоть трава не расти

Cf.: After us the deluge (Am., Br.)

1732. После пожара за водой не бегут. *See 1730 (П)*

Cf.: It is too late to throw water on the cinder when the house is burned down (Am.). When the house is burned down, you bring water (Br.)

1733. После поры не точат топоры. *See 1986 (С)*

Cf.: Don't set the net after the fish have gone by (Am.). When a fool has bethought himself, the market's over (Br.). When a fool has made up his mind, the market has gone by (Am.)

1734. После свадьбы в барабаны не бьют. *See 1986 (С)*

Cf.: Don't set the net after the fish have gone by (Am.). When a fool has bethought himself, the market's over (Br.). When a fool has made up his mind, the market has gone by (Am.)

1735. После смерти взятки гладки. *See 1940 (С)*

Cf.: Death pays all debts (Am., Br.).

Death quits all scores (squares all accounts) (Br.)

1736. После ужина горчица. *It has come too late and is not needed*

Cf.: After death, the doctor (Am., Br.). After meat comes mustard (Am.). After meat, mustard (Br.). Good that comes too late is good as nothing (Am.)

1737. Пословица не мимо молвится. *A proverb can always be used to the point*

Var.: Пословица недаром (не зря, не на ветер) молвится

Cf.: A good maxim is never out of season (Am., Br.)

1738. По службе—ни друга, ни недруга. *No concessions in business can be made on such grounds as friendship, family ties, etc. See 515 (Д)*

Cf.: Business is business (Am., Br.). Business is business, and love is love (Am.)

1739. Посмотрим ещё, чья возьмёт. *Now you are the winner, but we do not know which of us will be the one in the end*

Cf.: At the game's end we shall see who gains (Br.). It is a game at which two can play (Am., Br.). Two can play at that game (Am., Br.)

1740. По соломинке—сноп. *See 979 (К)*

Var.: По соломинке—сноп, по снопишку—копнишка, из копен—стог

Cf.: A bushel of wheat is made up of single grains (Br.). Though one grain fills not the sack, it helps (Am.)

1741. Поспешишь—людей насмешишь. *When trying to do something in a hurry, one ends up in making less progress or achieving a poor result. See 249 (В), 1609 (О), 1911 (С), 1912 (С), 1914 (С), 1979 (С), 2054 (Т)*

Cf.: Good and quickly seldom meet (Am.). The greater hurry, the worse the speed (Am.). Haste makes waste (Am., Br.). Haste may trip up its own heels (Am.). Haste trips over its own heels (Br.). The hasty bitch brings forth blind puppies (Am.). The hasty bitch btings forth blind whelps (Br.). The hasty burned his lips (Br.). Hasty climbers have sudden falls (Am., Br.). A hasty man is seldom out of trouble (Am.). A hasty man never wants woe (Br.). More haste, less speed (Am., Br.). What is done in a hurry is never done well (Br.). /Wisely and slowly / they stumble that run fast (Am.)

1742. Поспешность нужна только при ловле блох. *Never take an ill- considered step. See 1887 (С)*

Cf.: Hurry is only good for catching flies (Am.). Nothing should be done in haste but gripping a flea (Br.). Nothing to be done in haste but catching fleas (Br.)

1743. Постригся кот, намылся кот, а всё тот же кот. *See 827 (К)*

Cf.: A golden bit does not make a horse any better (Br.). A golden bit does not make the horse any better (Am.)

1744. Посуленный мерин не везёт. *See 1968 (С)*

Cf.: An acre of performance is worth the whole world of promise (Am.). Fair words butter no cabbage (Am.). Fair words butter no parsnips (Br.). One acre of performance is worth twenty of the Land of Promise (Br.). Promises don't fill the belly (Am.)

1745. По сытому брюху хоть обухом бей. *When a man is not hungry, he feels well and strong, and it is easier for him to bear any trouble. See 600 (Ж)*

Cf.: A full belly makes a brave heart (Am.). Stuffing holds out storm (Br.). When the belly is full, the bones are at rest (Am.). When the belly is full, the bones would be at rest (Br.). When the stomach is full, the heart is glad (Am.)

1746. Потерянного времени не воротишь. *Make use of the present time because it is irrevocable. See 445 (Д), 1847 (С)*

Var.: Потерянного времени не догонишь

Cf.: An hour wasted can never be regained (Am.). Lost time is never found again (Am., Br.). Time flies like an arrow, and time lost never returns (Am.)

1747. Потерянного не воротить. *See 2308 а (Ч)*

Cf.: Spilled water cannot be gathered up (Am.). What is lost is lost (Br.)

1748. По товарищам и слава. *See 1896 (С)*

Cf.: A man is known by the company he keeps (Am.). Man is known by the company he keeps (Br.)

1749. Потом и Семён умён. *See 620 (З)*

Cf.: After the danger everyone is wise (Am.). Everybody is wise after the event (Br.)

1750. Почин дороже денег. *In any undertaking it is the beginning that is of greatest importance*

Cf.: Begun is half done (Am., Br.). The first blow (stroke) is half the battle (Br.). A journey of a thousand miles begins with one step (Am.)

1751. Пошёл в попы, так служи и панихиды. *See 1201 (Н)*

Cf.: If you pledge, don't hedge (Br.). Once you pledge, don't hedge (Am.). You can't back out (Am., Br.)

1752. Пошёл за большим, не жалей малого. *It is worth sacrificing a little to gain much*

Cf.: He that would catch a fish must venture his bait (Am.). A hook's well lost to catch a salmon (Am., Br.). Risk (Set) a sprat to catch a whale (Am.). Throw out a sprat to catch a herring (a mackerel, a whale) (Br.). Venture a small fish to catch a great one (Am., Br.). You must lose a fly to catch a trout (Am., Br.)

1753. Пошла Настя по напастям. *See 1778 (П)*

Cf.: It never rains but it pours (Am., Br.). Misfortunes seldom come alone (Am.). One misfortune comes on (upon) the back (the neck) of another (Br.). Trouble never comes single-handed (Am.). Troubles come in crowds (Br.)

1754. Правая рука не знает, что делает левая. *The actions of one person or a group of people are inconsistent with those of another one*

Var.: Левая рука не ведает, что делает правая

Cf.: The left hand doesn't know what the right hand is doing (Am., Br.)

1755. Правда в огне не горит и в воде не тонет. *A deception will be found out and the just cause will triumph. See 1599 (О), 1758 (П), 1765 (П)*

Var.: Правду водой не зальёшь, огнём не сожжёшь

Cf.: Truth and oil always come to the top (Am.). Truth and oil are ever above (Br.). Truth, crushed to earth, will rise again (Am.). Truth is mighty and will prevail (Am., Br.). Truth may languish but never perish (Br.). Truth never perishes (Am., Br.). Truth will break out (will out, will come to light) (Br.). The truth will come out (will come to light, will out) (Am.). Truth will prevail (Am.)

1756. Правда глаза колет. *A man who is in the wrong does not like to hear the bitter truth about himself. See 1757 (П)*

Cf.: Home truths are hard to swallow (Br.). It is truth that makes a man angry (Am., Br.). No one wants to hear the truth (Am.). Nothing stings like the truth (Br.). The sting of a reproach is its truth (Br.). The sting of a reproach is the truth of it (Am.). Truth and roses have thorns /about them/ (Am.). The truth hurts (Am., Br.). Truth is (tastes) bitter (Am.). Truths and roses have thorns about them (Br.)

1757. Правда, как оса, лезет в глаза. *See 1756 (П)*

Cf.: No one wants to hear the truth (Am.). Truth and roses have thorns /about them/ (Am.). The truth hurts (Am., Br.). Truths and roses have thorns about them (Br.)

1758. Правда как солнце—ладонями не прикроешь. *See 1755 (П)*

Var.: Правда что шило—в мешке не утаишь

Cf.: The truth will come out (will come to light, will out) (Am.). Truth will come to light (will out) (Br.)

1759. Правда не боится света. *One should tell the truth openly. See 1230 (Н)*

Cf.: Truth fears nothing but concealment (Am.). Truth seeks no corners (Am., Br.)

1760. Правда сама себя очистит. *Truth can be blamed, but sooner or later it will triumph*

Cf.: A clean hand needs (wants) no washing (Am., Br.). A lie runs until it is overtaken by truth (Am.)

1761. Правду говорить—друга не нажить. *If you tell a man the truth he does not like, he will never be your friend. See 1762 (П)*

Cf.: Candor breeds hatred (Am.). Flattery begets friends, but the truth begets enmity (Am.)

1762. Правду говорить—себе досадить. *If you tell a man the truth about his faults or wrongdoings, you may suffer for it. See 1761 (П)*

Cf.: Candor breeds hatred (Am.). Flattery begets friends, but the truth begets enmity (Am.). Follow not truth too near the heels lest it dash out your teeth (Am., Br.). He who follows truth too closely will have dirt kicked in his face (Am., Br.). Truth breeds hatred (Br.). Truth finds foes, where it makes none (Am., Br.)

1763. Правду ищи на дне морском. *It is not easy to find the truth*

Var.: Ищи ветра в поле, а правду на дне морском

Cf.: Truth has always a fast bottom (Br.). Truth is at the bottom of a well (in a well) (Br.). Truth keeps to the bottom of her well (Am.). Truth lies at the bottom of a pit (Br.). Truth lies at the bottom of a well (Am., Br.)

1764. Правду красить нет нужды. *Truth must be told as it is without being embelished, for otherwise it is not truth*

Var.: Правду красить не нужно

Cf.: Craft must have clothes, but truth loves to go naked (Br.). The expression of truth is simplicity (Am.). Truth has a good face, but bad clothes (Br.). Truth has no need of figures (rhetoric) (Br.). Truth is a naked lady (Am.). Truth needs no colo(u)rs (Am., Br.). The truth shows best being naked (Br.)

1765. Правды не спрячешь. *See 1755 (П)*

Var.: Правду не скроешь

Cf.: Truth will break out (will come to light, will out) (Br.). The truth will come out (will come to light, will out) (Am.)

1766. Праздник бывает не каждый день. *We do not have a merry-making very often. See 1297 (Н)*

Cf.: Christmas comes but once a year (Am., Br.). Every day is not a holiday (Am.). Every day is not Sunday (Br.). We don't kill a pig every day (Br.)

1767. Прежде соберись, потом дерись. *Get everything ready before you undertake some action*

Cf.: Draw not your bow till your arrow is fixed (Am., Br.)

1768. Привычка—вторая натура. *We do things as we are accustomed to. See 2076 (Т)*

Var.: Привычка—вторая природа

Cf.: Custom is a second nature (Am., Br.). Custom surpasses nature (Am.). Habit is a cable (Am.). Habit is a second nature (Br.). Habits are hard to break (Am.). Old customs (habits) die hard (Am.). Use is a second nature (Br.)

1769. Привяжется сума, откажется и родня. *When a man becomes poor, people break up relations with him. See 27 (Б)*

Cf.: No one claims kindred (is akin) to the poor (Br.). No one claims kin to the fortuneless age (Am.). A poor man has no friends (Am.). Poverty has no kin (Am.)

1770. Придёт время, и мы ногой топнем. *See 106 (Б)*

Cf.: Every dog has his day (Am., Br.). We shall have our day /too/ (Br.)

1771. Придёт время, прорастёт и семя. *See 233 (В)*

Var.: Всё в свой срок: придёт времечко вырастет и семечко

Cf.: All in good time (Br.). There's a season for all things (Am.)

1772. Придёт солнышко и к нашим окошечкам. *See 106 (Б)*

Var.: Взойдёт солнце и перед нашими воротами. Взойдёт солнышко и на нашем подворье

Cf.: Better luck next time (Am., Br.). Every dog has his day (Am., Br.). The sun will shine down our street too (on our side of the fence) (Br.)

1773. Придорожная пыль неба не коптит. *See 399 (Г)*

Cf.: The sun is never the worse for shining on a dunghill (Br.). The sun is not less bright for sitting on a dunghill (Am.)

1774. Признание—сестра покаянию. *To acknowledge one's guilt means to feel sorry or self-reproachful for what one has done*

Cf.: Confession is good for the soul (Am., Br.). Confession is the first step to repentance (Br.). /An/ honest confession is good for the soul (Am.). Open confession is good for the soul (Br.)

1775. Природа не терпит пустоты. *No position will be left vacant, some person is always found to take it. See 1870 (С)*

Cf.: Nature abhors a vacuum (Am., Br.). A vacuum is always filled (Am.)

1776. Природа своё возьмёт. *You cannot change the nature of people. See 383 (Г)*

Cf.: Nature will take its course (Br.). What is bred in the bone will not /come/ out of the flesh (Am., Br.). What's in the bone is in the marrow (Am.)

1777. Пришёл, увидел, победил. *I or someone won an easy victory in love, career, war, etc.*

Cf.: I came, I saw, I conquered (Am., Br)

1778. Пришла беда—отворяй ворота. *Misfortunes always follow one another. See 22 (Б), 1753 (П), 2231 (П)*

Var.: Пришла беда, открывай (растворяй) ворота

Cf.: Bad luck comes in threes (Am.). Disasters come treading on each other's heel (Br.). Ill comes often on the back of worse (Br.). It never rains, but it pours (Am., Br.). Trouble comes in bunches (in twos) (Am.). Trouble never comes single (single-handed) (Am.). Troubles come in crowds (never come alone) (Br.). Troubles never come singly (Am., Br.)

1779. Пришло махом, ушло прахом. *See 993 (Л)*

Var.: Легко придёт—прахом пойдёт

Cf.: Easy come, easy go (Am.). Lightly come, lightly go (Am., Br.). Quickly come, quickly go (Am., Br.). Soon gained, soon gone (Br.). Soon got, soon spent (Am., Br.)

1780. Прогнило что-то в королевстве Датском. *Something is wrong in the state of things*

Cf.: Something is rotten in the state of Denmark (Br.). There's something rotten in the state of Denmark (Am.)

1781. Проголодаешься, так хлеба найти догадаешься. *See 378 (Г)*

Cf.: Hunger teaches us many things (Br.). Necessity is the mother of invention (Am., Br.). Poverty is the mother of all arts (Am.). Want makes wit (Br.)

1782. Прокукарекает петух или нет, а день будет. *No matter what, everything will change for the better. See 239 (В)*

Cf.: Daylight will come, though the cock does not crow (Br.). In the end, all will mend (Am.). In the end things will mend (Br.). It will all come out (come right) in the wash (Am., Br.). Let the cock crow or not, the day will come (Br.). The sunrise never failed us yet (Am.). The sun will always come up tomorrow (Am.)

1783. Пролитую воду не соберёшь. *See 2308 a (Ч)*

Cf.: Spilled water cannot be gathered up (Am.). What is lost is lost (Br.)

1784. Промедление смерти подобно. *Deferring things can result in disaster. See 583 (Ж)*

Cf.: Delay breeds loss (is dangerous) (Am.). Delays are dangerous (Br.). Delays have dangerous ends (Am., Br.). He who hesitates is lost (Am., Br.). He who lingers is lost (Am.). Kill time and time will kill you (Am.). Procrastination brings loss (Br.)

1785. Простота хуже воровства. *Man's simplicity or stupidity causes much trouble*

Cf.: The fools do more hurt in this world than rascals (Am.)

1786. Против рожна не попрёшь. *a) Power makes you submit to it. See a) 990 a (Л), 1647 a (П); b) Do not struggle against things which you cannot overcome. See 990 b (Л), 1647 b (П), 2082 (Т)*

Cf.: a) It is hard to live in Rome and strive against the Pope (Am.). It is hard to sit in Rome and strive against the Pope (Br.). There is no arguing with a large fist (Am.). What may the mouse do against the cat? (Am.). You cannot fight City Hall (Am., Br.)

b) Do not kick against the pricks (Br.). Don't kick aginst pricks (Am.). It is ill striving against the stream (Br.). Puff not against the wind (Br.). Strive not against the stream (Am.). You can't fight guns with sticks (Br.)

1787. Птица в руках стоит двух в кустах. *See 1421 (Н)*

Cf.: Better a sparrow in the hand than a vulture on the wing (Br.). A bird in the hand is better than two in the bush (Am.). A bird in the hand is worth two in the bush (Am., Br.). A carrot in the hand is worth two in the midden (Br.). A sparrow in the hand is better than a pigeon in the roof (in the sky) (Br.). A sparrow in the hand is worth a pheasant that flies by (Br.)

1788. Пуганая ворона и куста боится. *He who once had big troubles is afraid even of that which is not fraught with danger. See 68 (Б), 1507 (О), 1626 (О)*

Var.: Пуганый волк и кочки боится. Пуганый заяц и пенька боится

Cf.: Birds once snared fear all bushes (Br.). A bitten child dreads a dog (Am.). A bitten child dreads the dog (Br.). A burnt child dreads the fire (Am., Br.). He that hath been bitten by a serpent is afraid of a rope (Br.). A man once bitten by a snake will jump at the sight of a rope in his path (Am.). Once bitten (bit), twice shy (Am., Br.). Once wounded, twice as windy (Br.). Whom a serpent has bitten, a lizard alarms (Br.)

1789. Пуговички золочёные, а три дня не евши. *See 1178 (Н)*

Cf.: Great boast, small roast (Am., Br.)

1790. Пуля—дура, а виноватого найдёт. *See 1602 (О)*

Cf.: Punishment comes slowly, but it comes (Am.). Punishment follows hard upon crime (Br.)

1791. Пустая бочка пуще гремит. *Empty-headed men are most talkative and their manners are most demonstrative. See 332 (Г)*

Cf.: Deep rivers move with silent majesty; shallow brooks are noisy (Am.). An empty barrel (bowl, kettle) makes the most noise (Am.). Empty barrels make the greatest din (sound) (Br.). An empty can makes a lot of noise (Am.). Empty casks make the most noise (Am.). The empty pail (wagon) makes the most noise (Am.). Empty vessels make the most noise (sound) (Am., Br.). An empty wagon rattles /loudest/ (Am.). A hollow drum makes the most noise (Am.). A loaded wagon creaks, an empty one rattles (Br.)

1792. Пусти козла в огород, он всю капусту обдерёт. *See 185 (В)*

Cf.: Don't set a wolf to watch the sheep (Am.). Never trust a wolf with the care of lambs (Br.)

1793. Пусти свинью в мякину—она и в зерно заберётся. *See 406 (Д)*

Cf.: Give a dog a finger and he will want a whole hand (Am.). Give him an inch and he'll take a mile (an ell, a yard) (Am., Br.). Give knaves an inch and they will take a yard (Br.)

1794. Пуст карман, да красив кафтан. *See 1178 (Н)*

Cf.: Great boast, small roast (Am., Br.)

1795. Пустой колос голову кверху носит. *Unlike a clever person, a narrow-minded man is often self-conceited*

Var.: Порожний колос выше стоит

Cf.: The boughs that bear most, hang lowest (Am., Br.). A full ear of corn will bend its head; an empty ear will stand upright (Am.). The heaviest head of corn hangs its head lowest (Br.)

1796. Пустой мешок введёт в грешок. *See 30 (Б)*

Cf.: It is a hard task to be poor and leal (Br.). It is hard to be poor and honest (Br.). The lack of money is the root of all evil (Am.). Poverty is the mother of crime (Am.). Want of money is the root of all evil (Am.)

1797. Пустой мешок стоять не будет. *Poverty often deprives people of their spirit and dignity*

Cf.: An empty bag cannot stand (Am.). An empty bag (sack) cannot stand upright (Am., Br.). It is hard for an empty sack to stand upright (Br.). It's hard for an empty bag to stand upright (Am.). Pride is a luxury a poor man cannot afford (Am.)

1798. Пусть первым бросит камень, кто безгрешен. *Before condemning anyone, ask yourself whether you are blameless. See 511 (Д)*

Cf.: Cast not the first stone (Br.). He that is without sin among you, let him cast the first stone (Br.). He that is without sin among you, let him first cast a stone at her (Am., Br.). Let him that is without sin cast the first stone (Am.)

1799. Путному началу благой конец. *It is very important to begin everything right. See 477 (Д), 809 (К)*

Var.: У хорошего почина хороший конец

Cf.: A good beginning makes a good ending (Am., Br.)

1800. Путь к сердцу мужчины лежит через желудок. *A woman can gain a man's love by cooking food he enjoys*

Cf.: The way to a man's heart is through his belly (Br.). The way to a man's heart is through his stomach (Am., Br.). You can win a man through his stomach (Am.)

1801. Пушинка к пушинке—выйдет перинка. *See 979 (К)*

Cf.: Many a little (a pickle) makes a mickle (Br.). Many a mickle makes a muckle (Am.)

1802. Пчела жалит жалом, а человек—словом. *See 1932 (С)*

Cf.: There is no venom like that of the tongue (Br.). A word hurts more than a wound (Am.)

1803. Пьяница проспится, а дурак—никогда. *See 541 (Д)*

Var.: Пьяный проспится, а дурак—никогда

Cf.: A drunken man will get sober, but a fool will never get wise (Am.). Drunks sober up, fools remain fools (Am.). Fools will be fools (Br.)

1804. Пьяному и море по колено. *When a man is drunk, he does not fear anything*

Cf.: It's pot valour (Br.). It's the beer speaking (talking) (Am.). Whiskey make rabbit hug lion (Am.)

1805. Пьянство до добра не доведёт. *Hard drinking results in bad consequences. See 1806 (П)*

Cf.: Drink is the source of evil (Br.). Drunken days have all their tomorrow (Am., Br.). Drunken days have their tomorrow (Am.). A red nose makes a ragged back (Br.). Wine wears no breeches (Br.)

1806. Пьяный скачет, а проспался—плачет. *Bitter sobering comes after the excitement caused by strong drinks. See 1805 (П)*

Cf.: Drunken days have all their tomorrow (Br.). Drunken days have their tomorrow (Am.). Drunken joy brings sober sorrow (Br.). Sweet's the wine but sour's the payment (Am.). What you do drunk you must pay for sober (Br.)

1807. Пьяный—что малый: что на уме, то и на языке. *See 2312 (Ч)*

Cf.: Children and drunkards speak the truth (Am.). Children and drunk people speak the truth (Br.). Children, fools and drunkards tell the truth (Am.). Drunken heart won't lie (Am.)

Р

1808. Работа дураков любит. *You are given so much work to do just because you can never say no. (You say this to a man whose zeal you do not approve of.) See 1199 (Н)*

Cf.: All lay load (loads) on a willing horse (Br.). All lay the load on the willing horse (Am.). Only fools and horses work (Am.)

1809. Работает упорно и ест задорно. *See 820 (К)*

Cf.: Quick at meat, quick at work (Am., Br.). A swift eater, a swift worker (Am.)

1810. Рад бы в рай, да грехи не пускают. *I would like to do it, but I have no ability, power, means, right, etc.*

Cf.: I would if I could, but I can't (Am., Br.)

1811. Разбитому кораблю нет попутного ветра. *There is no help to a ruined enterprise or a person aiming at nowhere*

Cf.: A bad ship never casts anchor in port (Am.). Every wind is ill to a broken ship (Br.). No wind can do him good who steers for no port (Am.). No wind is of service to him who is bound for nowhere (Am.). To a crazy ship all winds are contrary (Br.)

1812. Разбитую чашу не склеишь. *See 1718 (П)*

Cf.: A cracked bell can never sound well (Am., Br.)

1813. Разверзлись хляби небесные. *It is raining heavily*

Cf.: It is raining cats and dogs (pitchforks) (Am., Br.). It is raining chicken coops (darling needles) (Am.). The rain comes down in sheets (in torrents) (Br.). The windows of the heaven have opened (Br.)

1814. Разделённая радость—двойная радость. *We are much happier if other people enjoy good time with us. See 390 (Г)*

Cf.: Happiness is not perfect until it is shared (Am.). Joy shared is joy doubled (Br.). Joys shared with others are more enjoyed (Br.). A joy that's shared is a joy made double (Am.). A pleasure shared is a pleasure doubled (Br.). A thing is the bigger of being shared (Br.)

1815. Разделяй и властвуй. *Achieve power by sowing dissension among people*

Cf.: Divide and conquer (Am.). Divide and govern (Br.). Divide and rule (Am., Br.)

1816. Разлука—враг любви. *See 1871 (С)*

Cf.: Far from eye, far from heart (Br.). Long absent, soon forgotten (Am., Br.). Out of sight, out of mind (Am., Br.). Salt water and absence wash away love (Br.)

1817. Раз на раз не приходится. *Things do not always go well. See 363 (Г), 1716 (П)*

Cf.: Every day is not yesterday (Br.). Some days are darker than others (Am.). There are no two years alike (Br.). Things are not always the same (Br.)

1818. Разом густо, разом пусто. *There is either an overabundance of food, money, work, etc. or a shortage of it. See 1880 (С), 2229 (Ч)*

Var.: Вдруг густо, вдруг пусто. Сегодня густо, завтра пусто. То густо, то пусто

Cf.: Chickens today, feathers tomorrow (Am.). Either a feast or a fast (Br.). Either too much or too little (Br.). It's either a feast or a famine (Am.). Rich today, poor tomorrow (Am., Br.). Stuff today and starve tomorrow (Br.)

1819. Раз украл, а навек вором стал. *Once you have committed a wrongdoing, your reputation is besmirched for ever. See 547 (Д)*

Cf.: He that has an ill name is half hanged (Br.). He who has a bad name is half hanged (Am.)

1820. Ранний смех—поздние слёзы. *See 1256 (Н)*

Cf.: He who laughs on Friday will weep on Sunday (Br.). Laugh before breakfast, cry before night (sunset, supper) (Am.). Laugh before breakfast, you'll cry before supper (Am., Br.). Laughter before sleep, tears when wakened (Am.). Rejoice today and repent tomorrow (Am.). Sing before breakfast, and you'll cry before supper (Br.). Sing before breakfast, you'll cry before night (supper) (Am.)

1821. Рано пташечка запела, как бы кошечка не съела. *You are happy too prematurely, everything may have a dismal end. See 1321 (Н)*

Cf.: Do not triumph before the victory (Br.). Don't sing your triumph before you have conquered (Am.)

1822. Раньше начнёшь, раньше поспеешь. *The earlier you begin your work, the easier it will be for you to cope with it sooner. See 252 (В), 954 (К)*

Cf.: Early start makes easy stages (Br.). He that would thrive must rise at five (Am.). Sooner begun, sooner done (Br.)

1823. Раньше смерти не умрёшь. *See 1527 (О)*

Cf.: A man can die but once (Am.). A man can only die once (Br.)

1824. Распутья бояться, так в путь не ходить. *See 186 (В)*

Cf.: He that fears every grass must not walk in the meadow (Br.). He that fears leaves must not come into the wood (Am.). He that is afraid of the wagging of feathers, must keep from among wild fowl (Br.). He that will not sail till all dangers are over must not put to sea (Am., Br.). He that would sail without danger must never come on the main sea (Br.)

1825. Расскажи другу—пойдёт по кругу. *See 232 (В)*

Cf.: A secret's a secret until it's told (Am.). A secret shared is no secret (Am., Br.). Two can keep a secret if one is dead (Am.). Two may keep counsel if one be away (if one of them's dead) (Br.)

1826. Рассказывай сказки. *See 1858 (С)*

Cf.: Carry me out and bury me decently (Br.). Don't give me that (Am., Br.). Don't (Never) tell me (Br.). Tell it to Sweeney (Am.). Tell it (that) to the horse-marines (to the marines) (Am., Br.). Tell me (us) another (Am., Br.). Tell that for a tale (Am., Br.)

1827. Редкого гостя милости просят, а частого гостя еле выносят. *If you want to be welcome, do not pay visits too often. See 1131 (М), 2186 (Х), 2232 (Ч)*

Var.: Редкому гостю—двери настежь

Cf.: A constant guest is never welcome (Am., Br.). A constant guest will wear out his visit (Am.). Short visits and seldom are best (Am.)

1828. Реже видишь—больше любишь. *You like people better if you do not see them very often. See 1667 (П)*

Cf.: Absence makes the heart grow fonder (Am., Br.). Absence sharpens love (Am., Br.). Men are best loved furthest off (Br.). Short visits and seldom are best (Am.)

1829. Река начинается с ручейка. *See 2008 (С)*

Cf.: The highest towers begin (rise) from the ground (Am.). Large streams from little fountains flow (Br.). Little streams grow into mighty (make big) rivers (Am.). Little streams make great rivers (Br.). The seeds of great things are often small (Am.)

1830. Ремесло—кормилец. *See 1396 (Н)*

Cf.: He that has a trade has a share everywhere (Am.). He who has an art, has everywhere a part (Br.). Learn a trade and earn a living (Am.). Trade is the mother of money (Br.). Who has a trade has a share everywhere (Br.)

1831. Решетом воду не носят. *There is no point in doing something with improper means, it is sheer waste of time. See 1894 (С)*

Var.: Решетом воду мерять—потерять время

Cf.: You cannot carry water in a sieve (Br.). You cannot draw water with a sieve (Br.). You can't measure water with a sieve (Am.)

1832. Решето сказало кувшину: дырявый! *See 2334 (Ч)*

Cf.: The pot calling (calls) the kettle black (Am., Br.)

1833. Ржа железо ест. *When a man is inactive, he degrades. See 1007 (Л), 2014 (С)*

Cf.: Iron not used soon rusts (Br.). Rust eats up iron (Br.). The rust rots the steel which use preserves (Am.)

1834. Риск—благородное дело. *You can obtain nothing if you do not run the chance of achieving your goal. See 945 (К)*

Cf.: No risk, no gain (Am.). Nothing dared, nothing gained (Am.). Nothing risk, nothing gain (Br.). Nothing stake, nothing draw (Br.). Nothing ventured, nothing gained (Am., Br.). Nothing venture, nothing gain (win) (Am., Br.). Who dares wins (Am.)

1835. Родителей не выбирают. *We have to put up with our parents, whether we like them or not*

Cf.: You may choose your friends; your family is thrust upon you (Am.)

1836. Ростом с Ивана, а умом с болвана. *See 97 (Б)*

Var.: Ростом с тебя, а разумом (умом) с теля

Cf.: Better fed than taught (Br.). A big head and little wit (Br.). Big head and little wit (Am.)

1837. Рубашка бела, да душа черна. *See 1859 (С)*

Cf.: A clean glove often hides a dirty hand (Am.). A fair face may hide a foul heart (Am., Br.). Fair without, foul within (Br.)

1838. Руби дерево по себе. *a) Do not take on yourself a task that you are unable to do. See 60 (Б); b) Do not marry your superior. See 80 (Б), 308 (В)*

Cf.: a) Don't bite off more than you can chew (Am., Br.). A man must not swallow more than he can digest (Am.). Undertake no more than you can perform (Am., Br.)

b) Everyone to his equal (Am.). Keep to your own kind (Am.). Marry above your match and you get a master (Am.). Marry a wife of thine own degree (Br.). Marry your equal (your like, your match) (Br.)

1839. Рукам работа—душе праздник. *The satisfaction you get when doing some work gives you a feeling of delight. See 337 (Г)*

Cf.: Busy hands are happy hands (Am.). Employment is enjoyment (Br.). It is neither wealth nor splendor, but tranquility and occupation, which give happiness (Am.). Labor is the law of happiness (makes life sweet) (Am.). Man was never so happy as when he was doing something (Am.). Work makes life pleasant (Am.)

1840. Рука руку моет, вор вора кроет. *Law-breakers and cheats protect one another. See 196 (В)*

Cf.: One hand claws (washes) another (Br.). One hand washes the other (Am.). There is honor /even/ among thieves (Am.). There is honour among thieves (Br.)

1841. Руки согрешили, а спина виновата. *One man is guilty, but quite a different person is blamed. See 65 (Б), 1392 (Н)*

Var.: Руки согрешат, а голова в ответе

Cf.: The dog bites the stone, not him that throws it (Am.). One does the scathe, and another has the scorn (Br.). The tongue offends and the ears get the cuffing (Am.)

1842. Рыбак рыбака видит издалека. *People of similar intellect and interests find one another and come to mutual understanding. See 1113 (М), 1672 (П)*

Var.: Дурак дурака видит издалека. Свояк свояка видит издалека

Cf.: Birds of a color flock together (Am.). Birds of a feather flock together (Am., Br.). Each kind attracts its own (Am.). It takes a fool to know a fool (Am.). It takes one to know one (Am.). Like attracts (will to) like (Am., Br.). Like calls to (draws to, knows, likes, seeks, sees) like (Br.). One after kind (Am., Br.). They that know one another salute afar off (Br.). A thief knows a thief, as a wolf knows a wolf (Am., Br.). Water finds its own level (Am., Br.). Water seeks its /own/ level (Am.)

1843. Рыба мелка, да уха сладка. *See 1099 (М)*

Cf.: An inch is as good as an ell

(Br.). Little bodies have great souls (Am.). Little fish are sweet (Br.). Little fish is sweet (Am.)

1844. Рыба с головы гниёт. *Decay of a community, government, office, etc. begins with those who are at the head of it*

Var.: Рыба с головы воняет (тухнет)

Cf.: The fish always stinks from the head downward (Br.). Fish begins to stink at the head (Am., Br.). The fish stinks first in the head (Am.)

1845. Рыбка золотая, да внутри гнилая. *See 1859 (С)*

Cf.: Fair without and false within (Br.). Fair without, foul within (Am.). Many a rosy apple is rotten to the core (Am.)

С

1846. Сама испекла пирожок, сама и кушай. *See 1848 (С)*

Cf.: You buttered your bread; now eat it (Am.). You made the broth, now sup it (Br.). You made your bed, now lie in it (Am., Br.)

1847. Самая большая трата—трата времени. *Time should not be wasted because it is irrevocable. See 445 (Д), 1746 (П)*

Cf.: Expense of time is the most costly of all expenses (Br.). The greatest expense we can be at is that of our time (Am.). Kill time and time will kill you (Am.). What greater crime than the loss of time? (Am., Br.)

1848. Сам кашу заварил, сам и расхлёбывай. *You have started all this trouble, you have made a mess of things, now you must bear the consequences. See 1846 (С)*

Cf.: He that feathers his nest must sleep in it (Am.). If you cook your own goose, you will have to eat it (Am.). Who breaks, pays (Br.). You made the broth, now sup it (Br.). You made your bed, now lie in it (Am., Br.)

1849. Сам поёт, сам слушает, сам и хвалит. *Conceited people are of great opinion of what they do. See 395 (Г)*

Cf.: Every ass likes to hear himself bray (Br.). Every ass loves to hear himself bray (Am.). /There is/ nothing like leather (Br.)

1850. Сам себя губит, кто гуляночки любит. *Frequent feasts ruin your health*

Cf.: Diseases are the interest of (the tax on) pleasures (Am.). Diseases are the interests of pleasure (Br.). Diseases are the price of ill pleasures (Br.)

1851. Сам чёрт не разберёт. *The problem or the situation is too complex to understand or to solve it*

Var.: Сам чёрт ногу сломает

Cf.: The deuce (devil and all, hell) to pay (Br.). Here is the devil to pay, and no pitch hot (Br.). Here's a fine (pretty) kettle of fish (Am., Br.). /It is/ enough to puzzle a Philadelphia lawyer (Br.). You can't get there from here (Am.)

1852. Сапог лаптю не брат. *See 402 (Г)*

Cf.: Everyone to his equal (Am.). Every sheep with its like (Am.). Geese with geese, and women with women (Br.). Tigers and deer do not stroll together (Am.)

1853. Сапог с сапогом, лапоть с лаптем. *See 308 (В), 1295 b (Н)*

Cf.: Everyone to his equal (Am.). Every sheep with its like (Am.). Geese with geese, and women with women (Br.). Keep to your own kind (Am.)

1854. Сапожки со скрипом, а каша без масла. *See 1178 (Н)*

Var.: Сапог-то скрипит, да в горшке не кипит

Cf.: Great boast, small roast (Am., Br.)

1855. Сапожник ходит без сапог. *A craftsman who does some kind of work for other people is short of time to do it for his family or himself. See 2136 (У), 2330 (Ч), 2331 (Ч)*

Var.: Портной без кафтана (порток), сапожник без сапог

Cf.: The blacksmith's horse and the shoemaker's family always go unshod (Am.). A cobbler's child is always the worst shod (Am.). The cobbler's children usually go unshod (Br.). The cobbler's wife is the worst shod (Br.). The door of the carpenter is loose (Am.). He who makes shoes goes barefoot (Am.). None more bare than the shoemaker's wife and the smith's mare (Br.). The shoemaker's child goes barefoot (Am.). The shoemaker's son always goes barefoot (Br.). The shoemaker's wife is the worst shod (Br.). The tailor's wife is the worst clad (Br.). The tailor's wife is worse (worst) clad (Am.)

1856. Сбережёшь—что найдёшь. *If you keep laying up some money, you will never be in want of it. See 638 (З), 2065 (Т)*

Cf.: A dollar saved is a dollar earned (Am.). Money saved is money earned (got) (Am.). Of saving comes having (Br.). A penny saved is a penny earned (Am., Br.). A penny saved is a penny gained (Br.). A penny saved is a penny made (Am.). Sparing is the first gaining (Br.)

1857. Свадьба скорая—что вода полая. *See 588 (Ж)*

Cf.: Marry in haste and repent at leisure (Am., Br.)

1858. Свежо предание, да верится с трудом. *Do not expect me to believe what you are telling. See 1826 (Р)*

Cf.: Carry me out and bury me decently (Br.). Come home with your knickers torn and say you found a shilling (the money)? (Br.). Don't give me that (Am., Br.). Tell it to Sweeney (Am.). Tell it to the horse-marines (to the marines) (Am., Br.). Tell me (us) another (Am., Br.). Tell that to the marines, the sailors won't believe it (Br.)

1859. Сверху мило, снизу гнило. *Meanness and dishonesty are often hidden beneath a pleasant appearance. See 341 (Г), 694 (И), 1027 (Л), 1181 (Н), 1301 (Н), 1415 (Н), 1837 (Р), 1845 (Р), 1926 (С)*

Var.: Сверху ясно, снизу грязно

Cf.: An angel on top but a devil underneath (Am.). Beauty may have fair leaves, but (yet) bitter fruit (Br.). A clean glove often hides a dirty hand (Am.). A fair face, a false heart (Br.). A fair face may hide a foul heart (Am., Br.). Fair without and false within (Br.). Foppish dressing tells the world the outside is the best of the puppet (Br.). Many a rosy apple is rotten to the core (Am.). The reddest apple may have a worm in it (Am.). There is many a fair thing full false (Br.)

1860. Свет не клином сошёлся. *Do not despair, you will find another opportunity, job or person equally good or even better. See 699 (И), 1010 (Л), 1136 (М), 1439 (Н), 1440 (Н)*

Var.: Белый свет не клином сошёлся (стал). Земля не клином сошлась

Cf.: The sea is full of other fish (Am.). There are as good fish in the sea as ever came out of it (Am., Br.). There are better fish in the sea than have ever been caught (Am.). There are more pebbles on the beach (Br.). There are plenty of pebbles on the shore (Br.). There is always the next train coming (Am.). There is more than one grain of sand on the seashore (Am.)

1861. Свои собаки грызутся, чужая не суйся. *Stay away when friends or relatives quarrel, they will make it up but you will suffer for it. See 1164 (М)*

Var.: Свои собаки дерутся, чужая не мешайся (не приставай). Свой со своим бранись, а чужой не вяжись

Cf.: Never interfere with family quarrels (Am.). Put not your finger (hand) between the bark and the tree (Br.)

1862. Свои сухари лучше чужих пирогов. *To have something of one's own, be it not the best, is preferable to being obliged to other people for a better thing. See 499 (Д), 500 (Д)*

Var.: Лучше свой кусок чем чужой пирог. Свой хлеб слаще чужого калача. Свой хлеб сытнее

Cf.: Better is a slice of bread and garlic eaten at one's own table than a thousand dishes eaten under another's roof (Am.). Dry bread at home is better than roast meat abroad (Am., Br.). I had rather ask of my fire brown bread than borrow of my neighbour white (Br.). A poor thing, but mine (my own) (Br.)

1863. Свой глаз—алмаз. *See 1614 (О)*

Var.: Свой глаз—алмаз, а чужой—стекло

Cf.: No eye like the eye of the master (Br.). No eye like the master's eye (Am.)

1864. Свой обычай в чужой дом не носи. *See 297 (В)*

Cf.: Follow the customs, or fly the country (Br.). When in Rome, do as the Romans /do/ (Am., Br.). When you are at Rome, do as Rome does (Am.)

1865. Свой своему поневоле брат. *See 896 (К)*

Var.: Свой своему поневоле друг

Cf.: Blood is thicker than water (Am., Br.). One ass (horse, mule) scrubs another (Br.)

1866. С волками жить, по-волчьи выть. *You have to adapt yourself to people you are with and to behave the way they do whether you like it or not. See 297 (В), 834 (К), 1710 (П)*

Cf.: He who kennels with wolves must howl (Br.). When you are with wolves, you must howl with them (Am.). With foxes one must play the fox (Br.)

1867. Своя ноша не тянет. *What you do for yourself and at your own will is not difficult or troublesome. See 1721 (П)*

Var.: Своя ноша не тяжела

Cf.: A burden of one's choice is not felt (Br.). The burden of one's own choice is not felt (Am.). The burden one likes is cheerfully borne (Br.). A burden which one chooses is not felt (Am.). A chosen burden is not felt (Am.). The ox is never weary of carrying its horns (Am.). A voluntary burden is no burden (Am.). A willing burden is no burden (Br.)

1868. Своя рубашка ближе к телу. *In the first place one takes care of himself and his own family. See 265 (В), 903 (К)*

Cf.: Charity begins at home (Am., Br.). Close sits my shirt, but closer my skin (Am., Br.). Every one rakes the fire under his own pot (Br.). The laundress washes her own smock first (Am.). Mind other men, but most yourself (Br.). Near is my coat, but nearer is my shirt (Br.). Number one is the first house in the row (Br.). Self comes first (Br.). Self loves itself best (Am., Br.). The shirt is nearer than the coat (Am.)

1869. Своя рука—владыка. *One acts only at his own will because one has power in his hands. See 829 (К), 2214 (Х)*

Cf.: As I will so I command (Br.). I do as I please (Am.)

1870. Свято место пусто не бывает. *A position will not stay vacant, there is always someone to take it. See 1342 (Н), 1775 (П)*

Cf.: Nature abhors a vacuum (Am., Br.). A vacuum is always filled (Am.)

1871. С глаз долой—из сердца вон. *Separation does not contribute to friendship or love. See 344 (Г), 1816 (Р)*

Cf.: Distance ends enchantment (Am.). Far from eye, far from heart (Br.). The heart soon forgets what the eye sees not (Am.). Long absent, soon forgotten (Am., Br.). Out of sight, out of mind (Am., Br.). Salt water and absence wash away love (Br.). Seldom seen, soon forgotten (Am., Br.). What the eye doesn't see the heart doesn't crave for (Br.)

1872. Сделанного не воротишь. *What has already been done cannot be changed. See 897 (K)*

Var.: Что сделано, того не переделаешь (то сделано)

Cf.: A bell, once rung, cannot be rerung (Am.). Once milk becomes sour, it can't be made sweet again (Am.). Things done cannot be undone (Am.). What is done cannot be undone (is done) (Am., Br.). You can't unscramble eggs (Am.)

1873. С деньгами мил, без денег постыл. *A happy relationship is often ruined when people get broke. See 1495 (H), 2223 (X)*

Cf.: Love in a hut with water and crust is cinders, ashes, dust (Br.). Love lasts as long as money endures (Am., Br.). Poverty breeds strife (Br.). Want makes strife (Br.). Want makes strife between man and wife (Am.). When money flies out the window, love flies out the door (Am.). When poverty comes in at the door, love flies out of the window (Br.). When poverty comes in the door, love flies out the window (Am.). When the wolf comes in at the door, love creeps out of the window (Am., Br.). When want comes in at the door, love flies out of the window (Am.)

1874. С доброй женой и горе—полгоря, а радость—вдвое. *A devoted wife is a comfort to her husband both in good and bad times*

Cf.: To him who has a good wife no evil can come which he cannot bear (Br.)

1875. С дураками не шутят. *It is not worth bantering a stupid man as humo(u)r is beyond his comprehension, and he may get angry*

Var.: С дураками шутить опасно

Cf.: Jest with an ass and he will flap you in the face with his tail (Br.). Jest with an ass and he will slap you in the face with his tail (Am.). Never joke with a fool (Am.)

1876. Себя жалеючи, кверху не плюй. *Do not raise your hand against those in power because you will be the worse for it*

Var.: Выше носа плюнешь—себя заплюёшь. Кверху плевать—свою бороду заплевать

Cf.: An arrow shot upright falls on the shooter's head (Am., Br.). Hew not too high, lest the chips fall in thine eye (Br.). The man who flings a stone up a mountain may have it rolled back upon himself (Am.). Who spits against the heaven (the wind), it falls in his face (Br.). Who spits against the wind spits in his own face (Am.)

1877. Себя не переделаешь. *You cannot change your character when it is already shaped. See 643 (З)*

Cf.: Once a crook, always a crook (Am.). Once a priest, always a priest (Am., Br.). Once a thief, always a thief (Am., Br.). You cannot change your skin (Br.)

1878. Сегодня здесь, а завтра там. *The person does not stay long in one and the same place*

Cf.: Here today and gone tomorrow (Am., Br.). Here today, gone tomorrow (Am., Br.)

1879. Сегодня пан, а завтра пропал. *Luck is so unstable that one day we can be at the top and the next day at the bottom. See 206 (B), 603 (Ж), 2056 (T)*

Var.: Сегодня в цветах, а завтра в слезах. Сегодня в чести, а завтра свиней пасти

Cf.: Fortune is changeable (Br.).

Fortune is fickle (Am.). Fortune is variant (Am., Br.). Life is a varied career (Br.). Life is subject to ups and downs (Am.). One abides not long on the summit of fortune (Br.). Rich today, poor tomorrow (Am., Br.). Today a man, tomorrow a mouse (none) (Br.). We all have our ups and downs (Br.). The wheel of fortune is forever in motion (Am.)

1880. Сегодня пир горой, а завтра пошёл с сумой. *He who squanders money will soon have none. See 1643 (П), 1818 (Р)*

Cf.: Chickens today, feathers tomorrow (Am.). Cookie today, crumb tomorrow (Am.). Fasting comes after feasting (Br.). Feast today, and fast tomorrow (Br.). Feast today, fast tomorrow (Am.). Feast today makes fast tomorrow (Am.). Who dainties love shall beggars prove (Br.)

1881. Седина в голову, а бес в ребро. *He is an elderly man but started a love affair at his age. (This is said ironically.)*

Cf.: Grey hairs are nourished with green thoughts (Br.). /There is/ no fool like an old fool (Am., Br.). /There is/ no fool to the old fool (Br.)

1882. Семеро капралов, да один рядовой. *There are many bosses but few workers to do the work*

Cf.: All chiefs and no Indians (Am.). Too many generals and no privates (Br.)

1883. Семеро одного не ждут. *There are many of us, we cannot wait or do not want to wait for one man who has not come and we will do what we are planning to without him*

Cf.: A dollar waiting on a dime (Am.). For one man that is missing there's no spoiling the wedding (Am.)

1884. Семь бед—один ответ. *As we have to bear punishment all the same, let us take this risky step too. See 323 (Г)*

Cf.: As good be hanged for a sheep as a goat (Am.). As good (well) be hanged (hung) for a sheep as /for/ a lamb (Br.). As well for the cow calf as for the bull (Br.). Might as well be hanged for a sheep as a lamb (Am.). Over shoes, over boots (Br.)

1885. Семь вёрст до небес и все лесом. *This is long and senseless talking. See 1139 (М)*

Cf.: Big talking, but little saying (Am., Br.)

1886. Семь дел в одни руки не берут. *If you start doing many things at the same time, you will spoil some or not accomplish any. See 617 (З)*

Cf.: Don't have too many irons in the fire (Am., Br.). He who begins many things finishes but few (Am.). He who undertakes too much seldom succeeds (Br.). If you have too many irons in the fire, some of them will burn (Am.). Who undertakes too much seldom succeeds (Am.)

1887. Семь раз отмерь, один раз отрежь. *Think well before you take a decision, do not act rashly. See 1742 (П), 1977 (С)*

Var.: Семь раз примерь, один раз отрежь

Cf.: Better twice measured than once wrong (Am.). Measure three times before you cut once (Br.). Measure thrice and cut once (Br.). Measure twice before you cut once (Am.). Measure your cloth ten times; you can cut it but once (Am., Br.). Score twice before you cut once (Br.). Second thoughts are best (Am., Br.). Think—then act (Am.). Think twice before you act (Am.)

1888. Сердце не лукошко, не прорежешь окошко. *See 2319 (Ч)*

Var.: Сердце не лукошко, не прошибёшь окошко

Cf.: The human heart is a mystery (Br.). You can look in the eyes but not in the heart (Am.)

1889. Сердце сердцу весть подаёт. *People in love do not need words to let one another know about their mutual feelings*

Cf.: What comes from the heart goes to the heart (Am., Br.)

1890. Сердцу любить не прикажешь. *See 1241 (Н)*

Cf.: Kissing goes by favour (Br.). Love can neither be bought nor sold; its only price is love (Am.). Love cannot be compelled (forced, ordered) (Br.)

1891. Серенькое утро—красненький денёк. *See 1725 (П)*

Cf.: Cloudy mornings may turn to clear evenings (Am.). Cloudy mornings turn to clear afternoons (evenings) (Am., Br.). Fair weather after foul (Br.). A foul morning may turn to a fair day (Br.). A foul morn turns into a fine day (Am.). A misty morn may have a fine day (Am.)

1892. Серого помянёшь, а серый здесь. *See 1513 (О)*

Cf.: Speak of the devil (Am., Br.). Speak of the devil and he is sure to appear (Br.). Speak of the devil and he'll appear (Am., Br.). Speak of the devil and in he walks (Am.)

1893. Сильному и мешок на плечи. *See 99 (Б)*

Cf.: Big ships require deep waters (Am.). The great man makes the great thing (Am.). A great ship asks (requires) deep waters (Br.). A great ship asks for deeper water (Am.)

1894. Ситом моря не черпают. *See 1831 (Р)*

Cf.: You cannot carry water in a sieve (draw water with a sieve) (Br.). You can't measure water with a sieve (Am.)

1895. Скажешь с уха на ухо, а узнают с угла на угол. *See 232 (В)*

Cf.: A secret's a secret until it's told (Am.). A secret shared is no secret (Am., Br.). Two can keep a secret if one is dead (Am.). Two may keep counsel if one be away (if one of them's dead) (Br.)

1896. Скажи мне, кто твой друг, и я скажу, кто ты. *You can judge of a man by his friends. See 1748 (П), 1903 (С)*

Var.: Скажи мне, с кем ты дружен, и я скажу, кто ты

Cf.: A man is known by his friends (by the company he keeps) (Am.). Man is known by the company he keeps (Br.). Show me your company, and I'll tell you who you are (Am.). Tell me whom you live with, and I will tell you who you are (Br.). Tell me with whom you go, and I'll tell you what you are (Am.)

1897. Сказала Настя, как удастся. *See 18 (Б)*

Cf.: There is many a slip twixt /the/ cup and /the/ lip (Am.). /There's/ many a slip between ('twixt) the cup and the lip (Br.)

1898. Сказал бы словечко, да волк недалечко. *See 2153 (У)*

Cf.: The wall has ears and the plain has eyes (Am.). Walls have ears (Am., Br.)

1899. Сказанное слово—серебряное, а несказанное—золотое. *See 1933 (С)*

Cf.: Silence is golden (Am., Br.). Speaking is silver; silence is golden (Am.). Speech is silvern, /but/ silence is golden (Br.). Speech is silver, /but/ silence is gold (Br.). Speech is silver; silence is golden (Am.)

1900. Сказано—сделано. *A promise to do something is kept, or an order is fulfilled without delay*

Cf.: No sooner said than done (Am. Br.). So said, so done (Br.)

1901. Скатерть со стола, и дружба сплыла. *While you have money and are generously treating people, they are* *on friendly relations with you; but once you cannot afford it, they break with you. See 204 (В), 572 (Е), 1215 (Н), 1645 (П), 2176 (Х)*

Cf.: As long as the pot boils, friendship lasts (Am., Br.). The bread eaten, the company dispersed (Br.). The dinner over, away go the guests (Am.). Feasting makes no friendship (Br.). Having finished the meal, the company leaves (Am.). In time of prosperity, friends will be plenty; in time of adversity, not one amongst twenty (Br.). In time of prosperity, friends will be plenty; in time of adversity, no one in twenty (Am.). When fortune frowns, friends are few (Am.)

1902. Скатертью дорога. *Go away and do not come back. See 201 (В)*

Cf.: Beat it! (Am.). Don't let us keep you (Br.). Here lies your way (Br.). If we never see you again, it'll be too soon (Br.). Never darken my door again (Am.). There's the door, use it (Am.)

1903. С кем живёшь, тем и слывёшь. *See 1896 (С)*

Cf.: A man is known by the company he keeps (Am.). Man is known by the company he keeps (Br.). Tell me whom you live with, and I will tell you who you are (Br.). Tell me with whom you live, and I will tell you who you are (Am.)

1904. С кем поведёшься, от того и наберёшься. *Close intercourse with people makes you behave and think like they do. See 551 (Д), 1905 (С), 1989 (С)*

Cf.: Associate with cripples and you learn to limp (Am.). Enter the mill and you come out floury (Am.). Evil communications corrupt good manners (Am., Br.). He that dwells next door to a cripple will learn to halt (Br.). He that lives with wolves will learn to howl (Br.). Live with the lame and you will limp (Am.). Who keeps company with a wolf learns to howl (Am.)

1905. С кем хлеб-соль водишь, на того и походишь. *See 1904 (С)*

Cf.: Associate with cripples and you learn to limp (Am.). He that lives with cripples learns /how/ to limp (Br.). Live with the lame and you will limp (Am.)

1906. Склеенная—не посуда. *See 1718 (П)*

Cf.: A cracked bell can never sound well (Am., Br.). A cracked bell is never sound (Br.)

1907. Сколько верёвочке ни виться, а конец будет. *Criminal acts are discovered in the end, and the guilty are punished. See 122 (Б), 780 (К), 1659 (П), 2037 (Т)*

Cf.: All thieves come to some bad end (Am.). Crime doesn't pay (Am.). The end of the thief is the gallows (Am.). He who steals will always fail (Am.). The jug goes to the well until it breaks (Am.). The pitcher goes often to the well /but is broken at last/ (Br.). A pitcher that goes to the well too often is broken at last (Am.). The pitcher went once too often to the well (Am., Br.). A pot oft sent to the well is broken at last (Br.)

1908. Сколько голов, столько и умов. *Every person thinks in his own way which is different from that of other people. See 2123 (У)*

Var.: Сколько людей, столько и мнений. Сто голов, сто умов

Cf.: As many men, so many opinions (Am.). Everybody to his own opinion (Br.). Every man to his own opinion (Am.). Opinions differ (Br.). So many heads, so many wits (Am., Br.). So many men, so many minds (Br.)

1909. Сколько лет, сколько зим! *I am so glad to meet you after such a long time has passed!*

Cf.: I haven't seen you for ages (Am., Br.). I haven't seen you in a month of Sundays (Am.). Long time no see (Am.)

1910. Сколько стран, столько и обычаев. *See 2300 (Ч)*

Cf.: Every country has its /own/ custom (customs) (Am., Br.). So many countries, so many customs (Am., Br.)

1911. Скоро—не споро. *See 1741 (П)*

Var.: Что скоро, то и не споро (то хворо)

Cf.: Good and quickly seldom meet (Am., Br.). The greater hurry, the worse the speed (Am.). Haste makes waste (Am., Br.). Quick and well-done do not agree (Br.). Things will never be bettered by an excess of haste (Br.)

1912. Скоро поедешь, не скоро доедешь. *Excessive haste is often the cause of delay. See 1741 (П)*

Cf.: Always in a hurry, always behind (Am.). /Fool's/ haste is no speed (Br.). The greater hurry, the worse the speed (Am.). Haste is slow (Am.). More haste, less (worse) speed (Am., Br.)

1913. Скоро сказка сказывается, да не скоро дело делается. *It is much easier to suggest some course of action than to carry it out. See 997 (Л), 1470 (Н), 1540 (О)*

Var.: Легко сказка сказывается, да нелегко дело делается

Cf.: Easier said than done (Am., Br.). Easy to say and hard to do (Br.). Saying and doing are two different things (Am.). Saying and doing are two things (Am., Br.). Sooner said than done (Am.). There is a difference between saying and doing (Br.)

1914. Скороспелка до поры загнивает. *What is done in a hurry is not durable enough. See 1741 (П)*

Cf.: Early ripe, early rotten (Am.). Quick ripe, quick rotten (Am.). Soon ripe, soon rotten (Br.)

1915. Скрипучее дерево стоит, а здоровое летит. *People complaining of bad health often outlive those who look strong. See 66 (Б)*

Var.: Скрипучая берёза дольше стоит. Скрипучее дерево два века живёт

Cf.: A creaking cart goes long on its wheels (Br.). A creaking door hangs long on its hinges (Am., Br.). A creaking gate hangs a long time (hangs long) (Br.). A creaking gate lasts long (swings a long time) (Am.). Creaking wagons are long in passing (Br.). The ill stake stands long (longest) (Br.). An ill stake stands the longest (Am.). The loose stake stands longest (Br.). Near dead never filled the kirkyard (Am.). The sickest is not the nearest the grave (Am.). A squeaking gate hangs the longest (Am.). A squeaking hinge lasts the longest (Am.)

1916. Скупой богач беднее нищего. *Rich but miserly people grudge themselves everything. See 162 (В), 2342 (Ш)*

Cf.: The ass loaded with gold still eats thistles (Br.). Even if the ass is laden with gold, he will seek his food among the thorns (Am.). He that hoardes up money pains for other men (Br.). Moles and misers live in their graves (Br.). A rich miser is poorer than a poor man (Am.)

1917. Славны бубны за горами. *That which is elsewhere and which we are only told about seems better and attractive. See 69 (Б), 2036 (Т)*

Var.: Звонки бубны за горами

Cf.: Blue are the hills that are far from us (Br.). Distance lends enchantment to the view (Am., Br.). Distant pastures are greener (Br.). Faraway birds have fine feathers (Am.). Faraway cows have (wear) long horns (Am.). Faraway fowls have fair feathers (Br.). Far folk fare best (Br.). Far hills look the bluest (Am.). Far-off cows have long horns (Br.). Hills are green far away (Br.). Hills look green far away (Am.)

1918. Сладко в рот, да горько в глот. *See 1075 (Л)*

Cf.: Honey is sweet, but bees sting (Am.). Honey is sweet, but the bee stings (Br.). No pleasure without repentance (Am.). Pleasure has a sting in its tail (Br.). What is sweet in the mouth is oft bitter in the stomach (Br.)

1919. Сладок мёд, да не по пуду в рот. *See 2187 (X)*

Cf.: Abundance of things engenders disdainfulness (Br.). Eat your honey, but stop when you are full (Am.). Even too much honey nothing else than gall (Br.). If in excess even nectar is poison (Br.). Nothing in excess is best (Am.). Too much honey cloys the stomach (Br.). Too much of a good thing (Am., Br.). Too much of a good thing is worse than none at all (Am.). Too much pudding chokes the dog (Br.)

1920. Слезами горю не поможешь. *a) It is no use indulging in sorrow that cannot be helped. See 2302 (Ч); b) Tears and complaints are of no help, to find a way out you must act, not cry. See 1157 (M)*

Var.: В слезах горя не утопишь. Плачем горю не поможешь

Cf.: a) Don't cry over spilled milk (Am.). Don't grieve over spilt milk (Am.). Never grieve for what you cannot help (Br.). No weeping for shed milk (Am., Br.). Tears bring nobody back from the grave (Am.). There is no use crying over spilt milk (Br.). What's gone and what's past help should be past grief (Am.)

b) Action is worry's worst enemy (Am.). Crying will not mend matters (Br.). A good relief for grief is action (Am.). The only cure for grief is action (Am.). Sorrow will pay no debts (Br.)

1921. Слепой курице всё пшеница. *Incompetent men cannot distinguish good from bad and right from wrong. See 1348 (H), 1924 (C)*

Cf.: A blind man can judge no (is no judge of) colors (Am.). Blind men can judge no colours (Br.). A pebble and a diamond are alike to a blind man (Am.). To the color-blind, all colors are alike (Am.)

1922. Слепой сказал: "Посмотрим". *We will see if it will be as you say, I doubt your prediction. See 18 (Б)*

Var.: "Посмотрим",—сказал слепой /, "как будет плясать хромой"/

Cf.: A blind man would be glad to see (Br.). Let me see, as a blind man said (Br.). We'll wait and see (Am.)

1923. Слепой слепого водит, а оба ни зги не видят. *When people with no adequate knowledge try to direct other ignorant men, the result is ruinous*

Var.: Слепой слепого далеко не уведёт. Слепой слепому не указчик

Cf.: If the blind lead the blind, both shall fall into the ditch (Am., Br.). When the blind lead the blind, they all go head over heels into the ditch (Am.)

1924. Слепому и свет темнота. *Even exceptional things seem ordinary to an ignorant person. See 1921 (C)*

Cf.: He is very blind who does not see the sun (Br.). A pebble and a diamond are alike to a blind man (Am.)

1925. С лица не воду пить. *A beautiful appearance of a person is not so significant as the innermost goodness. See 884 (K), 1356 (H)*

Var.: Не с лица воду пить /, можно с некрасивой жить/

Cf.: Beauty dies and fades away but ugly holds its own (Br.). Beauty is a fading flower (Am.). Beauty is only skin deep (Am., Br.). Beauty is only skin-deep; goodness goes to the bone (Am.). Beauty lasts only a day; ugly holds its own (Am.). Looks are not enough (Br.). Looks are not everything (Am.). Prettiness dies first (Br.). Prettiness dies quickly (Am.)

1926. С личика—яичко, а внутри—болтун. *See 1859 (C)*

Cf.: A fair face may hide a foul heart (Am., Br.). Fair thing full false (Br.).

Fair without and foul within (Br.). Fair without, false within (Am.)

1927. Слово бело, да дело черно. *See 1170 (М)*

Cf.: Fine words dress ill deeds (Br.). Too much courtesy, too much craft (Am.)

1928. Слово делом красно. *See 1503 (Н)*

Cf.: Beauty is as beauty does (Am.). Handsome is as handsome does (Am., Br.). It is not words that count but deeds (Br.). Pretty is as pretty does (Am.). Well is that well does (Br.)

1929. Словом человека не убьёшь. *See 103 (Б)*

Cf.: Hard words break no bones (Am., Br.). Sticks and stones may break my bones, but names will never hurt me (Am., Br.)

1930. Слово не воробей, вылетит—не поймаешь. *Once we have said something, we cannot get it back. See 303 (В), 865 (К), 1063 (Л), 1969 (С), 2296 (Ч)*

Cf.: Spoken words are like flown birds: neither can be recalled (Am.). A thing that is said is said, and forth it goes (Br.). Time and words can never be recalled (Am.). What is said can never be resaid (Am.). When the word is out it belongs to another (Br.). Words have wings and cannot be recalled (Br.). Words once spoken you can never recall (Am.). A word spoken is an arrow let fly (Br.)

1931. Слово не обух—в лоб не бьёт. *See 103 (Б)*

Cf.: Hard words break no bones (Am., Br.). Sticks and stones may break my bones, names will never hurt me (Am., Br.)

1932. Слово не стрела, а пуще стрелы разит. *Insulting words and unjust accusations inflict grave sufferings on people. See 582 (Ж), 667 (З), 669 (З), 1380 (Н), 1574 (О), 1575 (О), 1629 (П), 1802 (П)*

Cf.: The boneless tongue, so small and weak, can crush and kill (Am.). An evil tongue may do much (Br.). The hard words cut the heart (Am.). Man's tongue is soft and bone does lack, yet a stroke therewith may break a man's back (Am.). No sword bites so bitterly as an evil tongue (Am.). The tongue breaks the bone, and herself has none (Am., Br.). The tongue is more venomous than a serpent (Br.). The tongue is not steel, but (yet) it cuts (Am., Br.). The tongue is sharper than the sword (Am.). The tongue stings (Am., Br.). A word hurts more than a wound (Am.). Words cut (hurt) more than swords (Br.)

1933. Слово—серебро, молчание—золото. *To know what to say is good, but to know when to be silent is much more valuable. See 905 (К), 1899 (С)*

Var.: Молчание—золото

Cf.: Silence is a rare jewel (Am.). Silence is golden (Am., Br.). Silence is the best policy (Am.). Speaking is silver; silence is golden (Am.). Speech is silver, /but/ silence is gold (Br.). Speech is silvern, /but/ silence is golden (Br.). Speech is silver; silence is golden (Am.). Words are silver and silence is gold (Am.)

1934. Слухом земля полнится. *Someone told it to me, and I am reluctant to mention the name of the person. See 1972 (С)*

Cf.: A little bird told me (Am., Br.). A little bird whispered to me (Br.). My little finger told me (Br.). News flies fast (Am.). News flies quickly (Br.). There is a rumour abroad (in the wind) (Br.)

1935. Слушай ухом, а не брюхом. *You have to listen attentively to what is being told. See 354 (Г)*

Cf.: Open your ears (Am., Br.). Unplug your ears (Am.). Wake up and smell the coffee (Am.)

1936. Слышно было, как муха пролетит. *There wa dead silence*

Cf.: Not a breath was heard (Br.). You could have heard (could hear) a pin drop (Am.)

1937. Смелость города берёт. *People who act courageously deserve and get good luck. See 326 (Г), 966 (К), 1411 (Н), 1578 (О)*

Cf.: A bold heart is half the battle (Br.). Cheek brings success (Br.). Courage wins (Br.). Faint heart never won fair lady (Am., Br.). Fortune favo(u)rs the bold (the brave) (Am., Br.). Fortune is on the side of the bold (Am.). None but the brave deserves the fair (Am., Br.). Success is the child of audacity (Am.). To a valiant heart nothing is impossible (Br.)

1938. Смерть не разбирает чина. *All men must die, be they great or insignificant, rich or poor, good or bad. See 240 (В). 2149 (У)*

Cf.: Death and the grave make no distinction of persons (Am.). Death combs us all with the same comb (Br.). Death devours lambs as well as sheep (Am., Br.). Death is no respecter of persons (Am.). Graves are of all sizes (Br.). Kings and queens must die as well as you and I (Am.). A piece of churchyard fits everybody (Am., Br.)

1939. Смерть не спросит, придёт да скосит. *Not a single man knows when his death hour will come, but when it does, one must die. See 1607 (О)*

Cf.: Death does not blow a trumpet (Br.). Death has (keeps) no calendar (Am.). Death observes no ceremony (Am.). Death waits for no one (Am.). Death when it comes will have no denial (Br.). God comes to see us without a bell (Br.). There is nothing so certain as death and nothing so uncertain as the hour of death (Br.). There is no way of knowing when death will come; it just does (Am.)

1940. Смерть платит все долги. *When a man dies, all his obligations are wiped out. See 1735 (П)*

Cf.: Death pays all debts (Am., Br.). Death quits all scores (squares all accounts) (Br.). He that dies pays all debts (Am., Br.)

1941. Смех без причины—признак дурачины. *Stupid people laugh immoderately and without any reason. See 545 (Д)*

Cf.: A fool is known by his laughing (Br.). It's a trifle that makes fools laugh (Am.). Laugh and /you/ show your ignorance (Am.). Laughter is the hiccup of a fool (Am.). The louder the laugh, the more empty the head (Am.). A loud laugh bespeaks the vacant mind (Am.). Too much laughter discovers folly (Br.)

1942. С милым рай и в шалаше. *A man and a woman in love are happy though they may live in a poor dwelling*

Cf.: Love can make any place agreeable (Am.). Love converts a cottage into a palace of gold (Br.). Love lives in cottages as well as in courts (Am.). Love makes a cottage a castle (Br.)

1943. Смирение паче гордости. *Submission, in certain circumstances, means more than demonstration of pride*

Cf.: Pride apes humility (Br.). Pride often apes (borrows the cloak of) humility (Am.)

1944. Смирного волка и телята лижут. *See 899 (К)*

Cf.: He that makes himself a sheep shall be eaten by the wolves (Am.). He that maketh himself a sheep shall be eaten by the wolf (Br.)

1945. Смирную собаку и кочет побьёт. *See 899 (К)*

Var.: Смирную собаку и ястреб бьёт

Cf.: Don't make yourself a mouse, or the cat will eat you (Br.). Make yourself a sheep and the wolves will eat you (Am.)

1946. С миром и беда не убыток. *See 1209 (Н)*

Cf.: Company in distress makes trouble less (Am., Br.)

1947. С миру по нитке—голому рубашка. *Little help given by many people will eventually become great*

Cf.: Every knock is a boost (Am.). Every little counts (Am.). Every little helps (Am., Br.). Everything helps (Br.). A knock is as good as a boost (Am.). Though one grain fills not the sack, it helps (Am.)

1948. Сноп без перевясла—солома. *When there is no firm hand to unite people, they are not organized and good for nothing. See 13 (А)*

Cf.: A headless army fights badly (Am.). Thirteen staves and never a hoop will never make a barrel (Am.). When the chief fails, the host quails (Br.)

1949. Собака лает, ветер носит. *It is not worth paying attention to what people gossip or what rumo(u)rs they spread. See 1954 (С)*

Cf.: The braying of an ass does not reach heaven (Br.). The braying of an jackass never reaches heaven (Am.). Let the world wag (Br.). The moon does not heed the barking of dogs (Br.). The moon doesn't give a hoot when the dog barks (the dogs bark) at her (Am.)

1950. Собака на сене лежит, сама не ест и другим не даёт. *A niggardly person will not do, use or enjoy something nor let others do it. See 745 (И)*

Cf.: The dog in the manger won't eat the oats or let anyone else eat them (Am.). Like the dog in the manger he will neither eat himself nor let the horse eat (Br.). You will neither dance nor hold the candle (Br.)

1951. Собака собаку не ест. *See 196 (В)*

Cf.: Dog does (will) not eat dog (Am., Br.). Wolves never prey upon wolves (Am.)

1952. Собака, что лает, редко кусает. *Men who threaten much do no harm. See 1273 (Н), 1325 (Н)*

Var.: Брехливая собака лает, но не кусает

Cf.: A barking dog has no bite (Br.). A barking dog never bites (Am.). Barking dogs do not (seldom) bite (Br.). Dogs that bark at a distance don't (seldom) bite (Am.). Great barkers are no biters (Br.). The greatest barkers are not the greatest biters (Am.). He scolds most that can hurt the least (Am.). Those who threaten don't fight (Br.). A threatened blow is seldom given (Br.). When the thunder is very loud, there's very little rain (Am.)

1953. Собаке—собачья смерть. *The man was mean and his death is mean too. See 782 (К)*

Cf.: The dog shall die a dog's death (Br.). He that liveth wickedly can hardly die honestly (Br.). An ill life, an ill end (Am., Br.)

1954. Собаки лают, караван идёт. *No obstacle, gossip or slander can prevent determined men from pursuing their goal. See 1949 (С)*

Var.: Собака лает, а конь идёт. Собаки лают, караван проходит

Cf.: The dogs bark, but the caravan goes on (Br.). The parade goes on (Am.)

1955. Собачьего нрава не изменишь. *See 383 (Г)*

Cf.: Wash a dog, comb a dog: still a dog (Am.). What is bred in the bone will not /come/ out of the flesh (Am., Br.). You can't take the grunt out of a pig (Am.)

1956. Собирай по ягодке, наберёшь кузовок. *See 979 (К)*

Cf.: Drop by drop and the pitcher is full (Am.). Many a little (a pickle) makes a mickle (Br.). Many a mickle makes a muckle (Am.)

1957. Сова спит, а кур видит. *See 372 (Г)*

Cf.: The ass dreams of thistles (Br.). The hungry man often talks of bread (Am.)

1958. Совесть без зубов, а гложет. *See 1476 (Н)*

Var.: Совесть без зубов, а грызёт (загрызает)

Cf.: Conscience is an avenging angel in the mind (Am.). A guilty conscience is a self-accuser (Br.). A guilty conscience is its own accuser (needs no accuser) (Am., Br.). A guilty conscience needs no condemner (Am.)

1959. Совет да любовь. *We wish the newly-wed to love each other and have a happy life*

Cf.: All your future troubles be /but/ little ones! (Br.). Let your joys be many and your sorrows be few! (Am.). May all your troubles be little ones! (Am.). May your sun of happiness never set! (Am.). Peace and happiness! (Br.)

1960. Со вранья пошлины не берут. *See 2360 (Я)*

Var.: Со лжи пошлины не берут

Cf.: Lying pays no tax (Br.). Talking pays no toll (Am.)

1961. Соврёшь—не помрёшь, да вперёд не поверят. *See 914 (К)*

Cf.: A liar is not believed when he speaks the truth (Am., Br.). No one believes a liar when he tells the truth (Am.)

1962. Согласному стаду и волк не страшен. *See 130 (В)*

Var.: Согласного стада и волк не берёт

Cf.: Union is strength (Am., Br.)

1963. С огнём не шути и воде не верь. *See 1477 (Н)*

Var.: Огня бойся, воды берегись

Cf.: Fire and water are good servants but bad masters (Am., Br.)

1964. С одного вола две шкуры не дерут. *When you have taken from a man as much as he could possibly give, you cannot demand from him to give or pay you again. See 1668 (П)*

Cf.: Double charge will rive a cannon (Br.). You cannot flay the same ox twice (Br.). You can't charge the same man twice (Am.)

1965. С одного удара дуб не свалишь. *See 730 (И)*

Cf.: The first blow does not fell the tree (Am.). An oak is not felled at one stroke (Am.). An oak is not felled with one stroke (Br.). One stroke fells not an oak (Am.)

1966. С одной надежды не сшить одежды. *If you rely on hope only but do not work or act, you will gain nothing. See 1543 (О)*

Cf.: He that lives upon hope will die fasting (Am.). Hope is a good breakfast, but a bad supper (Br.). Hope is a good breakfast, but it is a bad supper (Am.). Hope is a slender reed for a stout man to lean on (Am.). Hope is the poor man's bread (Am.)

1967. Солдат спит, служба идёт. *A person, though doing nothing, still has good luck and profits*

Cf.: Good comes to some while they are sleeping (Am.). Interest runs on while you sleep (Am.). The net of the sleeper catches fish (Br.). While the fisher sleeps the net takes (Br.)

1968. Соловья баснями не кормят. *a) Mere promising never helps. See 614 (З), 710 (И), 1229 (Н), 1360 (Н), 1505 (О), 1744 (П), 2191 (Х); b) Let us stop talking and have some meal*

Var.: Баснями сыт не будешь. Соловья песнями не кормят

Cf.: a) The belly is not filled with fair words (Br.). Fair words butter no cabbage (Am.). Fair words butter no parsnips (will not make the pot boil) (Br.). Fine words butter no parsnips (Br.). He who gives fair words feeds you with an empty spoon (Br.). It's a good story that fills the belly (Am.). Many (Mere) words will not fill the bushel (Br.). Promises don't fill the belly (fill no sack) (Am.). Sweet words butter no parsnips (Am.). Talk does not cook rice (Am.). A thousand words won't fill a bushel (Am.). Words never filled a belly (Am.). Words pay no debts (Am., Br.)

b) The belly is not filled with fair words (Br.). Fair words fill not the belly (Br.). It's a good story that fills the belly (Am.)

1969. Сорвалось словцо—не схватишь за кольцо. *See 1930 (С)*

Cf.: Words once spoken you can never recall (Am.). A word spoken is past recalling (Am., Br.)

1970. Сор из избы не выносят. *Squabbles or quarrels going on in a family or in the office must be discussed only in private*

Var.: Из избы сору не выноси, а в уголок (под лавку) копи

Cf.: Dirty clothes are washed at home (Am.). Don't air your dirty linens in public (Am.). Don't tell tales out of school (Am., Br.). Don't wash your dirty linen in public (Am., Br.). Wash your dirty linen at home (Am., Br.)

1971. Сорока без причины не стрекочет. *See 231 (В)*

Cf.: Nothing ever comes to pass without a cause (Am.). There is reason in all things (Am.). There is reason in roasting of eggs (Br.). There's a reason for everything (Br.)

1972. Сорока на хвосте принесла. *See 1934 (С)*

Var.: Сорока на хвосте весть принесла

Cf.: A little bird told me (Am., Br.). My little finger told me (Br.)

1973. Со стороны всегда виднее. *A person who is not involved in an activity can better observe and judge what is going on*

Cf.: The looker-on (onlooker, outsider, spectator) sees more (most) of the game (Br.). Lookers-on see more than the players (Am., Br.). Outsiders see most of the game (Am.). Standers-by see more than the gamesters (Br.)

1974. С паршивой овцы хоть шерсти клок. *When you cannot take much from a person, you take what he can afford. See 1070 (Л)*

Var.: С лихого пса хоть шерсти клок. С лихой (паршивой) собаки хоть шерсти клок

Cf.: Anything is better than nothing (Am.). Better something than nothing (Am.). Better something than nothing at all (Am., Br.). Half a loaf is better than none (Am., Br.). Of a bad paymaster get what you can, though it be a straw (Am.). Of ill debtors men take oats (Br.). You can have no more of a cat but her skin (of a fox than the skin) (Br.)

1975. Спасение утопающего—дело рук самого утопающего. *One must cope with his problems himself. See 267 (В), 591 (Ж)*

Cf.: Every man must carry his own sack to the mill (Br.). Every man must stand on his own two feet (Am.). Every man must stand on his own two legs (Br.). Everyone for himself (Am., Br.). Every pot must stand upon its own bottom (Am.). Let every peddler carry his own pack (Am.). Let every pedlar carry his own burden (pack) (Br.). Let every pig dig for herself (Br.). Let every tub stand on its own bottom (Am., Br.). Let him save himself who can (Am.). Self-help is the best help (Am.). Self preservation is the first law of nature (Am., Br.)

1976. Спасиба в карман не положишь. *Mere thanking for something*

done for you is not enough, you must pay for it. See 648 (З)

Var.: Спасиба домой не принесёшь

Cf.: Keep your thanks to feed your cat (Br.). Thanks is a poor payment (Br.). Thanks is poor pay /on which to keep a family/ (Am.). Thanks killed the cat (Am.). Thanks would starve a cat to death (Br.). You can't put it in the bank (Br.). You can't put thanks into your pocket (Am.)

1977. Сперва подумай, потом говори. *Consider carefully what you are going to say not to express an erroneous opinion or say something irrelevant. See 95 (Б), 1887 (С)*

Cf.: Don't let your tongue run away with your brains (Am.). First think and then speak (Br.). Let not thy tongue run away with thy brains (Am., Br.). Second thoughts are best (Am., Br.). Think before you speak (Am., Br.). Think today and speak tomorrow (Br.). Think twice before you speak once (Am., Br.). Think twice; speak once (Am.). Turn your tongue seven times before speaking (Am.). Weigh well your words before you give them breath (Am.)

1978. Сперва проверь, потом поверь. *See 490 (Д)*

Cf.: First try and then trust (Am., Br.). If you trust before you try, you may repent before you die (Am.). Test before trusting (Am.). Trust, but not too much (Br.). Try before you trust (Am., Br.)

1979. Спех людям на смех. *See 1741 (П)*

Cf.: Haste makes waste (Am., Br.). What is done in a hurry is never done well (Br.). /Wisely and slowly/—they stumble that run fast (Am.)

1980. Спеши, да не торопись. *See 2054 (Т)*

Var.: Спеши медленно

Cf.: Easy does it (Am., Br.). Make haste but do not hurry (Am.). Make haste slowly (Am., Br.). Not too fast for /fear of/ breaking your shins (Br.). One step at a time (Am., Br.)

1981. С погляденья сыт не будешь. *Mere looking at food or something else does not content a person*

Cf.: Better fill a man's belly than his eye (Br.). The eye is not satisfied with seeing (Am.)

1982. Спорь до слёз, а об заклад не бейся. *It is foolish to bet when trying to prove something*

Cf.: Fools for argument use wagers (Am.). A wager is a fool's argument (Am., Br.)

1983. Спохватился, когда с горы свалился. *See 1730 (П)*

Var.: Спохватился, когда скатился

Cf.: After the danger everyone is wise (Am.). /We are all/ wise after the event (Br.)

1984. Спрос всё укажет. *See 2363 (Я)*

Cf.: He who has a tongue in his head can travel all the world over (Br.). He who uses his tongue will reach his destination (Am.)

1985. Спрос не беда. *You should not be too shy to inquire someone about the information you need. See 649 (З)*

Var.: Спрос в карман не лезет и карман не трёт

Cf: Nothing is lost for asking (Br.). There is no harm in asking (Am.)

1986. Спустя лето в лес по малину не ходят. *When the time has gone by, it is too late to undertake something. See 1733 (П), 1734 (П)*

Cf.: Don't set the net after the fish have gone by (Am.). When a fool has bethought himself, the market's over (Br.). When a fool has made up his mind, the market has gone by (Am.)

1987. С ребятами горе, а без ребят—вдвое. *It is not easy to bring up children,* *but it is much worse to have no children at all*

Cf.: It takes children to make a happy home (Am.). Many children, many cares; no children, no felicity (Br.)

1988. С ремеслом не пропадёшь. *See 1396 (Н)*

Var.: С руками нигде не пропадёшь

Cf.: He who has an art has a place everywhere (Am.). He who has an art, has everywhere a part (Br.)

1989. С собакой ляжешь, с блохами встанешь. *See 1904 (С)*

Cf.: He that lies down with dogs gets up with fleas (Br.). If you lie down with dogs, you'll get up with fleas (Am.)

1990. С соседом дружись, а забор городи. *If you want to be on friendly relations with your neighbo(u)rs, you should not be obtrusive*

Var.: С соседом дружись, а тын городи

Cf.: A fence between makes friends more keen (Am.). Good fences make good neighbo(u)rs (Am., Br.). A hedge between keeps fellowship green (Am.). A hedge between keeps friendship green (Am., Br.). Love your neighbor, but do not pull down the fence (yet pull not down your hedge) (Am.). Love your neighbour, yet pull not down your fence (Br.). A wall between preserves love (Am.)

1991. С суконным рылом в калачный ряд не суйся. *See 974 (К)*

Var.: С мякинным (суконным) рылом да в калачный ряд

Cf.: The bear wants a tail and cannot be lion (Br.). Every ass thinks himself worthy to stand with the king's horses (Am., Br.)

1992. Станешь лапти плесть, как нечего есть. *See 369 (Г)*

Var.: Станешь ворожить, когда нечего в рот положить

Cf.: The belly teaches all arts (Br.). He must needs go whom the devil drives (Am., Br.). Need makes the naked man run (Am.). Need makes the old wife trot (Br.)

1993. Станешь лежать на печи, так не будет ничего в печи. *See 1005 (Л), 1145 (М)*

Cf.: A lazy dog finds no bone (Am.). Sleeping cats catch no mice (Am.). The sleeping dog (fox) catches no poultry (Br.). When the fox sleeps no grapes fall in his mouth (Br.)

1994. Станешь лениться, будешь с сумой волочиться. *Laziness leads to poverty. See 1005 (Л)*

Cf.: Idleness is the key of beggary (Am.). Idleness is the key to beggary (Br.)

1995. Старая любовь не ржавеет. *We always remember the person we loved when we were young*

Cf.: The heart that once truly loves never forgets (Br.). No love like the first love (Br.). An old flame never dies (Am.). An old love does not fade (Br.). Old love does not rust (Am., Br.). Old love will not be forgotten (Br.)

1996. Старая собака на пустое дерево не лает. *An experienced man will not speak to no purpose. See 2010 (С)*

Var.: Добрый (Старый) пёс на ветер не лает

Cf.: An old dog barks not in vain (Br.). An old dog does not bark for nothing (Am., Br.). An old dog does not bark in vain (Am.)

1997. Старая солома жарко горит. *An elderly person can often love passionately*

Cf.: The older the fiddle, the better the tune (Am.). The older the fiddle, the sweeter the tune (Br.). Old ovens are soon heated (Br.). There's many a good tune played on an old fiddle (Am., Br.)

1998. Старого волка в тенета не загонишь. *See 1999 (C)*

Cf.: Old foxes are not easily caught (Am.). An old fox is not easily snared (is not to be caught with a trap) (Br.). An old fox understands the trap (Br.)

1999. Старого воробья на мякине не проведёшь. *Experienced people are not easily taken in and outwitted. See 1998 (C)*

Var.: Стреляного воробья на мякине не обманешь (не проведёшь)

Cf.: An old bird is not /to be/ caught by (with) chaff (Br.). Old foxes are not easily caught (Am.). An old fox is not easily snared (Br.). You cannot catch old birds with chaff (Am., Br.)

2000. Старого пономаря не перепономаришь. *See 2002 (C)*

Cf: It is hard to make an old dog stoop (Br.). You can't teach an old dog new tricks (Am., Br.). You can't teach an old horse new tricks (Am.)

2001. Старого пса к цепи не приучишь. *See 2002 (C)*

Cf.: It is hard to make an old dog stoop (Br.). An old dog will learn no tricks (Am.). You can't teach an old dog new tricks (Am., Br.)

2002. Старого учить, что мёртвого лечить. *You cannot make old people change their way of life, ideas, methods of work, etc. See 1153 (M), 2000 (C), 2001 (C)*

Cf.: It is hard to teach an old dog tricks (Br.). An old dog cannot alter his way of barking (Br.). An old dog will learn no new tricks (Am., Br.). An old dog will learn no tricks (Am.). You can't teach an old dog new tricks (Am., Br.). You can't teach an old horse new tricks (Am.). You might as well physic the dead as give advice to an old man (Br.)

2003. Старость не радость. *It is no pleasure to be old and weak and suffer from infirmities. See 364 (Г), 2004 (C)*

Var.: Старость не радость, не красные дни

Cf.: Age breeds aches (Am.). The feet are slow when the head wears snow (Am., Br.). Old age is a heavy burden (Br.). An old ass is never good (Br.). Old vessels must leak (Br.)

2004. Старость приходит не с радостью, а со слабостью. *See 2003 (C)*

Var.: Придёт старость, придёт и слабость

Cf.: Age breeds aches (Am.). The feet are slow when the head wears snow (Am., Br.). Old age is sickness of itself (Br.). An old ape has an old eye (Br.). Old churches have dim windows (Br.)

2005. Старую лису дважды не проведёшь. *People of experience are not liable to be cheated twice. See 178 (B)*

Var.: Старая лиса дважды поймать себя не даёт

Cf.: A fish never nibbles at the same hook twice (Am.). A fox is not caught twice in the same place (trap) (Am.). A fox is not taken twice in the same snare (trap) (Br.). It is a silly fish that is caught twice with the same bait (Am., Br.). An old fox does not run into the same snare a second time (Am., Br.). You can fool an old horse once, but you can't fool him twice (Am.)

2006. Старую лису хитростям не учат. *See 1466 (H)*

Cf.: An old fox needs not to be taught tricks (Am., Br.)

2007. Старые дураки глупее молодых. *A foolish act is most foolish when done by an old person*

Cf.: The older the fool, the worse he is (Am.). An old fool is worse than a young fool (Am.). /There is/ no fool like an old fool (Am., Br.). /There is/ no fool to the old fool (Br.)

2008. Старый бык тоже телёнком был. *No one starts at the top. See 1829 (P)*

Cf.: Big (Great, Tall) oaks from little acorns grow (Am., Br.). Big trees grow from little acorns (Am.). Every artist was first an amateur (Am.). A forest is in an acorn (Br.). Great things have a small beginning (Am., Br.)

2009. Старый волк знает толк. *An old experienced man can conduct his affairs competently. See 2012 (C)*

Cf.: The best wine comes out of an old vessel (Br.). The deuce (devil) knows many things because he is old (Br.). Good broth may be made in an old pot (Am., Br.). The old mule ploughs a straight furrow (Am.). An old ox makes (ploughs) a straight furrow (Br.). There's no head like an old head (Am.)

2010. Старый ворон даром не каркнет. *See 1996 (C)*

Var.: Старый ворон не мимо каркнет

Cf.: An old dog barks not in vain (Br.). An old dog does not bark for nothing (Am., Br.). An old dog does not bark in vain (Am.)

2011. Старый друг лучше новых двух. *No newly made friends can be so loyal and devoted as old ones. See 144 (B)*

Cf.: No friend is like an old friend (Am.). Old friends are better than new ones (Br.). Old friends are best (Am., Br.). Old friends wear well (Am.). Old shoes wear best (Am.). Old tunes are sweetest, old friends are surest (Am.). One old friend is better than two new (Am.)

2012. Старый конь борозды не портит. *An old experienced person will not spoil the work he undertakes to do. See 2009 (C)*

Var.: Старая кобыла борозды не испортит

Cf.: The old mule ploughs a straight furrow (Am.). An old ox makes (ploughs) a straight furrow (Br.)

2013. Сто друзей — мало, один враг — много. *The more friends you have, the better; but it is bad to have even one single enemy*

Cf.: One enemy is too many, and a hundred friends too few (Br.). One enemy is too much for a man, and a hundred friends are too few (Am.)

2014. Стоячее болото гниёт. *Ultimately, a man or community that is not active degrades. See 1218 (H), 1833 (P)*

Var.: Стоячая вода гниёт (плесенью покрывается, тухнет)

Cf.: If you rest, you rust (Am.). Inactivity breeds ignorance (Am.). Iron not used soon rusts (Br.). Rest, rust, rot (Am.). The rust rots the steel which use preserves (Am.). Standing pools gather filth (Am., Br.). A standing pool soon stagnates (Am.). Still water breeds vermin (Br.)

2015. Стоячему с сидячим трудно говорить. *See 2032 (C)*

Cf.: A full belly does not understand an empty one (Br.). The full do not believe the hungry (Am.). He that is warm thinks all are so (Am.). Little knows the fat man what the lean thinks (Am.). There is ill talk between a full man and a fasting (Br.)

2016. Стыдливый из-за стола голодный встаёт. *A shy man will never achieve anything*

Cf.: Bashfulness is an enemy to poverty (Br.). Bashfulness is no use to the needy (Am.). Dumb folks (men) get no lands (Br.). He that cannot ask, cannot live (Br.). It is only the bashful that lose (Am.). The lame tongue gets nothing (Br.). Modest dogs miss much meat (Am.)

2017. Суженого и на коне не объедешь. *See 102 (Б)*

Var.: Сужена на коне (на кривых оглоблях) ни обойти, ни объехать.

Сужена-ряжена не обойдёшь и на коне не объедешь

Cf.: Marriage and hanging go by destiny (Am., Br.). Marriage comes by (is) destiny (Br.). Marriages are made in heaven (Am., Br.)

2018. Суму нищего не наполнишь. *When a man is too poor, it is very difficult to improve his situation. See 40 (Б)*

Cf.: The beggar's bag has no bottom (Br.). A beggar's purse is always empty (is bottomless) (Br.). A beggar's scrip is never filled (Br.). The beggar's wallet has no bottom (Am.). The beggar's wallet is a mile to the bottom (Am.)

2019. Сухая ложка рот дерёт. *See 1387 (Н)*

Cf.: An empty hand is no lure for the hawk (Br.). Empty hands allure no hawks (Am.)

2020. Счастливые часов не наблюдают. *Time passes quickly when you are happy*

Cf.: All of our sweetest hours fly fast (Am.). Happiness takes no account of time (Br.). Love makes time pass (Br.). Lovers' time runs faster than the clock (Br.). Pleasant hours fly fast (Am., Br.)

2021. Счастье без ума—дырявая сума. *A foolish man always loses. See 2096 (У)*

Cf.: A fool and his money are soon parted (Am., Br.). Fools never prosper (Am.)

2022. Счастье едет в карете, а и с умом, да ходят пешком. *See 1403 (Н)*

Cf.: A pocketful of luck is better than a sackful of wisdom (Am.). 'Tis better to be born fortunate than wise (Br.). You don't need brains if you have luck (Am.)

2023. Счастье на деньги не купишь. *Money cannot make you happy. See 756 (И)*

Cf.: Money can't (won't) buy happiness (Am.)

2024. Счастье с бессчастьем—вёдро с ненастьем. *Nothing lasts for ever, neither good nor bad luck. See 330 (Г), 1481 (Н)*

Var.: Счастье и несчастье на одном коне ездят. Счастье с несчастьем близко живут (на одних санях ездят)

Cf.: Every flood has its ebb (Br.). Every flow must have its ebb (Br.). A flow will have an ebb (Am.). Fortune and misfortune are next-door neighbors (Am.). Joy and sorrow are next-door neighbors (Am.). Sadness a gladness succeeds (Am.). Sadness and gladness succeed each other (Br.). Sorrow treads upon the heels of mirth (Am., Br.)

2025. Счёт дружбе не помеха. *A right way of setting accounts does not hinder friendship. See 2234 (Ч)*

Var.: Счёт дружбы не портит

Cf.: Correct counting keeps good friends (Br.). Even reckoning makes lasting (long) friends (Br.). Pay your debts or lose your friends (Am.). Short reckonings make long friends (Am., Br.). Weight and measure take away strife (Br.)

2026. С чужого коня среди грязи долой. *You must leave the post to be taken by someone else because you are not qualified for it, be it very inconvenient for you*

Cf.: If you are on a strange horse, get off in the middle of the road (Am.)

2027. Съесть не могу, а оставить жаль. *See 570 (Е)*

Cf.: Better the belly burst than good drink (meat) lost (Br.). It's better a belly burst than good food wasted (Am.)

2028. Съешь и ржаного, коли нет никакого. *See 1174 (Н)*

Var.: Съешь и морковку, коли яблочка нет

Cf.: All is good in a famine (Am., Br.). They that have no other meat, bread and butter are glad to eat (Br.). They that have no other meat, gladly bread and butter eat (Am.)

2029. Сыпь коню мешком, не будешь ходить пешком. *See 2155 (У)*

Cf.: The belly carries the feet (the legs) (Br.). The stomach carries the feet (Am.)

2030. Сытое брюхо к учению глухо. *He who is satiated is reluctant to acquire new knowledge*

Cf.: A belly full of gluttony will never study willingly (Br.). Full stomachs make empty heads (Am.). When the belly is full, the mind is blank (Am.)

2031. Сытой мышке и сало не вкусно. *When a man is not hungry, he is hard to please*

Var.: Мышь сыта—мука горька. Сытая мышь и муки не ест

Cf.: Plenty makes daintiness (Am.). Plenty makes dainty (Am., Br.). To him that lost his taste sweet is sour (Br.). Too much plenty makes mouths dainty (Am.). When the cat is full, then the milk tastes sour (Am.)

2032. Сытый голодного не разумеет. *A man not suffering from want of money or food, difficulties or troubles cannot sympathise with another person who is in distress. See 81 (Б), 2015 (С)*

Var.: Богатый бедного не разумеет

Cf.: A full belly does not understand an empty one (Br.). The full do not believe the hungry (Am.). He that is warm thinks all are so (Am.). He whose belly is full believes not him who is fasting (Br.). It is ill speaking between a full man and a fasting (Br.). Little knows the fat man what the lean thinks (Br.). Little knows the fat sow what the lean does mean (Br.). Little knows the fat sow what the lean one thinks (Am.). A man with a full belly thinks no one is hungry (Br.)

2033. С этим не шутят. *It is a serious matter. See 2353 (Э)*

Cf.: It is not a laughing matter (Am., Br.). No laughing matter (Am.)

Т

2034. Та же щука, да под хреном. *See 225 (В)*

Var.: Тот же блин, да на другом блюде

Cf.: Another yet the same (Br.). It amounts to the same thing (Br.). It's six of one, half a dozen of the other (Am.)

2035. Такова жизнь. *That is life, and we must accept things as they are. See 199 (В)*

Cf.: Such is life (Am., Br.). That's about the size of it (Am.). That's how (the way) the cookie crumbles (Am., Br.). That's the way it goes (it is) (Am., Br.). That's the way the ball bounces (the bread rises, the doughnut rolls, the mop flops) (Am.). There you are (go) (Am.)

2036. Там хорошо, где нас нет. *See 1917 (С)*

Var.: Везде хорошо, где нас нет

Cf.: Far folk fare best (Br.). Far hills look the bluest (Am.). Grass is always greener away from home (Am.). The grass is always greener on the other side of the fence (Am., Br.). The grass is always greener on the other side of the hill (Br.)

2037. Таскал волк—потащили и волка. *The crafty is captured in the end. See 1042 (Л), 1907 (С)*

Cf.: At length the fox is brought to the furrier (Br.). The end of the thief is the gallows (Am.). Long runs the fox, but at last is caught (Am.). The old ape is taken at last (Am.). The old fox is caught at last (Br.)

2038. Твой дом—твоя и воля. *Nobody can order you what to do in your own house*

Cf.: Every man is a king (a master) in his own house (Br.). A man is king in his home (Am.)

2039. Тебе смешно, а мне к сердцу дошло. *One man's joy is another man's sorrow. See 879 (К)*

Cf.: It may be fun for you, but it is death to the frog (Br.). What is good for one man, may not be good for another (Am.)

2040. Тело заплывчиво, горе забывчиво. *Excessive grief cannot last without ever ending. See 211 (В)*

Cf.: A bawling calf soon forgets its mother (Am.). A bawling cow soon forgets her own calf (Am.). A bellowing cow soon forgets her calf (Am., Br.). A bletherin' coo soon forgets her calf (Br.). Earth has no sorrow that heaven cannot heal (Am.). Nothing dries sooner than tears (Am., Br.). Time cures all griefs (Br.). Time erases all sorrows (Am.)

2041. Темна вода во облацех. *The matter is incomprehensible or obscure*

Cf.: Dark are the waters in the clouds (Am., Br.)

2042. Тёмная ночь не навек. *Bad times will come to an end. See 1725 (П)*

Cf.: The darker hour is that before the dawn (Br.). The darkest hour is just before dawn (Am.). The darkest hour is nearest the dawn (Am., Br.). It is always darkest before /the/ dawn (Am., Br.). It's always dark before the sun shines (Am.). The longest night must end (Am.). The longest night will have an end (Br.)

2043. Тем не играют, от чего умирают. *See 1477 (Н)*

Cf.: Do not play with edged tools (Am.). It is ill jesting with edged tools (Br.)

2044. Терпенье и труд всё перетрут. *Success comes with endurance and tenacity. See 280 (В), 833 (К)*

Cf.: Care and diligence bring luck (Br.). Diligence is the mother of good luck (Am., Br.). Elbow grease gives the best polish (Am., Br.). He that's always shooting must sometimes hit (Br.). If at first you don't succeed, try, try again (Am.). If at first you don't succeed, try, try, try again (Br.). It is dogged as (that) does it (Am., Br.). Labour overcomes all things (Br.). Little by little and bit by bit (Am., Br.). Patience conquers (Am.). Perseverance conquers all things (Am.). Perseverance kills the game (wins) (Br.). Slow and steady wins the race (Am., Br.). Time and patience change the mulberry leaf to satin (Am.). With time and art the leaf of the mulberry-tree becomes satin (Br.)

2045. Терпение—лучшее спасение. *Do not complain, you will get over your griefs and overcome your difficulties in the end. See 2046 (Т)*

Cf.: No remedy but patience (Br.). Patience is a plaster for all sores (Am., Br.). Patience is a remedy for every sorrow (Am., Br.). Patience is the key of paradise (Am.). Patient men win the day (Br.). The remedy for hard times is to have patience (Am.)

2046. Терпи, казак, атаманом будешь. *If you bear the difficulties or pain without complaint, you will live up to better times. See 920 (К), 2045 (Т)*

Cf.: He conquers who endures (Am.). It's a great life if you do not weaken (Am., Br.). Patience brings everything about (Br.). Patience conquers (Am.). Patience is bitter, but its fruit is sweet (Am.). Patience is the key of paradise (Am.). Patient men win the day (Br.)

2047. Терпит брага долго, а через край пойдёт—не уймёшь. *See 286 (В)*

Cf.: Even a worm will turn (Am., Br.). A man may cause even his own dog to bite him (Am.). A man may provoke his own dog to bite him (Am., Br.). When the well is full, it will run over (Br.)

2048. Тесные сапоги разносятся, широкие осядутся. *See 239 (В)*

Cf.: Hard luck can't last one hundred years (Am.). In the end, all will mend (Am.). In the end things will mend (Br.)

2049. Тех же щей, да пожиже влей. *See 225 (В)*

Var.: Те же щи, да в другую тарелку

Cf.: Another yet the same (Br.). It amounts to the same thing (Br.). It's six of one, half a dozen of the other (Am.). The same stew only the name is new (Br.)

2050. Тихая вода берега подмывает. *See 294 (В)*

Cf.: Still waters have deep bottoms (Am., Br.)

2051. Тихие воды глубоки. *A quiet person can have strong emotions. See 93 (Б), 331 (Г)*

Cf.: The shallow brook warbles, while the still water is deep (Am.). Smooth waters run deep (Br.). The stiller the water, the deeper it runs (Br.). Still water flows (runs) deep (Am.). Still waters run deep (Am., Br.). Waters that are deep don't babble as they flow (Br.). Where the river is deepest it makes least noise (Am., Br.)

2052. Тихий ангел пролетел. *Silence has fallen. (This is said by one of those present when people gathered together suddenly stop talking.) See 1132 (М)*

Cf.: An angel is passing overhead (Am., Br.). It must be the ten minute lull (Am.). It must be twenty past the hour (Am.)

2053. Тихий воз скорее будет на горе. *See 2054 (Т)*

Cf.: He who treads softly goes far (Am.). Slow and steady wins the race (Am., Br.). Slow but certain wins the race (Am.). Slow but sure wins the race (Br.). Soft pace goes far (Br.)

2054. Тише едешь, дальше будешь. *The more care and thought you give to what you are doing, the better the result will be. See 1117 (М), 1741 (П), 1980 (С), 2053 (Т)*

Cf.: He who treads softly goes far (Am.). Slow and steady wins the race (Am., Br.). Slow but certain wins the race (Am.). Slow but sure wins the race (Br.). A slow fire makes sweet malt (Br.). Soft fire makes sweet malt (Am.). Soft pace goes far (Br.). Steady does it (Br.). Step by step one goes a long way (Am.). Step by step one goes far (Br.)

2055. Товар лицом кажут. *For somebody to take an interest in you or in a thing, show yourself or the thing to the best advantage*

Cf.: Always put your best foot forward (Am.). Put your best foot forward (Br.). Start off with the best foot (Am.)

2056. То вскачь, то хоть плачь. *See 1879 (С)*

Cf.: Our lives have ups and downs (Br.). We all have our ups and downs (Am.)

2057. Тогда пляши, когда играют. *Do things at the proper time. See 977 (К)*

Cf.: As the wind blows, set your sails (Am.). Fly your kite when it is windy (Am.). Hoist your sail when the wind is fair (Br.). Strike while the iron is hot (Am., Br.). Time to catch bears is when they're out (Am.). The time to pick berries is when they're ripe (Am.). When the iron is hot, it is time to strike (Am.)

2058. То ли ещё будет! *See 2352 (Э)*

Cf.: Cheer up—the worst is yet to come (Am.). Cheer up, things will get worse (Am.). The end is not yet (Br.). This is only the beginning (Am.). The worst is yet to come (Am., Br.)

2059. Только мёртвые не ошибаются. *See 2251 (Ч)*

Cf.: He is dead that is faultless (Am.). He is lifeless that is faultless (Am., Br.)

2060. Только тот, на чьей ноге башмак, знает, где он жмёт. *It is the person who is in trouble that knows where the difficulty, the cause of annoyance or discomfort lies*

Cf.: Each organism knows best where it itches (Am.). Every one knows best where his shoe pinches (Br.). Everyone knows where his shoe pinches (Am.). No one but the wearer knows where the shoe pinches (Br.). Only he who wears the shoe knows where it pinches (Am.). The wearer best knows where the shoe pinches (Am.)

2061. Только через мой труп. *By no means if I can prevent it. See 2356 (Э)*

Cf.: No way (Am.). /Only/ over my dead body (Am., Br.)

2062. Тому врать легко, кто был далеко. *A man who visited far-away places can tell fanciful stories as there are no witnesses to refute them*

Cf.: Liars have long legs (Am.). Long ways, long lies (Br.). A travelled man has leave to lie (Br.). A traveller may lie with authority (Br.). Travellers have leave to lie (Am., Br.)

2063. Топор виноват, что изба нехороша. *See 1111 (M)*

Cf.: A bad worker finds faults with his tools (Br.). A bad workman quarrels with his tools (Am., Br.). An ill workman quarrels with his tools (Br.). The losing horse blames the saddle (Am.)

2064. Торговали—веселились, подсчитали—прослезились. *What we got is not so great as we hoped we would have*

Cf.: Expectation always surpasses realization (Am.). Expectation is better than realization (Br.). Negotiation—celebration, calculation—consternation (Br.). Nothing is so good as it seems beforehand (Br.). Prospect is often better than possession (Br.). The realization is never as great as anticipation (Am.). There's more joy in anticipation than in realization (Am.)

2065. Тот без нужды живёт, кто деньги бережёт. *You will never lack money if you do not squander it. See 1856 (C)*

Cf.: Of saving comes having (Br.). Save and have (Am.). Save today, safe tomorrow (Am.). Sparing is the first gaining (Br.). Thrift is a great revenue (Br.). Waste not, want not (Am., Br.)

2066. Тот в нищету пошёл, на ком долг тяжёл. *A person who owes much money is in danger of becoming poor*

Cf.: Debt is the worst kind of poverty (Am.). Debt is the worst poverty (Am., Br.)

2067. Тот здоровья не знает, кто болен не бывает. *It is only after you get sick that you learn the real value of health*

Var.: Без болезни и здоровью не рад

Cf.: Health is not valued till sickness comes (Am., Br.)

2068. Тот человек пустой, кто полон самим собой. *Self-admiration or conceit speaks of lack of intellect*

Cf.: He that is full of himself is very empty (Am., Br.)

2069. Точность—вежливость королей. *A man's coming or fulfilling his promise in time is a noble streak in his character*

Cf.: Punctuality is a kingly virtue (is the politeness of kings) (Br.). Punctuality is the politeness of princes (Am.)

2070. Трещина в горшке скоро скажется. *Once friendly relations are impaired, you cannot restore them. See 1718 (П)*

Cf.: A broken egg cannot be put back together (Am.). A broken friendship may be soldered, but will never be sound (Am.). Broken friendships may be soldered, but never sound

(Br.). A cracked bell can never sound well (Am., Br.). A cracked bell is never sound (Br.)

2071. Труден только первый шаг. *See 1025 (Л)*

Cf.: The first step is always the hardest (Am.). The first step is the hardest (Am., Br.). The first step is the only difficulty (Br.)

2072. Трус в карты не играет. *See 186 (В)*

Cf.: He that fears leaves let him not go into the wood (Br.). He that fears leaves must not come into the wood (Am.)

2073. Трус и до смерти часто умирает. *Cravens are obsessed by the dread of passing away*

Cf.: The coward dies many times (Am.). The coward dies a thousand deaths, the brave but one (Am.). The coward often dies, the brave but once (Br.). Cowards die many times before their death (Am., Br.)

2074. Трутни горазды на плутни. *See 35 (Б)*

Cf.: The devil finds (makes) work for idle hands /to do/ (Am., Br.)

2075. Трутням праздник и по будням. *See 2113 (У)*

Cf.: Every day is holiday with sluggards (Br.). A lazy man always finds excuses (Am.). Sluggards work best when the sun's in the West (Am.)

2076. Трясёт козёл бороду, так привык смолоду. *See 1768 (П)*

Cf.: Custom is a second nature (Am., Br.). Dogs delight to bark and bite for God has made 'em so (Am.). Habit (Use) is a second nature (Br.)

2077. Ты—мне, я—тебе. *Do me a good turn, and I will do it to you too. See 2148 (У)*

Cf.: Ca me, ca thee (Br.). Claw me, and I'll claw thee (Br.). Scratch my breech and I'll claw your elbow (Am.). Tickle me, Bobby, and I'll tickle you (Br.). You play my game, and I'll play yours (Br.). You roll my log, and I'll roll yours (Br.). /You/ scratch my back, and I'll scratch yours (Am., Br.)

2078. Тяжела ты, шапка Мономаха. *A man in power has to cope with a lot of obligations connected with the high post he holds*

Cf.: Crowns have cares (Br.). Great honours are great burdens (Br.). Heavy (Uneasy) is the head that wears the crown (Am.). Uneasy lies the head that wears the crown (Am., Br.)

2079. Тяжёл крест, да надо несть. *We must endure our troubles and sorrows*

Cf.: Every man must bear his /own/ cross (Br.). Every man must bear his own burden (Am.). Every man shall bear his own burden (Br.). We must drink the cup (Br.). When we suffer a great loss, we must bear our cross (Am.)

2080. Тяжело в учении, легко в бою. *Knowledge and skill acquired by hard work will be of great help in difficult times. See 2166 (У)*

Cf.: Lessons hard to learn are sweet to know (Am., Br.). They that sow in tears shall reap in joy (Am.)

2081. Тяжело нагребёшь, домой не донесёшь. *Do not be greedy, do not take too much if you want it to be safe. See 580 (Ж), 1030 (Л)*

Var.: Тяжело накладёшь, не унесёшь. Тяжело понёс—и домой не донёс

Cf.: Avarice loses all in seeking to gain all (Am.). Covetousness breaks (bursts) the bag (brings nothing home) (Br.). Grasp a little and you may secure it; grasp too much and you will lose everything (Am.). Grasp all, lose all (Br.). Grasp no more than the hand will hold (Br.). Greediness bursts the bag (Br.). If you wish for too much, you will end up with nothing (Am.). Too much breaks the bag (Br.)

2082. Тяжело против воды плыть. *See 1786 b (П)*

Cf.; It is ill striving against the stream (Br.). Strive not against the stream (Am.)

У

2083. Увидеть Париж и умереть. *I want to achieve this much desired goal of mine and I do not care about the rest of my life*

Cf.: See Rome and die (Am.)

2084. У вора ремесло на лбу не написано. *A man's appearance does not always betray his wrongdoings*

Cf.: Every man's faults are not written on their foreheads (Am.). Every one's faults are not written in (on) their foreheads (Br.)

2085. У воров не бывает каменных домов. *Wealth got in a dishonest way will never make you rich. See 1475 (Н)*

Var.: Ни у одного вора нет каменного дома

Cf.: Cheaters never prosper (win) (Am.). Cheating play never thrives (Am.). Cheats never prosper (Br.)

2086. У всякого барона своя фантазия. *See 774 (К)*

Cf.: Every man has his delight (foible) (Br.). Everyone enjoys himself in his own way (Am.)

2087. У всякого свой вкус, а у осла ослиный. *See 1182 (Н)*

Cf.: Each to his own taste (Am.). Every man to his taste (Am., Br.). Every man to his own taste (Br.). A pig used to dirt turns up its nose at rice boiled in milk (Am.). A thistle is a fat salad for an ass's mouth (Br.)

2088. У всякого своя дурь в голове. *See 774 (К)*

Cf.: Every man is mad on some point (Br.). Everyone enjoys himself in his own way (Am.)

2089. У всякого скота своя пестрота. *See 270 (В)*

Cf.: All bread is not baked in one oven (Am., Br.). Every man after his fashion (Br.). Every man after his own heart (Am.). Every man in his own way (Am., Br.)

2090. У всякого таракана своя щёлка есть. *There is no man who would not have some kind of shelter*

Cf.: Every fox has its hole (Br.). Every rabbit has his hole (Am.). For every pea there is a pod (Am.)

2091. У всякого Федорки свои отговорки. *A lazy man will always find a pretext to excuse his idleness or shrinking from work. See 1034 (Л), 2113 (У)*

Var.: У всякого Федотки свои отговорки. У лентяя Федорки всегда отговорки

Cf.: Idle folks lack no excuses (Br.). A lazy man always finds excuses (Am.). The sluggard's convenient season never comes (Br.). Sluggards work best when the sun's in the west (Am.)

2092. У всякой песни есть свой конец. *See 2271 (Ч)*

Cf.: Everything has an end (Am., Br.)

2093. У всякой пташки свои замашки. *See 270 (В)*

Cf.: All bread is not baked in one oven (Am., Br.). Every man after his fashion (Br.). Every man after his own heart (Am.). Every man in his own way (Am., Br.)

2094. У всякой стряпки свои порядки. *All people have their own way of acting or doing something. See 2300 (Ч)*

Cf.: Every country has its /own/ custom (customs) (Am., Br.). Every man in his own way (Am., Br.)

2095. Уговор дороже денег. *Promises must be kept at any cost. See 412 (Д)*

Var.: Уговор—святое дело

Cf.: A bargain is a bargain (Am., Br.). A bet's a bet (Am.). A promise is a promise (Am., Br.)

2096. У дурака в горсти дыра. *A fool is wasteful with his money. See 1428 (Н), 2021 (С)*

Cf.: A fool and his gold are soon parted (Am.). A fool and his money are soon parted (Am., Br.). Fools never prosper (Am.). Without wisdom wealth is worthless (Br.)

2097. У дурака что на уме, то и на языке. *Fools cannot conceal what they think or what they know*

Cf.: Fools and children cannot lie (Am.). Fools and children speak (tell) the truth (Am.). Fools and madmen speak the truth (Br.)

2098. У дурака язык впереди ног бежит. *Fools talk very much without thinking first. See 2361 (Я)*

Cf.: An empty head, like a bell, has a long tongue (Am.). Foolish tongues talk by the dozen (Am.). A fool's bell is soon rung (Br.). Fools cannot hold their tongues (Am.). A fool's tongue runs before his wit (Br.). A loud mouth and a shallow brain go well together (Am.)

2099. У завтра нет конца. *See 1592 (О)*

Cf.: Tomorrow come never (Br.). Tomorrow may never come (Am.). Tomorrow never comes (Am., Br.)

2100. У злой Натальи все люди канальи. *See 161 (В)*

Cf.: Bad eyes never see any good (Am.). A crook thinks every man is a crook (Am.). Evil doers are evil dreaders (Br.). Evil will never said well (Br.). He who does evil suspects evil on the part of his fellow man (Am.). Ill-doers are ill thinkers (Am., Br.). Ill will never said well (Br.). Ill will never speaks well or does well (Am.). The thief thinks that everyone else is a thief (Am.)

2101. У каждого бывает светлый день. *See 106 (Б)*

Cf.: Every dog has his (its) day (Am., Br.). Fortune knocks at least once at every man's gate (Am., Br.). Fortune knocks once at every door (Am.). The saddest dog sometimes wags its tail (Am.)

2102. У каждого голубка своя горлица. *Every male gets a female in the end. See 46 (Б)*

Cf.: Every Jack has his Gill (Am., Br.). Every Jack has his Jill (Am.). Every kettle has a lid (Am.). For every Jack there is a Jill (Am.). There was never a shoe but had its mate (Am.)

2103. У каждого своё горе. *There is no man that would not have any kind of trouble, sorrow or grief*

Var.: У каждого свои горести

Cf.: Every heart has its own ache (Am., Br.). Every heart knows its bitterness (Br.). Every man bears his /own/ cross (Br.). The heart knows its own bitterness (Am.)

2104. У каждой избушки свои погремушки. *See 1670 (П)*

Var.: Во всякой избушке свои погремушки

Cf.: No house without mouse (Br.). There is a skeleton in every house (Am., Br.). There's a skeleton in everybody's closet (in every family /closet/) (Am.)

2105. У каждой медали есть обратная сторона. *A problem can be viewed and explained differently as it has contrary aspects*

Var.: Всякая медаль о двух сторонах

Cf.: Every medal has its reverse (Am., Br.). There are two sides to every question (Am., Br.). There are two sides to every story (to everything) (Am.)

2106. У каждой пичужки свой голосок. *See 270 (В)*

Cf.: All bread is not baked in one oven (Am., Br.). Every cock sings in his own manner (Br.). Every man after his own heart (Am.). Every man in his own way (Am., Br.)

2107. Укатали Сивку крутые горки. *Hard conditions of life or old age made one weak or deprived him of enthusiasm. See 120 (Б), 364 (Г)*

Var.: Укачали Бурку (Сивку) крутые горки. Умыкали Савраску горы да овражки

Cf.: The bloom is off the peach (Am., Br.). The bloom is off the rose (Am.). I have had my day (Br.). The old gray mare ain't what she used to be (Am.)

2108. У кого желчь во рту, тому всё горько. *Malicious people cannot but think or speak ill of others. See 161 (В)*

Cf.: He that is angry is seldom at ease (Am., Br.). No rest for the wicked (Am.). /There's/ no peace for the wicked (Br.). Who has bitter in his mouth spits not all sweet (Br.). Who has bitter in his mouth spits not /at/ all sweet (Am.)

2109. У кого жить, тому и служить. *See 1264 (Н)*

Cf.: Every man bows to the bush he gets bield of (Br.). Whose bread I eat, his song I sing (Am.)

2110. У кого совесть чиста, у того подушка под головой не вертится. *A man who committed no wrongdoings lives a peaceful life. See 1474 (Н)*

Var.: У кого совесть чиста, тот может спать спокойно. Чистая совесть—спокойный сон (хорошая подушка)

Cf.: A clean conscience is a good pillow (Am.). A good conscience is a continual feast (Br.). A good conscience is a soft pillow (Am., Br.). A good conscience knows no fear (Am.). A quiet conscience sleeps in thunder (Br.). A safe conscience makes a sound sleep (Am.). Sweet are the slumbers of the virtuous (Am.)

2111. У кого что болит, тот о том и говорит. *Men talk about what is worrying them. See 1577 (О)*

Cf.: A man in suffering finds relief in rehearsing his ills (Am.). A man lays his hand where he feels the pain (Br.). Nearest the heart comes first out (Am.). Nearest the heart, nearest the mouth (Br.). The tongue ever turns to the aching tooth (Br.). The tongue returns to the aching tooth (Am.). When the fire burns in the soul, the tongue cannot be silent (Am.)

2112. Укрыватель—тот же вор. *See 197 (В)*

Cf.: The receiver is as bad as the thief (Am., Br.)

2113. У ленивого Емели семь воскресений на неделе. *There is no time a lazy man would like to work. See 1003 (Л), 1035 (Л), 2075 (Т), 2091 (У)*

Cf.: Every day is holiday with sluggards (Br.). A lazy man always finds excuses (Am.). Sluggards work best when the sun's in the west (Am.)

2114. У лжи короткие ноги. *See 205 (В)*

Var.: Ложь на гнилых ногах (на тараканьих ножках) ходит

Cf.: A liar is sooner caught than a cripple (Am., Br.). A lie has no legs (Am.). A lie hath no feet (Br.). A lie only runs on one leg (Am.). Lies have short legs (Br.)

2115. Улита едет, когда-то будет. *It will take too much time to have it done, if at all. See 1506 (О), 1605 (О)*

Cf.: Between promising and performing a man may marry his daughter (Br.). Between saying and doing there is a long road (Am., Br.). From saying to doing is a long stride (Br.)

2116. Умей дело делать, умей и позабавиться. *See 1129 (М)*

Cf.: All work and no play makes Jack a dull boy (Am., Br.). All work and no play makes Johnny a dull boy (Am.)

2117. Умел взять, умей и отдать. *When you take something from someone, you must give it back. See 496 (Д)*

Var.: Любишь взять, люби и отдать

Cf.: A borrowed loan should come laughing home (should return with thankfulness) (Br.). Pay what you owe (Am.). Pay with the same dish you borrow (Br.)

2118. Умел дитя родить, умей и научить. *The parents' responsibility is to bring up their children properly. See 992 (Л)*

Cf.: The best colt needs breeding (Br.). Birth is much, but breeding is more (Am., Br.)

2119. Умел ошибиться—умей и поправиться. *When you are at fault or wrong, do your best to set the things right. See 1625 (О)*

Cf.: It is never too late to mend (Am., Br.)

2120. Умён, умён, а у себя под носом не видит. *People are often surprisingly ignorant of what is going on near them. See 646 (З)*

Cf.: The darkest place is under the candlestick (Br.). The darkest spot is just under the candle (Am.). It is always dark just under a lamp (Am.). It is always darkest under the lantern (Am.). It is dark at the foot of a lighthouse (Am.). Some people can't see beyond the tip of their nose (Am.)

2121. Уменье везде найдёт примененье. *See 1396 (Н)*

Cf.: He who has an art has a place everywhere (Am.). He who has an art, has everywhere a part (Br.)

2122. Умеренность—лучшее лекарство. *A moderate way of life gives better results than any medication*

Var.: Умеренность—мать здоровья

Cf.: Temperance is the best medicine (Br.). Temperance is the best physic (Am.)

2123. Ум на ум не приходится. *See 1908 (С)*

Cf.: As many men, so many opinions (Am.). Every man to his own opinion (Am.). Many men, many minds (Br.). So many men, so many opinions (Br.)

2124. Ум не в бороде, а в голове. *See 100 (Б)*

Var.: Борода уму не замена. Мудрость в голове, а не в бороде

Cf.: The beard does not make the doctor or philosopher (Am.). The brains don't lie in the beard (Br.). If a beard were a sign of smartness, the goat would be Socrates (Am.). If the beard were all, the goat might preach (Am., Br.). It is not the beard that makes the philosopher (Br.)

2125. Умница, как попова курица. *You are or someone is stupid*

Var.: Умная умница—что светлая пуговица

Cf.: If you had all the wit of the world, fools would fell you (Br.). Not all there (Am.). Nothing between the ears (Am.). Some men are wise and some are otherwise (Am., Br.). There is not much between the ears (Am.). There's nobody home (Am.). You haven't got the brains you were born with (Am.)

2126. Умному свистни, а он уже смыслит. *Give a covert suggestion to a clever man and he knows what to say or to do. See 1545 (О), 2130 (У)*

Var.: Умному—намёк, глупому—толчок

Cf.: Half a word is enough for a wise man (Br.). A hint is as good as a kick (Am.). A nod for a wise man, and a rod for a fool (Br.). A nod is as good as a wink (Br.). Send a wise man on an errand and say nothing to him (Br.). To one who understands, few words are needed (Am.). A word is enough to the wise (Am., Br.). A word to the wise (Br.). A word to the wise is sufficient (Am.)

2127. Умные речи приятно и слышать. *What you are saying now makes sense*

Cf.: Now you're talking (Am.)

2128. Умный в гору не пойдёт, умный гору обойдёт. *If you encounter some difficulties or obstacles, try to avoid or overcome them by way of making the least efforts. See 575 (E), 1060 (Л)*

Cf.: Better go about (around) than fall into the ditch (Am.). Better to go about than to fall into the ditch (Br.). A horse never goes straight up (Am.). A low hedge is easily leaped over (Am.). Men leap over where the hedge is lowest (Br.). The thread is cut where the thread is thinnest (Am.)

2129. Умный любит учиться, а дурак учить. *The clever realize that they need more knowledge, whereas the stupid think they have enough of it to instruct others*

Var.: Умный любит учиться, а глупый учить

Cf.: Every fool wants to give advice (Am.). Folly is wise in her own eyes (Br.). The fool doth think he is wise, but the wise man knows himself to be a fool (Br.). A fool is wise in his own conceit (Br.). A wise man will learn (Am.). The wise seek wisdom; the fool has found it (Am.)

2130. Умный понимает с полуслова. *See 2126 (У)*

Var.: Умный слышит (смыслит) с полуслова

Cf.: Half a word is enough for a wise man (Br.). To one who understands, few words are needed (Am.). A word is enough to the wise (Am., Br.). A word to the wise is sufficient (Am.)

2131. Умный совет всегда в пользу. *See 2193 (X)*

Cf.: Good advice never comes too late (Am.). Good counsel does no harm (never comes amiss) (Br.). Good counsel never comes too late (Am., Br.)

2132. Умный товарищ—половина дороги. *Talking with a nice fellow-traveller helps you to while away the time. See 63 (Б)*

Cf.: Cheerful company shortens the miles (Am.). Good company on the road is the shortest cut (Br.). Good company upon the road is shortest cut (Am.). A merry companion is a waggon in the way (Br.). No road is long with good company (Am.). Pleasant company shortens the miles Am.)

2133. Умрём, так всё останется. *We should be generous and enjoy life while we are alive, we will need nothing after death. See 1704 (П)*

Cf.: A dead man's shroud has no pockets (Am.). Naked we came, naked we go (Am.). No matter how much money you have, when you die, you must leave it (Am.). Our last garment is made without pockets (Br.). The richest man carries nothing away with him but his shroud (Am.). A shroud has no pockets (Am., Br.). You can't take it with you (Am., Br.). You can't take it (money) with you when you die (Br.). Your wooden overcoat won't have any pockets (Am.)

2134. У мужа жена всегда виновата. *Men always accuse their wives of all that goes wrong*

Cf.: Adam must have an Eve, to blame her for what he has done (Am., Br.). He took it like a man, he blamed it on his wife (Am.)

2135. Ум—хорошо, а два—лучше. *See 1531 (O)*

Var.: Ум—хорошо, а два—лучше того

Cf.: Many wits are better than one (Br.). Two heads are better than one (Am., Br.). Two minds are better than one (Am.)

2136. У нашей пряхи ни одежды, ни рубахи. *See 1855 (C)*

Cf.: He who makes shoes goes barefoot (Am.). The tailor's sons wear patched pants (Am.). The tailor's wife is the worst clad (Br.)

2137. У огня, да не погреться. *See 2160 a (У)*

Cf.: Every cook knows to lick her own fingers (Am.). Every honest miller has a golden thumb (a thumb of gold) (Br.). He is an ill cook that cannot lick his own fingers (Am., Br.)

2138. Упавшего не считай за пропавшего. *Even a loser has a chance. See 1308 (H)*

Cf.: All is not lost that is in danger (Am.). All is not lost that is in peril (Br.). He that falls today may rise tomorrow (Br.). A man may be down, but he's never out (Am.). Near dead never filled the kirkyard (Am.). No man is dead till he's dead (Am.)

2139. У плохого мастера всегда инструмент виноват. *See 1111 (M)*

Var.: У плохого косаря всегда серп виноват. У худого пильщика пила виновата

Cf.: A bad workman quarrels with his tools (Am., Br.)

2140. Упустишь огонь—не потушишь. *See 2341 (Ш)*

Cf.: A green wound is soon healed (Am., Br.). A little neglect may breed great mischief (Am.)

2141. У ремесла не без промысла. *See 1396 (H)*

Cf.: Learn a trade and earn a living (Am.). Trade is the mother of money (Br.). A useful trade is a mine of gold (Br.)

2142. У робкой кошки мышь резвится. *If you are bashful or servile, others will dominate you. See 899 (K)*

Cf.: A blate cat, a proud mouse (Br.). He that makes himself a sheep, shall be eaten by the wolves (Am.). Make yourself all honey and the flies will devour you (Br.). Make yourself honey and flies will devour you (Am.). A shy cat makes a proud mouse (Br.)

2143. У свекрови всегда невестка виновата. *We always blame people we dislike. See 203 (B)*

Cf.: Fault is thick, where love is thin (Am.). Faults are thick when love is thin (Am.). Faults are thick, where love is thin (Br.). When a man is not liked, whatever he does is amiss (Br.)

2144. У своего гнезда и ворон бьёт орла. *See 1238 (H)*

Var.: В своём гнезде и ворона коршуну глаза выклюет

Cf.: A cock is /always/ bold on his dunghill (Br.). A cock is mighty in his own backyard (Am.). A cock is valiant on his own dunghill (Br.). Every dog is brave in his own yard (Am.). Every dog is valiant at his own door (Am.)

2145. У семи нянек дитя без глазу. *When many people are responsible for doing one job, they spoil it. See 320 (Г)*

Var.: Где нянек много, там дитя безного. У семи мамок дитя без глаза (глазу)

Cf.: Everybody's business is nobody's business (Am., Br.). Many commanders sink the ship (Br.). Many physicians have killed the king (Br.). A pig that has two owners is sure to die of hunger (Br.). Too many cooks spoil the brew (the stew) (Am.). Too many cooks spoil the broth (Am., Br.). Too many fingers (hands) spoil the pie (Am.). Too many hands in the pot make poor soup (Am.). Two captains will sink the (wreck a) ship (Am.). Where every man is master, the world goes to wrack (Am., Br.). With seven nurses a child will be without eyes (Am.)

2146. Усердие не по разуму приносит вред. *See 650 (З)*

Cf.: Action without thought is like shooting without aim (Am.). Zeal without knowledge is a fire without light (Am., Br.). Zeal without knowledge is a runaway horse (Br.)

2147. У скупого в мороз снега не выпросишь. *You cannot get help from an uncharitable or greedy man*

Var.: Среди зимы льда не выпросишь у кумы

Cf.: Ask a kite for a feather and she will say she has but just enough to fly with (Br.). If he had the 'flu, he wouldn't give you a sneeze (Br.). You cannot get blood from (out of) a stone (Am., Br.). You cannot get blood from a turnip (Am.)

2148. Услуга за услугу. *Any favo(u)r or help you receive should be repaid. See 496 (Д), 622 (З), 2077 (Т)*

Cf.: One good deed deserves another (Am.). One good turn deserves another (Am., Br.). Scratch my breech and I'll claw your elbow (Am.). /You/ roll my log, and I'll roll yours (Br.). You scratch my back, and I'll scratch yours (Am., Br.)

2149. У смерти все равны. *Death makes all men equal, both the rich and the poor, the famous and the insignificant, the wise and the stupid, etc. See 605 (Ж), 744 (И), 1938 (С)*

Var.: Смерть всех равняет

Cf.: Death combs us all with the same comb (Br.). Death is a great leveler (Am.). Death is the grand leveler (Br.). The end makes all equal (Am., Br.). The grave levels all distinctions (Am.). Six feet of earth make all men equal (Br.). Six feet of earth (of underground, under) makes all men equal (Am.). We /shall/ all lie alike in our graves (Br.)

2150. У соседа занялось—гляди в оба. *You should be on your guard when someone next to you gets into trouble*

Cf.: My next neighbour's scathe is my present peril (Br.). When the house of your neighbour is on fire your own is in danger (Br.). When your neighbor's house is on fire, beware of your own (Am.)

2151. Усталому коню и сбруя тяжела. *When a man works hard, he gets very tired. See 1177 (Н)*

Cf.: On a long journey even a straw is heavy (Br.)

2152. Устами младенца глаголет истина. *Children are naïve and always tell the truth*

Cf.: Out of the mouth of babes speaks the truth (Br.). Out of the mouths of babes and sucklings come great truths (Am.). Truth comes out of the mouths of babes and sucklings (Br.)

2153. У стен есть уши. *There are overhearers everywhere, be careful when telling something in secret. See 1009 (Л), 1898 (С)*

Var.: /И/ стены имеют уши

Cf.: Even the corn has ears (Am.). Fields have eyes, and woods have ears (Am., Br.). /Hedges have eyes, and/ walls have ears (Am., Br.). Hedges have eyes, and woods have ears (Br.). The wall has ears and the plain has eyes (Am.)

2154. У страха глаза велики. *A man, who easily gives way to fear, exaggerates danger and sees it where there is none. See 908 (К)*

Cf.: Fear breeds terror (Br.). Fear has a hundred eyes (Br.). Fear has many eyes (Am.). The fear is greater than the reason for it (Am.)

2155. У сытого коня восемь ног. *Men will work hard if they are fed well. See 743 (И), 1208 (Н), 1327 (Н), 1359 (Н), 1379 (Н), 2029 (С)*

Cf.: An army goes on its belly (Am.). An army marches on its stomach (Am., Br.). An army travels on its stomach (Am.). The belly carries the feet (the legs) (Br.). A full belly makes a strong back (Br.). The stomach carries the feet (Am.)

2156. У сытого на уме гулянки. *When not hungry, people think not of working but of entertainment*

Cf.: Idleness and lust are bosom friends (Am.). Leisure breeds lust (Am.). Living in luxury begets lustful desires (Am.). When the belly is full, the mind is among the maids (Br.)

2157. Утопающий и за соломинку хватается. *A man in despair will use anything, be it ever helpless, to save himself from danger or difficulties*

Cf.: A drowning man clutches at a thread (grabs at a straw) (Am.). A drowning man will catch at a straw (Am., Br.). A drowning man will snatch at a straw (would catch at a razor) (Br.)

2158. Утро вечера мудренее. *Leave your worries for tomorrow; in the morning you will think the problem over again and solve it*

Cf.: The best advice is found on the pillow (Br.). Consult with your pillow (Br.). Have a sleep on it (Br.). Morning brings counsel (Am., Br.). Night brings counsel (Am.). The night brings (is the mother of) counsel (Br.). Sleep brings counsel (Br.). Sleep on it (Am.). Sleep over it (Am., Br.). Take counsel of your pillow (Br.). Things look brighter in the morning (Am.)

2159. У Фили были, у Фили пили, да Филю ж побили. *See 250 (В)*

Var.: У Фили пили, да Филю ж и били

Cf.: No good deed goes unpunished (Am.). Save a thief from the gallows and he'll be the first to cut your throat (Am.). Save a thief from the gallows and he'll cut your throat (Br.)

2160. У хлеба не без крох. *a) He who deals with what is profitable will take a share of it. See 314 (Г), 2137 (У); b) See 1011 (Л)*

Var.: У хлеба и крохи

Cf.: a) Every cook knows to lick her own fingers (Am.). Every honest miller has a thumb of gold (a golden thumb) (Br.). He is an ill cook that cannot lick his own fingers (Am., Br.) *b)* You cannot make an omelet (pancakes) without breaking eggs (Am., Br.)

2161. У хлеба не без крошек, у торговли не без урона. *When you have a business, you must lose sometimes*

Cf.: Every gain must have a loss (Am.). There is no trader who does not meet with losses (Br.)

2162. У хорошего мужа и жена хороша. *A good and honest man has a wholesome influence on his wife. See K-29*

Var.: За хорошим мужем и жена хороша

Cf.: A good husband makes a good wife (Am., Br.). A good Jack makes a good Jill (Am., Br.). Good wives and good plantations are made by good husbands (Am.). A good yeoman makes a good wife (Br.)

2163. Учат не только сказом, но и показом. *To teach effectively you have to show people how to do it rather than tell what to do*

Cf.: Demonstration is the best mode of instruction (Am.). Example is better than precept (Am., Br.). A good example is the best sermon (Am.)

2164. Учёного учить—только портить. *Competent people do not need your adivice. See 1466 (Н), 2368 (Я)*

Cf.: Old foxes want no tutors (Am., Br.)

2165. Ученье—свет, а неученье—тьма. *When you study, you know much; when you do not, you know nothing and are helpless*

Cf.: The lamp of knowledge burns brightly (Am.). Learning is the eye of the mind (Br.). Your ignorance is your worst enemy (Am.)

2166. Ученья корень горек, да плод сладок. *See 2080 (T)*

Cf.: Lessons hard to learn are sweet to know (Am., Br.). They that sow in tears shall reap in joy (Am.)

2167. Учи других—и сам поймёшь. *When explaining some complicated problem to other people, you comprehend it better too*

Cf.: Men learn while they teach (Am.). Teaching others teaches yourself (Am., Br.). We learn by (in) teaching (Br.). What Johnnie will not teach himself, Johnnie will never learn (Am.). While I teach, I learn (Am.)

2168. Учиться никогда не поздно. *No person is so old that he cannot profit by acquiring knowledge. See 1184 (H)*

Cf.: /It is/ never too late to learn (Am., Br.). Never too old to learn (Am., Br.). Never too old to turn; never too late to learn (Br.). You are never too old to learn (Am., Br.)

Ф

2169. Факты—упрямая вещь. *Facts are undeniable and cannot be ignored*

Cf.: Facts are facts (Am.). Facts are stubborn things (Am., Br.). Facts don't lie (Am.). There is no getting away from the facts (Br.)

2170. Федот, да не тот. *People, phenomena or things, though having some similar characteristics, are not identical. See 980 (K)*

Cf.: Every fish is not a sturgeon (Am.). Every like is not the same (Am., Br.). No like is the same (Br.). Right church but wrong pew (Am., Br.)

2171. Фома ему, а он всему селу. *See 232 (B)*

Cf.: A secret's a secret until it's told (Am.). A secret shared is no secret (Am., Br.). Two can keep a secret if one is dead (Am.). Two may keep counsel if one be away (if one of them's dead) (Br.)

Х

2172. Хвали горку, как перевалишься. *See 1321 (H)*

Cf.: Do not shout until you are out of the woods (Am.). Don't halloo (shout) till you are out of the wood (Br.). Don't halloo till you're out of the woods (Am.). Don't whistle before you leap (till you are out of the wood) (Br.). Never crow till you're out of the woods (Am.)

2173. Хвалилась синица море зажечь. *Great promise or boast but no performance. See 1143 (M)*

Var.: Пустила синица славу, а море не зажгла

Cf.: Good words and no deeds (Br.). Great boast, small roast (Am., Br.). Much talk, little work (Am.)

2174. Хвали утро днём, а день вечером. *It is only the end that can show if a man has been happy or successful. See 1321 (H)*

Var.: Вечер покажет, каков был день. Хвали жизнь при смерти, а день вечером. Хвали утро днём, а день вечером, не видав вечера, и хвалиться нечего

Cf.: Before the morning is away praise not the glory of the day (Br.). Boast not tomorrow, for you know not what a day may bring forth (Am.). Call no man happy till he dies (Br.). Call no man happy till he is dead (Am.). The evening crowns (praises) the day (Br.). No day is over until the sun has set (Am.). Praise a fair day at night /, and life at the end/ (Br.). Praise a fine day at night (Am.). Wait till night before saying that the day has been fine (Br.)

2175. Хватился шапки, когда головы не стало. *See 1730 (П)*

Cf.: After the danger everyone is wise (Am.). Wise after the event (Br.).

2176. Хлеба нет, так и друзей не бывало. *See 1901 (С)*

Cf.: As long as the pot boils, friendship lasts (Am., Br.). The bread eaten, the company dispersed (Br.). Poverty parts fellowship (friends) (Am.)

2177. Хлеб всему голова. *Bread supports life, and man cannot live without it. See 53 (Б)*

Cf.: Bread is the staff of life (Am., Br.). No such thing as brown bread (Br.)

2178. Хлеб за брюхом не ходит. *It is the man who needs something or somebody that has to be initiative. See 50 (Б)*

Cf.: God reaches us good things by our own hands (Br.). God sends every bird its food, but he does not throw it into the nest (Am.). Roasted ducks don't fly into your mouth (Am.)

2179. Хлеб-соль ешь, а правду режь. *Your conscience will be clear is you tell the truth, especially in circumstances when there seems to be a strong temptation not to do so. See 475 (Д), 1049 (Л)*

Cf.: Speak the truth and shame the devil (Am., Br.). Speak the truth bravely, cost as it may; hiding the wrong act is not the way (Am.). Tell it like it is (Am.). Tell the truth and shame the devil (Am., Br.). The truth shall set you free (Am.)

2180. Хода нет, ходи с червей. *Take a bold action*

Var.: Не с чего ходить, так с бубён

Cf.: Nothing stake, nothing draw (Br.). When in doubt, lead trumps (Am.)

2181. Хозяин—барин. *As the boss wants it, so you must do it or act. See 1265 (Н)*

Cf.: Orders are orders (Am.). Orders must not be challenged (Am.). Will is his law (Br.)

2182. Хозяйкою дом стоит. *It is the wife that keeps the house and makes a house into a home. See 469 (Д), 1265 (Н)*

Cf.: The eye of the housewife makes the cat fat (Am.). Men build houses, women build homes (Am.). Men get wealth and women keep it (Br.). Men make houses, women make homes (Am., Br.). The wife is the key of the house (Br.)

2183. Холодные руки, горячее сердце. *When a person has cold hands you say that it is a sign of him having a kind heart*

Cf.: A cold hand, a warm heart (Am., Br.)

2184. Хороша Маша, да не наша. *The woman is beautiful or the thing is good, and one would like to have them but he cannot. See 2207 (Х)*

Var.: Хорош кус, да не для наших уст

Cf.: It is good fish if it were but caught (Br.). You can look, but you cannot touch (Am.)

2185. Хороша рыба на чужом блюде. *See 296 (В)*

Cf.: The apples on the other side of the wall are sweetest (Am., Br.). The grass is always greener on the other side of the fence (Am., Br.). The next man's cows have the longest horns (Am.). Other people's eggs have two yolks (Am.). Our neighbour's ground yields better corn than ours (Br.). Your neighbour's apples are the sweetest (Br.). Your pot broken seems better than my whole one (Br.)

2186. Хорош гость, коли редко ходит. *See 1827 (Р)*

Cf.: A constant guest is never welcome (Am., Br.). Short visits and seldom are best (Am.)

2187. Хорошего понемножку. *Do not overindulge in doing anything not to spoil what you have done.See 75 (Б),*

246 (В), 467 (Д), 720 (И), 1110 (М), 1919 (С)

Var.: Хорошенького понемногу (понемножку)

Cf.: All sunshine makes a desert (Am.). Enough is as good as a feast (Am., Br.). Enough is enough, and too much spoils (Br.). Enough of a good thing is plenty (Am.). Lick honey with your little finger (Br.). More than enough is too much (Am.). Nothing in excess is best (Am.). Plenty is no dainty (Br.). There is a measure in all things (Am., Br.). Too much in the vessel bursts the lid (Am.). Too much of a good thing /is good for nothing/ (Br.). Too much of a good thing /is worse than none at all/ (Am.). Too much water drowned the miller (Br.). Without measure medicine will become poison (Am.)

2188. Хорошее дело два века живёт. *See 622 (З)*

Var.: Доброе дело на век

Cf.: A good deed is never forgotten (never dies) (Am.). A good deed is never lost (Br.)

2189. Хорошее лежит, а худое бежит. *See 550 (Д)*

Var.: Хорошее лежит, а худое далеко бежит

Cf.: Bad news travels fast /, good news is scarcely heard/ (Am.). Evil news rides post, while good news bates (Br.). Good news travels slow (Am.). Good news travels slowly; bad news travels fast (Am.). Ill news flies (Br.). Ill news travels fast (Am.)

2190. Хорошее лекарство никогда не бывает сладким. *Measures taken to improve the health or a state of affairs are often far from being pleasant*

Cf.: Bitter pills may have blessed effects (Am., Br.)

2191. Хорошие слова, а всё не пряники. *See 1969 (С)*

Cf.: Fair words butter no cabbage (Am.). Fair words fill not the belly (Br.). Flattery butters no parsnips (Am.). Good words fill not the sack (Br.). Many (Mere) words will not fill a bushel (Br.). Praise is no pudding (Br.). A thousand words won't fill a bushel (Am.). Words never filled a belly (Am.)

2192. Хороший совет дороже золота. *There is nothing more valuable than a sensible piece of advice. See 2193 (X)*

Var.: Доброму совету цены нет

Cf.: Good advice is beyond price (Am., Br.). A good counsel has no price (Br.). Good counsel is a pearl beyond price (Am.)

2193. Хороший совет не идёт во вред. *A sensible opinion should not be neglected. See 2131 (У), 2192 (X)*

Cf.: Counsel breaks not the head (Br.). Good counsel does no harm (Br.). Good counsel never comes amiss (Br.). We should never be too proud to take advice (Am.)

2194. Хороший товар не залежится. *Quality things will be sold; a nice unmarried girl will surely find her mate. See 1255 (Н)*

Cf.: Good things soon find a purchaser (Am.). Good ware makes a good (a quick) market (Br.). Good ware will off (will sell itself) (Br.). Pleasing ware is half sold (Am.. Br.)

2195. Хороший товар сам себя хвалит. *Good people and good things do not need to be praised*

Cf.: A good shop needs (wants) no sign (Am.). Good ware needs no chapman (Br.). Good wine needs no bush (Am., Br.). /A/ good wine needs no ivy bush (Br.). He whose own worth does speak need not speak his own worth (Am.)

2196. Хорошо беречь белую денежку на чёрный день. *Do not spend all your money, keep some for bad times*

Cf.: Lay by (off, up) for a rainy day (Br.). No morning sun lasts a whole day (Br.). Put something away for a rainy day (Am.). Save it for a rainy day (Am.)

2197. Хорошо дёшево не бывает. *To buy a quality thing you have to pay much money. See 458 (Д)*

Cf.: A bargain is a pinch-purse (Am.). A good bargain is a pick-purse (Am., Br.). Good things are seldom cheap (Am.)

2198. Хорошо смеётся тот, кто смеётся последним. *It is the man who succeeds at the end of a battle, argument, competition, etc., that is the winner*

Cf.: Better the last smile than the first laughter (Am., Br.). He laughs best who laughs last (Am., Br.). He who laughs last, laughs best (Am.). He who laughs last laughs longest (Am., Br.). Let them laugh that win (Am.). That's /good/ wisdom which is wisdom in the end (Br.)

2199. Хорошо тому жить, кому бабушка ворожит. *Men can do well when they have someone to support them, or when circumstances are favo(u)rable for them. See 721 (И), 861 (К)*

Cf.: A good fire makes a good cook (Am.). He dances well to whom fortune pipes (Am., Br.). He may well swim that is held up by the chin (Br.). He that is carried down the stream need not row (Am., Br.). He whose father is judge goes safely to court (Br.). It is good baking beside meal (Br.). It's easy going with the stream (Am.). It's easy to bake when the meal is beside you (Am.). Well thrives he whom God loves (Br.)

2200. Хорошо чужими руками жар загребать. *It is good to profit when other people do the hard or dirty work for you. See 1114 (М)*

Cf.: It's good to take the chestnuts out of the fire with the cat's (the dog's) paw (Br.). One man works, and another reaps the benefits (Am.)

2201. Хорош цветок, да остёр шипок. *The person looks beautiful but he is dangerous. See 877 (К), 982 (Л)*

Cf.: The bait hides the hook (Am., Br.). Cats hide their claws (Am., Br.)

2202. Хоть волком вой, хоть в прорубь головой. *See 975 (К)*

Cf.: Damned if you do, damned if you don't (Am.). There is no way out (Am., Br.)

2203. Хоть горшком назови, только в печку не ставь. *You may call me any names, but do not do any bodily harm to me. See 103 (Б)*

Var.: Хоть горшком назови, только в печь не сажай

Cf.: Sticks and stones may break my bones, but names will never hurt me (Am., Br.). Sticks and stones may break my bones, but words will never hurt me (Br.). Words may pass but blows fall heavy (Br.)

2204. Хоть лопни брюшко, да не останься добрецо. *See 570 (Е)*

Cf.: Better the belly burst than good drink (meat) lost (Br.). It's better a belly burst than good food wasted (Am.)

2205. Хоть падать, да не лежать. *Even when failing, go on acting*

Cf.: Our greatest glory consists not in never falling, but in rising every time we fall (Am.). Success comes in rising every time you fall (Am.)

2206. Хоть родной, да злой. *Men are unkind to their own relatives*

Cf.: Many kinsfolk, few friends (Am.). More kith than kind (Br.)

2207. Хоть хорош пирог, да в чужих руках. *See 2184 (Х)*

Cf.: It is good fish if it were but

caught (Br.). You can look, but you cannot touch (Am.)

2208. Хотя и гол, да не вор. *See 1043 (Л)*

Var.: Гол, да не вор, беден, да честен

Cf.: Better poor with honor than rich with shame (Am.). A penny by right is better than a thousand by wrong (Br.)

2209. Хочется рыбку съесть, да не хочется в воду лезть. *People are eager to obtain something but they are unwilling to do the required unpleasant job. See 755 (И)*

Var.: Лакома кошка до рыбки, да в воду лезть (лапки мочить) не хочет

Cf.: The cat loves fish but dares not wet his feet (Am.). The cat loves fish but hates water (Br.). The cat would eat fish, but she will not wet her feet (Am.). The cat would eat fish, but would not wet her paws (Br.)

2210. Хочешь—верь, хочешь—нет. *Incredible as it may seem to be, it is true*

Var.: Хотите—верьте, хотите—нет

Cf.: Believe it or not (Am., Br.)

2211. Хочешь дружбы—будь другом. *To maintain friendly relations with people you must be amiable. See 125 (В), 523 (З)*

Cf.: The best way to gain a friend is to be one (Am.). Friendship cannot always stand on one side (Br.). Friendship cannot stand all on one side (Am.). If you want a friend, you will have to be one (Am.). A man, to have friends, must show himself friendly (Am.). The way to have a friend is to be one (Br.)

2212. Хочешь есть калачи, так не лежи на печи. *See 1145 (М)*

Cf.: A lazy dog finds no bone (Am.). No sweat, no sweet (Am.). No sweet without /some/ sweat (Br.). Sleeping cats catch no mice (Am.). A (The) sleeping dog catches no poultry (Br.). The sleeping fox catches no poultry (Am., Br.)

2213. Хочешь мира, готовься к войне. *To prevent war you have to get well armed before it is unleashed*

Cf.: If you desire peace, be ever prepared for war (prepare for war) (Am.). If you want (wish for) peace, be prepared for war (Br.). One sword keeps another in its scabbard (Am.). One sword keeps another in the sheath (Br.). Prepare for war in time of peace (Am.)

2214. Хочу, с кашей ем, хочу, масло пахтаю. *I am more powerful than you are, so I will do as I prefer to. See 1869 (С)*

Cf.: As I will so I command (Br.). I do as I please (Am.)

2215. Хрен редьки не слаще. *There is little difference between two equally bad people, things, or events. See 225 (В), 728 (И), 2285 (Ч)*

Cf.: Another yet the same (Br.). Between two evils 'tis not worth choosing (Br.). Don't swap the witch for the devil (Am.). It is six of one and half a dozen of the other (Br.). It's six of one, half a dozen of the other (Am.). Neither barrel a (the) better herring (Br.)

2216. Худа та мышь, которая одну лазейку знает. *We must not depend on one way of salvation but have others in reserve*

Var.: Беззаботна та мышь, которая только одну лазейку знает. Плоха мышь, что один только лаз знает

Cf.: It is a poor mouse that has only one hole (Br.). A mouse never trusts its life to one hole only (Br.). The mouse that has but one hole is soon caught (Am.). The mouse that has but one hole is quickly taken (Am., Br.). The rat which has but one hole is soon caught (Am.). A smart mouse has more than one hole (Am.)

2217. Худая трава быстро растёт. *The number of unworthy people increases quickly*

Var.: Дурная трава в рост идёт (хорошо растёт). Сорная трава хорошо растёт. Худая трава в рост идёт

Cf.: Evil weed is soon grown (Br.). Ill customs grow apace (Am.). Ill weeds always grow apace (fast) (Br.). Ill weeds grow apace; folly runs a rapid race (Am.). Weeds need no sowing (Am.). Weeds want no sowing (Am., Br.). The wicked flourish as the green bay tree (Am.)

2218. Худое дворянство хуже пономарства. *It is very bad to be a once rich and noble but impoverished man*

Cf.: Gentility without ability is worse than plain beggary (Am., Br.). Noble ancestry makes a poor dish at the table (Am.)

2219. Худой мешок не наполнишь. *You can never give enough to a spendthrift*

Var.: На дырявый мешок не наберёшься

Cf.: A broken sack will hold no corn (Br.). A broken sack won't hold corn (Am.)

2220. Худой мир лучше доброй ссоры. *Any armistice or reconciliation is preferable to an open conflict*

Var.: Лучше плохой мир, чем добрая ссора

Cf.: A bad peace is better than a good quarrel (Am., Br.). A lean compromise is better than a fat lawsuit (Br.). There never was a good war or a bad peace (Am.). There was never a good war or a bad peace (Br.)

2221. Худо нажитое впрок не идёт. *Things gained in a dishonest way never bring lasting benefit. See 658 (З), 993 (Л), 2323 (Ч)*

Var.: Краденое добро впрок не идёт. Неправдой нажитое впрок не пойдёт. Чужая денежка впрок нейдёт: как придёт, так и уйдёт. Чужое добро впрок нейдёт

Cf.: Dishonest gains are losses (Am.). An evil gain is equal to a loss (Am.). Evil gotten, evil spent (Am.). Evil won is evil lost (Am.). He who steals will always fail (Am.). Ill got, ill spent (Am.). Ill-gotten gains are soon lost (Am.). Ill-gotten gains never prosper (Br.). Ill-gotten goods seldom prosper (Am., Br.). Ill-gotten, ill-spent (Br.). Ill-gotten wealth never thrives (Br.). Nothing goes over the devil's back that doesn't come back under the devil's belly (Am.). What goes over the devil's back comes under his belly (Am., Br.). What is got over the devil's back is spent under his belly (Br.)

2222. Худо начинается, худо и кончается. *See 1652 (П)*

Cf.: A bad beginning has a bad (makes a worse) ending (Br.). A bad day never has a good night (Am.). If you miss the first buttonhole, you will not succeed in buttoning up your coat (Am.). So goes Monday, so goes all the week (Am.)

2223. Худ Роман, когда пуст карман; хорош Мартын, когда есть алтын. *See 1873 (С)*

Cf.: Love lasts as long as money endures (Am., Br.). Poverty breeds strife (Br.). Want makes strife (Br.). Want makes strife between man and wife (Am.). When poverty comes in at the door, love flies out of the window (Am., Br.). When poverty comes in at the door, love leaps out of the window (Br.). When poverty comes in the door, love goes out the window (Am.). When want comes at the door, love flies out of the window (Am.)

2224. Хуже всякого слепого, кто не хочет видеть. *See 1444 (Н)*

Cf.: It is sure to be dark if you shut your eyes (Br.). A nod is as good as a wink to a blind horse (Am., Br.).

/There are/ none so blind as those who will not see (Am., Br.)

Ц

2225. Целовал ворон курочку до последнего пёрышка. *See 1677 (П)*

Var.: Целовал ястреб курочку до последнего пёрышка

Cf.: The crow bewails the sheep, and then eats it (Br.). Crows weep for the dead lamb and then devour him (Am.)

2226. Цель оправдывает средства. *If the result is good, it does not matter whether the methods used are unjust or violent*

Cf.: Choice of the end covers choice of the means (Br.). The devil can cite Scripture for his purpose (Am., Br.). The end justifies the means (Am., Br.)

2227. Цену вещи узнаешь, когда потеряешь. *See 2292 (Ч)*

Cf.: The cow knows not the value of her tail till she has lost it (Am.). The cow knows not what her tail is worth till she has lost it (Br.). One's blessings are not known until lost (Am.). We know the worth of a thing when we have lost it (Br.). We never know the value (the worth) of water till the well is dry (Br.). We only know the worth of water when the well is dry (Am.). You never miss the water till the well runs dry (Am., Br.)

2228. Цыплят по осени считают. *You should never be prematurely sure of being successful till you know the result. See 1115 (М), 1321 (Н), 1388 (Н), 1425 (Н), 1438 (Н)*

Cf.: Catch the fish before you fry it (Br.). Count not four, except you have them in the wallet (till they be in the bag) (Br.). Do not boast of a thing until it is done (Br.). Do not fish in front of a net (Am.). Don't clean your fish before you catch it (Am.). Don't count your chickens before they are hatched (Am., Br.). Don't eat the calf in the cow's belly (Br.). Draw your salary before spending it (Am.). First catch your hare (Am., Br.). First catch your hare, then cook him (Br.). First catch your hare, then cook it (Am.). First catch your rabbit and then make the stew (Am.). It is ill fishing before the net (Br.). It is ill prizing of green barley (Br.). Make not your sauce till you have caught your fish (Am.). Never spend your money before you have it (Am., Br.)

Ч

2229. Часом с квасом, порой с водой. *See 1818 (Р)*

Var.: Часом щи с мясом, а часом и хлеб с квасом

Cf.: Chickens today, feathers tomorrow (Am.). Either too much or too little (Br.). Feast today, and fast tomorrow (Br.). It's either a feast or a famine (Am.). Rich today, poor tomorrow (Am., Br.)

2230. Час от часу, а к смерти ближе. *As time goes on, the end of our life comes nearer and nearer*

Cf.: The more thy years, the nearer the grave (Am., Br.). They that live longest must die at last (Am., Br.)

2231. Час от часу не легче. *One trouble is on top of another. See 1778 (П)*

Cf.: Things are going from bad to worse (Am., Br.). When it rains, it pours (Am., Br.)

2232. Частый гость скорее наскучит. *See 1827 (Р)*

Cf.: A constant guest is never welcome (Am., Br.). A constant guest will wear out his welcome (Am.). Short visits and seldom are best (Am.)

2233. Чаша терпения переполнилась. *I cannot tolerate it any longer*

Cf.: Enough is enough (Am., Br.). I am fed up (Am., Br.). I've had it up to here (Am.). My cup is full (Br.). That's the last straw (the limit) (Am.). There's a limit to everything (Am.). This is the last straw (Br.)

2234. Чаще счёт—крепче дружба. *Paying a debt promptly promotes lasting friendship. See 2025 (C)*

Var.: Ближний счёт—дальняя дружба. Счёт чаще—дружба слаще

Cf.: Pay your debts or lose your friends (Am.). Short accounts (reckonings) make long friends (Am., Br.). Short debts make lasting (long) friends (Br.). Short reckonings make good friends (Br.)

2235. Чего на свете не бывает! *Unusual things can occur that are beyond our understanding, imagination or experience. See 1233 (Н)*

Cf.: Facts are stranger than fiction (Am.). There are more things in heaven and earth than are dreamt of in our philosophy (Br.). There are more things than are thought of in heaven and earth (Am.). There are stranger things in reality than can be found in romances (Am.). Truth is stranger than fiction (Am., Br.)

2236. Чего не дано, в аптеке не купишь. *See 541 (Д)*

Cf.: Folly is an incurable disease (Am.). There is no cure for folly (Br.)

2237. Чего не знаешь, за то не отвечаешь. *A man cannot be accused of wrongdoing if he knows nothing about it. See 680 (З)*

Cf.: It pays to be ignorant (Am.). What one doesn't know won't hurt him (Am.). What you don't hear will not hurt you (Am.). What you don't know won't hurt you (Br.). What you don't see you won't get hung for (Am.). Without knowledge there is no sin or sinner (Am.)

2238. Чего немножко, того не мечи в окошко. *When you have too little of what you need yourself, do not be wasteful of it*

Cf.: He who has but one coat cannot lend it (Br.). Lend only that which you can afford to lose (Am., Br.)

2239. Чего не чаешь, то получаешь. *Something you do not hope for, or anticipate, often occurs. See 1478 (Н)*

Cf.: The impossible always happens (Am.). It is the unforeseen that always happens (Br.). It's always the unexpected that happens (Am.). Least expected, sure to happen (Am.). Many things happen unlooked for (Br.)

2240. Чего хочется, тому и верится. *People are inclined to consider that things are or will be just as they would like them to*

Cf.: It is easy to believe what you want to (Am.). Men believe what they will to believe (Am.). We soon believe what we desire (Am., Br.). The wish is the father of the thought (Am.). The wish is the father to the thought (Am., Br.)

2241. Чей хлеб ешь, того и обычай тешь. *See 1264 (Н)*

Cf.: Every man bows to the bush he gets bield of (Br.). Whose bread I eat, his song I sing (Am.)

2242. Челном моря не переехать. *See 141 (В)*

Var.: челном океана не переехать

Cf.: It is hard to cross (to sail over) the sea in an egg-shell (Br.). You cannot catch the wind in the palm of your hand (Am.)

2243. Человек два раза глуп живёт—стар и мал. *Old people become silly and helpless and behave like children*

Cf.: An old man is twice a boy (Am.). An old man is twice a child (Br.). Old men are twice children (Am., Br.). Once a man and twice a child (Am., Br.). When the age is in the wit is out (Br.)

2244. Человек не камень: терпит да и треснет. *See 286 (В)*

Cf.: Even a worm will turn (Am., Br.). A man may bear till his back break (Br.). Rub a galled horse and he will kick (Am.)

2245. Человек познаётся в беде. *It is in hard times that men show their true, noble or mean, nature*

Var.: Золото огнём, человек бедой познаётся

Cf.: Calamity and prosperity are the touchstones of integrity (Am.). Calamity is the man's true touchstone (Br.). Difficulties are things that show what men are (Am.)

2246. Человек предполагает, а Бог располагает. *Men make plans which may not be accomplished because of unforseen circumstances. See 340 (Г)*

Var.: Человек гадает, а Бог располагает. Человек по-своему, а Бог по-своему

Cf.: Man proposes, and (but) God disposes (Br.). Man proposes, God disposes (Am.)

2247. Человек сам кузнец своего счастья. *It depends on one's will, energy and persistence if he is or will be successful or not*

Var.: Каждый человек—кузнец своего счастья

Cf.: Every man is master of his fortune (Am.). Every man is the architect of his own fortune (Am., Br.). Every man's destiny is in his own hands (Br.). Everyone is the maker of his own fate (Am.). Life is just what you make it (Am.). A man's best friend and worst enemy is himself (Am.). You make your own luck (Am.)

2248. Человек сам себе враг. *Some men act in such a way that they cause harm to themselves. See 1277 (H)*

Cf.: Beware of no man more than thyself (Br.). Each man makes his own shipwreck (Am.). Every man carries an enemy in his own bosom (Br.). Every man is his own worst enemy (Am., Br.). Evil is brought on by oneself (Am.). Man only from himself can suffer wrong (Am.). A man's best friend and worst enemy is himself (Am.). None is hurt (offended) but by himself (Br.). You dig your grave with your own hands (Am.)

2249. Человек сам себе не судья. *No man can be unbiased enough in his own case to give a just estimation of his own doings*

Var.: В своём деле никто сам себе не судья

Cf.: He who will have no judge but himself condemns himself (Br.). If you judge your own case, you are judged by a fool (Am.). Men are blind in their own cause (Am., Br.). No man ought to be judge in his own case (Br.)

2250. Человек сам себе плохой советчик. *When in predicament, you should not rely only on your own opinion to find a way out*

Cf.: He that is his own counsel (lawyer) has a fool for a client (Br.). A man who is his own lawyer has a fool for a client (Am.). Only a fool is his own lawyer (Am.). Self is a bad counsellor (Br.)

2251. Человеку свойственно ошибаться. *It is in the nature of man to err, hence we should be forgiving. See 136 (В), 738 (И), 1515 (О), 2059 (Т)*

Cf.: Every man makes mistakes (Am.). He is dead that is faultless (Am.). He is lifeless that is faultless (Am., Br.). He who makes no mistakes is a fool (Am.). He who makes no mistakes makes nothing (Br.). No man is without faults (Am.). No one is infallible (Am.). To err is human (Am., Br.)

2252. Человек человеку—волк. *People struggle mercilessly for existence or success*

Var.: Человек человеку зверь

Cf.: Man is a wolf to a man (Br.). Man is a wolf to man (Am.)

2253. Чем ближе знаешь, тем меньше почитаешь. *See 1450 (Н)*
Cf.: Familiarity breeds contempt (Am., Br.)

2254. Чем богаты, тем и рады. *You are welcome to share our food with us be it not plentiful or rich. See 1133 (М)*
Cf.: Come and have a pickle (Br.). Come and have (take) potluck with us (Am.). Come and have (take) pot-luck with us (Br.)

2255. Чем больше ешь, тем больше хочется. *See 7 (А)*
Cf.: The appetite comes while eating (Am.). /The/ appetite comes with eating (Br.). The more one has, the more one wants (Am., Br.). The more you eat (get), the more you want (Am.)

2256. Чем больше знаешь, тем больше сомневаешься. *See 949 (К)*
Cf.: Doubt grows up with knowledge (Am.). He that knows nothing, doubts nothing (Br.). He who knows most knows best how little he knows (Am.). Increase your knowledge and increase your grief (Am.). The more you know, the more you know what you don't know (Am.)

2257. Чем дальше в лес, тем больше дров. *As events develop or when you dig into some hard work, additional problems arise*
Cf.: As the days grow longer, the storms are stronger (Br.). The farther in, the deeper (Br.). Go farther and far worse (Am., Br.)

2258. Чем меньше говорить, тем здоровее. *The less one talks, the less harm is done. See 1029 (Л)*
Cf.: Few words are best (Am.). Least said is soonest mended (Am., Br.). Least said, soonest mended (Am.). The less said, the better (Am., Br.). Little said, soon amended (Am., Br.). A word that is not spoken never does any mischief (Am.)

2259. Чем раньше, тем лучше. *The matter is urgent and it has to be begun and fulfilled as soon as possible*
Cf.: The sooner, the better (Am., Br.)

2260. Чем сосуд наполнен, то из него и льётся. *People behave the way they were brought up. See 2284 (Ч)*
Cf.: The dogs bark as they are bred (Br.). Every cask smells of the wine it contains (Am., Br.). Every tub smells of the wine it contains (Br.). Every tub smells of the wine it holds (Am.). Garbage in, garbage out (Am.). One only brings to any place what is in himself (Br.). There comes nothing out of the sack but what was in it (Am.). There comes nought out of the sack but what was there (Br.)

2261. Чему бывать, того не миновать. *See 1610 (О)*
Cf.: No flying from fate (Br.). There's no flying from fate (Am.). What is to be, will be (Br.). What must be, must be (Am., Br.)

2262. Чему было начало, тому будет и конец. *Nothing is everlasting. See 1485 (Н), 2092 (У)*
Var.: Всему есть конец. Нет начала без конца
Cf.: All good things come to an end (Am., Br.). Every hour has its end (Br.). Everything has an end (Am., Br.). Nothing evil or good lasts a hundred years (Am.). There must be a beginning and an end to a thing (Am.). Time ends all things (Am.)

2263. Чему научишься в молодости, то знаешь и в старости. *Skill and knowledge you acquire when young are retained till you are old*
Cf.: What is learned in the cradle is carried to the tomb (Br.). What is learned in the cradle lasts to the tomb (till the grave) (Br.). What is learned in the cradle lasts to the grave (Am.). What we learn early we remember late (Am.). What youth is used to, age remembers (Br.)

2264. Чем ушибся, тем и лечись. *See 838 (K)*
Cf.: Desperate cuts (diseases) must have desperate cures (Am., Br.). Desperate evils require desperate remedies (Am.). Fight fire with fire (Am.). Fight the devil with his own tools, or fight the devil with fire (Am.). The hair of the dog is good for the bite (Am.). One poison drives out another (Br.). Poison quells poison (Am.). Seek your salve where you got your sore (Br.). Take the hair of the same dog that bit you, and it will heal the wound (Br.). You must fight fire with fire (Br.)

2265. Чем чёрт не шутит. *a) You never know, anything good or bad may happen quite unexpectedly; b) See 323 (Г)*
Var.: Чем чёрт не шутит, пока Бог спит
Cf.: a) You never can tell (Am., Br.)
b) I'll stick my head out (Br.). I'll stick my neck out (Am.). A man can die but once, go ahead and give it a try (Br.). What will be will be (Am., Br.)

2266. Через тернии к звёздам. *It is only by endurance and suffering that glory and beatitude are obtained. See 1424 (H)*
Cf.: Crosses are the ladders to heaven (Am.). The greater the obstacle, the more glory in overcoming it (Am.). No cross, no crown (Am., Br.). No path of flowers conducts to glory (Br.). No path of flowers leads to glory (Am.). Nothing great is easy (Br.). Through hardships to the stars (Br.)

2267. Чёрная курочка—белые яички. *See 870 (K)*
Cf.: Black fowl can lay white eggs (Am.). A black hen always lays (will lay) a white egg (Am.). A black hen lays a white egg (Br.)

2268. Чёрного кобеля не отмоешь добела. *See 383 (Г)*
Var.: Чёрного ворона не вымоешь добела
Cf.: Bad is the wool that cannot be dyed (Am.). Black will take no other hue (Am., Br.). A crow is never /the/ whiter for washing herself oft (often) (Br.). A crow is no whiter for being washed (Am.). Wash a dog, comb a dog: still a dog (Am.). You cannot wash a blackamoor (charcoal) white (Br.). You can't paint the devil white (Br.)

2269. Чёрное от стирки не белеет. *See 383 (Г)*
Cf.: Bad is the wool that cannot be dyed (Am.). It is a bad cloth that will take no colo(u)r (Am., Br.). It's ill wool that will take no dye (Br.)

2270. Чёрт попу не товарищ. *See 402 (Г)*
Cf.: Geese with geese, and women with women (Br.). Tigers and deer do not stroll together (Am.)

2271. Чёрт чёрту рога не обломает. *See 196 (B)*
Cf.: Dog does not eat dog (Am., Br.). The ravens don't peck one another's eyes out (Am.)

2272. Честный путь—лучший путь. *It is wiser to act righteously not to be conscience-stricken or have your dishonesty foud out*
Cf.: Honesty is the best policy (Am., Br.)

2273. Честь не в честь, как нечего есть. *Hono(u)r is of no use if it does not bring money*
Var.: Честь добра, да съесть нельзя. Что за (и) честь, коли нечего есть
Cf.: Honesty is praised and left to starve (Am.). Honour buys no beef in the market (Br.). Honour without maintenance is like a blue coat without a badge (Br.)

2274. Чинёная посуда два века живёт. *A well restored friendship or thing lasts long*

Var.: Склеенная посуда два века живёт

Cf.: Broken bones well set become stronger (Am., Br.)

2275. Чистого и огонь не обожжёт. *See 1474 (Н)*

Cf.: A clear conscience is a coat of mail (a sure card) (Am., Br.). A clear conscience is a wall of brass (Am.)

2276. Чистому—всё чисто. *Noble and honest people are least likely to see evil and indecency in a person or speak ill of him*

Cf.: From a pure spring, pure water flows (Am.). To the pure all things are pure (Am., Br.). Who has a clean heart, has also a clean tongue (Am.)

2277. Чистота—лучшая красота. *To be physically and morally clean is to possess most significant virtues*

Cf.: Cleanliness is akin to godliness (Am.). Cleanliness is next to godliness (Am., Br.)

2278. Чтоб не сглазить. *Let good luck stay or bad luck never come*

Cf.: Cross your fingers (Am.). Knock on wood (Am., Br.). Touch wood (Am., Br.)

2279. Что Бог ни делает, всё к лучшему. *Do not be so sorry, things, bad as they are at present, will change for the better. See 227 (В)*

Var.: Что ни делается, всё к лучшему

Cf.: All /is/ for the best (Am.). All's for the best in the best of all possible worlds (Am., Br.). All that happens, happens for the best (Am). All things happen for the best (Am.). Whatever happens will turn out for the better in the end (Br.)

2280. Что было, то видели, что будет, то увидим. *We know only what occurred, but we cannot foresee what will happen. See 1678 (П)*

Cf.: We'll wait and see (Am., Br.). We shall see what we shall see (Br.)

2281. Что было, то прошло и быльём поросло. *a) Do not sigh for the past, we cannot call it back. See 67 (Б), 2295 a (Ч), 2302 (Ч); b) Allow old causes of contention to be forgotten. See 970 (К)*

Var.: Было, да сплыло (да быльём (травой) поросло). Что было, то сплыло

Cf.: a) The mill cannot grind with the water that is past (Am., Br.). The mill grinds no corn with water that has passed (Br.). It is too late to grieve when the chance is past (Br.). What has been, has been (Br.). What's gone and what's past help should be past grief (Am.)

b) Let bygones be bygones (Am., Br.). Reopen not a wound once healed (Am.)

2282. Чтобы рыбку съесть, надо в воду лезть. *See 50 (Б)*

Cf.: The cat that would eat fish must wet her feet (Am.). Dry shoes won't catch fish (Br.). He who would catch fish must not mind getting wet (Am., Br.). You can't catch trout with dry trousers (Am.)

2283. Чтобы узнать человека, надо с ним пуд соли съесть. *You need much time to fully find out what a man is like*

Var.: Человека узнаешь, как из семи печек с ним щей похлебаешь (когда с ним пуд соли /ложкой/ расхлебаешь). Человека узнать -не котелок каши съесть

Cf.: Before you trust a man, eat a peck of salt with him (Br.). Eat a peck of salt with a man before you trust him (Am.). You have to hoe a row of corn with a man in order to know him (Am.). You have to winter and summer with people to know them (Am.)

2284. Что в котёл положишь, то и вынешь. *The result depends on the stuff used. See 805 (К), 821 (К), 2260 (Ч)*

Var.: Что положишь себе в котёл, то и будет в ложке

Cf.: Fat hens make rich soup (Am.).

Garbage in, garbage out (Am.). If you plant potatoes, you can't reap tomatoes (Am.). Such beef, such broth (Br.). You get out of something only what you put in (Am.)

2285. Что в лоб, что по лбу. *Either alternative is bad. See 225 (В), 728 (И), 1461 (Н), 2215 (Х)*

Var.: Всё одно, что в лоб, что в голову

Cf.: Between two evils 'tis not worth choosing (Br.). It is all one (Br.). /It is/ six of one and half a dozen of the other (Br.). It's six of one, half a dozen of the other (Am.). Whether the pitcher strikes the stone, or the stone the pitcher it is bad for the pitcher (Am.)

2286. Что ворам с рук сходит, за то воришек бьют. *Men are accused for insignificant offenses, but they are acquitted for great ones when they have money to pay off or are powerful. See 6 (А)*

Cf.: Laws are like cobwebs which may catch small flies, but let wasps and hornets break through (Br.). Laws catch flies and let hornets go free (Am.). Laws catch flies, but let hornets go free (Br.). Little thieves are hanged, but great ones escape (Am., Br.). We hang little thieves and take off our hats to great ones (Am.)

2287. Что в сердце варится, то в лице не утаится. *The feelings and emotions of a person can be seen in his face. See 1026 (Л)*

Cf.: The face is the index of the heart (Br.). What you wear in your heart shows in your face (Am.)

2288. Что говорит большой, слышит и малый. *Children often hear and pick up from adults what they are not supposed to know*

Cf.: Little children have long ears (Am.). Little pigs have long ears (Br.). Little pitchers have big ears (Am.). Little pitchers have great (long) ears (Am., Br.). Small pitchers have wide ears (Am., Br.)

2289. Что говорят взрослые, то и дети повторяют. *Kids repeat what their parents talk about in their presence*

Cf.: As young folks see, the young folks do; as they hear, they say (Am.). Children tell in the highway what they hear by the fireside (Br.). What children hear at home does soon fly abroad (Br.). What children hear at home soon flies abroad (Am.)

2290. Что за шум, а драки нет. *What is happening?*

Cf.: What's buzzing /cousin/? (Am.). What's cooking? (Am., Br.). What's doing? (Am.). What's going down? (Am.). What's going on /around here/? (Am., Br.). What's shaking? (Am.). What's the deal (the drill)? (Am.). What's the game? (Am., Br.). What's the scam? (Am.). What's up? (Am., Br.)

2291. Что знает кум, знает и кумова жена, а по ней и вся деревня. *See 232 (В)*

Var.: Знает кум, да кума, да людей полсела

Cf.: Confide in an aunt and the world will know (Br.). A secret shared is no secret (Am., Br.)

2292. Что имеем, не храним, потерявши, плачем. *We realize what love, friendship, things, etc. mean to us when we lose them. See 2227 (Ц)*

Cf.: The cow knows not the value of her tail till she has lost it (Am.). The cow knows not what her tail is worth till she has lost (loses) it (Br.). One's blessings are not known until lost (Am.). We know the worth of a thing when we have lost it (Br.). We never appreciate the sunshine and the rainbow until the storm clouds hang low (Am.). When the pinch comes you remember the old shoe (Br.). The worth of a thing is best known by its want (Am.). The worth of a thing is best known by the want of it (Br.). You never miss the water till the well runs dry (Am., Br.)

2293. Что летом родится, то зимой пригодится. *See 1015 (Л)*

Cf.: Winter discovers what summer conceals (Am.). Winter eats what summer gets (Am.). Winter eats what summer lays up (Br.). Winter finds out what summer lays up (Am.)

2294. Что людям желаешь, то и сам получаешь. *See 917 (К), 1598 (О)*

Cf.: Curses like chickens come home to roost (Br.). Curses, like chickens, come home to roost (Am.). Harm watch, harm catch (Am., Br.). He who does harm should expect harm (Am.). He who thinks evil wishes it on himself (Am.). If you curse others, you will be cursed (Am.)

2295. Что минуло, то сгинуло. *See a) 2281 a (Ч); b) 970 (К)*

Cf.: a) The mill cannot grind with the water that is past (Am., Br.). Things past cannot be recalled (Br.). What's gone and what's past help should be past grief (Am.)

b) Bury the past (Br.). Let bygones be bygones (Am., Br.). Let the dead bury the dead (Am.)

2296. Что молвишь. то не воротишь. *See 1930 (С)*

Cf.: Spoken words are like flown birds: neither can be recalled (Am.). A thing that is said is said, and forth it goes (Br.). What is said can never be resaid (Am.). When the word is out it belongs to another (Br.). A word spoken is past recalling (Am., Br.)

2297. Что можно одному, то нельзя другому. *That which is decent for one man to do is ridiculous for another*

Cf.: All things fit not all persons (Am.). Every shoe fits not every foot (Br.). One shoe does not fit every foot (will not fit all feet) (Br.). You can't put the same shoe on every foot (Am.)

2298. Что написано пером, того не вырубишь топором. *When what is on paper comes into effect, it cannot be changed*

Var.: Напишешь пером, не вырубишь и топором

Cf.: What is writ is writ (Br.). The written letter remains (Br.). The written word remains (Am.)

2299. Что на уме, то и на языке. *a) You must think before saying something you should be silent about. See 2361 (Я); b) A sincere man opens his mind frankly*

a) An empty head, like a bell, has a long tongue (Am.). The tongue runs before the wit (Br.)

b) What the heart thinks, the tongue speaks (Am., Br.)

2300. Что ни город, то норов, что ни деревня, то обычай. *Any community has its own traditions and way of life. See 158 (В), 172 (В), 1910 (С), 2094 (У)*

Var.: Что ни город, то обычай, что ни местечко, то свой нрав. Что ни двор (край), то свой обычай

Cf.: Different countries, different customs (Am., Br.). Every country has its /own/ custom (customs) (Am., Br.). Other countries, other customs (Br.). So many countries, so many customs (Am., Br.)

2301. Что обещание, что зарок — ненадёжны. *You can never be sure if someone will keep his word or not. See 1506 (О)*

Cf.: All promises are either broken or kept (Am., Br.). It's one thing to promise, another to perform (Am., Br.). Promises are like good piecrust: easily broken (Am.). Promises are like pie-crust, made to be broken (Br.). Promises are like piecrust: they are made to be broken (Am.)

2302. Что о том тужить, чего нельзя воротить. *See 1920 a (С), 2281 a (Ч)*

Var.: Что про то говорить, чего не можно воротить

Cf.: Don't cry over spilled milk (Am.). For a lost thing care not (Br.).

It is no good crying over spilt milk (Br.). Let the dead bury the dead (Am., Br.). Never grieve for what you cannot help (Br.). No weeping for shed milk (Am., Br.). Past cure, past care (Br.). Things without remedy should be without regard (Am.)

2303. Что посеешь, то и пожнёшь. *One will take the consequences of his actions. See 792 (К), 811 (К), 825 (К)*

Cf.: As you sow, so shall you reap (Am., Br.). He that plants thorns must never expect to gather roses (Br.). He that sows thistles shall reap prickles (Br.). He who sows brambles reaps thorns (Am.). He who sows thorns will never reap grapes (Am.). You must reap what you have sown (Br.). You shall reap what you sow (Am.)

2304. Что природа дала, того и мылом не отмоешь. *See 383 (Г)*

Var.: Чёрную душу /и/ мылом не отмоешь

Cf.: A crow is never the whiter for washing herself oft (often) (Br.). A crow is no whiter for being washed (Am.). Wash a dog, comb a dog: still a dog (Am.)

2305. Что прошло, поминать на что. *See 970 (К)*

Cf.: Let bygones be bygones (Am., Br.). Reopen not a wound once healed (Am.)

2306. Что прошло, то будет мило. *We enjoy recollecting hardships we overcame in the past*

Cf.: Pain past is pleasure (Am., Br.). The remembrance of past dangers is pleasant (Am.). Remembrance of past sorrow is joyful (Br.). Sorrows remembered sweeten present joy (Am.). That which was bitter to endure may be sweet to remember (Am., Br.). What is hard to bear is sweet to remember (Am.). When difficulties are over they become blessings (Br.)

2307. Что русскому здорово, то немцу смерть. *What is beneficial for some man may be very harmful for another*

Cf.: None so good that it's good to all (Br.). One man's breath, /is/ another man's death (Br.). One man's drink (gravy) is another man's poison (Am.). One man's meat is another man's poison (Am., Br.). One man's sweet is another man's sour (Am.). What is good for one man, may not be good for another (Am.)

2308. Что с возу упало, то пропало. *a) You cannot get back a thing that is gone or lost and is past recovery. See 1747 (П), 1783 (П); b) He who finds a lost thing becomes its owner*

Cf.: a) The mill cannot grind with the water that is past (Am., Br.). Spilled water cannot be gathered up (Am.). What is lost is lost (Br.). When the ewe is drowned she is dead (Br.)

b) Finders keepers /, losers weepers/ (Am.). Finding is keeping (Am., Br.). Losers seekers, finders keepers (Br.). Possession is nine points of the law (Am., Br.)

2309. Что стерпится, то и слюбится. *Habit brings liking. (We say it to console a person who has to do something against his will, especially to marry someone he does not love)*

Var.: Стерпится, слюбится

Cf.: It is nothing when you are used to it (Am.). Marry first, and love will come afterwards (Br.). Marry first, and love will follow (Am.)

2310. Что твёрдо выучишь, долго помнится. *Thorough knowledge is lasting. See 1242 (Н)*

Cf.: He who learns the hard way will never forget (Am.). Quickly learned, soon forgotten (Br.). What is well learned is not forgotten (Am.)

2311. Что у тебя болит, то у другого не свербит. *See 2325 (Ч)*

Cf.: It is easy to bear the misfortunes

of others (Br.). We can always bear the misfortunes of others (Am.)

2312. Что у трезвого на уме, то у пьяного на языке. *People when they are drunk tell things they are silent about when sober. See 750 (И), 1807 (П)*

Var.: Трезвого дума, пьяного речь

Cf.: Drunken heart won't lie (Am.). Drunkenness reveals what soberness conceals (Am., Br.). A drunken tongue tells what's on a sober mind (Am.). /Good/ ale will make a cat speak (Br.). Good liquor will make a cat speak (Am., Br.). What soberness conceals, drunkenness reveals (Am., Br.). When wine sinks, words swim (Am., Br.). Wine /is/ in, truth /is/ out (Br.). Wine is the discoverer of secrets (Am.)

2313. Что хорошо, то хорошо, а что лучше, то лучше. *There is no end to perfection*

Cf.: Nothing /is/ so good but it might have been better (Br.). There may be blue and better blue (Br.). There's always room for improvement (Am.)

2314. Чудеса в решете! *What an incredibly amazing thing!*

Cf.: If that don't beat all! (Am.). Miracles will never cease! (Br.). Surprises never cease (Am.). That beats cock-fighting (grandmother, the Dutch)! (Br.). That beats everything! (Am.). Will wonders never cease? (Br.). Wonders will never cease! (Am.)

2315. Чужая беда научит. *See 1221 (Н)*

Cf.: It is good to beware by other men's harms (Br.). Let another's shipwreck be your beacon (sea-mark) (Br.). Let another's shipwreck be your sea work (Am.). Profit by the folly of others (Am.)

2316. Чужая беда не весит. *See 2325 (Ч)*

Cf.: Another's cares will not rob you of sleep (Am.). It is easy to bear the misfortunes of others (Br.). We can always bear our neighbors' misfortunes (Am.)

2317. Чужая беда не даёт ума. *It is not from other men's failings, but from our own, that we gain experience how to avoid them*

Var.: Чужая беда не научит

Cf.: Experience keeps no school, she teaches her pupils singly (Br.). Other men's failures can never save you (Am.). Someone else's troubles don't make you wise (Am.). We don't learn by others' mistakes (Am.)

2318. Чужая болячка в боку не сидит. *See 2325 (Ч)*

Cf.: Another's cares will not rob you of sleep (Am.). It is easy to bear the misfortunes of others (Br.). We can always bear our neighbors' misfortunes (Am.)

2319. Чужая душа—потёмки. *You cannot know what other people think or feel. See 1454 (Н), 1888 (С)*

Var.: В чужую душу не влезешь. Чужая душа—тёмный лес

Cf.: The face is no index to the heart (Br.). The human heart is a mystery (Br.). You can look in the eyes but not in the heart (Am.). You don't know what's in the heart (Am.)

2320. Чужая ноша не тянет. *You are not depressed by someone else's difficulties. See 2325 (Ч)*

Var.: Ноша легка на чужом плече

Cf.: The burden is light on the shoulders of others (Am.). He carries well to whom it weighs not (Br.). No one knows the weight of another's burden (Am., Br.). Your neighbor's burden is always light (Am.)

2321. Чужая слеза, что с гуся вода. *See 2325 (Ч)*

Cf.: Another's cares will not rob you of sleep (Am.). It is easy to bear the misfortunes of others (Br.). We can always bear our neighbors' misfortunes (Am.)

2322. Чужая сторона прибавит ума. *You learn more when you see much of the world*

Cf.: He that travels much knows much (Am., Br.). Travel broadens the mind (Am.)

2323. Чужим добром не разживёшься. *See 2221 (X)*

Cf.: Dishonest gains are losses (Am.). An evil gain is equal to a loss (Am.). Ill-gotten goods seldom prosper (Am., Br.). What is got over the devil's back is spent under his belly (Br.)

2324. Чужим добром подноси ведром. *You take or give away willingly things that belong to other people. See 719 (И)*

Cf.: All men are free of other men's goods (Am.). Hens are free of horse corn (Br.). It is easy to be generous with what is another's (Br.). It is easy to spend someone else's money (Am.). Men cut large shives of another's loaf (Br.). Men cut large thongs of other men's leather (Br.). Somebody else's wealth is easy to dispose (Am.)

2325. Чужое горе не болит. *We take someone else's grief quite easy. See 386 (Г), 659 (З), 2311 (Ч), 2316 (Ч), 2318 (Ч), 2320 (Ч), 2321 (Ч)*

Var.: Чужое горе вполгоря горевать. Чужое горе оханьем пройдёт

Cf.: Another's cares will not rob you of sleep (Am.). The comforter's head never aches (Br.). It is easy to bear the misfortunes of others (Br.). One has always strength enough to bear the misfortunes of others (Br.). We all have strength enough to bear the misfortunes of others (Am.). We can always bear our neighbors' misfortunes (Am.)

2326. Чужой грех своего не искупит. *Your wrongdoings will not atone for another's. See 668 (З)*

Cf.: Two blacks do not make a white (Am., Br.). Two wrongs do not make a right (Am., Br.)

2327. Чужой дурак—смех, а свой—стыд. *Someone else's foolishness makes you laugh, but if it concerns your family, you take it close to heart. See 1092 (Л)*

Var.: Чужой дурак—веселье, а свой—бесчестье

Cf.: Everything is funny as long as it happens to someone else (Am.)

2328. Чужой обед похваляй, да и сам ворота открывай. *See 125 (В)*

Var.: По гостям гуляй, да и сам ворота отворяй

Cf.: The best way to gain a friend is to be one (Am.). Friendship cannot always stand on one side (Br.). Friendship cannot stand all on one side (Am.). He who would have friends must show himself friendly (Am.). One complimentary letter asks another (Br.). The way to have a friend is to be one (Br.)

2329. Чужой хлеб рот дерёт. *You have to pay off with humiliation or hard work for anything given to you out of pity. See 404 (Д)*

Var.: Чужой мёд горек

Cf.: Another's bread costs dear (Br.). The bitter bread of dependence is hard to chew (Am.). Bitter is the bread of charity (Am.). Bound is he that gifts taketh (Br.). Who receives a gift sells his liberty (Br.)

2330. Чужую кровлю кроешь, а своя каплет. *See 1855 (С)*

Var.: Чужую крышу кроешь, а своя течёт

Cf.: A cobbler's child is always the worst shod (Am.). The cobbler's children go unshod (never wear shoes) (Am.). The cobbler's children usually go unshod (Br.). The door of the carpenter is loose (Am.). You water the fields of others while your own are parched (Br.)

2331. Чужую пашню пашет, а своя в залежи. *See 1855 (С)*

Cf.: The cobbler's children go unshod (Am.). The cobbler's wife is the worst shod (Br.). Neglect not your own field to plough a neighbour's (Br.). You water the fields of others while your own are parched (Br.)

2332. Чуть не считается. *Even a narrow failure in doing or getting something is the same as failing completely*

Cf.: Almost never killed a fly (Am., Br.). Almost was never hanged (Am., Br.). The archer who overshoots the mark misses, as well as he that falls short of it (Br.). An inch in missing is as bad as a mile (Am.). A miss is as good as a mile (Am., Br.). Nearly never did any good (Am.)

2333. Чьё кушаю, того и слушаю. *See 1264 (Н)*

Cf.: Every man bows to the bush he gets bield of (Br.). Whose bread I eat, his song I sing (Am.)

2334. Чья бы корова мычала, а твоя бы молчала. *You do not have any right to judge or criticize other people because you are not faultless either. See 15 (А), 358 (Г), 511 (Д), 909 (К), 1406 (Н), 1562 (О), 1612 (О), 1832 (Р)*

Cf.: Blame not others for the faults that are in you (Am.). The devil rebukes sin (Br.). Fly pride, says the peacock (Br.). Ill may the kiln call the oven burnt-tail (Br.). It takes one to know one (Am.). The kiln calls the oven burnt ass (Am.). Look who's talking! (Am.). One ass calls another long ears (Am.). The pot calling (calls) the kettle black (Am., Br.). The raven chides blackness (Br.). The raven eludes blackness (Am.). The raven said to the rook: "Stand away, black-coat" (Br.). Satan (Vice) rebukes sin (Br.)

Ш

2335. Шапка в рубль, а щи без круп. *See 1178 (Н)*

Var.: Дома щи без круп, а в людях шапка в рубль

Cf.: Great boast and small roast (Am., Br.)

2336. Шила в мешке да любви в сердце не утаишь. *Love, like any other secret, will give itself away however hard you may try to keep it from others. See 243 (В), 1071 (Л), 2337 (Ш)*

Cf.: Love and a cough cannot be hidden (Am.). Love and cough cannot be hid (hidden) (Br.). Love and poverty are hard to hide (Br.). Love and smoke cannot be hidden (Am., Br.). There is nothing hidden that is not shown (Am.)

2337. Шила в мешке не утаишь. *A secret that is sure to give itself away cannot be concealed. See 243 (В), 2336 (Ш)*

Cf.: Fire cannot be hidden in a flax (in straw) (Br.). Murder will out (Am., Br.). There is nothing hidden that is not shown (Am.). Wicked deeds will not stay hid (Am.). You cannot hide an eel in a sack (Br.)

2338. Шила и мыла, гладила и катала, пряла и лощила, а всё языком. *See 1143 (М)*

Cf.: Good words and no deeds (Br.). Much talk, little work (Am.)

2339. Шилом моря не нагреть. *See 141 (В)*

Cf.: The wind cannot be caught in (with) a net (Br.). You cannot catch the wind in the palm of your hand (Am.)

2340. Шкодлив, как кошка, а труслив, как заяц. *Meanness always goes together with cowardice*

Cf.: A bully is always a coward (Am., Br.)

2341. Штопай дыру, пока невелика. *If you take instant actions when something starts going wrong, you will not have to face bad consequences. See 2140 (У)*

Cf.: A dropped stitch is soon a hole (Am.). A green wound is soon healed (Am., Br.). He that corrects not small faults will not control great ones (Br.). He that repairs not a part, builds all (Br.). A little neglect may breed great mischief (Am.). Nip the act while in the bud (Am.). A step in time saves nine (Am.). A stitch in time saves nine (Am., Br.). Who repairs not his gutters repairs the whole house (Br.)

2342. Шуба висит, а тело дрожит. *See 1916 (С)*

Var.: Шуба лежит, а шкура дрожит

Cf.: The ass loaded with gold still eats thistles (Br.). Even if the ass is laden with gold, he will seek his food among the thorns (Am.). Fools live poor to die rich (Br.). A miser is an ass that carries gold and eats thistles (Am.). Moles and misers live in their graves (Br.)

2343. Шумом праву не быть. *It is good reasons, but not talking at the top of the voice, that are convincing*

Cf.: Some people think that the louder they shout, the more persuasive their argument is (Am.). Those who are right need not talk loudly (Am.)

2344. Шути, да оглядывайся. *Do not go too far when rallying a man, be careful not to offend him. See 2345 (Ш)*

Cf.: Do not carry a joke too far (Am.). Leave a jest when it pleases lest it turn to earnest (Br.). Long jesting was never good (Br.). When your jest is at its best, let it rest (Am., Br.)

2345. Шутка в добро не введёт. *Very often people take a joke as an offence. See 940 (К), 2344 (Ш)*

Cf.: He makes a foe who makes a jest (Am.). If you give (make) a jest, you must take a jest (Br.). A joke never gains over an enemy, but often loses a friend (Am.). True jests breed bad blood (Am.)

Щ

2346. Щеголял с молоду, а под старость умирает с голоду. *If you do not work, but only squander your money when young, you will suffer when old*

Var.: Гулять с молоду—помирать под старость с голоду

Cf.: The excesses of our youth are draughts upon our old age (Am.). Idleness in youth makes way for a painful and miserable old age (Am.). An idle youth, a needy age (Br.). If you lie upon roses when young, you'll lie upon thorns when old (Am., Br.). Lie on roses when young, lie on thorns when old (Am.). Reckless youth makes rueful age (Am., Br.). A young man idle, an old man needy (Am.)

2347. Щенок лает, от больших слышит. *See 1101 (М)*

Var.: Маленькая собачка лает—от большой слышит

Cf.: As the old bird sings, so the young ones twitter (Am.). As the old cock crows, so crows the young (Br.). As the old cock crows, the young cock learns (Am.). The dogs bark as they are bred (Br.)

2348. Щеня злое от злой суки. *See 2357 (Я)*

Cf.: The fruit doesn't fall far from the tree (Am.). Like cow, like calf (Br.)

Э

2349. Эта беда не беда, только б больше не была. *If a more severe thing does not happen, this trouble can be endured. See 1147 (М)*

Cf.: Nothing so bad but it might have been worse (Am., Br.). Nothing so bad that it couldn't be worse (Am.)

2350. Этого ещё не хватало. *There is enough trouble without this one*

Cf.: Can you beat it (that)! (Am., Br.). It's a bit (rather, too) thick (Br.)

2351. Это ещё вилами по воде писано. *I do not believe it will come true, it is hardly probable. See 18 (Б)*

Cf.: If the sky falls, we shall catch larks (Am.). It is still quite in the air (Br.). That remains to be seen (Am.). There is many a slip twixt cup and lip (Am.). There's many a slip between ('twixt) the cup and the lip (Br.). We shall catch larks if (when) the sky falls (Br.)

2352. Это ещё цветочки, а ягодки впереди. *It is only the beginning of troubles, there are worse ones ahead. See 2058 (Т)*

Cf.: Cheer up—the worst is yet to come (Am., Br.). Cheer up, things will get worse (Am.). The end is not yet (Br.). The sting is in the tail (Br.). This is only the beginning (Am.). The worst is yet to come (Am., Br.)

2353. Это не шутка! *This is a very serious thing not to joke about. See 2033 (С)*

Cf.: It is not a laughing matter (Am., Br.)

2354. Это совсем другая история. *What you are telling me is not what I was told before*

Cf.: It's a different (another) story (Am., Br.). That's /quite/ a different story (Am., Br.)

2355. Это совсем другое дело. *What you are saying shows the matter in quite a different light*

Cf.: That's a horse of a different (another) colo(u)r (Am., Br.)

2356. Этот номер не пройдёт. *What is being planned or what you are telling me will never be done, I am flatly against it. See 2061 (Т)*

Cf.: The answer's a lemon (Am., Br.). /It's/ no go (Am., Br.). No way (Am.). That cat won't fight (jump) (Br.). That cock won't fight (Br.). That dog won't hunt (Am.). That horse will not jump (run) (Br.). That won't do (Am., Br.). That won't wash (Br.). That won't work (Am., Br.). You won't get away with this (Am.)

Я

2357. Яблочко от яблони недалеко падает. *Children are like their parents in character, habits, behavio(u)r, etc. See 783 (К), 789 (К), 790 (К), 800 (К), 806 (К), 807 (К), 810 (К), 812 (К), 815 (К), 953 (К), 1101 (М), 1560 (О), 1576 (О), 1587 (О), 1615 (О), 1616 (О), 1617 (О), 1619 (О), 1722 (П)*

Var.: Какая яблонька, такие и яблочки

Cf.: An apple does not fall (never falls) far from the tree (Am.). The apple never falls far from the tree (Br.). As the apple, so the fruit (Am.). As the tree, so the fruit (Am., Br.). The fruit doesn't fall far from the tree (Am.). Like cow, like calf (Br.). Like parents, like children (Br.). Like tree, like fruit (Br.). The litter is like to the sire and the dam (Br.). Such bird, such egg (Br.). The young ravens are beaked like the old (Am.)

2358. Я говорю про Ивана, а ты про болвана. *See 174 (В)*

Var.: Я говорю про попа, ты про попадью, а он про попову дочку. Я ему про ремень, а он мне про лыко. Я ему про Фому, а он про Ерёму. Я про сапоги, а он про пироги

Cf.: I talk of chalk and you of cheese (Br.). What's that got to do with the price of apples (eggs, horses)? (Am.)

2359. Я знаю, что я ничего не знаю. *Human knowledge is very limited*

Cf.: All that we know is that we know nothing (Am.)

2360. Язык без костей. *One can say what he likes. See 1270 (Н), 1960 (С)*

Var.: Язык без костей, что хочет, то и лопочет

Cf.: Lying pays no tax (Br.). The tongue is an unruly member (Am.)

2361. Язык болтает, а голова ничего не знает. *Windbags never think of what they are talking about. See 2098 (У), 2299 а (Ч)*

Var.: Язык говорит (лепечет), а голова не ведает

Cf.: A fool's bell is soon rung (Br.). Fools cannot hold their tongues (Am.). He who talks much says many foolish things (Am.). The tongue runs before the wit (Br.)

2362. Язык до добра не доведёт. *See 2364 (Я)*

Var.: Язык до добра не доведёт болтуна

Cf.: Don't cut off your head with your tongue (Am.). Let not your tongue cut your throat (Am.). Many words, many buffets (Br.). Nothing ruins a duck but (like) his bill (Am.). An ox is taken by the horns, and a man by the tongue (Am., Br.). Tongue double brings trouble (Am.). The tongue talks at the head's cost (Br.)

2363. Язык до Киева доведёт. *You have only to ask and people will give you the directions. See 1984 (С)*

Cf.: He who has a tongue in his head can travel all the world over (Br.). He who has a tongue in his mouth can find his way anywhere (Br.). He who has a tongue may go to Rome (Br.). He who uses his tongue will reach his destination (Am.)

2364. Язык мой—враг мой. *A man who talks too much often does harm to himself. See 1028 (Л), 1120 (М), 2362 (Я)*

Var.: Язык наш—враг наш

Cf.: Birds are entangled by their feet, and men by their tongues (Br.). A bleating sheep loses her bit (Br.). The crying cat always gets the scratch (Am.). Don't cut off your head with your tongue (Am.). A fish wouldn't get caught if it kept its mouth shut (Am.). A fool's tongue is long enough to cut his own throat (Br.). A fool's tongue is long enough to cut his throat (Am.). Let not your tongue cut your throat (Am.). The mill that is always going grinds coarse and fine (Br.). More have repented speech than silence (Am., Br.). Nothing ruins a duck but (like) his bill (Am.). An ox is taken by the horns, and a man by the tongue (Am., Br.). The sheep that bleats loses a mouthful (Am.). Tongue double brings trouble (Am.). The tongue talks at the head's cost (Br.)

2365. Языком не спеши, а делом не ленись. *See 412 (Д)*

Cf.: Be slow to promise and quick to perform (Am., Br.)

2366. Язычок введёт в грешок. *See 931 (К)*

Cf.: He cannot speak well that cannot hold his tongue (Am.). He who talks much errs much (makes many mistakes) (Am.). In a multitude of words there wants not sin (Am.). Much talking, much erring (Am.). Talk much and err much (Am.). Talk much, err much (Br.)

2367. Яичница без яиц не бывает. *Nothing can be made without the necessary material*

Cf.: You cannot make bricks without straw (Am., Br.)

2368. Яйца курицу не учат. *Young or less experienced people should not instruct those who have more experience. See 1466 (Н), 2164 (У)*

Cf.: Don't teach your grandmother to suck eggs (Am., Br.). Eggs can't teach the hen (Am.). Teach your father to get children (Br.). You have to be smarter than the dog to teach him tricks (Am.)

2369. "Я не дурак"—сказал дурак. *A fool is of a high opinion of himself*

Cf.: Folly is wise in her own eyes (Br.). A fool is wise in his own conceit (Br.). Ignorance is the mother of conceit (Am.)

2370. Я не первый, и я не последний. *Other people did this before me and will do it after me*

Cf.: I am not the first, and I won't be

the last (Am.). I am not the first and shall not be the last (Br.)

2371. Я не тот ребёнок, что вчера из пелёнок. *I am wiser than you think; I am not to be tricked or deceived*

Cf.: I didn't come over on the last boat (Am.). I didn't come up in the last bucket (with the last boat) (Br.). I didn't fall off a Christmas tree (Br.). I was not born yesterday (Am., Br.)

2372. Я не я, и лошадь не моя, и я не извозчик. *See 1159 (M)*

Var.: Я не я, и котомка не моя

Cf.: Am I my brother's keeper? (Am., Br.). I am not my brother's keeper (Am.). I'm a stranger here (Br.). It's no skin off my back (Am., Br.). It's no skin off my tail (Am.)

2373. Яркий огонь быстро горит. *People living a very intense life are exhausted quickly*

Cf.: It is the pace that kills (Br.). The more light a torch gives, the shorter it lasts (Br.). 'Tis pace that kills (Am.)

2374. Ясно, как дважды два—четыре. *It is absolutely obvious, there is no mistake about it, it is a matter of fact*

Cf.: It sticks out a mile (Br.). Two and two make four (Am., Br.)

2375. Ящерка маленька, да зубы востреньки. *See 1140 (M)*

Cf.: No viper so little but has its venom (Br.). A thorn is small, but he who has felt it doesn't forget it (Am.)

Russian Proverb and Saying Key Word Index

Указатель ключевых слов русских пословиц и поговорок

A

АВОСЬ
Авось да небось—хоть вовсе брось—1 (А)

АЗ
Аз да буки, а там и науки—2 (А)
Сперва аз да буки, а потом науки—2 (А)

АКСЁН
Всяк Аксён про себя умён—255 (В)

АЛМАЗ
Алмаз алмазом режется—4 (А)
Алмаз и в грязи виден—5 (А)

АЛТЫН
Не жалей алтына—отдашь полтину—1339 (Н)

АМ
И сам не ам, и другому не дам—745 (И)

АМЕРИКА
Открыл Америку!—1590 (О)

АНАНИЙ
Каков Ананий, такова у него и Маланья—787 (К)

АНГЕЛ
В людях ангел, а дома чёрт—164 (В)
В людях—ангел, не жена, дома с мужем—сатана—164 (В)
Тихий ангел пролетел—2052 (Т)

АППЕТИТ
Аппетит приходит во время еды—7 (А)

АПРЕЛЬ
Апрель с водою, а май с травою—8 (А)
Апрель тёплый, май холодный—год плодородный—9 (А)

АПТЕКА
Аптека и лечит, так калечит—10 (А)
Аптека не прибавит века—10 (А)
Чего не дано, в аптеке не купишь—2236 (Ч)

АРТЕЛЬ
Артель атаманом крепка—11 (А)
Артель воюет, а один горюет—12 (А)
Артелью хорошо и недруга бить—14 (А)

АРШИН
Не мерь всех на свой аршин—1367 (Н)

АТАМАН
Не всем казакам в атаманах быть—1298 (Н)
По ватаге атаман, по овцам пастух—1660 (П)

АУКНУТЬСЯ
Как аукнется, так и откликнется—778 (К)

АХАТЬ
Ахал бы дядя, на себя глядя—15 (А)

Б

БАБА
Баба—бабе, баба—борову, а потом по всему городу—16 (Б)
Баба с воза—кобыле легче—17 (Б)
Бил дед жабу, грозясь (сердясь) на бабу—65 (Б)
Не было у бабы хлопот, купила баба порося—1277 (Н)
Не знала баба горя (хлопот), так купила баба порося—1277 (Н)

БАБКА
Бабка надвое сказала—18 (Б)

БАБУШКА
Бабушка ещё надвое гадала (сказала)—18 (Б)
Кабы бабушка не бабушка, то была б она дедушкой—759 (К)
Хорошо тому жить, кому бабушка ворожит—2199 (Х)

БАРАН
Куда один баран, туда и всё стадо—976 (К)

БАРИН
По барину и говядина—1723 (П)
Хозяин—барин—2181 (Х)

БАРОН
У всякого барона своя фантазия—2086 (У)

БАСНЯ
Соловья баснями не кормят—1968 (С)
Баснями сыт не будешь—1968 (С)

БАШМАК
Только тот, на чьей ноге башмак, знает, где он жмёт—2060 (Т)

БЕДА
Беда—глупости сосед—19 (Б)
Беда к нам приходит верхом, а от нас уходит пешком—20 (Б)
Беда мучит, да беда и выучит—33 (Б)
Беда не ходит одна—22 (Б)
Беда никогда не приходит одна: сама идёт и другую ведёт—22 (Б)
Беда приходит пудами, а уходит золотниками—23 (Б)
Беды мучат, уму учат—33 (Б)
Берегись бед, пока их нет—1555 (О)
Большая беда молчит, а малая кричит—92 (Б)
Как ни ликовать, а беды не миновать—786 (К)
Лиха беда не живёт одна—22 (Б)
Не до Бога, когда беда у порога—1330 (Н)
Не ищи беды, беда сама тебя сыщет—1354 (Н)
Одна беда не беда—1530 (О)
Опасайся бед, пока их нет—1555 (О)
Пришла беда—отворяй (открывай, растворяй) ворота—1778 (П)
Семь бед—один ответ—1884 (С)
Чужая беда научит—2315 (Ч)
Чужая беда не весит—2316 (Ч)
Чужая беда не даёт ума (не научит)—2317 (Ч)
Эта беда не беда, только б больше не была—2349 (Э)

БЕДНОСТЬ
Бедность не грех, а до греха доводит—30 (Б)
Бедность не порок—31 (Б)

Бедность не порок, а большое свинство—32 (Б)

БЕДНЫЙ
Бедному все сапоги по ноге—25 (Б)
Бедному жениться и ночь коротка—26 (Б)
Бедному зятю и тесть не рад—27 (Б)
Бедному нужно многое, жадному—всё—28 (Б)

БЕДНЯК
Лучше быть (жить) бедняком, чем разбогатеть с грехом—1052 (Л)

БЕЖАТЬ
Кто бежит, тот и догоняет—906 (К)

БЕЗДЕЛЬЕ
Бездельс—мать пороков—35 (Б)
Безделье ум притупляет—36 (Б)
Нет тяжелее бремени, чем безделье—1455 (Н)

БЕЗДЕЛЬНИК
За бездельника язык работает—608 (З)

БЕЗДНА
Бездна бездну призывает—39 (Б)

БЕЗЛЮДЬЕ
На безлюдье и сидни в чести (и Фома дворянин)—1173 (Н)

БЕЗРЫБЬЕ
На безрыбье и рак рыба—1174 (Н)

БЕЗУМЬЕ
Безумье и на мудрого бывает—51 (Б)

БЕЛО
Бело, да не серебро—56 (Б)

БЕРЕЖЁНЫЙ
Бережёного Бог бережёт—59 (Б)

БЕРЁЗА
Скрипучая берёза дольше стоит—1915 (С)

БЕРЕЧЬ
Береги бровь, глаз цел будет—57 (Б)

БЕРЕЧЬСЯ
Берегись тихой собаки да тихой воды—58 (Б)

БЕСЕДА
Беседа дорогу коротает—63 (Б)

БЕСПТИЧЬЕ
На бесптичье и ворона соловей—1175 (Н)

БЕСЧЕСТЬЕ
Бесчестье хуже смерти—64 (Б)

БИСЕР
Не мечи бисер перед свиньями—1368 (Н)

БЛИЖНИЙ
Ближняя—ворона, а дальняя—соколёна—69 (Б)

БЛИН
Горяч блин, да скоро остыл—393 (Г)
Первый блин комом—1639 (П)
Тот же блин, да на другом блюде—2034 (Т)

БЛОХА
Ни одна блоха не плоха—1480 (Н)
Осердясь на блох, да и шубу в печь—1564 (О)
Рассердясь на блох, да и одеяло (шубу) в печь—1564 (О)

БОГ
Бог дал, Бог и взял—82 (Б)
Бог его знает—1518 (О)
Бог-то Бог, да и сам не будь плох—85 (Б)
Все под Богом ходим—240 (В)
На кого Бог, на того и добрые люди—1204 (Н)
Не боги города строят (горшки обжигают)—1271 (Н)
Один Бог знает—1518 (О)
Чего Бог не дал, того за деньги не купишь—78 (Б)

БОГАТСТВО
Богатство—вода, пришла и ушла—446 (Д)
Богатством ума не купишь—78 (Б)

Богатство родителей—кара (порча) детям—79 (Б)
Залез в богатство, забыл и братство—628 (Б)

БОГАТЫЙ
Богатому как хочется, а бедному как можется—76 (Б)
Богатому деньги, а бедному дети—77 (Б)
Богатому телята, а бедному ребята—77 (Б)
Богатую взять—станет попрекать—80 (Б)
Богатый бедному не брат (товарищ)—81 (Б)
Всё может случиться—и богатый к бедному стучиться—229 (В)
Кабы не кабы да не но, были бы мы богаты давно—763 (К)
Не тем богат, что есть, а тем богат, что рад—1433 (Н)
Богатый бедного не разумеет—2032 (С)
Чем богаты, тем и рады—2254 (Ч)

БОГАЧ
Скупой богач беднее нищего—1916 (С)

БОЛЕЗНЬ
Болезнь приходит пудами, а уходит золотниками—90 (Б)
Не всякая болезнь к смерти—1308 (Н)

БОЛЕТЬ
У кого что болит, тот о том и говорит—2111 (У)
Что у тебя болит, то у другого не свербит—2311 (Ч)

БОЛОТО
Стоячее болото гниёт—2014 (С)

БОЛТАТЬ
Кто много болтает, тот много врёт—931 (К)

БОЛТУН
Болтун—находка для врага—91 (Б)
Возьмётся болтун болтать—ничем не унять—180 (В)

БОЛЬНОЙ
Не рад больной и золотой кровати—1398 (Н)

БОЛЬШОЕ
Пошёл за большим, не жалей малого—1752 (П)

БОЛЬШОЙ
Большой, да дурной—97 (Б)
Что говорит большой, слышит и малый—2288 (Ч)

БОЛЯЧКА
Чужая болячка в боку не сидит—2318 (Ч)

БОРОДА
Борода не в честь, а усы и у кошки есть—100 (Б)
Борода уму не замена—2124 (У)
Мудрость в голове, а не в бороде—2124 (У)
Ум не в бороде, а в голове—2124 (У)

БОТВИНЬЯ
Какова Аксинья, такова и ботвинья—795 (К)

БОЧКА
Бездонную бочку водой не наполнишь—40 (Б)
Пустая бочка пуще гремит—1791 (П)

БОЯТЬСЯ
Кто боится, у того в глазах двоится—908 (К)
Кто ничего не имеет, тот ничего не боится—950 (К)
Не бойся собаки, что лает, а бойся той, что молчит да хвостом виляет—1273 (Н)

БРАК
Браки заключаются на небесах—102 (Б)

БРАНИТЬ
Кто кого за глаза бранит, тот того боится—923 (К)

БРАНЬ
Брань на вороту не виснет—103 (Б)

Брань—не дым, глаза не ест—103 (Б)

БРАТ
Всем брат—никому не брат—230 (В)

БРАТЬСЯ
Берись за то, к чему ты годен—62 (Б)
За всё браться—ничего не сделать—612 (З)
За всё браться—ничего не уметь—613 (З)
Кто /сразу/ за всё берётся, тому ничего не удаётся—612 (З)

БРЕВНО
Всё одно, что дерево, что бревно—225 (В)

БРОВЬ
Не в бровь, а в глаз—1279 (Н)

БРОД
Не зная (спросясь) броду, не суйся в воду—1347 (Н)

БРУТ
И ты, Брут!—752 (И)

БРЮХО
Брюхо сыто, да глаза голодны—104 (Б)
Голодное брюхо ко всему глухо—370 (Г)
Голодное брюхо к учению глухо—371 (Г)
На брюхе шёлк, а в брюхе-то щёлк—1178 (Н)
Не ноги кормят брюхо, а брюхо ноги—1379 (Н)
По сытому брюху хоть обухом бей—1745 (П)
Сытое брюхо к учению глухо—2030 (С)
У голодного брюха нет уха—370 (Г)

БРЮШКО
Хоть лопни брюшко, да не останься добрецо—2204 (Х)

БУБЕН
Звонки бубны за горами—1917 (С)
Славны бубны за горами—1917 (С)

БУМАГА
Бумага всё терпит—111 (Б)
Бумага от стыда не краснеет—111 (Б)
Бумага терпит, перо пишет—111 (Б)

БУРКА
Укачали Бурку крутые горки—2107 (У)

БУРЯ
Буря только рощу валит, а кусты к земле гнёт—112 (Б)
После бури наступает затишье—1724 (П)

БЫВАТЬ
Бывает, что и корова летает (вошь кашляет, курица петухом поёт)—113 (Б)

БЫК
Как (Сколько) с быком ни биться, а молока от него не добиться—826 (К)
Старый бык тоже телёнком был—2008 (С)

БЫЛЬ
Быль молодцу не укор—121 (Б)

БЫЛЬЁ
Было, да сплыло, да быльём поросло—2281 (Ч)
Что было, то прошло и быльём поросло—2281 (Ч)

БЫТЬ
Будь, что будет—110 (Б)
То ли ещё будет!—2058 (Т)
Что будет, то и будет—110 (Б)
Что было, то видели, что будет, то увидим—2280 (Ч)

БЫЧОК
Быть бычку на верёвочке—122 (Б)

В

ВАНЬКА
Не валяй Ваньку!—1278 (Н)

ВАРВАРА
Любопытчой Варваре нос оторвали—1086 (Л)

ВЕЗЕНИЕ
Не было б везения, кабы не было умения—1275 (Н)

ВЕЗТИ
Если не везёт, так не везёт—565 (Е)
Кто везёт, на того и накладывают—910 (К)
Кто везёт, того и погоняют—911 (К)

ВЕК
Век долог, всем полон—133 (В)
Век живи, век надейся—134 (В)
Век живи, век учись—135 (В)
Век живучи, споткнёшься идучи—136 (В)
Век изжить—не рукавицей тряхнуть (не рукой махнуть)—137 (В)
Век не поле—вдруг не перескочишь—602 (Ж)
Век прожить—не поле перейти—602 (Ж)
Век протянется, всего (всем) достанется—603 (Ж)
На веку—не на боку, всего будет—1179 (Н)
На веку, что на долгой ниве (долгом волоку)—1180 (Н)

ВЕЛИЧАТЬ
От кого чают, того и величают—1589 (О)

ВЕНИК
Веника не переломишь, а по пруту весь веник переломаешь—139 (В)

ВЕРЁВКА
В доме повешенного не говорят о верёвке—129 (В)
Порванную верёвку как ни вяжи, а всё узел будет—1718 (П)

ВЕРЁВОЧКА
Завивай горе верёвочкой—610 (З)
Завяжи горе верёвочкой—610 (В)
Сколько верёвочке ни виться, а конец будет—1907 (С)

ВЕРИТЬ
Кто легко верит, тот легко и погибает—926 (К)
Не верь козлу в капусте, а волку в овчарне—1284 (Н)
Не верь словам, а верь делам—1285 (Н)
Не верь ушам, а верь /своим/ глазам—1286 (Н)
Не верь чужим речам, верь своим очам—1286 (Н)
Хотите—верьте, хотите—нет—2210 (Х)
Хочешь—верь, хочешь—нет—2210 (Х)

ВЕРСТА
Где мило, семь вёрст не криво—318 (Г)
Для друга и семь вёрст не околица—464 (Д)
Если мил друг, и десять вёрст—не круг—464 (Д)
К милому и семь вёрст не околица—464 (Д)
Семь вёрст до небес и все лесом—1885 (С)

ВЕРТЕТЬСЯ
И всё-таки она вертится!—691 (И)

ВЕРШИНА
Залезают на дерево не с вершины—627 (З)

ВЕСЁЛЫЙ
Не всяк весел, кто поёт—1311 (Н)

ВЕСТЬ
Добрые вести не лежат на месте—483 (Д)
Дурная весть имеет крылья—550 (Д)
Дурные вести не лежат на месте—550 (Д)
Нет вестей—добрые вести—1429 (Н)
Худые вести не лежат на месте—550 (Д)

ВЕТЕР
Ветра в рукавицу не поймаешь—141 (В)
Ищи ветра в поле—757 (И)
Кто сеет ветер, пожнёт бурю—964 (К)
Посеешь ветер—пожнёшь бурю—964 (К)

Руками ветра не поймаешь—141 (В)

ВЕЧЕР
Вечер покажет, каков был день—2174 (Х)
Каков ни будь грозен день, а вечер настанет—804 (К)
Хвали жизнь при смерти, а день вечером—2174 (Х)
Хвали утро днём, а день вечером /не видав вечера, и хвалиться нечего/—2174 (Х)

ВЕЧНЫЙ
Ничто не вечно под луной—1485 (Н)

ВЕЩЬ
Вешь вещи рознь—142 (В)
Вещь вещи рознь, человек человеку рознь—143 (В)
Вещь хороша, пока новая, а друг—когда старый—144 (В)

ВЕЯТЬ
Надо веять, пока ветер веет—1198 (Н)

ВЗГЛЯД
Ласковый взгляд, да на сердце яд—988 (Л)

ВЗМАХ
За один взмах дерева не срубишь—636 (З)

ВЗРОСЛЫЙ
Что говорят взрослые, то и дети повторяют—2289 (Ч)

ВЗЫСКАТЬСЯ
Кому много дано, с того много и взыщется—855 (К)

ВЗЯТЬ
Взял топор—возьми и топорище—149 (В)

ВИД
На вид пригож, а внутри на чёрта похож—1181 (Н)

ВИДЕТЬ
Не вижу, так и не верю—1289 (Н)
Реже видишь—больше любишь—1828 (Р)

ВИЛЫ
Это ещё вилами по воде писано—2351 (З)

ВИНА
Была бы спина, найдётся и вина—118 (Б)

ВИНО
Вино уму не товарищ—156 (В)

ВИНОВАТЫЙ
Виноватому всё кажется, что про него говорят—155 (В)
Топор виноват, что изба нехороша—2063 (Т)
У мужа жена всегда виновата—2134 (У)

ВИНОГРАД
Зелен виноград—662 (З)

ВКУС
На вкус, на цвет товарища нет—1182 (Н)
Не разжевав, вкуса не узнаешь—1401 (Н)
О вкусах не спорят—1512 (О)
У всякого свой вкус, а у осла ослиный—2087 (У)
У кого какой вкус: кто любит дыню, а кто арбуз—927 (К)
У кого какой вкус, один другому не указчик: кто любит арбуз, а кто свиной хрящик—927 (К)

ВЛАДЫКА
Вольно псу и на владыку брехать—189 (В)

ВЛАСТВОВАТЬ
Разделяй и властвуй—1815 (Р)

ВЛАСТЬ
Где сила, там и власть—333 (Г)

ВНЕШНОСТЬ
Внешность обманчива—168 (В)

ВОДА
В мутной воде хорошо рыбу ловить—167 (В)
Вода не мутит ума—175 (В)
Воду варить (толочь)—вода и будет—253 (В)
В ступе воду варить—вода и будет—253 (В)

Далёкая вода жажды не утолит—410 (Д)
Если вода не течёт за тобою, иди ты за водою—563 (Е)
Мутная вода течёт не из чистого озера—1166 (М)
Пора придёт и вода пойдёт—1717 (П)
Пролитую воду не соберёшь—1783 (П)
Темна вода во облацех—2041 (Т)
Тихая вода берега подмывает—2050 (Т)
Тихие воды глубоки—2051 (Т)

ВОДОПУСК
Не высок водопуск, а реку держит—1320 (Н)

ВОЗ
На чьём возу сижу, того и песенку пою—1264 (Н)
Не мой воз, не мне его и везти—1372 (Н)
Тихий воз скорее будет на горе—2053 (Т)
Что с возу упало, то пропало—2308 (Ч)

ВОЗВРАЩАТЬСЯ
Всё возвращается на круги своя—222 (В)

ВОЗДУХ
В запас воздухом не надышишься—147 (В)

ВОИН
Один воин тысячу водит—1519 (О)

ВОЙНА
Война кровь любит—181 (В)
Война не лечит, а калечит—181 (В)
Ни моря без волны, ни войны без крови—1479 (Н)

ВОЛК
Волка ноги кормят—182 (В)
Волк волка не съест—183 (В)
Волк каждый год линяет, а всё сед бывает—184 (В)
Волк каждый год линяет, да обычая не меняет—184 (В)
Волк не пастух, свинья не огородник—185 (В)
Волков бояться—в лес не ходить—186 (В)
Голодный волк и завёртки рвёт—374 (Г)
Из волка пастух не выйдет—702 (И)
Как волка ни корми, а он всё в лес глядит—779 (К)
Лезет в волки, а хвост собачий—1002 (Л)
Ловит волк, да ловят и волка—1033 (Л)
Не всё, что серо, волк—1305 (Н)
О волке толк, а тут и волк—1513 (О)
Плохого волка и телята лижут—1650 (П)
Пожалел волк кобылу, оставил хвост да гриву—1677 (П)
Помяни волка, а волк тут—1513 (О)
Про волка речь, а он навстречь—1513 (О)
Пуганый волк и кочки боится—1788 (П)
С волками жить, по-волчьи выть—1866 (С)
Сколько волка ни корми, /а/ он всё в лес смотрит—779 (К)
Смирного волка и телята лижут—1944 (С)
Старого волка в тенета не загонишь—1998 (С)
Старый волк знает толк—2009 (С)
Таскал волк—потащили и волка—2037 (Т)
Хоть волком вой, хоть в прорубь головой—2202 (Х)

ВОЛОКНО
Каково волокно, таково и полотно—805 (К)

ВОЛОС
Волос долог, да ум короток—187 (В)
У бабы волос долог, а (да) ум короток—187 (В)
Дай чёрту волос, а он и за всю голову—409 (Д)

ВОЛОСОК

По волоску всю бороду выщиплешь—1662 (П)

ВОЛЬНЫЙ

Вольному воля /, спасённому рай/—188 (В)

ВОЛЯ

Воля птичке лучше золотой клетки—682 (З)

Дай волю на ноготок—он возьмёт на весь локоток—406 (Д)

По своей воле лучше неволи—1721 (П)

Своя воля страшней неволи—1620 (О)

ВОР

Вора миловать—доброго губить—190 (В)

Вор вора не обидит—191 (В)

Вор вора скорее поймает—192 (В)

Вор вором губится—193 (В)

Вор крадёт деньги, а друг время—194 (В)

Вору потакать, что самому воровать—197 (В)

Где кража, там и вор—315 (Г)

Где плохо лежит, туда и вор глядит—328 (Г)

Гол, да не вор, беден, да честен—2208 (Х)

Два вора в одном лесу не уживутся—420 (Д)

Два вора дерутся—честному польза—418 (Д)

Доброму вору всё впору—479 (Д)

Как вор ни ворует, а тюрьмы не минует—780 (К)

На воре шапка горит—1183 (Н)

На дороге не клади, вора в грех не вводи—1655 (П)

Не пойман—не вор—1390 (Н)

Не там вор ворует, где много, а там, где лежит плохо (где оплошно)—1427 (Н)

Не там вор крадёт, где много, а там, где лежит плохо—1427 (Н)

Не только тот вор, что крадёт, а и тот, кто лестницу подаёт—1441 (Н)

Не тот вор, кто украл, а тот, кто попался—1443 (Н)

Ни у одного вора нет каменного дома—2085 (У)

Плохой тот вор, что около себя грабит—1653 (П)

Плохо не клади, вора в грех не вводи—1655 (П)

Раз украл, а навек вором стал—1819 (Р)

У воров не бывает каменных домов—2085 (У)

У вора ремесло на лбу написано—2084 (У)

Хотя и гол, да не вор—2208 (Х)

Худой вор, который в своей деревне ворует—1653 (П)

Что ворам с рук сходит, за то воришек бьют—2286 (Ч)

Что самому воровать, что вору стремянку держать—197 (В)

ВОРОБЕЙ

Лучше воробей в руке, чем петух на кровле—1066 (Л)

Старого воробья на мякине не проведёшь—1999 (С)

Стреляного воробья на мякине не обманешь (не проведёшь)—1999 (С)

ВОРОГ

Не вспоя, не вскормя, ворога не наживёшь—1307 (Н)

Не поя, не кормя, ворога не наживёшь—1307 (Н)

ВОРОЖИТЬ

Станешь ворожить, когда нечего в рот положить—1992 (С)

Хорошо тому жить, кому бабушка ворожит—2199 (Х)

ВОРОН

Ворон ворону глаз не выклюет—196 (В)

Вскорми ворона—он тебе глаза (очи) выклюет—250 (В)

Старый ворон даром не (не мимо) каркнет—2010 (С)

Чёрного ворона не вымоешь добела—2268 (Ч)

ВОРОНА

Ворона за море летала, а умнее не стала — 195 (В)

Ворона за море летала, да вороной и вернулась — 195 (В)

К воронам попал, по-вороньи каркай — 834 (К)

Пуганая ворона и куста боится — 1788 (П)

С воронами летать — по-вороньи каркать — 834 (К)

ВОРОТА

Мети всяк перед своими воротами — 1128 (М)

По гостям гуляй, да и сам ворота отворяй — 2328 (Ч)

Чужой обед похваляй, да и сам ворота открывай — 2328 (Ч)

ВОРОТИТЬ

Битого, пролитого да прожитого не воротишь — 67 (Б)

Вчерашнего дня не воротишь — 67 (Б)

Прожито, что пролито — не воротишь — 67 (Б)

Прошлого не воротишь — 67 (Б)

Что о том тужить, чего нельзя воротить — 2302 (Ч)

Что про то говорить, чего не можно воротить — 2302 (Ч)

ВПЕЧАТЛЕНИЕ

Первое впечатление обманчиво — 1637 (П)

ВПРОК

Краденое добро впрок не идёт — 2221 (Х)

Неправдой нажитое впрок не идёт — 2221 (Х)

Худо нажитое впрок не идёт — 2221 (Х)

Чужая денежка впрок нейдёт: как придёт, так и уйдёт — 2221 (Х)

Чужое добро впрок нейдёт — 2221 (Х)

ВРАГ

Не сробеешь, так врага одолеешь — 1411 (Н)

Не ставь врага овцою, ставь волком — 1413 (Н)

Подшучивать над другом — нажить врага — 1674 (П)

Человек сам себе враг — 2248 (Ч)

ВРАНЬЁ

Вранью короткий век — 205 (В)

Со вранья пошлины не берут — 1960 (С)

ВРАТЬ

Ври, да знай меру — 219 (В)

Ври, да не завирайся — 219 (В)

Ври, да помни — 220 (В)

Люди врут, так и мы врём — 1088 (Л)

Тому врать легко, кто был далеко — 2062 (Т)

ВРЕМЯ

Время бежит, как вода — 207 (В)

Время всему научит — 208 (В)

Время всё излечит — 211 (В)

Время — деньги — 209 (В)

Время дороже золота — 209 (В)

Время красит, а безвременье сушит — 210 (В)

Время красит, безвременье старит — 210 (В)

Время — лучший врач (исцелитель, лекарь) — 211 (В)

Время на время не приходится — 1716 (П)

Время — не деньги, потеряешь — не найдёшь — 445 (Д)

Время не ждёт (не терпит) — 212 (В)

Время никого не ждёт — 213 (В)

Время подойдёт, так и лёд пойдёт — 214 (В)

Время покажет — 215 (В)

Время пройдёт — слёзы утрёт — 216 (В)

Время работает на нас — 217 (В)

Время рассудит — 218 (В)

Время — судья — 218 (В)

Всему своё время — 233 (В)

Всему своё время и место — 234 (В)

Всё хорошо в своё время — 247 (В)

Деньги пропали — ещё наживёшь, время пропало — его не вернёшь — 445 (Д)

Не время волос белит, а кручина — 1294 (Н)
Нет ничего такого, чего бы не поглотило время — 1437 (Н)
Потерянного времени не воротишь (не догонишь) — 1746 (П)

ВСЁ
Или всё, или ничего — 725 (И)

ВСКАЧЬ
Вскачь не напашешься — 249 (В)
То вскачь, то хоть плачь — 2056 (Т)

ВСТАТЬ
Встать пораньше, шагнуть подальше — 252 (В)

ВСТРЕЧНЫЙ
Не всякий встречный — друг сердечный — 1312 (Н)

ВЫБИРАТЬ
Долго выбирать — замужем не бывать — 495 (Д)
Много выбирать — женатым не бывать — 495 (Д)

ВЫРАСТИ
Выше себя не вырастешь — 304 (В)

ВЫРОДОК
И в хорошей семье выродок бывает — 237 (В)

ВЫУЧИТЬ
Что твёрдо выучишь, долго помнится — 2310 (Ч)

ВЯЗАТЬСЯ
Вяжись лычко с лычком, ремешок с ремешком — 308 (В)
Свой со своим бранись, а чужой не вяжись — 1861 (С)

Г

ГАЛКА
Бей галку и ворону: руку набьёшь, сокола убьёшь — 55 (Б)

ГАРЦЕВАТЬ
Гарцевал пан, да с коня упал — 309 (Г)

ГВОЗДЬ
На один гвоздь всего не вешают — 1217 (Н)
На одном гвозде всего не повесишь — 1217 (Н)

ГЕНЕРАЛ
Кабы не кабы да не но, был бы генералом давно — 763 (К)

ГЕРБОВАЯ
За неимением гербовой пишут на простой — 633 (З)

ГЛАДКИЙ
И гладок, да гадок — 694 (И)

ГЛАЗ
Брюхо сыто, да глаза голодны — 104 (Б)
В кривом глазу всё криво — 161 (В)
Выше лба глаза не растут — 305 (В)
Глаза — бирюза, а душа — сажа — 341 (Г)
Глаза — зеркало души — 343 (Г)
Глаза не видят — сердце не болит — 344 (Г)
Глаза страшатся, а руки делают — 345 (Г)
Завистливые глаза всегда не сыты — 611 (З)
Зоб полон, а глаза голодны — 104 (Б)
Одному глазом мигни, а другого дубиной толкни — 1545 (О)
От хозяйского глаза скотина жиреет — 1614 (О)
Свой глаз — алмаз /, а чужой — стекло/ — 1863 (С)
С глаз долой — из сердца вон — 1871 (С)

ГЛАС
Глас народа — глас божий — 346 (Г)

ГЛИНА
Глину не мять — горшков не видать — 347 (Г)

ГЛУПЕЦ
Осла узнают по ушам, а глупца по речам — 1566 (О)

ГЛУПОСТЬ
Глупость заразительна—349 (Г)

ГЛУПЫЙ
Глупый болтает, а умный думает—350 (Г)
Глупый да малый всегда правду говорят—351 (Г)
Глупый ищет большого места—352 (Г)
И глупый иногда молвит слово в лад—739 (И)
Один глупый камень в море бросит, а сто умных не вынут—535 (Д)

ГЛУХОЙ
Не тот глухой, кто глух, а тот, кто не желает слышать—1444 (Н)
Хуже всякого глухого, кто не хочет слышать—1444 (Н)

ГНЕВ
Гнев—плохой советчик—356 (Г)

ГНЕЗДО
В своём гнезде и ворона коршуну глаза выклюет—2144 (У)
Мало-помалу птичка гнездо свивает—1107 (М)
У своего гнезда и ворон бьёт орла—2144 (У)

ГНИЛУШКА
В темноте и гнилушка светит—291 (В)

ГНУТЬ
Гни дерево, пока гнётся; учи дитятко, пока слушается—357 (Г)
Гни дерево, пока молодо; учи ребёнка, пока мал—357 (Г)

ГНУТЬСЯ
Лучше гнуться, чем переломиться—1048 (Л)

ГОВОРИТЬ
Говори меньше, умнее будешь—359 (Г)
Говорит бело, а делает черно—360 (Г)
Говорить, так договаривать—361 (Г)
Говорят, что в Москве кур доят, а коровы яйца несут—362 (Г)
Говорят, что за морем кур доят—362 (Г)
Кто бы говорил, а ты бы помалкивал—909 (К)
Кто говорит без умолку, в том мало толку—915 (К)
Лишнее говорить—себе вредить—1028 (Л)
Лишнее говорить—только делу вредить—1029 (Л)
Меньше говори, да больше делай—1122 (М)
Не хитро говорить, хитро дело творить—1470 (Н)
Одно дело говорить, другое дело—делать—1540 (О)
Чем меньше говорить, тем здоровее—2258 (Ч)

ГОД
Год году не равен—363 (Г)
Год на год не приходится—363 (Г)
Годы хребет горбят—364 (Г)

ГОЛОВА
Была бы голова здорова, а на голове шапка будет—114 (Б)
Высоко голову несёшь—споткнёшься да упадёшь—301 (В)
Выше головы волосы не растут—305 (В)
Выше головы не прыгнешь—304 (В)
Выше голову!—307 (В)
Голова не колышек, не шапку на неё вешать—365 (Г)
Голова с короб, а ум с орех—366 (Г)
Голова с лукошко, а мозгу ни крошки—366 (Г)
Голова-то есть, а в голове-то нет—366 (Г)
Голова что чан, а ума ни на капустный качан—366 (Г)
Даю голову на отсечение—415 (Д)
Дурная голова ногам покоя не даёт—624 (З)
За глупой головою и ногам нет покою—624 (З)
За дурной головой и ногам непокой—624 (З)

Лучше быть головой кошки, чем хвостом льва—1045 (Л)
Лучше быть головой осла, чем хвостом лошади—1045 (Л)
Лучше быть головой собаки, чем хвостом льва—1045 (Л)
На голове густо, да в голове пусто—1192 (Н)
Не для шапки только голова на плечах—365 (Г)
Нет в голове, нет и в мошне—1428 (Н)
Одна голова хорошо, а две лучше—1531 (О)
Повинную голову и меч не сечёт—1661 (П)
Сколько голов, столько умов—1908 (С)

ГОЛОД
Владеет городом, а помирает голодом—162 (В)
Голод гонит на холод—1496 (Н)
Голод и волка из лесу гонит—367 (Г)
Голод—лучший повар—368 (Г)
Голод не тётка, калачика не подложит—369 (Г)
Голод не тётка, пирожка не подсунет—369 (Г)
Голод не тёща, блины не поднесёт—369 (Г)
Гонит голод и волка из колка—367 (Г)

ГОЛУБОК
У каждого голубка своя горлица—2102 (У)

ГОЛУБЬ
Лучше голубь в тарелке, чем глухарь на току—1066 (Л)

ГОЛЫЙ
Голому разбой не страшен—377 (Г)
Голый разбоя не боится—377 (Г)
Голый—что святой, не боится беды—377 (Г)

ГОЛЬ
Голь на выдумки хитра—378 (Г)
Голь хитра, голь мудра, голь на выдумки пошла—378 (Г)

ГОП
Не говори "гоп", пока не перепрыгнешь (не перескочишь)—1321 (Н)

ГОРА
Гора родила мышь—381 (Г)
Гора с горой не сходится, а человек с человеком сойдётся—382 (Г)
Если гора не идёт к Магомету, то Магомет идёт к горе—564 (Е)

ГОРБАТЫЙ
Горбатого могила исправит—383 (Г)

ГОРДИТЬСЯ
Гордись не ростом, а умом—384 (Г)

ГОРДЫНЯ
Гордыня до добра не доведёт—385 (Г)

ГОРЕ
Где радость, там и горе—330 (Г)
Горе ваше, что без масла каша—386 (Г)
Горе да беда с кем не была—387 (Г)
Горе заставит—бык соловьём запоёт—388 (Г)
Горе на двоих—полгоря—389 (Г)
Горе на двоих—полгоря, радость на двоих—две радости—390 (Г)
Горе не молодит, а голову белит—391 (Г)
Горе только одного рака красит—392 (Г)
Лёгкое горе болтливо, тяжёлое—молчаливо—994 (Л)
На людях горе вполгоря—1209 (Н)
Натерпишься горя—научишься (узнаешь, как) жить—1250 (Н)
Не узнав горя, не узнаешь и радости (счастья)—1458 (Н)
От горя бежал, да в беду попал—1582 (О)
Тело заплывчиво, горе забывчиво—2040 (Т)
У каждого своё горе—2103 (У)

Чужое горе вполгоря горевать—2325 (Ч)
Чужое горе не болит—2325 (Ч)
Чужое горе оханьем пройдёт—2325 (Ч)

ГОРЕСТЬ
Без горести нет радости—34 (Б)
Горесть не принять, радость не видать—34 (Б)

ГОРКА
Временем в горку, а временем в норку—206 (В)
Хвали горку, как перевалишься—2172 (Х)

ГОРШОК
Хоть горшком назови, только в печку не ставь (в печь не сажай)—2203 (Х)

ГОРЬКИЙ
Не вкусив (отведав) горького, не узнаешь и сладкого—1291 (Н)

ГОСПОДИН
Двум господам не служат—422 (Д)

ГОСТИТЬ
Любишь гостить, люби и к себе звать—1074 (Л)

ГОСТЬ
Бойся гостя стоячего—89 (Б)
В гости ходить, к себе водить—125 (В)
В гостях хорошо, а дома лучше /того/—126 (В)
Кто гостю рад, тот и собачку его накормит—916 (К)
Мил гость, что недолго гостит (сидит)—1131 (М)
На незваного гостя не припасена и ложка—1212 (Н)
Не вовремя гость хуже недруга (татарина)—1345 (Н)
Незваного гостя с пира долой—1212 (Н)
Незваный гость хуже татарина—1345 (Н)
Первому гостю—первое место—1638 (П)
Позднему гостю—кости—1680 (П)
Поздние гости глодают кости—1680 (П)
Пора гостям и честь знать—1715 (П)
Пора гостям по своим дворам—1715 (П)
Хорош гость, коли редко ходит—2186 (Х)
Частый гость скоро наскучит—2232 (Ч)

ГОТОВИТЬ
Готовь сани с весны, а колёса с осени—394 (Г)
На троих готовили—и четвёртый сыт—1252 (Н)

ГРЕХ
Все мы не без греха—236 (В)
От греха подальше—1583 (О)
Чужой грех своего не искупит—2326 (Ч)

ГРЕШИТЬ
Грешить легко, трудно каяться—396 (Г)

ГРЕШНЫЙ
Кто Богу не грешен, царю не виноват?—907 (К)

ГРИБ
Грибы ищут—по лесу рыщут—397 (Г)
На окошке грибы не растут—1220 (Н)

ГРИВА
Кабы сивому коню чёрную гриву, был бы буланый—765 (К)
Кабы хвост да грива, так бы цела кобыла—765 (К)
Куда грива, туда и хвост—973 (К)

ГРОЗА
После грозы—вёдро—1725 (П)

ГРОЗИТЬ
Много грозит, да мало вредит—1140 (М)
Не грози попу кадилом—1326 (Н)

ГРОЗИТЬСЯ
Не горазд биться, а горазд грозиться—1325 (Н)

ГРОМ
Гром не грянет—мужик не перекрестится—398 (Г)

ГРУДЬ
Или (Либо) грудь в крестах, или (либо) голова в кустах—726 (И)

ГРЯЗНОЕ
Грязное к чистому не пристаёт—399 (Г)

ГРЯЗЬ
Грязью играть—руки марать—400 (Г)
Из грязи да в князи—703 (И)

ГУЖ
Взялся за гуж, не говори, что не дюж—150 (В)

ГУЛЯНОЧКА
Сам себя губит, кто гуляночки любит—1850 (С)

ГУЛЯТЬ
Гулять с молоду—помирать под старость с голоду—2346 (Щ)
Гулять так гулять, работать так работать—401 (Г)
Пить будем, гулять будем, а смерть придёт—помирать будем—1646 (П)

ГУСЬ
Гусь свинье не товарищ—402 (Г)
Полетели гуси за море, а прилетели тоже не лебеди—1696 (П)

Д

ДАВАТЬ
Дают—бери, а бьют—беги—416 (Д)

ДАНАЙЦЫ
Боюсь данайцев и дары приносящих—101 (Б)

ДАНЬ
С одного тягла по две дани не берут—1668 (П)

ДАТЬ
Лучше дать, чем взять—1050 (Л)

ДВАЖДЫ
Дважды даёт, кто скоро даёт—419 (Д)
Кто скоро помог, тот дважды помог—419 (Д)

ДВОРЯНСТВО
Худое дворянство хуже пономарства—2218 (Х)

ДЕВУШКА
Все девушки хороши, но откуда злые жёны берутся?—223 (В)

ДЕЛАТЬ
Не делай другим того, чего себе не желаешь—1328 (Н)
Чего сам не любишь, того и другому не делай—1328 (Н)

ДЕЛО
Всякое дело до мастера—277 (В)
Дела идут—контора пишет—426 (Д)
Дела, как сажа бела—427 (Д)
Делами славен человек—428 (Д)
Дело в шляпе—429 (Д)
Дело делу учит—430 (Д)
Дело мастера боится—431 (Д)
Дело не медведь—в лес не уйдёт—432 (Д)
Дело не сено, пять лет не сгниёт—432 (Д)
Дело не сокол, не улетит—432 (Д)
Дело с бездельем не смешивай—433 (Д)
Дело сделано—434 (Д)
Дело—табак—435 (Д)
Делу—время, потехе—час—436 (Д)
Доброе дело на век—2188 (Х)
Доброе дело—правду говорить смело—475 (Д)
Доброе дело само себя хвалит—476 (Д)
Кто не в своё дело суётся, тому достаётся—942 (К)
Маленькое дело лучше большого безделья—1104 (М)
Начатого дела не бросай—1257 (Н)
Начатое дело доводи до конца—1257 (Н)

Начиная дело, о конце думай—1258 (Н)
Наше дело—сторона (телячье) /, поел да в закут/—1265 (Н)
Не за своё дело не берись—1344 (Н)
Не по словам судят, а по делам—1393 (Н)
Нужны дела, а не слова—1503 (Н)
Одно дело говорить, другое дело—делать—1540 (О)
О человеке судят не по словам, а по его делам—1621 (О)
Семь дел в одни руки не берут—1886 (С)
Славен человек не словами, а делами—428 (Д)
Умей дело делать, умей и позабавится—2116 (У)
Хорошее дело два века живёт—2188 (Х)
Это совсем другое дело—2355 (З)

ДЁМА
Каков Дёма, таково у него и дома—797 (К)

ДЕМИД
Всякий Демид для себя норовит—268 (В)

ДЕНЕЖКА
Денежки—крылышки—442 (Д)
Денежки труд любят—438 (Д)
Хорошо беречь белую денежку на чёрный день—2196 (Х)

ДЕНЁЧЕК
Дал Бог денёчек, даст и кусочек—83 (Б)

ДЕНЬ
Бог даст день, Бог даст и пищу—83 (Б)
Весенний день целый год кормит—140 (В)
Вешний день весь год кормит—140 (В)
День да ночь и сутки прочь /- так и отваливаем/—447 (Д)
День долог, а век короток—448 (Д)
День мой—век мой—449 (Д)
День наш—век наш—449 (Д)
День придёт и заботу принесёт—450 (Д)
У каждого бывает светлый день—2101 (У)

ДЕНЬГА
Беднее всех бед, как денег нет—24 (Б)
Без денег—везде худенек—37 (Б)
Без денег сон крепче—38 (Б)
Где вода была, там и будет; куда деньга пошла, там и скопится—319 (Г)
Где много воды, там больше будет; где много денег—ещё прибудет—319 (Г)
Денег ни гроша, да слава хороша—437 (Д)
Деньги все двери открывают—439 (Д)
Деньги к деньгам идут (льнут)—441 (Д)
Деньги—крылья—442 (Д)
Деньги не пахнут—443 (Д)
Деньги не щепки, на полу не подымешь—444 (Д)
Деньги приходят и уходят, как вода—446 (Д)
Деньги, что вода—446 (Д)
За деньги и кляча поскачет—618 (З)
За деньги и поп пляшет—618 (З)
Когда деньги говорят, тогда правда молчит—842 (К)
Меньше денег, меньше хлопот—1123 (М)
Много денег—много забот (и хлопот)—1141 (М)
Не в деньгах счастье—1280 (Н)
С деньгами мил, а без денег постыл—1873 (С)
Хуже всех бед, когда денег нет—24 (Б)

ДЕРЕВО
Гни дерево, пока гнётся; учи дитятко, пока слушается—357 (Г)
Гни дерево, пока молодо; учи ребёнка, пока мал—357 (Г)
Дерево славится плодами, а человек делами—451 (Д)
Дерево смотри в плодах, а человека в делах—451 (Д)

Дерево ценят по плодам, а человека по делам—451 (Д)
Какова дерево, таковы и сучья—807 (К)
Криво дерево, да яблоки сладки—891 (К)
Кривое дерево не разогнётся прямо—892 (К)
Куда дерево клонилось, туда и повалилось—972 (К)
Куда дерево клонится, туда и повалится—972 (К)
Неказисто дерево, да вкусен плод—1358 (Н)
Одно дерево ещё не сад—1541 (О)
От доброго дерева добрый и плод—1615 (О)
От хорошего дерева—хороший плод—1615 (О)
Павшее дерево рубят на дрова—1627 (П)
Руби дерево по себе—1838 (Р)
Скрипучее дерево два века живёт—1915 (С)
Скрипучее дерево стоит, а здоровое летит—1915 (С)
Упавшее дерево рубят на дрова—1627 (П)

ДЕРЖАТЬ
Держи голову в холоде, живот в голоде, а ноги в тепле—452 (Д)

ДЕТИ
Все одного отца дети—238 (В)
Дети есть дети—456 (Д)
Дети не в тягость, а в радость—457 (Д)
Малые дети—малая печаль, большие дети—большая печаль—1103 (М)

ДЕТКА
Маленькие детки—маленькие бедки, а вырастут велики—большие будут—1103 (М)
Малые детки—малые бедки, а большие детки—большие и бедки—1103 (М)
С малыми детками горе, а с большими—вдвое—1103 (М)

ДЁШЕВО
Дёшево, да гнило; дорого, да мило—458 (Д)
Хорошо дёшево не бывает—2197 (Х)

ДЕШЁВЫЙ
Дешёвому товару—дешёвая цена—459 (Д)

ДИТЯ
Дитя не плачет—мать не разумеет—460 (Д)
Малое дитя грудь сосёт, а большое—сердце—1106 (М)

ДИТЯТКО
Дитятко, что тесто: как замесил, так и выросло—461 (Д)
Легко дитятко нажить, нелегко вырастить—992 (Л)

ДОБРО
Добро век не забудется—472 (Д)
Добро добро покрывает—474 (Д)
Добро помни, а зло забывай—481 (Д)
Добро скоро забывается—482 (Д)
За добро добром и платят—622 (З)
За моё же добро да мне же поломали ребро—631 (З)
Лихо помнится, а добро забывается—482 (Д)
От добра добра не ищут—1584 (О)
Твоим же добром тебя же челом—631 (З)
Чужим добром не разживёшься—2323 (Ч)
Чужим добром подноси ведром—2324 (Ч)

ДОБРОДЕТЕЛЬ
Добродетель—сама себе награда—473 (Д)

ДОБРОТА
Не ищи красоты, ищи доброты—1356 (Н)

ДОБРЫЙ
Доброму добрая память—480 (Д)

ДОВЕРЯТЬ
Доверяй, да проверяй—490 (Д)

ДОВОЛЬСТВОВАТЬСЯ
Довольствуйся тем, что имеешь—491 (Д)

ДОГАДАТЬСЯ
Догадался, как проигрался—492 (Д)

ДОЖДИК
Либо дождик, либо снег, либо будет, либо нет—1018 (Л)

ДОЖДИЧЕК
После дождичка будет солнышко—1728 (П)
После дождичка в четверг—1729 (П)
После дождичка солнце выглянет—1728 (П)

ДОЖДЬ
Будет дождь, будет и вёдро—105 (Б)

ДОЛГ
В долг брать легко, да отдавать тяжело—991 (Л)
В долг давать—дружбу терять—128 (В)
Долги помнит не тот, кто берёт, а кто даёт—493 (Д)
Долг не ревёт, а спать не даёт—494 (Д)
Долг платежом красен—496 (Д)
Заплатишь долг скорее, так будет веселее—639 (З)
Легко в долг брать, отдавать трудно—991 (Л)

ДОМ
Дом с детьми—базар, без детей—могила—501 (Д)
Каждый дом имеет свой содом—773 (К)
Мой дом—моя крепость—1149 (М)
Твой дом—твоя и воля—2038 (Т)

ДОМА
Дома и солома едома (съедобна)—497 (Д)
Дома и стены помогают—498 (Д)

ДОРОГА
Все дороги ведут в Рим—224 (В)
Всякая дорога вдвоём веселей—256 (В)
Дорога в ад вымощена благими намерениями—502 (Д)
Дороги не ищут, а спрашивают—505 (Д)
Дорогу осилит идущий—507 (Д)
Нет дороги без изъяна—1430 (Н)

ДРАКА
После драки кулаками не машут—1730 (П)

ДРОВА
Когда дрова горят, тогда и кашу варят—843 (К)
Кривы дрова, да прямо горят—894 (К)
Обед тогда варят, когда дрова горят—843 (К)

ДРУГ
Будь друг, да не вдруг—108 (Б)
Вдруг не станешь друг—108 (Б)
Добрый друг лучше ста родственников—485 (Д)
Друга иметь—себя не жалеть—508 (Д)
Друга узнать—вместе куль (пуд) соли съесть—509 (Д)
Друг до поры—тот же недруг—510 (Д)
Друг до поры хуже недруга—510 (Д)
Друг не испытанный—что орех не расколотый (не сколотый)—512 (Д)
Друг познаётся в беде—521 (Д)
Друг спорит, а недруг поддакивает—513 (Д)
Друзей-то много, да друга нет—520 (Д)
Друзья познаются в беде (несчастье)—521 (Д)
Замиренный друг ненадёжен—630 (З)
Легче друга потерять, чем найти—998 (Л)
Не держи сто рублей, /а/ держи сто друзей—1350 (Н)
Не имей сто рублей, а имей сто друзей—1350 (Н)

Не тот друг, кто на пиру гуляет, а тот, кто в беде помогает—1446 (Н)
Не узнавай друга в три дня, узнавай в три года—1457 (Н)
Новых друзей наживай, а старых не теряй—1492 (Н)
Раздружится друг—хуже недруга—510 (Д)
Сердечный друг не родится вдруг—108 (Б)
Скажи мне, кто твой друг (с кем ты дружен), и я скажу, кто ты—1896 (С)
Старый друг лучше новых двух—2011 (С)
Сто друзей—мало, один враг—много—2013 (С)

ДРУЖБА
Дружба—дружбой, а денежкам счёт (а денежки врозь)—514 (Д)
Дружба—дружбой, а служба—службой—515 (Д)
Дружба как стекло: разобьёшь—не сложишь—516 (Д)
Дружба что стекло: сломаешь—не починишь—516 (Д)
За дружбу дружбой платят—623 (З)
Не в службу, а в дружбу—1306 (Н)
Хочешь дружбы—будь другом—2211 (Х)

ДРУЖНО
Дружно—не грузно, а врозь—хоть брось—517 (Д)

ДРУЖНЫЙ
Скажи мне, с кем ты дружен, и я скажу, кто ты—1896 (С)

ДРУЖОК
Для (Ради) милого дружка и серёжка из ушка—466 (Д)

ДУБ
Не срубишь дуба, не отдув губы—1412 (Н)

ДУМАТЬ
Больше думай, меньше говори—95 (Б)

ДУПЛО
И в сосне дупло есть—692 (И)

ДУРАК
Дуракам везёт—522 (Д)
Дуракам всё счастье—522 (Д)
Дуракам закон не писан—523 (Д)
Дуракам полработы не показывают—524 (Д)
Дуракам счёту нет—525 (Д)
Дурака учить, что мертвого лечить—526 (Д)
Дурак в воду камень закинет, десятеро умных не вытащат—535 (Д)
Дурак времени не знает—527 (Д)
Дурак врёт, врёт, да и правду скажет (соврёт)—528 (Д)
Дурак дом построил, а умный купил—529 (Д)
Дурак думой богатеет—548 (Д)
Дурак дурака видит издалека—1842 (Р)
Дурак-дурак, а себе на уме—531 (Д)
Дурак дурака хвалит—530 (Д)
Дурак-дурак, а хитрый—531 (Д)
Дурак дураком останется—532 (Д)
Дурак завяжет узел—умный не скоро развяжет—533 (Д)
Дураки о добыче спорят, а умные её делят—534 (Д)
Дурак кинет в воду камень, а десять умных не вынут—535 (Д)
Дурак кричит, умный молчит—536 (Д)
Дурак, кто с дураком свяжется—537 (Д)
Дурак не дурак, а от роду так—538 (Д)
Дураков не орут, не сеют—сами родятся—539 (Д)
Дураков не сеют, не жнут—сами родятся—539 (Д)
Дураком на свете жить—ни о чём не тужить—540 (Д)
Дураком родился—дураком и помрёшь—541 (Д)
Дурак родился—1132 (М)
Дурак сам скажется—542 (Д)
Дурак спит, а счастье /у него/ в головах лежит (сидит, стоит)—543 (Д)

Дураку всегда компания найдётся—544 (Д)
Дураку всё смех на уме—545 (Д)
Дураку семь вёрст не крюк—546 (Д)
Заставь дурака Богу молиться, он и лоб расшибёт—650 (З)
Иной раз и дурак молвит слово в лад—739 (И)
Мёртвого не вылечишь, а дурака не выучишь—526 (Д)
На дураках воду возят—1199 (Н)
На наш век дураков хватит—1211 (Н)
Не валяй дурака!—1278 (Н)
Осла знать по ушам, медведя—по когтям, а дурака—по речам—1566 (О)
Свяжись с дураком, сам дурак будешь—537 (Д)
С дураками не шутят (шутить опасно)—1875 (С)
С дураком связаться—не развязаться—537 (Д)
Старые дураки глупее молодых—2007 (С)
Счастье дураков любит—522 (Д)
У дурака в горсти дыра—2096 (У)
У дурака что на уме, то и на языке—2097 (У)
Чужой дурак—веселье, а свой бесчестье—2327 (Ч)
Чужой дурак—смех, а свой—стыд—2327 (Ч)
"Я не дурак"—сказал дурак—2369 (Я)

ДУРЕНЬ
Дурни думкой богатеют—548 (Д)

ДУРЬ
У всякого своя дурь в голове—2088 (У)

ДУХ
Дух бодр, да плоть немощна—552 (Д)

ДУША
В чужую душу не влезешь—2319 (Ч)
Чужая душа—потёмки (тёмный лес)—2319 (Ч)

ДЫМ
Дым столбом, а огня не видно—553 (Д)
Дым с чадом сошёлся—554 (Д)
Много дыму, да мало пылу—1143 (М)
Нет дыма без огня—1432 (Н)
Огонь без дыма не живёт—325 (Г)
По дыму над баней пару не угадаешь—1675 (П)

ДЫРА
Штопай дыру, пока невелика—2341 (Ш)

ДЫШАТЬ
Дышите глубже (глубоко)—555 (Д)

ДЬЯВОЛ
Дьявол гордился, да с неба свалился—556 (Д)

ДЯДЯ
Дядя, достань (поймай) воробышка—557 (Д)
Каков дядя до людей, таково дяде от людей—798 (К)

ДЯТЕЛ
Дятел и дуб продалбливает—558 (Д)

Е

ЕДИНЕНИЕ
В единении—сила—130 (В)

ЕДИНСТВО
В единстве—сила—130 (В)

ЕМЕЛЯ
У ленивого Емели семь воскресений на неделе—2113 (У)

ЕСТЬ
Горько есть, да жалко покинуть—570 (Е)
Ест тихо и работает не лихо—567 (Е)
Есть—горько, бросить—жалко—570 (Е)
Кто ест скоро, тот и работает споро—919 (К)

Мы едим, чтобы жить, а не живём, чтобы есть—1167 (М)
Чем больше ешь, тем больше хочется—2255 (Ч)

ЕХАТЬ
Ехал прямо, да попал в яму—575 (Е)
Тише едешь, дальше будешь—2054 (Т)

Ж

ЖАДНОСТЬ
Жадность фраера сгубила—580 (Ж)

ЖАЛЕТЬ
Жалеет—значит любит—581 (Ж)

ЖАЛО
Жало остро, а язык острей того—582 (Ж)

ЖАР
Хорошо чужими руками жар загребать—2200 (Х)

ЖДАТЬ
Ждать да гадать—только время терять—583 (Ж)
Кто ждёт, тот дождётся—920 (К)

ЖЕЛАТЬ
Много желать, добра (ничего) не видать—1142 (М)
Не делай другим того, чего себе не желаешь—1328 (Н)
Чего сам не любишь, того и другому не желай—1328 (Н)
Что людям желаешь, то и сам получаешь—2294 (Ч)

ЖЕЛАЮЩИЙ
Желающего судьба ведёт, нежелающего—тащит—584 (Ж)

ЖЕЛЕЗО
Куй железо, пока горячо—977 (К)

ЖЕЛУДОК
Не до пляски, не до шутки, когда пусто в желудке—1333 (Н)

ЖЕЛЧЬ
У кого желчь во рту, тому всё горько—2108 (У)

ЖЕМЧУГ
И на жемчуге бывает царапина—735 (И)

ЖЕНА
Добрая жена да жирные щи—другого добра не ищи—468 (Д)
Добрая жена дом сбережёт—469 (Д)
Жена—в доме глава—586 (Ж)
Жена Цезаря должна быть выше подозрений—587 (Ж)
За хорошей женой и муж пригож—653 (З)
Муж—голова, жена—шея, куда захочет, туда и повернёт—1161 (М)
С доброй женой и горе—полгоря, а радость—вдвое—1874 (С)
У мужа жена всегда виновата—2134 (У)
У хорошей жены и мужу нет цены (и плохой муж будет молодцом)—653 (З)

ЖЕНИТЬСЯ
Женился на скорую руку, да на долгую муку—588 (Ж)
Кто на бодром коне жениться поскачет, тот скоро поплачет—939 (К)
Лучше на убогой жениться, чем с богатой браниться—1059 (Л)
На резвом коне жениться не езди—1232 (Н)
Не торопись жениться, чтобы потом на себя не сердиться—1442 (Н)
Один женился—свет увидал, другой женился—с головой пропал—1521 (О)

ЖЕНЩИНА
Женщине столько лет, на сколько она выглядит—589 (Ж)

ЖИВОЙ
Живой о живом и думает—597 (Ж)
Живой смерти боится (не ищет)—598 (Ж)
Живому именины, мёртвому помины—599 (Ж)
Мёртвому помины, живому именины—599 (Ж)

ЖИВОТ
Живот крепче, на сердце легче—600 (Ж)
И поджарый живот без еды не живёт—743 (И)

ЖИЗНЬ
Жизнь бьёт ключом—601 (Ж)
Жизнь прожить—не поле перейти—602 (Ж)
Жизнь протянется—всего достанется—603 (Ж)
Жизнь—зто движение—604 (Ж)
Такова жизнь—2035 (Т)

ЖИТЬ
Живи всяк своим умом да своим горбом—591 (Ж)
Живи для людей, поживут и люди для тебя—592 (Ж)
Живи и жить давай другим—593 (Ж)
Живи не скупись, с друзьями веселись—594 (Ж)
Живи не так, как хочется, а так, как можется—595 (Ж)
Как живёшь, так и слывёшь—781 (К)
Как жил, так и умер—782 (К)
Не тот живёт больше, кто живёт (чей век) дольше—1445 (Н)

ЖРЕБИЙ
Жребий брошен—607 (Ж)

ЖУК
В поле и жук мясо—202 (В)

ЖУРАВЛЬ
Не сули журавля в небе, а дай синицу в руки—1421 (Н)

З

ЗАВИСТЛИВЫЙ
Железо ржа съедает, а завистливый от зависти сохнет—585 (Ж)
Завистливого и сон неймёт—585 (Ж)
Завистливый от зависти по чужому счастью сохнет—585 (Ж)

ЗАВИСТЬ
В зависти нет ни проку, ни радости—145 (В)
Где несчастье, там зависти нет—324 (Г)

ЗАВТРА
У завтра нет конца—2099 (У)

ЗАВТРАК
Завтраками сыт не будешь—614 (З)
Завтрак съешь сам, обедом поделись с другом, а ужин отдай врагу—615 (З)
Не корми завтраками, а сделай сегодня—1360 (Н)

ЗАГЛЯДЕНЬЕ
Всяк сам себе загляденье—289 (В)

ЗАКЛАД
Спорь до слёз, а об заклад не бейся—1982 (С)

ЗАКОН
Закон—дышло: куда хочешь, туда и воротишь—626 (З)
Закон, что дышло: куда повернёшь, туда и вышло—626 (З)
Незнание закона не есть оправдание—1346 (Н)

ЗАНИМАТЬ
Кто любит занимать, тому не сдобровать—928 (К)

ЗАПАС
Запас кармана не дерёт /и каши не просит/—637 (З)
Запас кармана не трёт (места не пролежит, мешка не дерёт)—637 (З)
Запас не ноша, рук не оттянет—637 (З)
Запас ни пить, ни есть не просит (плеч не тянет)—637 (З)

ЗАПАСЛИВЫЙ
Запасливый нужды не знает (не терпит)—638 (З)

ЗАПЕРЕТЬ
Крепче запрёшь—вернее найдёшь—890 (К)

ЗАПРОС
Запрос в карман не лезет—642 (З)

ЗАРЯ
Заря денежку берёт (куёт, родит)—645 (З)
Заря деньгу даёт—645 (З)
Заря золотом осыпает—645 (З)

ЗАСЛУГА
По заслугам и почёт (честь)—1679 (П)
По заслугам молодца и жалуют—1679 (П)

ЗАУЧИТЬ
Наскоро заучишь—скоро забудешь—1242 (Н)

ЗАХАР
По бедному Захару всякая щепа бьёт—1658 (П)

ЗАЧИН
Зачин дело красит—656 (З)

ЗАЯЦ
За двумя зайцами погонишься, ни одного не поймаешь—617 (З)
Не ищи зайца в бору—на опушке сидит—1355 (Н)
Пуганый заяц и пенька боится—1788 (П)

ЗВОН
Звону много, /да/ дела (толку) мало—1143 (М)

ЗВЯКНУТЬ
Есть чем звякнуть, так можно и крякнуть—573 (Е)

ЗДЕСЬ
Сегодня здесь, а завтра там—1878 (С)

ЗДОРОВЬЕ
Без болезни и здоровью не рад—2067 (Т)
Здоровье всего дороже—660 (З)
Здоровье дороже богатства (золота)—660 (З)
Здоровью цены нет—660 (З)
Здоровья на деньги не купишь—661 (З)
Тот здоровья не знает, кто болен не бывает—2067 (Т)

ЗЕМЛЯ
Земля на трёх китах стоит—663 (З)
Земля не клином сошлась—1860 (С)
Не поклонясь до земли, и грибка не подымешь—1391 (Н)

ЗЕРКАЛО
Лицо—зеркало души—1026 (Л)
Нечего на зеркало пенять, коли рожа крива—1473 (Н)

ЗЕРНО
Не то зерно, что в поле, а то, что в амбаре—1438 (Н)

ЗЁРНЫШКО
Зёрнышко к зёрнышку—будет мешок—664 (З)

ЗИМА
Зима—не лето, пройдёт и это—665 (З)

ЗЛО
Злом зла не поправишь—668 (З)
Зло на зло—добра не будет—706 (И)
Из двух зол выбирают меньшее—704 (И)
Из зла добро не родится—706 (И)

ЗМЕЙКА
Выкормил змейку на свою шейку—300 (В)

ЗМЕЯ
Змею обойдёшь, а от клеветы не уйдёшь—670 (З)
Змея змее на хвост не наползёт—671 (З)
Змея, меняя шкуру, не меняет натуру—672 (З)

ЗНАНИЕ
Знание лучше богатства—677 (З)
Знание—сила—678 (З)
Знания на плечи не давят—679 (З)

ЗНАТЬ
Всё будешь знать, скоро состаришься—1138 (М)
Знать не знаешь, так и вины нет—680 (З)

Много будешь знать, скоро состаришься—1138 (М)
Наперёд не знаешь, где найдёшь, где потеряешь—1224 (Н)
Чего не знаешь, за то не отвечаешь—2237 (Ч)
Я знаю, что я ничего не знаю—2359 (Я)

ЗОЛОТНИК
Мал золотник, да дорог—1105 (М)

ЗОЛОТО
Золото и в болоте видно (светится)—683 (З)
Золото и в грязи блестит—683 (З)
Золото железо переедает—685 (З)
Золото не в золото, не побывав под молотом—686 (З)
Золото не говорит, да много творит—687 (З)
Не всё то золото, что блестит—1301 (Н)
Не всякая блёстка—золото—1301 (Н)

ЗОЛОТОЙ
Рыбка золотая, да внутри гнилая—1845 (Р)

ЗУБ
Где волчьи зубы, а где лисий хвост—310 (Г)
Не волчьи зубы, так лисий хвост—310 (Г)
Око за око, зуб за зуб—1550 (О)

И

ИВАН
Я говорю про Ивана, а ты про болвана—2358 (Я)

ИВАШКА
По Ивашке и рубашка—1681 (П)

ИГЛА
Игла в стог сена попала—пиши пропало—693 (И)
Игла в стог сена упала—считай пропала—693 (И)
Иглой дороги не меряют—695 (И)

ИГОЛКА
Куда иголка, туда и нитка—973 (И)
На сто вёрст и иголка тяжела—1177 (Н)

ИГРА
Игра игрою, а дело делом—696 (И)
Игра не доведёт (не доводит) до добра—697 (И)
Игра не стоит свеч—698 (И)

ИГРАТЬ
Тем не играют, от чего умирают—2043 (Т)

ИЗБАВИТЬ
Избави меня, Боже, от друзей, а с врагами я сам справлюсь—700 (И)

ИЗБУШКА
Во всякой избушке свои погремушки—2104 (У)
У каждой избушки свои погремушки—2104 (У)

ИЗНОСИТЬ
Каково сошьёшь, таково и износишь—811 (К)

ИНСТРУМЕНТ
У плохого мастера всегда инструмент виноват—2139 (У)

ИНТЕРЕС
Каждый свой интерес знает—775 (К)

ИСКАТЬ
Ищи да обрящешь—758 (И)
Кто ищет, тот всегда найдёт—922 (К)

ИСКЛЮЧЕНИЕ
Исключение подтверждает правило—746 (И)

ИСКРА
Искру туши до пожара, беду отводи до удара—747 (И)
Мала искра, да великий пламень родит—1096 (М)
От малой искры, да большой пожар—1096 (М)

ИСПЕЧЬ
Каково испечёшь, таково и съешь—811 (К)
Сама испекла пирожок, сама и кушай—1846 (С)

ИСТИНА
Истина в вине—750 (И)

ИСТОРИЯ
История повторяется—751 (И)
Это совсем другая история—2354 (Э)

К

КАЛАЧ
И калачи приедаются—720 (И)
Не мявши, не тёрши, не будет калач—1376 (Н)
Хочешь есть калачи, так не лежи на печи—2212 (Х)

КАМЕНЬ
В камень стрелять—только стрелы терять—160 (В)
И камень лёжа обомшится—1218 (Н)
На одном месте и камень мохом обрастает—1218 (Н)
Под лежачий камень вода не течёт—1671 (П)
Пусть первым бросит камень, кто безгрешен—1798 (П)

КАМЫШ
Пока зацветут камыши, у нас не будет души—1685 (П)

КАНОНЕР
Всяк канонер на свой манер—274 (В)

КАПАТЬ
Над нами не каплет—1196 (Н)

КАПЕЛЬКА
По капельке—море, по зёрнышку—ворох (, по былинке (травинке)—стог)—1686 (П)

КАПЛЯ
Из крошек—кучка, из капель—море—1686 (П)
Капля и камень долбит (точит)—830 (К)
Капля по капле и камень долбит—830 (К)
По капле—дождь, по росинке—роса—1686 (П)
Последняя капля переполняет чашу—1727 (П)

КАРАВАЙ
На чужой каравай рот не разевай—1260 (Н)

КАРАСЬ
Карась сорвётся, щука навернётся—1389 (Н)
Не поймал карася, поймаешь щуку—1389 (Н)

КАРМАН
Держи карман шире—453 (Д)
Из чужого кармана платить легко—719 (И)
Карман сух—и поп глух—831 (К)
Карман сух, так и судья глух—831 (К)

КАРТА
Везёт в картах—не везёт в любви—131 (В)
Кому везёт в картах, тому не везёт в любви—131 (В)
Не везёт в картах, повезёт в любви—1282 (Н)
Не ставь всё на одну карту—1414 (Н)

КАТАНЬЕ
Не мытьём, так катаньем—1375 (Н)

КАТАТЬСЯ
Любишь кататься, люби и саночки возить—1075 (Л)

КАФТАН
Пуст карман, да красив кафтан—1794 (П)

КАША
Гречневая каша сама себя хвалит—395 (Г)
Заварил кашу—не жалей масла—609 (З)
Кашу маслом не испортишь—832 (К)

Сам кашу заварил, сам и расхлёбывай—1848 (С)
Хочу, с кашей ем, хочу, масло пахтаю—2214 (Х)

КВАС
Часом с квасом, порой с водой—2229 (Ч)

КЕСАРЬ
Кесарю кесарево—835 (К)

КИВАТЬ
На соседа не кивай—за собой примечай—1087 (Л)

КЛАД
Зачем и клад, коли в семье лад—655 (З)
На что и клад, когда дети идут в лад—1259 (Н)
На что и клад, коли в семье лад—655 (З)

КЛАНЯТЬСЯ
Занимает, кланяется, а отдаёт, так чванится—634 (З)

КЛАСТЬ
Плохо не клади, вора в грех не вводи—1655 (П)

КЛЕВЕТА
Клевета что уголь: не обожжёт, так замарает—837 (К)

КЛЕТКА
Золотая клетка соловью не потеха—682 (З)
Не нужна соловью золотая клетка, а нужна золотая ветка—682 (З)
Птичке ветка дороже золотой клетки—682 (З)

КЛИН
Как ни кинь, /а/ всё клин—975 (К)
Клин клином вышибают—838 (К)
Куда ни кинь, везде (всё) клин—975 (К)

КЛИЧКА
Не смотри на кличку—смотри на птичку—1407 (Н)

КЛОБУК
Не всяк игумен (монах), на ком клобук—1314 (Н)

КЛЮЧИК
Золотой ключик все двери открывает—684 (З)

КЛЯЧА
Кляча и в золотой узде не конь—839 (К)
Неказиста кляча, да в беге хороша—1358 (Н)

КНУТ
На послушного коня кнута не надо—1228 (Н)
На ретивого коня (ретивую лошадь) не кнут, а вожжи—1228 (Н)

КОБЕЛЬ
Чёрного кобеля не отмоешь добела—2268 (Ч)

КОБЫЛА
Старая кобыла борозды не испортит—2012 (С)

КОГОТОК
Гладка шёрстка, да коготок остёр—877 (К)
Коготок увяз—всей птичке пропасть—852 (К)
Кошачья лапка мягка, да коготок востёр—877 (К)

КОЖА
Из ежовой кожи шубы не сошьёшь—714 (Е)

КОЗЁЛ
Зарекался козёл в огород ходить—643 (З)
Козла сколько ни корми, а он всё в огород лезет—853 (К)
Пусти козла в огород, он всю капусту обдерёт—1792 (П)
Трясёт козёл бороду, так привык смолоду—2076 (Т)

КОЗЯВКА
Всякая козявка лезет в букашки—257 (В)

КОЛЕСО
Плохое колесо больше хорошего скрипит—1651 (П)
Худое колесо больше (громче) скрипит—1651 (П)

КОЛОДЕЗЬ
Не плюй в колодезь, пригодится /воды/ напиться — 1386 (Н)

КОЛОДЕЦ
Не плюй в колодец, пригодится воды напиться — 1386 (Н)

КОЛОКОЛЬНЯ
Каждый смотрит со своей колокольни — 776 (К)

КОЛОС
Порожний колос выше стоит — 1795 (П)
Пустой колос голову кверху носит — 1795 (П)

КОЛЫБЕЛЬКА
Каков в колыбельку, таков и в могилку — 796 (К)

КОМАР
За комаром не с топором — 632 (З)
За семь вёрст комара искали, а комар на носу — 646 (З)
И комар лошадь свалит, коли волк подсобит — 721 (И)
И комары кусают до поры — 722 (И)

КОНЕЦ
Всему есть конец — 2262 (Ч)
И у самого длинного дня есть конец — 753 (И)
Конец — делу венец — 863 (К)
Конец венчает дело — 863 (К)
Не стращай началом, покажи конец — 1416 (Н)
Нет начала без конца — 2262 (Ч)
Путному началу благой конец — 1799 (П)
У хорошего почина хороший конец — 1799 (П)
Чему было начало, тому будет и конец — 2262 (Ч)

КОНЧАТЬ
Не мудрено начать, мудрено кончать — 1374 (Н)

КОНЧИТЬ
Когда не можешь кончить, не начинай — 846 (К)

КОНЬ
Бережливого коня и зверь в поле не берёт — 1571 (О)
Был конь, да заезжен, был молодец, да подержан — 120 (Б)
Был конь, да изъездился — 120 (Б)
Дарёному коню в зубы не смотрят — 414 (Д)
И на доброго коня бывает спотычка — 866 (К)
Конь вырвется — догонишь, а слова сказанного не воротишь — 865 (К)
Конь о четырёх ногах, да и тот спотыкается — 866 (К)
Конь узнаётся при горе, а друг при беде — 867 (К)
Который конь пал, тот рысак был — 875 (К)
Кто в кони пошёл, тот и воду070 вози — 913 (К)
Куда конь с копытом, туда и рак с клешнёй — 974 (К)
Не давай коню тощать — в дороге не станет — 1327 (Н)
Ночью все кони вороные — 1493 (Н)
Осторожного коня и зверь не берёт — 1571 (О)
Собака лает, а конь идёт — 1954 (С)
Старый конь борозды не портит — 2012 (С)
С чужого коня среди грязи долой — 2026 (С)
Сыпь коню мешком, не будешь ходить пешком — 2029 (С)
Усталому коню и сбруя тяжела — 2151 (У)
У сытого коня восемь ног — 2155 (У)

КОПЕЕЧКА
Ближняя копеечка дороже дальнего рубля — 70 (Б)

КОПЕЙКА
Без копейки рубль не живёт (рубля не бывает) — 869 (К)
Домашняя копейка лучше заезжего рубля — 499 (Д)
Копейка к копейке — проживёт и семейка — 868 (К)
Копейками рубль держится — 869 (К)

Копейка рубль бережёт—869 (К)

КОРАБЛЬ
Большому кораблю—большое и плаванье—99 (Б)
Разбитому кораблю нет попутного ветра—1811 (Р)

КОРЕНЬ
Каков корень, таков и плод (отпрыск)—800 (К)
Каков корень, таково и семя—800 (К)

КОРЕШОК
Какие корешки, такие и ветки, какие родители, такие и детки—783 (К)

КОРМ
Не в коня корм—1290 (Н)

КОРОВА
Бодливой корове Бог рог не даёт—88 (Б)
Бывает, что и корова летает—113 (Б)
Взял корову—возьми и подойник—149 (В)
Корова черна, да молоко у неё бело—870 (К)
От чёрной коровы, да белое молочко—870 (К)
Которая корова пала, та по два удоя давала—875 (К)
Чья бы корова мычала, а твоя бы молчала—2334 (Ч)

КОРОВКА
Некрасива коровка, да молочко даёт—870 (К)
От чёрной коровки, да белое молочко—870 (К)

КОРОЛЬ
Король и в рубище король—871 (К)
Кривой среди слепых—король—893 (К)
Среди слепых и одноглазый король—893 (К)

КОРОТКО
Коротко да ясно, от того и прекрасно—872 (К)

КОСА
Коси коса, пока роса—873 (К)
Нашла коса на камень—1267 (Н)

КОСМАТЫЙ
И космато, да не медведь—723 (И)

КОСОЙ
Не говори с косым о кривом—1322 (Н)
С кривым о косом не беседуют—1322 (Н)

КОСТЬ
Наскочила кость на кость—1243 (Н)
Около кости мясо слаще—1552 (О)
Поздно пришёл—одни кости нашёл—1680 (П)

КОТ
Без кота мышам масленица (раздолье)—41 (Б)
Видит кот молоко, да в кувшине глубоко (да рыло коротко)—152 (В)
Кота в мешке не покупают (покупать нельзя)—874 (К)
Кот скребёт на свой хребет—876 (К)
Мыши танцуют, когда кота не чуют—41 (Б)
Ошпаренный кот боится холодной воды—1626 (О)
Постригся кот, намылся кот, а всё тот же кот—1743 (П)

КОТЁЛ
Что в котёл положишь, то и вынешь—2284 (Ч)
Что положишь себе в котёл, то и будет в ложке—2284 (Ч)

КОТЕЛОК
Говорил горшку котелок: Уж больно ты чёрен, дружок!—358 (Г)

КОТОМКА
Я не я, и котомка не моя—2372 (Я)

КОШКА
Знает кошка, чьё мясо съела—673 (З)
Знай, кошка, своё лукошко—674 (З)

Кошка скребёт на свой хребет—876 (К)
Кошка спит, а всё мышей (а мышку) видит—878 (К)
Кошке игрушки, а мышке слёзки—879 (К)
Кошке смех, а мышке слёзы—879 (К)
Кошки дома нет—мышам воля (раздолье)—41 (Б)
Кошку бьют, а невестке знак подают (наветки дают)—880 (К)
Кошку девятая смерть донимает—881 (К)
Любит и кошка мышку—1072 (Л)
Ночью все кошки серы—1493 (Н)
У робкой кошки мышь резвится—2142 (У)
Чует кошка, чьё мясо съела—673 (З)

КРАЙНОСТЬ
Крайности сходятся—883 (К)

КРАСА
Была бы краса, кабы не дождь да осенняя роса—115 (Б)

КРАСИВЫЙ
Не красивая красива, а любимая—1361 (Н)

КРАСИТЬ
Не одежда красит человека—1381 (Н)
Человека красит голова, а не шляпа—1381 (Н)

КРАСОТА
Красота до венца, а ум до конца—884 (К)
Красота до вечера, а доброта навек—885 (К)
Красотой сыт не будешь—886 (К)

КРАТКОСТЬ
Краткость—сестра таланта—887 (К)

КРАЮШКА
За краюшкой погонишься, каравай потеряешь—629 (З)

КРЕДИТ
Кредит портит отношения—888 (К)

КРЕМЕНЬ
Кремень на кремень—искра—889 (К)

КРЕСТ
Тяжёл крест, да надо несть—2079 (Т)

КРИК
Много крику, мало толку—1143 (М)

КРИЧАТЬ
Не кричи о себе—пусть другие о тебе хоть тихо скажут—1364 (Н)

КРОВЛЯ
Чужую кровлю кроешь, а своя каплет—2330 (Ч)

КРОВЬ
Голос крови не заглушить—376 (Г)
Кровь за кровь—895 (К)
Кровь не вода—896 (К)

КРОЁНОЕ
Кроёного не перекроить—897 (К)

КРОХА
Обрадовался крохе, да ломоть потерял—1510 (О)
Погнался за крохою, потерял ломоть—1510 (О)

КРОШКА
Где едят, там крошки падают—314 (Г)
Кинь в окошко крошки, в дверь придёт лепёшка—836 (К)

КРУГ
Для друга нет круга—464 (Д)

КРУПИЦА
По крупице и птица собирает, а сыта бывает—979 (К)

КРУЧИНА
Кручина иссушит в лучину—900 (К)

КРЫЛО
Без крыльев не улетишь—42 (Б)

КРЫСА
Крысы бегут с тонущего корабля—901 (К)

КРЫША
Под каждой крышей свои мыши—1670 (П)
Чужую крышу кроешь, а своя течёт—2330 (Ч)

КРЯХТЕТЬ
Кряхти, да гнись, а упрёшься—переломишься—902 (К)

КУВШИН
До поры кувшин воду носит: оторвётся—разобьётся—1659 (П)
Повадился кувшин по воду ходить, там ему и голову сложить—1659 (П)

КУДРИ
В хорошем житье кудри вьются, а в плохом секутся—295 (В)

КУЗНЕЦ
Каждый человек—кузнец своего счастья—2247 (Ч)
Человек сам кузнец своего счастья—2247 (Ч)

КУЛИК
Всяк кулик на своём болоте велик—275 (В)
Всяк кулик своё болото хвалит—276 (В)

КУМ
Знает кум, да кума, да людей полсела—2291 (Ч)
Что знает кум, знает и кумова жена, а по ней и вся деревня—2291 (Ч)

КУМА
Кума с воза—возу (кобыле, куму) легче—17 (Б)

КУПЕЦ
Всякий купец свой товар хвалит—269 (В)

КУПИТЬ
За ничто ничего не купишь—635 (З)
За что купил, за то и продаю—657 (З)

КУРА
Ложись с курами, а вставай с петухами—1036 (Л)
Сова спит, а кур видит—1957 (С)

КУРИЛКА
Жив курилка—596 (Ж)

КУРИЦА
Всякая курица своим голосом поёт—258 (В)
Каждая курица свой насест хвалит—276 (В)
Голодной курице просо снится—372 (Г)
Дай курице гряду—изроет весь огород—408 (Д)
Пусти курицу на грядку—исклюёт весь огород—408 (Д)
Кому что, а курице просо—862 (К)
Курица соседа всегда выглядит гусыней—978 (К)
От худой курицы худые яйца—1617 (О)
Петух скажет курице, а она—всей улице—1642 (П)
Скажешь курице, а она—всей улице—1642 (П)
Слепой курице всё пшеница—1921 (С)

КУРОЧКА
Курочка по зёрнышку клюёт, да сыта бывает—979 (К)

КУС
Хорош кус, да не для наших уст—2184 (Х)

КУСАТЬСЯ
Попался, который кусался—1711 (П)

КУСОК
В чужих руках кусок больше кажется—296 (В)
Лучше свой кусок, чем чужой пирог—1862 (С)

КУСТ
Куст тот, да не та ягода—980 (К)

КУШАТЬ
Чьё кушаю, того и слушаю—2333 (Ч)

Л

ЛАД
Где лад, там и клад—655 (З)

ЛАПОТЬ
И мы не на руку лапоть обуваем—731 (И)
Станешь лапти плесть, как нечего есть—1992 (С)

ЛАРЧИК
А ларчик просто открывался—3 (А)

ЛАСКА
Ласка вернее таски—983 (Л)

ЛАСТОЧКА
Одна ласточка весны не делает—1533 (О)
Первая ласточка весны не делает (лста нс приносит)—1533 (О)

ЛГАТЬ
Кто привык лгать, тому трудно отвыкать—957 (К)

ЛЕВ
Лев мышей не ловит—1559 (О)

ЛЕГИОН
Имя им легион—734 (И)

ЛЕГКО
Легко добыто (нажито), легко и прожито—993 (Л)
Что без труда (легко) наживается, легко и проживается—993 (Л)

ЛЁД
Среди зимы льда не выпросишь у кумы—2147 (У)

ЛЕЖАТЬ
Лёжа пищи (хлеба) не добудешь—1000 (Л)
Станешь лежать на псчи, так нс будет ничего в печи—1993 (С)

ЛЕЖАЧИЙ
Лежачего не бьют—1001 (Л)

ЛЕКАРСТВО
Есть болезнь, есть и лекарство—568 (Е)
На всякую хворь найдётся лекарство—568 (Е)
Хорошее лекарство никогда не бывает сладким—2190 (Х)

ЛЁН
Каков лён, такова и пряжа—801 (К)

ЛЕНИВЫЙ
Ленивому всегда некогда—948 (К)
Ленивому всегда (и в будни) праздник—1003 (Л)
Ленивый к работе—ретивый к обеду—1004 (Л)

ЛЕНИТЬСЯ
Станешь лениться, будешь с сумой волочиться—1994 (С)

ЛЕНОСТЬ
Леность наводит на бедность—1005 (Л)

ЛЕНЬ
Лень добра не делает—1006 (Л)
Лень до добра не доводит—1006 (Л)
Лень—мать всех пороков—1006 (Л)
Лень человека портит—1007 (Л)

ЛЕПЕТАТЬ
Ешь калачи, да поменьше лепечи—577 (Е)

ЛЕС
В лес дров не возят, в колодец воду не льют—163 (В)
Из-за деревьев леса не видать—705 (И)
Кто в лес, кто по дрова—912 (К)
Лес без лешего не живёт—1008 (Л)
Лес видит, а поле слышит—1009 (Л)
Лес не без шакала—1008 (Л)
Лес по дереву не плачет, море по рыбе не тужит—1010 (Л)
Лес рубят—щепки летят—1011 (Л)
Чем дальше в лес, тем больше дров—2257 (Ч)

ЛЕСТЬ
Лесть без зубов, а с костьми ест—1012 (Л)

ЛЕТА
Сколько лет, сколько зим!—1909 (С)

ЛЕТАТЬ
Высоко летаешь, да низко садишься—302 (В)
Кто высоко летает, тот низко падает—302 (В)
Летала пташка высоко, а села недалеко—302 (В)

ЛЕТЕТЬ
Высоко летишь—где-то сядешь—302 (В)

ЛЕТО
Лето пролежишь, зимой с сумой побежишь—1014 (Л)
Лето собирает, а зима подбирает—1015 (Л)
Спустя лето в лес по малину не ходят—1986 (С)

ЛЕТОМ
Готовь летом сани, а зимой телегу—394 (Г)
Летом дома сидеть—зимой хлеба не иметь—1013 (Л)
Летом с удочкой, зимой с сумочкой—1014 (Л)
Что летом родится, то зимой пригодится—2293 (Ч)

ЛЖИВЫЙ
Лживый человек правды боится—1016 (Л)

ЛИСА
И лиса хитра, да шкуру её продают—1042 (Л)
Лиса и во сне кур считает—1022 (Л)
Лиса кур не сбережёт—1023 (Л)
Лиса семерых волков проведёт—1024 (Л)
Лукава лисица, да в капкан попадает—1042 (Л)
Спит лиса, а во сне кур считает—1022 (Л)
Старая лиса дважды поймать себя не даёт—2005 (С)
Старую лису дважды не проведёшь—2005 (С)
Старую лису хитростям не учат—2006 (С)
Уж на что лиса хитра, да и её ловят—1042 (Л)
Хитра лиса, а в силки попадает—1042 (Л)

ЛИСИЦА
Всякая лисица свой хвост хвалит—259 (В)
Лукава лисица, да в капкан попадает—1042 (Л)

ЛИХО
Не буди лихо, пока оно тихо—1274 (Н)

ЛИХОЙ
От лихого не услышишь доброго слова—1591 (О)

ЛИЦО
В хорошем житье лицо белится—295 (В)
Лицо—зеркало души—1026 (Л)
Не с лица воду пить /, можно с некрасивой жить/—1925 (С)
С лица не воду пить—1925 (С)

ЛИЧИКО
Личиком бел, да душою чёрен—1027 (Л)
Личиком гладок, а делами гадок—694 (И)
С личика—яичко, а внутри—болтун—1926 (С)

ЛИШИТЬСЯ
Лучше глаза лишиться, чем доброго имени—1054 (Л)
Лучше лишиться жизни, чем доброго имени—1054 (Л)
Лучше лишиться яйца, чем курицы—1055 (Л)

ЛОБ
Всё одно, что в лоб, что в голову—2285 (Ч)
Выше лба уши не растут—305 (В)
Лбом стены не прошибёшь—990 (Л)

Лоб что лопата, а ума небогато — 1031 (Л)
Что в лоб, что по лбу — 2285 (Ч)

ЛОВЕЦ
На ловца и зверь бежит — 1207 (Н)

ЛОВЛЯ
Какова от пса ловля, такова ему и кормля — 791 (К)

ЛОВУШКА
В одну ловушку два раза зверя не заманишь — 178 (В)

ЛОДЫРЬ
Лодырь всегда найдёт причину, лишь бы не работать — 1034 (Л)
Лодырь и бездельник празднуют и в понедельник — 1035 (Л)

ЛОЖИТЬСЯ
Ложись с курами, а вставай с петухами — 1036 (Л)

ЛОЖКА
Ложка дёгтя испортит бочку мёда — 1037 (Л)
Ложкой море не исчерпаешь — 1038 (Л)
Море ложкой не наполнишь — 1038 (Л)
Новая ложка в чести, а отхлебается — и под лавкой валяется — 1489 (Н)
Одна ложка дёгтя испортит бочку мёда — 1037 (Л)
Сухая ложка рот дерёт — 2019 (С)

ЛОЖЬ
И ложь правдой статься может — 729 (И)
Ложь ложью погоняет — 1039 (Л)
Ложь на гнилых ногах (на тараканьих ножках) ходит — 2114 (У)
Люди ложь, и мы то ж — 1088 (Л)
Маленькая ложь за собой большую ведёт — 1100 (М)
Одна ложь тянет за собой другую — 1535 (О)
Со лжи пошлины не берут — 1960 (С)
У лжи короткие ноги — 2114 (У)

ЛОКОТЬ
Близок локоть, да не укусишь — 73 (Б)

ЛОМАТЬ
Ломать не делать (не строить) — 1040 (Л)

ЛОМОТОК
На чужой ломоток не разевай роток — 1260 (Н)

ЛОМОТЬ
В чужих руках ломоть велик — 296 (В)
Дадут ломоть, да заставят неделю молоть — 404 (Д)
Погнался за ломтем, да хлеб потерял — 1510 (О)

ЛОШАДЬ
Дай глупому лошадь, он на ней и к чёрту уедет — 407 (Д)
Когда лошадь бежит, не надобно шпор — 844 (К)
Куда лошадь, туда и телега — 973 (К)
Лошадей на переправе не меняют — 1041 (Л)
Не гоняй лошадь к воде, если ей пить не хочется — 1324 (Н)
Ночью все лошади вороные — 1493 (Н)
Я не я, и лошадь не моя, и я не извозчик — 2372 (Я)

ЛУКОШКО
Каково лукошко, такова и покрышка — 808 (К)

ЛУЧШЕЕ
Всё к лучшему в зтом лучшем из миров — 227 (В)
Лучшее — часто враг хорошего — 1051 (Л)
Что Бог ни делает, всё к лучшему — 2279 (Ч)
Что ни делается, всё к лучшему — 2279 (Ч)

ЛЫКО
И мы не лыком шиты /, не лаптем щи хлебаем/ — 731 (И)
Не всякое (каждое) лыко в строку — 1315 (Н)

ЛЮБИТЬ
Кто любит арбуз, а кто свиной хрящик, никто никому не указчик—927 (К)
Кто любит попа, кто попадью, кто попову дочку—929 (К)
Любишь меня, так люби и мою родню (и собачку мою)—1076 (Л)

ЛЮБОВЬ
Гони любовь хоть в дверь, она влетит в окно—379 (Г)
Любовь всё побеждает—1078 (Л)
Любовь за деньги не купишь—1079 (Л)
Любовь зла—полюбишь и козла—1080 (Л)
Любовь—кольцо, а у кольца нет конца—1081 (Л)
Любовь лечит или калечит—1082 (Л)
Любовь на замок не закроешь (не запрёшь)—1083 (Л)
Любовь не картошка, не выбросишь в окошко—1084 (Л)
Любовь слепа—1085 (Л)
Не дорог подарок, дорога любовь—1334 (Н)
От любви до ненависти один шаг—1593 (О)
От любви нет лекарства—1594 (О)
Совет да любовь—1959 (С)
Старая любовь не ржавеет—1995 (С)
Шила в мешке да любви в сердце не утаишь—2336 (Ш)

ЛЮБОПЫТНЫЙ
Любопытному на базаре нос прищемили—1086 (Л)

ЛЮДИ
Все мы люди, все мы человеки—235 (В)
И за горами люди—699 (И)
И за рекой люди живут—699 (И)
Люди разные бывают—1089 (Л)
На людях горе вполгоря (и смерть красна, умирать легче)—1209 (Н)
Не только людей что Фома да Фаддей—1439 (Н)
Сколько людей, столько и мнений—1908 (С)

ЛЯГУШКА
Лягушка квакает в своё время—1093 (Л)

М

МАВР
Мавр сделал своё дело, мавр может уходить—1095 (М)

МАГОМЕТ
Если гора не идёт к Магомету, то Магомет идёт к горе—564 (Е)

МАЙ
В мае дождь—родится рожь—165 (В)
Май холодный—не будешь голодный—9 (А)

МАКАР
На бедного Макара все шишки валятся /- и с сосен, и с ёлок/—1172 (Н)

МАЛАНЬЯ
Какова Маланья, таковы у ней и оладьи—788 (К)

МАЛО
Лучше мало, чем совсем ничего—1056 (Л)

МАЛОЕ
За малым погонишься, большое потеряешь—629 (З)
Малое пожалеешь, большое потеряешь—629 (З)

МАМКА
У семи мамок дитя без глаза (глазу)—2145 (У)

МАРТ
Март сухой да мокрый май, будет каша и каравай—1108 (М)
Сухой март, а май мокрый делают хлеб добрый—1108 (М)

МАСЛЕНИЦА
Не всё коту масленица /, будет (бывает) и великий пост/—1297 (Н)
Не житьё, а масленица—1340 (Н)

МАСЛО
Всё идёт как по маслу—226 (В)
Маслом огонь не заливают—1109 (М)
Масло по маслу не приправа—1110 (М)
Огонь маслом заливать—лишь огня прибавлять—1109 (М)

МАСТЕР
Видно мастера по работе—154 (В)
Каков мастер, такова и работа—802 (К)
Мастер глуп—нож туп—1111 (М)
Не испортив дела, мастером не будешь—1352 (Н)
По мастеру и закрой—1702 (П)
По работе и мастера знать—154 (В)
Работа мастера хвалит—154 (В)

МАСТЬ
Масть к масти подбирается—1113 (М)

МАТКА
Какова матка, таково и ягнятко (таковы и детки)—789 (К)

МАТЬ
Какова мать, такова и дочь—790 (К)

МАША
Хороша Маша, да не наша—2184 (Х)

МАШКА
Живёт и на Машку промашка—736 (И)
И на Машку бывает промашка—736 (И)

МЁД
Будь лишь мёд, много мух нальнёт—109 (Б)
Где мёд, там и мухи—316 (Г)
Где мёд, там и пчёлы—317 (Г)
Ешь мёд, да берегись жала—576 (Е)
Либо мёд пить, либо биту быть—1019 (Л)
Мёд есть—в улей лезть—1116 (М)
Мёдом больше мух наловишь, чем уксусом—1118 (М)
На устах мёд, а на сердце лёд—1269 (Н)
На языке мёд, а в сердце (на уме, под языком) лёд—1269 (Н)
Сладок мёд, да не по пуду в рот—1919 (С)

МЕДАЛЬ
Всякая медаль о двух сторонах—2105 (У)
У каждой медали есть обратная сторона—2105 (У)

МЕДВЕДЬ
Два медведя в одной берлоге не живут—420 (Д)
Медведь пляшет, а поводырь деньги берёт—1114 (М)
От волка бежал, да на медведя напал—1582 (О)
От волка ушёл—на медведя набрёл—1582 (О)

МЕДЛЕННО
Медленно, да верно—1117 (М)

МЕДОК
На словах (языке) медок, а на сердце ледок—1269 (Н)

МЕЛЬНИЦА
Мельница мелет—мука будет, язык мелет—беда будет—1120 (М)

МЕНА
Мена—не грабёж—1121 (М)

МЕНЬШЕ
Лучше меньше, да лучше—1057 (Л)

МЕРА
Во всём надо знать меру—246 (В)
Всё хорошо в меру—246 (В)
Выше меры и конь не скачет—306 (В)

МЕРИН
Посуленный мерин не везёт—1744 (П)

МЁРТВЫЙ
Мёртвые не вредят—1125 (М)
Мёртвый не выдаст (не расскажет)—1126 (М)
Мёртвых с погоста не носят—1127 (М)

МОЛВА
Людская молва что морская волна—1090 (Л)
Мирская молва что морская волна—1090 (Л)
От молвы не уйдёшь—670 (З)
Плохая молва на крыльях летит—1648 (П)
Худая молва на крыльях летит—1648 (П)

МОЛВИТЬ
В добрый час молвить, в худой промолчать—127 (В)
Что молвишь, то не воротишь—2296 (Ч)

МОЛОДЕЦ
Всякий молодец на свой образец—270 (В)
Знать птицу по перьям, а молодца по речам—681 (З)
Молодец на (против) овец, а на (против) молодца и сам овца—1150 (М)

МОЛОДО
Молодо—зелено, погулять велено—1151 (М)

МОЛОДОЙ
Из молодых, да ранний—707 (И)
Молод—перебесится, а стар—не переменится—1153 (М)

МОЛОДОСТЬ
Если бы молодость знала, если бы старость могла—561 (Е)
Если бы молодость умела, а старость могла—561 (Е)
Чему научишься в молодости, то знаешь и в старости—2263 (Ч)

МОЛОЧКО
Захотел молочка от бычка—654 (З)

МОЛЧАНИЕ
Молчание—знак согласия—1154 (М)
Молчание—золото—1933 (С)

МОЛЧАТЬ
Кто молчит, тот двух научит—936 (К)
Лучше молчать, чем пустое врать—1058 (Л)
Молчи—за умного сойдёшь—1155 (М)
Не стыдно молчать, коли нечего сказать—1501 (Н)
Нужно молчать, коли нечего сказать—1501 (Н)

МОМЕНТ
Лови момент!—1032 (Л)

МОНАСТЫРЬ
В чужой монастырь со своим уставом не ходят—297 (В)

МОНОМАХ
Тяжела ты, шапка Мономаха—2078 (Т)

МОРЕ
Кабы не кабы, так и было бы море, а не пруды—763 (К)
На море овин горит, по небу медведь летит—1210 (Н)

МОРОЗ
Если бы на горох не мороз, он бы давно через тын перерос—762 (К)
Если бы не мороз, так овёс бы до неба дорос—762 (К)
Кабы на хмель не мороз, так он бы и тын перерос—762 (К)

МОСКВА
И Москва не вдруг строилась—730 (И)
Москва от искры загорелась (копеечной свечки сгорела)—1156 (М)
От копеечной свечи Москва сгорела—1156 (М)
Москва слезам не верит—1157 (М)
Не сразу Москва строилась—730 (И)

МОТАТЬ
Кто мотает, в том пути не бывает—938 (К)

МОШНА
Есть в мошне, так будет и в квашне—569 (Е)

Мошна туга—всяк ей слуга—1158 (М)

МУДРЕЦ
На всякого мудреца довольно простоты—1187 (Н)

МУДРОСТЬ
Мудрость в голове, а не в бороде—2124 (У)

МУДРЫЙ
Каждый для себя мудрый—772 (К)

МУЖ
Всякому мужу своя жена мила—283 (В)
За хорошим мужем и жена хороша—2162 (У)
Муж без жены—что гусь без воды (конь без узды)—1160 (М)
Муж—голова, жена—шея, куда захочет, туда и повернёт—1161 (М)
Муж и жена—одна сатана—1162 (М)
Муж с женой бранятся, чужой не вяжись—1164 (М)
У хорошего мужа и жена хороша—2162 (У)

МУЖИК
Мужик тонул—топор обещал, вытащили—топорища жаль—1163 (М)
Русский мужик задним умом крепок—620 (З)

МУЖЧИНА
Путь к сердцу мужчины лежит через желудок—1800 (П)

МУЗЫКА
Кто платит музыканту, тот и заказывает музыку—955 (К)
Помирать, так с музыкой—1703 (П)

МУ'КА
Без муки нет науки—43 (Б)

МУКА'
Всё перемелется, мука будет—239 (В)

МУРАВЕЙ
Мал муравей, да горы копает—1165 (М)
Муравей невелик, а горы копает—1165 (М)

МУХА
За мухой не с обухом, за комаром не с топором—632 (З)
Слышно было, как муха пролетит—1936 (С)

МЫЛО
Мыло серо, да моет бело—1169 (М)
Чёрную душу /и/ мылом не отмоешь—2304 (Ч)
Что природа дала, того и мылом не отмоешь—2304 (Ч)

МЫШКА
Невелика мышка, да зубок остёр—1098 (М)
Сытой мышке и сало не вкусно—2031 (С)

МЫШЬ
Беззаботна та мышь, которая только одну лазейку знает—2216 (Х)
И мышь в свою норку тащит корку—733 (И)
Мышь сыта—мука горька—2031 (С)
Плоха мышь, что один только лаз знает—2216 (Х)
Сытая мышь и муки не ест—2031 (С)
Худа та мышь, которая одну лазейку знает—2216 (Х)

МЯКИНА
Во всяком хлебе мякина есть—173 (В)
Всё едино, что хлеб, что мякина—225 (В)
И в мякине зёрна находятся—689 (И)

МЯСО
Как нет мяса, и жук мясо—202 (В)
Мяса без костей не бывает—1171 (М)

Н

НАВАР
От воды навару не будет—1581 (О)

НАВЕТКА
Одного бьют, а другому наветки дают—880 (К)

НАВЫК
Навык мастера ставит—1190 (Н)

НАГОЙ
Мокрый дождя, а нагой разбоя не боится—377 (Г)

НАГРЕСТИ
Тяжело нагребёшь, домой не донесёшь—2081 (Т)

НАДЕЖДА
Надеждой жив человек—1195 (Н)
Одной надеждой не проживёшь—1543 (О)
Сердце надеждой живо—1195 (Н)
С одной надежды не сшить одежды—1966 (С)

НАДЕЯТЬСЯ
На Бога надейся, а сам не плошай—1176 (Н)
Пока дышу (живу), надеюсь—1682 (П)

НАЖИВА
Лакома нажива, да востёр крючок—982 (Л)

НАЖИВАТЬ
Кто рано ложится и рано встаёт, здоровье, богатство и ум наживёт—962 (К)

НАЗЛО
Назло мужу сяду в лужу—1203 (Н)

НАКЛАСТЬ
Тяжело накладёшь, не унесёшь—2081 (Т)

НАКЛОНИТЬСЯ
Надо наклониться, чтобы из пруда (ручья) напиться—1502 (Н)
Нужно наклониться, чтоб из ручья воды напиться—1502 (Н)

НАПАДЕНИЕ
Нападение—лучший вид защиты—1249 (Н)

НАПЛЕВАТЬ
Наплюй в глаза, скажет: божья роса—1225 (Н)

НАПРАСЛИНА
Как себя ни поведёшь, от напраслин не уйдёшь—828 (К)

НАПРЯМИК
Напрямик—ближе, кругом—скорее—1231 (Н)

НАПРЯМКИ
Напрямки ездить—дома не ночевать—959 (К)

НАРОД
В каком народе живёшь, того обычая и держись—159 (В)

НАРУЖНОСТЬ
Наружность обманчива—168 (В)

НАРЯДИТЬ
Наряди пенёк в вешний денёк, так и пенёк будет паренёк—1234 (Н)
Наряди пень /в вешний день/, и пень будет хорош—1234 (Н)
Наряди свинью хоть в серьги, а она всё в навоз пойдёт—1235 (Н)

НАСЕДКА
Знала бы наседка, узнает и соседка—676 (З)

НАСТУПЛЕНИЕ
Наступление—лучший вид обороны—1249 (Н)

НАСТЯ
Пошла Настя по напастям—1753 (П)
Сказала Настя, как удастся—1897 (С)

НАТАЛЬЯ
У злой Натальи все люди канальи—2100 (У)

НАУКА
Науке учиться—старости нет—1254 (Н)

НАЧАЛО
Без начала нет конца—44 (Б)
Всякое начало трудно—278 (В)
Доброе начало полдела откачало—477 (Д)
Доброе начало—половина дела—477 (Д)
Каково начало, таков и конец—809 (К)

Не бойся начала, а бойся конца—1272 (Н)
Плохое начало не к доброму концу—1652 (П)
Плохое начало—плохой и конец—1652 (П)
Путному началу благой конец—1799 (П)
Хорошее начало полдела откачало—477 (Д)

НАЧАТЬ
Легко начать, да нелегко кончить—995 (Л)
Не начавши—думай, а начавши—делай—1378 (Н)
Раньше начнёшь, раньше поспеешь—1822 (Р)

НЕВЕСТА
Все невесты хороши, но откуда злые жёны берутся?—223 (В)
Всякая невеста для своего жениха родится—260 (В)

НЕВЕСТКА
Невестке в отместку—1287 (Н)
У свекрови всегда невестка винована—2143 (У)

НЕДОСТАТОК
Нет людей без недостатков—1436 (Н)

НЕДОУЧЕННЫЙ
Недоученный хуже неучёного—1336 (Н)

НЕДРУГ
Недруг дарит, зло мыслит—1338 (Н)

НЕЗАМЕНИМЫЙ
Незаменимых людей нет—1342 (Н)

НЕКОГДА
Кто ничего не делает, тому всегда некогда—948 (К)

НЕМНОЖКО
Чего немножко, того не мечи в окошко—2238 (Ч)

НЕМОЙ
Немой караул закричал, безногий на пожар побежал—1373 (Н)

НЕНАСТЬЕ
Не всегда ненастье, не всегда и несчастье—1296 (Н)
Не всё ненастье—проглянет и красное солнышко—1296 (Н)

НЕНАСЫТНЫЙ
Ненасытному всё мало—1377 (Н)

НЕОБЪЯТНОЕ
Нельзя объять необъятное—1366 (Н)

НЕСЧАСТЬЕ
Несчастья бояться—счастья не видать—1424 (Н)

НЕТЕРПЕНИЕ
Кто с нетерпением ждёт, тот долго ждёт—967 (К)

НЕЧЕСТНО
Нечестно живёшь—себя подведёшь—1475 (Н)

НИТКА
Длинная нитка—ленивая швея—463 (Д)
С миру по нитке—голому рубашка—1947 (С)

НИЧЕГО
Всё лучше того, как нет ничего—1070 (Л)
Из ничего ничего не сделаешь—708 (И)

НИЩЕТА
Нищета не отнимает ни чести, ни ума—1488 (Н)
Тот в нищету пошёл, на ком долг тяжёл—2066 (Т)

НИЩИЙ
Суму нищего не наполнишь—2018 (С)

НОВОЕ
Новое—это хорошо забытое старое—1491 (Н)

НОВЫЙ
Ничто не ново под луной—1486 (Н)

НОГА
В ногах правды нет—169 (В)

Придёт время, и мы ногой топнем — 1770 (П)

НОГОТОК

В чужих руках ноготок с локоток — 296 (В)

Гладка шёрстка, да ноготок остёр — 877 (К)

Мал ноготок, да остёр — 1098 (М)

НОМЕР

Этот номер не пройдёт — 2356 (Э)

НОРА

Близ норы лиса на промысел не ходит — 72 (Б)

Каждый в свою нору тянет — 771 (К)

НОС

Выше головы носа не поднимешь — 304 (В)

Вышс нос! — 307 (В)

Заруби себе зто на носу — 644 (З)

Не задирай нос кверху, а то упадёшь — 1341 (Н)

Не суй носа в чужое просо — 1419 (Н)

Не суй свой нос в чужой вопрос — 1419 (Н)

Не тычь носа в чужое просо — 1419 (Н)

Умён, умён, а у себя под носом не видит — 2120 (У)

НОЧЬ

Тёмная ночь не навек — 2042 (Т)

НОША

Каждому своя ноша тяжела — 770 (К)

На большом пути и малая ноша тяжела — 1177 (Н)

Ноша легка на чужом плече — 2320 (Ч)

Своя ноша не тяжела (не тянет) — 1867 (С)

Чужая ноша не тянет — 2320 (Ч)

НРАВ

Иные времена, иные нравы — 740 (И)

Нет таких трав, чтоб знать чужой нрав — 1454 (Н)

Нрав на нрав не приходится — 1494 (Н)

Под всякую песню не подпляшешь, под всякие нравы не подладишь — 1669 (П)

Собачьего нрава не изменишь — 1955 (С)

НУЖДА

В нужде и кулик соловьём свищет — 170 (В)

В нужде с кем ни поведёшься — 171 (В)

Для нужды нет закона — 1497 (Н)

Кто нужды не видал, тот и счастья не знает — 951 (К)

Лучше нужду неси, а взаймы не проси — 1061 (Л)

Нужда всему научит — 1498 (Н)

Нужда горюет, нужда воюет — 1495 (Н)

Нужда да голод выгоняют (прогоняют) на холод — 1496 (Н)

Нужда закона не знает, а через шагает — 1497 (Н)

Нужда научит ворожить, когда нечего в рот положить — 1498 (Н)

Нужда научит горшки обжигать (калачи есть, решетом воду носить) — 1498 (Н)

Нужда свой закон пишет — 1497 (Н)

Нужда скачет, нужда пляшет, нужда песенки поёт — 1499 (Н)

Нужда цены не знает — 1500 (Н)

От нужды волк лисой запел — 1595 (О)

Тот без нужды живёт, кто деньги бережёт — 2065 (Т)

НЯНЬКА

Где нянек много, там дитя безного — 2145 (У)

У семи нянек дитя без глаза (глазу) — 2145 (У)

О

ОБЕД

На обеде — все соседи, кончился обед — соседа нет — 1215 (Н)

На обеде — все соседи, а пришла

беда—они прочь, как вода—1215 (Н)
От доброго обеда и к ужину останется—1585 (О)

ОБЕДНЯ
Глухому поп по две обедни не служит—354 (Г)

ОБЕЩАНИЕ
Что обещание, что зарок—ненадёжны—2301 (Ч)

ОБЕЩАННОЕ
Обещанного три года ждут—1506 (О)

ОБЕЩАТЬ
Кто много обещает, тот ничего не сделает—933 (К)

ОБЖЕЧЬСЯ
Обжёгшись на горячем, дуешь на холодное—1507 (О)
Обжёгшись на молоке (ухе), дуют на воду—1507 (О)

ОБИДА
Не в обиду будь сказано—1292 (Н)

ОБИДЕТЬ
Кто кого обидит, тот того и ненавидит—924 (К)

ОБЛИЧЬЕ
Обличье—уличье—1508 (О)

ОБОЙТИСЬ
Обойдётся, оботрётся—всё постарому пойдёт—1509 (О)

ОБРАЗЧИК
По образчику узнают и сукно—1705 (П)

ОБЫЧАЙ
В каком народе живёшь, того обычая и держись—159 (В)
В чужой стране жить—чужой обычай любить—159 (В)
Обычай крепче (сильнее) закона—1511 (О)
Свой обычай в чужой дом не носи—1864 (С)
Сколько стран, столько и обычаев—1910 (С)
Что ни город, то норов, что ни деревня, то обычай—2300 (Ч)
Что ни город, то обычай, что ни местечко, то свой нрав—2300 (Ч)
Что ни двор (край), то свой обычай—2300 (Ч)

ОВЁС
На лошадь не плеть покупай, а овёс—1208 (Н)
Не кони везут, а овёс—1359 (Н)

ОВОЩ
Всякому овощу своё время—284 (В)

ОВЦА
Глядит овцой, а пахнет волком—355 (Г)
Голой овцы не стригут—375 (Г)
И от доброго отца родится бешенная овца—741 (И)
Кроткая овца всегда волку по зубам—899 (К)
Куда одна овца, туда и всё стадо—976 (К)
Не будь овцой, так и волк не съест—899 (К)
/Одна/ паршивая овца всё стадо портит—1536 (О)
Смирная овца волку по зубам—899 (К)
С паршивой овцы хоть шерсти клок—1974 (С)
Шелудивая овца всё стадо портит—1536 (О)

ОВЧИНКА
Овчинка выделки не стоит—1514 (О)

ОГЛОБЛЯ
Не по коню, так по оглобле—1392 (Н)

ОГОНЬ
Где дым, там и огонь—1432 (Н)
Где огонь, там и дым—325 (Г)
Из огня да в полымя—709 (И)
Ляжешь подле огня, не хотя, обожжёшься—1094 (Л)
Не шути с огнём—обожжёшься—1477 (Н)
Огонь огнём не погасишь—1516 (О)

Огня бойся, воды берегись — 1963 (С)
С огнём не шути и воде не верь — 1963 (С)
У огня, да не погреться — 2137 (У)
Упустишь огонь — не потушишь — 2140 (У)
Яркий огонь быстро горит — 2373 (Я)

ОГОРОД
В огороде бузина, а в Киеве дядька — 174 (В)

ОДЕЖДА
На чужую одежду плохая надежда — 1263 (Н)
Одежда красит человека — 1517 (О)
По одежде встречают — 1706 (П)

ОДЁЖКА
По одёжке встречают, по уму провожают — 1707 (П)
По одёжке протягивай ножки — 1708 (П)

ОДИН
Один в поле не воин — 1520 (О)
Один за всех, все за одного — 1522 (О)
Один и дома горюет, а двое в поле воюют — 12 (А)
Один и камень не поднимешь, а миром и город передвинешь — 1523 (О)
Один — камень не сдвинешь, артелью — гору подвинешь — 1523 (О)
Одному и у каши не споро — 1547 (О)

ОДНО
Одно и то же, что отказать, что поздно дать — 1542 (О)

ОЖИДАТЬ
Никто не знает, что его ожидает — 1478 (Н)

ОЗЕРО
В озере два чёрта не живут — 179 (В)

ОКО
Видит око, да зуб неймёт — 153 (В)
Око за око, зуб за зуб — 1550 (О)

ОМУТ
В тихой воде омуты глубоки — 294 (В)
В тихом омуте черти водятся — 294 (В)
Тиха вода, да омуты глубоки — 294 (В)

ОПОЗДАТЬ
Кто опоздает, тот воду хлебает — 952 (К)
Опоздаешь — воду хлебаешь — 952 (К)

ОПЫТ
Опыт — лучший учитель — 1557 (О)
Опыт полезнее тысячи советов — 1558 (О)

ОРЁЛ
Орёл мух не ловит — 1559 (О)
Орёл орла плодит, а сова сову родит — 1560 (О)
Орлом комара не травят — 1561 (О)

ОРЕХ
Дали орехи белке, когда зубов не стало — 411 (Д)
Когда зубов не стало, тогда и орехи принесли — 411 (Д)
Не разгрызёшь ореха — не съешь и зерна (ядра) — 1400 (Н)

ОСЁЛ
Осёл осла длинноухим обзывает — 1562 (О)
Осёл ослом остаётся и в орденах, и в лентах — 1563 (О)
Осёл ослом остаётся, хоть обсыпь его звёздами — 1563 (О)
Осла хоть в Париж, а он всё будет рыж — 1567 (О)

ОСКОМИНА
Отцы тёрпкое поели, а у деток оскомина — 1618 (О)

ОСТАТОК
Остатки — сладки — 1568 (О)

ОСТОРОЖНОСТЬ
Осторожность и зверя бережёт — 1572 (О)
Осторожность — мать мудрости — 1573 (О)

ОСТУПИТЬСЯ
Лучше оступиться, чем оговориться — 1063 (Л)

ОСУЖДАТЬ
Людей не осуждай, а за собою примечай — 1087 (Л)

ОТВАГА
Где отвага, там и победа — 326 (Г)
Отвага мёд пьёт — 1578 (О)
Отвага — половина спасения — 1578 (О)

ОТВЕДАТЬ
Не изведаешь, пока не отведаешь — 1349 (Н)

ОТГОВОРКА
У всякого Федорки (Федотки) свои отговорки — 2091 (У)

ОТДАТЬ
Легко взять, да трудно отдать — 991 (Л)
Любишь взять, люби и отдать — 2117 (У)
Умел взять, умей и отдать — 2117 (У)

ОТЕЦ
Какова хата, таков и тын, каков отец, таков и сын — 806 (К)
Каков отец, таков и молодец — 812 (К)
Отец накопил, а сын раструсил — 1586 (О)
Отец — рыбак, и дети в воду смотрят — 1587 (О)

ОТЗВОНИТЬ
Отзвонил, да и с колокольни долой — 1588 (О)

ОТКАЗАТЬ
Одно и то же, что отказать, что поздно дать — 1542 (О)

ОТКЛАДЫВАТЬ
Не откладывай на завтра то, что можно сделать сегодня — 1382 (Н)
Оттягивать да откладывать — только время терять — 583 (Ж)

ОТЛОЖИТЬ
Отложил на осень, а там и вовсе бросил — 1592 (О)

ОХОТА
Без охоты неспоро у работы — 45 (Б)
Была бы охота — заладится всякая работа — 116 (Б)
Как на охоту ехать, так собак кормить — 785 (К)
Не тогда собак кормить, как на охоту идти — 785 (К)
Охота пуще неволи — 1620 (О)

ОЧЕРНИТЬ
Легко очернить, нелегко обелить — 996 (Л)

ОШИБАТЬСЯ
Не ошибается тот, кто ничего не делает — 1384 (Н)
Ошибайся, да сознавайся — 1623 (О)
Человеку свойственно ошибаться — 2251 (Ч)

ОШИБИТЬСЯ
Не ошибёшься — не поумнеешь — 1385 (Н)
Умел ошибиться — умей и поправиться — 2119 (У)

ОШИБКА
На ошибках других учимся — 1221 (Н)
На ошибках учатся — 1222 (Н)
Ошибка в фальшь не ставится — 1624 (О)
Ошибка красна поправкой — 1625 (О)
Ошибка не обман — 1624 (О)

П

ПАВА
Какова пава, такова ей и слава — **818 (К)**

ПАВУШКА
По Павушке и славушка — 1709 (П)

ПАДАЛЬ
На падаль и собака бежит — 1223 (Н)

ПАДАТЬ
Не всё то падает, что шатается — 1302 (Н)

Хоть падать, да не лежать—2205 (Х)

ПАЛАТА
Oт трудов праведных не наживёшь палат каменных—1613 (О)
Правдою жить, палат каменных не нажить—1613 (О)

ПАЛЕЦ
Не указывай на людей пальцем, не указали б на тебя и всей рукой—1459 (Н)
Один палец не кулак—1524 (О)
Подай палец, а за руку сам возьму—1665 (П)

ПАЛКА
Была бы собака, а палка найдётся—117 (Б)
Коли быть собаке битой, найдётся и палка—117 (Б)
Кому надо собаку ударить, тот и палку сыщет—117 (Б)
Палка о двух концах—1628 (П)
Палка по мясу бьёт, а слово до костей достаёт—1629 (П)
Сердитому палка найдётся—117 (Б)

ПАН
Или пан, или пропал—727 (И)
Паны дерутся, а у хлопцев чубы летят—1630 (П)
Паны дерутся, а у холопов чубы трещат (трясутся)—1630 (П)

ПАР
Пар костей не ломит—1631 (П)
Пар любить—баню топить—1632 (П)
Пару бояться—в баню не ходить—1633 (П)

ПАРА
Без пары не живут и гагары—46 (Б)

ПАРИЖ
Увидеть Париж и умереть—2083 (У)

ПАСТУХ
Где много пастухов, там овцы дохнут—320 (Г)
Пастуху дремать, так стада не видать—1634 (П)

ПАСТУШОК
Куда пастушок, туда и посошок—973 (К)

ПАСТЫРЬ
Каков пастырь, таковы и овцы—813 (К)

ПАХАТЬ
И мы пахали—732 (И)
Пахать, так в дуду не играть—1635 (П)

ПАХОМ
Каков Пахом, такова и шапка на нём—814 (К)

ПАШНЯ
Чужую пашню пашет, а своя в залежи—2331 (Ч)

ПЕНЬ
Или пень об сову, или сову об пень—всё равно ей больно—728 (И)
Пень—так пень, хоть золотое платье надень—1636 (П)

ПЕПЕЛ
И в пепле искра бывает—690 (И)

ПЕПЕЛИЩЕ
На своём пепелище и курица бьёт—1239 (Н)

ПЕРВЫЙ
Кто первый пришёл, первый /муку/ смолол—954 (К)
Лучше быть первым в деревне, чем последним в городе—1046 (Л)
Я не первый, и я не последний—2370 (Я)

ПЕРЕДЕЛАТЬ
Себя не переделаешь—1877 (С)

ПЕРЕСОЛ
Недосол на столе, пересол на спине—1335 (Н)
Пересол хуже недосола—1335 (Н)

ПЕРО
В одно перо и птица не родится—749 (И)

И сорока в одно перо не родится—749 (И)
Напишешь пером, не вырубишь и топором—2298 (Ч)
Что написано пером, того не вырубишь топором—2298 (Ч)

ПЁС
Битому псу только плеть покажи—68 (Б)
Добрый пёс на ветер не лает—1996 (С)
Околевший пёс не укусит—1551 (О)
Старого пса к цепи не приучишь—2001 (С)
Старый пёс на ветер не лает—1996 (С)

ПЕСЕНКА
Доведётся и нам свою песенку спеть—489 (Д)
По которой реке плыть, той и песенки петь—1693 (П)

ПЕСНЯ
Вся свадьба песни не стоит—1514 (О)
Затянул песню, так веди до конца—652 (З)
Из песни слова не выкинешь—712 (И)
Наладил песню—пой, хоть тресни—652 (З)
У всякой песни есть свой конец—2092 (У)

ПЕСОК
Из песка верёвки не вьют—711 (И)
Песком моря не засыплешь—1038 (Л)

ПЕТУХ
В своём курятнике петух хозяин—287 (В)
Всяк петух на своём пепелище хозяин—287 (В)
Прокукарекает петух или нет, а день будет—1782 (П)

ПЕЧАЛЬ
Ни печали без радости, ни радости без печали—1481 (Н)

ПЕЧЬ
На своей печи сам себе голова—1237 (Н)

ПИЛА
У худого пильщика пила виновата—2139 (У)

ПИР
Где пиры да чаи, там и немочи—327 (Г)

ПИРОГ
Вот такие пироги—199 (В)
В чужих руках пирог велик—296 (В)
Не могу, а ем по пирогу—1369 (Н)
Один пирог два раза не съешь—1525 (О)
Пирог в чужом рту всегда слаще—296 (В)
Пироги да блины, а там сиди да гляди—1643 (П)
Пироги на кустах не растут—1644 (П)
Пироги со стола, друзья со двора—1645 (П)
Хоть хорош пирог, да в чужих руках—2207 (Х)

ПИРОЖОК
Есть пирожки—есть и дружки, нет пирожков—нет и дружков—572 (Е)

ПИТЬ
Ешь вволю, пей в меру—574 (Е)

ПИЧУЖКА
У каждой пичужки свой голосок—2106 (У)

ПЛАКАТЬ
Одни плачут, а другие скачут—1539 (О)

ПЛАТА
Каков молебен, такова и плата—794 (К)

ПЛАЧ
Плачем горю не поможешь—1920 (С)

ПЛЕВАТЬ
Бесстыжему хоть плюй в глаза—всё божья роса—1225 (Н)

Выше носа плюнешь — себя заплюёшь — 1876 (С)
Кверху плевать — свою бороду заплевать — 1876 (С)
Не плюй в водицу: сгодится (случится) напиться — 1386 (Н)
Не плюй в колодезь (колодец), пригодится /воды/ напиться — 1386 (Н)
Себя жалеючи, кверху не плюй — 1876 (С)

ПЛЕТЬ
Плетью обуха не перешибёшь — 1647 (П)

ПЛЕШЬ
Кабы не плешь, так бы не голо — 764 (К)

ПЛОД
Запретный плод сладок — 640 (З)
Каков плод, таков и приплод — 815 (К)

ПЛОШАТЬ
На Бога надейся (уповай), а сам не плошай — 1176 (Н)

ПЛУТ
Бог плута метит — 87 (Б)

ПЛЫТЬ
Тяжело против воды плыть — 2082 (Т)

ПЛЯСАТЬ
Тогда пляши, когда играют — 2057 (Т)

ПОБЕДИТЕЛЬ
Победителей не судят — 1657 (П)

ПОБЕДИТЬ
Пришёл, увидел, победил — 1777 (П)

ПОВАР
Добрый повар стоит доктора — 486 (Д)
Не все те повара, у кого ножи долгие — 1300 (Н)

ПОВЕЗТИ
Коли повезёт, так и бык телёнка принесёт — 854 (К)

ПОВЕСТИСЬ
С кем поведёшься, от того и наберёшься — 1904 (С)

ПОВТОРЕНИЕ
Повторение — мать учения — 1663 (П)

ПОГОСТ
Мёртвых с погоста не носят — 1127 (М)
На погосте жить — всех не оплачешь — 1226 (Н)

ПОДВОРЬЕ
Во всяком подворье своё поверье — 172 (В)

ПОДМАЗАТЬ
Не подмажешь — не поедешь — 1387 (Н)

ПОДОБНЫЙ
Подобный подобного любит — 1672 (П)

ПОДОЙНИК
Осерчав на корову, да подойник оземь — 1565 (О)

ПОДУМАТЬ
Сперва подумай, потом говори — 1977 (С)

ПОЕЗД
Поезд ушёл — 1676 (П)

ПОЕХАТЬ
Каков поехал, таков и приехал — 816 (К)

ПОЖАЛЕТЬ
Пожалел волк кобылу, оставил хвост да гриву — 1677 (П)

ПОЖАР
После пожара за водой не бегут — 1732 (П)

ПОЖЕЛАТЬ
Лишнее пожелаешь — последнее потеряешь — 1030 (Л)

ПОЗДНО
Кто поздно приходит, тот ничего не находит — 956 (К)
Кто поздно пришёл, тому обглоданный мосол — 956 (К)

Лучше поздно, чем никогда—1064 (Л)
Поздно пришёл, одни кости нашёл—956 (К)

ПОЙМАТЬ
Не поймав, не щиплют—1388 (Н)

ПОКЛОН
Поклоном поясницы не переломишь (спины не надсадишь, шеи не свихнёшь)—1690 (П)

ПОКЛОНИТЬСЯ
Поклониться—голова не отвалится—1689 (П)

ПОКОЙ
Покой нам только снится—1691 (П)

ПОКОЙНИК
Жил—полковник, помер—покойник—605 (Ж)
О покойнике плохо не говорят—1554 (О)

ПОКРЫШКА
Каково лукошко, такова ему и покрышка—1664 (П)
По горшку (кубышке) и покрышка—1664 (П)

ПОЛАТИ
На полатях лежать—ломтя не достать—1227 (Н)
На полатях лежать, так и ломтя (хлеба) не видать—1227 (Н)

ПОЛЕНО
Полено к полену—костёр—1694 (П)

ПОЛКОВНИК
Или полковник, или покойник—727 (И)

ПОЛОЖИТЬ
Подальше положишь—поближе возьмёшь—1666 (П)

ПОЛУЗНАНИЕ
Полузнание хуже незнания—1699 (П)

ПОЛЮБИТЬСЯ
Полюбится сова—не надо райской птички—1701 (П)

ПОМЕРЕТЬ
Помрёшь—ничего с собой не возьмёшь—1704 (П)

ПОНЕСТИ
Тяжело понёс—и домой не донёс—2081 (Т)

ПОНОМАРЬ
И пономарь, и владыка в земле равны—744 (И)
Старого пономаря не перепономаришь—2000 (С)

ПОП
Всякий поп по-своему поёт—271 (В)
Глупый поп свенчает, умному не развенчать—353 (Г)
Каков поп, таков и приход—817 (К)
Пошёл в попы, так служи и панихиды—1751 (П)
Чёрт попу не товарищ—2270 (Ч)
Я говорю про попа, ты про попадью, а он про попову дочку—2358 (Я)

ПОПАДЬЯ
Кому попадья, а кому попова дочка—929 (К)

ПОПИСАТЬ
Ничего не попишешь—1484 (Н)

ПОПУСТУ
Ешь капусту, да не мели попусту—577 (Е)

ПОПЫТКА
Попытка не пытка—1713 (П)

ПОРА
Жнут поле в пору—606 (Ж)
Пора на пору не приходится—1716 (П)

ПОРОГ
Вот Бог, а вот порог—201 (В)

ПОРОСЁНОК
Краденый поросёнок в ушах визжит—882 (К)

П0РОХ
Держи порох сухим—454 (Д)
Есть ещё порох в пороховницах—571 (Е)

ПОРТИТЬ
Ничего не портит тот, кто ничего не делает — 1384 (Н)

ПОРТНОЙ
Всяк портной на свой покрой — 288 (В)
Портной без кафтана (порток), сапожник без сапог — 1855 (С)

ПОРЯДОК
Порядок — душа всякого дела — 1719 (П)

ПОСАД
В каждом посаде в своём наряде — 158 (В)
Во всяком посаде в своём наряде — 158 (В)

ПОСЕЯТЬ
Что посеешь, то и пожнёшь — 2303 (Ч)

ПОСЛЕДНИЙ
Последнего и собаки рвут — 1726 (П)

ПОСЛОВИЦА
Пословица недаром (не зря, не мимо, не на ветер) молвится — 1737 (П)

ПОСМЕЯТЬСЯ
Над другим посмеёшься, над собой поплачешь — 1194 (Н)

ПОСМОТРЕТЬ
Посмотрим ещё, чья возьмёт — 1739 (П)

ПОСПЕШИТЬ
Поспешишь — людей насмешишь — 1741 (П)

ПОСПЕШНОСТЬ
Поспешность нужна только при ловле блох — 1742 (П)

ПОСТЕЛИТЬ
Как постелешь, так и поспишь — 825 (К)
На весь мир мягко не постелешь — 1184 (Н)

ПОСТЕЛЬ
Какова постель, таков и сон — 792 (К)

ПОСТЫЛЫЙ
В постылом всё немило — 203 (В)

ПОСУДА
Битая посуда два века живёт — 66 (Б)
Склеенная — не посуда — 1906 (С)
Склеенная посуда два века живёт — 2274 (Ч)
Чинёная посуда два века живёт — 2274 (Ч)

ПОСУЛ
На посуле, как на стуле: посидишь и встанешь — 1229 (Н)
Не держи посулом, одолжи отказом — 1329 (Н)

ПОТЕРЯННОЕ
Потерянного не воротить — 1747 (П)

ПОТЕРЯТЬ
На одном потеряешь, на другом найдёшь — 1219 (Н)

ПОТЕХА
Одному потеха, а другому не до смеха — 1548 (О)

ПОТОП
После нас хоть потоп — 1731 (П)

ПОТОПАТЬ
Не потопаешь, не полопаешь — 1394 (Н)

ПОХОДКА
Не стоит гроша, да походка хороша — 1415 (Н)

ПОЧИН
Почин дороже денег — 1750 (П)
У хорошего почина хороший конец — 1799 (П)

ПОЧИТАТЬ
Чем ближе знаешь, тем меньше почитаешь — 2253 (Ч)

ПОШЛИНА
По две пошлины с одного товара не берут — 1668 (П)

ПРАВДА
Ищи ветра в поле, а правду на дне морском — 1763 (П)

Лучше горькая правда, чем красивая ложь—1049 (Л)
Не всё то правда, что люди говорят—1303 (Н)
Не всякую правду сказывай—1318 (Н)
На правду суда нет—1230 (Н)
От правды не уйдёшь (никуда не денешься)—1599 (О)
Правда в огне не горит и в воде не тонет—1755 (П)
Правда глаза колет—1756 (П)
Правда, как оса, лезет в глаза—1757 (П)
Правда как солнце—ладонями не прикроешь—1758 (П)
Правда не боится света—1759 (П)
Правда сама себя очистит—1760 (П)
Правда суда не боится—1230 (Н)
Правда что шило—в мешке не утаишь—1758 (П)
Правду водой не зальёшь, огнём не сожжёшь—1755 (П)
Правду говорить—друга не нажить—1761 (П)
Правду говорить—себе досадить—1762 (П)
Правду ищи на дне морском—1763 (П)
Правду красить не нужно (нет нужды)—1764 (П)
Правду не скроешь—1765 (П)
Правды не спрячешь—1765 (П)
Хлеб-соль ешь, а правду режь—2179 (Х)
Худая правда лучше хорошей лжи—1049 (Л)

ПРАВИЛО
Нет правил без исключения—1448 (Н)

ПРАВИТЬ
Кто едет, тот и правит—918 (К)

ПРАЗДНИК
Будет и на нашей улице праздник—106 (Б)
Праздник бывает не каждый день—1766 (П)

ПРАХ
Легко придёт—прахом пойдёт—1779 (П)
Пришло махом, ушло прахом—1779 (П)

ПРЕДАНИЕ
Свежо предание, да верится с трудом—1858 (С)

ПРИВЕТ
Какой привет, такой и ответ—824 (К)
На добрый привет и добрый ответ—1197 (Н)
Не дорог обед, дорог привет—1334 (Н)
По привету и ответ—824 (К)

ПРИВЫКНУТЬ
Ко всему привыкаешь—841 (К)

ПРИВЫЧКА
Привычка—вторая натура (природа)—1768 (П)

ПРИГЛАШЕНИЕ
Кто пришёл без приглашения, тот уйдёт без угощения—958 (К)
Пришёл без приглашения, не жди угощения—958 (К)

ПРИДУМАТЬ
Нарочно не придумаешь—1233 (Н)

ПРИЗНАНИЕ
За признание—половина наказания—641 (З)
Признание—сестра покаянию—1774 (П)

ПРИМЕР
Дурные примеры заразительны—551 (Д)
Плохие примеры заразительны—551 (Д)

ПРИРОДА
Гони природу в дверь, она влетит в окно—380 (Г)
Природа не терпит пустоты—1775 (П)
Природа своё возьмёт—1776 (П)

ПРИСТАВАТЬ
Грязное к чистому не пристанет—399 (Г)
К доброму плохое не пристанет—399 (Г)

ПРИСУТСТВУЮЩИЙ
О присутствующих не говорят—1556 (О)

ПРИЧИНА
Без причины нет кручины—47 (Б)
Всему есть своя причина—231 (В)

ПРОВЕРИТЬ
Сперва проверь, потом поверь—1978 (С)

ПРОВЕРЯТЬ
Доверяй, да проверяй—490 (Д)

ПРОЙТИ
Что прошло, то будет мило—2306 (Ч)

ПРОМЕДЛЕНИЕ
Промедление смерти подобно—1784 (П)

ПРОМОЛЧАТЬ
Кстати промолчать, что большое слово сказать—905 (К)

ПРОПАДАТЬ
Где наше не пропадало—323 (Г)

ПРОРОК
Не славен пророк в своём отечестве—1450 (Н)
Нет пророка без порока—1449 (Н)
Нет пророка в своём отечестве—1450 (Н)

ПРОСЁЛОЧНЫЙ
Не ищи просёлочной, когда есть столбовая—1357 (Н)

ПРОСТОТА
Простота хуже воровства—1785 (П)

ПРОТИВ
Кто не с нами, тот против нас—946 (К)

ПРОШЛОЕ
Кто прошлое вспомянёт, тому глаз вон—970 (К)

ПРУТИК
По прутику всю метлу переломить можно—139 (В)

ПРЯМО
Кто прямо ездит, в поле ночует (дома не ночует)—959 (К)
Прямо ворона летает, да дома не ночует—959 (К)

ПРЯХА
Какова пряха, такова на ней и рубаха—793 (К)
У нашей пряхи ни одежды, ни рубахи—2136 (У)

ПТАШЕЧКА
Рано пташечка запела, как бы кошечка не съела—1821 (Р)

ПТАШКА
По пташке и клетка—1723 (П)
У всякой пташки свои замашки—2093 (У)

ПТИЦА
Видать птицу по полёту—151 (В)
Всякая птица своё гнездо любит—261 (В)
Всякая птица своим голосом (свои песни) поёт—258 (В)
Глупа та птица, которой гнездо своё не мило—348 (Г)
Птица в руках стоит двух в кустах—1787 (П)

ПТИЧКА
Мала птичка, да ноготок востёр—1098 (М)
Невелика птичка, да ноготок остёр—1098 (М)

ПУГОВИЧКА
Пуговички золочёные, а три дня не евши—1789 (П)

ПУЛЯ
Всякая пуля грозит, но не всякая разит—262 (В)
Выстрелив, пулю не схватишь, а слово, сказав, не поймаешь—303 (В)

От пули не уйдёшь—1600 (О)
Пуля—дура, а виноватого найдёт—1790 (П)

ПУСТО
Где работают, там густо, а в ленивом доме—пусто—329 (Г)

ПУСТОЙ
Тот человек пустой, кто полон самим собой—2068 (Т)

ПУТЬ
Неисповедимы пути господни—1351 (Н)
Честный путь—лучший путь—2272 (Ч)

ПУХ
Ни пуха, ни пера!—1482 (Н)

ПУШИНКА
Пушинка к пушинке—выйдет перинка—1801 (П)

ПУШКА
Из пушки по воробьям не стреляют—713 (И)

ПЧЕЛА
Одна пчела не много мёду натаскает—1537 (О)
Плохие пчёлы—плохой и мёд—1649 (П)
Пчела жалит жалом, а человек—словом—1802 (П)

ПЫЛЬ
Придорожная пыль неба не коптит—1773 (П)

ПЬЯНИЦА
Пьяница проспится, а дурак—никогда—1803 (П)

ПЬЯНСТВО
Пьянство до добра не доведёт—1805 (П)

ПЬЯНЫЙ
Пьяному и море по колено—1804 (П)
Пьяный проспится, а дурак—никогда—1803 (П)
Пьяный скачет, а проспался—плачет—1806 (П)
Пьяный—что малый: что на уме,, то и на языке—1807 (П)

ПЯТНО
И на солнце есть пятна—737 (И)

Р

РАБОТА
Какова работа, такова и плата—794 (К)
От работы кони дохнут—1601 (О)
По работе и деньги—1714 (П)
Работа дураков любит—1808 (Р)
Работа—не волк, в лес не убежит—432 (Д)
Рукам работа—душе праздник—1839 (Р)

РАБОТАТЬ
Ест тихо и работает не лихо—567 (Е)
Кто не работает, тот не ест—944 (К)
Работает упорно и ест задорно—1809 (Р)

РАВНЫЙ
Все равны под солнцем—242 (В)

РАДОВАТЬСЯ
Не радуйся нашедши, не плачь потерявши—1399 (Н)

РАДОСТЬ
В радости сыщут, в горе забудут—204 (В)
Где горе, там и радость—311 (Г)
Разделённая радость—двойная радость—1814 (Р)

РАЗ
Два раза не умирать—1527 (О)
За один раз дерева не срубишь—636 (З)
Один раз живём—1526 (О)
Один раз мать родила, один раз и умирать—1527 (О)
Один раз не в счёт—1528 (О)
Раз на раз не приходится—1817 (Р)
Семь раз отмерь (примерь), один раз отрежь—1887 (С)

РАЗЛУКА
Разлука—враг любви—1816 (Р)

РАЗУМ
Если Бог хочет наказать, он разума лишает—851 (К)
Кого Бог захочет погубить, у того сначала отнимет разум—851 (К)

РАЙ
Рад бы в рай, да грехи не пускают—1810 (Р)
С милым рай и в шалаше—1942 (С)

РАК
Когда рак свистнет и рыба запоёт—847 (К)

РАНА
Зажила рана, а всё рубцы есть—625 (З)

РАНО
Кто рано встаёт, тому Бог даёт (подаёт)—961 (К)
Кто рано ложится и рано встаёт, здоровье, богатство и ум наживёт—962 (К)
Кто раньше на мельницу придёт, раньше смелет—963 (К)
Чем раньше, тем лучше—2259 (Ч)

РАСПЛАТА
От расплаты не уйдёшь—1602 (О)

РАСПУТЬЕ
Распутья бояться, так в путь не ходить—1824 (Р)

РАССЕРДИТЬСЯ
Когда рассердишься, сосчитай до ста—848 (К)

РАСХОД
По приходу и расход держи—1712 (П)

РЕБЁНОК
Гни дерево, пока молодо; учи ребёнка, пока мал—357 (Г)
С ребятами горе, а без ребят—вдвое—1987 (С)
Я не тот ребёнок, что вчера из пелёнок—2371 (Я)

РЕВЕТЬ
Не реви раньше смерти—1402 (Н)

РЕКА
Большая река течёт спокойно—93 (Б)
Где река глубже, там она меньше шумит—331 (Г)
Где река мельче, там она больше шумит—332 (Г)
Каждая река к морю течёт—766 (К)
Река начинается с ручейка—1829 (Р)

РЕМЕНЬ
Я ему про ремень, а он мне про лыко—2358 (Я)

РЕМЕСЛО
Не просит ремесло хлеба, а само кормит—1396 (Н)
Ремесло пить-есть не просит, а само кормит—1396 (Н)
Ремесло—кормилец—1830 (Р)
С ремеслом не пропадёшь—1988 (С)
У ремесла не без промысла—2141 (У)

РЕЧЬ
Людским речам вполовину верь—1091 (Л)
Твои бы речи да Богу в уши—716 (И)
Умные речи приятно и слышать—2127 (У)

РЕШЕТО
Решетом воду мерять—потерять время—1831 (Р)
Решетом воду не носят—1831 (Р)
Решето сказало кувшину: дырявый!—1832 (Р)

РЖА
Ржа железо ест—1833 (Р)

РИЗА
Не суйся в ризы, коль не поп—1420 (Н)

РИСК
Риск—благородное дело—1834 (Р)

РИСКОВАТЬ
Кто не рискует, тот не пьёт шампанского—945 (К)

РИСОВАТЬ
Кто не умеет рисовать, должен краски растирать—947 (К)

РОГОЖА
Из рогожи не сделаешь кожи—714 (И)

РОД
Каков род, таков и приплод—815 (К)

РОДИТЕЛЬ
Какие корешки, такие и ветки, какие родители, такие и детки—783 (К)
Родителей не выбирают—1835 (Р)

РОДИТЬ
Не родит верба груши—1608 (О)
Умел дитя родить, умей и научить—2118 (У)

РОДИТЬСЯ
От ивы (осины) яблочко не родится—1608 (О)
От совы не родятся соколы—1608 (О)

РОДНОЙ
Подальше—роднее, пореже—милее—1667 (П)
Хоть родной, да злой—2206 (Х)

РОЖОН
Против рожна не попрёшь—1786 (П)

РОЗА
Нет розы без шипов—1452 (Н)

РОМАН
Худ Роман, когда пуст карман; хорош Мартын, когда есть алтын—2223 (Х)

РОСТ
Гордись не ростом, а умом—384 (Г)
Ростом с Ивана, а умом с болвана—1836 (Р)
Ростом с тебя, а разумом (умом) с теля—1836 (Р)

РОТ
В закрытый рот муха не залетит—146 (В)
В чужой рот не поставишь ворот—1261 (Н)
Держи рот на замке, а гляди в оба—455 (Д)
К своему рту ложка ближе—903 (К)
На чужой рот пуговицы не нашьёшь—1261 (Н)
Рот не огород, не затворишь ворот—1261 (Н)
Сладко в рот, да горько в глот—1918 (С)

РОТОК
Бог даст роток, так даст и кусок—84 (Б)
Будет роток, будет и кусок—84 (Б)
На чужой роток не накинешь платок—1261 (Н)
Чужой роток не свой хлевок, не затворишь—1261 (Н)

РУБАШКА
Рубашка бела, да душа черна—1837 (Р)
Своя рубашка ближе к телу—1868 (С)

РУКА
Всякая рука к себе загребает—263 (В)
Дающего рука не оскудеет—417 (Д)
Когда рук много, работа спорится—849 (К)
Левая рука не ведает, что делает правая—1754 (П)
Мастерские руки от доброй науки—1112 (М)
Одной рукой и узла не завяжешь—1544 (О)
От больного места рука не отходит—1577 (О)
Правая рука не знает, что делает левая—1754 (П)
Рукам работа—душе праздник—1839 (Р)
Рука руку моет, вор вора кроет—1840 (Р)
Руки согрешат, а голова в ответе—1841 (Р)
Руки согрешили, а спина виновата—1841 (Р)

Своя рука—владыка—1869 (С)
С руками нигде не пропадёшь—1988 (С)
Холодные руки—горячее сердце—2183 (Х)

РУССКИЙ
Что русскому здорово, то немцу смерть—2307 (Ч)

РЫБА
Большая рыба маленькую целиком глотает—94 (Б)
Всякая рыба хороша, коли на удочку пошла—264 (В)
Ни рыба, ни мясо /, ни кафтан, ни ряса/—1483 (Н)
Рыба мелка, да уха сладка—1843 (Р)
Рыба с головы воняет (гниёт, тухнет)—1844 (Р)
Хороша рыба на чужом блюде—2185 (Х)

РЫБАК
Рыбак рыбака видит издалека—1842 (Р)

РЫБКА
В чужой лодке всегда больше рыбки—296 (В)
Лакома кошка до рыбки, да в воду лезть (лапки мочить) не хочет—2209 (Х)
Либо рыбку съесть, либо на мель сесть—1020 (Л)
Рыбка золотая, да внутри гнилая—1845 (Р)
Хочется рыбку съесть, да не хочется в воду лезть—2209 (Х)
Чтобы рыбку съесть, надо в воду лезть—2282 (Ч)

РЫЛО
С мякинным (суконным) рылом да в калачный ряд—1991 (С)
С суконным рылом в калачный ряд не суйся—1991 (С)

РЯБЧИК
Лучше рябчик в руках, чем два на ветке—1066 (Л)

С

САВВА
Каков Савва, такова ему и слава—818 (К)

САВКА
По Савке и свитка—1723 (П)

САВРАСКА
Умыкали Савраску горы да овражки—2107 (У)

САЖА
Не трись возле сажи—сам замараешься—1451 (Н)

САНИ
Каковы сами, таковы и сани—823 (К)
Не в свои сани не садись—1295 (Н)

САПОГ
Гусь да гагара—два сапога пара—421 (Д)
Два сапога—пара—421 (Д)
На ногах сапоги скрипят, а в горшке мухи кипят—1214 (Н)
Сапог лаптю не брат—1852 (С)
Сапог с сапогом, лапоть с лаптем—1853 (С)
Тесные сапоги разносятся, широкие осядутся—2048 (Т)
Я про сапоги, а он про пироги—2358 (Я)

САПОЖНИК
Сапожник ходит без сапог—1855 (С)

САТАНА
Покажется сатана лучше ясного сокола—1684 (П)
Полюбится сатана лучше ясного сокола—1684 (П)
Сатана гордился—и с неба свалился—556 (Д)

СБЕРЕЧЬ
Сбережёшь—что найдёшь—1856 (С)

СВАДЬБА
Вся свадьба песни не стоит—1514 (О)

На двух свадьбах сразу не танцуют—1193 (Н)
После свадьбы в барабаны не бьют—1734 (П)
Свадьба скорая—что вода полая—1857 (С)

СВЕКРОВЬ
Свекровь дочку бранит—невестке науку даёт—880 (К)
Свекровь кошку бьёт, а невестке наветки даёт—880 (К)

СВЕРХУ
Сверху мило, снизу гнило—1859 (С)
Сверху ясно, снизу грязно—1859 (С)

СВЕРЧОК
Всяк сверчок знай свой шесток—290 (В)

СВЕТ
Белый свет не клином сошёлся (стал)—1860 (С)
Не только света, что в окошке—1440 (Н)
Свет не без добрых людей—1136 (М)
Свет не клином сошёлся—1860 (С)
Чего на свете не бывает!—2235 (Ч)

СВИНКА
Всякая свинка лезет в скотинки—257 (В)

СВИНЬЯ
Как свинью в кафтан ни ряди, она свиньёй останется—827 (К)
На свинью хоть седло надень—всё конём не будет—1236 (Н)
Не дал Бог свинье рогов, а бодуща была б—88 (Б)
От бобра—бобрёнок, от свиньи—поросёнок—1576 (О)
От лося—лосята, от свиньи—поросята—1576 (О)
Посади свинью за стол, она и ноги на стол—1720 (П)
Пусти свинью в мякину—она и в зерно заберётся—1793 (П)
Свинья скажет борову, а боров всему городу—16 (Б)

СВОЁ
Каждому своё—767 (К)

СВОЙ
Свой своему поневоле брат (друг)—1865 (С)

СВОЯК
Свояк свояка видит издалека—1842 (Р)

СГЛАЗИТЬ
Чтоб не сглазить—2278 (Ч)

СДЕЛАНО
Сказано—сделано—1900 (С)
Что сделано, того не переделаешь (то сделано)—1872 (С)

СДЕЛАННОЕ
Сделанного не воротишь—1872 (С)

СЕБЯ
Всяк за себя—267 (В)
Сова о сове, а всяк о себе—267 (В)

СЕГОДНЯ
Лучше сегодня яичко, чем курица завтра—1065 (Л)
Сегодня в цветах, а завтра в слезах—1879 (С)
Сегодня в чести, а завтра свиней пасти—1879 (С)
Сегодня пан, а завтра пропал—1879 (С)
Сегодня пир горой, а завтра пошёл с сумой—1880 (С)

СЕДИНА
Седина в голову, а бес в ребро—1881 (С)

СЕКРЕТ
Большой секрет—знает весь свет—98 (Б)
Всему свету по секрету—232 (В)
Говоришь по секрету, а пойдёт по всему свету—232 (В)
Я ему по секрету, а он по всему свету—232 (В)

СЕМЁН
Потом и Семён умён—1749 (П)

СЕМЕРО
Семеро капралов, да один рядовой—1882 (С)
Семеро одного не ждут—1883 (С)

СЕМЕЧКО
Всё в свой срок: придёт времечко вырастет и семечко—1771 (П)

СЕМЬЯ
В своей семье и сам большой—221 (В)
И в хорошей семье выродок бывает—237 (В)

СЕМЯ
Всякое семя знает своё время—279 (В)
Доброе семя—добрый и всход—478 (Д)
Каково семя, таков и плод (таково и племя)—810 (К)
От худого семени не жди доброго племени—1616 (О)
По семени и плод—1722 (П)
Придёт время, прорастёт и семя—1771 (П)
Яблочное семя знает своё время—279 (В)

СЕНО
Либо сена клок, либо вилы в бок—1021 (Л)

СЕНЬКА
По Сеньке и шапка—1723 (П)
По Сеньке—шапка, по Ерёме—кафтан (колпак)—1723 (П)

СЕРДИТЫЙ
На сердитых воду возят—1240 (Н)

СЕРДЦЕ
Сердце не лукошко, не прорежешь (не прошибёшь) окошко—1888 (С)
Сердце сердцу весть подаёт—1889 (С)
Сердцу любить не прикажешь—1890 (С)
Что в сердце варится, то в лице не утаится—2287 (Ч)

СЕРП
У плохого косаря всегда серп виноват—2139 (У)

СЕРЫЙ
Серого помянёшь, а серый здесь—1892 (С)

СЖАЛИТЬСЯ
Сжалился волк над ягнёнком—оставил кости да кожу—1677 (П)

СИВКА
Укатали Сивку крутые горки—2107 (У)
Укачали Сивку крутые горки—2107 (У)

СИЛА
Через силу и конь не скачет—306 (В)

СИЛЬНЫЙ
Кто сильнее, тот и правее—965 (К)
Чья сторона сильнее, та и правее—965 (К)

СИНИЦА
Лучше синица в руках, чем журавль в небе—1066 (Л)

СИТО
Ситом моря не черпают—1894 (С)

СКАЗАТЬ
Легко сказать, да нелегко орла поймать—997 (Л)
Легко сказать, да тяжело сделать—997 (Л)
Легче сказать, чем сделать—997 (Л)

СКАЗКА
Легко сказка сказывается, да нелегко дело делается—1913 (С)
Рассказывай сказки—1826 (Р)
Скоро сказка сказывается, да не скоро дело делается—1913 (С)

СКАТЕРТЬ
Скатерть со стола, и дружба сплыла—1901 (С)
Скатертью дорога—1902 (С)

СКОРО
Скоро—не споро—1911 (С)

Скоро поедешь, не скоро доедешь—1912 (С)
Что скоро, то и не споро (то хворо)—1911 (С)

СКОРОСПЕЛКА
Скороспелка до поры загнивает—1914 (С)

СКОТ
У всякого скота своя пестрота—2089 (У)

СКУПОЙ
У скупого в мороз снега не выпросишь—2147 (У)

СЛАВА
Добрая слава в углу сидит, а худая по дорожке (свету) бежит—471 (Д)
Добрая слава до порога, а худая за порог—471 (Д)
Добрая слава дороже богатства—470 (Д)
Добрая слава за печкой сидит, а худая по свету бежит—471 (Д)
Добрая слава лежит, а худая бежит—471 (Д)
Добрая слава лучше мягкого пирога—470 (Д)
Хорошая слава шагом плетётся, а худая вскачь несётся—471 (Д)

СЛЕЗА
В слезах горя не утопишь—1920 (С)
В слезах никто не видит, а в песне всяк слышит—251 (В)
Всякому своя слеза солона—285 (В)
И через золото слёзы текут—756 (И)
Отольются волку овечьи (медведю коровьи) слёзы—1598 (О)
От слёз ничего не прибудет—1604 (О)
Слезами горю не поможешь—1920 (С)
Чужая слеза, что с гуся вода—2321 (Ч)

СЛЁЗКА
Отольются кошке мышкины слёзки—1598 (О)

СЛЕПОЙ
В царстве слепых и кривому честь—893 (К)
Меж слепых и кривой в чести (зрячий)—893 (К)
Хуже всякого слепого, кто не хочет видеть—2224 (Х)

СЛОВЕЧКО
Острое словечко колет сердечко—1574 (О)
Сказал бы словечко, да волк недалечко—1898 (С)

СЛОВО
Выстрелив, пулю не схватишь, а слово, сказав, не поймаешь—303 (В)
Где много слов, там мало дела—321 (Г)
Давши слово, держись, а не давши—крепись—412 (Д)
Дал слово, держись, а не дал—крепись—412 (Д)
Добрые слова лучше мягкого (сладкого) пирога—484 (Д)
Дурное слово, что смола: пристанет—не отлепится—549 (Д)
Из одних слов шубы не сошьёшь—710 (И)
Конь вырвется—догонишь, а слова сказанного не воротишь—865 (К)
Коня на вожжах не удержишь, а слово с языка не воротишь—865 (К)
Кроткое слово гнев побеждает—1692 (П)
Ласковое слово и буйную голову смиряет (и бурю укрощает, и кость ломит)—984 (Л)
Ласковое слово не трудно, да споро—985 (Л)
Ласковое слово пуще дубины—986 (Л)
Много слов, а мало дела—1143 (М)
На одних словах далеко не уедешь—1216 (Н)
На словах и так и сяк, а на деле никак—1244 (Н)
От одних слов толку мало—1596 (О)

От слова до дела—бабушкина верста—1605 (О)
От слова до дела—сто перегонов (целая верста)—1605 (О)
Покорное слово гнев укрощает—1692 (П)
Сказанное слово—серебряное, а несказанное—золотое—1899 (С)
Слово бело, да дело черно—1927 (С)
Слово делом красно—1928 (С)
Словом человека не убьёшь—1929 (С)
Слово не воробей, вылетит—не поймаешь—1930 (С)
Слово не обух—в лоб не бьёт—1931 (С)
Слово не стрела, а пуще стрелы разит—1932 (С)
Слова—серебро, молчание—золото—1933 (С)

СЛУЖБА
Не в службу, а в дружбу—1306 (Н)
По службе—ни друга, ни недруга—1738 (П)

СЛУЖИТЬ
Кому служу, тому и пляшу—858 (К)
У кого жить, тому и служить—2109 (У)

СЛУХ
Не всякому слуху верь—1316 (Н)
Слухом земля полнится—1934 (С)

СЛУШАТЬ
Больше слушай, меньше говори—96 (Б)

СЛЫТЬ
С кем живёшь, тем и слывёшь—1903 (С)

СЛЫШАТЬ
От такого же слышу—1612 (О)

СЛЮБИТЬСЯ
Стерпится, слюбится—2309 (Ч)

СМЕЛОСТЬ
Где смелость, там и победа—326 (Г)
Смелость города берёт—1937 (С)

СМЕЛЫЙ
Кто смел, тот два съел—966 (К)
Кто смел, тот и на коня сел (и съел, наперёд поспел)—966 (К)

СМЕРТНЫЙ
Все люди смертны—228 (В)

СМЕРТЬ
Двум смертям не бывать, а одной не миновать—423 (Д)
Кровь за кровь, смерть за смерть—895 (К)
Кроме смерти от всего вылечишься—898 (К)
Лучше смерть, нежели позор—1067 (Л)
Лучше смерть славная, чем жизнь позорная—1067 (Л)
На людях и смерть красна—1209 (Н)
На миру и смерть красна—1209 (Н)
На одну смерть лекарства нет—1606 (О)
На смерть поруки нет—1246 (Н)
От смерти бегством не избавишься—1607 (О)
От смерти зелья (лекарства) нет—1606 (О)
От смерти не откупишься (не отмолишься, не уйдёшь)—1607 (О)
Перед смертью не надышишься—1640 (П)
После смерти взятки гладки—1735 (П)
Раньше смерти не умрёшь—1823 (С)
Смерть всех равняет—2149 (У)
Смерть лучше бесчестья—1067 (Л)
Смерть не разбирает чина—1938 (С)
Смерть не спросит, придёт да скосит—1939 (С)
Смерть платит все долги—1940 (С)
У смерти все равны—2149 (У)

Час от часу, а к смерти ближе—2230 (Ч)

СМЕХ

Начал смехами, кончил слезами—1256 (Н)

Ранний смех—поздние слёзы—1820 (Р)

Смех без причины—признак дурачины—1941 (С)

СМЕШНО

Тебе смешно, а мне к сердцу дошло—2039 (Т)

СМЕЯТЬСЯ

Не смейся, братец, чужой сестрице: своя в девицах—1405 (Н)

Не смейся, горох, не лучше бобов—1406 (Н)

Не смейся, квас, не лучше нас—1406 (Н)

Не смейся, хрен, не слаще редьки—1406 (Н)

Хорошо смеётся тот, кто смеётся последним—2198 (Х)

СМИРЕНИЕ

Смирение паче гордости—1943 (С)

СМОРОДИНА

Любишь смородину, люби и оскомину—1077 (Л)

СМОЧЬ

Кто кого смог, тот того и с ног—925 (К)

Кто кого сможет, тот того и гложет—925 (К)

СНЕГ

Много снега—много хлеба—1144 (М)

Не всё, что бело, снег—1304 (Н)

СНОП

Сноп без перевясла—солома—1948 (С)

СНОСИТЬ

Лучше сносить, чем сгноить—1068 (Л)

СОБАКА

Брехливая собака лает, но не кусает—1952 (С)

Вот где собака зарыта—198 (В)

Двум собакам одной кости не поделить—424 (Д)

Живая собака лучше мёртвого льва—590 (Ж)

За то собаку кормят, что она лает—651 (З)

Из собаки блох не выбьешь (не выколотишь)—715 (И)

Не бойся собаки брехливой, а бойся молчаливой—1273 (Н)

Не бойся собаки, что лает, а бойся той, что молчит да хвостом виляет—1273 (Н)

Не дразни собаку, так не укусит—1337 (Н)

Не та собака кусает, что лает, а та, что молчит да хвостом виляет—1273 (Н)

Одна лающая собака всполошила всю улицу—1534 (О)

Свои собаки грызутся, чужая не суйся—1861 (С)

Свои собаки дерутся, чужая не мешайся (не приставай)—1861 (С)

Смирную собаку и кочет побьёт (и ястреб бьёт)—1945 (С)

Собака лает, а конь идёт—1954 (С)

Собака лает, ветер носит—1949 (С)

Собака на сене лежит, сама не ест и другим не даёт—1950 (С)

Собака собаку не ест—1951 (С)

Собака, что лает, редко кусает—1952 (С)

Собаке собачья смерть—1953 (С)

Собаки лают, караван идёт (проходит)—1954 (С)

С собакой ляжешь, с блохами встанешь—1989 (С)

Старая собака на пустое дерево не лает—1996 (С)

СОБАЧКА

Маленькая собачка лает—большой подражает (от большой слышит)—1101 (М)

СОБРАТЬСЯ

Прежде соберись, потом дерись—1767 (П)

СОВА
Видать сову по полёту—151 (В)
Не видит сова, какова сама—1288 (Н)
От совы не родятся соколы—1608 (О)
Полюбится сова—не надо райской птички—1701 (П)
Сова о сове, а всяк о себе—267 (В)
Что совою об печь, что печью о сову—всё больно—728 (И)

СОВЕСТЬ
Нечего тому бояться у кого совесть чиста—1474 (Н)
Нечистая совесть спать не даёт—1476 (Н)
Совесть без зубов, а гложет (грызёт, загрызает)—1958 (С)
У кого совесть чиста, тот может спать спокойно—2110 (У)
У кого совесть чиста, у того подушка под головой не вертится—2110 (У)
Чистая совесть—спокойный сон (хорошая подушка)—2110 (У)

СОВЕТ
Доброму совету цены нет—2192 (Х)
Добрый совет ко времени хорош—487 (Д)
Добрый совет на примету бери—488 (Д)
На чужой совет без зову не ходи—1262 (Н)
Совет хорош вовремя—487 (Д)
Умный совет всегда в пользу—2131 (У)
Хороший совет дороже золота—2192 (Х)
Хороший совет не идёт во вред—2193 (Х)

СОВЕТЧИК
Человек сам себе плохой советчик—2250 (Ч)

СОВРАТЬ
Раз соврал, в другой раз не поверят—914 (К)
Соврёшь—не помрёшь, да вперёд не поверят—1961 (С)

СОГЛАШАТЬСЯ
Кто молчит, тот соглашается—937 (К)

СОГНУТЬ
Кто кого согнёт, тот того и бьёт—925 (К)

СОКОЛ
Знать сокола по полёту, а доброго молодца по походке—151 (В)
И сокол выше солнца не летает—748 (И)
Подстреленного сокола и ворона носом долбит—1673 (П)

СОЛГАТЬ
Кто вчера солгал, тому и завтра не поверят—914 (К)
Раз солгал, а навек лгуном стал—914 (К)
Солжёшь сегодня, не поверят и завтра—914 (К)

СОЛДАТ
Плох тот солдат, который не надеется быть генералом—1656 (П)
Солдат спит, служба идёт—1967 (С)

СОЛНЦЕ
Взойдёт солнце и перед нашими воротами—1772 (П)
И на солнце есть пятна—737 (И)
Пока солнце взойдёт, роса очи выест—1687 (П)

СОЛНЫШКО
Взойдёт солнышко и на нашем подворье—1772 (П)
И красное солнышко на всех не угождает—724 (И)
Придёт солнышко и к нашим окошечкам—1772 (П)

СОЛОВЕЙ
Мал соловей, да голос (голосом) велик—1105 (М)
Соловья баснями (песнями) не кормят—1968 (С)

СОЛОМА
Старая солома жарко горит—1997 (С)

СОЛОМИНКА
По соломинке—сноп /, по снопишку—копнишка, из копен—стог/—1740 (П)

СОЛОМКА
Ближняя соломка лучше дальнего сенца—70 (Б)
Кабы знал, где упасть, так соломки б подостлал—760 (К)
Кабы знал, где упасть, так соломки бы постлал (припасть)—760 (К)

СОЛЬ
Добра соль, а переложишь—рот воротит—467 (Д)
Человека узнаешь, когда с ним пуд соли /ложкой/ расхлебаешь—2283 (Ч)
Чтобы узнать человека, надо с ним пуд соли съесть—2283 (Ч)

СОМНЕВАТЬСЯ
Кто ничего не знает, тот ни в чём не сомневается—949 (К)
Чем больше знаешь, тем больше сомневаешься—2256 (Ч)

СОР
Из избы сору не выноси, а в уголок (под лавку) копи—1970 (С)
Сор из избы не выносят—1970 (С)

СОРИНКА
В чужом глазу и соринка видна, а в своём и бревна не видно—298 (В)

СОРОКА
Бей сороку и ворону—добьёшься до ясного сокола—55 (Б)
Дружные сороки и гуся съедят (утащут)—518 (Д)
Знай сорока сороку, ворона ворону—675 (З)
И сорока в одно перо не родится—749 (И)
Каждая сорока своё гнездо хвалит—276 (В)
Сорока без причины не стрекочет—1971 (С)
Сорока на хвосте /весть/ принесла—1972 (С)

СОСЕД
Близкий сосед лучше дальней родни—71 (Б)
Лучше добрые соседи, чем далёкая родня—71 (Б)
На соседа не кивай—за собой примечай—1247 (Н)
Не кивай на соседа, а погляди на себя—1247 (Н)
Не купи двора, а купи соседа—1365 (Н)
Не купи дом (места), купи соседа—1365 (Н)
Не меняй ближнего соседа на дальнюю родню—71 (Б)
С соседом дружись, а забор (тын) городи—1990 (С)
У соседа занялось—гляди в оба—2150 (У)

СОСНА
Всякая сосна своему бору шумит—265 (В)

СОСУД
Чем сосуд наполнен, то из него и льётся—2260 (Ч)

СПАСИБО
За спасибо шубу не сошьют—648 (З)
Из спасиба шапки не сошьёшь—648 (З)
Спасиба в карман не положишь 1976 (С)
Спасиба домой не принесёшь—1976 (С)

СПАТЬ
Дурак спит, а счастье /у него/ в головах лежит (сидит, стоит)—543 (Д)
Долго спать—добра не видать (с долгом встать)—1145 (М)
Кто спит весною, плачет зимою—969 (К)
Много спать—добра не видать—1145 (М)

СПЕХ
От спеху чуть не наделал смеху—1609 (О)

Спех людям на смех—1979 (С)

СПЕШИТЬ
Не спеши, куманёк, не вздут огонёк—1408 (Н)
Спеши, да не торопись—1980 (С)
Спеши медленно—1980 (С)

СПЛЫТЬ
Было, да сплыло—2281 (Ч)
Что было, то сплыло—2281 (Ч)

СПОТЫКАТЬСЯ
Кто не бежит, тот не спотыкается—941 (К)

СПОТЫЧКА
Без спотычки и конь не пробежит—866 (К)
Кабы на коня не спотычка, ему бы и цены не было—761 (К)

СПОХВАТИТЬСЯ
Спохватился, когда с горы свалился (когда скатился)—1983 (С)

СПРАШИВАТЬ
Не спрашивай старого (умного), /а/ спрашивай бывалого—1410 (Н)

СПРОС
За спрос денег не берут (не бьют в нос)—649 (З)
Спрос в карман не лезет и карман не трёт—1985 (С)
Спрос всё укажет—1984 (С)
Спрос не беда—1985 (С)

СПРОСИТЬСЯ
Кому много дано, с того много и спросится—855 (К)

СРАВНЕНИЕ
Всё познаётся в сравнении—241 (В)

СТАДО
Согласного стада и волк не берёт—1962 (С)
Согласному стаду и волк не страшен—1962 (С)

СТАРОЕ
Кто старое помянёт, тому глаз вон—970 (К)

СТАРОСТЬ
Не старость калечит, а горе—1323 (Н)
Придёт старость, придёт и слабость—2004 (С)
Старость не радость /, не красные дни/—2003 (С)
Старость приходит не с радостью, а со слабостью—2004 (С)

СТАРУХА
И на старуху бывает проруха—738 (И)

СТАРУШКА
У всякой старушки свои прорушки—738 (Н)

СТАРЫЙ
На старого и немочи валятся—1248 (Н)
Старого учить, что мёртвого лечить—2002 (С)

СТАЯ
Попал в стаю, лай не лай, а хвостом виляй—1710 (П)

СТЕЛИТЬ
Мягко стелет, да жёстко спать—1170 (М)

СТЕНА
И стены имеют уши—2153 (У)
У стен есть уши—2153 (У)

СТЕРПЕТЬСЯ
Что стерпится, то и слюбится—2309 (Ч)

СТОРОНА
Всякому мила своя сторона—282 (В)
Со стороны всегда виднее—1973 (С)
Чужая сторона прибавит ума—2322 (Ч)

СТОЯЧИЙ
Стоячая вода гниёт (плесенью покрывается, тухнет)—2014 (С)
Стоячему с сидячим трудно говорить—2015 (С)

СТРАХ
У страха глаза велики—2154 (У)

СТРЕМЯ
Либо в стремя ногой, либо в пень головой—1017 (Л)

СТРОИТЕЛЬ
Каков строитель, таков и дом—819 (К)

СТРЯПКА
У всякой стряпки свои порядки—2094 (У)

СТУЛ
Между двумя стульями не усидишь—1119 (М)

СТЫД
Людской стыд—смех, а свой—смерть—1092 (Л)

СТЫДЛИВЫЙ
Стыдливый из-за стола голодный встаёт—2016 (С)

СУД
В суд ногой, в карман рукой—254 (В)
На нет и суда нет—1213 (Н)

СУДИТЬ
Не зная дела, не суди—1348 (Н)
Не суди об арбузе по корке, а о человеке—по платью—1417 (Н)
Не судите, да не судимы будете—1418 (Н)

СУДЬБА
От судьбы не уйдёшь—1610 (О)

СУДЬЯ
В своём деле никто сам себе не судья—2249 (Ч)
Человек сам себе не судья—2249 (Ч)

СУЖДЕНО
Кому суждено быть повешенным, тот не утонет—859 (К)

СУЖЕНЫЙ
Сужена на коне (кривых оглоблях) ни обойти, ни объехать—2017 (С)
Сужена-ряжена не обойдёшь и на коне не объедешь—2017 (С)
Суженого и на коне не объедешь—2017 (С)

СУК
На крепкий сук—острый топор—1205 (Н)
Налетел /острый/ топор на /острый/ сук—1206 (Н)
Не руби сук, на котором сидишь—1404 (Н)

СУЛИТЬ
Кто много сулит, тот мало даёт (делает)—934 (К)
Не сули бычка, а дай стакан (чашку) молочка—1421 (Н)
Не сули журавля в небе, дай синицу в руки—1421 (Н)
Не сули с гору, а подай в пору—1422 (Н)
Не сули собаке пирога, а кинь краюху—1423 (Н)

СУМА
От сумы да от тюрьмы не зарекайся (не отказывайся, не отрекайся)—1611 (О)
Привяжется сума, откажется и родня—1769 (П)

СУХАРЬ
Свои сухари лучше чужих пирогов—1862 (С)

СУЧОК
В чужом глазу сучок велик—298 (В)

СЧАСТЛИВЫЙ
Счастливые часов не наблюдают—2020 (С)

СЧАСТЬЕ
Где счастье поведётся, там и петух несётся—335 (Г)
У кого счастье поведётся, у того и петух несётся—335 (Г)
Кому счастье служит, тому и люди—860 (К)
Кому счастье служит, тот ни о чем не тужит—861 (К)
Легче счастье найти, нежели (чем) удержать—999 (Л)
Не было бы счастья, да несчастье помогло—1276 (Н)
Полного счастья не бывает—1698 (П)

Счастье без ума — дырявая сума — 2021 (С)
Счастье едет в карете, а и с умом, да ходят пешком — 2022 (С)
Счастье и несчастье на одном коне ездят — 2024 (С)
Счастье на деньги не купишь — 2023 (С)
Счастье с бессчастьем — вёдро с ненастьем — 2024 (С)
Счастье с несчастьем близко живут (на одних санях ездят) — 2024 (С)

СЧЁТ
Ближний счёт — дальняя дружба — 2234 (Ч)
Счёт дружбе не помеха — 2025 (С)
Счёт дружбы не портит — 2025 (С)
Счёт чаще — дружба слаще — 2234 (Ч)
Чаще счёт — крепче дружба — 2234 (Ч)

СЪЕСТЬ
Съесть не могу, а оставить жаль — 2027 (С)
Съешь и морковку, коли яблочка нет — 2028 (С)
Съешь и ржаного, коли нет никакого — 2028 (С)

СЫН
Каково дерево, таков и клин, каков батька, таков и сын — 806 (К)

СЫТЫЙ
Сытый голодного не разумеет — 2032 (С)
У сытого на уме гулянки — 2156 (У)

Т

ТАБАК
Дело — табак — 435 (Д)

ТАБУН
Дружный табун волков не боится — 519 (Д)

ТАЗ
Лучше в нас, чем в таз — 1047 (Л)

ТАЙНА
Один — тайна, два — полтайны, три — нет тайны — 1529 (О)

ТАЙНОЕ
Всё тайное становится явным — 243 (В)
Нет ничего тайного, что не стало бы явным — 243 (В)

ТАМ
Все там будем — 244 (В)

ТАНЦЕВАТЬ
Если танцевать не умеешь, не говори, что каблуки кривые — 566 (Е)

ТАРАКАН
У всякого таракана своя щёлка есть — 2090 (У)

ТЕЛЁНОК
Домашний телёнок лучше заморской коровы — 500 (Д)
К мокрому телёнку все мухи льнут — 840 (К)

ТЕЛО
В здоровом теле — здоровый дух — 148 (В)

ТЕЛЯ
Ласковое теля двух маток сосёт — 987 (Л)

ТЕПЛО
Любить тепло — и дым терпеть — 1073 (Л)
Любишь тепло — терпи и дым — 1073 (Л)

ТЕРНИИ
Через тернии к звёздам — 2266 (Ч)

ТЕРПЕНИЕ
Без терпения нет и умения — 833 (К)
Всякому терпению приходит конец — 286 (В)
К большому терпению придёт и умение — 833 (К)
На всякое хотение есть терпение — 1188 (Н)
Чаша терпения переполнилась — 2233 (Ч)

ТЕРПЕНЬЕ
Терпенье и труд всё перетрут—2044 (Т)

ТЕРПЕТЬ
Терпи, казак, атаманом будешь—2046 (Т)
Терпит брага долго, а через край пойдёт—не уймёшь—2047 (Т)

ТЕСНОТА
В тесноте, да не в обиде—293 (В)

ТЕЧЬ
Всё течёт, всё изменяется—245 (В)

ТОВАР
На запретный товар весь базар—1200 (Н)
На опальный товар много купцов—1200 (Н)
На хороший товар и купцов много—1255 (Н)
Товар лицом кажут—2055 (Т)
Хороший товар не залежится—2194 (Х)
Хороший товар сам себя хвалит—2195 (Х)

ТОВАРИЩ
Волк свинье не товарищ—402 (Г)
Гусь свинье не товарищ—402 (Г)
Пеший конному не товарищ—402 (Г)
По товарищам и слава—1748 (П)
Умный товарищ—половина дороги—2132 (У)

ТОЛКИ
Где много толков, там мало толку—321 (Г)

ТОНКО
Где тонко, там и рвётся—336 (Г)

ТОНУТЬ
Когда тонул—топор сулил, а когда вытащили—топорища не дал—1163 (М)
Мужик тонул—топор обещал, вытащили—топорища жаль—1163 (М)

ТОПОР
Без топора—не плотник, без иглы—не портной (без лопаты—не огородник)—48 (Б)
Без топора по дрова не ходят—49 (Б)
Налетел топор на сук—1206 (Н)
Остёр топор, да и сук зубаст—1569 (О)
После поры не точат топоры—1733 (П)

ТОРГОВАТЬ
Торговали—веселились, подсчитали—прослезились—2064 (Т)

ТОРГОВЛЯ
У хлеба не без крошек, у торговли не без урона—2161 (У)

ТОТ
Кто от кого, тот и в того—953 (К)

ТОЧНОСТЬ
Точность—вежливость королей—2069 (Т)

ТРАВА
Было, да сплыло, да травой поросло—2281 (Ч)
Дурная трава в рост идёт (хорошо растёт)—2217 (Х)
На битой (прохожей, торной) дороге /и/ трава не растёт—1251 (Н)
Пока трава вырастет, кобыла сдохнет—1688 (П)
После нас хоть трава не расти—1731 (П)
Сорная трава хорошо растёт—2217 (Х)
Худая трава быстро растёт (в рост идёт)—2217 (Х)

ТРАТА
Самая большая трата—трата времени—1847 (С)

ТРЕЗВЫЙ
Трезвого дума, пьяного речь—2312 (Ч)
Что у трезвого на уме, то у пьяного на языке—2312 (Ч)

ТРЕТИЙ
Где двое, там третий лишний—312 (Г)
Двум любо, третий не суйся—312 (Г)

ТРЕЩИНА
Трещина в горшке скоро скажется—2070 (Т)

ТРОИЦА
Бог троицу любит—86 (Б)

ТРУД
Без труда и в саду нет плода—50 (Б)
Без труда не вытащишь и рыбку из пруда—50 (Б)
Без труда ничего не даётся—50 (Б)
Где труд, там и счастье—337 (Г)
От трудов праведных не наживёшь палат каменных—1613 (О)

ТРУП
Только через мой труп—2061 (Т)

ТРУС
Всякий трус о храбрости беседует—272 (В)
Трус в карты не играет—2072 (Т)
Трус и до смерти часто умирает—2073 (Т)

ТРУСЛИВЫЙ
На смелого собака лает, а трусливого рвёт—1245 (Н)
Шкодлив, как кошка, а труслив, как заяц—2340 (Ш)

ТРУТЕНЬ
Трутни горазды на плутни—2074 (Т)
Трутням праздник и по будням—2075 (Т)

ТРЯПИЦА
Всякая тряпица в три года пригодится—266 (В)

ТУЖИТЬ
О чём тому тужить, кому есть чем жить—1622 (О)
Что о том тужить, чего нельзя воротить—2302 (Ч)

ТУЧА
Большая туча, да малый дождь—701 (И)
Из большой тучи, да малый дождь—701 (И)
Не всякая туча грозовая—1310 (Н)

ТЫ
Ты—мне, я—тебе—2077 (Т)

ТЯЖЁЛЫЙ
На большом пути и малая ноша тяжела—1177 (Н)
На сто вёрст и иголка тяжела—1177 (Н)

У

УБОГИЙ
На убогого всюду каплет—1253 (Н)

УВИДЕТЬ
Лучше один раз увидеть, чем сто раз услышать—1062 (Л)
Поживём—увидим—1678 (П)
Что было, то видели, что будет, то увидим—2280 (Ч)

УГОВОР
Уговор дороже денег—2095 (У)
Уговор—святое дело—2095 (У)

УГОДИТЬ
На весь мир не угодишь—1184 (Н)
На всех не угодишь—1184 (Н)
На всех угодить—себя истомить—1185 (Н)
На всякий нрав не угодишь—1184 (Н)

УГОДЛИВЫЙ
Всем угодлив, так никому не пригодлив—230 (В)

УДАЛЫЙ
Мал, да удал—1099 (М)

УДАР
С одного удара дуб не свалишь—1965 (С)

УДАЧА
Одна удача идёт, другую ведёт—1538 (О)

УЖИН
Завтрак съешь сам, обедом поделись с другом, а ужин отдай врагу—615 (З)
Ужин отдай врагу—615 (З)

УКРАСТЬ
Кто может украсть телёнка, украдёт и корову—935 (К)
Кто украдёт яйцо, тот украдёт и лошадь—935 (К)
Кто украл яйцо, украдёт и курицу—935 (К)

УКРЫВАТЕЛЬ
Укрыватель—тот же вор—2112 (У)

УЛИТА
Улита едет, когда-то будет—2115 (У)

УЛОЧКА
На своей улочке храбра и курочка—1238 (Н)

УМ
Задний ум хорош, да никуда не гож—619 (З)
Задним умом всяк крепок—620 (З)
Задним умом дела не поправишь—621 (З)
Каждый по-своему с ума сходит—774 (К)
На всякого дурака ума не напасёшься—1186 (Н)
Обед узнают по кушанью, а ум по слушанью—1504 (О)
Один ум хорошо, а два—лучше—1531 (О)
По одёжке (платью) встречают, по уму провожают—1707 (П)
Ума на деньги не купишь—78 (Б)
Ум за деньги не купишь—78 (Б)
Ум на ум не приходится—2123 (У)
Ум не в бороде, а в голове—2124 (У)
Ум—хорошо, а два—лучше /того/—2135 (У)

УМЕНИЕ
Всякое умение трудом даётся—280 (В)

УМЕНЬЕ
Уменье везде найдёт примененье—2121 (У)

УМЕРЕННОСТЬ
Умеренность—лучшее лекарство—2122 (У)
Умеренность—мать здоровья—2122 (У)

УМЕРЕТЬ
Как жил, так и умер—782 (К)
Не умер Данило—болячка задавила—1461 (Н)
Умрём, так всё останется—2133 (У)

УМИРАТЬ
На людях умирать легче—1209 (Н)
Не всяк умирает, кто хворает—1317 (Н)
Один раз мать родила, один раз и умирать—1527 (О)

УМНИЦА
Умная умница—что светлая пуговица—2125 (У)
Умница, как попова курица—2125 (У)

УМНЫЙ
Лучше с умным потерять, чем с глупым найти—1069 (Л)
Не всякий умён, кто богато (хорошо) наряжён—1313 (Н)
Умному—намёк, глупому—толчок—2126 (У)
Умному свистни, а он уже смыслит—2126 (У)
Умный любит учиться, а глупый (дурак) учить—2129 (У)
Умный не всегда развяжет /то/, что глупый завяжет—533 (Д)
Умный понимает (слышит, смыслит) с полуслова—2130 (У)

УПАВШИЙ
Упавшего не считай за пропавшего—2138 (У)

УПРАВИТЬ
Кто собою не управит, тот и другого на разум не наставит—968 (К)

Не управишь собой, не управишь и другими — 968 (К)

УРОД
В семье не без урода — 237 (В)

УС
Мы и сами с усами — 1168 (М)

УСЕРДИЕ
Усердие не по разуму приносит вред — 2146 (У)

УСЕСТЬСЯ
Ладно уселся, так и сиди — 981 (Л)

УСЛУГА
Услуга за услугу — 2148 (У)

УСОЛ
Каков усол, таков и вкус — 821 (К)

УСТА
Вашими бы устами да мёд пить — 123 (В)
Из твоих уст да Богу в уши — 716 (И)
Устами младенца глаголет истина — 2152 (У)

УСТИНЬЯ
Какова Устинья, такова у ней и ботвинья — 795 (К)

УТАИТЬ
Любви, огня да кашля от людей не утаишь — 1071 (Л)

УТЁНОК
Не считай утят, пока не вылупились — 1425 (Н)

УТОНУТЬ
Когда не везёт, утонешь и в ложке воды — 845 (К)

УТОПАЮЩИЙ
Спасение утопающего — дело рук самого утопающего — 1975 (С)
Утопающий и за соломинку хватается — 2157 (У)

УТОПЛЕННИК
Везёт как утопленнику — 132 (В)

УТРО
Серенькое утро — красненький денёк — 1891 (С)
Утро вечера мудренее — 2158 (У)

УХО
В одно ухо влетает, а в другое вылетает — 177 (В)
В одно ухо входит, а в другое выходит — 177 (В)
Скажешь с уха на ухо, а узнают с угла на угол — 1895 (С)
Слушай ухом, а не брюхом — 1935 (С)

УЧЕНИЕ
Тяжело в учении, легко в бою — 2080 (Т)

УЧЁНЫЙ
Учёного учить — только портить — 2164 (У)

УЧЕНЬЕ
Ученье — свет, а неученье — тьма — 2165 (У)
Ученья корень горек, да плод сладок — 2166 (У)

УЧИТЬ
Не учила сына, когда кормила, а тебя кормить станет — не научишь — 1463 (Н)
Не учили, покуда поперёк лавки укладывался, а во всю вытянулся — не научишь — 1463 (Н)
Не учи рыбу плавать, а собаку лаять — 1464 (Н)
Не учи учёного /есть хлеба печёные (хлеба есть печёного)/ — 1466 (Н)
Учат не только сказом, но и показом — 2163 (У)
Учи дитя, пока поперёк лавки ложится (укладывается) — 1463 (Н)
Учи других — и сам поймёшь — 2167 (У)

УЧИТЬСЯ
Не учись до старости, а учись до смерти — 1465 (Н)
Учиться никогда не поздно — 2168 (У)

УШИБИТЬСЯ
Чем ушибся, тем и лечись — 2264 (Ч)

Ф

ФАДДЕЙ
Не только людей что Фома да Фаддей—1439 (Н)

ФАКТ
Факты—упрямая вещь—2169 (Ф)

ФЕДОРА
Велика Федора, да дура—138 (В)

ФЕДОРКА
У всякого Федорки свои отговорки—2091 (У)
У лентяя Федорки всегда отговорки—2091 (У)

ФЕДОТ
Голодному Федоту и репа в охоту—373 (Г)
Федот, да не тот—2170 (Ф)

ФЕДОТКА
У всякого Федотки свои отговорки—2091 (У)

ФИГУРА
Велика фигура, да дура—138 (В)

ФИЛЯ
У Фили были, у Фили пили, да Филю ж побили—2159 (У)
У Фили пили, да Филю ж и били—2159 (У)

ФОМА
На безлюдье и Фома дворянин—1173 (Н)
Фома ему, а он всему селу—2171 (Ф)
Я ему про Фому, а он про Ерёму—2358 (Я)

Х

ХАМ
Из хама не сделаешь пана—717 (И)

ХАТА
В своей хате и углы помогают—498 (Д)
Какова хата, таков и тын, каков отец, таков и сын—806 (К)
Когда хата сгорит, сажи не трусят—850 (К)
Моя хата с краю—1159 (М)

ХВАЛИТЬ
Всякий купец свой товар хвалит—269 (В)
Всякий цыган свою кобылу хвалит—269 (В)
Всяк своё хвалит—269 (В)
Каждая сорока своё гнездо хвалит—276 (В)
Не хвали себя сам, пусть тебя другие (люди) похвалят—1467 (Н)
Хвали горку, как перевалишься—2172 (Х)

ХВАЛИТЬСЯ
Не хвались в поле едучи, хвались с поля—1468 (Н)
Не хвались едучи на рать, а хвались едучи с рати—1468 (Н)
Не хвались идучи на рать, а хвались идучи с рати—1468 (Н)
Не хвались отъездом, а хвались приездом—1469 (Н)

ХВАСТАТЬ
Собой не хвастай, дай наперёд похвалить тебя людям—1467 (Н)

ХВАТАТЬ
Этого ещё не хватало—2350 (Э)

ХВОСТ
Без хвоста и ворона не красна—52 (Б)
Отсеки собаке хвост—не будет овца—1603 (О)

ХИТРОСТЬ
Где силой не возьмёшь, там хитрость на подмогу—334 (Г)
Хитростью силу берут—334 (Г)

ХЛЕБ
Без хлеба не обойдёшься—53 (Б)
Во всяком хлебе мякина есть—173 (В)
Едешь на день, хлеба бери на неделю—559 (Е)
Ешь хлеб, коли пирогов нет—578 (Е)
Ешь щи с мясом, а нет, так и хлеб с квасом—579 (Е)

Каков у дела, таков и у хлеба—820 (К)
Не от хлеба ходят, а к хлебу—1383 (Н)
Не спится—хлеб снится—1409 (Н)
Не то хлеб, что в поле, а то, что в амбаре—1438 (Н)
Не хлебом единым жив (сыт) человек—1471 (Н)
От хлеба хлеба не ищут—1383 (Н)
Пока есть хлеб да вода, всё не беда—1683 (П)
Проголодаешься, так и хлеба найти догадаешься—1781 (П)
Свой хлеб слаще чужого калача—1862 (С)
Свой хлеб сытнее—1862 (С)
С кем хлеб-соль водишь, на того и походишь—1905 (С)
У хлеба и крохи (не без крох)—2160 (У)
Хлеба нет, так и друзей не бывало—2176 (Х)
Хлеб всему голова—2177 (Х)
Хлеб за брюхом не ходит—2178 (Х)
Чей хлеб ешь, того и обычай тешь—2241 (Ч)
Чужой хлеб рот дерёт—2329 (Ч)

ХМЕЛЬНОЕ
Кто пьёт хмельное, тот говорит дурное—960 (К)

ХОД
Хода нет, ходи с червей—2180 (Х)

ХОДИТЬ
Не с чего ходить, так с бубён—2180 (Х)

ХОЗЯИН
Где хозяин ходит, там земля родит—338 (Г)
Каков хозяин, таков и слуга—822 (К)
Не дом хозяина красит, а хозяин дом—1332 (Н)
Хозяин—барин—2181 (Х)

ХОЗЯЙКА
Хозяйкою дом стоит—2182 (Х)

ХОМУТ
Была бы шея, а хомут найдётся—119 (Б)

ХОРОШЕЕ
Хорошего понемножку—2187 (Х)
Худое долго помнится, а хорошее скоро забудется—482 (Д)

ХОРОШЕНЬКОЕ
Хорошенького понемногу (понемножку)—2187 (Х)

ХОРОШИЙ
Всяк сам себе хорош—289 (В)
Не по хорошему мил, а по милу хорош—1395 (Н)
Не тот хорош, кто лицом пригож, а кто на дело гож (а тот хорош, кто для дела гож)—1447 (Н)

ХОРОШО
Везде хорошо, где нас нет—2036 (Т)
Всё хорошо, что хорошо кончается—248 (В)
Не то мило, что хорошо, а то хорошо, что мило—1395 (Н)
Там хорошо, где нас нет—2036 (Т)
Что хорошо, то хорошо, а что лучше, то лучше—2313 (Ч)

ХОТЕНЬЕ
Где хотенье, там и уменье—339 (Г)

ХОТЕТЬ
Как хочу, так и ворочу—829 (К)

ХОТЕТЬСЯ
И хочется, да не можется—754 (И)
И хочется, и колется /, и мама (матушка) не велит/—755 (И)
Чего хочется, тому и верится—2240 (Ч)

ХРАБРИТЬСЯ
Не храбрись на медведя, а храбрись при медведе—1472 (Н)

ХРАНИТЬ
Что имеем, не храним, потерявши, плачем—2292 (Ч)

ХРЕН
Хрен редьки не слаще—2215 (Х)

ХУДО
Без худа добра не бывает—54 (Б)
Нет худа без добра—1456 (Н)
Худо начинается, худо и кончается—2222 (Х)

ХУДОЕ
За худым пойдёшь—худое найдёшь—921 (К)
Из худого не сделаешь хорошее—718 (И)
Кто за худым пойдёт, тот добра не найдёт—921 (К)
Хорошее лежит, а худое /далеко/ бежит—2189 (Х)

ХУЖЕ
Могло быть и хуже—1147 (М)

Ц

ЦАРАПИНА
И на жемчуге бывает царапина—735 (И)

ЦАРЬ
Близ царя—близ смерти—74 (Б)
За глаза и царя ругают—616 (З)

ЦВЕТОК
Хорош цветок, да остёр шипок—2201 (Х)

ЦВЕТОЧЕК
Это ещё цветочки, а ягодки впереди—2352 (З)

ЦЕЛОВАТЬ
Целовал ворон (ястреб) курочку до последнего пёрышка—2225 (Ц)

ЦЕЛЬ
Цель оправдывает средства—2226 (Ц)

ЦЕНА
Каждый человек свою цену имеет—777 (К)
Цену вещи узнаешь, когда потеряешь—2227 (Ц)

ЦЫПЛЁНОК
Цыплят по осени считают—2228 (Ц)

Ч

ЧАЙКА
Дружные чайки и ястреба забьют—518 (Д)

ЧАС
Всему свой час—233 (В)
Час от часу не легче—2231 (Ч)

ЧАША
Да минует меня чаша сия—413 (Д)
Чаша терпения переполнилась—2233 (Ч)

ЧАЯТЬ
Чего не чаешь, то получаешь—2239 (Ч)

ЧЁЛН
Челном моря (океана) не переехать—2242 (Ч)

ЧЕЛОВЕК
Злой человек не проживёт в добре век—666 (З)
Золото огнём, человек бедой познаётся—2245 (Ч)
Не место человека красит, а человек место—1332 (Н)
Человека узнаешь, как из семи печек с ним щей похлебаешь—2283 (Ч)
Человек гадает, а Бог располагает—2246 (Ч)
Человек два раза глуп живёт—стар и мал—2243 (Ч)
Человек не камень: терпит да и треснет—2244 (Ч)
Человек познаётся в беде—2245 (Ч)
Человек по-своему, а Бог по-своему—2246 (Ч)
Человек предполагает, а Бог располагает—2246 (Ч)
Человек человеку—волк (зверь)—2252 (Ч)

ЧЕЛОВЕЧЕСКОЕ
Ничто человеческое нам не чуждо—1487 (Н)

ЧЕРЁД
Всему свой черёд—233 (В)

ЧЁРНЕНЬКИЙ
Полюбите нас чёрненькими, а беленькими всякий (красненькими всяк) полюбит—1700 (П)

ЧЁРНОЕ
Чёрное от стирки не белеет—2269 (Ч)

ЧЁРТ
Два чёрта в одном болоте не живут—420 (Д)
Не так страшен чёрт, как его малюют—1426 (Н)
Около святых черти водятся—1553 (О)
Сам чёрт не разберёт (ногу сломает)—1851 (С)
Чем чёрт не шутит /, пока Бог спит/—2265 (Ч)
Чёрт попу не товарищ—2270 (Ч)
Чёрт чёрту рога не обломает—2271 (Ч)

ЧЕСНОК
Кто чесноку поел—сам скажется—971 (К)

ЧЕСТНОСТЬ
Лучше бедность да честность, нежели прибыль да стыд—1044 (Л)

ЧЕСТНЫЙ
Беден, да честен—1043 (Л)
Лучше беднее, да честнее—1043 (Л)

ЧЕСТЬ
Дадут дураку честь, так не знает, где и сесть—403 (Д)
Дай Бог тому честь, кто умеет её несть—405 (Д)
Каков есть, такова и честь—799 (К)
Честь добра, да съесть нельзя—2273 (Ч)
Честь не в честь, как нечего есть—2273 (Ч)
Что за (и) честь, коли нечего есть—2273 (Ч)

ЧИСТОТА
Чистота—лучшая красота—2277 (Ч)

ЧИСТЫЙ
Чистого и огонь не обожжёт—2275 (Ч)
Чистому—всё чисто—2276 (Ч)

ЧИХ
На всякий чих не наздравствуешься—1189 (Н)

ЧИХАНЬЕ
На всякое чиханье не наздравствуешься—1189 (Н)

ЧТО-НИБУДЬ
Лучше хоть что-нибудь, чем ничего—1070 (Л)

ЧУДО
Чудеса в решете!—2314 (Ч)

ЧУЖОЕ
За чужим погонишься, своё потеряешь—658 (З)
Кто чужого желает, скоро своё потеряет—658 (З)

ЧУЖОЙ
В чужой прудок не кидай неводок—1260 (Н)
На чужую кучу нечего глаза пучить—1260 (Н)

ЧУТЬ
Чуть не считается—2332 (Ч)

Ш

ШАГ
От великого до смешного один шаг—1580 (О)
Труден только первый шаг—2071 (Т)

ШАЛАШ
Милости прошу к нашему шалашу—1133 (М)
С милым рай и в шалаше—1942 (С)

ШАПКА
Дома щи без круп, а в людях шапка в рубль—2335 (Ш)
И под дырявой шапкой живёт голова—742 (И)
Обещанная шапка на уши не лезет—1505 (О)
Хватился шапки, когда головы не стало—2175 (Х)
Шапка в рубль, а щи без круп—2335 (Ш)

Щ

Часом щи с мясом, а часом и хлеб с квасом—2229 (Ч)

ЩУКА
Не учи плавать щуку, щука знает свою науку—1462 (Н)
Та же щука, да под хреном—2034 (Т)

Ю

ЮРЬЕВ
Вот тебе, бабушка, и Юрьев день—200 (В)

Я

Я
Я говорю про Ивана, а ты про болвана—2358 (Я)
Я говорю про попа, ты про попадью, а он про попову дочку—2358 (Я)
Я ему про ремень, а он мне про лыко—2358 (Я)
Я ему про Фому, а он про Ерёму—2358 (Я)
Я знаю, что я ничего не знаю—2359 (Я)
"Я не дурак"—сказал дурак—2369 (Я)
Я не первый, и я не последний—2370 (Я)
Я не тот ребёнок, что вчера из пелёнок—2371 (Я)
Я не я, и котомка не моя—2372 (Я)
Я не я, и лошадь не моя, и я не извозчик—2372 (Я)
Я про сапоги, а он про пироги—2358 (Я)

ЯБЛОКО
От одного порченого яблока целый воз загнивает—1597 (О)

ЯБЛОНЬКА
Какая яблонька, такие и яблочки—2357 (Я)
От яблони яблоко родится, от ели—шишка—1619 (О)

ЯБЛОЧКО
Яблочко от яблони недалеко падает—2357 (Я)

ЯГОДКА
Собирай по ягодке, наберёшь кузовок—1956 (С)

ЯЗЫК
Держи язык за зубами (на привязи)—577 (Е)
Ешь пирог с грибами, да держи язык за зубами—577 (Е)
Злой язык убивает—667 (З)
Злые языки—острый меч—669 (З)
Злые языки страшнее пистолета—669 (З)
На язык пошлин нет: что хочет, то и лопочет—1270 (Н)
Не ножа бойся, а языка—1380 (Н)
Острый язык, что бритва—1575 (О)
От вежливых слов язык не отсохнет—1579 (О)
От доброго слова язык не отсохнет—1579 (О)
От ласковых слов язык не отсохнет—1579 (О)
У дурака язык впереди ног бежит—2098 (У)
Что на уме, то и на языке—2299 (Ч)
Шила и мыла, гладила и катала, пряла и лощила, а всё языком—2338 (Ш)
Язык без костей /, что хочет, то и лопочет/—2360 (Я)
Язык болтает, а голова ничего не знает—2361 (Я)
Язык говорит, а голова не ведает—2361 (Я)
Язык до добра не доведёт /болтуна/—2362 (Я)
Язык до Киева доведёт—2363 (Я)
Язык лепечет, а голова не ведает—2361 (Я)
Язык мой—враг мой—2364 (Я)
Язык мягок: что хочет, то и лопочет—1270 (Н)
Язык наш—враг наш—2364 (Я)
Языком не спеши, а делом не ленись—2365 (Я)

ЯЗЫЧОК
Язычок введёт в грешок—2366 (Я)

ЯИЧКО
Дорого яичко к великому (светлому, Христову) дню—506 (Д)

ЯИЧНИЦА
Яичница без яиц не бывает—2367 (Я)

ЯЙЦО
Засиженное яйцо всегда болтун, занянченное дитя всегда дурак—647 (З)
Засиженное яйцо всегда болтун, занянченный сын (сынок)—всегда шалун—647 (З)
Яйца курицу не учат—2368 (Я)

ЯМА
Кто другому яму копает, тот сам в неё попадает—917 (К)
Не копай (рой) другому яму, сам в неё попадёшь—917 (К)

ЯСНО
Ясно, как дважды два—четыре—2374 (Я)

ЯЩЕРКА
Ящерка маленька, да зубы остреньки—2375 (Я)

English Proverb and Saying Key Word Index

Указатель ключевых слов английских пословиц и поговорок

A

ABDAB
Don't give me the old abdabs!—1590 (О)

ABILITY
Ability, not luck, conquers—1275 (Н)

ABSENCE
Absence makes the heart grow fonder—1667 (П), 1828 (Р)
Absence sharpens love—1828 (Р)
Salt water and absence wash away love—1816 (Р), 1871 (С)

ABSENT
Long absent, soon forgotten—1816 (Р), 1871 (С)

ABUNDANCE
Abundance of things engenders disdainfulness—1919 (С)

ABUSE
Best things may be abused (The)—670 (З), 828 (К)
Everything may be abused—670 (З), 828 (К)

ACCEPT
Accept us as we are—1700 (П)

ACCIDENT
Accidents /will/ happen in the best of families—1670 (П)
Accidents will happen in the best regulated families—1670 (П)

ACCOMPLICE
Accomplice is as bad as the thief (The)—197 (В)

ACCOUNT
Short accounts make long friends—2234 (Ч)

ACHE
Every heart has its own ache—2103 (У)

ACHIEVE
We learn by doing, achieve by pursuing—507 (Д)

ACQUAINTANCE
Of chance acquaintance beware—108 (Б), 1312 (Н)
Short acquaintance brings repentance—1312 (Н)
Sudden short acquaintances bring repentance—1312 (Н)

ACRE
Acre of performance is worth the whole world of promise (An)—1421 (Н), 1423 (Н)
One acre of performance is worth twenty of the Land of Promise—1421 (Н), 1423 (Н)

ACT
Act proves the intention (The)—1285 (Н)
Good acts are better than good intentions—1503 (Н)

ACTION
Action is worry's worst enemy—1920 b (С)
Actions are mightier than words—1503 (Н)
Actions, not words—1503 (Н)
Actions speak louder than words—428 (Д), 1285 (Н), 1393 (Н), 1503 (Н)
Action without thought is like shooting without aim—407 (Д), 650 (З), 2146 (У)
Good actions speak for themselves, they need no tin horn—476 (Д)
Words don't mean a thing; it's the action that counts—1285 (Н)

ADAM
Adam ate the apple and our teeth still ache—1618 (О)
Adam must have an Eve, to blame her for what he has done—2134 (У)
We are all Adam's children—238 (В)

ADIEU
Never say adieu to the devil until you have met him—1468 (Н)

ADMONISH
Admonish your friends in private, praise then in public—124 (В)

ADO
Much ado about nothing—1146 (М)

ADVANTAGE
Every advantage has its disadvantage—54 (Б)

ADVERSITY
Adversity flatters no man—210 (В), 391 (Г), 392 (Г), 900 (К), 1294 (Н), 1323 (Н), 1397 (Н)
Adversity has no friends—204 (В)
Adversity is a good discipline (a good teacher, a great schoolmaster—33 (Б), 170 (В), 388 (Г), 1595 (О)
Adversity is the test of friendship—521 (Д)
Adversity is the touchstone of virtue—686 (З)
Adversity makes men wise—33 (Б), 1250 (Н)
Adversity makes strange bedfellows—171 (В)
Adversity tries virtue—686 (З)
Sweet are the uses of adversity—1276 (Н)
There is no education like adversity—33 (Б), 170 (В), 388 (Г)

ADVICE
Advice after mischief is taken like medicine after death—487 (Д)
Advice comes too late when a thing is done—487 (Д)
Advice is handy only before trouble comes—487 (Д)
Advice should precede the act—487 (Д)
Give neither salt nor advice till asked for it—1262 (Н)
Good advice is beyond price—2192 (Х)
Good advice never comes too late—2131 (У)
We should never be too proud to take advice—2193 (Х)
When a thing is done, advice comes too late—487 (Д)
You might as well physic the dead as give advice to an old man—2002 (С)

AFFECTION
Affection blinds reason—1085 (Л)

AFFLICTION
Afflictions are best blessings—1276 (Н)

Afflictions are blessings in disguise—1276 (Н)

AFRAID

He that is afraid of the wagging of feathers, must keep from among wild fowl—1824 (Р)

He that is afraid of wounds must not come near (nigh) a battle—186 (В)

He who is afraid of every nettle must not walk through the tall grass—186 (В)

AFTERNOON

Cloudy mornings turn to clear afternoons—1891 (С)

AFTER-WIT

After-wit is dear bought—619 (З), 621 (З)

After-wit is everybody's wit—620 (З)

AGAINST

He that is not with me is against me—946 (К)

AGE

Age breeds aches—364 (Г), 1248 (Н), 2003 (С), 2004 (С)

If youth but knew and (,if) age but could—561 (Е)

Old age is a heavy burden—2003 (С)

Old age is sickness of itself—2004 (С)

What youth is used to, age remembers—2263 (Ч)

When the age is in the wit is out—2243 (Ч)

AGUE

Agues come on horseback but go away on foot—20 (Б), 90 (Б)

AIM

Well-aimed—1279 (Н)

AIR

It is still quite in the air—2351 (З)

Man cannot live on air (А)—743 (И)

AKIN

No man is akin to the poor—1769 (П)

ALE

Ale in, truth out—750 (И)

/Good/ ale will make a cat speak—2312 (Ч)

When /the/ ale is in, wit is out—156 (В), 960 (К)

ALIKE

Not everything is alike—142 (В)

There are no two alike—142 (В), 143 (В)

ALIVE

Alive and kicking—571 (Е), 596 (Ж)

ALL

All for one, /and/ one for all—1522 (О)

All fouled up—435 (Д)

All's lost—435 (Д)

All or nothing /at all/—725 (И)

It's all over but the shouting—429 (Д)

It's all up—427 (Д), 434 (Д), 435 (Д)

Not all there—2125 (У)

ALLOY

No joy without alloy—34 (Б), 1698 (П)

ALMOST

Almost never killed a fly—2332 (Ч)

Almost was never hanged—2332 (Ч)

ALMS

Alms never make poor—417 (Д)

Giving alms never lessens the stock—417 (Д)

No one becomes poor through giving alms—417 (Д)

ALMSGIVING

No one ever impoverished himself by almsgiving—417 (Д)

ALONG

Little along is better than a long none (А)—1104 (М)

ALWAYS

Always at it wins the day—833 (К)

AMATEUR

Amateur tactics cause grave wounds—1336 (Н), 1699 (П)

AMISS
Nothing comes amiss to a hungry man (stomach)—25 (Б)
When a man is not liked, whatever he does is amiss—2143 (У)

ANGEL
Angel is passing overhead (An)—1132 (М), 2052 (Т)
Angel on top but a devil underneath (An)—341 (Г), 694 (И), 1181 (Н), 1859 (С)
Angel on the street, a devil at home (An)—164 (В)
Men are not angels—235 (В)
Speak of angels and you'll hear the rustling of their wings—1513 (О)
Talk of the angel and you'll hear the fluttering of his wings—1513 (О)

ANGER
Anger and haste hinder /a/ good counsel—356 (Г)
Anger and love give bad counsel—356 (Г)
Anger is a sworn enemy—1240 (Н)
Anger profits nobody—1240 (Н)
Anger punishes itself—1240 (Н)
Good remedy for anger is delay (A)—848 (К)
Sleep with your anger—356 (Г), 848 (К)
When in anger, count to ten before you speak—848 (К)
When in anger, say the alphabet—848 (К)

ANGRY
Angry beggar gets a stone instead of a hand (The)—1240 (Н)
Angry man never wants woe (An)—1240 (Н)
He that is angry is seldom at ease—2108 (У)
If you are angry, count to ten /, if very angry count to ten again/—848 (К)
If you are angry, you may turn the buckle of your girdle behind you—848 (К)
Two to one in all things against the angry man—1240 (Н)
When angry count a hundred (recite the alphabet)—848 (К)

ANNOY
Every inch of joy has an ell of annoy—1698 (П)
/There is/ no joy without annoy—1698 (П)

ANOTHER
You are another—1612 (О)

ANSWER
Answer a fool according to his folly—1191 (Н)
Answer's a lemon (The)—2356 (З)
Ask a silly question and you'll get a silly answer—1191 (Н)
Like question, like answer—1191 (Н)
No answer is also an answer—1154 (М)
Silly question, silly answer—1191 (Н)
Soft answer turns away wrath (A)—984 (Л), 1692 (П)
Such answer as a man gives, such will he get—824 (К)

ANTICIPATION
There's more joy in anticipation than in realization—2064 (Т)

ANVIL
Iron anvil should have a hammer of feathers (An)—983 (Л), 986 (Л)

ANYTHING
Anything is better than nothing—1070 (Л), 1974 (С)

ANYTIME
Anytime is (means) no time—1592 (О)

APE
Ape is an ape, a varlet is a varlet, though they be clad in silk and scarlet (An)—827 (К)
Ape's an ape, a varlet's a varlet, though they be clad in silk or scarlet (An)—827 (К)
Old ape has an old eye (An)—2004 (С)
Old ape is taken at last (The)—2037 (Т)

APPAREL
Apparel makes the man—1517 (О)

APPEARANCE

Appearances are deceiving (deceptive)—168 (В), 723 (И), 1300 (Н), 1304 (Н), 1305 (Н), 1314 (Н)

Appearances go a great ways—1706 (П)

Judge not according to appearances—168 (В), 1417 (Н)

Never judge by (from) appearances—168 (В), 1417 (Н)

APPETITE

Appetite comes while (with) eating (The)—7 (А), 2255 (Ч)

Appetite furnishes the best sauce—368 (Г)

For a good appetite there is no hard bread—368 (Г)

APPLE

Adam ate the apple and our teeth still ache—1618 (О)

Apple does not fall far from the tree (An)—953 (К), 2357 (Я)

Apple never falls far from the tree (An/The)—2357 (Я)

Apples don't grow on monkey-trees—1220 (Н), 1644 (П)

Apples on the other side of the wall are sweetest (The)—2185 (Х)

As the apple, so the fruit—2357 (Я)

How we apples swim!—703 (И), 732 (И)

Many a rosy apple is rotten to the core—692 (И), 1845 (Р), 1859 (С)

No good apple on a sour stock—1616 (О)

One bad apple spoils the lot—1597 (О)

One rotten apple can spoil a lot of good ones (a whole barrel full, the whole bunch)—1597 (О)

One rotten apple decays the (will spoil a) bushel—1597 (О)

Prize apple can have a worm inside (A)—692 (И), 737 (И)

Reddest apple may have a worm in it (The)—692 (И), 737 (И), 1859 (С)

Rotten apple injures its companion (neighbours) (The)—1597 (О)

There is at least one rotten apple in every barrel—237 (В)

There's a bad apple in every box—237 (В)

Your neighbour's apples are the sweetest—2185 (Х)

APPRECIATE

We never appreciate the sunshine and the rainbow until the storm clouds hang low—2292 (Ч)

APRIL

April and May are the keys of the year—140 (В)

April showers bring /forth/ May flowers—8 (А)

Cold April and a wet May fill the barn with grain and hay (A)—9 (А), 1108 (М)

Dry March, wet April and cool May fill barn and cellar and bring much hay (A)—9 (А), 1108 (М)

When April blows its horn, it's good for the hay and corn—140 (В)

ARCHER

Archer who overshoots the mark misses, as well as he that falls short of it (The)—2332 (Ч)

ARGUMENT

Some people think that the louder they shout, the more persuasive their argument is—2343 (Ш)

ARK

Ark rested on Mt. Ararat (The)—1590 (О)

ARM

Stretch your arm no farther than your sleeve will reach—1708 (П)

ARMY

Army of hogs led by a lion is more formidable than an army of lions led by a hog (An)—11 (А)

Army of stags led by a lion would be more formidable than one of lions led by a stag (An)—11 (А)

Headless army fights badly (A)—11 (А), 1948 (С)

ARROW

Arrow shot upright falls on the shooter's head (An)—1876 (С)

Draw not your bow till your arrow is fixed—1767 (П)

ART

He that sips many arts drinks none—613 (З)

He who has an art has a place everywhere—1396 (Н), 1988 (С), 2121 (У)

He who has an art, has everywhere a part—1396 (Н), 1830 (Р), 1988 (С), 2121 (У)

ARTIST

Every artist was first an amateur—2008 (С)

ASK

Better ask than lose your way—505 (Д)

Better ask twice than lose yourself once—505 (Д)

Better to ask than go astray—505 (Д)

Don't ask me—1518 (О)

He that cannot ask, cannot live—2016 (С)

It costs nothing to ask—649 (З)

It is better to ask twice than to go wrong once—505 (Д)

It never hurts to ask—649 (З)

Lose nothing for asking—649 (З)

No one can ask for more than your best—1213 (Н)

Nothing is lost for asking—642 (З), 649 (З), 1985 (С)

There is no harm in asking—642 (З), 649 (З), 1985 (С)

ASS

Ass dreams of thistles (The)—372 (Г), 878 (К), 1409 (Н), 1957 (С)

Ass endures his burden, but no more than his burden (An)—60 (Б)

Asses fetch the oats and the horses eat them—529 (Д), 1114 (М)

Ass is beautiful to an ass, and a pig to a pig (An)—1672 (П)

Ass is /but/ an ass, though laden with gold (An)—827 (К), 1236 (Н), 1563 (О)

Ass is known by his ears (An)—1566 (О)

Ass laden with gold climbs to the top of the castle (An)—439 (Д)

Ass loaded with gold still eats thistles (The)—162 (В), 1916 (С), 2342 (Ш)

Ass to an ass is beautiful (An)—1672 (П)

Braying of an ass does not reach heaven (The)—1949 (С)

Even if the ass is laden with gold, he will seek his food among the thorns—162 (В), 1916 (С), 2342 (Ш)

Every ass likes (loves) to hear himself bray—1849 (С)

Every ass thinks himself worthy to stand with the king's horses—257 (В), 974 (К), 1002 (Л), 1991 (С)

He is an ass that brays against another ass—537 (Д)

He that cannot beat the ass, beats the saddle—880 (К), 1392 (Н)

He that makes himself an ass must not complain if men ride him—1199 (Н)

If an ass bray at you, don't bray at him—537 (Д)

If an ass goes a-traveling, he'll not come back a horse—195 (В), 1696 (П)

If an ass goes a-travelling, he will not come home a horse—195 (В), 1696 (П)

It's a sorry ass that will not bear his own burden—465 (Д)

Jest with an ass and he will flap (slap) you in the face with his tail—1875 (С)

Living ass is better than a dead lion (A)—590 (Ж)

Make yourself an ass and everyone will lay a sack on you—910 (К)

Old ass is never good (An)—120 (Б), 364 (Г), 1248 (Н), 2003 (С)

One ass calls another long ears—1406 (Н), 2334 (Ч)

One ass scrubs another—1865 (С)

What good can it do to an ass to be called a lion?—1407 (Н)

When the ass dreams it is of thistles—1022 (Л)

Where ever an ass falls there will he never fall again—1222 (Н)

ASSOCIATE
Associate with cripples and you learn to limp—1904 (С)

ATTACK
Attack is the best /form (method) of/ defence—1249 (Н)

ATTRACT
Each kind attracts its own—1113 (М), 1672 (П), 1842 (Р)

AUDACITY
Success is the child of audacity—1578 (О), 1937 (С)

AUNT
If my aunt had been a man, she'd have been my uncle—560 (Е)
So's your aunt Susie—1612 (О)

AUTHOR
Like author, like book—802 (К)

AVARICE
Avarice is never satisfied—28 (Б), 1377 (Н)
Avarice is the old man's sin—166 (В)
Avarice loses all in seeking to gain all—580 (Ж), 2081 (Т)
Poverty is in want of much, avarice of everything—28 (Б)
Poverty wants many things and avarice all—28 (Б)
Poverty wants some things, luxury many things, avarice all—28 (Б)

AXE
Little axe cuts down big trees (A)—1099 (М)
Smallest axe may fell the hugest oak (The)—1098 (М), 1165 (М)

B

BABE
Babe in the house is a wellspring (well-spring) of pleasure (A)—457 (Д)

BABY
It's the crying baby that gets the milk—460 (Д)
Rich get richer, and the poor get babies (The)—77 (Б)
Rich man for dogs and a poor man for babies (A)—77 (Б)

BACK
Back is shaped to the load (The)—119 (Б)
God fits the back to the burden—119 (Б)
God shapes the back for the burden—119 (Б)
You can't back out—150 (В), 1201 (Н), 1751 (П)

BAD
Bad is called good when worse happens—241 (В)
Bad is never good until worse happens—241 (В)
Good for the liver may be bad for the spleen—10 (А)
It's never so bad that it can't be worse—1147 (М)
Nothing so bad but it might have been worse—1147 (М), 2349 (Э)
Nothing so bad in which there is not something good—1456 (Н)
Nothing so bad that it couldn't be worse—1147 (М), 2349 (Э)
That which is good for the back, is bad for the head—10 (А)
There's good and bad in everything—54 (Б)

BAG
Empty bag cannot stand /upright/ (An)—1797 (П)
It's hard for an empty bag to stand upright—1797 (П)

BAIT
Bait hides the hook (The)—982 (Л), 2201 (Х)
Fish will soon be caught that nibbles at every bait (The)—1086 (Л)
He that would catch a fish must venture his bait—1752 (П)
Without bait you can't catch fish—1387 (Н)

BALL
Ball comes to the player (The)—1207 (Н)

If the ball does not stick to the wall, it will at least leave a mark—837 (К)
That's the way the ball bounces—2035 (Т)

BANANA
If you want roasted bananas, you must burn your fingers first—1116 (М)

BANK
You can't put it in the bank—1976 (С)

BANQUET
There's no great banquet but some fare ill—1539 (О)

BARBER
Barber learns to shave by shaving (A)—1190 (Н)
Every barber knows that—98 (Б)

BARGAIN
Bargain is a bargain (A)—2095 (У)
Bargain is a pinch-purse (A)—458 (Д), 2197 (Х)
Good bargain is a pick-purse (A)—458 (Д), 2197 (Х)
Make the best of a bad bargain—307 (В)

BARK
Barking dog has no bite (A)—1952 (С)
Barking dog never bites (A)—1952 (С)
Barking dogs do not (seldom) bite—1952 (С)
Dog's bark is worse than his bite (A)—1140 (М)
His bite isn't as bad as his bark—1140 (М)
More bark than bite—701 (И), 1140 (М)

BARKER
Great barkers are no biters—1952 (С)
Greatest barkers are not the greatest biters (The)—1952 (С)
Slowest barker is the surest biter (The)—1273 (Н)

BARLEY
Barley-corn is better than a diamond to a cock (a rooster) (A)—862 (К), 927 (К)
It is ill prizing of green barley—2228 (Ц)

BARREL
Empty barrels make the greatest din (sound)—1791 (П)
Neither barrel is a (the) better herring—2215 (Х)

BASHFUL
It is only the bashful that lose—2016 (С)

BASHFULNESS
Bashfulness is an enemy to poverty—2016 (С)
Bashfulness is no use to the needy—2016 (С)

BE
Be as it may—110 (Б)
Be off with you—201 (В)
Be that as it may—110 (Б)
That which hath been is now; and that which is to be hath already been—1486 (Н)
What has been, has been—2281 a (Ч)
What is to be, will be—2261 (Ч)
What must be, must be—1610 (О), 2261 (Ч)
What used to be will be again—1486 (Н)
What will be, will be—110 (Б), 423 a (Д), 2265 b (Ч)

BEAM
Cast the beam out of your own eye before you try to cast the mole from the eyes of your neighbor—1459 (Н)

BEAN
Every bean has its black—735 (И)

BEAK
It's better to be the beak of a hen than the tail of an ox—1045 (Л)

BEAR
As a bear has no tail, for a lion he will fail—1295 b (Н)

Bear wants a tail and cannot be lion (The)—290 (В), 674 (З), 974 (К), 1002 (Л), 1991 (С)
Catch the bear before you cook him—1115 (М)
Catch the bear before you sell his skin—1115 (М)
Don't sell the bear's skin before you have caught the bear (you've caught him)—1388 (Н)
If it had been a bear, it would have bitten you—646 (З), 1355 (Н)
If it were a bear, it would bite you—646 (З), 1355 (Н)
I was not born yesterday—2371 (Я)
Man may bear till his back break (A)—286 (В), 2244 (Ч)
Take no more on you than you're able to bear—60 (Б)
Time to catch bears is when they're out—2057 (Т)

BEARD
Beard creates lice, not brains—100 (Б)
Beard does not make the doctor or philosopher (The)—2124 (У)
Beard well lathered is half a shave (A)—656 (З)
Brains don't lie in the beard (The)—100 (Б), 2124 (У)
If a beard were a sign of smartness, the goat would be Socrates—2124 (У)
If the beard were all, the goat might preach—2124 (У)
It is not the beard that makes the philosopher—2124 (У)
Old goat is never more revered for his beard (An)—100 (Б)

BEAST
Beast that goes always never wants blows (The)—844 (К)
Who goes a beast to Rome, a beast returns—195 (В)
Willful beast must have his own way (A)—188 (В)

BEAT
Beat it!—201 (В), 1902 (С)
Beats me—1518 (О)
Can you beat it (that)!—2350 (З)
He that cannot beat the ass (the horse), beats the saddle—880 (К), 1392 (Н)
Many beat the sack and mean the miller—65 (Б), 880 (К)
That beats cock-fighting (everything, grandmother, the Dutch)—2314 (Ч)

BEAUTY
Beauty and folly are old companions—1415 (Н)
Beauty and folly go often together—1415 (Н)
Beauty dies and fades away but ugly holds its own—1925 (С)
Beauty doesn't make the pot boil—886 (К)
Beauty is a fading flower—1925 (С)
Beauty is a fine thing, but you can't live on it—886 (К)
Beauty is as beauty does—1447 (Н), 1928 (С)
Beauty is but skin-deep; common sense is thicker than water—884 (К)
Beauty is in the beholder's eyes—769 (К)
Beauty is in the eye of the beholder—769 (К), 1361 (Н), 1395 (Н), 1701 (П)
Beauty is no inheritance—884 (К), 886 (К)
Beauty is only skin-deep—884 (К), 885 (К), 1356 (Н), 1925 (С)
Beauty is only skin-deep; goodness goes to the bone—885 (К), 1356 (Н), 1925 (С)
Beauty is skin-deep; it is the size of the heart that counts—885 (К), 1356 (Н)
Beauty lasts only a day; ugly holds its own—1925 (С)
Beauty lies in the lover's eyes—769 (К)
Beauty may have fair leaves but (yet) bitter fruit—1301 (Н), 1859 (С)
Beauty will buy no beef—886 (К)
Beauty won't buy groceries—886 (К)
One cannot live on beauty alone—886 (К)

BED

As you make your bed, so you must (will) lie in it—792 (К), 825 (К)

Go to bed with the lamb and rise with the lark—1036 (Л)

Too much bed makes a dull head—36 (Б), 1007 (Л)

You made your bed, now lie in it—1846 (С), 1848 (С)

BEE

Bees that have honey in their mouths have stings in their tails—1170 (М)

Bee that gets the honey doesn't hang around the hive (The)—182 (В)

Look for the honey where you see the bee—317 (Г)

No bees, no honey; no work, no money—329 (Г)

Where there are bees, there is honey—317 (Г)

Where there is honey to be found, there will be bees—317 (Г)

While honey lies in every flower, no doubt, it takes a bee to get the honey out—50 (Б), 317 (Г)

BEEF

Such beef, such broth—821 (К), 2284 (Ч)

BEER

It's the beer speaking (talking)—1804 (П)

BEGGAR

Beggar can never be bankrupt (A)—377 (Г)

Beggar ennobled does not know his own kinsman (A)—628 (З)

Beggar may sing before a footpad (a pickpocket, the thief) (The)—377 (Г), 950 (К)

Beggar's bag has no bottom (The)—40 (Б), 2018 (С)

Beggars cannot (can't) be choosers—25 (Б), 76 (Б)

Beggars mounted run their horses to death—407 (Д)

Beggar's purse is always empty (is bottomless) (A)—2018 (С)

Beggar's scrip is never filled (A)—2018 (С)

Beggar's wallet has no bottom (is a mile to the bottom) (The)—40 (Б), 2018 (С)

Give a beggar a horse and he'll ride it to death—407 (Д)

Let beggar match with beggar—308 (В)

Small change is riches to a beggar—1331 (Н)

Sue a beggar and get (you'll get) a louse—375 (Г)

There is no pride like that of a beggar grown rich—628 (З)

BEGIN

Bad beginning makes a good ending (A)—1639 (П)

Begin nothing until you have considered how it is to be finished—1258 (Н)

Begun is half done—1750 (П)

Better never begin than never make an end—846 (К)

Better never to begin than never to make an end—846 (К)

Good to begin well, better to end well—995 (Л), 1272 (Н), 1374 (Н), 1416 (Н)

He who begins many things finishes but few—1886 (С)

Ill begun, ill done—1652 (П)

Let him that begins the song make an end—361 (Г), 652 (З)

Poor beginning makes a good ending (A)—1639 (П)

Well begun is half done—477 (Д), 656 (З)

BEGINNING

Bad beginning has a bad ending (A)—809 (К), 1652 (П), 2222 (Х)

Bad beginning makes a good ending (A)—1639 (П)

Bad beginning makes a worse ending (A)—1652 (П), 2222 (Х)

Beginning is not everything (The)—995 (Л), 1272 (Н), 1374 (Н), 1416 (Н)

Beginning is the hardest (The)—1025 (Л)

Beware beginnings—1025 (Л)

Every beginning is hard—1025 (Л)

Everything has (must have) a beginning—44 (Б)
Good beginning is half the battle (the business, the task) (A)—477 (Д)
Good beginning makes a good ending (A)—809 (K), 1799 (П)
Ill beginning, (has) an ill ending (An)—1652 (П)
In every beginning think of the end—1258 (Н)
Poor beginning makes a good ending (A)—1639 (П)
Such beginning, such end—809 (K)
This is only the beginning—2058 (Т), 2352 (Э)

BEHIND
All behind—like a fat woman—1064 (Л)

BELIEVE
Believe it or not—2210 (X)
Believe not all that you see nor half what you hear—1091 (Л), 1303 (Н), 1316 (Н)
Believe only half of what you hear—1303 (Н)
Believe only half of what you see and nothing you hear—1091 (Л), 1303 (Н), 1316 (Н)
He who believes easily is easily deceived—926 (K)
It is easy to believe what you want to—2240 (Ч)
Men believe what they will to believe—2240 (Ч)
We soon believe what we desire—2240 (Ч)

BELL
Bell, once rung, cannot be rerung (A)—1872 (C)
Cracked bell can never sound well (A)—1718 (П), 1812 (P), 1906 (C), 2070 (Т)
Cracked bell is never sound (A)—1718 (П), 1906 (C), 2070 (Т)
Fool's bell is soon rung (A)—2098 (У), 2361 (Я)
God comes to see us without a bell—1939 (C)

BELLY
Army goes on its belly (An)—2155 (У)
Belly carries the feet (the legs) (The)—176 (В), 743 (И), 1208 (Н), 1327 (Н), 1359 (Н), 1379 (Н), 2029 (C), 2155 (У)
Belly full of gluttony will never study willingly (A)—2030 (C)
Belly has no ears (The)—370 (Г), 371 (Г)
Belly is not filled with fair words (The)—614 (З), 1360 (Н), 1968 a, b (C)
Belly teaches all arts (The)—1498 (Н), 1992 (C)
Belly wants ears (The)—370 (Г)
Better belly burst than good victuals wasted—570 (Е)
Better fill a man's belly than his eye—1981 (C)
Better the belly burst than good drink (meat) lost—570 (Е), 1047 (Л), 1369 (Н), 2027 (C), 2204 (X)
Full belly does not understand an empty one (A)—2015 (C), 2032 (C)
Full belly makes a brave heart (A)—600 (Ж), 1745 (П)
Full belly makes a strong back (A)—743 (И), 2155 (У)
He whose belly is full believes not him who is fasting—81 (Б), 2032 (C)
Hungry bellies have no ears—370 (Г)
It's better a belly burst than good food wasted—570 (Е), 1047 (Л), 1369 (Н), 2027 (C), 2204 (X)
Lean belly never feeds a fat brain—371 (Г)
Man with a full belly thinks no one is hungry (A)—2032 (C)
Promises don't fill the belly—614 (З), 710 (И), 1229 (Н), 1360 (Н), 1505 (О), 1744 (П), 1968 a (C)
Way to a man's heart is through his belly (The)—1800 (П)
When the belly is full, the bones are (would be) at rest—600 (Ж), 743 (И), 1745 (П)
When the belly is full, the mind is among the maids—2156 (У)

When the belly is full, the mind is blank—2030 (С)

BEND
Better bend than break—902 (К), 1048 (Л)
Better bend the neck than bruise the forehead—1048 (Л)
Better bent than broken—1048 (Л)
It is better to bend than break—902 (К), 1048 (Л)

BENEFIT
One man works, and another reaps the benefits—529 (Д), 2200 (Х)

BERRY
Time to pick berries is when they're ripe (The)—2057 (Т)

BEST
All is for the best—2279 (Ч)
All is for the best in the best of /all/ possible worlds—227 (В), 2279 (Ч)
All that happens, happens for the best—2279 (Ч)
All things happen for the best—2279 (Ч)
Best is the enemy of the good (The)—1051 (Л)
If you cannot have the best, make the best of what you have—633 (З)
Rest is the best (The)—1568 (О)
That which is last is best—1568 (О)

BET
Bet's a bet (A)—2095 (У)
I'll bet my boots (my bottom dollar, my life)—415 (Д)
You bet /your boots (your /sweet/ life)—415 (Д)
You can bet your shirt—415 (Д)

BETTER
Better fed than taught—97 (Б), 138 (В), 1836 (Р)
Whatever happens will turn out for the better in the end—2279 (Ч)
You're no better than I am—1612 (О)

BETTY
It's all Betty—435 (Б)

BEWAIL
He who bewails himself has the cure in his hands—460 (Д)

BEWARE
Beware of a silent man and a dog that does not bark—1273 (Н)
Beware of no man more than thyself—2248 (Ч)

BIG
Bigger they are (come), the harder they fall (The)—302 (В)

BILL
Nothing ruins a duck but (like) his bill—1028 (Л), 2362 (Я), 2364 (Я)

BIRD
As the old bird sings, so the young ones twitter—2347 (Щ)
Bad bird, bad eggs—807 (К), 1616 (О), 1617 (О)
Bird has flown /the coop/ (The)—757 (И)
Bird in the hand is better than two in the bush (A)—1787 (П)
Bird in the hand is worth two in the bush (A)—70 (Б), 1065 (Л), 1066 (Л), 1421 (Н), 1787 (П)
Bird in the sack is worth two on the wing (A)—1421 (Н)
Bird is known by his note and a man by his talk (A)—681 (З)
Bird is known by its flight (A)—151 (В)
Bird is known by its note, and the man by his words (The)—681 (З)
Bird is known by its song (A)—681 (З)
Birds of a color flock together—1842 (Р)
Birds of a feather flock together—1113 (М), 1842 (Р)
Birds once snared fear all bushes—1788 (П)
Each bird likes his own nest best—261 (В), 276 (В)
Each bird loves to hear himself sing—289 (В)
Early bird catches (gets) the worm (The)—961 (К)
Every bird likes its own nest—276 (В)
Every bird likes to hear himself sing—289 (В)

Every bird thinks her /own/ nest beautiful (his nest best)—261 (В), 276 (В)
Faraway birds have fine feathers—1917 (С)
God gives (sends) every bird its food, but he does not throw it into the nest—1644 (П)
It is a foolish bird that defiles (fouls) its own nest—348 (Г)
It is an ill bird that fouls its own nest—348 (Г)
It is the early bird that catches the worm—961 (К)
It's a poor bird that will dirty its own nest—348 (Г)
Little bird told me (A)—1934 (С), 1972 (С)
Little bird whispered to me (A)—1934 (С)
Old bird is not /to be/ caught by (with) chaff (An)—1999 (С)
One bird in the cage is worth two in the bush—1421 (Н)
One bird in the net is better than a hundred flying—1421 (Н)
Old birds are hard to pluck—166 (В)
Older the bird, the more unwillingly it parts with its feathers (The)—166 (В)
Such /a/ bird, such /a/ nest—793 (К), 797 (К), 802 (М), 819 (К)
Such bird, such egg—2357 (Я)
There are no birds in the last year's nest—67 (Б)
You cannot catch old birds with chaff—1999 (С)

BIT
Bit in the morning is better than nothing all day (A)—1056 (Л)
Golden bit does not make a (the) horse any better (A)—827 (К), 839 (К), 1235 (Н), 1636 (П), 1743 (П)

BITCH
Whom God loves, his bitch brings forth pigs—335 (Г), 854 (К)

BITE
Bite on that—644 (З)
Don't bite off more than you can chew—60 (Б), 1838 a (Р)
His bite isn't as bad as his bark—1140 (М)
Once bitten (bit), twice shy—1788 (П)

BITER
Biter is /often (sometimes)/ bit (The)—921 (К), 1598 (О), 1711 (П)

BITTER
Bitter must come before the sweet (The)—34 (Б)
Every bitter has its sweet—1456 (Н)
That which was bitter to endure may be sweet to remember—2306 (Ч)
Those who have not tasted the bitterest of life's bitters can never appreciate the sweetest of life's sweets—951 (К), 1458 (Н)
We know the sweet when we have tasted the bitter 951 (К), 1291 (Н)
What is sweet in the mouth is oft bitter in the stomach—1918 (С)
Who has bitter in his mouth spits not /at/ all sweet—2108 (У)
Who has never tasted bitter knows not what is sweet—951 (К), 1291 (Н), 1458 (Н)

BITTERNESS
Every heart knows its bitterness—2103 (У)
Heart knows its own bitterness (The)—2103 (У)

BLACK
Black will take no other hue—2268 (Ч)
Every black has its white 1456 (Н)
Every white has its black—54 (Б), 735 (И)
I am black, but I am not the devil—1305 (Н)
Two blacks do not make a white—668 (З), 2326 (Ч)
You can't rub on a black pot without getting black—1451 (Н)

BLACKAMOOR
You cannot wash a blackamoor white—2268 (Ч)

BLACKSMITH
Blacksmith's horse and the shoemaker's family always go unshod (The)—1855 (C)

BLAME
Blame not others for the faults that are in you—1087 (Л), 2334 (Ч)
Praise publicly; blame privately—124 (B)

BLESSING
Blessings brighten as they take their flight—875 (K)
One's blessings are not known until lost—2227 (Ц), 2292 (Ч)

BLIND
Among the blind the one-eyed man is king—1173 (H), 1175 (H)
Blind man can judge no colors (A)—1921 (C)
Blind man is no judge of colors (A)—1348 (H), 1921 (C)
Blind man should not judge colo(u)rs (A)—1348 (H)
Blind man would be glad to see (A)—1922 (C)
Blind men can judge no colours—1921 (C)
He is very blind who does not see the sun—1924 (C)
If the blind lead the blind, both shall fall into the ditch—1923 (C)
In the land of the blind the one-eyed are kings—1173 (H), 1175 (H)
Nod is as good as a wink to a blind horse (A)—2224 (X)
Pebble and a diamond are alike to a blind man (A)—1921 (C), 1924 (C)
There are none so blind as those who will not see—2224 (X)
To the color-blind, all colors are alike—1921 (C)
When the blind lead the blind, they all go head over heels into the ditch—1923 (C)

BLOOD
Blood asks blood, and death must (will) death requite—895 (K)
Blood is blood—896 (K)
Blood is thicker than water—376 (Г), 896 (K), 1865 (C)
Blood will have blood—895 (K)
Human blood is all one color—238 (B)
You cannot get blood from a flint—826 (K)
You cannot get blood from (out of) a stone—654 (З), 826 (K), 2147 (У)
You cannot get blood from a turnip—654 (З), 2147 (У)
You can't get blood from a flint—826 (K)

BLOOM
Bloom is off the peach (the rose) (The)—2107 (У)

BLOT
Blot is no blot till (unless) it be hit (A)—1390 (H), 1443 (H)

BLOW
First blow does not fell the tree (The)—1965 (C)
First blow is half the battle (The)—1750 (П)
It will soon blow over—239 (B)

BLUE
There may be blue and better blue—142 (B), 143 (B), 1089 (Л), 2313 (Ч)

BOAST
Boast not of tomorrow, for you know not what a day may bring forth—2174 (X)
Do not boast of a thing until it is done—2228 (Ц)
Do not boast until you see the enemy dead—1468 (H)
Great boast, (and) small roast—1178 (H), 1214 (H), 1789 (П), 1794 (П), 1854 (C), 2173 (X), 2335 (Ш)

BOASTER
Great boaster, little doer—932 (K)

BOAT
Don't embark on two boats, for you'll be split and thrown on your back—422 (Д)
Every person should row his own boat—267 (B), 591 (Ж), 1419 (H)
I didn't come over on (come up with) the last boat—2371 (Я)

BODY
Deformed body may have a beautiful soul (A)—1362 (H)
Little bodies /may/ have great souls—1099 (M), 1105 (M), 1843 (P)
Only over my dead body—2061 (T)
When the head aches, all the body is the worse—11 (A)

BONE
Bones bear the beef home (The)—1171 a (M)
Bones bring meat to town—1171 a (M)
Broken bones well set become stronger—2274 (Ч)
Closer to the bone, the sweeter the meat (The)—1552 (O)
Dog will not cry (howl) if you beat him with a bone (A)—1326 (H)
For the last the bones—956 (K)
Nearer the bone, the sweeter the flesh (the meat) (The)—1552 (O), 1568 (O)
One bone, one flesh—1162 (M)
Sweetest meat is closest the bone (The)—1552 (O), 1568 (O)
To those who come late the bones—952 (K), 956 (K), 1680 (П)
Were it not for the bone in the leg, all would be carpenters—560 (E)
What is bred in the bone will not /come (go)/ out of the flesh—380 (Г), 383 (Г), 779 (K), 796 (K), 853 (K), 892 (K), 1776 (П), 1955 (C)
What's in the bone is in the marrow—383 (Г), 1776 (П)

BOOK
You cannot (can't) judge a book by its binding (cover)—168 (B), 1417 (H)

BOOR
Boor remains a boor though he sleeps on a silken bolster (A)—827 (K)

BORROW
Borrow and borrow adds up to sorrow—928 (K)
Borrowing brings sorrowing—928 (K)
He borrows like an angel and pays back like the devil himself—634 (З)
He that borrows must pay again with shame and loss—928 (K)
He that goes a-borrowing, goes a-sorrowing—928 (K)
He who likes borrowing dislikes paying—634 (З)
If you want to keep a friend, never borrow, never lend—888 (K)
Quick to borrow are always slow to pay—634 (З)

BORROWER
Borrower runs in his own debt (The)—928 (K)

BOTTOM
If you cannot see the bottom, do not cross the river—1347 (H)

BOUGH
Boughs that bear most, hang lowest (The)—1795 (П)

BOW
Better bow than break—902 (K), 1048 (Л)
Bow long bent at last waxes weak (A)—286 (B)
Bow too much bent will break (A)—286 (B)
Don't cut the bow you are standing on—1404 (H)
Draw not your bow till your arrow is fixed—1408 (H), 1767 (П)
Fiddle cannot play without the bow (The)—42 (Б)

BOWELS
Keep the bowels open, the head cool, and the feet warm and a fig for the doctors—452 (Д)

BOY
Boys will be boys—456 (Д)

BRAG
Brag is a good dog, but Holdfast is better—1503 (H)
Old brag is a good dog, but hold fast is a better one—1503 (H)
They brag most that can do least—932 (K)

BRAGGART
Great braggarts are little doers—932 (K)

Greatest braggarts are generally the greatest cowards (The)—272 (В)

BRAIN

Brains in the head saves blisters on the feet—624 (З)

Idle brain is the devil's workshop (An)—1006 (Л)

Money spent on the brain is never spent in vain—677 (З)

You haven't got the brains you were born with—2125 (У)

BRAMBLE

He who sows brambles reaps brambles—1598 (О)

BRANCH

Don't saw off the branch you are sitting on—1404 (Н)

BRAVE

None but the brave deserves the fair—966 (К), 1937 (С)

BRAY

Braying of an ass does not reach heaven (The)—1949 (С)

Braying of an jackass never reaches heaven (The)—1949 (С)

BRAZEN

Brazen it out!—307 (В)

BREAD

All bread is not baked in one oven—142 (В), 143 (В), 270 (В), 1089 (Л), 1494 (Н), 2089 (У), 2093 (У), 2106 (У)

All sorrows are less with bread—600 (Ж), 1683 (П)

Another's bread costs dear—404 (Д), 2329 (Ч)

Better is a slice of bread and garlic eaten at one's own table than a thousand dishes eaten under another's roof—1862 (С)

Bitter bread of dependence is hard to chew (The)—2329 (Ч)

Bitter is the bread of charity—404 (Д), 2329 (Ч)

Bread always falls buttered side down—132 (В), 565 (Е)

Bread always falls on the buttered side (The)—565 (Е)

Bread is the staff of life—53 (Б), 2177 (Х)

Bread never falls but on its buttered side (The)—132 (В), 565 (Е)

Bread today is better than cake tomorrow—1065 (Л), 1423 (Н)

Cast thy bread upon the waters, for thou shalt find it after many days—472 (Д), 836 (К)

Cast your bread upon the water; it will return to you a hundredfold—472 (Д), 836 (К)

Don't quarrel with your bread and butter—1383 (Н), 1584 (О)

Dry bread at home is better than roast meat abroad—499 (Д), 500 (Д), 1862 (С)

Eaten bread is soon forgotten—482 (Д)

Griefs with bread are less—600 (Ж), 1683 (П)

If you have bread, don't look for cake—1383 (Н), 1584 (О)

I had rather ask of my fire brown bread than borrow of my neighbour white—1862 (С)

Man cannot (does not, shall not) live by bread alone—1471 (Н)

No such thing as brown bread—53 (Б), 2177 (Х)

Not by bread alone—1471 (Н)

That's the way the bread rises—2035 (Т)

They that have no other meat, bread and butter are glad to eat (gladly bread and butter eat)—578 (Е), 579 (Е), 633 (З), 1174 (Н), 2028 (С)

What bread men break is broke to them again—824 (К)

Who goes for a day into the forest should take bread for a week—559 (Е)

Whose bread I eat, his song I sing—858 (К), 1264 (Н), 1589 (О), 1693 (П), 2109 (У), 2241 (Ч), 2333 (Ч)

You buttered your bread; now eat it—1846 (С)

You can't eat the same bread twice—1525 (О)

BREAK
It that lies not in your gate breaks not your shin—1419 (Н)
Never be breaking your shin on a stool that is not in your way—1419 (Н)
Who breaks, pays—1848 (С)

BREATH
Don't hold your breath—453 (Д)
Keep your breath to cool your porridge (soup)—577 (Е)
One man's breath is another man's death—2307 (Ч)
Save your breath to cool your broth (porridge)—577 (Е)
Take a deep breath—555 (Д)

BREATHE
Breathe easy—555 (Д)

BREEDING
Best colt needs breeding (The)—992 (Л), 2118 (У)
Birth is much, but breeding is more—992 (Л), 2118 (У)

BREVITY
Brevity is the soul of wit—872 (К), 887 (К)

BRIDGE
Don't cross the bridge before you get (till you come) to it—1402 (Н)
Let every man praise the bridge he goes over—1386 (Н)
Let every man speak well of the bridge that carries him over—1386 (Н)
Praise the bridge that carries you over 1386 (Н)
There is no building a bridge across the ocean—305 (В)

BRIGHT
None too bright, could be better—427 (Д)

BRING
One only brings to any place what is in himself—2260 (Ч)

BROAD
It is as broad as it's long (as long as it's broad)—225 (В)

BROOK
Deep rivers move with silent majesty; shallow brooks are noisy—1791 (П)

BROOM
New broom sweeps clean (A)—1490 (Н)
New brooms sweep clean—1490 (Н)

BROTH
You made the broth, now sup it—1846 (С), 1848 (С)

BRUTUS
You too, Brutus!—752 (И)

BUCKET
I didn't come up in the last bucket—2371 (Я)

BUD
Nip the act while in the bud—2341 (Ш)

BUDGE
Don't budge if you are at ease where you are—1584 (О)

BULL
You may play with the bull till you get his horn in your eye—1477 (Н)

BULLET
Every bullet finds (has) its billet—1600 (О)
If the bullet has your name on it, you'll get it—1600 (О)

BULLY
Bullies are always (generally) cowards—1325 (Н)
Bully is always a coward (A)—1325 (Н), 2340 (Ш)

BURDEN
Ass endures his burden, but no more than his burden (An)—60 (Б)
Burden is light on the shoulders of others (The)—2320 (Ч)
Burden of one's choice is not felt (A)—1721 (П), 1867 (С)
Burden of one's own choice is not felt (The)—1721 (П), 1867 (С)
Burden one likes is cheerfully borne (The)—1867 (С)

Burden which one chooses is not felt (A)—1867 (C)
Chosen burden is not felt (A)—1867 (C)
Don't burden today's strength with tomorrow's load—432 (Д)
Every man must (shall) bear his own burden—2079 (T)
Every man thinks his own burden the heaviest—770 (K)
Every one thinks his own burden heavy—770 (K)
It is not the burden, but the overburden that kills the beast—60 (Б)
No one knows the weight of another's burden—2320 (Ч)
Too long burden makes weary bones—1177 (H)
Voluntary (willing) burden is no burden (A)—1867 (C)
Your neighbor's burden is always light—2320 (Ч)

BURN
Burn not your house to frighten the mouse /away/—1564 (O), 1565 (O)
Burn not your house to rid of the mouse—1564 (O), 1565 (O)
Burn not your house to scare away the mice—1564 (O), 1565 (O)
Once burned, twice shy—1507 (O)
Once burnt, twice cautious—1507 (O)

BURY
Bury the past—970 (K), 2295 b (Ч)
Let the dead bury the dead—970 (K), 2295 b (Ч)

BUSH
Bad bush is better than an open field (A)—1174 (H)
Every man bows to the bush he gets bield of—858 (K), 1264 (H), 1589 (O), 1693 (П), 2109 (У), 2241 (Ч), 2333 (Ч)
One beats the bush, and another catches the birds (has the hare, takes the bird)—529 (Д), 1114 (M)

BUSHEL
Bushel of wheat is made up of single grains (A)—664 (З), 1686 (П), 1740 (П)

BUSINESS
Business before pleasure—436 (Д), 864 (K)
Business comes before pleasure—864 (K)
Business first, pleasure afterwards—436 (Д), 864 (K)
Business is business—515 (Д), 1738 (П)
Business is business, and love is love—515 (Д), 1738 (П)
Business is the salt of life—337 (Г)
Everybody's business is nobody's business—320 (Г), 2145 (У)
Mind your own business—1419 (H)
That's no business of mine—1159 (M), 1372 (H)
You can't mix business and pleasure—433 (Д), 696 (И)

BUSY
Ever busy, ever bare—1613 (O)
Who is more busy than he who has least to do?—948 (K)

BUTCHER
Butcher looked for his knife and it was (while he had it) in his mouth (The)—646 (З), 1355 (H)

BUTTER
Butter is good for anything but to stop an oven—1109 (M)
Butter to butter is no relish—1110 (M)
No butter will stick to my (his) bread—132 (B), 1172 (H)

BUTTONHOLE
If you miss the first buttonhole, you will not succeed in buttoning up your coat—809 (K), 1652 (П), 2222 (X)

BUY
Do not buy a pig in a poke—874 (K)
Never buy anything before you see it—874 (K)
Try it before you buy it—874 (K)

BUZZ
What's buzzing /cousin/?—2290 (Ч)

BYGONES
Let bygones be bygones—121 (Б), 970 (K), 2281 b (Ч), 2295 b (Ч), 2305 (Ч)

C

CA
Ca me, ca thee—2077 (Т)

CACKLE
Cackling hen does not always lay (A)—608 (З)
Don't cackle till your egg is laid—1321 (Н)
He that would have eggs must endure the cackling of hens—1073 (Л), 1077 (Л)
'Tis not the hen that cackles most that lays the most eggs—608 (З), 915 (К), 932 (К), 1143 (М)

CAESAR
Caesar's wife must be above suspicion—587 (Ж)
Render to (unto) Caesar the things that (which) are Caesar's—767 b (К), 835 (К)

CAGE
Fine cage does not fill a bird's belly (A)—1363 (Н)
Fine cage won't feed the /hungry/ bird (A)—1363 (Н)
Golden cage is still a cage (A)—682 (З)
Nightingales will not sing in a cage—682 (З)
Nightingale won't sing in a cage (A)—682 (З)

CAKE
Cake never falls but on its buttered side (The)—132 (В), 565 (Е)
You can't eat your cake and have it /too/—1525 (О)

CALAMITY
Calamity and prosperity are the touchstones of integrity—2245 (Ч)
Calamity is the man's true touchstone—2245 (Ч)

CALF
As well for the cow calf as for the bull—1884 (С)
Bawling calf soon forgets its mother (A)—2040 (Т)
Don't eat the calf in the cow's belly—2228 (Ц)
Give a calf rope enough and it will hang itself—407 (Д), 650 (З)
He who has carried the calf will be able by and by to carry the ox—55 (Б)
When the calf is drowned, we cover the well—850 (К)

CALM
After a storm comes a calm—804 (К), 1724 (П), 1725 (П)
After the storm comes the calm—804 (К), 1724 (П), 1725 (П)

CAN
I would if I could, but I can't—1810 (Р)

CANDLE
Game is not worth the candle (The)—698 (И), 1514 (О)
You cannot burn the candle at two ends—1525 (О)

CANDOR
Candor breeds hatred—1761 (П), 1762 (П)

CANOE
Paddle your own canoe—1419 (Н)

CANYON
Before you go into a canyon, know how you'll get out—1347 (Н)

CAP
Cap fits (The)—1279 (Н)
Cap in hand never harmed anyone—1689 (П), 1690 (П)
If the cap fits, put it on (wear it)—673 (З), 1183 b (Н)

CAPER
Cut your capers—201 (В)

CAPTAIN
Every ship needs a captain—11 (А), 1519 (О)
Such captain, such retinue—817 (К)
Two captains will sink the (will wreck a) ship—320 (Г), 2145 (У)

CARAVAN
Dogs bark, but the caravan goes on (The)—1954 (С)

CARCASS
Wheresoever the carcass is, there will eagles (ravens) be gathered—1223 (Н)
Where the carcass is, there the buzzards gather (the ravens will collect together, will the eagles be gathered)—1223 (Н)

CARD
Cards are the devil's books (tools)—697 (И)
Lucky at (in) cards, unlucky in love—131 (В)
Unlucky at cards, lucky in love—1282 (Н)

CARE
Another's cares will not rob you of sleep—386 (Г), 659 (З), 2316 (Ч), 2318 (Ч), 2321 (Ч), 2325 (Ч)
Care brings grey hair—210 (В), 900 (К), 1294 (Н), 1323 (Н), 1397 (Н)
Care is beauty's thief—1294 (Н), 1323 (Н), 1397 (Н)
Care is no cure—1397 (Н)
Care killed the cat—900 (К), 1397 (Н)
Hang care—610 (З)
Leave your cares to the wind—610 (З)
Little goods (wealth), little care—38 (Б), 1123 (М)
Many cares make the head white—1397 (Н)

CAREFUL
You cannot be too careful—57 (Б)

CARPENTER
Door of the carpenter is loose (The)—1855 (С), 2330 (Ч)
Like carpenter, like chips—802 (К), 1649 (П)
Such carpenter, such chips—802 (К), 1649 (П)

CARRION
Carrion crows bewail the dead sheep, and then eat them—1677 (П)

CARROT
Carrot in the hand is worth two in the midden (A)—1787 (П)

CARRY
Carry me out and bury me decently—1826 (Р), 1858 (С)
He carries well to whom it weighs not—2320 (Ч)
He who has carried the calf will be able by and by to carry the ox—55 (Б)
If you agree to carry the calf, they'll make you carry the cow—910 (К)

CART
Best cart may overthrow (The)—866 (К)
Unhappy man's cart is easy to overthrow (An)—840 (К), 845 (К), 857 (К), 1172 (Н), 1253 (Н), 1658 (П)
Unhappy man's cart is easy to tumble (An)—1172 (Н)

CASK
Every cask smells of the wine it contains—2260 (Ч)

CASKET
None can guess the jewel by the casket—168 (В)

CASTLE
House is a castle which the king cannot enter (The)—1149 (М)
Man's home (house) is his castle (A)—1149 (М)
My house is my castle—1149 (М)

CAT
All cats are alike (black) at night—1493 (Н)
All cats are gray (grey) in the dark—1493 (Н)
All cats look alike in the dark—1493 (Н)
All cats love fish but fear to wet their paws—755 (И)
Bad cat deserves a bad rat (A)—799 (К), 808 (К), 814 (К), 823 (К), 1664 (П), 1679 (П), 1681 (П), 1723 (П)
Blate cat, a proud mouse (A)—2142 (У)
Cat has nine lives (A)—881 (К)
Cat in gloves catches no mice (A/The)—50 (Б)

Cat is absent, the mice dance (The)—41 (Б)
Cat is mighty dignified until the dog comes along (by) (The)—272 (В), 1150 (М)
Cat knows whose butter he has eaten (The)—673 (З), 1183 b (Н)
Cat loves fish but dares not wet his feet (The)—2209 (Х)
Cat loves fish but hates water (The)—2209 (Х)
Cat may look at a king (A)—189 (В)
Cat may look at the queen (The)—189 (В)
Cats hide their claws—877 (К), 2201 (Х)
Cat would eat fish, but she will (would) not wet her feet (paws) (The)—755 (И), 2209 (Х)
Crying cat always gets the scratch (The)—2364 (Я)
He who plays with a cat must expect to be scratched—1477 (Н)
Mouse lordships where a cat is not (The)—41 (Б)
Muffled cats are not good mousers (catch no mice)—50 (Б)
Never was a mewing cat a good mouser—932 (К)
Put not the cat near the goldfish—1023 (Л)
Rats will play while the cat's away—41 (Б)
Scalded cat fears cold water (A/The)—1507 (О), 1626 (О)
Scalded cats fear even cold water—1507 (О), 1626 (О)
Send not a cat for lard—185 (В)
Shy cat makes a proud mouse (A)—2142 (У)
Singed cat dreads the fire (A)—1507 (О), 1626 (О)
Sleeping cats catch no mice—1145 (М), 1993 (С), 2212 (Х)
Son of the cat pursues the rat (The)—1587 (О)
So's your sister's cat—1612 (О)
That cat won't fight (won't jump)—2356 (З)
That that comes of a cat will catch mice—1587 (О)
To a good cat a good rat—1679 (П)
To a good rat a good cat—1205 (Н)
When the cat is full, then the milk tastes sour—2031 (С)
Well kens the mouse when the cat's out of the house—41 (Б)
When candles are out all cats are gray (grey)—1493 (Н)
When (While) the cat is away, the mice will play—41 (Б)
You can have no more of a cat but her skin—1974 (С)

CATCH
Catch before hanging—1115 (М), 1388 (М)
Catch no more fish than you can salt—60 (Б)
It's catch as catch can—1032 (Л)
You can't catch trout with dry trousers—50 (Б)

CAUSE
Men are blind in their own cause—2249 (Ч)
Nothing ever comes to pass without a cause—231 (В), 1971 (С)

CAUTION
Caution is the eldest child of wisdom—1573 (О)
Caution is the parent of safety—59 (Б), 1571 (О), 1572 (О)
Don't throw caution to the wind—59 (Б)

CAUTIOUS
Cautious seldom cry (The)—59 (Б), 1571 (О)

CAVIAR(E)
It is caviar(e) to the general—1290 (Н)

CELEBRATE
Don't celebrate victories before you have conquered—1321 (Н)

CEMETERY
From the cemetery no one is brought back—1127 (М)

CERTAINTY
Never leave (quit) certainty for hope—1383 (Н), 1584 (О)

CHAFF
No corn without chaff—54 (Б), 173 (В)
There is no wheat without chaff—173 (В)
There's no corn without chaff—173 (В)

CHAIN
Chain bursts at its weakest link (The)—336 (Г)

CHAIR
If you try to sit on two chairs, you'll sit on the floor—422 (Д)

CHANCE
Evil chance seldom comes alone (An)—22 (Б)
Let chance decide—110 (Б)

CHANGE
Change of pasture makes fat calves—182 (В)
In this world nothing is permanent except change—604 (Ж)
Nothing is permanent except changes—604 (Ж)
Small change is riches to a beggar—1331 (Н)
Time changes all things (everything)—245 (В)

CHARACTER
Brave and gentle character is often found under the humblest clothes (A)—742 (И), 1488 (Н)

CHARCOAL
You cannot wash charcoal white—2268 (Ч)

CHARGE
Double charge will rive a cannon—1668 (П), 1964 (С)
You can't charge the same man twice—1668 (П), 1964 (С)

CHARITY
Charity begins at home—265 (В), 903 (К), 1868 (С)

CHARLIE
Lots of luck, Charlie!—453 (Д), 847 (К)

CHARON
Charon waits for all—240 (В)

CHEAP
Best is best cheap—458 (Д)
Best is cheapest /in the end/ (The)—458 (Д)
Cheap goods are not good, good things are not cheap—458 (Д), 459 (Д)
Dear is cheap, and cheap is dear—458 (Д)
Dirt is cheat; it takes money to buy wool—458 (Д)
Good things are seldom cheap—2197 (Х)

CHEAT
Cheating play never thrives—1475 (Н), 2085 (У)
Cheats never prosper—1475 (Н), 2085 (У)

CHEATER
Cheaters never prosper (win)—1475 (Н), 2085 (У)

CHEEK
Cheek brings success—966 (К), 1937 (С)

CHEER
Cheer up—the worst is yet to come—2058 (Т), 2352 (Э)
Cheer up, things will get worse—2058 (Т), 2352 (Э)

CHEESE
Brotherly love for brotherly love, but cheese for money—514 (Д)

CHEST
Righteous man sins before an open chest (The)—328 (Г)

CHESTNUT
It's good to take the chestnuts out of the fire with the cat's (the dog's) paws—2200 (Х)

CHICKEN
Chicken has flown the coop (The)—757 (И)
Chickens today, feathers tomorrow—1643 (П), 1818 (Р), 1880 (С), 2229 (Ч)

Don't count your chickens before they are hatched—1425 (Н), 1438 (Н), 2228 (Ц)

CHIEF

All chiefs and no Indians—1882 (С)
When the chief fails, the host quails—11 (А), 1948 (С)

CHILD

Bitten child dreads a (the) dog (A/The)—1788 (П)
Bring up your beloved child with a stick—647 (З)
Burnt child dreads the fire (A)—68 (Б), 1507 (О), 1626 (О), 1788 (П)
Child may have too much of his mother's blessing (A)—647 (З)
Children and fools cannot lie—351 (Г)
Children and fools speak (tell) the truth—351 (Г)
Children are poor man's riches—77 (Б)
Children are the parents' riches—1697 (П)
Children are what their mothers are—789 (К)
Children tell in the highway what they hear by the fireside—2289 (Ч)
Children will be children—456 (Д)
Happy is he who is happy in his children—1259 (Н)
He that has no children knows not what is love—501 (Д)
House without children is a cemetery (The)—501 (Д)
If you want the truth, go to a child or a fool—351 (Г)
It takes children to make a happy family—457 (Д), 1259 (Н), 1697 (П), 1987 (С)
Little children have long ears—2288 (Ч)
Little children, little sorrows; big children, great sorrows—1102 (М), 1103 (М), 1106 (М)
Little children, little troubles, big children, big troubles—1102 (М), 1103 (М), 1106 (М)
Little children step on your toes, big children step on your heart—1102 (М), 1106 (М)
Many children, many cares; no children, no felicity—1987 (С)
Once a man and twice a child—2243 (Ч)
Rich get richer, and the poor have children (The)—77 (В)
Spare the rod and spoil the child—647 (З)
What children hear at home does soon fly (soon flies) abroad—2289 (Ч)
When a child is little, it pulls at your apron strings; when it gets older, it pulls at your heart strings—1102 (М)

CHIN

Keep your chin up!—307 (В)

CHIP

Carpenter is known by his chips (A)—154 (В)
/Good/ workman is known by his chips (A)—154 (В)
Little chips light great fires—1099 (М)
You can tell a woodsman by his chips—154 (В)

CHOICE

Quick choice, long repentance—588 (Ж)
There is little choice in a barrel of rotten apples—1174 (Н)
There is small choice in rotten apples—1174 (Н)
There's no choice among stinking fish—1174 (Н)

CHRISTMAS

After a Christmas comes a Lent—1297 (II)
Christmas comes but once a year—1766 (П)
Coming, and so is Christmas—453 (Д)
I didn't fall off a Christmas tree—2371 (Я)

CHURCH

No church is so handsome that a man would desire straight to be buried—598 (Ж)
Old churches have dim windows—2004 (С)

Right church but wrong pew—2170 (Ф)

CHURCHYARD
Piece of churchyard fits everybody (A)—1938 (C)

CIVILITY
Civility costs nothing—985 (Л)
Mouth civility is no great pains but may turn to a good account—484 (Д)
Nothing costs less than civility—985 (Л)

CLAW
Claw me, and I'll claw thee—2077 (T)
Scratch my breech and I'll claw your elbow—2077 (T)

CLEAN
There's no one so clean that somebody doesn't think they're dirty—670 (З), 828 (К)
Who has a clean heart, has also a clean tongue—2276 (Ч)

CLEANLINESS
Cleanliness is akin (next) to godliness—2277 (Ч)

CLEAR
Rain before seven, clear before eleven—1296 (H)

CLIMB
Climb not too high lest the chips fall in thine eye—302 (B)
He that never climbed, never fell—941 (К), 1384 (H)
He who climbs too high is near a fall (to fall)—302 (B), 309 (Г)
Higher you climb, the harder you fall (The)—302 (B)
One who climbs high falls low—309 (Г)
Who never climbed never fell—941 (К), 1384 (H)

CLOAK
Although the sun shine, leave not thy (your) cloak at home—59 (Б)
Don't have thy cloak to make when it begins to rain—398 (Г), 785 (К)
Fool wants his cloak on a rainy day (A)—398 (Г)
Have not the cloak to be made when it begins to rain—398 (Г), 785 (К)
It is good to have a cloak for a rainy day—59 (Б)
Though the sun shine, leave not your cloak at home—59 (Б)

CLOCK
One cannot put back the clock—67 (Б)

CLOTH
Best cloth may have a moth in it (The)—735 (И)
It is a bad cloth that will take no colo(u)r—2269 (Ч)

CLOTHE
Clothe thee in war, arm thee in peace—394 (Г)

CLOTHES
Borrowed clothes never fit—1263 (H)
Clothes do not make the man—1313 (H), 1381 (H), 1707 (П)
Clothes make the man—1517 (O)
Dirty clothes are washed at home—1970 (C)
Fine clothes make the man—1517 (O)
Good clothes open all doors—1706 (П)

CLOUD
All clouds bring not rain—262 (B), 1310 (H)
Every cloud engenders not a storm—1309 (H), 1310 (H)
Every cloud has a silver lining—1456 (H)
Every cloud is not a sign of storm—262 (B), 1309 (H), 1310 (H)
Inner side of every cloud is bright and shining (The)—1456 (H)

CLUE
I haven't the clue—1518 (O)

COACH
We got the coach /up the hill/—732 (И)

COAL
Don't carry coals to Newcastle—163 (B)

If coals don't burn, they blacken—837 (К)

COAT

Cut the coat according to the cloth—595 (Ж), 1370 (Н), 1708 (П), 1712 (П)

Cut your coat according to your cloth—1370 (Н), 1708 (П), 1712 (П)

He who has but one coat cannot lend it—2238 (Ч)

It is not the gay coat that makes the gentleman—1381 (Н), 1707 (П)

No man can make a good coat with bad cloth—714 (И)

Ragged coat may cover an honest man (A)—1488 (Н)

Smart coat is a good letter of introduction (A)—1706 (П)

You can't always tell what is under a worn coat—742 (И)

You can't get warm on another's fur coat—1263 (Н)

COBBLE

They that can cobble and clout shall have work when others go without—1396 (Н)

COBBLER

Cobbler must not go beyond his last (A)—21 (Б)

Cobbler must stick to his last (The)—1295 a (Н)

Cobbler's child is always the worst shod (A)—1855 (С), 2330 (Ч)

Cobbler's children go unshod (The)—2330 (Ч), 2331 (Ч)

Cobbler's children never wear shoes (The)—2330 (Ч)

Cobbler's children usually go unshod (The)—1885 (С), 2330 (Ч)

Cobbler's wife is the worst shod (The)—1855 (С), 2331 (Ч)

Let not the cobbler go beyond his last—1295 a (Н)

Let the cobbler stick to his last—1295 a (Н), 1344 (Н), 1420 (Н)

COCK

As the old cock crows, so crows the young—1101 (М), 2347 (Щ)

As the old cock crows, the young cock learns (so the young bird chirrups)—1101 (М), 2347 (Щ)

Cock is /always/ bold on his own dunghill (A)—1238 (Н), 1239 (Н), 2144 (У)

Cock is master of (on) his own dunghill (The)—275 (В), 287 (В)

Cock is mighty in his own backyard (A)—275 (В), 287 (В), 1237 (Н), 1238 (Н), 1239 (Н), 2144 (У)

Cock is valiant on his own dunghill (A)—1238 (Н), 2144 (У)

Every cock crows the loudest upon his own dunghill—275 (В), 287 (В)

Every cock is proud on his own dunghill—275 (В)

Every cock sings in his own manner—258 (В), 270 (В), 2106 (У)

If you are a cock, crow; if a hen, lay eggs—62 (Б), 989 (Л), 1295 a (Н)

It will be a forward cock that crows in the shell—707 (И)

Let the cock crow or not, the day will come—1782 (П)

That cock won't fight—2356 (З)

Young cock crows as he hears the old one (The)—1101 (М)

COCONUT

That accounts for the milk in the coconut—3 (А), 198 a (В)

COFFEE

Wake up and smell the coffee—354 (Г), 1935 (С)

COIN

Much coin, much care—1141 (М)

COLD

Feed a cold and starve a fever—452 (Д)

Is it cold up there?—557 (Д)

COLOR

All colors will agree in the dark—1493 (Н)

COLT

Best colt needs breeding (The)—992 (Л), 2118 (У)

Young colts will canter—456 (Д)

COME

Come and eat your mutton with me—1133 (М)

Come and have a pickle—1133 (М), 2254 (Ч)
Come and have (take) pot luck (pot-luck) with us—1133 (М), 2254 (Ч)
Come hell or high water—110 (Б)
Come high, come low—110 (Б)
Come home with your knickers torn and say you found a shilling (the money)?—1858 (С)
Come what may (might)—110 (Б)
Coming, and so is Christmas—453 (Д)
Who doesn't come at the right time must take what is left—952 (К), 956 (К), 1680 (П)

COMEDY
Cut the comedy!—1278 (Н)

COMFORTER
Comforter's head never aches (The)—2325 (Ч)

COMMAND
As I will so I command—829 (К), 1869 (С), 2214 (Х)
He is not fit to command others that cannot command himself—968 (К)
If you can't command yourself, you can't command others—968 (К)
There is a great force hidden in sweet command—983 (Л), 986 (Л)

COMMANDER
Many commanders sink the ship—2145 (У)

COMMEND
Reprove your friend privately; commend him publicly—124 (В)

COMMUNICATION
Evil communications corrupt good manners—551 (Д), 1904 (С)

COMPANION
Merry companion is a wagon in the way (A)—63 (Б), 2132 (У)

COMPANY
Bread eaten, the company dispersed (The)—1215 (Н), 1645 (П), 1901 (С), 2176 (Х)
Cheerful company shortens the miles—63 (Б), 2132 (У)
Company in distress makes trouble less—1209 (Н), 1946 (С)
Company in misery makes it light—1209 (Н)
Good company on the road is the shortest cut—63 (Б), 256 (В), 1546 (О), 2132 (У)
Good company upon the road is shortest cut—63 (Б), 256 (В), 1546 (О), 2132 (У)
Having finished the meal, the company leaves—1215 (Н), 1645 (П), 1901 (С)
Man is known by the company he keeps (/A/)—1748 (П), 1896 (С), 1903 (С)
No road is long with good company—2132 (У)
Pleasant company shortens the miles—63 (Б), 2132 (У)
Present company excepted—1556 (О)
Show me your company, and I'll tell you who you are—1896 (С)

COMPARISON
It is /the/ comparison that makes men happy or miserable—241 (В)
Nothing is good or bad but by comparison—241 (В)

COMPLAIN
One who complains the most suffers less—92 (Б)
They complain most who suffer least—92 (Б), 994 (Л)

COMPROMISE
Lean compromise is better than a fat lawsuit (A)—2220 (Х)

CONFESSION
Confession is good for the soul—1774 (П)
Confession is the first step to repentance—1774 (П)
Honest confession is good for the soul (/An/)—1774 (П)
Open confession is good for the soul—1774 (П)

CONFIDE
Confide in an aunt and the whole world knows it (and the world will know)—232 (В), 676 (З), 2291 (Ч)

CONQUER
He conquers who endures—2046 (Т)
I came, I saw, I conquered—1777 (П)

CONSCIENCE
Clean conscience is a good pillow (A)—2110 (У)
Clear conscience fears no accuser (A)—1474 (Н), 2275 (Ч)
Clear conscience fears not false accusations (A)—1474 (Н)
Clear conscience is a coat of mail (a sure card) (A)—1474 (Н), 2275 (Ч)
Clear conscience is a wall of brass (A)—1474 (Н), 2275 (Ч)
Clear conscience laughs at false accusations (A)—1474 (Н)
Conscience does make (makes) cowards of us all—155 (В)
Conscience is the avenging angel in the mind—1476 (Н), 1958 (С)
Good conscience is a continual feast (A)—2110 (У)
Good conscience is a soft pillow (A)—2110 (У)
Good conscience knows no fear (A)—2110 (У)
Guilty conscience feels continuous fear (A)—155 (В), 1476 (Н)
Guilty conscience gives itself away—971 (К), 1183 а (Н)
Guilty conscience is a self-accuser (A)—882 (К), 1476 (Н), 1958 (С)
Guilty conscience is its own accuser (A)—882 (К), 1476 (Н), 1958 (С)
Guilty conscience needs no accuser (condemner) (A)—882 (К), 1476 (Н), 1958 (С)
No whip cuts so sharply as the lash of conscience—1476 (Н)
Quiet conscience sleeps in thunder (A)—2110 (У)
Safe conscience makes a sound sleep (A)—2110 (У)
There is no hell like a bad conscience—1476 (Н)
You cannot hide from your conscience—1476 (Н)

CONTENT
Be content with what you have—491 (Д)
Contented mind is a continual feast (A)—491 (Д)
Content is all—1433 (Н)
Content is better than riches—1433 (Н)
Content is happiness—1433 (Н)
Content is more than a kingdom—1433 (Н)
Happy is he who is content—1433 (Н)
He is not rich that possesses much, but he that is content with what he has—1433 (Н)
He is rich enough who is contented with little—491 (Д)
He who is content has enough—1433 (Н)
They need much whom nothing will content—1377 (Н)
To be content with little is true happiness—491 (Д)
Where content is there is a feast—1433 (Н)

CONTENTMENT
Contentment is better than riches—491 (Д)
Greatest wealth is contentment with a little (The)—491 (Д)

CONVERSATION
Conversation makes the man—681 (З), 1504 (О)
Fool is known by his conversation (A)—1566 (О)

COO
Bletherin' coo soon forgets her calf (A)—2040 (Т)

COOK
All are not cooks who sport white caps and carry long knives—1300 (Н), 1314 (Н)
Cooks are not to be taught in their own kitchen—1466 (Н)
Every cook knows to lick her own fingers—2137 (У), 2160 а (У)
Every cook praises his own broth (stew)—259 (В), 269 (В), 395 (Г)
He is an ill cook that cannot lick his own fingers—314 (Г), 2137 (У), 2160 а (У)

Salt cooks bear blame, but fresh bear shame—1335 (Н)
Too many cooks spoil the broth (the brew, the stew)—2145 (У)
What's cooking?—2290 (Ч)

COOKIE
Cookie today, crumb tomorrow—1643 (П), 1880 (С)
That's how (the way) the cookie crumbles—199 (В), 2035 (Т)

CORAL
Right coral needs no colouring—871 (К)
True coral needs no painter's brush—871 (К)

CORD
Cord breaks at the last but weakest pull (The)—1727 (П)
When one reknots a broken cord, it holds, but one feels the knot—1718 (П)

CORN
In much corn is some cockle—173 (В)
Much corn lies under the straw that is not seen—689 (И)
You have to hoe a row of corn with a man in order to know him—2283 (Ч)

CORPSE
Don't count your corpses before they are cold—1321 (Н), 1468 (Н)

COST
What costs nothing is worth nothing—458 (Д), 459 (Д)

COUNSEL
Come not to counsel uncalled—1262 (Н)
Counsel breaks not the head—2193 (Х)
Counsel must be followed not praised—488 (Д)
Give neither counsel nor salt till you are asked for /it/—1262 (Н)
Good counsel does no harm—2131 (У), 2193 (Х)
Good counsel has no price (A)—2192 (Х)
Good counsel is a pearl beyond price—2192 (Х)
Good counsel never comes amiss—2131 (У), 2193 (Х)
Good counsel never comes too late—2131 (У)
He that is his own counsel has a fool for a client—2250 (Ч)
If the counsel is good, take it, even from a fool—488 (Д)
Three may keep counsel if two be away—232 (В), 1529 (О)
Two may keep counsel if one be away (if one of them's dead)—232 (В), 676 (З), 1529 (О), 1642 (П), 1825 (Р), 1895 (С), 2171 (Ф)

COUNSELLOR
Self is a bad counsellor—2250 (Ч)

COUNT
Count not four, except you have them in the wallet (till they be in the bag)—2228 (Ц)

COUNTENANCE
Countenance is the index of the mind (The)—1026 (Л)

COUNTING
Correct counting keeps good friends—2025 (С)

COUNTRY
Different countries, different customs—2300 (Ч)
Every country has its /own/ custom (customs)—158 (В), 172 (В), 1910 (С), 2094 (У), 2300 (Ч)
Other countries, other customs—2300 (Ч)
So many countries, so many customs—1910 (С), 2300 (Ч)
You can get the man out of the country, but you can't get the country out of the man—717 (И), 1567 (О)

COURAGE
Courage wins—1411 (Н), 1937 (С)

COURTESY
All doors /are/ open to courtesy—484 (Д)
Courtesy costs nothing—985 (Л)

Courtesy never broke one's crown—1579 (О), 1690 (П)
Fox is all courtesy and all craft (The)—988 (Л)
Full of courtesy, full of craft—988 (Л), 1170 (М)
Too much courtesy, too much craft—360 (Г), 988 (Л), 1170 (М), 1269 (Н), 1927 (С)

COVER
Every pot has its cover—46 (Б)

COVET
All covet, all lose—1030 (Л), 1142 (М)
Covet not which belongs to others—1260 (Н)

COVETOUSNESS
Covetousness breaks the bag—2081 (Т)
Covetousness brings nothing home—580 (Ж), 2081 (Т)
Covetousness bursts the bag—1030 (Л), 2081 (Т)
Covetousness is always filling a bottomless vessel—1377 (Н)
Envy and covetousness are never satisfied—1377 (Н)
Poverty wants many things and (but) covetousness all—28 (Б)
Too much covetousness breaks (bursts) the bag (the sack)—580 (Ж), 1142 (М)

COW
Bawling (bellowing) cow soon forgets her /own/ calf (A)—2040 (Т)
Bring a cow into the hall and she'll run to the byre—779 (К), 853 (К)
Cow knows not the value of her tail till she has lost (loses) it (The)—2227 (Ц), 2292 (Ч)
Cow knows not what her tail is worth till she has lost it (The)—2227 (Ц), 2292 (Ч)
Cow that moos the most gives the least milk (A)—932 (К)
Cursed cow has short horns (A)—88 (Б)
Curst cows have curt horns—88 (Б)
Cussed cows have short horns—88 (Б)
Faraway cows have (wear) long horns—1917 (С)
Far-off cows have long horns—69 (Б), 1917 (С)
God sends a cursed cow short horns—88 (Б)
Good cow may have a bad (a black, an evil, an ill) calf (A)—741 (И)
If you can't get a horse, ride a cow—633 (З)
If you sell the cow, you sell her (the) milk /too/—1525 (О)
Like cow, like calf—953 (К), 2348 (Щ), 2357 (Я)
Many a good cow has a bad calf—741 (И)
Next man's cows have the longest horns (The)—296 (В), 978 (К), 2185 (Х)
Old brown cow laid an egg (The)—1138 (М)
Our neighbour's cow yields more milk than ours—978 (К)
When the cows come home—847 (К)
You cannot sell the cow and drink (have, sup) the milk—1525 (О)

COWARD
Better a live coward than a dead hero—590 (Ж)
Coward dies many times (The)—2073 (Т)
Coward dies a thousand deaths, the brave but one (The)—2073 (Т)
Coward often dies, the brave but once (The)—2073 (Т)
Cowards die many times before their death—2073 (Т)
Greatest braggarts are generally the greatest cowards (The)—272 (В)
Live coward is better than a dead hero (A)—590 (Ж)

CRAB
Older the crab, the tougher the claws (The)—166 (В)
You cannot make a crab walk straight—383 (Г)

CRACKED
Cracked plate always lasts longer than a new one (A)—66 (Б)

Cracked pot lasts the longest (The)—66 (Б)
Cracked pots last longer—66 (Б)
Cracked saucer lasts longest (The)—66 (Б)

CRAFTSMAN
Use makes the craftsman—280 (В), 1190 (Н)

CRAP
Cut the crap—219 (В)

CREAK
Creaking cart goes long on its wheels (A)—1915 (С)
Creaking door hangs long on its hinges (A)—1915 (С)
Creaking gate hangs a long time (hangs long, lasts long, swings a long time) (A)—1915 (С)
Creaking wagons are long in passing—1915 (С)

CREDIT
Credit makes enemies—128 (В), 888 (К)
Give credit to whom credit is due—405 (Д)
Give every man the credit that he deserves (has earned)—767 b (К), 835 (К)

CREDITOR
Creditors have better memories than debtors—493 (Д)

CRIMINAL
Mercy to the criminal may be cruelty to the people—190 (В)

CRIPPLE
Associate with cripples and you learn to limp—1904 (С), 1905 (С)
He that dwells next door to a cripple will learn to halt—1904 (С)
He that lives with cripples learns /how/ to limp—1905 (С)
He that mocks a cripple, ought to be whole—1087 (Л), 1405 (Н)
It's ill halting before a cripple—129 (В)

CROCK
Put not all your crocks on one shelf—1414 (Н)

CROOK
Crook thinks every man is a crook (A)—161 (В), 2100 (У)
Once a crook, always a crook—1877 (С)
There is a crook in the lot of everyone—387 (Г)

CROOKED
Crooked furrows grow straight grain—891 (К)
Crooked log makes a good fire (A)—894 (К)
Crooked logs make a straight fire (straight fires)—894 (К)
Crooked stick makes a straight fire (A)—894 (К)
Crooked tree will never straighten its branches (A)—892 (К)
Crooked wood makes an even fire—894 (К)
That which is crooked cannot be made straight—892 (К)

CROSS
After crosses and losses, men grow humbler and wiser—33 (Б)
Crosses are the ladders to heaven—2266 (Ч)
Cross on the breast, and the devil in the heart (The)—355 (Г)
Devil lurks (sits) behind the cross (The)—355 (Г)
Each cross has its inscription—1610 (О)
Every man bears his /own/ cross—2103 (У)
Every man must bear his /own/ cross—2079 (Т)
Every one thinks his own cross the hardest to bear—285 (В), 768 (К), 770 (К)
No cross, no crown—2266 (Ч)
To everyone his own cross is heaviest—285 (В), 768 (К), 770 (К)
When we suffer a great loss, we must bear our cross—2079 (Т)

CROW
Breed up a crow and he will peck out your eyes—250 (В), 300 (В), 631 (З), 1307 (Н)

Crow bewails the sheep, and then eats it (The)—1072 (Л), 1677 (П), 2225 (Ц)
Crow does not pull out the eye of another crow (A)—196 (В)
Crow is never /the/ whiter for washing herself oft (often) (A)—2268 (Ч), 2304 (Ч)
Crow is no whiter for being washed (A)—2268 (Ч), 2304 (Ч)
Crows weep for the dead lamb and then devour him—1072 (Л), 1677 (П), 2225 (Ц)
Crow thinks her own bird /the/ fairest (The)—462 (Д)
Each old crow thinks her young are the blackest—462 (Д)
Evil crow, an evil egg (An)—1617 (О)
Never crow till you're out of the woods—2172 (Х)
Of an evil crow an evil egg—1616 (О)
Old one crows, the young one learns (The)—1101 (М)

CROWN
Crowns have cares—2078 (Т)
Heavy is the head that wears the crown—2078 (Т)
Near the death he stands that stands near the crown—74 (Б)
Uneasy is (lies) the head that wears the crown—2078 (Т)

CRUST
Crust is better than no bread (A)—1070 (Л)

CRY
Crying does not pay—1157 (М)
Crying will not mend matters—1157 (М), 1604 (О), 1920 b (С)
Don't cry before (till) you are hurt—1402 (Н)
Don't cry over spilled milk—1920 a (С), 2302 (Ч)
Great cry and (but) little wool—1143 (М)
It is no good crying over spilt milk—2302 (Ч)
It's the crying baby that gets the milk—460 (Д)
Laugh and the world laughs with you; cry and you cry alone—204 (В)
Much cry and little wool—1143 (М)
There is no use crying over spilt milk—1920 a (С)
When we laugh, everyone sees; when we cry, no one sees—204 (В), 251 (В)

CUDGEL
Man that will fight may find a cudgel in every hedge (A)—117 (Б)

CUNNING
Cunning is more than (surpasses) strength—310 (Г), 334 (Г), 1024 (Л)
He that is not strong should be cunning—310 (Г), 334 (Г)

CUP
Between the cup and the lip a morsel may slip—18 (Б)
Let this cup pass from me—413 (Д)
Like cup, like cover—823 (К), 1664 (П), 1679 (П), 1681 ((П), 1723 (П)
My cup is full—2233 (Ч)
Such cup, such cover—808 (К), 814 (К), 1664 (П), 1679 (П), 1681 (П), 1723 (П)
There is many a slip twixt /the/ cup and /the/ lip—18 (Б)
There's many a slip between ('twixt) the cup and the lip—18 (Б)
We must drink the cup—2079 (Т)

CURE
Cure is worse than the disease (The)—10 (А)
Cure the disease and kill the patient—10 (А)
Desperate cures to desperate ills apply—838 (К)
Desperate cuts must have desperate cures—2264 (Ч)
Desperate diseases must have desperate cures—838 (К), 2264 (Ч)
Desperate diseases require desperate cures—838 (К)
He who bewails himself has the cure in his hands—460 (Д)
Kill or cure—726 (И)
Only cure for grief is action (The)—1157 (М), 1920 b (С)
Past cure, past care—2302 (Н)

Physicians kill more than they cure—10 (A)
What can't be cured must be endured—1641 (П)

CURIOSITY
Curiosity has a spiteful way of turning back on the curious—1086 (Л)
Curiosity killed the cat—1086 (Л), 1138 (M), 1419 (H)
Too much curiosity killed the cat—1138 (M)
Too much curiosity lost Paradise—1086 (Л)

CURSE
Curses /, like chickens ,/ come home to roost—917 (K), 2294 (Ч)
Curse sticks to the tongue of the curser (The)—917 (K)
If you curse others, you will be cursed—2294 (Ч)

CUSTOM
Custom is a second nature—1768 (П), 2076 (T)
Custom makes the thing easy—1190 (H)
Customs are stronger than law—1511 (O)
Customs rule the law—1511 (O)
Custom surpasses nature—1768 (П)
Different countries, different customs—2300 (Ч)
Every country has its /own/ custom (customs)—158 (B), 172 (B), 1910 (C), 2094 (У), 2300 (Ч)
Follow the customs, or fly the country—297 (B), 1864 (C)
Ill customs grow apace—2217 (X)
Old customs die hard—1768 (П)
Other countries, other customs—2300 (Ч)
So many countries, so many customs—1910 (C), 2300 (Ч)

CUT
It cuts both ways—1628 (П)
Short cut is not always the fastest way (A)—959 (K)
Short cut is often a (the) wrong cut (A)—959 (K)
Short cuts are roundabout ways—959 (K)

D

DAGGER
There are daggers behind men's smiles—360 (Г), 1170 (M), 1269 (H)

DAINTY
Dainties of the great are tears of the poor (The)—879 (K)
Who dainties love shall beggars prove—1643 (П), 1880 (C)

DAMAGE
Damage is done (The)—434 (Д)

DAMN
Damned if you do, damned if you don't—975 (K), 2202 (X)

DANCE
If you dance, you must pay the fiddler—1075 (Л)
If you don't know how to dance, you say that the drum is bad—566 (E), 1111 (M), 1654 (П)
If you want to dance, you must pay the fiddler—1075 (Л)
You will neither dance nor hold the candle—745 (И), 1950 (C)

DANGER
After the danger everyone is wise—492 (Д), 620 (З), 1983 (C), 2175 (X)
All is not lost that is in danger—1308 (H), 2138 (У)
Better face danger than be always in fear—1371 (H)
Better pass danger once than always be in fear—1371 (H)
Danger foreseen is half avoided (/A/)—747 (И), 760 (K), 1555 (O)
Danger makes men devout—1163 (M)
Danger past and God forgotten—1163 (M)
Danger past, God is forgotten—1163 (M)
Dangers are conquered by dangers—838 (K)

DARE
Nothing dared, nothing gained—1834 (P)
Who dares wins—1834 (P)

DARK
Darker hour is that before the dawn (The)—2042 (Т)
Darkest hour is just before (nearest the) dawn (The)—2042 (Т)
Darkest place is under the candlestick (The)—2120 (У)
Darkest spot is just under the candle (The)—2120 (У)
It is always darkest before /the/ dawn—2042 (Т)
It is always dark just under the lamp—2120 (У)
It is always darkest under the lantern—2120 (У)
It is dark at the foot of a lighthouse—2120 (У)
It's always dark before the sun shines—2042 (Т)
What goes on in the dark must come out in the light—243 (В)

DARLING
Mothers' darlings make but milksop heroes—647 (З)

DAWN
Darker hour is that before the dawn (The)—2042 (Т)
Darkest hour is just before (is nearest the) dawn (The)—2042 (Т)
It is always darkest before /the/ dawn—2042 (Т)

DAY
Another day, another dollar—83 (Б)
As the days grow longer, the storms are stronger—2257 (Ч)
Bad day never has a good night (A)—809 (К), 1652 (П), 2222 (Х)
Be the day never so long, at length comes evensong—753 (И), 804 (К)
Blustering night, a fair day (A)—1725 (П), 1728 (П)
Come day, go day /, God send Sunday/—447 (Д)
Days of our pride are gone (The)—120 (Б)
Every day brings bread with it—83 (Б)
Every day has its night, every weal its /own/ woe—34 (Б), 1148 (Н), 1453 (Н)
Every day is not a holiday (Sunday)—1297 (Н), 1766 (П)
Every day is not yesterday—1716 (П), 1817 (Р)
Foul morning may turn to a fair day (A)—1891 (С)
Foul morn turns into a fine day (A)—1891 (С)
Go day, come day, God send Sunday—447 (Д)
I have had my day—120 (Б), 2107 (У)
Lay by (off, up) for a rainy day—2196 (Х)
Let the cock crow or not, the day will come—1782 (П)
Long as the day may be, the night comes at last—753 (И)
Longest day has an end (The)—753 (И)
Misty morn may have a fine day (A)—1891 (С)
New day, a new dollar (A)—83 (Б)
No day is over until the sun has set—2174 (Х)
No day passes without /some/ grief—450 (Д)
One day does not a summer make—1528 (О), 1533 (О)
One of these days is none of these days—1592 (О)
One of these days is no time—1592 (О)
Other days, other ways—740 (И)
Put something away for a rainy day—2196 (Х)
Save it for a rainy day—2196 (Х)
Some days are darker than others—363 (Г), 1716 (П), 1817 (Р)
There are no two days alike—1716 (П)
We have known (seen) better days—120 (В)
We shall have our day too—106 (Б), 489 (Д), 1770 (П)
What is done in the night appears in the day—243 (В)
Yesterday is past; tomorrow may never come; this day is ours—1526 (О)
You can tell the day by the morning—809 (К)

DAYLIGHT
Daylight will come, though the cock does not crow—1782 (П)

DEAD
Dead dog never bites (A)—1125 (M)
Dead dogs bark not—1126 (M)
Dead dogs don't bite—1125 (M), 1551 (O)
Dead dogs never bite—1551 (O)
Dead dog tells no tales (A)—1126 (M)
Dead men do no harm—1125 (M)
Dead men don't bite—1125 (M), 1551 (O)
Dead men don't talk—1126 (M)
Dead men don't walk again—1127 (M)
Dead men never bite—1125 (M), 1551 (O)
Dead men tell no tales—1126 (M)
He is dead that is faultless—136 (B), 1515 (O), 2059 (T), 2251 (Ч)
Let the dead bury the dead—2295 b (Ч), 2302 (Ч)
Near dead never filled the kirkyard—1308 (H), 1317 (H), 1915 (C), 2138 (У)
Never speak ill of the dead—1554 (O)
No man is dead till he's dead—1308 (У), 2138 (У)
Say nothing but good of the dead—1554 (O)
Slander not the dead—1554 (O)
Speak well of the dead—1554 (O)
You might as well physic the dead as give advice to an old man—2002 (C)

DEAF
No ear is so deaf as one which wishes not to hear—1444 (H)
None so deaf as he (those) who won't hear—1444 (H)
There's none so deaf as they (those) who won't listen—1444 (H)

DEAL
What's the deal?—2290 (Ч)

DEATH
After death, the doctor—1736 (П)
Better a glorious death than a shameful life—1067 (Л)
Better death than dishono(u)r—1054 (Л), 1067 (Л)
Death and the grave make no distinction of persons—1938 (C)
Death combs us all with the same comb—1938 (C), 2149 (У)
Death comes to us all—244 (B), 1607 (O)
Death defies the doctor—1606 (O)
Death devours lambs as well as sheep—1938 (C)
Death does not blow a trumpet—1939 (C)
Death has no calendar—1939 (C)
Death is a black camel which kneels at every man's gate—1607 (O)
Death is a great leveler—605 (Ж), 744 (И), 2149 (У)
Death is but death, and all in time shall die—1607 (O)
Death is deaf and will hear no denial—1607 (O)
Death is no respecter of persons—1938 (C)
Death is the grand leveler—605 (Ж), 744 (И), 2149 (У)
Death keeps no calendar—1939 (C)
Death observes no ceremony—1939 (C)
Death pays all debts—1735 (П), 1940 (C)
Death quits all scores—1735 (П), 1940 (C)
Death squares all accounts—1735 (П), 1940 (C)
Death takes all—1607 (O)
Death takes no denial—1246 (H), 1607 (O)
Death waits for no one—1939 (C)
Death when it comes will have no denial—1939 (C)
Good life makes a good death (A)—782 (K)
It may be fun for you, but it is death to the frog—879 (K), 2039 (T)
Men fear death as children do going in the dark—598 (Ж)
Near the death he stands that stands near the crown—74 (Б)
Nothing is so sure as death—1607 (O)
Such a life, such a death—782 (K)

There is a remedy for all dolours (things) but death—898 (К), 1606 (О)
There is nothing so certain as death and nothing so uncertain as the hour of death—1939 (С)
There is no way of knowing when death will come; it just does—1939 (С)
This may be play to you, 'tis death to us—879 (К), 1548 (О)
When death knocks at your door, you must answer it—1607 (О)

DEBT
Better /to/ go to bed supperless than rise in debt—1061 (Л)
Death pays all debts—1735 (П), 1940 (С)
Debt is a heavy burden to an honest man—494 (Д)
Debt is the worst /kind of/ poverty—2066 (Т)
Debts make the cheek black—494 (Д)
He that dies pays all debts—1940 (С)
He who pays his debts enriches himself—639 (З)
Man in debt is caught in a net (A)—494 (Д)
Out of debt, out of danger—639 (З)
Pay your debts or lose your friends—2025 (С), 2234 (Ч)
Rather go to bed supperless than rise in debt for a breakfast—1061 (Л)
Rather than run into debt, wear your old coat—1061 (Л)
Short debts make lasting (long) friends—2234 (Ч)
Without debt, without care—639 (З)
You can run into debt, but you have to crawl out—991 (Л)

DEBTOR
Of ill debtors men take oats—1974 (С)

DECEIT
Deceit breeds deceit—957 (К)

DECEIVE
He that once deceives is ever suspected—914 (К)

DEED
Bad deed never dies (A)—471 (Д)
Bad deeds follow you; the good ones flee—471 (Д), 482 (Д)
Best of the sport is to do the deed and say nothing (The)—1122 (М)
Deeds are fruits, words are /but/ leaves—1503 (Н)
Deeds, not words—1122 (М), 1503 (Н)
Deeds not words are the test—1393 (Н)
Deeds speak louder than words—1285 (Н), 1393 (Н)
Deed will praise itself (The)—476 (Д)
Deeds will show themselves, and words will pass away—1503 (Н)
Few words and many deeds—1122 (М)
Good deed comes back a thousandfold (A)—836 (К)
Good deed is never forgotten (lost) (A)—622 (З), 2188 (Х)
Good deed never dies (A)—2188 (Х)
It is not words that count but deeds—1393 (Н), 1928 (С)
Judge a man by his deeds, not by his words—428 (Д), 1621 (О)
Judge a man by what he does, not by what he says—1621 (О)
Man is known by his deeds—428 (Д), 451 (Д), 1621 (О)
No good deed goes unpunished—250 (В), 631 (З), 1307 (Н), 2159 (У)
One good deed brings forth another—1197 (Н)
One good deed deserves another—622 (З), 1197 (Н), 2148 (У)
Ten good turns lie dead, and one ill deed report abroad does spread—471 (Д)
There is a big difference between word and deed—1540 (О)

DEEP
Deep calls unto /the/ deep (/The/)—39 (Б)

DEER
Tigers and deer do not stroll together—402 (Г), 1295 b (Н), 2270 (Ч)

DEFECT
Every man has the defects of his /own/ qualities (his virtues)—235 (В), 737 (И), 1436 (Н), 1449 (Н)

DELAY
Delay breeds loss (is dangerous)—1784 (П)
Delays are dangerous—1784 (П)
Delays have dangerous ends—1784 (П)
To delay may mean to forget—1592 (О)

DELIGHT
Every man has his delight—2086 (У)

DELUGE
After us the deluge—1731 (П)

DEMONSTRATION
Demonstration is the best mode of instruction—2163 (У)

DENMARK
Something is rotten in the state of Denmark—1780 (П)
There's something rotten in the state of Denmark—1780 (П)

DEPTH
You cannot tell the depth of the well by the length of the handle of the pump—1675 (П)

DESERVE
He deserves not sweet that will not taste of sour—1424 (Н)
He deserves not the sweet that will not taste the sour—1424 (Н)

DESTINY
Every man's destiny is in his own hands—2247 (Ч)

DEUCE
Deuce knows many things because he is old (The)—2009 (С)
Deuce to pay (The)—1851 (С)

DEVIL
Cross on the breast, and the devil in the heart (The)—355 (Г)
Devil and all to pay (The)—1851 (С)
Devil can cite Scripture for his purpose (The)—2226 (Ц)
Devil dances in an empty pocket (The)—30 (Б)
Devil finds (makes) work for idle hands /to do/ (The)—35 (Б), 2074 (Т)
Devil is dead (The)—429 (Д)
Devil is ever kind to (is fond of, is good to, is kind to, looks after, protects, takes care of) his own (The)—904 (К)
Devil is not as (so) black as he is painted (The)—1426 (Н)
Devil knows many things because he is old (The)—2009 (С)
Devil looks after his own (The)—904 (К)
Devil lurks behind the cross (The)—355 (Г)
Devil protects his own (The)—904 (К)
Devil rebukes sin (The)—2334 (Ч)
Devil sits behind the cross (The)—355 (Г)
Devil takes care of his own (The)—904 (К)
Devil was sick, the devil a monk (a saint) would be; the devil was well, the devil of a monk (a saint) was he (The)—1163 (М)
Don't bid the devil good morning until you have met him—1402 (Н)
Fight the devil with his own tools, or fight the devil with fire—838 (К), 2264 (Ч)
Give the devil an inch and he will take an ell—406 (Д), 408 (Д), 409 (Д)
Here is the devil to pay, and no pitch hot—1851 (С)
He that takes the devil into his boat must carry him over the sound—150 (В)
It is easier to raise the devil than to lay him—20 (Б), 23 (Б)
Nothing goes over the devil's back that doesn't come back under the devil's belly—2221 (Х)
Pull devil, pull baker—593 (Ж)
Speak of the devil /and he is sure to appear/—1892 (С)
Speak of the devil, and he'll appear—1207 (Л), 1513 (О), 1892 (С)
Speak of the devil and in he walks—1892 (С)

Talk about the devil and his imps will appear—1513 (О)
Talk of the devil and his imp appears—1513 (О)
Talk of the devil and you'll see his horns—1513 (О)
What goes over the devil's back comes under his belly—2221 (Х)
What is got over the devil's back is spent under his belly—2221 (Х), 2323 (Ч)
When the devil was sick, a monk was he; when the devil was well, the devil of a monk was he—1163 (М)
Where God has a church, the devil has a chapel—1553 (О)
Where God has his church (temple), the devil will have his chapel—1553 (О)
You can't paint the devil white—2268 (Ч)

DEXTERITY
Dexterity comes with experience—1190 (Н)

DIAMOND
Diamond cut (cuts) diamond—4 (А), 554 (Д), 1205 (Н), 1206 (Н), 1243 (Н), 1267 (Н), 1569 (О)
Diamond is valuable though it lie on a midden (A)—5 (А), 683 (З)
Diamond on a dunghill is a precious diamond still (A)—5 (А), 683 (З), 871 (К)
There is a diamond in the rough—689 (И)

DIE
All men must die—228 (В), 240 (В), 244 (В)
As a man lives, so shall he die; as a tree falls, so shall it lie—782 (К)
Better die standing than live kneeling—1067 (Л)
Better die with honour than live in shame—1067 (Л)
Better to die on one's feet than to live on one's knee—1067 (Л)
Die is cast (thrown) (The)—607 (Ж)
He that dies pays all debts—1940 (С)
He that liveth wickedly can hardly die honestly—1953 (С)
It's better to die with honor than to live in infamy—64 (Б), 1054 (Л), 1067 (Л)
Kings and queens must die, as well as you and I—240 (В), 1938 (С)
Man can die but (only) once (A)—423 b (Д), 1527 (О), 1823 (Р)
Never say die—134 (В)
No matter how much money you have, when you die, you must leave it—2133 (У)
Once born, once must die—240 (В)
They die well that live well—782 (К)
They that live longest must die—1246 (Н), 2230 (Ч)
We die as we live—782 (К)
You can't take it (money) with you when you die—2133 (У)

DIET
Diet cures more than the doctor (the knife, the lancet)—486 (Д)

DIFFICULT
All things are difficult before they are easy—1025 (Л)

DIFFICULTY
Difficulties are things that show what men are—2245 (Ч)
When difficulties are over they become blessings—2306 (Ч)

DIG
Things turn out for the man who digs—317 (Г)

DILIGENCE
Care and diligence bring luck—2044 (Т)
Diligence is the mother of good luck—2044 (Т)
Few things are impossible to diligence and skill—277 (В), 431 (Д)

DILIGENT
Diligent working makes an expert workman—280 (В), 833 (К)

DIME
Take care of the dimes, and the dollars will take care of themselves—869 (К)

DINNER
Dinner over, away go the guests (The)—1215 (О), 1645 (П), 1901 (С)

DIRT
Cast no dirt in (into) the well that gives you water—1386 (Н)
Don't throw dirt into the well that gives you water—1386 (Н)
Every man must eat a peck of dirt before he dies—137 (В)
Fling dirt enough and some will stick—837 (К)
It's no dirt down my neck—1159 (М)
Never cast dirt in the fountain that has given you refreshing drink—1386 (Н)
Never cast dirt into that fountain of which thou hast sometimes drunk—1386 (Н)
We must eat a peck of dirt before we die—137 (В)
Who deals in dirt has foul fingers—400 (Г)

DISASTER
Disasters come treading on each other's heel—1778 (П)
Meet success like a gentleman and disaster like a man—1399 (Н)

DISCOMMODITY
Every commodity has its discommodity—1073 (Л)

DISCRETION
Discretion is the better part of valo(u)r—59 (Б)
Discretion is the mother of other virtues—1573 (О)
Ounce of discretion is worth a pound of knowledge (learning, wit) (An)—1573 (О)

DISEASE
Cure is worse than the disease (The)—10 (А)
Cure the disease and kill the patient—10 (А)
Diseases are the interest (interests) of pleasures—1850 (С)
Diseases are the price of ill pleasures—1850 (С)
Diseases are the tax on pleasure—1850 (С)

DISH
Many a fine dish has nothing on it—1301 (Н)
Many dishes /make/ many diseases—327 (Г)
No dish pleases all palates alike—1182 (Н)

DESPISE
It is easy to despise what you cannot get—662 (З)

DISTANCE
Distance ends enchantment—1871 (С)
Distance lends enchantment to the view—1917 (С)

DITCH
If you dig a ditch for your neighbor, you will fall into it yourself—917 (К)

DIVE
He who would search for pearls must dive below—50 (Б)

DIVIDE
Divide and conquer (govern, rule)—1815 (Р)

DO
As we do unto others, so it is done unto us—798 (К), 824 (К)
As you do to others, expect others to do to you—798 (К)
Best of the sport is to do the deed and say nothing (The)—1122 (М)
Be the labor great or small, do it well or not at all—1 (А)
By doing nothing we learn to do ill—35 (Б)
Do as you may if you cannot as you would—595 (Ж), 1370 (Н)
Do as you would be done by—1328 (Н)
Doing is better than saying—1503 (Н)
Doing everything is doing nothing—612 (З)
Doing nothing is doing ill—1006 (Л)
Do it right (well) or not at all—1 (А)
Don't do to others what you would not have done to you—1328 (Н)
Do or die—726 (И), 727 (И), 1017 (Л), 1021 (Л)
Double or quits—727 (И)

Do unto others as they do unto you—778 (К), 798 (К)
Do unto others as you would have them do unto you—1328 (Н)
Do well, (and) have well—1197 (Н), 622 (З)
He who can't do what he wants must want what he can do—1370 (Н)
I do as I please—829 (К), 1869 (С), 2214 (Х)
If a thing is worth doing, it is worth doing well—1 (А)
If there isn't any, one (we) must do without /it/—1213 (Н)
In doing we learn—280 (В), 430 (Д)
It is better to do well than to say well—1503 (Н)
It is dogged as (that) does it—507 (Д)
It is one thing to say and another to do—1540 (О)
Let every man do what he was made for—1295 (Н)
Man was never so happy as when he was doing something—337 (Г), 1839 (Р)
One can only do by doing—507 (Д)
Say well and do well end with one letter; say well is good, but do well is better—1503 (Н)
"Say well" is good, but "do well" is better—1503 (Н)
Speak little; do much—1122 (М)
That won't do—2356 (З)
Things done cannot be undone—897 (К), 1872 (С)
To do, one must be doing—507 (Д)
We learn to do by doing—1190 (Н)
Whatever man has done man may do—1271 (Н)
What is done cannot be undone (is done)—897 (К), 1872 (С)
What man has done man can do—1271 (Н)
What's doing?—2290 (Ч)
When you are done, you can go—1095 (М)
You can do anything you want to if you want to bad enough—339 (Г)

DOCUMENT
Document does not blush (A)—111 (Б)

DOG
All dogs bite the bitten dog—1204 (Н)
As the dog barks, the young ones learn—1101 (М)
Barking dog has no bite (never bites) (A)—1952 (С)
Beaten dog is afraid of the stick's shadow (A)—68 (Б)
Beware of a silent man and a dog that does not bark—1273 (Н)
Cut off a dog's tail and he will be a dog still (and he will still be a dog)—1603 (О)
Dead dogs bite not—1125 (М)
Dog bites the stone, not him that throws it (The)—65 (Б), 1392 (Н), 1841 (Р)
Dog does not eat dog—183 (В), 191 (В), 196 (В), 671 (З), 1951 (С), 2271 (Ч)
Dog eat dog—193 (В)
Dog in the kitchen desires no company (A)—628 (З)
Dog in the manger won't eat the oats or let anyone else eat them (The)—745 (И), 1950 (С)
Dog is a lion at home (A)—275 (В)
Dog is bold on his own dunghill (A)—1238 (Н)
Dog is brave in his own yard (A)—1238 (Н)
Dogs are barking in the street (The)—98 (Б)
Dogs bark as they are bred (The)—2260 (Ч), 2347 (Щ)
Dogs delight to bark and bite for God has made 'em so—2076 (Т)
Dogs don't kill sheep at home—72 (Б), 1653 (П)
Dog shall die a dog's death (The)—1953 (С)
Dogs that bark at a distance don't (seldom) bite—1952 (С)
Dogs that put up many hares kill none—617 (З)
Dog that barks much is never a good hunter (A)—932 (К)
Dog that trots about finds a (the) bone (The)—182 (В), 397 (Г), 1394 (Н)
Dog will not cry (howl) if you beat him with a bone (A)—1326 (Н)

Dog will not eat dog—1951 (С)
Dog with a bone knows no friend (A)—628 (З)
Dog without teeth barks the most (The)—1325 (Н)
Don't keep a dog and bark yourself—651 (З)
Don't teach a dog to bark—1464 (Н)
Dumb dogs /and still waters/ are dangerous—294 (В), 1273 (Н)
Every dog has his day /and every man his hour/—106 (Б), 489 (Д), 1770 (П), 1772 (П), 2101 (У)
Every dog is a lion at home—1238 (Н), 2144 (У)
Every dog is brave in his own yard—1238 (Н), 2144 (У)
Every dog is valiant at his own door—1238 (Н), 2144 (У)
Foremost dog catches the hare (The)—954 (К)
Give a dog a finger and he will take (want) a hand—1665 (П), 1793 (П)
Good dog deserves a good bone (A)—799 (К), 808 (К), 814 (К), 823 (К), 1664 (П), 1679 (П), 1681 (П), 1723 (П)
He that lies down with dogs gets up with fleas—1989 (С)
If it had been a dog, it would have bitten you—646 (З), 1355 (Н)
If you lie down with dogs, you'll get up with fleas—1989 (С)
It is hard to make an old dog stoop—2000 (С), 2001 (С)
It is hard to teach an old dog tricks—2002 (С)
It is ill to waken sleeping dogs—1337 (Н), 1354 (Н)
I will not keep a dog and bark myself—651 (З)
Lazy dog catches no meat (A)—1000 (Л)
Lazy dog finds no bone (A)—1000 (Л), 1145 (М), 1227 (Н), 1993 (С), 2212 (Х)
Lean dog is all fleas (The)—840 (К), 1172 (Н), 1253 (Н)
Let sleeping dogs (the sleeping dog) lie—1274 (Н), 1337 (Н)
Life is a matter of dog eat dog—193 (В)
Like the dog in the manger he will neither eat himself not let the horse eat—745 (И), 1950 (С)
Live (living) dog is better than a dead lion (A)—590 (Ж)
Man may cause even his own dog to bite him (A)—2047 (Т)
Man may provoke his own dog to bite him (A)—286 (В), 2047 (Т)
No sense in keeping a dog when doing your own barking—651 (З)
Old dog barks not in vain (An)—1996 (С), 2010 (С)
Old dog cannot alter his way of barking (An)—1153 (М), 2002 (С)
Old dog does not bark for nothing (in vain) (An)—1996 (С), 2010 (С)
Old dog will learn no /new/ tricks (An)—2001 (С), 2002 (С)
One dog can drive a flock of sheep—1519 (О)
One barking dog sets all the street a-barking—1534 (О)
One dog barks at nothing; the rest bark at him—1534 (О)
One house cannot keep two dogs—420 (Д)
Saddest dog sometimes wags its tail (The)—2101 (У)
Scalded dog fears cold water (A/The)—1507 (О), 1626 (О)
Scalded dog thinks cold water hot (A)—1507 (О), 1626 (О)
Scornful dogs will eat dirty puddings—1499 (Н)
Silent dog is first to bite (The)—294 (В), 1273 (Н)
Sleeping dog catches no poultry (A/The)—1145 (М), 1993 (С)
That dog won't hunt—2356 (З)
Two dogs fight for a bone, and a third runs away with it—534 (Д)
Two dogs fight over a bone, while the third always runs away with the bone—534 (Д)
Two dogs over one bone seldom agree—424 (Д)
Two dogs strive for a bone, and a third runs away with it—534 (Д)
Wash a dog, comb a dog: still a dog—715 (И), 1955 (С), 2268 (Ч), 2304 (Ч)

"We hounds killed the hare," quoth the lap dog—732 (И)
When a dog is drowning every one (everyone) offers him drink—411 (Д)
When one dog barks, another at once barks too—1534 (О)
While the dog gnaws a bone companions would be none—628 (З)
You can never scare a dog from a greasy hide—383 (Г)
You can't teach an old dog new tricks—1153 (М), 2000 (С), 2001 (С), 2002 (С)
You have to be smarter than the dog to teach him tricks—2368 (Я)
You kick the dog—65 (Б), 880 (К), 1392 (Н)

DOGGED
It is dogged as (that) does it—2044 (Т)

DOLLAR
Dollar saved is a dollar earned (A)—638 (З), 1856 (С)
Dollar waiting on a dime (A)—1883 (С)
In for a dime, in for a dollar—150 (В), 609 (З)
One dollar in your hand beats the promise of two in somebody else's—70 (Б), 1066 (Л), 1421 (Н)

DONKEY
Donkey looks beautiful to a donkey (A)—1672 (П)
Donkey means one thing and the driver another (The)—776 (К)
If a donkey brays at you, don't bray at him—537 (Д)
Living donkey is better than a dead lion (A)—590 (Ж)
Send a donkey to Paris, he'll return no wiser than he went—195 (В), 1567 (О)

DOOR
At open doors dogs come in—328 (Г), 1427 (Н)
Every door may be shut but death's door—1607 (О)
Here's the door and there's the way—201 (В)
Never darken my door again—201 (В), 1902 (С)
Open door may tempt a saint (An)—328 (Г), 1655 (П)
Shut the door on your way out—201 (В)
There's the door—1902 (С)
There's the door the carpenter made—201 (В)
There's the door, use it—201 (В), 1902 (С)
When one door closes, another one opens—1219 (Н)
When one door shuts, another opens—1219 (Н)

DOORSTEP
Keep your own doorstep clean—1128 (М)
People don't see things on their own doorstep—646 (З), 1355 (Н)

DOUBT
Doubt grows up with knowledge—2256 (Ч)
He that knows nothing, doubts nothing—949 (К), 2256 (Ч)
He who knows nothing never doubts—949 (К)

DOUGHNUT
That's the way the doughnut rolls—2035 (Т)

DOWRY
Great dowry is a bed full of brambles (A)—80 (Б), 1059 (Л)

DRAW
Draw it mild!—219 (В)

DRESS
Keep a dress long enough and it will come back in style—1491 (Н)
Keep a dress seven years and it will come back into style—1491 (Н)

DRESSING
Foppish dressing tells the world the outside is the best of the puppet—1859 (С)

DRILL
What's the drill?—2290 (Ч)

DRINK
Drink is the source of evil—1805 (П)

Drink only with the duck—175 (B)
It is all right to drink like a fish if you drink what a fish drinks—175 (B)
One man's drink is another man's poison—2307 (Ч)
Water is the only drink for a wise man—175 (B)
When drink is in, wit is out—156 (B), 960 (П)
Where drink goes in, wit goes out—156 (B)

DRINKING
Drinking and thinking don't mix—156 (B), 960 (K)

DRIPPING
Constant dripping wears away a stone—830 (K)

DRIVE
If you cannot drive the engine, you can clear the road—947 (K), 1460 (H)

DRIVER
Stubborn driver to a stubborn ass (A)—1205 (H)

DROP
Drop by drop and the pitcher is full—979 (K), 1956 (C)
Drop by drop the lake is drained—830 (K)
Falling drops at last will wear the stone (The)—830 (K)
Last drop makes the cup run (turn) over (The)—1727 (П)
Little drops of water, little grains of sand, make a (the) mighty ocean and a (the) pleasant land—1686 (П)
Little drops produce a shower—1686 (П)
Many drops make a flood (a shower)—1686 (П)
Many drops of water make an ocean—1686 (П)
Many drops of water will sink a ship—830 (K)
Steady drop makes a hole in a rock (A)—830 (K)

DROPPING
Constant dropping wears away a (the) stone—830 (K)

DROWN
Drowning man clutches at a thread (A)—2157 (У)
Drowning man grabs (will catch, will snatch) at a straw (A)—2157 (У)
Drowning man would catch at a razor (A)—2157 (У)
Man who was born to drown will drown on a desert (A)—1610 (O)

DROWSINESS
Drowsiness shall clothe (dresses) a man in rags—1145 (M)

DRUM
Hollow drum makes the most noise (A)—1791 (П)

DRUNK
Children and drunk people speak the truth—1807 (П)
Drunks sober up, fools remain fools—1803 (П)
What you do drunk you must pay for sober—1806 (П)

DRUNKARD
Children and drunkards speak the truth—1807 (П)
Children, fools and drunkards tell the truth—1807 (П)

DRUNKEN
Drunken days have /all/ their tomorrow—1805 (П), 1806 (П)
Drunken heart won't lie—1807 (П), 2312 (Ч)
Drunken joy brings sober tomorrow—1806 (П)
Drunken tongue tells what's on a sober mind (A)—2312 (Ч)

DRUNKENNESS
Drunkenness reveals what soberness conceals—2312 (Ч)
What soberness conceals, drunkenness reveals—2312 (Ч)

DUCK
Every duck thinks it is a swan—974 (K)
Every mother's duck is a swan—462 (Д)
It's better to be a big duck in a little puddle than be a little duck in a big puddle—1046 (Л)

Roasted ducks don't fly into your mouth—50 (Б), 2178 (Х)

DUE
Give every man his due—767 b (К), 835 (К), 1679 (П)

DULE
Talk of the Dule and he'll put out his horns—1513 (О)

DUMB
Dumb folks (men) get no lands—2016 (С)

DUNGHILL
Risen from the dunghill—703 (И)

DUST
Fly sat upon the axle-tree of the chariot-wheel and said, What a dust do I raise (The)!—732 (И)
He that blows dust fills his own eyes—964 (К)
He that blows in the dust fills his eyes with it—964 (К)

DUTCH
Dutch are in (have taken) Holland (The)—1590 (О)

DUTY
Duty before pleasure—436 (Д), 864 (К)
I have done my duty to God and country—1588 (О)

E

EACH
To each his own—767 a (К), 862 (К), 927 (К), 1182 (Н)

EAGLE
Attempt not to fly like an eagle with the wings of a wren—974 (К)
Eagle does not hawk at flies (An/The)—1559 (О)
Eagles do not breed doves—1608 (О)
Eagles don't catch flies—1559 (О)
When the eagle is dead, the crows pick out his eyes—1124 (М), 1650 (П)

EAR
Even the corn has ears—2153 (У)
Full ear of corn will bend its head; an empty ear will stand upright (A)—1795 (П)
Give every man thine (your) ear, but few thy (your) voice—96 (Б)
Have a long (a wide) ear and a short tongue—96 (Б)
He who has ears let him hear—354 (Г)
In at one ear and out of the other—177 (В)
It is better to play with the ears than with the tongue—96 (Б)
Keep your mouth shut and your ears open—96 (Б)
Must I tell you a tale and find your ears too?—354 (Г)
Nothing between the ears—2125 (У)
Open your ears—1935 (С)
There is not much between the ears—2125 (У)
Unplug your ears—1935 (С)
Wall has ears and the plain has eyes (The)—2153 (У)

EARLY
Better early than late—747 (И)
Early bird catches (gets) the worm (The)—961 (К)
Early start makes easy stages—252 (В), 1822 (Р)
Early to bed, early to rise makes a man healthy, wealthy and wise—962 (К), 1036 (Л)
He who gets up early has gold in his mouth—961 (К)
It is the early bird that catches the worm—961 (К)

EARTH
Six feet of earth make (makes) all men equal—2149 (У)

EASE
Take thine ease, eat, drink, and be merry—1526 (О)

EAST
Too far East is West—883 (К)

EASY
Breathe easy—555 (Д)

Easy come, easy go—993 (Л), 1779 (П)
Easy does it—1980 (С)
Nothing is easy to the unwilling—45 (Б)
Take it easy—555 (Д), 610 (З)

EAT
Eat, drink and be merry /, for tomorrow we (you) die/—594 (Ж), 1526 (О), 1646 (П)
Eat, drink, and be merry, for tomorrow we may die—594 (Ж), 1526 (О), 1646 (П)
Eating and scratching, it's all in the beginning—7 (А)
Eating and scratching wants but a beginning—7 (А)
He that will eat the kernel must crack the nut—50 (Б)
He that would eat the fruit must climb the tree—50 (Б)
I'll eat my boots (my hat, my head)—415 (Д)
Let him that earns eat—107 (Б)
Let him that earns the bread eat it—107 (Б)
Man eats so he works (A)—567 (Е), 820 (К)
More you eat, the more you want (The)—7 (А)
Who eats with heart is a worker smart—820 (К), 919 (К)
You cannot eat for tomorrow—147 (В)

EATER
Greedy eaters dig their graves with their teeth—327 (Г)
Swift eater, a swift worker (A)—820 (К), 919 (К), 1809 (Р)

ECHO
As the call, so the echo—778 (К), 824 (К)

EDGE
Thin edge of the wedge is dangerous (The)—1477 (Н)

EDUCATION
Education is a gift that none can take away—677 (З)
Silver and gold tarnish away, but a good education will never decay—677 (З)

EFFORT
It's not worth the effort—698 (И)

EGG
Better an egg today than a hen tomorrow—1065 (Л)
Broken egg cannot be put back together (A)—1718 (П), 2070 (Т)
Don't carry (put) all your eggs in one basket—1217 (Н), 1414 (Н)
Don't put all your eggs in (into) one basket—1217 (Н), 1414 (Н)
Eggs can't teach the hen—2368 (Я)
Egg today is worth a hen tomorrow (An)—1065 (Л)
Half an egg is better than an empty shell (than the shell)—1056 (Л)
It is very hard to shave an egg—375 (Г), 654 (З), 826 (К)
Other people's eggs have two yolks—2185 (Х)
Rotten egg spoils the pudding (A)—1037 (Л), 1536 (О)
Show him an egg and instantly the whole air is full of feathers—548 (Д)
There's always a bad egg in every crowd—237 (В)
'Tis very hard to shave an egg—654 (З)
You can't unscramble eggs—1872 (С)

ELBOW
Elbow grease gives the best polish—2044 (Т)
Elbow is near, but try and bite it (The)—73 (Б), 152 (В), 153 (В)

ELEPHANT
Elephant does not catch flies (The)—1559 (О)

EMPLOYMENT
Employment is enjoyment—1839 (Р)

EMPTY
Empty bag cannot stand /upright/ (An)—1797 (П)
Empty barrel (bowl, kettle) makes the most noise (An)—1791 (П)

Empty barrels make the greatest din (sound)—1791 (П)
Empty can makes a lot of noise (An)—1791 (П)
Empty casks make the most noise—1791 (П)
Empty pail makes the most noise (The)—1791 (П)
Empty sack cannot stand upright (An)—1797 (П)
Empty vessels make the most noise (sound)—1791 (П)
Empty wagon makes the most noise (The)—1791 (П)
Empty wagon rattles /loudest/ (An)—1791 (П)
He that is full of himself is very empty—2068 (Т)
It is hard for an empty sack to stand upright—1797 (П)
It's hard for an empty bag to stand upright—1797 (П)
Loaded wagon creaks, an empty one rattles (A)—1791 (П)

END
All good things come to an end—2262 (Ч)
All's well that ends well—248 (В)
Better is the end of a thing than the beginning thereof—1374 (Н)
Choice of the end covers choice of the means—2226 (Ц)
End crowns all (the work) (The)—863 (К)
End is not yet (The)—2058 (Т), 2352 (Э)
End justifies the means (The)—2226 (Ц)
Every hour has its end—2262 (Ч)
Everything has an end—1485 (Н), 2092 (У), 2262 (Ч)
Good to begin well, better to end well—995 (Л), 1272 (Н), 1374 (Н), 1416 (Н)
Ill life, an ill end (An)—782 (К), 1953 (С)
In the end, all (things) will mend—239 (В), 665 (З), 1509 (О), 1782 (П), 2048 (Т)
It'll all come right in the end—239 (В)
It's not the end of the world—1147 (М)
It will all work out in the end—239 (В)
Longest night must end (The)—2042 (Т)
Longest night will have an end (The)—2042 (Т)
Look to the end—1258 (Н)
Mark the end—1258 (Н)
Nothing is ill that ends well—248 (В)
There must be a beginning and an end to a thing—2262 (Ч)
Think of the end before you begin—1258 (Н)

ENEMY
Despise not your enemy—1413 (Н)
Every man carries an enemy in his own bosom—2248 (Ч)
Every man is his worst enemy—2248 (Ч)
Little enemies and little wounds must not be despised—1413 (Н), 1480 (Н)
Man's best friend and worst enemy is himself (A)—2248 (Ч)
One enemy is too many, and a hundred friends too few—2013 (С)
One enemy is too much for a man, and a hundred friends are too few—2013 (С)
There is no little enemy—1413 (Н), 1480 (Н)

ENJOY
Enjoy yourself: it's later than you think—449 (Д), 1526 (О)
Everyone enjoys himself in his own way—774 (К), 2086 (У), 2088 (У)

ENOUGH
Cook enough to feed an army—1585 (О)
Enough is enough—2233 (Ч)
Enough is as good as a feast—246 (В), 2187 (Х)
Enough is enough, and too much spoils—2187 (Х)
Enough is great riches—491 (Д)
Enough of a good thing is plenty—2187 (Х)

It is enough to puzzle a Philadelphia lawyer—1851 (C)
More than enough is too much—2187 (X)
Of enough men leave—1585 (O)
There is enough where there is not too much—246 (B)
There'll always be enough—1252 (H)
There was never enough where nothing was left—1585 (O)
What's enough for one is enough for two—1252 (H)

ENQUIRE
Enquire not what boils in another's pot—1419 (H)

ENVIOUS
Envious man grows lean (The)—145 (B), 585 (Ж)
Envious man shall never want woe (The)—145 (B), 585 (Ж)

ENVY
Better be envied than pitied—1053 (Л)
Envy and covetousness are never satisfied—611 (З)
Envy does not enter an empty house—324 (H)
Envy eats nothing but its own heart—585 (Ж)
Envy envies itself—585 (Ж)
Envy has no holiday—611 (З)
Envy is a two-edged sword—585 (Ж)
Envy never enriched any man—145 (B)
Envy never has a holiday—611 (З)
Envy shoots at others and wounds itself—585 (Ж)

EQUAL
All men are created equal—242 (B)
End makes all equal (The)—2149 (У)
Everyone to his equal—290 (B), 308 (B), 402 (Г), 674 (З), 675 (З), 1295 b (H), 1838 b (P), 1852 (C), 1853 (C)
Six feet of earth make (makes) all men equal—2149 (У)
Six feet of underground (under) makes all men equal—2149 (У)

ERR
Erring is not cheating—1624 (O)
To err is human—2251 (Ч)

ERRAND
Send a wise man on an errand and say nothing to him—2126 (У)

ERROR
Admitting error clears the score and proves you wiser than before—1623 (O)
From errors of others a wise man corrects his own—1221 (H)
It is no disgrace to acknowledge an error—1623 (O)

ETHIOPIAN
Can the Ethiopian change his colour (skin)?—383 (Г)

EVENING
Cloudy mornings /may/ turn to clear evenings—1891 (C)
Evening crowns (praises) the day (The)—2174 (X)
Morning to the mountain, the evening to the fountain (The)—233 (B)

EVENT
Great events from little causes spring—1156 (M)

EVERYONE
Everyone for himself—267 (B), 591 (Ж), 1975 (C)

EVERYTHING
Everything will turn out (work out) for the best—239 (B)

EVENSONG
Be the day never so long, at length comes evensong—804 (K)

EVIL
Avoid evil and it will avoid you—1274 (H)
Avoid the evil and it will avoid thee—1274 (H)
Between two evils 'tis not worth choosing—728 (И), 2215 (X), 2285 (Ч)
Choose the lesser of two evils—704 (И)

Desperate evils require desperate remedies—838 (К)
Evil be to him who evil thinks—666 (З), 921 (К)
Evil comes in by ells and goes away (out) by inches—23 (Б)
Evil doers are evil dreaders—2100 (У)
Evil doer weeps (The)—666 (З)
Evil does not cure evil—668 (З)
Evil gotten, evil spent—2221 (Х)
Evil is brought on by oneself—2248 (Ч)
Evil lesson is soon learnt (An)—551 (Д), 1202 (Н)
Evil that comes out of (goeth out of, issues from) thy mouth flieth into thy bosom (The)—917 (К)
Evil to him who evil does (thinks)—666 (З), 921 (К)
Evil will never said well—161 (В), 1591 (О), 2100 (У)
Evil won is evil lost—2221 (Х)
He knows best what good is that has endured evil—951 (К), 1291 (Н), 1458 (Н)
He who does evil suspects evil on the part of his fellow man—161 (В), 2100 (У)
He who thinks evil wishes it on himself—2294 (Ч)
If you help the evil, you hurt the good—190 (В)
Never do evil for evil—668 (З), 706 (И)
Never do evil hoping that good will come of it—668 (З), 706 (И)
Of two evils choose the least (the lesser, the prettier)—704 (И), 1055 (Л)
One evil breeds (brings) another—852 (К)
That which is evil is soon learned—551 (Д), 1202 (Н)
That which is good for the head, is evil for the neck and the shoulders—10 (А)
You cannot fight evil with evil—668 (З)

EWE
When the ewe is drowned she is dead—2308 а (Ч)

EXAMPLE
Example is better than precept—2163 (У)
Good example is the best sermon (A)—2163 (У)
Nothing is so infectious as example—551 (Д)

EXCEPTION
Exception proves the rule (The)—746 (И)
There is an exception to every rule—1448 (Н)
There is no general rule without exception—1448 (Н)
There's no rule without an exception—1448 (Н)

EXCESS
Excesses of our youth are draughts upon our old age (The)—2346 (Щ)
If in excess even nectar is poison—1919 (С)
Nothing in excess is best—1919 (С), 2187 (Х)

EXCHANGE
Exchange is no robbery—1121 (М)

EXCUSE
Excuse my French (my language)—712 (И)
Idle folks lack no excuses—1034 (Л), 2091 (У)
Lazy man always finds excuses (A)—1003 (Л), 1034 (Л), 1035 (Л), 2075 (Т), 2091 (У), 2113 (У)

EXPECT
Least expected, sure to happen—2239 (Ч)

EXPECTATION
Expectation always surpasses realization—2064 (Т)
Expectation is better than realization—2064 (Т)

EXPERIENCE
Believe one who has had experience—1410 (Н)
Experience is a hard master but a good teacher—1557 (О)
Experience is the best teacher—1557 (О)

Experience is the father of wisdom—1557 (O)
Experience is the mother of knowledge (of wisdom)—1557 (O)
Experience keeps no school, she teaches her pupils singly—2317 (Ч)
Experience teaches—1557 (O)
Profit by the experience of others—1221 (H)
Thorn of experience is worth a wilderness of advice (A)—1558 (O)
Troubles bring experience, and experience brings wisdom—33 (Б)
With experience comes knowledge—1557 (O)

EXPERT
Diligent working makes an expert workman—280 (B)

EXTREME
Extremes meet—883 (K)
No extreme will hold long—1570 (O)

EYE
Bad eyes never see any good—161 (B), 2100 (У)
Better eye out than always ache—1371 (H)
Better eye sore than all blind—704 (И)
Eye for an eye /, a tooth for a tooth/ (An)—1550 (O)
Eye is bigger than the belly (the mouth) (The)—104 (Б)
Eye is not satisfied with seeing (The)—1981 (C)
Eye is the mirror of the soul (the window of the heart, the window of the mind) (The)—343 (Г)
Eye of the master fattens the herd (The)—1614 (O)
Eye of the master will do more work than both his hands (The)—1614 (O)
Eyes are bigger than the stomach (The)—104 (Б)
Eyes are larger than the belly (The)—104 (Б)
Eyes are the mirror of the mind (The)—343 (Г)
Eyes are the mirrors (the windows) of the soul (The)—343 (Г)
Far from eye, far from heart—1816 (P), 1871 (C)
Four eyes are better (see more) than one—1531 (O)
Heart's letter is read in the eye (The)—343 (Г)
If the owner keeps his eye on the horse, it will fatten—1614 (O)
In the forehead and the eye the lecture of the mind doth lie—343 (Г)
It is better to trust the eye than the ear—1062 (Л), 1286 (H)
It is sure to be dark if you shut your eyes—2224 (X)
Keep your mouth shut and your eyes open—455 (Д)
Master's eye makes the horse fat (The)—1614 (O)
Men's ears are less reliable than their eyes—1286 (H)
One eye has more faith than two ears—1062 (Л)
No eye like the eye of the master (the master's eye)—338 (Г), 1614 (O), 1863 (C)
One eye of the master sees more than ten of the servants—1614 (O)
What the eye does not see, the heart cannot grieve (does not grieve over)—344 (Г)
What the eye doesn't see the heart doesn't crave for—1871 (C)
What the eye doesn't see, the heart doesn't grieve for (doesn't feel)—344 (Г)
What the eye sees not the heart rues not—344 (Г)

EYE-WITNESS
One eye-witness is better than ten hearsays—1062 (Л)
One eyewitness is better than two hear-so's—1062 (Л)

F

FACE
Empty purse fills the face with wrinkles (An)—295 (B)

Fancy may kill or cure—1082 (Л)
Fancy passes (surpasses) beauty—1080 (Л)

FAR
Farther in, the deeper (The)—2257 (Ч)
Go farther and far worse—2257 (Ч)
So near and yet so far—73 (Б), 152 (В), 153 (В)

FAST
Clean fast is better than a dirty breakfast (A)—1043 (Л), 1044 (Л)
Either a feast or a fast—1818 (Р)
Fast enough is well enough—503 (Д), 504 (Д)
Fasting comes after feasting—1643 (П), 1880 (С)
Feast today, /and/ fast tomorrow—1880 (С), 2229 (Ч)
Feast today makes fast tomorrow—1643 (П), 1880 (С)
Not too fast for /fear of/ breaking your shins—1980 (С)
Wisely and slowly—they stumble that run fast—1741 (П), 1979 (С)

FAT
Fat is in the fire (The)—434 (Д)
Little knows the fat man what the lean thinks—2015 (С), 2032 (С)
Little knows the fat sow what the lean does mean (the lean one thinks)—2032 (С)

FATE
Everyone is the maker of his own fate—2247 (Ч)
Fated will happen (The)—1610 (О)
Fate leads the willing and drags the unwilling—584 (Ж)
Fate leads the willing but drives the stubborn (The)—584 (Ж)
Fates lead the willing man; the unwilling they drag (The)—584 (Ж)
For whom ill is fated, him it will strike—1610 (О)
/There's/ no flying from fate—1610 (О), 2261 (Ч)

FATHER
As father, as son (so the son)—806 (К), 812 (К)
As mother and father, so is daughter and son—783 (К), 800 (К), 810 (К)
He whose father is judge goes safely to court—2199 (Х)
Like father, like child—800 (К), 812 (К)
Like father, like son—800 (К), 806 (К), 812 (К)
Many a good father has a bad son—741 (И)
Miserly father makes a prodigal son (A)—1586 (О)
Such a father, such a son—806 (К), 812 (К)
Such is the father, such is the son—806 (К), 812 (К)
Teach your father to get children—2368 (Я)
Thrifty father rarely has a thrifty son (thrifty sons) (A)—1586 (О)

FAULT
Blame not others for the faults that are in you—1473 (Н)
By others' faults wise men correct their own—1221 (Н)
Confessed faults are half mended—1661 (П)
Confession of a fault makes half amends for it—1661 (П)
Don't blame your faults on others—1473 (Н)
Don't lay your own faults at another person's (other persons') door—1473 (Н)
Every man has his faults—235 (В), 737 (И)
Every man's faults are not written on their foreheads—2084 (У)
Every man's faults are written on their foreheads—87 (Б), 971 (К), 1183 (Н), 1508 (О)
Every one's faults are not written in (on) their foreheads—2084 (У)
Every one's faults are written in (on) their foreheads—87 (Б), 971 (К), 1183 (Н), 1508 (О)
Fault confessed is half forgiven (half redressed) (A)—641 (З), 1661 (П)
Fault is thick, where love is thin—2143 (У)

Faults are thick when (where) love is thin—203 (В), 2143 (У)
He that commits a fault thinks everybody is speaking of it—155 (В)
He that corrects not small faults will not control great ones—2341 (Ш)
He who wants a mule without fault, must walk on foot—735 (И)
In every fault there is a folly—19 (Б)
It is difficult to admit your faults—396 (Г)
Know your own faults before blaming others for theirs—1087 (Л)
No one is without faults—1436 (Н), 2251 (Ч)
One man's fault is another man's lesson—1221 (Н)
When love cools all faults are seen—203 (В)
Where love fails, we espy all faults—203 (В)
Where there is no love, all are faults (all faults are seen)—203 (В)
Wink at small faults—1315 (Н)
You can find faults in an angel if you look hard enough—236 (В)

FAULT-FINDER
Nothing is safe from fault-finders—670 (З)

FAULTLESS
He is dead that is faultless—136 (В), 235 (В), 236 (В), 907 (К), 1436 (Н), 1515 (О), 2059 (Т), 2251 (Ч)
He is lifeless that (who) is faultless—235 (В), 236 (В), 907 (К), 1436 (Н), 1515 (О), 2059 (Т), 2251 (Ч)

FAULTY
Faulty stands on his guard (The)—155 (В)

FAVO(U)R
Do it as a personal favo(u)r—1306 (Н)

FEAR
Fear breeds terror—2154 (У)
Fear has a hundred (many) eyes—908 (К), 2154 (У)
Fear is greater than the reason for it (The)—2154 (У)
He that fears every bush must never go a-birding—186 (В)
He that fears every grass must not walk in the meadow—1824 (Р)
He that fears leaves, let him not go (must not come) into the wood—186 (В), 2072 (Т)
He that (who) fears you present, will hate you absent—616 (З), 923 (К)

FEAST
Feast and your halls are crowded—204 (В), 572 (Е), 1215 (Н)
Feasting is the physician's harvest—327 (Г)
It's either a feast or a famine—1818 (Р), 2229 (Ч)

FEATHER
Fair feathers make fair fowls—1517 (О)
Feather by feather a (the) goose is plucked—1662 (П)
Feather in the hand is better than a bird in the air (A)—1421 (Н)
Fine feathers do not make fine birds—1381 (Н)
Fine feathers make fine birds (fowl)—52 (Б), 1234 (Н), 1517 (О)
You can't get (pick, take) feathers off a toad—375 (Г), 826 (К)

FEED
I am fed up—2233 (Ч)

FEIGN
Nothing is lasting that is feigned—205 (В)

FENCE
Fence between makes friends more keen (A)—1990 (С)
Good fences make good neighbo(u)rs—1990 (С)
Love your neighbor, but do not pull down the fence—1990 (С)
Love your neighbour, yet pull not down your fence—1990 (С)
No fence against ill fortune—786 (К), 1611 (О)
There is no fence against ill fortune—1610 (О), 1611 (О)

FETTERS
No man loves /his/ fetters, be they made of gold—682 (З)

FEVER
Feed a cold and starve a fever—452 (Д)

FIDDLE
Fiddle cannot play without the bow (The)—42 (Б)
Older the fiddle, the better (the sweeter) the tune (The)—1997 (С)
There's many a good tune played on an old fiddle—1997 (С)
You can't play a fiddle without a fiddle-stick—42 (Б), 48 (Б), 49 (Б)

FIDDLER
If you dance (want to dance), you must pay the fiddler—1075 (Л)

FIDDLESTICK
Devil rides on a fiddlestick (The)—1146 (М)

FIELD
Distant fields look greener (greenest)—69 (Б)
Faraway fields look greenest—69 (Б)
Fields have eyes, and woods have ears—2153 (У)
Neglect not your own field to plough a neighbour's—2331 (Ч)
You water the fields of others while your own are parched—2330 (Ч), 2331 (Ч)

FIG
Figs do not grow on thistles—1608 (О)
One cannot gather grapes of thorns or figs of thistles—1608 (О)
You can't grow figs from thorns—1608 (О)

FIGHT
You cannot fight City Hall—990 a (Л), 1647 a (П), 1786 a (П)
You can't fight guns with sticks—990 a (Л), 1647 a (П), 1786 a (Р)

FIND
Fast bind, fast find—890 (К)
Finding is keeping—2308 b (Ч)
He that hides can find—890 (К)
Safe bind, safe find—890 (К), 1666 (П)
Sure bind, sure find—890 (К), 1666 (П)
Them that hides can find—890 (К), 1666 (П)
Those who hide know how to find—890 (К)

FINDER
Finders keepers /, losers weepers/—2308 b (Ч)

FINE
Rain before seven, fine before eleven—1296 (Н)

FINGER
Better a finger off than aye wagging—1371 (Н)
Cross your fingers—2278 (Ч)
Give a dog a finger and he will want a whole hand—1665 (П), 1793 (П)
Give him a finger and he will take a hand—406 (Д), 1665 (П)
He has a finger in every pie—1268 (Н)
My little finger told me—1934 (С), 1972 (С)
Point not at others' spots with a foul finger—1247 (Н), 1405 (Н), 1459 (Н)
Put not your finger between the bark and the tree—1164 (М), 1861 (С)
Scamp has a finger in every pie (The)—1268 (Н)
Too many fingers spoil the pie—2145 (У)
Where the pain is, the finger will be—1577 (О)

FIRE
Add not fire to fire—1516 (О)
Don't fire until you see the white of his eye—1408 (Н)
Don't play with fire—1477 (Н)
Fight fire with fire—838 (К), 2264 (Ч)
Fire and water are good servants but bad masters—1963 (С)
Fire burns brightest on one's own hearth (The)—126 (В)

Fire in the flint shows not till it's (until it is) struck (The)—1293 (Н)
Fire in the heart sends smoke into the head—356 (Г), 1085 (Л)
Fire is a good servant but a bad master—1477 (Н)
Fire which warms us at a distance will burn us when near (The)—1094 (Л)
Good fire makes a good cook (A)—2199 (Х)
Hidden fires are always the hottest—1293 (Н)
If you would enjoy fire, you must put up with the smoke—1073 (Л)
Little fire burns up a great deal of corn (A)—1156 (М)
Little fire is quickly trodden out (A)—747 (И)
Much smoke, little fire—553 (Д)
Nearer the fire, the hotter it is (The)—1094 (Л)
No fire without smoke—325 (Г)
Skeer your own fire—1419 (Н)
Slow fire makes sweet malt (A)—2054 (Т)
Soft fire makes sweet malt—2054 (Т)
Strike a flint and you get fire—690 (И), 1293 (Н)
There is no fire without smoke—325 (Г)
There is no jesting with fire—1477 (Н)
Two kitchen fires burn not on one hearth—420 (Д)
Violent fires soon burn out—722 (И)
When the fire burns in the soul, the tongue cannot be silent—2111 (У)
Where there is fire there is smoke—325 (Г)
You must fight fire with fire—2264 (Ч)

FIRST

All men can't be first—1298 (Н)
Be content in your lot; one cannot be first in everything—1298 (Н)
Better be first in a village than second at Rome—1046 (Л)
Cow that's first up, gets the first of the dew (The)—954 (К)
Everyone can't be first—1298 (Н)
First come, first served—954 (К), 963 (К), 1638 (П)
First there, first served—954 (К), 963 (К), 1638 (П)
First winner, last loser—952 (К), 956 (К), 1638 (П)
He that comes first to the mill may sit where he will—963 (К)
He who comes first grinds first—954 (К), 963 (К), 1638 (П)
I am not the first and I won't be the last—2370 (Я)
I am not the first, and shall not be the last—2370 (Я)

FISH

All is fish that comes to the net—264 (В), 479 (Д)
All's fish that comes to his net—264 (В), 479 (Д)
Best fish smell when they are three days old (/The/)—1131 (М)
Better a big fish in a little pond than a little fish in a big pond—1046 (Л)
Better a big fish in a little puddle than a little fish in a big puddle—1046 (Л)
Better a small fish than an empty dish—1056 (Л)
Big fish eat the little ones (The)—94 (Б), 925 (К)
Catch the fish before you fry it—2228 (Ц)
Cat that would eat fish must wet her feet (The)—2282 (Ч)
Do not fish in front of a net—2228 (Ц)
Don't clean your fish before you catch it—1388 (Н), 2228 (Ц)
Dry shoes won't catch fish—2282 (Ч)
Every fish is not a sturgeon—143 (В), 2170 (Ф)
Fish always stinks from the head downward (The)—1844 (Р)
Fish and callers (company, visitors) smell in three days—1131 (М)

Fish begins to stink at the head—1844 (Р)
Fish never nibbles at the same hook twice (A)—2005 (С)
Fish stinks first in the head (The)—1844 (Р)
Fish that escapes is the biggest fish of all (The)—875 (К)
Fish will soon be caught that nibbles at every bait (The)—1086 (Л)
Fresh fish and new-come guests smell in three days—1131 (М)
Great fish eat up the small (The)—94 (Б), 925 (К)
Gut no fish till you get them—1388 (Н)
He that would catch a fish must venture his bait—1752 (П)
He who would catch fish must not mind getting wet—1343 (Н), 2282 (Ч)
It is a silly fish that is caught twice with the same bait—178 (В), 2005 (С)
It is better to be the biggest fish in a small puddle than the smallest fish in a big puddle—1045 (Л)
It is good fish if it were but caught—2184 (Х), 2207 (Х)
Little fish are (is) sweet—1843 (Р)
Make not your sauce till you have caught the fish—1115 (М), 1388 (Н), 2228 (Ц)
Neither fish, flesh, nor fowl—1483 (Н)
Neither fish, nor flesh, nor good red herring—1483 (Н)
Never fry a fish till it's caught—1115 (М)
Never offer to teach fish to swim—1462 (Н), 1464 (Н), 1466 (Н)
Sea is full of other fish (The)—1136 (М), 1860 (С)
That fish is soon caught who nibbles at every bait—942 (К), 1086 (Л)
There are as good fish in the sea as ever came out of it—699 (И), 1010 (Л), 1439 (Н), 1440 (Н), 1860 (С)
There are better fish in the sea than have ever been caught—699 (И), 1010 (Л), 1439 (Н), 1440 (Н), 1860 (С)
There is as good fish in the sea as ever came out of it—1440 (Н)
Venture a small fish to catch a great one—1752 (П)

FISHING
It is ill fishing before the net—2228 (Ц)
It's good fishing in troubled waters—167 (В)

FIST
There is no arguing with a large fist—990 a (Л), 1647 a (П), 1786 a (П)

FIT
All things fit not all persons—2297 (Ч)

FLAME
Flame is not far from the smoke (The)—1432 (Н)
Old flame never dies (An)—1995 (С)

FLATTERER
Flatterer's bite is poisonous (The)—1012 (Л)

FLATTERY
Flattery butters no parsnips—2191 (Х)
Flattery is sweet poison—1012 (Л)

FLAY
You cannot flay the same ox twice—1964 (С)

FLEA
Even a flea can bite—1480 (Н)

FLESH
Spirit is willing, but the flesh is weak (The)—552 (Д), 754 (И)

FLINT
In the coldest flint there is hot fire—690 (И), 1293 (Н)

FLOCK
Flock follow the bell-wether (The)—976 (К)

FLOOD
Every flood has its ebb—2024 (С)
What the ebb takes out, the flood brings in—1219 (Н)

FLOURISH
It's one thing to flourish and another to fight—1325 (Н), 1472 (Н)
To flourish is one thing, to fight another—1325 (Н), 1472 (Н)

FLOW
Every ebb has its flow—1219 (Н)
Every flow must have its ebb—2024 (С)
Flow will have its ebb (A)—2024 (С)

FLOWER
April showers bring May flowers—8 (А), 1725 (П)
Handsomest flower is not the sweetest (The)—1301 (Н)
March wind and April showers bring forth May flowers—8 (А)
March winds and April showers bring /forth/ May flowers—8 (А)
One flower makes no garland—1533 (О), 1541 (О)

FLUX
All things are in the flux—245 (В)

FLY
Don't fly till your wings are fledged—1408 (Н)
Fly follows the honey (A)—316 (Г)
Fly sat upon the axle-tree of the chariot-wheel and said, What dust do I raise (The)!—732 (И)
You must lose a fly to catch a trout—1752 (П)

FOG
Fog cannot be dispelled with a fan (A)—141 (В), 688 (И), 1038 (Л)

FOIBLE
Every man has his foible—774 (К), 2086 (У)

FOLK
As the young folks see, the young folks do; as they hear, they say—2289 (Ч)
Far folk fare best—1917 (С), 2036 (Т)

FOLLY
Folly is an incurable disease—541 (Д), 2236 (Ч)
Folly is the most incurable of maladies—541 (Д)
Folly is wise in her own eyes—2129 (У), 2369 (Я)
Folly of one man is the fortune of another (The)—1221 (Н)
In every fault there is a folly—19 (Б)
Learn wisdom by the follies of others—1221 (Н)
Profit by the folly of others—1221 (Н)
Too much laughter discovers folly—545 (Д), 1941 (С)
There is no cure for folly—541 (Д), 2236 (Ч)

FOOD
God gives (sends) every bird its food, but he does not throw it into the nest—1220 (Н), 1644 (П), 2178 (Х)
More die of food than famine—327 (Г)

FOOL
Arguing with a fool shows there are two—537 (Д)
As the fool thinks, so the bell clinks—548 (Д)
Children and fools cannot lie—351 (Г)
Children and fools have merry lives—540 (Д)
Children and fools speak (tell) the truth—351 (Г)
Dreams give wings to fools—548 (Д)
Drunken man will get sober, but a fool will never get wise (A)—1803 (П)
Drunks sober up, fools remain fools—1803 (П)
Even a fool, when he holds his peace, is counted wise—1155 (М)
Every fool wants to give advice—2129 (У)
Every man has a fool in (up) his sleeve—51 (Б), 736 (И), 738 (И), 1187 (Н)

Fool always finds a bigger fool to praise him (A)—530 (Д)
Fool always finds another fool (A)—544 (Д)
Fool always rushes to the fore (A)—352 (Г), 527 (Д)
Fool and his gold are soon parted (A)—2096 (У)
Fool and his money are soon parted (A)—1428 (Н), 2021 (С), 2096 (У)
Fool can ask more questions in a minute than a wise man can answer in an hour (A)—1186 (Н)
Fool can ask more questions in an hour than a wise man can answer in seven years (A)—1186 (Н)
Fool can ask questions that wise men cannot answer (A)—1186 (Н)
Fool doth think he is wise, but the wise man knows himself to be a fool (The)—2129 (У)
Fool is born every minute (A)—525 (Д), 1211 (Н)
Fool is he who deals with a fool—537 (Д)
Fool is he who deals with other fools (A)—537 (Д)
Fool is known by his conversation (speech) (A)—542 (Д), 1566 (О)
Fool is known by his laughing (A)—542 (Д), 1941 (С)
Fool is wise in his own conceit (A)—2129 (У), 2369 (Я)
Fool may ask more questions /in an hour/ than a wise man can answer /in seven years/ (A)—1186 (Н)
Fool may give a wise man counsel (A)—528 (Д), 739 (И)
Fool may sometimes speak to the purpose (A)—528 (Д), 739 (И)
Fool may throw a stone into a well which a hundred wise men cannot pull out (A)—353 (Г), 535 (Д)
Fools and bairns should not see half-done work (things half-done)—524 (Д)
Fools and children cannot lie—2097 (У)
Fools and children speak (tell) the truth—2097 (У)
Fools and madmen speak the truth—2097 (У)
Fools are born not made—538 (Д), 539 (Д)
Fools are fain of nothing—548 (Д)
Fools are lucky—522 (Д)
Fool's bolt is soon shot (A)—542 (Д)
Fool's bolt may sometimes hit the mark (A)—528 (Д), 739 (И)
Fools build houses and wise men buy them—529 (Д)
Fools build houses for wise men to live in—529 (Д)
Fools cannot hold their tongues—2098 (У)
Fools do more hurt in this world than rascals (The)—1785 (П)
Fools for luck—522 (Д)
Fools go in crowds—525 (Д), 544 (Д)
Fools grow of themselves without sowing or planting—539 (Д)
Fools grow without watering—539 (Д)
Fools have fortune—543 (Д)
Fool's head never grows white (A)—540 (Д)
Fools lade the water, and wise men catch the fish—529 (Д)
Fools live poor to die rich—2342 (Ш)
Fools make feasts and wise men eat them—529 (Д), 1114 (М)
Fools multiply folly—349 (Г)
Fool's name appears everywhere (is seen in many places) (A)—352 (Г)
Fools' names and fools' faces are always seen in public places—352 (Г)
Fools need no passport—542 (Д)
Fools never prosper—1428 (Н), 2021 (С), 2096 (У)
Fools rush in where angels fear to tread—523 (Д)
Fools set stools for wise folks to stumble—353 (Г), 535 (Д)
Fools set stools for wise men to fall over (to stumble)—353 (Г), 535 (Д)
Fools tie knots, and wise men loosen (loose) them—353 (Г), 535 (Д)

Fool's tongue runs before his wit (A)—2098 (У)
Fool talks when he should be listening (A)—527 (Д)
Fool talks while a wise man thinks (A)—350 (Г)
Fools will be fools /still/—526 (Д), 532 (Д), 541 (Д), 1803 (П)
Fool when he is silent is counted wise (A)—1155 (M)
Fortune favo(u)rs fools—522 (Д), 543 (Д)
God sends fortune to fools—522 (Д)
Half a fool, half a knave—531 (K)
He is not the fool that the fool is but he that with the fool deals—537 (Д)
He who is born a fool is never cured—541 (Д)
If all fools wore feathers, we should seem a flock of geese—525 (Д)
If all fools wore white caps, we'd all look like (we should seem a flock of) geese—525 (Д), 1211 (H)
If every fool held a bauble, fuel would be dear—525 (Д)
If you argue with a fool, that makes two fools arguing—537 (Д)
If you want the truth, go to a child or a fool—351 (Г)
It's a trifle that makes fools laugh—545 (Д), 1941 (C)
It takes a fool to know a fool—1842 (P)
Let a fool hold his tongue, and he can pass for a sage—1155 (M)
Live a fool, die a fool—541 (Д)
Never joke with a fool—1875 (C)
Never show a fool half-done job—524 (Д)
No man is always a fool, but every man is sometimes—738 (И)
Older the fool, the worse he is (The)—2007 (C)
Old fool is worse than a young fool (An)—2007 (C)
Once a fool, always a fool—538 (Д), 541 (Д)
One fool makes a hundred (many)—349 (Г)
One fool praises another—530 (Д)
Only fools and horses work—1601 (O), 1808 (P)
Send a fool to France and he'll come a fool back—195 (B)
Send a fool to the market, and a fool he'll return—195 (B), 816 (K), 1567 (O)
There is no fool like an (to the) old fool—1881 (C), 2007 (C)
When a fool has bethought himself, the market's over—1733 (П), 1734 (П), 1986 (C)
When a fool has made up his mind, the market has gone by—1733 (П), 1734 (П), 1986 (C)
When a fool made up his mind, the market's over—1733 (П), 1734 (П), 1986 (C)
Wise men have their mouth in their heart, fools their heart in their mouth—350 (Г), 536 (Д)
Wise men silent, fools talk—350 (Г), 536 (Д)
Wise seek wisdom; the fool has found it (The)—2129 (У)
World is full of fools (The)—525 (Д), 1211 (H)
You can fool an old horse once, but you can't fool him twice—2005 (C)

FOOLING
Stop fooling around—1278 (H)

FOOLISHNESS
Foolishness grows by itself—no need to sow it—538 (Д), 539 (Д)

FOOT
Always put your best foot forward—2055 (T)
Better a bare foot than none at all—1070 (Л)
Cool mouth and warm feet live long (A)—452 (Д)
Feet are slow when the head wears snow (The)—364 (Г), 2003 (C), 2004 (C)
Foot at rest meets nothing (The)—1671 (П)
Going foot always gets something, if it is only a thorn (A)—182 (B)
Keep the bowels open, the head cool, and the feet warm and a fig for the doctors—452 (Д)

Little wit in the head makes much work for the feet—546 (Д), 624 (З)
My silly head will never save my feet—624 (З)
One foot is better than two crutches—1070 (Л)
Put your best foot forward—2055 (Т)
Six feet under makes all men equal—2149 (У)
Stand on your own two feet—267 (В)
Start off with the best foot—2055 (Т)
Take the load (the weight) off your feet—169 (В)
What you haven't got in your head, you have in your feet—624 (З)
Where the will is ready, the feet are light—318 (Г)
Willing heart carries a weary pair of feet a long way (A)—318 (Г)
Willing mind makes a light foot (A)—318 (Г)
Witless head makes weary feet (A)—624 (З)

FOOTSTEP
Master's footsteps fatten the soil (The)—338 (Г)

FORBID
Everything forbidden is sweet—640 (З)
Forbidden fruit is sweet (/the/ sweetest)—640 (З), 1200 (Н)

FORCE
Accusing is proving where malice and force sit judges—965 (К)
Where force prevails, right perishes—333 (Г), 965 (К)

FORESIGHT
If a man's foresight were as good as his hindsight, we would all get somewhere—619 (З)

FOREST
Forest is in an acorn (A)—2008 (С)
Some men go through a forest and see no firewood—1695 (П)
You can't see the forest for the trees—705 (И)

FOREWARNED
Forewarned is forearmed—760 (К)

FORGET
Quickly learned, soon forgotten—1242 (Н)
Seldom seen, soon forgotten—1871 (С)
Soon learnt, soon forgotten—1242 (Н)

FORGIVE
Forgive and forget—121 (Б), 970 (К)
He that does you an ill turn will never forgive you—924 (К)
Injured often forgive but those who injure neither forgive nor forget (The)—924 (К)

FORK
You dig your grave with your fork—327 (Г)

FORTUNATE
'Tis better to be born fortunate that wise—1403 (Н), 2022 (С)

FORTUNE
Fortune and misfortune are next-door neighbors—2024 (С)
Fortune comes to him who seeks her—922 (К)
Fortune favo(u)rs the bold (the brave)—326 (Г), 966 (К), 1411 (Н), 1578 (О), 1937 (С)
Fortune helps them that help themselves—1176 (Н)
Fortune is changeable—206 (В), 1879 (С)
Fortune is easily found, but hard to be kept—999 (Л)
Fortune is easy to find, but hard to keep—999 (Л)
Fortune is fickle—206 (В), 1879 (С)
Fortune is on the side of the bold—1937 (С)
Fortune is variant—1879 (С)
Fortune knocks at least once at every man's gate—2101 (У)
Fortune knocks once at every door—2101 (У)
Give a man fortune and cast him into the sea—861 (К)

Great fortune is a great slavery (servitude) (A)—1141 (M)
He dances well to whom fortune pipes—861 (K), 2199 (X)
One abides not long on the summit of fortune—1879 (C)
Wheel of fortune is forever in motion (The)—1879 (C)
When fortune knocks, open the door—1032 (Л)
When fortune smiles, embrace her (it)—1032 (Л)

FOUL
All fouled up—435 (Д)
He that has to do with what is foul never comes away clean—400 (Г), 1451 (H)
No man fouls his hands in his own business—72 (Б)

FOWL
Black fowl can lay white eggs—870 (K), 2267 (Ч)
Faraway fowls have fair feathers—69 (Б), 1917 (C)

FOX
At length the fox is brought to the furrier—2037 (T)
Don't put the fox to guard the henhouse—185 (B), 1023 (Л)
Even foxes are outwitted and caught—1042 (Л)
Every fox must pay with his skin to the flayer (furrier)—122 (Б), 780 (K), 1033 (Л)
Fox changes his skin but keeps his knavery (but not his habits) (The)—184 (B)
Fox knows much, but more he that catches him (The)—1042 (Л)
Fox may grow gray (grey), but never good—(The) 184 (B)
Fox is not caught twice in the same place (trap) (A)—178 (B), 2005 (C)
Fox is not taken twice in the same snare (trap) (A)—178 (B), 2005 (C)
Fox preys farthest from his home (The)—72 (Б), 1653 (П)
If the lion's skin cannot, the fox's shall—310 (Г)
Let every fox take care of his own brush—591 (Ж)
Long runs the fox, but at last is caught—780 (K), 1033 (Л), 1042 (Л), 2037(T)
Old fox does not run into the same snare a second time (An)—178 (B), 2005 (C)
Old foxes are not easily caught—1998 (C), 1999 (C)
Old foxes want no tutors—1462 (H), 1466 (H), 2164 (У)
Old fox is caught at last (The)—1042 (Л), 2037 (T)
Old fox is not easily snared (to be caught with a trap) (An)—1998 (C), 1999 (C)
Old fox needs learn no craft (An)—1466 (H)
Old fox needs not to be taught tricks (An)—1462 (H), 1464 (H), 1466 (H), 2006 (C)
Old fox understands the trap (An)—1998 (C)
Sleeping fox catches no chickens (The)—1145 (M)
Sleeping fox catches no geese (A)—1227 (H)
Sleeping fox catches no poultry (The)—1000 (Л), 1145 (M), 1227 (H), 1993 (C), 2212 (X)
Smartest fox is caught at last (The)—122 (Б), 1042 (Л)
When the foxes pack the jury box, the chicken is always found guilty as accused—965 (K)
When the fox sleeps no grapes fall in his mouth—1145 (M), 1227 (H), 1993 (C)
Wise fox will never rob his neighbour's hen-roost (A)—72 (Б), 1653 (П)
With foxes one must play the fox—1866 (C)
You can have no more of a fox than her skin—1974 (C)

FREE
Hens are free of horse corn—2324 (Ч)

FRIEND
Adversity has no friends—204 (B)

All are not friends that speak us fair—513 (Д)
Anything for a friend—466 (Д), 508 (Д)
Before you choose (make) a friend, eat a bushel of salt with him—108 (В), 509 (Д), 1457 (Н)
Before you make a friend, eat a peck of salt with him—108 (Б), 509 (Д), 1457 (Н)
Be slow in choosing a friend, but slower in changing him—1431 (Н)
Best way to gain a friend is to be one (The)—125 (В), 1074 (Л), 2211 (Х), 2328 (Ч)
Don't trade /in/ old friends for new—1492 (Н)
Faithful friend is better than gold (A)—1350 (Н)
False friends are worse than bitter (open) enemies—510 (Д)
Forsake not old friends for new—1492 (Н)
Friend in need is a friend indeed (A)—521 (Д), 867 (К), 1446 (Н)
Friend in power is a friend lost (A)—628 (З)
Father is a treasure, brother is a comfort but a friend is both—485 (Д)
Friend is best found in adversity (A)—521 (Д)
Friend is easier lost than found (A)—998 (Л)
Friend is never known till a man has (have) need (till (until) needed) (A)—512 (Д), 521 (Д), 867 (К), 1353 (Н)
Friend is not so soon gotten as lost (A)—998 (Л)
Friends are made in wine and proved in tears—521 (Д), 1446 (Н)
Friends are thieves of time—194 (В)
Friends are to be preferred to relatives—485 (Д)
Friends tie their purses with a spider's web—466 (Д)
Friends tie their purse with a cobweb thread—466 (Д)
Friend to all is a friend to none (A)—230 (В)
Friend to everybody is a friend to nobody (A)—230 (В)
God defend (deliver) me from my friends, from my enemies I can (will) defend myself—700 (И)
God protect me from my friends /; my enemies I know enough to watch/—700 (И)
God save me from my friends—700 (И)
Good friend is better than a hundred relatives (A)—485 (Д)
Good friend is my nearest relation (A)—485 (Д)
Good friend is worth more than a hundred relatives (A)—485 (Д)
He is a good friend who speaks well of us behind our back—124 (В)
He is my friend who speaks well behind my back—124 (В)
He that ceases to be a friend, never was one—510 (Д)
He who has many friends has no friends—520 (Д)
He who would have friends must show himself friendly—2328 (Ч)
I cannot be your friend and your flatterer—513 (Д)
If he is your flatterer, he can't be your friend—513 (Д)
If you want a friend, you will have to be one—2211 (Х)
Injured friend is the bitterest of foes (An)—630 (З)
In time of prosperity, friends will be plenty; in time of adversity not one amongst (in) twenty—204 (В), 1645 (П), 1901 (С)
It takes years to make a friend, but minutes to lose one—998 (Л)
It takes years to make a friend, but you can lose one in an hour—998 (Л)
Keep old friends with the new—1492 (Н)
Make new friends but keep the old /, for one is silver and the other is gold/—1492 (Н)
Man is known by his friends (A)—1896 (С)
Many acquaintances, but few friends—520 (Д)
Many kinsfolk, few friends—2206 (Х)

New things are the best things, but old friends are the best friends—144 (B)
No friend is like an old friend—144 (B), 2011 (C)
Old fish, old oil and an old friend are best—144 (B)
Old friends and old wine /and old gold/ are best—144 (B)
Old friends are best—144 (B), 2011 (C)
Old friends are better than new ones—2011 (C)
Old friends wear well—2011 (C)
Old tunes are sweetest, old friends are surest—144 (B), 2011 (C)
One old friend is better than two new—2011 (C)
Poverty parts friends—2176 (X)
Prosperity makes friends, and adversity tries them—521 (Д), 1446 (H)
Prosperity makes friends; adversity tries them—521 (Д), 1446 (H)
Reconciled friend is a double enemy (A)—630 (З)
Save me from my friends—700 (И)
They are rich who have true friends—1350 (H)
To have a friend, be one—623 (З)
To keep a new friend, never break with the old—1492 (H)
Treacherous friend is the most dangerous enemy (A)—510 (Д)
Way to have a friend is to be one (The)—125 (B), 1074 (Л), 2211 (X), 2328 (Ч)
When a friend asks, there is no tomorrow—508 (Д)
When fortune frowns, friends are few—1901 (C)
When good cheer is lacking, our friends will be packing—204 (B)

FRIENDLY

Be friendly and you will never want friends—125 (B)
He who would have friends must show himself friendly—2328 (Ч)
Man, to have friends, must show himself friendly (A)—1074 (Л), 2211 (X)

FRIENDSHIP

As long as the pot boils, friendship lasts—572 (E), 1215 (H), 1645 (П), 1901 (C), 2176 (X)
Broken friendship may be soldered but will never be sound (A)—516 (Д), 630 (З), 1718 (П), 2070 (T)
Broken friendships may be soldered, but never sound—516 (Д), 630 (M), 1718 (П), 2070 (T)
Feasting makes no friendship—1446 (H), 1901 (C)
Friendship cannot always stand on one side—125 (B), 623 (З), 1074 (Л), 2211 (X), 2328 (Ч)
Friendship cannot stand /all/ on one side—125 (B), 1074 (Л), 2211 (X), 2328 (Ч)
Friendship made in a moment is of no moment—108 (Б)
Friendship stands not on one side—623 (З), 1074 (Л)
Once a torn friendship, a patch can't be sewn—630 (З)
Sudden friendship, sure repentance—108 (Б), 1312 (H)
True friendship is a plant of slow growth—108 (Б), 1457 (H)

FROG

Better to be a big frog in a little pool than a little frog in a big pool—1046 (Л)
Frog cannot out of her bog (The)—779 (K)
You can't tell how far a frog will jump or a horse will run by the color of his hide—1417 (H)

FRUIT

By their fruits you shall know them—451 (Д)
Fruit doesn't fall far from the tree (The)—953 (K), 2348 (Щ), 2357 (Я)
Fruit of a good tree is also good (The)—478 (Д), 783 (K), 1615 (O)
Good fruit never comes from a bad tree—1616 (O)
He that would eat (have) the fruit must climb the tree—50 (Б)
Tree is known by its fruit (A)—451 (Д)

FRYING-PAN
Don't jump from the frying pan into the fire—709 (И), 1582 (О)
Out of the frying-pan (frying pan) into the fire—709 (И), 1582 (О)

FUEL
Add not fuel to flames (the fire)—1109 (М)

FULL
Full do not believe the hungry (The)—81 (Б), 2015 (С), 2032 (С)
It is ill speaking between a full man and a fasting—2032 (С)
There is little talk between a full man and a fasting—2015 (С)
When the pot's full, it runs over (it will boil over)—1727 (П)
When the well is full, it will run over—286 (В), 1727 (П), 2047 (Т)

FUN
Have fun in this life: you'll never get out of it alive—449 (Д), 1526 (О)
Have fun while you are young—1151 (М)

FUNNY
Everything is funny as long as it happens to someone else—1092 (Л), 2327 (Ч)

FUSS
Great fuss about nothing—1146 (М)

FUTURE
All the future exists in the past—1486 (Н)
Future is a sealed book (The)—1478 (Н)

G

GAIN
Dishonest gains are losses—2221 (Х), 2323 (Ч)
Everyone fastens where there is gain—316 (Г)
Evil gain is equal to a loss (An)—2221 (Х), 2323 (Ч)
Ill-gotten gains are soon lost—658 (З), 2221 (Х)
Ill-gotten gains never prosper—2221 (Х)
Light gains make a heavy purse (heavy purses, heavy profits)—868 (К)
Little gain, little pain—1123 (М)
No great loss without some small gain—1219 (Н)

GALE
No gale can equally serve all passengers—1184 (Н)

GALLOWS
End of the thief is the gallows (The)—122 (Б), 780 (К), 1042 (Л), 1659 (П), 1907 (С), 2037 (Т)
Near the king, near the gallows—74 (Б)

GAMBLER
Unlucky gambler, lucky lover—1282 (Н)

GAMBLING
Gambling is the son of avarice and the father of despair—697 (И)
Gambling is the son of avarice, the brother of iniquity and the father of mischief—697 (И)

GAME
At the game's end we shall see who gains—1739 (П)
First game is kid's game—1528 (О)
Game is lost (The)—434 (Д)
Game is not worth the candle (the money) (The)—698 (И), 1514 (О)
Game is up (The)—434 (Д)
Game walks into the bag (The)—1207 (Н)
It is a game at which two can play—1739 (П)
Two can play at that game—1739 (П)
What's the game?—2290 (Ч)
You play my game, and I'll play yours—2077 (Т)

GANDER
As is the gander, so is the goose—787 (К), 1162 (М)
There is no goose so grey in the lake that cannot find a gander for her make—46 (Б)

There's never a goose so old and gray but what a gander would wonder her way—46 (Б)

GAP
Some have the hap, others stick in the gap—1539 (О)
Some of us have the hap; some stick in the gap—1539 (О)

GARBAGE
Garbage in, garbage out—2260 (Ч), 2284 (Ч)

GARDEN
As is the garden, such is the gardener—154 (В)
Good garden always has weeds (A)—1452 (Н)
No garden without its weeds—1452 (Н)
Weed your own garden first—1128 (Н)

GARDENER
As is the gardener so is the garden—793 (К), 797 (К), 802 (К)
Bad gardener quarrels with his rake (A)—1111 (М)

GARMENT
Borrowed garments fit not (never fit /well/)—1263 (Н)
Garment makes the man (The)—1517 (О)
Our last garment is made without pockets—2133 (У)
You must cut your garment according to the cloth—1708 (П)

GAS
All is gas and gaiters—226 (В), 426 (Д)

GATE
It that lies not in your gate breaks not your shin—1419 (Н)

GAY
Be gay today, for tomorrow you may die—449 (Д), 1526 (О)

GEAR
Little gear, less care—1123 (М)

GENERAL
Too many generals and no privates—1882 (С)

GENEROUS
It is easy to be generous with what is another's—719 (И), 2324 (Ч)

GENTILITY
Gentility without ability is worse than plain beggary—2218 (Х)

GEORGE
Everything is George—226 (В)
That's real George—226 (В)

GET
Since we cannot get what we like, let us like what we can get—491 (Д)
You can't get there from here—1851 (С)
You get what you give—824 (К)
You get what you pay for—458 (Д), 459 (Д)
You won't get away with this—2356 (Э)

GIFT
Beware of the Greeks bearing gifts (of the gift-bearing Greeks)—101 (Б), 1338 (Н)
Bound is he that gifts taketh—2329 (Ч)
Enemy's gifts are no gifts (An)—1338 (Н)
Gift in the hand is better than two promises (A)—1421 (Н), 1423 (Н)
Gift is better than a promise (A)—1421 (Н)
Gift long waited for is sold, not given (A)—1542 (О)
Gifts from enemies are dangerous—1338 (Н)
I fear the Greeks, even when bringing gifts—101 (Б)
Throw no gift again at the giver's head—416 (Д)
Who receives a gift sells his liberty—404 (Д), 2329 (Ч)

GIRL
Every girl has her day—260 (В)
Girls will be girls—456 (Д)
Girl that thinks no man is good enough for her is right, but she's left (The)—495 (Д)

GIVE
Better give than receive—1050 (Л)

Better to give than to take—1050 (Л)
Don't give me that—1826 (Р), 1858 (С)
Give and take—622 (З)
Give and you shall receive—622 (З)
He gives twice who gives in a trice—419 (Д)
He gives twice who gives promptly (quickly)—419 (Д), 1422 (Н)
I give it for what it is worth—657 (З)
I'll give my head for it—415 (Д)
It is better to give than to receive—1050 (Л)
It is more blessed to give than to receive—1050 (Л)
No one can give what he hasn't got—375 (Г)
What we gave we have—824 (К)

GIVE UP
Never give up once you have started—652 (З), 1257 (Н)

GLASS
He whose windows are of glass should never throw stones—1087 (Л)
People living in glass houses should not throw stones—1087 (Л), 1405 (Н), 1459 (Н)

GLORY
Greater the obstacle, the more glory in overcoming it (The)—2266 (Ч)
No path of flowers conducts (leads) to glory—2266 (Ч)

GLOVE
Clean glove often hides a dirty hand (A)—1837 (Р), 1859 (С)

GLUTTONY
Gluttony kills more than the sword—327 (П)

GO
Better go around (to go about) than fall into the ditch—575 (Е), 1060 (Л), 2128 (У)
Come easy, go easy—993 (Л)
Come light, go light—993 (Л)
Come with the wind, go with water—993 (Л)
Easy come, easy go—993 (Л)
Go along with you—1278 (Н)
Go home and say your prayers—1419 (Н)
Gone for a holiday—693 (И)
Gone with the wind—693 (И)
Here today and gone tomorrow—1878 (С)
Here today, gone tomorrow—1878 (С)
If you are going down, go down in a blaze of glory—1703 (П)
If you are going out, go out in style—1703 (П)
If you are going to go, go all the way (go in style)—1703 (П)
If you must go down, go down in flames—1703 (П)
It's no go—2356 (Э)
Light come, light go—993 (Л)
Lightly come, lightly go—993 (Л), 1779 (П)
Lightly won, lightly gone—993 (Л)
No go—2356 (Э)
Quickly come, quickly go—1779 (П)
Soon gained, soon gone—1779 (П)
That's the way it goes—2035 (Т)
There you go—2035 (Т)
What goes around comes around—778 (К), 798 (К), 824 (К)
What's going down (on /around here/, up)?—2290 (Ч)
What's gone and what's past help should be past grief—2295 a (Ч)
You can't go far in a rowboat without oars—42 (Б), 48 (Б)

GOAT
Don't play the giddy goat—1278 (Н)

GOD
God gives every bird its food, but he does not throw it into the nest—1644 (П)
God helps those who help themselves—85 (Б), 1176 (Н)
God is too good for a desperate mood—1330 (Н)
God never sends a mouth but he feeds it—84 (Б)
God never sends a mouth (mouths) but he sends meat—84 (Б)
God reaches us good things by our own hands—85 (Б), 1176 (Н), 2178 (Х)

God sends every bird its food, but he does not throw it into the nest—1644 (П), 2178 (Х)
God speed!—1482 (Н)
Man proposes, /and (but)/ God disposes—2246 (Ч)

GOLD
All is not gold that glitters—56 (Б), 1301 (Н)
All that glistens is not gold—1301 (Н)
Fire is the test of gold—686 (З)
Fire proves the gold—686 (З)
Gold dust blinds the eyes—440 (Д)
Gold grows not on trees—438 (Д)
Gold is but muck—1280 (Н)
Gold is tried in the fire—686 (З)
Gold must be tried by fire—686 (З)
Gold rules the world—439 (Д), 687 (З)
Man may buy gold too dear (A)—756 (И)
Much gold, much care—1141 (М)
No ear is deaf to the song that gold sings—618 (З), 684 (З)
No gold without his dross—737 (И)
No lock will hold against the power of gold—439 (Д)
When gold speaks, everyone is silent—842 (К)
When gold speaks other tongues are dumb—842 (К)
You may speak with your gold and make other tongues dumb (silent)—842 (К)

GONG
All gong and no action—1143 (М)

GOOD
All good things come (must come) to an end—1297 (Н)
Do no good and you shall find no evil—1307 (Н)
Good can never grow out of bad (evil)—706 (И), 1616 (О)
Good comes to some while they are sleeping—543 (Д), 1967 (С)
Good for the liver may be bad for the spleen—10 (А)
Good that comes too late is good as nothing—411 (Д), 503 (Д), 504 (Д), 506 (Д), 1736 (П)
Good that men do lives after them (The)—472 (Д)
Good things do not last for ever—1297 (Н)
Good things soon find a purchaser—1255 (Н), 2194 (Х)
Good ware makes a good (quick) market—1255 (Н), 2194 (Х)
Good we confer on others recoils on ourselves (The)—1197 (Н)
Good you do to others will always come back to you (The)—474 (Д), 622 (З), 1197 (Н)
I am as good as the next person—731 (И), 1168 (М)
Never do evil hoping that good will come of it—668 (З), 706 (И)
None so good that it's good to all—2307 (Ч)
None's so good that's good at all—737 (И), 1436 (Н)
Nothing but is good for something—266 (В)
Nothing is so good as it seems beforehand—2064 (Т)
Nothing /is/ so good but it might have been better—2313 (Ч)
So far, so good—1266 (Н)
That which is good for the back, is bad for the head—10 (А)
That which is good for the head, is evil for the neck and the shoulders—10 (А)
Too good is stark nought—75 (Б), 1110 (М)
What is good for one man, may not be good for another—1548 (О), 2039 (Т), 2307 (Ч)

GOODBYE
Everyone who says goodbye is not gone—89 (Б)

GOODS
All men are free of other men's goods—2324 (Ч)
Ill-gotten goods seldom prosper—658 (З), 2221 (Х), 2323 (Ч)
Little goods, little care—38 (Б), 1123 (М)

GOOSE
All is well and the goose hangs high—226 (В), 426 (Д)

All one's geese are swans—462 (Д)
As is the goose so is the gander—1162 (М)
Everything is lovely and the goose hangs high—226 (В), 426 (Д)
Geese with geese, and women with women—290 (В), 308 (В), 402 (Г), 674 (З), 675 (З), 1295 b (Н), 1852 (С), 1853 (С), 2270 (Ч)
Goose hangs high (The)—226 (В), 426 (Д)
He that has a goose will get a goose—319 (Г), 441 (Д)
If you cook your own goose, you will have to eat it—1848 (С)
Older the goose, the harder to pluck (The)—166 (В)
Setting goose has no feathers on her breast (A)—1394 (Н)
There is no goose so grey in the lake, that cannot find a gander for her make—46 (Б), 260 (В)
There's never a goose so old and gray but what a gander would wander her way—46 (Б), 260 (В)
Wild goose never laid a tame egg (A)—1616 (О), 1617 (О)

GOSSIP
Gossip needs no carriage—1090 (Л), 1261 (Н)
Gossips are frogs, they drink and talk—1090 (Л), 1261 (Н)
Gossips drink and talk; frogs drink and squawk—1090 (Л), 1261 (Н)

GRAIN
Grain by grain and the hen fills her belly—979 (К)
Of evil grain no good seed can come—706 (И), 1616 (О)
One grain fills not the sack but it helps his fellow—664 (З), 979 (К)
There is more than one grain of sand on the seashore—1439 (Н), 1860 (С)
Though one grain fills not the sack, it helps—664 (З), 1740 (П), 1947 (С)

GRANDMOTHER
Don't teach your grandmother to suck eggs—2368 (Я)
So is your sister's cat's grandmother—1612 (О)

GRAPES
Black grape is as sweet as a white (A)—1182 (Н)
Foxes, when they cannot reach the grapes, say they are not ripe—662 (З)
Grapes are sour (The)—662 (З)
One cannot gather grapes of thorns or figs of thistles—1608 (О)
Sour grapes can never make sweet wine—714 (И), 718 (И)
"Sour grapes," said the fox when he could not reach them—662 (З)

GRASP
Grasp a little, and you may secure it; grasp too much, and you will lose everything—1030 (Л), 1142 (М), 2081 (Т)
Grasp all, lose all—2081 (Т)
Grasp no more than the hand will hold—2081 (Т)
He that (who) grasps at too much holds nothing fast—1142 (М)

GRASS
Grass doesn't grow on a busy street—1251 (Н)
Grass grows not at the market cross—1251 (Н)
Grass grows not upon the highway—1251 (Н)
Grass is always greener away from home—2036 (Т)
Grass is always greener on the other side of the fence (hill) (The)—296 (В), 978 (К), 2036 (Т), 2185 (Х)
Grass is always greener on the other side of the street (The)—978 (К)
Trodden path bears no grass (A)—1251 (Н)
While the grass grows the horse starves—1685 (П), 1687 (П), 1688 (П)
While the grass grows the steed starves—1687 (П)

GRAVE
Graves are of all sizes—244 (В), 1938 (С)
Grave levels all distinctions (The)—2149 (У)

Grave will receive us all (The)—244 (В)
He who digs a grave for another falls in himself—917 (К)
More thy years, the nearer the grave (The)—2230 (Ч)
Only in the grave is there rest—292 (В), 1691 (П)
We /shall/ all lie alike in our graves—2149 (У)
You dig your grave with your own hands—2248 (Ч)

GRAVEYARD
Peace is found only in the graveyard—292 (В), 1691 (П)

GRAVY
One man's gravy is another man's poison—2307 (Ч)

GREASE
He who greases well drives well—1387 (Н)

GREAT
Great man makes the great thing (The)—1893 (С)
Nothing great is easy—2266 (Ч)

GREED
Greed killed the wolf—580 (Ж)

GREEDINESS
Greediness bursts the bag—1030 (Л), 2081 (Т)

GREEDY
Greedy folk (folks) have long arms—342 (Г)
Greedy never know when they have had enough (The)—342 (Г), 1377 (Н)

GREEK
Beware of the Greeks bearing gifts (of the gift bearing Greeks)—101 (Б), 1338 (Н)
I fear the Greeks, even when bringing gifts—101 (Б)
When Greek meets Greek, then comes the tug of war—554 (Д), 889 (К), 1267 (Н)

GRIEF
All griefs are less with bread—600 (Ж), 1683 (П)
Great griefs are mute—92 (Б)
Grief divided is made lighter—389 (Г)
Grief is lessened when imparted to others—389 (Г), 1209 (Н)
Grief often treads upon the heels of pleasure—330 (Г)
Little griefs are loud, great griefs (sorrows) are silent—92 (Б), 994 (Л)
Good relief for grief is action (A)—1920 b (С)
Only cure for grief is action (The)—1157 (М), 1920 b (С)
Secret griefs are the sharpest—994 (Л)
Time erases all griefs—216 (В)
What's gone and what's past help should be past grief—1920 a (С), 2281 a (Ч)

GRIEVANCE
Never rip up old grievances—970 (К)

GRIEVE
Don't grieve over spilt milk—1920 a (С)
It is too late to grieve when the chance is past—2281 a (Ч)
Never grieve for what you cannot help—1920 a (С), 2302 (Ч)

GRIN
Grin and bear it!—307 (В), 1484 (Н)
You must grin and bear it—1484 (Н)

GRIST
All is grist /that comes (goes)/ to the mill—264 (В), 479 (Д)
No grist is ground with the water that is passed—67 (Б)

GROAN
One man's laugh is another man's groan—879 (К)

GROOM
Every groom is a king at home—275 (В)

GROUND
Our neighbour's ground yields better corn than ours—2185 (Х)

GRUDGE
Do not grudge others what you cannot enjoy yourself—745 (И)

GRUNT
You can't take the grunt out of a pig—383 (Г), 715 (И), 1955 (С)

GUESS
Your guess is as good as mine—1518 (О)

GUEST
Be my guest—188 (В)
Constant guest is never welcome (A)—1827 (Р), 2186 (К), 2232 (Ч)
Constant guest will wear out his visit (A)—1827 (Р), 2232 (Ч)
Dinner over, away go the guests (The)—572 (Е), 1215 (Н), 1645 (П), 1901 (С)
Fresh fish and new-come guests smell in three days—1131 (М)
Speed the parting guest—89 (Б)
Unbidden guest is a bore and a pest (The)—1345 (Н)
Unbidden guest knows not where to sit (An)—958 (К), 1212 (Н)
Unbidden guest must bring his stool with him (An)—1212 (Н)
Unbidden guests are most welcome when they are gone—1212 (Н), 1345 (Н)
Unbidden guests are welcome when they are gone—1345 (Н)
Unbidden guests quickly outstay their welcome—1345 (Н)

GUILT
Guilt makes the bravest man a coward—155 (В)

GUILTY
Guilty flee when no man pursues (The)—155 (В)
Guilty men see guilt written on the faces of saints—161 (В)
He is as guilty who holds the bag as he who puts in—197 (В)
He that hinders not a mischief is guilty of it—197 (В)
Suspicion always haunts the guilty party—155 (В)
Truest jester sounds worst in guilty ears (The)—155 (В)
Truest jests sound worst in guilty ears (The)—155 (В)

GUNNER
Gunner to the linstock, and the steersman to the helm (The)—62 (Б), 989 (Л)

GUTTER
Who repairs not his gutters repairs the whole house—2341 (Ш»)

H

HABIT
Habit cures habit—838 (К)
Habit is a cable—1768 (П)
Habit is a second nature—1768 (П), 2076 (Т)
Habit is overcome by habit—838 (К)
Habits are hard to break—1768 (П)
Old habits die hard—1768 (П)

HAIR
Bush natural; more hair than wit—1192 (Н)
Grey hairs are nourished with green thoughts—1881 (С)
Hair by hair you pull out the horse's tail—1662 (П)
Hair long, wisdom little—187 (В)
Hair of the dog is good for the bite (The)—838 (К), 2264 (Ч)
Hair of the dog is the cure of his bite (The)—838 (К)
It's no hair off my head—1159 (М)
Long hair and short sense—187 (В)
Long hair, short wit—187 (В)
Take the hair of the dog that bit you—838 (К)
Take the hair of the same dog that bit you, and it will heal the wound—838 (К), 2264 (Ч)
Women have long hair and short brains—187 (В)
You can't grow hair and brains in the same head—187 (В)

HALF
Do nothing by halves—652 (З), 1257 (Н)

Do what you do with all your might: things done half are never done right—652 (З)
Half is better (more) than the whole (/The/)—1057 (Л)
Never do things by halves—652 (З), 1257 (Н)
Things done half are never done right—652 (З)

HALL
Public hall is never swept (A)—320 (Г)

HALLOO
Don't halloo till you are out of the wood—1321 (Н), 1469 (Н), 2172 (Х)
Don't halloo till you're out of the woods—1321 (Н), 1469 (Н), 2172 (Х)

HALT
It's ill halting before a cripple—129 (В), 1322 (Н)

HALTER
Name not a halter in his house that hanged himself (that was hanged)—129 (В), 1322 (Н)

HAMMER
You can't saw wood with a hammer—695 (И)

HAND
Busy hands are happy hands—1839 (Р)
By the hands of many a great work is made light—1135 (М), 1523 (О)
Clean hand needs (wants) no washing (A)—1760 (П)
Cold hand, a warm heart (A)—2183 (Х)
Don't bite the hand that feeds you—1404 (Н)
Don't bite the hand that butters your bread—1404 (Н)
Empty hand is no lure for the hawk (An)—831 (К), 1387 (Н), 2019 (С)
Empty hands allure no hawks—831 (К), 1387 (Н), 2019 (С)
Hand that gives gathers (The)—474 (Д), 592 (Ж), 622 (З)
It's the new hand who always gets the short-handed rake—1639 (П)
Left hand doesn't know what the right hand is doing (The)—1754 (П)
Man lays his hand where he feels the pain (A)—1577 (О), 2111 (У)
Many hands make light (quick) work—13 (А), 61 (Б), 849 (К), 1135 (М), 1523 (О)
Many hands make work light—1523 (О)
Nothing enters into a closed (close) hand—1387 (Н)
One hand claws another—1840 (Р)
One hand washes another (the other)—1840 (Р)
One hand will not clasp—1524 (О)
Put not your hand between the bark and the tree—1164 (М), 1861 (С)
Put your hand no farther than your sleeve will reach—1708 (П)
Scatter with one hand, gather with two—622 (З), 836 (К)
Too many hands in the pot make poor soup—2145 (У)
Too many hands spoil the pie—2145 (У)
Two hands are better than one—517 (Д)

HANDFUL
You may know by a (the) handful the whole sack—1705 (П)

HANDSOME
Handsome is as (that, who) handsome does—1447 (Н), 1621 (О), 1928 (С)

HANG
As good be hanged for a sheep as a goat (a lamb)—1884 (С)
As well be hung for a sheep as /for/ a lamb—1884 (С)
He that is born to be hanged shall never be drowned—859 (К)
He whose destiny is to be hanged will never be drowned—859 (К)
If you're born to be hanged, then you'll never be drowned—859 (К)
Let us all hang together or hang separately—12 (А), 139 (В), 517 (Д)
Might as well be hanged for a sheep as a lamb—1884 (С)

HAPPEN
It didn't happen by itself—315 (Г)

HAPPINESS
Happiness is not perfect until it is shared—390 (Г), 1814 (Р)
Happiness takes no account of time—2020 (С)
May your sun of happiness never set—1959 (С)
Money can't (won't) buy happiness—756 (И), 2023 (С)
One does not appreciate happiness unless one has known sorrow—1291 (Н), 1458 (Н)
Peace and happiness—1959 (С)

HAPPY
Better be happy than wise—1403 (Н)
Call no man happy till he dies (he is dead)—2174 (Х)
He is happy who finds peace in his home—655 (З)
Just because a man sings, it's no sign he's happy—1311 (Н)
Not everyone who dances is happy—1311 (Н)

HARD
Hardest job is no job (The)—1455 (Н)
Hardest work is to do nothing (The)—1455 (Н)
He has hard work indeed who has nothing to do—1455 (Н)
He has hard work (works hard) who has nothing to do—1455 (Н)
Lazy man works the hardest (A)—1455 (Н)
What is hard to bear is sweet to remember—2306 (Ч)

HARDSHIP
Through hardships to the stars—2266 (Ч)

HARE
Don't run with the hound and hold on to the hare—422 (Д)
Even hares insult a dead lion—1650 (П), 1673 (П)
First catch your hare—1115 (М), 2228 (Ц)
First catch your hare before you skin it—1115 (М)
First catch your hare, then cook him (it)—2228 (С)
Hares can gambol over the body of a dead lion—1650 (П)
Hares may pluck (pull) dead lions by the beard—1124 (М), 1650 (П)
He who chases two hares catches neither—617 (З)
He who hunts two hares leaves one and loves the other—617 (З)
If you run after two hares, you will catch neither—617 (З)
Lions in peace, hares in war—272 (В)
Timid hare dares to pluck the dead lion by the beard (The)—1124 (М), 1650 (П), 1673 (П)
You cannot run with the hare and hunt with the hounds—422 (Д)

HARM
Harm watch, harm catch—921 (К), 2294 (Ч)
He who does harm should expect harm—2294 (Ч)
It is good to beware by other men's harms—2315 (Ч)
Keep out of harm's way—1583 (О)
Of two harms choose the least—704 (И)
Stay out of harm's way—1583 (О)

HASTE
/Fool's/ haste is no speed—1912 (С)
Haste is slow—1912 (С)
Haste makes waste—249 (В), 1609 (О), 1741 (П), 1911 (С), 1979 (С)
Haste may trip up (trips over) its own heels—1741 (П)
Make haste but do not hurry—1980 (С)
Make haste slowly—1980 (С)
Make haste while the sun shines—606 (Ж)
More haste, less (worse) speed—1741 (П), 1912 (С)
Nothing should be done in haste but gripping a flee—1742 (П)
Nothing to be done in haste but catching fleas—1742 (П)

Things will never be bettered by an excess of haste—1911 (С)

HASTY
Hasty bitch brings forth blind puppies (whelps) (The)—1741 (П)
Hasty burned his lips (The)—1741 (П)
Hasty climbers have sudden falls—1741 (П)
Hasty man is seldom out of trouble (A)—1741 (П)
Hasty man never wants woe (A)—1741 (П)

HAT
Broad hat does not always cover a venerable head (A)—1313 (Н)
What counts most is what you've got under your hat—1381 (Н)

HATCHET
Don't take a hatchet to break eggs—632 (З), 713 (И), 1561 (О)
Send not for a hatchet to break open an egg with—713 (И)

HATE
Folks often injure all they fear and hate all they injure—924 (К)
Greatest hate comes (springs) from the greatest love (The)—1593 (О)
Love and hate are the two closest emotions—1593 (О)
Men hate where they hurt—924 (К)
Thinnest line is between love and hate (The)—1593 (О)
We hate those whom we have done wrong—924 (К)

HAVE
If you cannot have the best, make the best of what you have—1370 (Н)
To him that has shall be given—319 (Г), 441 (Д)
What we gave we have—824 (К)

HAW
When /all/ fruit (the fruit) fails, welcome haws—1174 (Н)

HAWK
Hawks will not pick hawks' eyes out—196 (В)

HAY
Make hay while the sun shines—606 (Ж), 873 (К), 977 (К)

HEAD
Better be the head of a dog (a fox, a lizard, a mouse) than the tail of a lion—1045 (Л)
Better be the head of an ass than the tail of a horse—1045 (Л)
Better be the head of the yeomanry than the tail of the gentry—1046 (Л)
Big head and little wit (/A/)—97 (Б), 138 (В), 366 (Г), 1031 (Л), 1836 (Р)
Big head, little sense—97 (Б), 366 (Г)
Good head does not want a hat (A)—114 (Б)
Hat will never be worn without a head (A)—114 (Б)
Heads I win, tails you lose—1148 (М)
Heaviest head of corn hangs its head lowest (The)—1795 (П)
I'll stick my head out—323 (Г), 2265 b (Ч)
Keep the bowels open, the head cool, and the feet warm and a fig for the doctors—452 (Д)
Keep your head up!—307 (В)
Many heads are better than one—1531 (О)
Mickle (Muckle) head, little wit—97 (Б), 366 (Г)
Small head, big ideas—1099 (М), 1105 (М)
So many heads, so many wits—1908 (С)
There's no head like an old head—2009 (С)
Two heads are better than one—1531 (О), 2135 (У)
Use your head for something besides a hat rack—365 (Г)
When the head aches, all the body is the worse—11 (А)
Who has a head will not want a hat—114 (Б)

HEAL
Before healing others, heal yourself—511 (Д)

Man (One) is not so soon healed as hurt (A)—90 (Б)

HEALTH
Find health better than gold—660 (З), 1398 (Н)
First wealth is health (The)—660 (З)
Good health is above wealth—660 (З)
Good health is priceless—660 (З)
Health is better than wealth (great riches)—660 (З)
Health is not valued till sickness comes—2067 (Т)
Health is /the best/ wealth—660 (З), 1398 (Н)
He that wants health wants all—660 (З)
Wealth can buy no health—661 (З)
Wealth is nothing without health—660 (З), 1398 (Н)
Without health no one is rich—660 (З)

HEAR
Be swift to hear, slow to speak—96 (Б)
Half is false of what you hear—1091 (Л)
Hear all, /and/ say nothing—96 (Б)
Hear much, speak little—96 (Б)
Not a breath was heard—1936 (С)
Season all you hear with salt—1091 (Л), 1303 (Н), 1316 (Н)
What you don't hear will not hurt you—2237 (Н)
When we sing everybody hears us, when we sigh nobody hears us—204 (В), 251 (В)
You could have heard (could hear) a pin drop—1936 (С)

HEART
Bold heart is half the battle (A)—1937 (С)
Cold hand, a warm heart (A)—2183 (Х)
Drunken heart won't lie—1807 (П), 2312 (Ч)
Every man after his own heart—258 (В)
Faint heart never won fair lady—1937 (С)
Heart soon forgets what the eye sees not (The)—1871 (С)
Human heart is a mystery (The)—1454 (Н), 1888 (С), 2319 (Ч)
Nearest the heart comes first out—2111 (У)
Nearest the heart, nearest the mouth—2111 (У)
To a valiant heart nothing is impossible—1937 (С)
What comes from the heart goes to the heart—1889 (С)
What the eye does not see, the heart cannot grieve (does not grieve over)—344 (Г)
What the eye doesn't see the heart doesn't crave for—1871 (С)
What the eye doesn't see, the heart doesn't grieve for (doesn't feel)—344 (Г)
What the heart thinks, the tongue speaks—2299 b (Ч)
You can look in the eyes but not in the heart—1454 (Н), 1888 (С), 2319 (Ч)
You don't know what's in the heart—2319 (Ч)

HEARTH
Fire burns brightest on one's own hearth (The)—126 (В)

HEAT
Heat breaks no bones—1631 (П)
If you can't stand the heat, get (stay) out of the kitchen—1633 (П)
No reek without heat—231 (В)
Same heat that melts the wax will harden the clay (The)—1628 (П)

HEAVEN
Heaven helps those that (who) help themselves—85 (Б)
Help yourself and heaven will help you—85 (Б), 1176 (Н)

HEDGE
Hedge between keeps fellowship green (A)—1990 (С)
Hedge between keeps friendship green (A)—1990 (С)

Hedges have eyes, and walls (woods) have ears—1009 (Л), 2153 (У)
Low hedge is easily leaped over (A)—1060 (Л), 2128 (У)
Men leap over where the hedge is lowest—1060 (Л), 2128 (У)
Once you pledge, don't hedge—150 (В)

HEEL
Forgetful head makes a weary pair of heels (A)—624 (З)

HELL
Hell is paved with good intentions—502 (Д)
Hell to pay (The)—1851 (С)
Road to hell is paved with good intentions (The)—502 (Д)
This is a day (a week) from hell—427 (Д)
Use your head and save your heels—624 (З)
Way to hell is paved with good intentions (The)—502 (Д)
What your head forgets, your heels must remember—624 (З)

HELP
Everything helps—1947 (С)
Help which is long on the road is no help—1542 (О)
Help yourself and heaven will help you—1176 (Н)
Self-help is the best help—1176 (Н), 1975 (С)
Slow help is no help—504 (Д), 1542 (О)
What can't be helped must be endured—1641 (П)
What's gone and what's past help should be past grief—2295 а (Ч)

HEN
Bad hen, bad eggs—1617 (О)
Black hen /always/ lays (will lay) a white egg (A)—870 (К), 891 (К), 1169 (М), 1358 (Н), 2267 (Ч)
Cackling hen does not always lay (A)—608 (З)
Fat hens make rich soup—821 (К), 2284 (Ч)
Hen of our neighbour appears to us as a goose (The)—978 (К)
He that comes of a hen, must scrape—1587 (О)
He that is born by a hen must scrape for a living—1587 (О)
Like hen, like chicken (children)—789 (К)
Setting hen gathers no feathers (A)—1000 (Л), 1671 (П)
Setting hen never gets fat (A)—1394 (Н), 1671 (П)
'Tis not the hen that cackles most that lays the most eggs—608 (З), 915 (К), 932 (К)

HERB
No herb will cure love—1084 (Л), 1594 (О)

HERE
I've had it up to here—2233 (Ч)

HERO
No man is a hero in his hometown (to his valet, to his wife or his butler)—1450 (Н)

HERRING
Every herring must hang by its own gill—591 (Ж)
Let every herring hang by its own tail—591 (Ж)
What we lose in hake, we shall have in herring—1219 (Н)

HESITATE
He who hesitates is lost—1784 (П)

HEW
Hew not too high, lest the chips fall in thine eye—1876 (С)

HIDE
Fire cannot be hidden in a flax (in straw)—2337 (Ш)
Love and /a/ cough cannot be hidden—2336 (Ш)
Love and poverty are hard to hide—2336 (Ш)
Love and smoke cannot be hidden—2336 (Ш)
Them that hides can find—890 (К), 1666 (П)
There is nothing hidden that is not shown—243 (В), 2336 (Ш), 2337 (Ш)

Those who hide know how to find—890 (К)
Wicked deeds will not stay hid—2337 (Ш)
You cannot hide an eel in a sack—2337 (Ш)

HIDER
Hiders are good finders—890 (К), 1666 (П)
Hiders make the best finders—890 (К), 1666 (П)

HIGH
Climb not too high lest the chips fall in thine eye—302 (В)
He sits not sure that sits high—74 (Б), 302 (В)
He who climbs too high is near a fall (to fall)—302 (В), 309 (Г)
Higher standing, the lower fall (The)—302 (В), 309 (Г)
Higher the mountain, the greater descent (The)—302 (В)
Higher the place, the harder the fall (The)—302 (В)
Higher they go, the lower they fall (The)—302 (В), 309 (Г)
Higher you climb, the harder you fall—302 (В)
Highest branch is not the safest roost (The)—74 (Б)
Highest in court, nearest the widdie—74 (Б)
Highest tree has the greatest fall (The)—302 (В)
High places have their precipices—74 (Б), 309 (Г)
Look high and fall in the dirt—302 (В)
Look high and fall low—302 (В)

HIGHWAY
Don't quit the highway for a short cut—1357 (Н)
He that leaves the highway to cut short, commonly goes about—1231 (Н)
Highway is never about (The)—1231 (Н), 1357 (Н)

HILL
Blue are the hills that are far from us—69 (Б), 322 (Г), 1917 (С)
Don't climb the hill before (until) you get to it—1402 (Н)
Faraway hills are green—69 (Б)
Far hills look the bluest—1917 (С), 2036 (Т)
Hills are (look) green far away—322 (Г), 1917 (С)

HINDMOST
Devil takes (take) the hindmost (The)—1726 (П)
Each for himself, and the devil take the hindmost—1726 (П)
Every man (fellow) for himself, and the devil take the hindmost—1726 (П)

HINDSIGHT
Hindsight is better than foresight—619 (З), 621 (З)

HINT
Hint is as good as a kick (A)—1545 (О), 2126 (У)

HISTORY
History repeats itself—751 (И), 1486 (Н)

HIT
Don't hit a man when he is down—1001 (Л)
Never hit a man when he is down—1001 (Л)

HOE
Hoe your own row—1419 (Н)

HOG
Better my hog dirty than no hog at all—1070 (Л)
Eat whole hog or die—725 (И), 726 (И), 1019 (Л), 1020 (Л)
If you talk with a hog, don't expect anything but a grunt—1591 (О)
It is hard to break a hog of an ill custom—715 (И)
Stillest hog gets the most swill (The)—987 (Л)
What can you expect from a hog but a grunt?—1591 (О)

HOIST
It is impossible to hoist oneself by one's own boots' straps—305 (В)

HOLE
Every fox has its hole—2090 (У)
Every rabbit has his hole—2090 (У)
I've got a bit of string with a hole in it—453 (Д)
Hole calls (invites) the thief (The)—328 (Г)
Little hole will sink a ship (A)—1156 (М)

HOLIDAY
Gone for a holiday—757 (И)

HOME
At home everything is easy—498 (Д)
Be it ever so humble there's no place like home—126 (В)
Dry bread at home is better than roast meat abroad—497 (Д)
East or West home is best—126 (В), 282 (В)
Go home and say your prayers—1419 (Н)
Home is home be it (though it be) ever so homely—126 (В), 497 (Д)
There is no place like home—126 (В), 497 (Д), 498 (Д)
There's nobody home—2125 (У)

HOMER
Homer sometimes nods (sleeps)—738 (И)

HONESTY
Honesty is praised and let to starve—2273 (Ч)
Honesty is the best policy—2272 (Ч)

HONEY
Cover yourself with honey and the flies will fasten on you—109 (Б), 899 (К)
Daub yourself with honey and you will have plenty of flies—899 (К)
Drop of honey catches more flies than a hogshead of vinegar (A)—1118 (М)
Eat your honey, but stop when you are full—1919 (С)
Flies are easier caught with honey than with vinegar—983 (Л), 1118 (М)
Fly follows the honey (A)—316 (Г)
He has honey in his mouth and razor at his girdle—1269 (Н)
Honey attracts more flies than vinegar—986 (Л), 1118 (М)
Honey catches more flies than vinegar—983 (Л), 986 (Л), 1118 (М)
Honey gathers more flies than vinegar—986 (Л)
Honey is not for the ass's mouth—1290 (Н)
Honey is sweet, but bees sting (the bee stings)—576 (Е), 1918 (С)
Honey tongue, a heart of gall (A)—1269 (Н)
If you want to gather honey, you must bear the stings of bees—1073 (Л), 1116 (М)
Lick honey with your little finger—2187 (Х)
Make yourself /all/ honey and /the/ flies will devour you—109 (Б), 899 (К), 2142 (У)
More flies are caught with honey than vinegar—1118 (М)
More wasps are caught by honey than by vinegar—1118 (М)
Ounce of honey draws more flies than a gallon of gall (An)—1118 (М)
Sweet as honey, bitter as gall—1269 (Н)
While honey lies in every flower, no doubt, it takes a bee to take the honey out—50 (Б), 317 (Г)

HONO(U)R
Great honours are great burdens—2078 (Т)
Honour and profit lie not in one sack—1613 (О)
Honour buys no beef in the market—2273 (Ч)
Hono(u)s change manners—628 (З)
Hono(u)r to whom hono(u)r is due—405 (Д), 1679 (П)
Honour without maintenance is like a blue coat without a badge—2273 (Ч)
It's better to die with honor than to live in infamy—64 (Б), 1054 (Л), 1067 (Л)
Lip-honour costs little, yet may bring in much—985 (Л)

HOOK
Fish never nibbles at the same hook twice (A)—2005 (C)
Hook's well lost to catch a salmon (A)—1752 (П)

HOOP
Thirteen staves and never a hoop will never make a barrel—1948 (C)

HOP
Don't say "hop" until you've jumped over—1321 (H)

HOPE
All hope is gone—435 (Д)
As long as I breathe I hope—1682 (П)
Don't feed yourself on false hopes—1543 (O)
Don't give up hope till hope is dead—134 (B), 1195 (H)
He that lives upon hope will die fasting—1543 (O), 1966 (C)
Hope is a good breakfast, but /it is/ a bad supper—1543 (O), 1966 (C)
Hope is a slender reed for a stout man to lean on—1543 (O), 1966 (C)
Hope is the poor man's bread—1543 (O), 1966 (C)
Hope keeps a man from hanging and drowning himself—1195 (H)
Hope keeps man alive—1195 (H)
Hope keeps the heart from breaking—1195 (H)
Hope springs eternal /in the human heart/—1195 (H)
If it were not for (without) hope, the heart would break—1195 (H)
To hope is to live—1195 (H)
Where there's life there's hope—1682 (П)
While I breathe I hope—1682 (П)
While there's life there's hope—1195 (H), 1682 (П)
While the sick man has life, there is hope—1682 (П)
Who lives by hope will die by hunger—1543 (O)

HORN
Let the horns go with the hide—149 (B)
One cannot make a horn of a pig's tail—714 (И)

HORSE
All lay /the/ load (loads) on a (the) willing horse—910 (K), 1199 (H), 1808 (P)
Boisterous horse must have a rough bridle (A)—1228 (H)
Common horse is worst shod (The)—320 (Г)
Do not look a gift (given) horse in the mouth—414 (Д), 416 (Д)
Don't change horses in the middle of the stream—1041 (Л)
Don't spur a willing horse—844 (K), 1228 (H)
Don't swap horses crossing a stream (in midstream, in the middle of the road, in the middle of the stream, while crossing the stream)—1041 (Л)
Don't whip the horse that is pulling—844 (K)
Either lose the horse or win the saddle—726 (И)
Every horse thinks his (its own) pack heaviest—770 (K)
Everyone lays a burden on the willing horse—910 (K), 1199 (H)
Flies go to (hunt) the lean horse—840 (K), 1172 (H), 1253 (H)
Good horse should be seldom spurred (A)—844 (K), 1228 (H)
He is a gentle horse that never cast his rider—54 (Б)
He that cannot beat the horse, beats the saddle—880 (K), 1392 (H)
Horse can't pull while kicking (A)—1193 (H)
Horse never goes straight up (A)—2128 (У)
Horse stumbles that has four legs (A)—866 (K)
Horse that draws best is most whipped (The)—911 (K)
Horse that will not carry a saddle must have no oats (A)—944 (K)
If you are on a strange horse, get off in the middle of the road—2026 (C)
It is a good horse that (who) never stumbles—866 (K)

Losing horse blames the saddle (The)—1111 (М), 1654 (П), 2063 (Т)
Never change horses in midstream—1041 (Л)
One horse scrubs another—1865 (С)
One man can lead a horse to water, but ten men can't make him drink—1324 (Н)
One man may lead a horse to the river (the water), but twenty cannot make him drink—1324 (Н)
Only fools and horses work—1601 (О), 1808 (Р)
Rub a galled horse and he will kick—286 (В), 2244 (Ч)
Running horse needs no spur (A)—844 (К)
That horse will not jump (run)—2356 (З)
That's a horse of a different (another) colo(u)r—2355 (Э)
When the horse is starved, you bring him oats—411 (Д)
Willing horse carries the load (The)—910 (К), 1199 (Н)
Willing horse gets the whip (The)—911 (К)
You can fool an old horse once, but you can't fool him twice—2005 (С)
You can lead a horse to water, but you can't make him drink—1324 (Н)
You can take (may lead) a horse to the water, but you cannot make him drink—1324 (Н)
You cannot judge the horse by its harness—168 (В)
You can't judge a horse by its harness, nor people by their clothing—1417 (Н)
You can't ride two horses at the same time—1193 (Н)
You can't teach an old horse new tricks—2000 (С), 2002 (С)

HORSEBACK
Set a beggar (a rogue) on horseback, and he'll ride to the devil—407 (Д)

HOUND
"We hounds killed the hare," quoth the lap dog—732 (И)
While the hound gnaws a bone companions would be none—628 (З)

HOUR
All of our sweetest hours fly fast—2020 (С)
Hour in the morning is worth two in the afternoon (in the evening) (An)—645 (З), 961 (К)
Hour wasted can never be regained (An)—445 (Д), 1746 (П)
It must be twenty past the hour—1132 (М), 2052 (Т)
It's an eleventh hour try—1640 (П)
Only way to save an hour is spend it wisely (The)—147 (В)
Pleasant hours fly fast—2020 (С)

HOUSE
Grace your house, and not let that grace you—1332 (Н)
House divided against itself cannot stand (A)—139 (В)
House is a fine house when good folks are within (The)—1332 (Н), 1363 (Н)
No house without mouse /; no throne without thorn/—1452 (Н)
Owner should bring honor to the house, not the house to the owner (The)—1332 (Н)
When the house is burned down you bring water—850 (К), 1730 (П), 1732 (П)
When the house is open, the honest man sins—328 (Г), 1655 (П)
When the house of your neighbour is on fire your own is in danger—2150 (У)
When your neighbor's house is on fire, beware of your own—2150 (У)

HOUSEKEEPING
Start housekeeping in your own house—1128 (М)

HOUSEWIFE
Eye of the housewife makes the cat fat (The)—2182 (Х)

HOW-DE-DO
Here's (That's) a fine (nice, pretty) how-de-do (how-d-ye-do)—200 (В)

HOWL
Never howl till you are bit (hit)—1402 (Н)
One must howl with the wolves—1710 (П)

HUMAN
I am a man and nothing human is alien to me—1487 (Н)
We are all human beings—235 (В), 1487 (Н)
We are only human—235 (В)

HUMBLE
Humble suffer from the folly of the great (The)—1630 (П)

HUMILITY
Life is a long lesson of humility—137 (В)

HUNGER
Hunger breaks (will break through) stone walls—1499 (Н)
Hunger causes the wolf to sally from the wood—367 (Г), 1496 (Н)
Hunger drives (fetches) the wolf out of the wood—367 (Г), 1496 (Н)
Hunger finds no fault with cookery—368 (Г)
Hunger is a good cook—368 (Г)
Hunger is a good kitchen—368 (Г), 374 (Г)
Hunger is good meat—368 (Г)
Hunger is the best cook (pickle, relish)—368 (Г)
Hunger is the best sauce—368 (Г), 374 (Г)
Hunger makes hard beans sweet—368 (Г), 374 (Г)
Hunger never saw bad bread—368 (Г), 373 (Г), 374 (Г)
Hunger sweetens what is bitter—368 (Г), 373 (Г)
Hunger teaches us many things—1781 (П)
They must hunger in frost that will not work in heat—969 (К), 1013 (Л), 1014 (Л)
They must hunger in winter that will not work in summer—969 (К), 1013 (Л), 1014 (Л)

HUNGRY
Hungry bellies have no ears—370 (Г)
Hungry dogs will eat dirty puddings—368 (Г)
Hungry horse makes a clean manger (A)—368 (Г), 373 (Г)
Hungry man, (is) an angry man (A)—1333 (Н)
Hungry man often talks of bread (The)—372 (Г), 878 (К), 1022 (Л), 1409 (Н), 1957 (С)
Hungry stomach has no ears (A)—370 (Г)
It is no use preaching to a hungry man—370 (Г)
To the hungry soul, every bitter thing is sweet—373 (Г)

HUNTER
All are not hunters that dogs bark at—1305 (Н)
All are not hunters who blow the horn—1305 (Н)

HURRY
Always in a hurry, always behind—1912 (С)
Greater hurry, the worse the speed (The)—1741 (П), 1911 (С), 1912 (С)
Hurry is only good for catching flies—1742 (П)
What is done in a hurry is never done well—1741 (П), 1979 (С)

HURT
He who hurts gets hurt—917 (К)
None is hurt but by himself—2248 (Ч)

HUSBAND
Good husband makes a good wife (A)—787 (К), 2162 (У)

I

ICE
Don't skate on thin ice—1477 (Н)
Enjoy your ice cream while it's on your plate—977 (К), 1032 (Л)
Try the ice before you venture upon it—1347 (Н)

IDIOT
Idiot—they happen in the best of families (An)—237 (В)

IDLE
Devil finds work for idle hands /to do/ (The)—35 (Б), 2074 (Т)
Devil some mischief finds for idle hands to do (The)—35 (Б)
Idle folk (folks) have the least leisure—948 (К)
Idle hands are the devil's tools—35 (Б)
Idle mind is the devil's workshop (An)—35 (Б)
Idle people have the least leisure—948 (К)
Idle youth, a needy age (An)—2346 (Щ)
Satan finds mischief (has some mischief /still /) for idle hands to do—35 (Б)
Young man idle, an old man needy (A)—2346 (Щ)

IDLENESS
Idleness and lust are bosom friends—2156 (У)
Idleness breeds trouble—1006 (Л)
Idleness dulls the wit—36 (Б), 1007 (Л)
Idleness goes in rags—1005 (Л)
Idleness in youth makes way for a painful and miserable old age—2346 (Щ)
Idleness is the Dead Sea that swallows all virtues—1007 (Л)
Idleness is the devil's workshop—35 (Б)
Idleness is the key of (to) beggary—1005 (Л), 1994 (С)
Idleness is the mother of /all/ evil (of mischief, of sin, of vice)—35 (Б), 1006 (Л)
Idleness is the mother of want—1005 (Л)
Idleness is the parent of many vices—35 (Б), 1006 (Л)
Idleness is the parent of vice—35 (Б), 1006 (Л)
Idleness is the root of all evil—35 (Б)
Idleness makes the wit rust—36 (Б), 1007 (Л)
Idleness rusts the mind—36 (Б), 1007 (Л)
Idleness turns the edge of wit—36 (Б)
No good comes of idleness—1006 (Л)
Of idleness comes no goodness—1006 (Л)
Trouble springs from idleness—1006 (Л)

IF
If "ifs" and "ands" were pots and pans, there would be no need for tinkers /tinkers' hands/—115 (Б), 560 (Е), 562 (Е), 759 (К), 762 (К), 763 (К), 764 (К), 765 (К)
If ifs and ans were pots and pans /there'd be no trade for tinkers/—115 (Б), 560 (Е), 562 (Е), 762 (К), 763 (К), 765 (К)
If my aunt had been a man, she'd have been my uncle—560 (Е), 759 (К), 764 (К)
If pigs had wings, they would be angels—560 (Е)
"Ifs" and "buts" butter no bread—560 (Е)
If the sky falls (fall), we shall catch larks—453 (Д), 562 (Е)
If turnips were watches, I would wear one by my side—762 (К)
If wishes were butter cakes, beggars might bite—115 (Б)
If wishes were horses, beggars could (might, would) ride—115 (Б), 560 (Е), 761 (К), 765 (К)

IGNORANCE
Ignorance is the mother of conceit—2369 (Я)
Your ignorance is your worst enemy—2165 (У)

IGNORANT
It pays to be ignorant—2237 (Ч)

ILL
He knows best what good is that has endured ill—951 (К), 1291 (Н), 1458 (Н)
Ill be to him that thinks ill—917 (К), 921 (К)
Ill comes in by ells and goes away (out) by inches—23 (Б)
Ill comes often on the back of worse—1778 (П)

Ill-doers are ill thinkers—161 (В), 2100 (У)
Ill got, ill spent—2221 (Х)
Ill-gotten, ill-spent—2221 (Х)
Ill stake stands long (/the/ longest) (An/The)—66 (Б), 1915 (С)
Ill will never said well—161 (В), 2100 (У)
Ill will never speaks well or does well—161 (В), 2100 (У)
Of one ill come many—852 (К)
Of two ills choose the least—704 (И)
'Tis a good ill that comes alone—1530 (О)
Who would do ill, ne'er wants occasion—118 (Б)

IGNORANCE
Knowledge talks lowly; ignorance talks loudly—350 (Г), 536 (Д)

IMPOSSIBLE
Impossible always happens (The)—2239 (Ч)

IMPRESSION
First impressions are untrustworthy—1637 (П)
Never judge by first impressions—1637 (П)

IMPROVEMENT
There's always room for improvement—2313 (Ч)

INACTIVITY
Inactivity breeds ignorance—2014 (С)

INCH
Give him an inch and he'll take a mile (an ell, a yard)—403 (Д), 406 (Д), 408 (Д), 409 (Д), 1665 (П), 1793 (П)
Give knaves an inch and they will take a yard—403 (Д), 406 (Д), 408 (Д), 409 (Д), 1665 (П), 1793 (П)
Inch breaks no square (An)—1315 (Н)
Inch in missing is as bad as a mile (An)—2332 (Ч)
Inch is as good as an ell (An)—1099 (М), 1320 (Н), 1843 (Р)
Man is not measured by inches—384 (Г)
Men are not /to be/ measured by inches—384 (Г)

INCOME
Men with the smallest income have the largest families—77 (Б)

INCONSTANCY
There is nothing constant but inconstancy—604 (Ж)

INCONVENIENCE
Conveniences have their inconveniences and comforts their crosses—1073 (Л)
No convenience without inconvenience—1073 (Л)

INDISPENSABLE
No man (one) is indispensable—1342 (Н)

INFALLIBLE
No one is infallible—738 (И), 1436 (Н), 2251 (Ч)

INIQUITY
He that sows iniquity shall reap sorrow—964 (К)

INJURE
He injures the good who spares the bad—190 (В)
Injure others, injure yourself—921 (К)
Pardoning the bad is injuring the good—190 (В)

INJURY
He does injury to the good who spares the bad—190 (В)
Injuries are written in brass—471 (Д)
Neglect will kill an injury sooner than revenge—481 (Д)
Remedy for injuries is not to remember them—481 (Д)
Write injuries in dust, but kindness in marble—481 (Д)

INNOCENT
Every one is held to be innocent until he is proved to be guilty—1390 (Н)

/One is/ innocent until proven guilty—1390 (Н)

INSTRUCT
Things which hurt, instruct—33 (Б)

INTENTION
Hell is paved with good intentions—502 (Д)
Road (way) to hell is paved with good intentions (The)—502 (Д)

INTEREST
Everyone speaks for his own interest—255 (В), 531 (Д), 772 (К), 775 (К)
Interest runs on while you sleep—1967 (С)
It is in his own interest that the cat purrs—775 (К)

INTERFERE
Never interfere with family quarrels—1164 (М), 1861 (С)

INTIMACY
Intimacy breeds contempt—1450 (Н)
Intimacy lessens fame—1450 (Н)

IRON
Don't have too many irons in the fire—1886 (С)
If you have too many irons in the fire, some of them will burn—1886 (С)
Iron cuts iron—4 (А), 554 (Д), 1205 (Н), 1206 (Н), 1267 (Н), 1569 (О)
Iron not used soon rusts—1833 (Р), 2014 (С)
Iron whets iron—1205 (Н)
Strike while the iron is hot—843 (К), 977 (К), 1198 (Н), 2057 (Т)
When the iron is hot, it is time to strike—2057 (Т)

J

JACK
Bad Jack may have a bad Jill (A)—787 (К)
Every Jack has his Gill (Jill)—46 (Б), 2102 (У)
For every Jack there is a Jill—46 (Б), 2102 (У)
Good Jack makes a good Jill (A)—787 (К), 2162 (У)
If Jack's in love, he's no judge of Jill's beauty—1085 (Л)
Jack is as good as Jill—653 (З)
There's a Jack for every Jill (Jane, Jean, Jenny)—46 (Б), 260 (В)

JACKASS
Braying of an jackass never reaches heaven (The)—1949 (С)

JADE
Better a lean jade than an empty halter—1070 (Л)

JAYBIRD
Jaybirds don't rob their own nest—72 (Б), 1653 (П)

JEERER
Jeerers must be content to taste of their own broth—1406 (Н)

JENNIE
There's never a Jennie but there's a Johnny—46 (Б)

JEST
Better lose a jest than a friend—943 (К), 1674 (П)
Half in jest, whole in earnest—157 (В)
He makes a foe who makes a jest—940 (К), 1194 (Н), 2345 (Ш)
If you give (make) a jest, you must take a jest—940 (К), 2345 (Ш)
Jesting lies bring serious sorrows—940 (К), 1194 (Н)
Leave a jest when it pleases lest it turn to earnest—2344 (Ш)
Long jesting was never good—2344 (Ш)
Many a true word (a truth) is spoken in jest—157 (В)
There's many a true word said in jest—299 (В)
True jests breed bad blood—940 (К), 2345 (Ш)
When your jest is at its best, let it rest—2344 (Ш)
Worst jests are the truest ones (The)—299 (В)

JILL
There is always a Jill as bad as a Jack—787 (К)
There's no so bad a Jill, but there's as bad a Jack (a Will)—787 (К)

JOAN
Joan's as good as my lady in the dark—1493 (Н)

JOB
Hardest job is no job (The)—1455 (Н)
Job started right is a job half done (A)—477 (Д)
When the job is well done, you can hang up the hammer—864 (К)

JOHNNY
Johnny is as Johnny does—1393 (Н), 1621 (О)

JOIN
If you can't beat (lick) them, join them—1375 (Н)

JOINT
Joint is jumping (The)—601 (Ж)

JOKE
Do not carry a joke too far—2344 (Ш)
Joke never gains over an enemy but often loses a friend (A)—1674 (П), 2345 (Ш)
Rich man's joke is always funny (A)—573 (Е)

JOURNEY
For a good friend the journey is never too long—318 (Г), 464 (Д)
It is (It's) a great journey to life's end—602 (Ж), 1180 (Н)
Journey of a thousand miles begins with one step (A)—1750 (П)
On a long journey even a straw is heavy (weighs)—1177 (Н), 2151 (У)

JOY
Every inch of joy has an ell of annoy—1698 (П)
Joy shared is joy doubled—1814 (Р)
Joys shared with others are more enjoyed—1814 (Р)
Joy that's shared is a joy made double (A)—1814 (Р)
Let your joys be many and your sorrows be few!—1959 (С)
No joy without alloy—34 (Б)
No joy without annoy—1453 (Н), 1698 (П)
Of thy sorrow be not too sad, of thy joy be not too glad—1399 (Н)
Shared joys are doubled; shared sorrows are halved—390 (Г)
Sorrow shared is half a trouble, /but/ a joy that is shared is a joy made double (A)—390 (Г)
There is no joy without affliction—1698 (П)
There is no joy without alloy—1453 (Н), 1698 (П)

JUDGE
Ask the judge—1410 (Н)
Don't judge a horse by its harness—1417 (Н)
Don't judge a man by the coat he wears—1417 (Н)
Don't judge others by yourself—1367 (Н)
Don't judge others according to your measures—1367 (Н)
He who will have no judge but himself condemns himself—2249 (Ч)
If you judge your own case, you are judged by a fool—2249 (Ч)
Judge a man by his deeds, not by his words—428 (Д), 1621 (О)
Judge a man by what he does, not by what he says—1621 (О)
Judge a tree by its fruit—451 (Д), 1621 (О)
Judge not according to appearances—168 (В), 1417 (Н)
Judge not and you shall not (won't) be judged—1418 (Н)
Judge not lest you be judged—1418 (Н)
Judge not of men and (or) things at first sight—1637 (П)
Judge not that ye (you) be not judged—1418 (Н)
Never judge before you see—1062 (Л)
Never judge by (from) appearances—168 (В), 1417 (Н)

Never judge others' corn by your own bushel (half-bushel) — 1367 (Н)
No man ought to be judge in his own case — 2249 (Ч)
You cannot judge a book by its binding (a sausage by its shin, /of/ a tree by its bark, the horse by the harness) — 168 (В)
You can't judge a book by its cover (binding) — 1417 (Н)
You can't judge a horse by its harness, nor people by their clothing — 1417 (Н)

JUDY
Don't make a Judy of yourself — 1278 (Н)

JUG
Jug goes to the well until it breaks (The) — 1659 (П), 1907 (С)

K

KEEP
Don't let us keep you — 1902 (С)
It will keep — 432 (Д)
Keep a thing for seven years and it will come in handy — 266 (В)
Keep a thing long enough — 266 (В)
Keep a thing seven years and you will find a use for it — 266 (В)
Keep the rake near the scythe, and the cart near the rake — 454 (Д)
Keep your powder dry — 454 (Д)
Keep your sails trimmed — 454 (Д)

KEEPER
Am I my brother's keeper? — 1159 (М), 1372 (Н), 2372 (Я)
I am not my brother's keeper — 1159 (М), 2372 (Я)

KERNEL
He that will eat the kernel must crack the nut — 50 (Б)

KETTLE
Every kettle has a lid — 2102 (У)
Every kettle has to sit on its own bottom — 267 (В)
Here's a fine (pretty) kettle of fish — 1851 (С)
It's a fine (nice, pretty) kettle of fish — 199 (В)
Kettle called the pot smutty (The) — 358 (Г)
Kettle calls the pot black (The) — 358 (Г)
Kettle should not call the pot black (The) — 15 (А), 358 (Г)
No matter how black the kettle, there is always a lid to fit it — 46 (Б)

KEY
All the keys are not at one man's girdle — 699 (И), 1136 (М)
All the keys hang not at one's girdle — 699 (И), 1136 (М)
Golden key opens every door (The) — 439 (Д), 684 (З)
Gold key opens every door (A) — 439 (Д), 684 (З)
Little key will open a large door (A) — 1099 (М)
Silver key can open an iron lock (A) — 439 (Д)

KICK
Do not kick against the pricks — 990 b (Л), 1647 b (П), 1786 b (П)
Don't kick a dog (a fellow, a man) when he is down — 1001 (Л)
Don't kick against pricks — 990 b (Л), 1647 b (П), 1786 b (П)
When a man is down, don't kick him lower — 1001 (Л)

KID
You kid me! — 1590 (О)

KILL
I kill the boars, another enjoys their flesh — 1114 (М)
I must have killed a Chinaman — 132 (В)
We killed the bear — 732 (И)

KILN
Ill may the kiln call the oven burnt-tail — 2334 (Ч)
Kiln calls the oven burnt ass (The) — 2334 (Ч)

KIN
No one claims kin to the fortuneless age — 27 (Б), 1769 (П)
Poverty has no kin — 1769 (П)

KIND
Each kind attracts its own—1113 (М), 1672 (П)
Keep to your own kind—290 (В), 402 (Г), 675 (З), 1295 b (Н), 1853 (С)
One after kind—1842 (Р)

KINDNESS
Act of kindness is well repaid (An)—472 (Д), 474 (Д), 622 (З)
Acts of kindness are soon forgotten, but the memory of an offence remains—482 (Д)
Kindness always begets kindness—622 (З), 1197 (Н)
Kindness is lost upon an ungrateful man—1368 (Н)
Kindness is never lost (wasted) (A)—622 (З)
Kindness is the noblest weapon to conquer with—983 (Л), 986 (Л), 1692 (П)
No one has ever been killed by kindness—1579 (О), 1689 (П), 1690 (П)
One kindness deserves another—622 (З), 1197 (Н)
One kindness is the price of another—622 (З)
Repay kindness with kindness—622 (З), 1197 (Н)
Write injuries in dust, but kindness in marble—481 (Д)

KINDRED
No one claims kindred to the poor—1769 (П)

KING
Every man is a king in his own house—221 (В), 275 (В), 287 (В), 1237 (Н), 2038 (Т)
I'd rather be king among dogs than a dog among kings—1046 (Л)
Kings go mad, and the people suffer for it—1630 (П)
Like king, like people—813 (К), 817 (К)
Man is king in his home (A)—221 (В), 275 (В), 1237 (Н), 2038 (Т)
Near the king, near the gallows—74 (Б)
Two kings in one kingdom cannot reign—420 (Д)

KINGDOM
Kingdom divided against itself cannot stand (A)—139 (В)

KINSFOLK
Many kinsfolk, few friends—2206 (Х)

KISS
Kissing goes by favour—1890 (С)
Kiss the hand you cannot bite—1375 (Н)
Many kiss the hand they wish to cut off (to see cut off)—1170 (М)

KITCHEN
Kitchen physic is the best physic—486 (Д)

KITE
Ask a kite for a feather and she will say she has but just enough to fly with—2147 (У)
Fly your kite when it is windy—2057 (Т)

KITH
More kith than kin—2206 (Х)

KNAVE
Worse knave, the better luck (The)—522 (Д)
When a knave is in a plum-tree, he hath neither friend nor kin—628 (З)
When knaves fall out, honest men come by their own—418 (Д)

KNIFE
Same knife cuts both bread and fingers (The)—1628 (П)
There never was a good knife made of bad steel—714 (И), 801 (К), 803 (К), 805 (К)

KNOCK
Every knock is a boost—1947 (С)
Knock is as good as a boost (A)—1947 (С)

KNOW
All that we know is that we know nothing—2359 (Я)
Christ knows—1518 (О)

God knows /and (but) he won't tell/—1518 (О)
God only knows—1518 (О)
Goodness (Heaven, Hell, Lord, Who) knows—1518 (О)
He who knows most knows best how little he knows—2256 (Ч)
It takes one to know one—1842 (Р)
Knowing is power—678 (З)
More you know, the more you know what you don't know (The)—2256 (Ч)
One never knows what a day may bring forth—1478 (Н)
What one doesn't know won't hurt him—680 (З), 2237 (Ч)
What you don't know won't hurt you—680 (З), 2237 (Ч)
When three know it, all know it—232 (В), 1529 (О)
You cannot know the wine by the barrel—168 (В), 1417 (Н)
You never know what you'll lose and what you'll gain—1224 (Н), 1478 (Н)

KNOWLEDGE
Increase your knowledge and increase your grief—2256 (Ч)
He who has knowledge has force—678 (З)
If you want knowledge, you must toil for it—43 (Б)
Investment in knowledge pays the best interest (An)—677 (З)
Knowledge has bitter roots but sweet fruits—43 (Б)
Knowledge is better than riches—677 (З)
Knowledge is no burden—679 (З)
Knowledge is power—678 (З)
Knowledge is the treasure of the mind—677 (З)
Lamp of knowledge burns brightly (The)—2165 (У)
Little knowledge is a dangerous thing (A)—1336 (Н), 1699 (П)
Too much knowledge makes the head bold—1138 (М)
Weight of knowledge is never measured (The)—679 (З)
Without knowledge there is no sin or sinner—680 (З), 2237 (Ч)

L

LABO(U)R
By labor comes wealth—317 (Г)
Labor is the law of happiness—337 (Г), 1839 (Р)
Labor makes life sweet—337 (Г), 1839 (Р)
Labour overcomes all things—2044 (Т)

LABO(U)RER
Labo(u)rer is worthy of his hire (The)—791 (К), 794 (К), 1714 (П)

LADDER
He that climbs a ladder must begin at the first round—627 (З)
He who holds the ladder is as bad as the thief—197 (В), 1441 (Н)
He who would climb the ladder must begin at the bottom—627 (З)
One begins to climb the ladder from the bottom—627 (З)
World is a ladder for some to go up and some down (The)—1539 (О)

LAIRD
New lairds, new laws—1490 (Н)

LAMB
God's lambs will play—456 (Д)

LAME
Live with the lame and you will limp—1904 (С), 1905 (С)

LAND
No land without stones, no meat without bones—54 (Б), 1171 b (М)
On fat land grow foulest weeds—79 (Б)

LANE
It's a long lane that has no turning—311 (Г), 753 (И)

LARK
If the sky falls, we shall catch larks—453 (Д)

LAST
Cord breaks at the last but weakest pull (The)—1727 (П)
It is the last feather that breaks the camel's back—1727 (П)
Last drop wobbles; the cup flows over (The)—1727 (П)
Morning sun never lasts a day (The)—1485 (Н)
Nothing can last forever—1485 (Н)
Nothing evil or good lasts a hundred years—2262 (Ч)

LATE
Better come late to church than never—1064 (Л)
Better late than never (not at all)—1064 (Л)
Good that comes too late is good as nothing—411 (Д), 1736 (П)
It is too late to cast anchor when the ship's on the rocks—850 (К)
It is too late to close the barn door after the horse has bolted—1730 (П)
It is too late to cover the well when the child is drowned—850 (К)
It is too late to lock the stable door when the steed is stolen—850 (К), 1730 (П)
It is too late to spare when the bottom is bare—1730 (П)
It is too late to throw water on the cinders when the house is burned down—850 (К), 1730 (П), 1732 (П)
When the devil comes, it is too late to pray—1730 (П)
Who comes late lodges ill—956 (К)

LATHER
Good lather is half a shave (A)—477 (Д)
Well lathered is half shaved—477 (Д)

LAUGH
He is not laughed at that laughs at himself first—1435 (Н)
He laughs best who laughs last—2198 (Х)
He who laughs at crooked men should need walk very straight—1405 (Н)
He who laughs last, laughs best (longest)—2198 (Х)
He who laughs on Friday will weep on Sunday—1256 (Н), 1820 (Р)
Laugh and /you/ show your ignorance—1941 (С)
Laugh before breakfast and you'll cry before supper—1256 (Н)
Laugh before breakfast, cry before supper (night, sunset)—1256 (Н), 1820 (Р)
Laugh before breakfast, you'll cry before supper—1256 (Н), 1820 (Р)
Laugh before seven, cry before eleven—1256 (Н)
Let them laugh that win—2198 (Х)
Louder the laugh, the more empty the head (The)—1941 (С)
Loud laugh bespeaks the vacant mind (A)—1941 (С)
To laugh at someone is to be laughed back at—940 (К)

LAUGHING
It is not a laughing matter—2033 (С), 2353 (Э)
No laughing matter—2033 (С)

LAUGHTER
Better the last smile than the first laughter—2198 (Х)
Laughter before sleep, tears when wakened—1820 (Р)
Laughter is the hiccup of a fool—1941 (С)
Too much laughter discovers folly—545 (Д), 1941 (С)

LAUNDRESS
Laundress washes her own smock first (The)—1868 (С)

LAW
Every law has a loophole—626 (З)
Ignorance of the law excuses no man—1346 (Н)
Ignorance of the law is no excuse—1346 (Н)
Law is a bottomless pit /; keep far from it/—254 (В)
Law is like an axle: you can turn it whichever way you please if you give it plenty of grease (The)—626 (З)

Laws are like cobwebs which may catch small flies, but let wasps and hornets break through—2286 (Ч)
Laws are made to be broken (evaded)—626 (З)
Laws catch flies and (, but) let hornets go free—2286 (Ч)
One law for the rich and another for the poor—29 (Б)
There is one law for the rich and another for the poor—29 (Б)
Will is his law—2181 (Х)

LAWYER
He that is his own lawyer has a fool for a client—2250 (Ч)
Lawyers are thieves—254 (В)
Man who is his own lawyer has a fool for a client (A)—2250 (Ч)
Only a fool is his own lawyer—2250 (Ч)

LAZINESS
Laziness travels so slow that poverty overtakes him—1005 (Л)
There is no luck in laziness—1005 (Л)

LAZY
Lazy man takes the most pain (The)—1455 (Н)
Lazy man works the hardest (A)—1455 (Н)

LEAK
Little leak will sink a big (great) ship (A)—1283 (Н)
Small leaks sink big ships—1283 (Н)
Small leak will sink a great ship (A)—1156 (М), 1283 (Н)

LEARN
As long as you live you must learn how to live—135 (В)
By writing we learn to write—1190 (Н)
Child must learn to crawl before it can walk (A)—2 (А)
Children learn to creep ere they can go—2 (А)
He who learns the hard way will never forget—2310 (Ч)
In doing we learn—280 (В), 430 (Д)
It is never too late to learn—1254 (Н), 2168 (У)
Learn to creep before you leap (walk)—2 (А)
Learn to say before you sing—2 (А)
Learn to walk before you run—2 (А)
Learn weeping and you shall gain laughing—43 (Б)
Live and learn—135 (В), 1465 (Н)
Never too late to learn—1254 (Н), 2168 (У)
Never too old to learn—1254 (Н), 2168 (У)
Never too old to turn; never too late to learn—2168 (У)
Old one crows, the young one learns (The)—1101 (М)
Quickly learned, soon forgotten—1242 (Н), 2310 (Ч)
Soon learnt, soon forgotten—1242 (Н)
We learn to do by doing—430 (Д), 1190 (Н)
What is learned in the cradle is carried to the tomb—2263 (Ч)
What is learned in the cradle lasts till (to) the grave (to the tomb)—2263 (Ч)
What is well learned is not forgotten—2310 (Ч)
What we learn early we remember late—2263 (Ч)
You are never too old to learn—2168 (У)
You have to learn to walk before you can run—2 (А)

LEARNING
Learning is the eye of the mind—2165 (У)
Little learning is a dangerous thing (A)—1336 (Н), 1699 (П)
There is no royal road to learning—43 (Б)

LEATHER
/There is/ nothing like leather—395 (Г), 1849 (С)

LEECH
While men go after a leech, the body is buried—1687 (П)

LEG
If you don't use your head, you must use your legs—624 (З)
Stretch your legs according to the length of your blanket—1708 (П)
Stretch your legs according to your coverlet—1708 (П)

LEGION
Their name is legion—734 (И)

LEISURE
Leisure breeds lust—2156 (У)

LEND
If you want to keep a friend, never borrow, never lend—888 (К)
Lend a dollar, lose a friend—128 (В)
Lend and lose the loan, or gain an enemy—128 (В)
Lend money and you get an enemy—128 (В), 634 (З)
Lend money, lose a friend—888 (К)
Lend only that which you can afford to lose—2238 (Ч)
Lend your money and lose your friend—128 (В), 888 (К)
Not so good to borrow as to be able to lend—1050 (Л)
When I lent I had a friend, when I asked he was unkind—128 (В), 634 (З)

LEOPARD
Can the leopard change his spots?—383 (Г)
Leopard cannot change (does not change, never changes) his spots (A/The)—184 (В), 383 (Г)

LESSON
Lessons hard to learn are sweet to know—2080 (Т), 2166 (У)

LETTER
Letters blush not—111 (Б)
One complimentary letter asks another—125 (В), 1074 (Л), 2328 (Ч)
Written letter remains (The)—2298 (Ч)

LIAR
Biggest liar in the world is they say (The)—362 (Г)
Liar is not believed when he speaks (tells) the truth (A)—914 (К), 1961 (С)
Liar is sooner caught than a cripple (A)—205 (В), 2114 (У)
Liar needs a good memory (A)—220 (В)
Liars have long legs—2062 (Т)
Liars have need of good memories—220 (В)
No one believes a liar when he tells the truth—914 (К), 1961 (С)
"They say" is a /tough old/ liar—362 (Г)
"They say so" is half a liar—362 (Г)

LID
Lid is off (The)—98 (Б)
No matter how black the kettle, there is always a lid to fit it—46 (Б)
There's a lid for every pot—46 (Б)
There's a pot for every lid—46 (Б)

LIE
He that tells a lie must invent twenty more to maintain it—1039 (Л), 1535 (О)
He who lies once is never believed again—914 (К)
Lie begets a lie (A)—957 (К), 1039 (Л)
Lie begets a lie until they become a generation (A)—957 (К), 1039 (Л), 1100 (М), 1535 (О)
Lie has no legs (A)—205 (В), 2114 (У)
Lie hath no feet (A)—2114 (У)
Lie not in the mire and say "God help"—1176 (Н)
Lie only runs on one leg (A)—2114 (У)
Lie runs until it is overtaken by truth (A)—205 (В)
Lies have short legs—205 (В), 2114 (У)
Lies hunt in packs—1039 (Л)
Long ways, long lies—2062 (Т)
Nothing stands in need of lying but a lie—1039 (Л)
One lie calls for many—1039 (Л), 1100 (М)
One lie leads to another—957 (К), 1039 (Л), 1100 (М)

One lie makes many—1039 (Л), 1100 (М), 1535 (О)
One lie needs seven lies to wait upon it—1535 (О)
One seldom meets a lonely lie—1535 (О)
Tell a lie and find a truth—729 (И)
"They say so" is half a lie—362 (Г)
Those who live on lies choke on truth—1016 (Л)
Travelled man has leave to lie (A)—2062 (Т)
Traveller may lie with authority (A)—2062 (Т)
Travellers have leave to lie—2062 (Т)
We must not lie down and die—1157 (М)
You can get far with a lie, but not come back—205 (В)

LIFE
Good life keeps away wrinkles (A)—295 (В)
Ill life, an ill end (An)—782 (К)
Into each (every) life some rain must fall—387 (Г)
It's a great life if you do not weaken—2046 (Т)
Life and misery begin together—603 (Ж)
Life brims over the edge—601 (Ж)
Life for /a/ life (/A/)—1550 (О)
Life has its ups and downs—603 (Ж)
Life is a bed of roses—1340 (Н)
Life is a varied career—1879 (С)
Life is but a bowl of cherries—1340 (Н)
Life is but a dream (but a span)—448 (Д)
Life is hell—427 (Д)
Life is just one damned thing after another—603 (Ж)
Life is movement—604 (Ж)
Life is no (not a) bed of roses—603 (Ж), 1180 (Н)
Life is not all beer and skittles (all clear sailing in calm water, all honey, wholly beer and skittles)—603 (Ж), 1180 (Н)
Life is short—448 (Д), 1526 (О)
Life is subject to ups and downs—1879 (С)
Life is what you make it—2247 (Ч)
No life without pain—603 (Ж)
Live your own life, for you die your own death—597 (Ж)
Our lives have ups and downs—206 (В), 2056 (Т)
Road of life is lined with many milestones (The)—602 (Ж)
Such is life—2035 (Т)
There is always life for a living one (for the living)—597 (Ж), 599 (Ж)
There is aye life for a living man—597 (Ж), 599 (Ж)
There is life in the old dog yet—571 (Е), 596 (Ж)
There is life in the old horse yet—571 (Е)

LIFETIME
It's all in a lifetime—133 (В), 603 (Ж)

LIGHT
Every light has its shadow—54 (Б), 737 (И)
Every light is not the sun—784 (К)
More light a torch gives, the shorter it lasts (The)—2373 (Я)
What goes on in the dark must come out in the light—243 (В)

LIKE
Every like is not the same—980 (К), 2170 (Ф)
If you like the sow, you like her litter—1076 (Л)
Like attracts like—1672 (П), 1842 (Р)
Like begets (breeds) like—815 (К), 1560 (О), 1576 (О), 1619 (О)
Like breeds the like (The)—815 (К), 1560 (О), 1576 (О), 1619 (О)
Like calls to like—1842 (Р)
Like cures like—838 (К)
Like draws to like—1672 (П), 1842 (Р)
Like knows like—1842 (Р)
Like likes like—1672 (П), 1842 (Р)
Like seeks (sees, will to) like—1842 (Р)
No like is the same—980 (К), 2170 (Ф)

LIKENESS
Likeness causes liking—1672 (Р)

LIKING
Every one to his liking—927 (К)

LIMB
Don't cut the limb which bears your weight—1404 (Н)

LIMIT
That's the limit—2233 (Ч)
There's a limit to everything—286 (В), 2233 (Ч)

LINE
It's a long line that has no turning—753 (И)

LINEN
Don't air your dirty linens in public—1970 (С)
Don't wash your dirty linen in public—1970 (С)
Wash your dirty linen at home—1970 (С)

LINGER
He who lingers is lost—1784 (П)

LION
Lion is not so fierce as he is painted (The)—1426 (Н)
Lion may come to be beholden to a mouse (A)—229 (В)
Lions in peace, hares in war—272 (В)
Man is a lion in his own house (A)—275 (В), 1238 (Н)
Who takes a lion when he is absent, fears a mouse present—1150 (М)

LIP
Between the cup and the lip a morsel may slip—18 (Б)
Even rosy lips must be fed—743 (И)
From your lips to God's ears—123 (В), 716 (И)
Keep a stiff upper lip!—307 (В)
Loose lips sink ships—91 (Б)
Scald not your lips in another man's porridge—1260 (Н)
Slip of the lip will sink a ship (A)—91 (Б)
There is many a slip twixt /the/ cup and /the/ lip—18 (Б)
There's many a slip between ('twixt) the cup and the lip—18 (Б)

LIQUOR
Good liquor will make a cat speak—2312 (Ч)

LISTEN
Listen much and speak little—96 (Б)

LITTER
Litter is like to the sire and the dam (The)—2357 (Я)

LITTLE
Add little to little and there will be a great heap—1686 (П)
Every little counts (helps)—1947 (С)
Every little makes a mickle (a nickel)—868 (К)
Little and good fills the trencher (A)- 1057 (Л)
Little and often fills the purse—868 (К), 979 (К)
Little and often makes a heap in time—664 (З), 979 (К)
Little by little and bit by bit—1107 (М), 2044 (Т)
Little by little one goes (travels) far—1107 (М)
Little by little the bird builds his (its) nest—730 (И), 1107 (М)
Little is better than none (A)—1056 (Л)
Little makes a lot (A)—979 (К)
Many a little makes a mickle—664 (З), 979 (К), 1694 (П), 1801 (П), 1956 (С)
Many a little makes a nickel—868 (К)

LIVE
Eat to live /; do not live to eat/—1167 (М)
He lives longest who lives best—1445 (Н)
He lives long that lives well—1445 (Н)
He lives twice who lives well—1445 (Н)
It matters not how long we live, but how—1445 (Н)
It's not how long but how well we live—1445 (Н)

Live and let live—593 (Ж)
Live and well—571 (Е), 596 (Ж)
Live not to eat, but eat to live—1167 (М)
Live today, for tomorrow may not come (for tomorrow you may die)—449 (Д)
Live today; tomorrow may be too late—449 (Д), 1526 (О)
We must live by the living, not by the dead—597 (Ж), 599 (Ж)
We must eat to live and not live to eat—1167 (М)
We only live once—1526 (О)

LOAF
Half a loaf is better than none—1056 (Л), 1070 (Л), 1974 (С)
Set not your loaf /in/ till the oven's hot—1408 (Н)

LOAN
Borrowed loan should come laughing home (A)—2117 (У)
Borrowed loan should return with thankfulness (A)—2117 (У)
Loan oft loses both itself and a friend (A)—128 (В)

LOG
You roll my log, and I'll roll yours—2077 (Т), 2148 (У)

LOOK
Don't look upon the vessel but upon that which it contains—1356 (Н)
It's all in the way you look at it—776 (К)
Long looked for comes at last—922 (К)
Look and you shall find—758 (И), 922 (К)
Look before you leap—1347 (Н), 1378 (Н)
Look before you leap, but having leapt never look back—1378 (Н)
Looks are deceiving—168 (В)
Looks are not enough—1381 (Н), 1925 (С)
Looks are not (aren't) everything—884 (К), 885 (К), 886 (К), 1381 (Н), 1925 (С)
Look who's talking!—909 (К), 1406 (Н), 1612 (О)
You can look, but you cannot touch—2184 (Х), 2207 (Х)

LOOKER-ON
Looker-on sees more (most) of the game (The)—1973 (С)
Lookers-on see more than the players—1973 (С)

LOOP
Every loop has a hole—626 (З)

LORD
Every man cannot be a lord—1298 (Н)
Like lord, like chaplain—822 (К)
Lord gives and the Lord takes (The)—82 (Б)
Lord helps those who help themselves (/The/)—85 (Б), 1176 (Н)
Lord knows—1518 (О)
Lord who gave can take away (The)—82 (Б)
Lord will provide (The)—83 (Б)
New lords, new laws—1490 (Н)

LOSE
All's lost—435 (Д)
Better lose the saddle than the horse—1055 (Л)
Better the fruit lost than the tree—1055 (Л)
It is not lost that comes at last—1064 (Л)
It is no use losing a sheep for a halfpenny worth of tar—629 (З), 1339 (Н)
One never loses by doing a good turn—417 (Д)
What is lost is lost—1747 (П), 1783 (П), 2308 a (Ч)

LOSER
First winner, last loser—952 (К), 956 (К)
Finders keepers, losers weepers—2308 b (Ч)
Losers seekers, finders keepers—2308 b (Ч)

LOSS
After crosses and losses, men grow humbler and wiser—33 (Б)
Every gain must have a loss—2161 (У)

There is no trader who does not meet with losses—2161 (У)

LOUD

Some people think that the louder they shout, the more persuasive their argument is—2343 (Ш)

LOUDLY

Those who are right need not talk loudly—2343 (Ш)

LOVE

Blind love makes a harelip for a dimple—1085 (Л)

Brotherly love for brotherly love, but cheese for money—514 (Д)

Falling out of lovers is the renewal (the renewing) of love (The)—1134 (М)

Fanned fire and forced love never did well yet—1241 (Н)

Forced love does not last—1241 (Н)

Hasty love is soon hot and soon cold—588 (Ж)

Heart that truly loves never forgets (The)—1995 (С)

He that has love in his breast, has spurs in his side—464 (Д)

He that (who) loves the tree, loves the branch—1076 (Л)

He who has love in his heart, has spurs in his heels—318 (Г), 464 (Д)

If you love the boll, you cannot hate the branches—1076 (Л)

Love and /a/ cough (smoke) cannot be hidden—1071 (Л)

Love can be a blessing or a curse—1082 (Л)

Love can make any place agreeable—1942 (С)

Love can neither be bought, nor sold /; its only price is love/—1079 (Л), 1241 (Н), 1890 (С)

Love cannot be compelled, (forced, ordered)—1241 (Н), 1890 (С)

Love conquers all—1078 (Л), 1083 (Л)

Love converts a cottage into a palace of gold—1942 (С)

Love covers many faults—1080 (Л), 1085 (Л)

Love covers many infirmities—1080 (Л)

Love in a hut with water and crust is cinders, ashes, and dust—1873 (С)

Love is a thirst that is never slaked—1081 (Л)

Love is blind—1080 (Л), 1085 (Л), 1684 (П)

Love is deaf as well as blind—1080 (Л)

Love is neither bought nor sold—1079 (Л), 1241 (Н)

Love is not found in the market—1079 (Л)

Love is without reason—1080 (Л)

Love lasts as long as money endures—1873 (С), 2223 (Х)

Love laughs at locksmiths—1083 (Л)

Love lives in cottages as well as in courts—1942 (С)

Love locks no cupboard—466 (Д)

Love makes a cottage a castle—1942 (С)

Love makes time pass—2020 (С)

Love me, love my dog—916 (К), 1076 (Л)

Love's anger is fuel to love—1134 (М)

Love sees no faults—1085 (Л), 1684 (П)

Love triumphs over all—1078 (Л)

Love will creep where it cannot go—379 (Г), 1083 (Л)

Love will find a way—1083 (Л)

Love will go through stone walls—1083 (Л)

Love without end has no end—1081 (Л)

Lucky at (in) cards (play), unlucky in love—131 (В)

Marry first, and love will come afterwards—2309 (Ч)

Marry first, and love will follow—2309 (Ч)

Men are best loved furthest off—1828 (Р)

Money cannot buy love—1079 (Л)

No love like the first love—1995 (С)

Old love does not fade (An)—1995 (С)

Old love does not rust—1995 (С)

Old love will not be forgotten—1995 (С)

They love us truly who correct us freely—513 (Д)
Unlucky at cards, lucky in love—1282 (Н)
You can't buy love—1079 (Л)

LOVELY
Everything in the garden is lovely—226 (В)

LOVER
In the eye (eyes) of the lover, pockmarks are dimples—1085 (Л)
Lover's anger is short-lived (A)—1134 (М)
Lovers' quarrels are soon mended—1134 (М)
Lovers' time runs faster than the clock—2020 (С)
Unlucky gambler, lucky lover—1282 (Н)

LUCK
As good luck as had the cow that struck herself with her own horn—132 (В)
Bad luck comes in threes—22 (Б), 1778 (П)
Bad luck often brings good luck—1456 (Н)
Behind bad luck comes good luck—311 (Г), 1276 (Н), 1456 (Н), 1725 (П)
Better luck next time—106 (Б), 1772 (П)
Give a man luck enough and throw him into the sea—861 (К)
Good luck!—1482 (Н)
Hard luck can't last one hundred years—239 (В), 2048 (Т)
If luck is with you, even your ox will give birth to a calf—335 (Г), 854 (К)
Ill luck is good for something—1456 (Н)
Just bad luck—132 (В)
Lots of luck, Charlie—453 (Д), 847 (К)
Luck goes in cycles—1538 (О)
Pocketful of luck is better that a sackful of wisdom (A)—2022 (С)
That's the beginner's luck—1528 (О)
What is worse than ill luck?—132 (В), 1172 (Н)
When a man has luck, even his ox calves—335 (Г), 854 (К)
Worse luck now, the better another time (The)—106 (Б)
You don't need brains if you have luck—522 (Д), 1403 (Н), 2022 (С)
You make your luck—2247 (Ч)

LUCKY
Better to be born lucky than rich—1403 (Н)
If you are lucky, even your rooster will lay eggs—345 (Г), 854 (К)

LULL
It must be the ten minute lull—1132 (М), 2052 (Т)

LUNCH
No such thing as a free lunch—635 (З)
There's no /such thing as a/ free lunch—635 (З)

LUSTRE
Good name keeps its lustre in the dark (A)—5 (А)

LUXURY
Living in luxury begets lustful desires—2156 (У)

LYING
Lying pays no tax—1270 (Н), 1960 (С), 2360 (Я)

M

MAD
Every man is mad on some point—774 (К), 2088 (У)
Whom God would destroy He first makes mad—851 (К)
Whom the gods would destroy they first make mad—851 (К)

MAID
All meat to be eaten and all maids to be wed—260 (В)
All meats to be eaten, all maids to be wed—260 (В)

MAIDEN
If one will not, another will, so are all maidens wed—260 (В)

MAKE
Make /it/, or break /it/—727 (И)
Make or mar—727 (И)

MAKER
Everyone is the maker of his own fate—2247 (Ч)

MALICE
Malice seldom wants a mark to shoot at—118 (Б)

MAN
All men are mortal—228 (В), 240 (В)
All men must die—228 (В), 240 (В), 244 (В)
As the man, so his cattle—813 (К), 817 (К)
Best of men are but men afterward (The)—235 (В)
Don't hit (kick, strike) a man when he is down—1001 (Л)
Even a wise man stumbles—1187 (Н)
Every man after his fashion (own heart)—270 (В), 1494 (Н), 2089 (У), 2093 (У), 2106 (У)
Every man as his business lies—1295 a (Н), 1420 (Н)
Every man has a fool in (up) his sleeve—51 (Б), 736 (И), 738 (И), 1187 (Н)
Every man in his /own/ way—143 (В), 258 (В), 270 (В), 271 (В), 273 (В), 274 (В), 288 (В), 1494 (Н), 2089 (У), 2093 (У), 2094 (У), 2106 (У)
Every man is exceptional—143 (В)
Every man is master of his fortune—2247 (Ч)
Every man is nearest himself—265 (В)
Every man is the architect of his own fortune—2247 (Ч)
Every man likes his own thing best—276 (В)
Every man must labour in his own trade—1344 (Н)
Every man must pay his Scot—267 (В)
Every man must skin his own skunk—267 (В), 591 (Ж)
Every man must stand on his own two feet—1975 (С)
Every man must stand on his own two legs—267 (В), 1975 (С)
Every man must walk in his own calling—1344 (Н)
Every man to his business (craft)—1295 a (Н)
Every man to his trade—62 (Б), 989 (Л), 1295 a (Н), 1344 (Н)
Every man will have his own turn served—265 (В)
Great men are not always wise—738 (И)
He that has not got a wife is not yet a complete man—1160 (М)
Let every man skin his own eel—267 (В)
Little man may have a large heart (A)—1099 (М), 1105 (М)
Look out for the man that does not talk and the dog that does not bark—1273 (Н)
Man born to misfortune will fall on his back and fracture his nose (A)—565 (Е), 845 (К), 857 (К), 1172 (Н)
Man can be led but he can't be driven (A)—1324 (Н)
Man can die but (only) once (A)—423 b (Д), 1527 (О)
Man can die but once, go ahead and give it a try (A)—423 a (Д), 2265 b (Ч)
Man can do no more than he can (A)—304 (В), 306 (В), 748 (И), 1366 (Н)
Man cannot live on air (A)—743 (И)
Man cannot reel and spin together (A)—1193 (Н)
Man cannot whistle and drink (and eat a meal) at the same time (A)—1193 (Н)
Man in passion rides a mad (wild) horse (A)—356 (Г)
Man is born into trouble—1611 (О)
Man is himself again (The)—596 (Ж)
Man is only half a man without a wife (A)—1160 (М)
Man may be down, but he's never out (A)—2138 (У)

MARKSMAN
Good marksman may miss (A)—738 (И)

MARRIAGE
Marriage and hanging go by destiny—102 (Б), 2017 (С)
Marriage comes by destiny—102 (Б), 2017 (С)
Marriage is a lottery—1521 (О)
Marriage is destiny—102 (Б), 2017 (С)
Marriage is heaven or hell—1521 (О)
Marriage makes or mars a man—1521 (О)
Marriages are made in heaven—102 (Б), 2017 (С)

MARRY
Before you marry 'tis well to tarry—1232 (Н)
Day you marry, it is either kill or cure (The)—1521 (О)
He that marries for wealth, sells his liberty—80 (Б)
He who marries for wealth, loses his liberty—80 (Б)
If you always say "No", you will never be married—495 (Д)
If you marry for money, you sell your freedom—80 (Б)
Marry above your match and you get a master—80 (Б), 1059 (Л), 1838 b (Р)
Marry a wife of thine own degree—1838 b (Р)
Marry in haste and repent at leisure—588 (Ж), 939 (К), 1442 (Н), 1857 (С)
Marry your equal (your like, your match)—1838 b (Р)

MASTER
As the master is, so is his dog—822 (К)
Bad master makes a bad servant (A)—822 (К)
Every man cannot be a master—1298 (Н)
Every man is a master in his own house—221 (В), 275 (В), 287 (В), 1237 (Н), 2038 (Т)
Everyone is master in his own shop—287 (В)
Good masters make good servants—822 (К)
In every art it is good to have a master—277 (В), 431 (Д)
Jack is as good as his master—822 (К)
Like master, like dog—822 (К)
Like master, like land—797 (К)
Like master, like man—822 (К)
Masters two will not do—420 (Д)
No man can serve two masters—422 (Д)
No man is his craft's master the first day—1639 (П)
We can't all be masters—1298 (Н)
Where every man is master, the world goes to wrack—2145 (У)

MATCH
If you play with matches, you will get burned—1477 (Н)

MATCH-MAKER
Match-makers often burn their fingers—921 (К)

MATE
Every rag meets its mate—46 (Б)
There was never a shoe but had its mate—46 (Б), 2102 (У)

MAY
April and May are the keys of the year—140 (В)
Cold April and a wet May fill the barn with grain and hay (A)—9 (А), 165 (В), 1108 (М)
Cold May and a windy makes a full barn and findy (A)—9 (А), 165 (В)
Dry March, wet April and cool May fill barn and cellar and bring much hay (A)—9 (А), 1108 (М)
Fall of snow in May is worth a ton of hay (A)—9 (А), 165 (В), 1108 (М)
May makes or mars the wheat—165 (В)

MAXIM
Good maxim is never out of season (A)—1737 (П)

MEAL
It is good baking beside meal—2199 (X)
It's easy to bake when the meal is beside you—2199 (X)
To lengthen your life, lessen your meals—615 (З)

MEAN
Many beat the sack and mean the miller—65 (Б), 880 (К)

MEASURE
Better twice measured than once wrong—1887 (С)
Bread at pleasure, drink by measure—574 (Е)
Don't measure another man's foot by your own last—1367 (Н)
Don't measure other men by your own yardstick—1367 (Н)
Don't measure other people's corn by your own bushel—1367 (Н)
Eat at pleasure; drink by (in, with) measure—574 (Е)
Man is not measured by inches (A)—384 (Г)
Measure for measure—1550 (О)
Measure is a treasure—246 (В)
Measure three times before you cut once—1887 (С)
Measure thrice and cut once—1887 (С)
Measure twice before you cut once—1887 (С)
Measure your cloth ten times; you can cut it but once—1887 (С)
Men are not /to be/ measured by inches—384 (Г)
There is a measure in all things—246 (В), 2187 (X)
Weight and measure take away strife—2025 (С)
Without measure medicine will become poison—246 (В), 2187 (X)

MEAT
All meat pleases not all mouths—1182 (Н)
Much meat, much malady—327 (Г)
No land without stones, or meat without bones—54 (Б), 1171 b (М)
One man's meat is another man's poison—2307 (Ч)
Quick at meat, quick at work—820 (К), 919 (К), 1809 (Р)
Slow at meat, slow at work—567 (Е), 820 (К)
Sweet meat will have its sour sauce—1453 (Н)
They that have no other meat, bread and butter are glad to eat (gladly bread and butter eat)—1174 (Н)

MEDAL
Every medal has its reverse—2105 (У)

MEDDLE
He who meddles smarts (will smart) for it—942 (К), 1086 (Л)
Meddle not with another man's matter—1419 (Н)

MEDICINE
There is a medicine for all things except death and taxex—1606 (О)

MEMORY
No man has a good enough memory to be a successful liar—220 (В)

MEND
In the end all (things) will mend—239 (В), 665 (З), 1509 (О), 1782 (П), 2048 (Т)
It is never too late to mend—1625 (О), 2119 (У)

MERCY
Mercy to the criminal may be cruelty to the people—190 (В)

MERRY
All are not merry that dance lightly—1311 (Н)
Every man is not merry that dances—1311 (Н)
More, the merrier (The)—293 (В)

MICE
No larder but has its mice—1670 (П)

MICKLE
Many a mickle makes a muckle—664 (З), 979 (К), 1694 (П), 1801 (П), 1956 (С)

MIGHT
Either by might or by slight—310 (В), 334 (Г)
Might beats right—333 (Г), 965 (К)
Might goes before (is) right—333 (Г), 965 (К)
Might knows no right—965 (К)
Might makes right—333 (Г), 918 (К), 965 (К)
Might overcomes right—333 (Г), 965 (К)

MILE
Make short miles with talk and smiles—63 (Б)

MILK
Milk is spilled (The)—434 (Д)
No weeping for shed milk—1920 a (С), 2302 (Ч)
Once milk becomes sour, it can't be made sweet again—1872 (С)
That accounts for the milk in the coconut—3 (А)
You cannot get (wring) milk from a flint—826 (К)

MILL
Enter the mill and you come out floury—1904 (С)
God's mills grind slowly, but sure—1602 (О)
Mill cannot grind with the water that is passed (past) (A/The)—67 (Б), 2281 a (Ч), 2295 a (Ч), 2308 a (Ч)
Mill grinds no corn with water that has passed (The)—2281 a (Ч)
Mills of God grind slowly (The)—1602 (О)
Mills of the gods grind slowly /, but they grind exceedingly fine (small)/ (The)—1602 (О)
Mills will not grind if we (you) give them no water—1387 (Н)
Mill that is always going grinds coarse and fine (The)—1120 (М), 2364 (Я)
No mill, no meal—944 (К)

MILLER
Every honest miller has a thumb of gold (a golden thumb)—314 (Г), 2160 a (У), 2137 (У)
Every miller drags (draws) water to his own mill—263 (В), 268 (В), 733 (И), 771 (К), 876 (К)

MILLION
In for a mill, in for a million—150 (В), 609 (З)

MILLSTONE
Lower millstone (mill-stone) grinds as well as the upper (The)—1520 (О), 1537 (О), 1544 (О)

MIND
Many men, many minds—2123 (У)
Mind other men, but most yourself—1868 (С)
So many men, so many minds—1908 (С)
Sound mind in a sound body (A)—148 (В)
Strong body makes the mind strong (A)—148 (В)
Two minds are better than one—1531 (О), 2135 (У)

MINE
What's yours is mine, and what's mine I am keeping—1148 (М)
What's yours is mine, and what's mine is mine (is my own)—1148 М)

MIRE
There was never a good town but had a mire at one end of it—54 (Б)

MISCHIEF
He that mischief hatches, mischief catches—921 (К), 1598 (О)
Mischief comes by the pound and goes /away/ by the ounce—23 (Б)
Of two mischiefs choose the least—704 (И)
When you plot mischief for others, you're preparing trouble for yourself—917 (К)

MISER
Miser is an ass that carries gold and eats thistles (A)—2342 (Ш)
Miser's son is a spendthrift (A)—1586 (О)
Moles and misers live in their graves—162 (В), 1916 (С), 2342 (Ш)

Rich miser is poorer than a poor man (A)—162 (B), 1916 (C)

MISERY
Misery makes strange bedfellows—171 (B)
Misery never comes singly—22 (Б)

MISFORTUNE
Blessed is the misfortune that comes alone—1530 (O)
It is easy to bear the misfortunes of others—386 (Г), 659 (З), 2311 (Ч), 2316 (Ч), 2318 (Ч), 2321 (Ч), 2325 (Ч)
Misfortune arrives on horseback but departs on foot—20 (Б)
Misfortune comes by the yard and goes by the inch—23 (Б)
Misfortune comes in bunches—22 (Б)
Misfortunes cause queer bedfellows—171 (B)
Misfortunes come on wings and depart on foot—20 (Б)
Misfortunes make us wise—33 (Б)
Misfortunes never come alone (singly)—22 (Б)
Misfortunes seldom come alone—1753 (П)
Misfortunes tell us what fortune is—1291 (H)
No man shall pass his whole life free from misfortune—786 (K)
One has always strength enough to bear the misfortunes of others—2325 (Ч)
One misfortune comes on (upon) the back (the neck) of another—1753 (П)
We all have strength enough to bear the misfortunes of others—2325 (Ч)
We can always bear our neighbors' misfortunes—386 (Г), 659 (З), 2311 (Ч), 2316 (Ч), 2318 (Ч), 2321 (Ч), 2325 (Ч)

MISS
Miss is as good as a mile (A)—2332 (Ч)

MISTAKE
Don't mistake an old goat for a preacher because of his beard—723 (И)
Every man makes mistakes—2251 (Ч)
He who makes no mistakes is a fool—2251 (Ч)
He who makes no mistakes makes nothing—1384 (H), 2251 (Ч)
He who never made a mistake never made anything—1384 (H)
It is difficult to own up to your own mistakes—396 (Г)
It is easy to make a mistake, hard to ask forgiveness—396 (Г)
Learn from the mistakes of others—1221 (H)
Mistakes are often the best teachers—1222 (H)
Show me the man that does not make a mistake, and I will show you the man that does not do anything—1384 (H)
We don't learn by others' mistakes—2317 (Ч)
We learn by our mistakes—1222 (H)
We profit by mistakes—1222 (H)

MISTRESS
Like mistress, like maid—822 (K)

MOCK
He that mocks a cripple, ought to be whole—511 (Д)

MODERATION
Moderation in all things—246 (B)

MODEST
Modest dogs miss much meat—2016 (C)

MOLASSES
Molasses catches more flies than vinegar—1118 (M)
You can catch more flies with molasses than vinegar—983 (Л)

MOMENT
Enjoy the present moment and don't grieve for tomorrow—1402 (H)
Never a dull moment—601 (Ж)

MONDAY
On Monday morning don't be looking for Saturday night—67 (Б)
So goes Monday, so goes all the week—809 (K), 1652 (П), 2222 (X)

MONEY
Abundance of money ruins youth (/The/)—79 (Б)
All things are obedient to money—1158 (М)
He that has money in his purse cannot want a head for his shoulders—573 (Е)
He that hordes up money pains for other men—1916 (С)
If money go before, all ways lie open—439 (Д)
It is easy to spend someone else's money—719 (И), 2324 (Ч)
Lack of money is the root of all evil (The)—30 (Б), 1796 (П)
Love of money is the root of all evil (The)—440 (Д)
Money begets (breeds, comes to, draws, gets, makes) money—319 (Г), 441 (Д)
Money calls but does not stay; it is round and rolls away—442 (Д), 446 (Д)
Money can't buy happiness—756 (И)
Money doesn't get dirty—443 (Д)
Money doesn't grow on trees—438 (Д), 444 (Д)
Money greases the axle—1387 (Н)
Money has no smell—443 (Д)
Money has wings—442 (Д)
Money is a universal language speaking any tongue—439 (Д)
Money is not everything—1280 (Н)
Money isn't everything in life—1280 (Н)
Money is power—439 (Д), 685 (З), 687 (З), 1158 (М)
Money is round and rolls away—442 (Д), 446 (Д)
Money is round—it truckles—442 (Д)
Money makes the man—573 (Е)
Money makes the mare go—618 (З)
Money makes the pot boil—569 (Е)
Money makes the wheels (the world) go round—439 (Д)
Money masters all things—439 (Д), 685 (З), 687 (З)
Money runs the world—439 (Д), 687 (З)
Money saved is money earned (got)—1856 (С)
Money speaks—439 (Д)
Money spent on the brain is never spent in vain—677 (З)
Money talks—439 (Д)
Never spend your money before you have it—2228 (Ц)
That's money down the drain—1290 (Н)
Those who have money have trouble about it—1141 (М)
Want of money is the root of all evil—30 (Б), 1796 (П)
When money flies out the window, love flies out the door—1873 (С)
When money speaks, truth keeps its mouth shut (keeps silent)—842 (К)
You can't take money with you when you die—2133 (Х)
You pay your money and you take your choice—955 (К)

MONK
Cowl (hood) does not make the monk (The)—1314 (Н)

MONKEY
Dress a monkey as you will, it remains a monkey still—827 (К)
Monkeys in hard times eat red peppers—373 (Г)

MOON
Moon does not heed the barking of dogs (The)—1949 (С)
Moon doesn't give a hoot when the dog barks (the dogs bark) (The)—1949 (С)
Moon is made of green cheese (The)—663 (З)

MOOR
Moor has done his duty, let him go (The)—1095 (М)

MOP
That's the way the mop flops—2035 (Т)

MORN
Let the morn come, and the meat with it—83 (Б)

MORNING
Morning brings counsel—2158 (У)

Morning /hour/ has gold in its mouth (The)—961 (К)
Morning to the mountain, the evening to the fountain (The)—233 (В)
Things look brighter in the morning—2158 (У)
You can tell the day by the morning—809 (К)

MORSEL
Between the cup and the lip a morsel may slip—18 (Б)
Morsel always looks big in other people's hands (A)—296 (В)

MORTAL
All men are mortal—228 (В), 240 (В)
Grass and hay, we are all mortal—240 (В)
Man is mortal—240 (В)

MOST
Make the most of what you have—1174 (Н)

MOTHER
As is the mother, so is the daughter—790 (К)
As mother and father, so is daughter and son—783 (К), 800 (К), 810 (К)
Every mother's duck is a swan—462 (Д)
Every mother thinks her own gosling a swan—462 (Д)
Like mother, like child (daughter)—790 (К)
There's only one pretty child in the world and every mother has it—462 (Д)

MOUNTAIN
Friends may meet but mountains never greet—382 (Г)
If the mountain will not come (won't go) to Mahomet (Mohammed),
Mahomet (Mohammed) must go to the mountain—563 (Е), 564 (Е)
Men may meet but mountains never greet—382 (Г)
Men may meet, though mountains cannot—382 (Г)
Mohammed has to go to the mountain—the mountain will not come to him—563 (Е), 564 (Е)
Mountain in labor brought forth a mouse (A)—381 (Г)
Mountain in labour has brought forth a mouse (The)—381 (Г)
Mountain labored and brought forth a mouse (A)—381 (Г)
Two men may meet, but never two mountains—382 (Г)

MOUSE
Better a mouse in the pot than no flesh at all—1070 (Л)
Don't make yourself a mouse, or the cat will eat you—899 (К), 1945 (С)
It is a poor mouse that has only one hole—2216 (Х)
Mouse never trusts its life to one hole only (A)—2216 (Х)
Mouse that has but one hole is quickly taken (soon caught) (The)—2216 (Х)
No house without mouse—773 (К), 1670 (П), 2104 (У)
Smart mouse has more than one hole (A)—2216 (Х)
Today a man, tomorrow a mouse—1879 (С)
What may the mouse do against the cat?—990 a (Л), 1647 a (П), 1786 a (П)

MOUTH
Closed (close) mouth catches no flies (A)—146 (В)
Cool mouth and warm feet live long (A)—452 (Д)
Fish who keeps his mouth shut will never get caught (A)—146 (В)
Fish wouldn't get caught if it kept its mouth shut (A)—2364 (Я)
He that will stop every man's mouth must have a great deal of meal—1261 (Н)
Into a mouth shut (a shut mouth) flies fly not—146 (В)
Keep your mouth shut and your eyes open—455 (Д)
Loud mouth and a shallow brain go well together (A)—2098 (У)
Out of the mouth of babes speaks the truth—2152 (У)

Out of the mouths of babes and sucklings come great truths—2152 (У)
Out of thy mouth into God's ears—123 (В), 716 (И)
Roasted ducks don't fly into your mouth—50 (Б)
Still mouth makes a wise head (A)—359 (Г)
Truth comes out of the mouths of babes and sucklings—2152 (У)
Wise head makes a close mouth (A)—536 (Д)

MOVE
And /yet/ it does move!—691 (И)
But it does move!—691 (И)

MUCH
Either too much or too little—1818 (Р), 2229 (Ч)
Even too much honey nothing else than gall—1919 (С)
For all those to whom much is given, much is required—855 (К)
Much is expected where much is given—855 (К)
Much will have more—441 (Д)
Never too much of a good thing—832 (К)
Too much breaks the bag—2081 (Т)
Too much honey cloys the stomach—1919 (С)
Too much of a good thing /is good for nothing/—75 (Б), 720 (И), 1919 (С), 2187 (Х)
Too much of a good thing is worse than none at all—75 (Б), 720 (И), 1110 (М), 1919 (С), 2187 (Х)
Too much of one thing is good for nothing—1110 (М)
Too much pudding chokes the dog—1919 (С)
Too much water drowned the miller—2187 (Х)
Whomsoever much is given, of him shall be much required—855 (К)
You can never (can't) have too much of a good thing—832 (К)

MUCK
Muck and money go together—1613 (О)

MUD
If you throw mud enough, some of it will stick—837 (К)
/There is/ no mud without a puddle—1432 (Н)
Throw mud enough, and some will stick—837 (К)

MULE
He who wants a mule without fault, must walk on foot—735 (И)
Old mule ploughs a straight furrow (The)—2009 (С), 2012 (С)
One mule scrubs another—2077 (Т)
When a mule is kicking, he is not pulling; and when he is pulling, he is not kicking—1193 (Н)
You may lead a mule to water, but you can't make him drink—1324 (Н)

MURDER
Murder will out—2337 (Ш)

MUSK
Look not for musk in a dog's kennel—654 (З)

MUSKET
Take not a musket to kill a butterfly—632 (З), 713 (И), 1561 (О)

MUSTARD
After meat comes mustard—1736 (П)
After meat, mustard—1736 (П)

MUTTON
When the shoulder of mutton is going, 'tis good to take a slice—1032 (Л)

N

NAIL
Don't hang all on one nail—1217 (Н)
Nail can go no farther than its head will let it (A)—304 (В)
One nail drives out another—838 (К)
Peg is driven out by a peg, a nail by a nail (A)—838 (К)
You hit the nail on the head—1279 (Н)

NAKED

Naked men never lose anything—377 (Г)

Naked we came, naked we go—2133 (У)

NAME

Bad wound is cured, /but/ not a bad name (A)—996 (Л)

Evil wound is cured, not an evil name (An)—996 (Л)

Give a dog a bad name and hang him (and his work is done)—547 (Д), 549 (Д), 996 (Л)

Give a dog a bad name, and it will stay with him—547 (Д)

Give a dog an ill name, and hang him—996 (Л)

Good name is a golden girdle (A)—437 (Д), 470 (Д)

Good name is a rich heritage (A)—470 (Д)

Good name is better than riches (gold) (A)—437 (Д), 470 (Д)

Good name is sooner lost than won (A)—996 (Л)

Good name keeps its lustre in the dark (A)—5 (A), 683 (З)

Good name will shine forever (A)—480 (Д)

He that has an ill name is half hanged—547 (Д), 1819 (Р)

He who has a bad name is half hanged—547 (Д), 1819 (Р)

Ill wound, but not an ill name, may be healed (An)—996 (Л)

Ill wound is cured, /but/ not an ill name (An)—996 (Л)

Names break no bones—103 (Б)

Rose by any other name would smell as sweet (A)—1407 (Н)

Sticks and stones may break my bones, but names will never hurt me—103 (Б), 1929 (С), 1931 (С), 2203 (Х)

What's in a name?—1407 (Н)

NATURE

Drive nature out of the door and it will return by the window—380 (Г), 779 (К)

Nature is deeper than nurture—779 (К)

Nature will take its course—1776 (П)

Though you cast out nature with a fork, it will still return—380 (Г)

Throw nature out of the door, it will come back /again/ (it will return) through the window—380 (Г), 779 (К)

NEARLY

Nearly never did any good—2332 (Ч)

NECESSARY

No man is necessary—1342 (Н)

NECESSITY

Necessity has no law—1497 (Н)

Necessity is a good teacher—1498 (Н)

Necessity is the mother of invention—1498 (Н), 1781 (П)

Necessity is the mistress of all arts—1498 (Н)

Necessity knows no law—1497 (Н)

Necessity never made a good bargain—1500 (Н)

NECK

I'll stick my neck out—323 (Г), 2265 b (Ч)

Neck or nothing—727 (И)

NEED

He must needs go whom the devil drives—1499 (Н), 1992 (С)

Need has no law—1497 (Н)

Need makes a (the) naked man run—369 (Г), 1499 (Н), 1992 (С)

Need makes the naked man run and sorrow makes websters spin—388 (Г)

Need makes the old wife trot—369 (Г), 1499 (Н), 1992 (С)

Need must when necessity drives—369 (Г), 1499 (Н)

Needs must when the devil drives—1499 (Н)

When in great need, everything will do—25 (Б)

NEEDLE

It's like looking for a needle in a haystack—693 (И)

Lost like a needle in a bundle of hay (in a haystack)—693 (И)

NEGLECT
Little neglect may breed great mischief (A)—2140 (У), 2341 (Ш)

NEGOTIATION
Negotiation—celebration, calculation—consternation—2064 (Т)

NEIGHBO(U)R
Better a neighbor near than a brother far—71 (Б)
Better is a neighbour that is near than a brother far off—71 (Б)
Close neighbor is better than a faraway relative (A)—71 (Б)
Good neighbor is a precious thing (A)—1365 (Н)
Good neighbour, a good morrow (A)—1365 (Н)
Near neighbour is better than a far-dwelling kinsman (A)—71 (Б)
We can live without our friends, but not without our neighbours—1365 (Н)
When you buy a house you buy a neighbour—1365 (Н)

NEST
He that feathers his nest must sleep in it—1848 (С)

NET
Don't set the net after the fish have gone by—1733 (П), 1734 (П), 1986 (С)
Net of the sleeper catches fish (The)—1967 (С)
Rough net is not the best catcher of birds (The)—983 (Л)

NETTLE
Grasp the nettle and it won't sting you—1578 (О)
He who handles a nettle tenderly is soonest stung—1245 (Н)
Stroke a nettle and it will sting you; grasp it and it is as soft as silk—1245 (Н)

NEW
Everything new is fine—1489 (Н)
Everything old is new again—1491 (Н)
New is what has been forgotten (The)—1491 (Н)
There is nothing new under the sun—1486 (Н)

NEWS
Bad news has wings—550 (Д)
Bad news travels fast—550 (Д), 2189 (Х)
Bad news travels fast, good news is scarcely heard—2189 (Х)
Evil news rides post, while good news bates—2189 (Х)
Good news travels fast—483 (Д)
Good news travels slowly /, bad news travels fast/—2189 (Х)
Ill news comes apace—550 (Д)
Ill news flies—550 (Д), 2189 (Х)
Ill news travels apace—550 (Д)
Ill news travels fast—550 (Д), 2189 (Х)
News flies fast (quickly)—1934 (С)
No news, good news—1429 (Н)
No news is good news—1429 (Н)

NICKEL
Take care of the nickels, and the dollars will take care of themselves—869 (К)

NIGHT
Every day has its night, every weal its /own/ woe—34 (Б)
Longest night must end (will have an end) (The)—2042 (Т)
Night brings counsel (/The/)—2158 (У)
Night is the mother of counsel (The)—2158 (У)
Wait till night before saying that the day has been fine—2174 (Х)
What is done in the night appears in the day—243 (В)

NOBLE
Noble ancestry makes a poor dish at the table—2218 (Х)

NOD
Nod for a wise man, and a rod for a fool (A)—1545 (О), 2126 (У)
Nod is as good as a wink (A)—2126 (У)
Nod is as good as a wink to a blind horse (A)—2224 (Х)

NOSE
Don't bite (cut) off your nose to spite your face—1203 (Н), 1287 (Н)
He that has a great nose thinks everybody is speaking of it—155 (В)
Keep your nose clean—1583 (О)
Keep your nose out of other people's business—1419 (Н)
Man should not stick his nose in his neighbor's pot (A)—1419 (Н)
Red nose makes a ragged back (A)—1805 (П)

NOTHING
From nothing, nothing is made—253 (В), 708 (И), 1581 (О)
He that has nothing need fear to lose nothing—377 (Г)
He who has nothing fears nothing—377 (Г)
If you have nothing, you've nothing to lose—377 (Г)
Nothing comes from (of) nothing—708 (И), 1581 (О)
Nothing doing—1484 (Н)
Nothing for nothing /, and very little for halfpenny/—635 (З)
Nothing happens for nothing—231 (В)
Nothing is gained without work—1376 (Н)
Nothing produces nothing—708 (И)
Nothing seek, nothing find—1671 (П)
Nothing to be got without pains—1376 (Н)
Nothing ventured, nothing gained—1671 (П)
Nothing venture, nothing gain (win)—1671 (П)
What costs nothing is worth nothing—458 (Д), 459 (Д)
You can't make something out of nothing—708 (И), 1581 (О)
You get nothing for nothing—635 (З)

NOVELTY
Novelty of noon is out of date by night (The)—1489 (Н)

NUMBER
Number one is the first house in the row—1868 (С)

NURSE
With seven nurses a child will be without eyes—2145 (У)

NUT
Gods send nuts to those who have no teeth (The)—411 (Д), 1676 (П)
He that will eat the kernel must crack the nut—1400 (Н)
He that will have the kernel must crack the shell—1400 (Н)
He who would eat the nut must first crack the shell—1400 (Н)

O

OAK
Big oaks from little acorns grow—2008 (С)
Great oaks from little acorns grow—2008 (С)
Oak is not felled at (with) one stroke (An)—636 (З), 730 (И), 1965 (С)
Oaks may fall when reeds stand the storm—112 (Б)
Reed before the wind lives on, while mighty oaks do fall (A)—112 (Б)
Tall oaks from little acorns grow—2008 (С)
When an oak falls every one gathers wood—1627 (П)

OAR
Forsaken by the wind, you must use the oars—1375 (Н)
You can't go far in a rowboat without oars—42 (Б), 48 (Б)

OAT
Every man must sow his wild oats—1151 (М)
Young will sow their wild oats (The)—1151 (М)

OCCUPATION
It is neither wealth nor splendor, but tranquility and occupation, which give happiness—1839 (Р)

OFFENCE
No offence /meant/—1292 (Н)
Offence is the best defence—1249 (Н)

OFFEND
None is offended but by himself—2248 (Ч)

OFFENDER
Offender never pardons (The)—924 (К)
Offenders never pardon—924 (К)

OFFENSE
Good offense is the best defense (A)—1249 (Н)
No offense meant—1292 (Н)

OFFER
Never refuse a good offer—416 (Д)

OIL
Add not oil to the fire—1109 (М)
Oil not, neither will you spin—1387 (Н)
Pour not oil on flame (on the fire)—1109 (М)
Spoonful of oil on the troubled waters goes farther than a quart of vinegar (A)—983 (Л), 984 (Л)
To pour oil on the fire is not the way to quench it—1109 (М)

OLD
Best wine comes out of an old vessel (The)—2009 (С)
Deuce (devil) knows many things because he is old (The)—2009 (С)
Good broth may be made in an old pot—2009 (С)
If the young knew, if the old could, there's nothing but would be done—561 (Е)
If the young man would and the old man could, there would be nothing undone—561 (Е)
Old man is twice a boy (a child) (An)—2243 (Ч)
Old men are twice children—2243 (Ч)
Old mule ploughs a straight furrow (The)—2009 (С), 2012 (С)
Old ox makes (ploughs) a straight furrow (An)—2009 (С), 2012 (С)

OMELET(TE)
You cannot make an omelet(te) (pancakes) without breaking eggs—313 (Г), 1011 (Л), 2160 b (У)
You can't have an omelette unless you break the eggs—1011 (Л)

ONCE
Once is no custom (rule)—1528 (О)
Once is not enough—1528 (О)

ONE
It is all one—225 (В), 2285 (Ч)
It takes one to know one—1842 (Р)
One beats the bush, and another catches the birds (has the hare, takes the bird)—529 (Д), 1114 (М)
One by one the spindles are made—1107 (М)
One does the scathe, and another has the scorn—1841 (Р)
One for all, and all for one—1522 (О)
One is no number—1520 (О)
One is too few, three /is/ too many—975 (К)
There is one born every minute—525 (Д), 1211 (Н)

ONE-EYED
Among the blind the one-eyed man is king—291 (В), 893 (К), 1174 (Н)
Better one-eyed than stone-blind—704 (И)
Blessed are the one-eyed among those who are blind—893 (К)
In the country (kingdom) of the blind the one-eyed man is king—893 (К)
In the land of the blind the one-eyed are kings—893 (К)

ONION
If thou hast not a capon, feed on an onion—579 (Е)

ONLOOKER
Onlooker sees more (most) of the game (The)—1973 (С)

OPINION
As many men, so many opinions—1908 (С), 2123 (У)
Everybody to his own opinion—1908 (С)
Every man to his own opinion—1908 (С), 2123 (У)
Opinions differ—1908 (С)

OPPORTUNITY
If opportunity knocks, let her in—1032 (Л)
Opportunity knocks but once—1032 (Л)
Opportunity makes a (the) thief—328 (Г), 1427 (Н), 1655 (П)

OPPOSITE
Opposites attract /each other/—883 (К)

ORDER
Order and method render things easily—1719 (П)
Order is heaven's first law—1719 (П)
Orders are orders—2181 (Х)
Orders must not be challenged—1265 (Н), 2181 (Х)

ORGANISM
Each organism knows where it itches—2060 (Т)

OUNCE
Last ounce breaks the camel's back (The)—1727 (П)

OUTSET
Good outset is half the voyage (the way) (A)—477 (Д)

OUTSIDER
Outsider sees more (most) of the game (The)—1973 (С)
Outsiders see most of the game—1973 (С)

OVEN
Old ovens are soon heated—1997 (С)

OVER
It's all over but the shouting—429 (Д)

OWE
Sleep without supping, and wake without owing—1061 (Л)

OWL
Don't send owls to Athens—163 (В)
Owl thinks all her young ones beauties (The)—462 (Д)
Owl thinks her own young fairest (The)—462 (Д)

OX
Fat ox in the stall gives no thought to the hungry as they pass by (The)—81 (Б)
God gives the vicious ox short horns—88 (Б)
Man must plough with such oxen as he has—1370 (Н)
Old ox makes (ploughs) a straight furrow (An)—2009 (С), 2012 (С)
Ox is never weary of carrying its horns (The)—1867 (С)
Ox remains an ox, even if driven to Vienna (An)—195 (В)
When the ox is down, many are the butchers—1627 (П)
Young ox learns to plough from the older (The)—1587 (О)

P

PACE
It is the pace that kills—2373 (Я)
Soft pace goes far—2053 (Т), 2054 (Т)
'Tis pace that kills—2373 (Я)

PACK
Every horse (one) thinks his pack heaviest—770 (К)

PADLOCK
Bad padlock invites a picklock (A)—328 (Г)

PAIN
It is more pain to do nothing that /to do/ something—1455 (Н)
Lazy man takes the most pain (The)—1455 (Н)
Pain past is pleasure—2306 (Ч)
There is no pleasure without pain—34 (Б)

PAINS
No pains, no gains /; no sweat, no sweet/—50 (Б), 1116 (М), 1220 (Н), 1391 (Н), 1412 (Н), 1502 (Н)
Nothing can be got without pains—347 (Г)

PAIR
They make a pair—421 (Д)

PALM
Every palm likes to be greased—1387 (Н)
Let him who deserves the palm carry it—405 (Д)

PANTS
Pants don't make the man—1381 (Н)

PAPER
It sounded (sounds) right on paper—340 (Г)
Paper bleeds little—111 (Б)
Paper does not blush—111 (Б)
Paper is patience; you can put anything on it—111 (Б)

PARADE
Parade goes on (The)—1954 (С)

PARDON
If you'll pardon the expression—712 (И)
Offender never pardons (The)—924 (К)
Offenders never pardon—924 (К)
Pardoning the bad is injuring the good—190 (В)
Pardon my French—712 (И)
They never pardon who have done the wrong—924 (К)

PARENT
If the parents are good, the children follow in their footsteps—783 (К)
Like parents, like children—783 (К), 807 (К), 810 (К), 2357 (Я)
Parents are patterns—783 (К)

PARIS
Paris was not built in a day—730 (И), 1281 (Н)

PARISH
Mad parish must have a mad priest (A)—1660 (П)

PARSON
Parson always christens his own children first (The)—265 (В)

PART
He that repairs not a part, builds all—2341 (Ш)

PARTRIDGE
Look where the partridge were last year—757 (И)

PASS
This, too, shall (will) pass—239 (В), 665 (З)

PAST
Things past cannot be recalled—1127 (М), 2295 а (Ч)

PASTURE
Distant pastures are greener—69 (Б), 1917 (С)
Greenest pasture is just over the fence (The)—69 (Б)
Other man's pasture always looks the greenest (The)—296 (В)

PATERNOSTER
No paternoster, no penny—944 (К)

PATH
Beaten path is a safe one (A)—1357 (Н)
Every path has a (its) puddle—1299 (Н), 1430 (Н)
Trodden path bears no grass (A)—1251 (Н)
You can't follow two paths—1193 (Н)

PATIENCE
He that can have patience can have what he will—1188 (Н)
No remedy but patience—2045 (Т)
Patience brings everything about—2046 (Т)
Patience conquers—1188 (Н), 2044 (Т), 2046 (Т)
Patience is a plaster for all sores—2045 (Т)
Patience is a remedy for every sorrow—2045 (Т)
Patience is a stout horse, but it will tire at last—286 (В)
Patience is bitter, but its fruit is sweet—2046 (Т)
Patience is the key of paradise—2045 (Т), 2046 (Т)
Remedy for hard times is to have patience (The)—2045 (Т)
Time and patience change the mulberry leaf to satin—833 (К), 2044 (Т)

PATIENT
Patient men win the day—2046 (Т)

Patient waiters are no losers—920 (К)

PAW

Velvet paws hide sharp claws—877 (К)

PAY

As the work, so the pay—791 (К), 794 (К), 1714 (П)

Everything that is worth having must be paid for—635 (З)

He who calls the tune must pay the piper—1075 (Л)

He who pays the piper calls (may call) the tune—955 (К)

If you dance (want to dance), you must pay the fiddler—1075 (Л)

Laugh when you borrow and you'll cry when you pay—991 (Л)

No pay, no play—635 (З)

Once paid and never craved—639 (З)

Pay the piper his due—794 (К)

Pay what you owe—2117 (У)

Pay with the same dish you borrow—2117 (У)

PAYMASTER

Of a bad paymaster get what you can, though it be a straw—1974 (С)

PAYMENT

Sweet is the wine, but sour is the payment—1806 (П)

PEACE

Bad peace is better than a good quarrel (A)—2220 (Х)

There never was (was never) a good war or a bad peace—2220 (Х)

PEACH

Rose has its thorn, the peach its worm (The)—1452 (Н)

PEACOCK

Fly pride, says the peacock—2334 (Ч)

PEARL

Don't cast pearls before swine—1290 (Н), 1368 (Н)

He who would search for pearls must dive below—50 (Б)

Pearl is often hidden in an ugly shell (A)—871 (К), 1362 (Н), 1488 (Н)

PEBBLE

There are more pebbles on the beach—1136 (М), 1439 (Н), 1860 (С)

There are plenty of pebbles on the shore—1439 (Н), 1860 (С)

PECKER

Keep your pecker up!—307 (В)

PEDDLER

Let every peddler carry his own pack—267 (В), 591 (Ж), 1975 (С)

PEDLAR

Every pedlar praises his needles—269 (В)

Let every pedlar carry his own burden (pack)—267 (В), 1975 (С)

PEG

Peg is driven out by a peg, a nail by a nail (A)—838 (К)

PEN

Pens may blot, but they cannot blush—111 (Б)

PENKNIFE

You cannot chop wood with a penknife—695 (И)

PENNY

Don't be penny- wise and dollar-foolish—1339 (Н)

In for a penny, in for a pound—609 (З)

Look after the pennies and the pounds will take care of themselves—869 (К)

No penny, no paternoster—635 (З)

One penny is better than none—1056 (Л)

Pennies make dollars—868 (К)

Penny and penny laid up will be many—868 (К)

Penny by right is better than a thousand by wrong (A)—1043 (Л), 1052 (Л), 2208 (Х)

Penny saved is a penny earned (gained) (A)—638 (З), 1856 (С)

Penny saved is a penny made (A)—1856 (С)

Penny soul never came to ('came) twopence (A)—629 (З), 1339 (Н)

Penny today is worth two tomorrow (A)—1549 (О)

Penny-wise and pound foolish—629 (З), 1510 (О)
Penny-wise, pound foolish—629 (З), 1510 (О)
Take care of the pence (pennies) and the pounds will take care of themselves—869 (К)
Take care of your pennies and the dollars will take care of themselves—869 (К)
Touch pot, touch penny—635 (З)
Two pennies will creep together—441 (Д)
Who will not keep a penny never shall (shall never) have many—869 (К)
You can tell a bad penny by its ring—1566 (О)

PEOPLE
Behind the mountains there are people to be found—699 (И)
People create their own problems—1277 (Н), 1620 (О)
People don't see things on their doorsteps—646 (З), 1355 (Н)
People living in glass houses should not throw stones—511 (Д)
People who live in glass houses shouldn't throw stones—511 (Д)
There are always other people and other places—699 (И)

PERFECT
None of us are perfect—235 (В), 737 (И), 1436 (Н), 1449 (Н)
Nothing is perfect—173 (В), 735 (И), 737 (И), 1008 (Л), 1171 b (М)
Not one is perfect—1487 (Н)
There is nothing perfect in the world—54 (Б), 737 (И)

PERFORMANCE
Acre of performance is worth the whole world of promise (An)—1421 (Н), 1423 (Н), 1744 (П)
One acre of performance is worth twenty of the Land of Promise—1421 (Н), 1423 (Н), 1744 (П)

PERIL
All is not lost that is in peril—1308 (Н), 2138 (У)

PERMANENT
There is nothing permanent under the moon (the sun)—1485 (Н)

PERSEVERANCE
Perseverance conquers all things—833 (К), 2044 (Т)
Perseverance kills the game—2044 (Т)
Perseverance wins—833 (К), 2044 (Т)

PERSON
Every person should row his own boat—267 (В), 591 (Ж), 1419 (Н)
/Here's/ just the person I need—1207 (Н)

PEW
Right church but wrong pew—2170 (Ф)

PHYSICIAN
Many physicians have killed the king—2145 (У)
Physician, heal thyself—511 (D)
Physicians kill more than the cure—10 (А)

PICK
Pick yourself up and dust yourself off—1157 (М)

PICKLE
Many a pickle makes a mickle—664 (З), 979 (К), 1694 (П), 1801 (П), 1956 (С)

PIG
He who scrubs every pig he sees will not long be clean himself—400 (Г)
If a pig had wings, he might fly—113 (Б), 1210 (Н), 1373 (Н)
Lead a pig to Rhine, it remains a pig—195 (В)
Let every pig dig for himself—267 (В), 1975 (С)
Little pigs have long ears—2288 (Ч)
Pig in the parlo(u)r is still a pig (A)—1720 (П)
Pigs are pigs—1235 (Н), 1720 (П)
Pigs grunt about everything and nothing—1261 (Н)

Pigs might fly /if they had wings/ (, but they are very unlikely birds)—113 (Б), 1210 (Н), 1373 (Н)
Pig that has two owners is sure to die of hunger (A)—2145 (У)
Pig used to dirt turns up its nose at rice boiled in milk (A)—862 (К), 2087 (У)
Still pig gets all the slop (The)—987 (Л)
We don't kill a pig every day—1297 (Н), 1766 (П)
What can you expect from a pig but a grunt?—1591 (О)
When a pig is proffered, hold up the poke—416 (Д)
When pigs fly—847 (К), 1729 (П)
Young pig grunts as the old sow (The)—1101 (М)

PIGEON
It's not my pigeon—1372 (Н)
Little pigeons can carry great messages—1099 (М)

PILL
Bitter pills may have blessed effects—2190 (Х)

PILLOW
Best advice is found on the pillow (The)—2158 (У)
Consult with your pillow—2158 (У)
Take counsel of your pillow—2158 (У)

PILOT
Every plane has its pilot—11 (А), 1519 (О)

PIN
Pin a day is a groat a year (A)—979 (К)
There's not a pin to choose between them—421 (Д)

PINCH
When the pinch comes you remember the old shoe—2292 (Ч)

PIPE
Put it in (into) your pipe and smoke it!—644 (З)
Put that (this) in your pipe and smoke it!—644 (З)

PIPER
He who calls the tune must pay the piper—1075 (Л)
He who pays the piper calls (may call) the tune—955 (К)

PIPKIN
Cracked pipkins are discovered by their sound—1566 (О)

PIT
He that diggeth a pit for another should look that he fall not into it himself—917 (К)
If you dig a pit for someone else, you will fall into it yourself—917 (К)
It's the pits—427 (Д), 435 (Д)
Whoso digs a pit, he shall fall therein—917 (К)

PITCH
He who touches pitch will get black—400 (Г)
If you throw enough pitch, some of it is sure to stick—837 (К)
Touch pitch and you'll be defiled—400 (Г), 1451 (Н)

PITCHER
Little pitchers have big (great, long) ears—2288 (Ч)
Pitcher goes often to the well /but is broken at last/ (The)—122 (Б), 1659 (П), 1907 (С)
Pitcher that goes to the well too often is broken at last (A)—1659 (П), 1907 (С)
Pitcher went once too often to the well (The)—122 (Б), 1659 (П), 1907 (С)
Small pitchers have wide ears—2288 (Ч)
Whether the pitcher strikes the stone, or the stone the pitcher it is bad for the pitcher—728 (И), 2285 (Ч)

PITY
If you pity rogues, you are no great friend of honest men—190 (В)
Pity is akin to love—581 (Ж)

PLACE
Everything is good in its place—281 (В)

It is not the place that honours the man, but the man that honours the place—1332 (Н)
One cannot be in two places at the same time—1193 (Н)
There is a place for everything, and everything in its place—281 (В)

PLAN
Best-laid plans of mice and men often go astray (The)—340 (Г)

PLANT
Plant often removed cannot thrive (A)—856 (К)

PLASTER
Plaster thick, and some will stick—837 (К)

PLATTER
Platter kills more than the sword (The)—327 (Г)

PLAY
He who plays with a cat must expect to be scratched—1477 (Н)
If you play with matches, you will get burned—1477 (Н)
Play while you play; work while you work—401 (Г), 696 (И)
You may play with the bull till you get his horn in your eye—1477 (Н)
Work is work, and play is play—401 (Г), 433 (Д), 696 (И), 1635 (П)

PLEASE
He labors in vain who tries to please everybody—1184 (Н), 1185 (Н)
He that all men will please shall never find ease—1185 (Н)
He that would please all and himself too, takes more in hand than he is like to do—1184 (Н)
He who pleased everybody died before he was born—1184 (Н)
He who tries to please everybody pleases nobody—230 (В)
If you try to please all, you will please none—230 (В)
It is hard to please all parties—1184 (Н)
Not even Jupiter can please everybody—1184 (Н)
One cannot please all the world and his wife—724 (И), 1184 (Н), 1189 (Н), 1669 (П)
You cannot please everybody (everyone)—724 (И), 1184 (Н), 1189 (Н), 1669 (П)
You can't please the whole world and his wife—724 (И), 1184 (Н), 1189 (Н), 1669 (П)

PLEASURE
No pleasure without repentance—1918 (С)
Pleasure has a sting in its tail—1918 (С)
Pleasure shared is a pleasure doubled (A)—1814 (Р)
Pleasures of the mighty are the tears of the poor (The)—879 (К)
Shared pleasures are doubled; shared griefs are halved—390 (Г)
There is no pleasure without pain—34 (Б), 1453 (Н)

PLEDGE
If you pledge, don't hedge—913 (К), 1201 (Н), 1751 (П)
Once you pledge, don't hedge—913 (К), 1201 (Н), 1751 (П)

PLENTY
Plenty is no dainty—2187 (Х)
Plenty is no plague—832 (К)
Plenty makes daintiness (dainty)—2031 (С)
Too much plenty makes mouths dainty—2031 (С)

PLOD
Plodding wins the race—507 (Д)

PLOUGH
Man must plough with such oxen as he has (A)—633 (З)

PLOW
Plow deep while sluggards sleep /, and you shall have corn to sell and to keep/—961 (К)

PLUCK
Pluck not where you never planted—1260 (Н)

PLUM
Black plum is as sweet as a white (A)—1182 (H)

POACHER
Old poacher makes the best game keeper (An)—192 (B)

POCKET
Your wooden overcoat won't have any pockets—2133 (У)

POCKMARK
In the eye (eyes) of the lover, pockmarks are dimples—1085 (Л)

POD
For every pea there is a pod—2090 (У)

POINT
Point not at others' spots with a foul finger—511 (Д)

POISON
One drop of poison can affect the whole—1037 (Л)
One drop of poison infects the whole tun of wine—1037 (Л)
One man's fancy (pleasure) is another man's poison—879 (К)
One poison drives out another—2264 (Ч)
Poison quells poison—2264 (Ч)

POLECAT
Polecat is a polecat, no matter what you call it (A)—1407 (H)

POLITENESS
One never loses anything by politeness—1579 (O), 1689 (П)
Politeness costs nothing and (but) gains everything—985 (Л)

POOL
Standing pools gather filth—1218 (H), 2014 (C)
Standing pool soon stagnates (A)—2014 (C)

POOR
Better poor with honor than rich with shame—1043 (Л), 1044 (Л), 1052 (Л), 2208 (X)
Children are poor man's riches—77 (Б)
He becomes poor that deals with a slack hand, but the hand of diligence makes rich—329 (Г)
He who works with a slack hand becomes poor—329 (Г)
If rich, be not elated; if poor, be not dejected—1399 (H)
It is a hard task (hard) to be poor and honest—30 (Б), 1796 (П)
It's hell to be poor—32 (Б)
It's no disgrace to be poor, but a terrible inconvenience—32 (Б)
It's no disgrace to be poor, but it may as well be—32 (Б)
No one claims kindred to the poor—27 (Б), 1769 (П)
No one is akin to the poor—27 (Б), 1769 (П)
Poor always pay (The)—1630 (П)
Poor do penance for the sins of the rich (The)—1630 (П)
Poor folks are glad of porridge—1331 (H)
Poor is hated even of his own neighbors (neighbour) (The)—27 (Б), 37 (Б)
Poor man always pays for all (The)—1630 (П)
Poor man has no friends (A)—27 (Б), 37 (Б), 1769 (П)
Poor man pays for all (The)—1630 (П)
Poor man wants some things, a covetous man all things (A)—28 (Б)
Poor suffer all the wrong (The)—1630 (П)
Poor thing, but mine (my own) (A)—1862 (C)
Rich get richer, and the poor have children (get babies) (The)—77 (Б)
Rich man for dogs and a poor man for babies (A)—77 (Б)

POPE
It is hard to live (to sit) in Rome and strive against the Pope—1786 a (П)

POSSESSION
Great possessions are great cares—1141 (M)
Possession is nine points of the law—2308 b (Ч)

POT
Every pot must stand upon its own bottom—1975 (С)
Every pot has its cover—46 (Б)
Good broth may be made in an old pot—2009 (С)
Let a good pot have a good lid—1723 (П)
Like pot, like pot-lid—787 (К)
Pot calling (calls) the kettle black (The)—15 (А), 358 (Г), 909 (К), 1406 (Н), 1562 (О), 1832 (Р), 2334 (Ч)
Pot goes so long to the water that it is broken at last (The)—1659 (П)
Pot oft sent to the well is broken at last (A)—1907 (С)
Pot that belongs to many is ill stirred and worse boiled (A)—320 (Г)
Such pot, such pot-lid—787 (К)
There is never a pot too crooked but what there's a lid to fit it—260 (В)
When the pot's full, it runs (will boil) over—1727 (П)
Your pot broken seems better than my whole one—296 (В), 2185 (Х)

POTATO
If you plant potatoes, you can't reap tomatoes—2284 (Ч)
Potatoes don't grow by the side of the pot—1220 (Н), 1644 (П)

POTTAGE
When it rains pottage you must hold up your dish—453 (Д)

POUND
In for a penny, in for a pound—150 (В), 609 (З)
Pound in the purse is worth two in the book (A)—70 (Б)

POVERTY
Poverty and hunger have many learned disciples—378 (Г), 1498 (Н)
Poverty breeds strife—1495 (Н), 1873 (С), 2223 (Х)
Poverty has no kin—27 (Б), 1769 (П)
Poverty is crafty; it outwits even a fox—378 (Г)
Poverty is in want of much, avarice of everything—28 (Б)
Poverty is no crime (no disgrace, no sin, not a crime, no vice)—31 (Б)
Poverty is no disgrace /, but it is a great inconvenience/—32 (Б)
Poverty is no sin /, but it is terribly inconvenient/—32 (Б)
Poverty is not a sin but something much worse—32 (Б)
Poverty is the mother of all arts (art)—378 (Г), 1498 (Н), 1595 (О), 1781 (П)
Poverty is the mother of crime—30 (Б), 1796 (П)
Poverty is the mother of invention—378 (Г)
Poverty is the sixth sense—378 (Г)
Poverty is the worst guard to chastity—30 (Б)
Poverty makes strange bedfellows—171 (В)
Poverty obstructs the road to virtue—30 (Б)
Poverty parts friends (fellowship)—27 (Б), 2176 (Х)
Poverty wants some things, luxury many things, avarice all—28 (Б)
There is no virtue that poverty does not destroy—30 (Б)
When poverty comes in /at/ the door, love flies out /of/ the window—1873 (С), 2223 (Х)
When poverty comes in at the door, love leaps out of the window—2223 (Х)
When poverty comes in the door, love goes out the window—2223 (Х)

POWDER
Keep your powder dry—454 (Д)

POWER
Accusation is proof where malice and power sit in judge—965 (К)

PRACTICE
Ounce of practice is worth a pound of preaching (An)—1558 (О)
Practice is the best master—1190 (Н)
Practice makes perfect—280 (В), 430 (Д), 1112 (М), 1190 (Н)

PRAISE
Admonish your friends in private, praise them in public—124 (В)

Before the morning is away praise not the glory of the day—2174 (Х)
He that praises himself spatters himself—1467 (Н)
It is not good praising a ford till a man be over—1321 (Н)
Let another man praise you /, and not your mouth (not yourself)/—1364 (Н), 1467 (Н)
Man's praise in his own mouth stinks—1467 (Н)
Praise a fair day at night /, and life at the end/—2174 (Х)
Praise a fine day at night—2174 (Х)
Praise is no pudding—2191 (Х)
Praise publicly; blame privately—124 (В)

PRAY
Pray to God, but keep hammering—1176 (Н)
Pray to God, but keep the hammer going—1176 (Н)
Pray to God, sailor, but pull for the shore—1176 (Н)

PRECAUTION
Precaution is better than repentance—57 (Б)

PRESENT
There is no future like the present—1382 (Н)
There is no time like the present—1382 (Н)

PRESERVATION
Self preservation is the first law of nature—1975 (С)

PRESS
Press not a falling man too hard—1001 (Л)

PRESUME
All are presumed good till found at fault—1390 (Н)
All are presumed good till (until) they are found in a fault—1396 (Н)

PRETENCE
If you want a pretence to whip a dog, say that he ate the frying pan—118 (Б)

PRETENSE
If you want a pretense to whip a dog, it is enough to say he ate up a frying pan—118 (Б)

PRETTINESS
Prettiness dies first (quickly)—1925 (С)
Prettiness makes no pottage—886 (К)

PRETTY
Pretty is as pretty does—1447 (Н), 1928 (С)

PREVENT
Prevent rather than repent—747 (И)

PREVENTION
Ounce of prevention is worth a pound of cure (An)—1555 (О)
Prevention is better than cure—747 (И), 1555 (О)

PRICE
Every man has his price—777 (К)
There is no good that does not cost a price—635 (З)
What's that got to do with the price of apples (eggs, horses)?—174 (В), 2358 (Я)

PRICKLE
No rose without prickles—1452 (Н)

PRIDE
Pride and poverty are ill met, yet often seen together—1488 (Н)
Pride apes humility—1943 (С)
Pride borrows the cloak of humility—1943 (С)
Pride goes before a fall—301 (В), 385 (Г), 556 (Д), 1341 (Н)
Pride goes before, and shame follows after—556 (Д)
Pride goes before destruction—301 (В), 385 (Г), 556 (Д)
Pride goes forth on horseback grand and gay, and comes back on foot and begs its way—556 (Д)
Pride is a luxury a poor man cannot afford—1797 (П)
Pride may lurk under a threadbare coat—1488 (Н)

Pride must suffer pain—556 (Д)
Pride often apes humility—1943 (С)

PRIEST
Each priest praises his own relics—269 (В), 395 (Г)
Like priest, like people—813 (К), 817 (К)
Once a priest, always a priest—1877 (С)
Such as the priest, such is the clerk—822 (К)

PRINCE
Like prince, like people—817 (К)

PROBLEM
People create their own problems—1277 (Н), 1620 (О)

PROCRASTINATION
Procrastination brings loss—583 (Ж), 1784 (П)
Procrastination is the thief of time—583 (Ж)

PROFIT
No great loss but some small profit—1219 (Н)
Profit by the folly of others—2315 (Ч)
We profit by mistakes—1222 (Н)

PROMISE
All promises are either broken or kept—2301 (Ч)
Bad promise is better broken than kept (A)—1329 (Н)
Be slow to make a promise, but swift to keep it—412 (Д), 2365 (Я)
Be slow to promise and quick to perform—412 (Д)
Better deny at once than promise long—1329 (Н)
Between promising and performing a man may marry his daughter—1506 (О), 2115 (У)
Expect nothing from him who promises a great deal—933 (К), 934 (К)
Great promises and small performances—933 (К), 934 (К)
He that promises much means nothing—934 (К)
It's one thing to promise, another to perform—1506 (О), 2301 (Ч)
Long on promises, short on performance—933 (К), 934 (К)
Perform whatever you promise—412 (Д)
Promise is a debt (A)—412 (Д)
Promise is a promise (A)—412 (Д), 2095 (У)
Promise little but do much—1503 (Н)
Promise made is a debt unpaid (A)—412 (Д)
Promises are like good piecrust: easily broken—2301 (Ч)
Promises are like pie-crust, /they are/ made to be broken—2301 (Ч)
Promises don't fill the belly—614 (З), 710 (И), 1229 (Н), 1360 (Н), 1505 (О), 1744 (П), 1968 a (С)
Promises fill no sack—1505 (О), 1968 a (С)
You can't live on promises—1505 (О)

PROMISER
No greater promisers than those who have nothing to give—934 (К)

PROPHESY
It is easy to prophesy after the event—620 (З)

PROPHET
No prophet is accepted in his own country—1450 (Н)
Prophet is not without hono(u)r, save in his own country /and his own house/ (A)—1450 (Н)
Prophet is without honor in his own country (A)—1450 (Н)

PROSPECT
Prospect is often better than possession—2064 (Т)

PRY
He that pries into every cloud may be stricken by a thunderbolt (with a thunder)—1086 (Л)
He that pries into the clouds may be struck with a thunderbolt—1086 (Л)

PUDDING
Better some of the pudding than none of the pie—1070 (Л)

Make your pudding according to your plums—1708 (П)
Proof (test) of the pudding is in the eating (The)—1349 (Н), 1401 (Н)
Too much pudding chokes the dog—1919 (С)

PUDDLE
/There is/ no mud without a puddle—1432 (Н)

PUFF
Puff not against wind—1786 b (П)

PULL
It is easier to pull down than to build /up/—1040 (Л)

PULLET
Pullet in the pen is worth a hundred in the fen (A)—1066 (Л)

PUNCH
You don't pull any punches—1279 (Н)

PUNCTUALITY
Punctuality is a kingly virtue—2069 (Т)
Punctuality is the politeness of kings (princes)—2069 (Т)

PUNISHMENT
Every sin brings its punishment with it—1602 (О)
Every sin carries its own punishment—1602 (О)
Punishment comes slowly, but it comes—1790 (П)
Punishment follows hard upon crime—1602 (О), 1790 (П)
Punishment is lame, but it comes—1602 (О)

PURE
From a pure spring, pure water flows—2276 (Ч)
To the pure all things are pure—2276 (Ч)

PURSE
Ask your purse what you should buy—1708 (П), 1712 (П)
Better an empty purse than an empty head—677 (З)
Empty purse fills the face with wrinkles (An)—295 (В)
Full purse has many friends (A)—860 (К)
Full purse makes a mouth speak (A)—573 (Е)
Full purse never lacks friends (A)—860 (К)
Heavy purse makes a light heart (A)—1622 (О)
He that has a full purse never wanted a friend—860 (К)
If a man empties his purse into his head, no one can take it from him—677 (З)
Light purse, a heavy heart (A)—24 (Б)
Light purse is a heavy curse (A)—24 (Б)
Light purse makes a heavy heart (A)—24 (Б)
Wrinkled purses make wrinkled faces—295 (В)
You cannot make a silk purse out of a sow's ear—714 (И), 717 (И), 718 (И)
You can't make a silk purse out of a pig's ear—714 (И)

PUZZLE
It is enough to puzzle a Philadelphia lawyer—1851 (С)

Q

QUALITY
It is quality rather than quantity which counts—1057 (Л)
Quality is better than quantity—1057 (Л)

QUARREL
Never quarrel with your bread and butter—1383 (Н)

QUEEN
Queen Ann (Anne, Bess, Elizabeth) is dead—1590 (О)

QUESTION
Ask a silly question and you'll get a silly answer—1191 (Н)
Like question, like answer—1191 (Н)

Ours is not to question why, ours is to do or die—1265 (Н)
Silly question, silly answer—1191 (Н)
Yours is not to question why; yours is but to do or die—1265 (Н)

QUICK
Quick and well-done do not agree—1911 (С)

QUICKLY
Good and quickly seldom meet—1741 (П), 1911 (С)
What is quickly done is quickly undone—1242 (Н)

QUIET
All is quiet along (on) the Potomac—1266 (Н)
All quiet on the Western front—1266 (Н)
All's quiet in the Shipka Pass—1266 (Н)
There's always a quiet after a storm—804 (К), 1724 (П), 1725 (П)

QUIETNESS
There's always quietness after a storm—1724 (П), 1725 (П)

R

RABBIT
First catch your rabbit and then make your stew—1115 (М), 2228 (Ц)
It is better to be a live rabbit than a dead tiger—590 (Ж)

RACE
Plodding wins the race—507 (Д)
Race is got by running (The)—507 (Д), 906 (К)
Slow and steady wins the race—2044 (Т)
You must run to win the race—507 (Д), 906 (К)

RAG
Better go to heaven in rags than to hell in embroidery—1043 (Л)
Every rag meets its mate—46 (Б)
From rags to riches—703 (И)

RAIN
Although it rain, throw not away your watering-pot—59 (Б)
Into each (every) life some rain must fall—137 (В)
It is raining cats and dogs (chicken coops, darling needles, pitchforks)—1813 (Р)
It never rains, but it pours—1753 (П), 1778 (П)
Little rain stills a great wind (A)—1097 (М), 1098 a (М), 1099 (М), 1165 (М), 1320 (Н)
Rain comes down in sheets (in torrents) (The)—1813 (Р)
Small rain allays a great wind—1097 (М), 1098 a (М)
Small rain lays /a/ great dust (/A/)-1097 (М), 1098 a (М)
Small rain may allay a great storm (A)—1098 a (М)
Small rain will lay great dust—1097 (М), 1098 a (М)
When it is raining gold (soup), I am caught with a leaky teaspoon—26 (Б)
When it rains, it pours—2231 (Ч)
When it rains porridge, the beggar has no spoon—26 (Б)
When it rains pottage you must hold up your dish—453 (Д)
Why is it when it rains good things we've left our slickers at the wagon?—26 (Б)

RAKE
Every one rakes the fire under his own pot—1868 (С)
Keep the rake near the scythe, and the cart near the rake—454 (Д)

RANK
Risen from the ranks—703 (И)

RAISIN
Black raisin is as sweet as a white (A)—1182 (Н)

RAT
Good rat to match a good cat (A)—1679 (П), 1723 (П)
Rats abandon (always leave, desert) a sinking ship—901 (К)

Rats forsake (leave) a falling house (a sinking ship)—901 (К)
Rats know the way of rats—192 (В)
Rat which has but one hole is soon caught (The)—2216 (Х)

RAVEN
Bring up a raven, he will pick out your eyes—250 (В)
One raven will not pluck another's eyes—196 (В)
Raven chides (eludes) blackness (The)—2334 (Ч)
Raven said to the rook: "Stand away, black-coat" (The)—2334 (Ч)
Ravens don't peck one another's eyes out (The)—183 (В), 196 (В), 2271 (Ч)
Young ravens are beaked like the old (The)—783 (К), 2357 (Я)

RAZOR
You cannot cut blocks with a razor—695 (И)

REACH
Out of reach is not worth having—410 (Д)

REALIZATION
Realization is never as great as anticipation (The)—2064 (Т)

REAP
They that sow in tears shall reap in joy—2080 (Т), 2166 (У)

REASON
There is reason in all things—1971 (С)
There is reason in roasting of eggs—1971 (С)
There's a reason for everything—1971 (С)
Whom God would ruin He first deprives of reason—851 (К)

RECALL
Things past cannot be recalled—1127 (М), 2295 а (Ч)

RECEIVER
Receiver is as bad as the thief (The)—197 (В), 1441 (Н), 2112 (У)

RECKONING
After dinner (the feast) comes the reckoning—1075 (Л)
Even reckoning makes lasting (long) friends—2025 (С)
Short reckonings make good friends—2234 (Ч)
Short reckonings make long friends—2025 (С), 2234 (Ч)

REED
Oaks may fall when reeds stay the storm—112 (Б)
Reed before the wind lives on, while mighty oaks do fall (A)—112 (Б)
Where there are reeds there is water—1432 (Н)

REEK
Where there's reek, there's heat—1432 (Н)

REJOICE
Rejoice today and repent tomorrow—1256 (Н), 1820 (Р)

RELAX
Relax and enjoy—555 (Д)

REMEDY
Desperate evils require desperate remedies—2264 (Ч)
Remedy is worse than the disease (The)—10 (А)
There is a remedy for all dolours (things) but death—898 (К), 1606 (О)
There is a remedy for all things except death and taxes—898 (К)
Things without remedy should be without regard—2302 (Ч)

REMEMBRANCE
Remembrance of past dangers is pleasant (The)—2306 (Ч)
Remembrance of past sorrow is joyful—2306 (Ч)

REPENTANCE
Repentance costs very dear—396 (Г)

REPETITION
Repetition is the mother of learning (of skill)—1663 (П)

REPROVE
Reprove your friend privately; commend him publicly—124 (В)

REPUTATION
Glass, china, and reputations are easily cracked and never well mended—547 (Д), 996 (Л)
Good reputation is more valuable than money (A)—437 (Д), 470 (Д)
Good reputation stands still; a bad one runs (A)—471 (Д), 1648 (П)
Wounded reputation is seldom cured (A)—547 (Д), 996 (Л)

REQUIRE
For all those to whom much is given, much is required—855 (К)
Whomsoever much is given, of him shall be much required—855 (К)

RESPECT
Respect is greater from a distance—1450 (Н)

REST
If you rest, you rust—1218 (Н), 2014 (С)
No rest for the weary—1691 (П)
Rest, rust, rot—2014 (С)
Too much rest is rust—1007 (Л)

RICH
Everyone is akin to the rich—860 (К)
He is rich enough that wants nothing (who is contented with little)—491 (Д)
He is rich who does not desire more—491 (Д), 1433 (Н)
If rich, be not elated; if poor, be not dejected—1399 (Н)
Richest is he who wants least—491 (Д)
Rich folk have many friends—860 (К)
Rich has many friends (The)—860 (К)
Rich man has the world by the tail (A)—439 (Д)
Rich man never lacks relatives (A)—860 (К)
Rich today, poor tomorrow—1818 (Р), 1879 (С), 2229 (Ч)
You can't be too rich or too thin—832 (К)

RICHARD
Richard is himself again—596 (Ж)

RICHES
Enough is great riches—491 (Д)
Riches and cares are inseparable—1141 (М)
Riches bring care /and fears/—1141 (М)
Riches have wings—442 (Д), 446 (Д)
Small riches hath most rest—38 (Б), 1123 (М)

RIDDANCE
Good riddance /to (of) bad rubbish/ (/A/)—17 (Б)

RIDE
He that never rode, never fell—941 (К)

RIGHT
God's in the heaven; all's right with the world—226 (В)
Right is with the strongest (The)—965 (К)

RIND
Under the coarsest rind, the sweetest meat—1362 (Н)

RING
Give him a ring, and he'll want your whole arm—406 (Д), 1665 (П)

RIP
Never a rip without a tear—231 (В)

RIPE
Early ripe, early rotten—1914 (С)
Quick ripe, quick rotten—1914 (С)
Soon ripe, soon rotten—1914 (С)

RISE
He that will (would) thrive must rise at five—252 (В), 645 (З), 961 (К), 1822 (Р)
Our greatest glory consists not in never falling, but in rising every time we fall—2205 (Х)
Success comes in rising every time you fall—2205 (Х)

RISK
Don't take unnecessary risks—1357 (Н)
No risk, no gain—945 (К), 1834 (Р)
Nothing risk, nothing gain—945 (К), 1834 (Р)

RIVER
All rivers run into (to) the sea—766 (К)
Deep rivers move with silent majesty; shallow brooks are noisy—332 (Г)
Don't cross your rivers before you get to them—1402 (Н)
Even the weariest river winds somewhere safe to the sea—1296 (Н)
River past, and God forgotten (The)—1163 (М)
Where the river is deepest it makes least noise—93 (Б), 2051 (Т)

ROAD
All roads lead to Rome—224 (В)
Beaten road is the safest (The)—1357 (Н)
Don't leave a travelled road to follow a trail—1357 (Н)
Every road has hills to be climbed—1299 (Н)
Hard by the road called "by and by" there stands a house called "never"—1592 (О)
He who wishes to know the road through the mountains must ask those who have already trodden it—1410 (Н)
It is a long road that does not end (has no ending)—753 (И)
It's a long road that has no turning—311 (Г), 753 (И)
Keep the common road and you are safe—1357 (Н)
Other side of the road always looks cleanest (The)—296 (В)

ROBIN
It takes more than a robin to make a spring—1533 (О)
One robin doesn't make a spring—1533 (О)

ROD
Spare the rod and spoil the child—647 (З)

ROGUE
It takes a rogue to catch a rogue—192 (В)
Little rogues easily become great ones—935 (К)
When rogues fall out, honest men come by their own—418 (Д)

ROLAND
Roland for an Oliver (A)—1550 (О)

ROLL
You roll my log, and I'll roll yours—2077 (Т), 2148 (У)

ROME
Rome was not built in a day—730 (И), 1281 (Н)
See Rome and die—2083 (У)
When at Rome, live as the Romans live—297 (В)
When in Rome, do as the Romans /do/—159 (В), 297 (В), 1864 (С)
When you are at Rome, do as Rome /does/—297 (В), 1864 (С)

ROOF
Thatch your roof before rainy weather; dig your well before you are thirsty—398 (Г)
Thatch your roof before the rain begins—398 (Г)

ROOM
There is always room for one more—293 (В)

ROOT
Root, hog, or die—727 (И)

ROPE
Give a fool (a man, a thief, him) rope enough and he'll hang himself—407 (Д), 650 (З)
If you don't touch the rope, you won't ring the bell—1671 (П)
Name not a rope in his house that hanged himself (that was hanged)—129 (В), 1322 (Н)
Never talk of a rope in the house of a man who has been hanged—129 (В), 1322 (Н)

ROSE
Always a thorn among roses—1452 (Н)

Every rose has its thorn—1452 (Н)
If you lie upon roses when young, you'll lie upon thorns when old—2346 (Щ)
Lie on roses when young, lie on thorns when old—2346 (Щ)
No rose without prickles (thorns)—1452 (Н)
Rose by any other name would smell as sweet (A)—1407 (Н)
Rose has its thorn, the peach its worm (The)—1452 (Н)

ROSEBUD
Gather ye rosebuds while ye may—449 (Д), 1151 (М), 1526 (О)

ROSY
Everything in the garden is rosy—226 (В)

ROUGH
You must take the rough with the smooth—133 (В), 1299 (Н)

ROUNDABOUT
What we lose on the roundabouts we will make up on the swings—1219 (Н), 1389 (Н)
What you lose on the swings you gain (make up, win) on the roundabouts—1219 (Н), 1389 (Н)

RUB
There lies the rub—198 b (В)
There's the rub—198 b (В)

RUBBISH
Dealer in rubbish sounds the praise of rubbish (A)—269 (В)

RULE
Rule or ruin—727 (И)

RUM
When the rum is in, wit is out—156 (В)

RUMO(U)R
Anyone can start a rumor, but none can stop one—1090 (Л)
Rumour grows as it goes—1090 (Л)
Rumour is a bubble that soon bursts—1090 (Л)
There is a rumour abroad (in the wind)—1934 (С)

RUN
Race is got by running (The)—507 (Д)
'Tis a long run that never turns—753 (И)
You must run to win the race—507 (Д)

RUST
If you rest, you rust—1218 (Н), 2014 (С)
Rust eats up iron—1833 (Р)
Rust rots the steel which use preserves (The)—1833 (Р), 2014 (С)
Too much rest is rust—1007 (Л)

S

SACK
Broken sack will hold no (won't hold) corn (A)—2219 (Х)
Every horse thinks its own sack heaviest—770 (К)
Every man must carry his own sack to the mill—1975 (С)
Every one thinks his sack heaviest—770 (К)
Everyone thinks his sack heaviest—770 (К)
It is hard for an empty sack to stand upright—1797 (П)
More sacks to the mill—293 (В)
Standing sack fills quicker (The)—441 (Д)
There comes nothing out of the sack but what was in it—2260 (Ч)
There comes nought out of the sack but what was there—2260 (Ч)

SADDLE
Either win the saddle or lose the horse—726 (И), 1017 (Л)

SADNESS
Sadness a gladness succeeds—1481 (Н), 2024 (С)
Sadness and gladness succeed each other—1481 (Н), 2024 (С)

SAFE
Highest branch is not the safest roost (The)—74 (Б)

It is best to be on the safe side—59 (Б)
It is better to be on the safe side—59 (Б), 1571 (О), 1572 (О)
It is better to be safe than sorry—57 (Б)

SAFETY
Safety first—59 (Б)
Safety lies in the middle course—246 (В)
There is safety in crowds (multitude, numbers)—14 (А)

SAIL
As the wind blows, set your sails—2057 (Т)
He that will not sail till all dangers are over must not put to sea—186 (В), 1824 (Р)
He that would sail without danger must never come on the main sea—1824 (Р)
Hoist up the sail while the gale does last—977 (К), 1198 (Н)
Hoist your sail when the wind is fair—2057 (Т)
Hoist your sail while the wind is fair—977 (К), 1198 (Н), 2057 (Т)
Keep your sails trimmed—454 (Д)
While it is fine weather mend your sails—977 (К)
You may hoist your sail—201 (В)

SAILOR
Good sailor may mistake in a dark night (A)—1187 (Н)

SAINT
Saint abroad, a devil at home (A)—164 (В)
Saint abroad and devil at home—164 (В)

SALARY
Draw your salary before spending it—2228 (Ц)

SALT
Before you trust a man, eat a peck of salt with him—2283 (Ч)
Eat a peck of salt with a man before you trust him—2283 (Ч)
Every man must eat a peck of salt before he dies—137 (В)

SALUTE
As you salute, you will be saluted—824 (К)
They that know one another salute afar off—1113 (М), 1842 (Р)

SALVE
Every sore has its salve—568 (Е)
Seek your salve where you got your sore—2264 (Ч)
There's a salve for every sore—568 (Е)

SAME
Another yet the same—225 (В), 2034 (Т), 2049 (Т), 2215 (Х)
It amounts to the same thing—2034 (Т), 2049 (Т)
It will be all the same a hundred years hence (in a hundred years)—222 (В)
More it changes, the more it remains the same (The)—1486 (Н)
Same old seven and six (The)—427 (Д)
Same to you /with brass knobs on!/ (The)—1612 (О)
Things are not always the same—1716 (П), 1817 (Р)

SAMPLE
By a small sample we may judge the whole piece—1705 (П)
Sack is known by the sample (The)—1705 (П)

SAND
If you play with sand, you'll get dirty—400 (Г)
Sands are running out (The)—212 (В)
Walls of sand are sure to crumble—711 (И)
You cannot make ropes of sand—711 (И)

SAPLING
You may bend a sapling, but never a tree—357 (Г), 1463 (Н)

SATAN
Satan finds mischief (work) for idle hands—35 (Б)
Satan rebukes sin—2334 (Ч)
Speak of Satan and you'll see his horns—1513 (О)

SATURDAY
On Monday morning don't be looking for Saturday night—67 (Б)

SAUCE
Make not your sauce till you have caught your fish—1388 (Н)

SAUSAGE
You cannot judge a sausage by its shin—168 (В)

SAVE
Let him save himself who can—1975 (С)
Of saving comes having—869 (К), 1856 (С), 2065 (Т)
Save and have—2065 (Т)
Save today, safe tomorrow—638 (З), 2065 (Т)
Save up for a rainy day—637 (З)

SAY
Better say nothing than not to the purpose—1058 (Л), 1501 (Н)
Between saying and doing there is a long road—1506 (О), 1540 (О), 1605 (О), 2115 (У)
Easier said than done—997 (Л), 1470 (Н), 1913 (С)
Easy to say and hard to do—1913 (С)
From saying to doing is a long stride—1605 (О), 2115 (У)
If it isn't worth saying, don't say it at all—1058 (Л), 1501 (Н)
It is not with saying "honey, honey" that sweetness comes (will come) into the mouth—1596 (Н)
Least said is soonest mended—1029 (Л), 2258 (Ч)
Least said, soonest mended—1029 (Л), 2258 (Ч)
Less said, the better (The)—2258 (Ч)
Little said is soonest mended—1029 (Л)
Little said, soon amended—2258 (Ч)
Never say A without saying B—361 (Г), 652 (З), 1257 (Н)
No sooner said than done—1900 (С)
Nothing is said now that has not been said before—1486 (Н)
Nothing said is soonest mended—1029 (Л)
Say well or be still—1501 (Н)
Sooner said than done—1913 (С)
So said, so done—1900 (С)
Thing that is said is said, and forth it goes (A)—1930 (С), 2296 (Ч)
What is said can never be resaid—1930 (С), 2296 (Ч)
When you have nothing to say, say nothing—1501 (Н)

SAYING
Between saying and doing there is a long road—1540 (О)
From saying to doing is a long stride—2115 (У)
Saying and doing are two /different/ things—1540 (О), 1913 (С)
Saying goes good cheap—997 (Л)
Sayings go cheap—997 (Л)
Saying is one thing, and doing is another—997 (Л), 1540 (О)
There is a difference between saying and doing—1540 (О), 1913 (С)

SCALD
Scald not your lips in another man's porridge—1260 (Н)

SCAM
What's the scam?—2290 (Ч)

SCATHE
My next neighbour's scathe is my present peril—2150 (У)
One does the scathe, and another has the scorn—1841 (Р)

SCHEME
Best-laid schemes of mice and men gang aft agley (The)—340 (Г)

SCOFF
He that scoffed at the crooked had need to go very upright himself—1087 (Л)
He that scoffs at the crooked had need go very upright himself—1087 (Л)

SCOLD
He scolds most that can hurt the least—1952 (С)

SCORE
Score twice before you cut once—1887 (С)

SCRATCH
If one cannot bite, he scratches—1375 (Н)
Scratch my breech and I'll claw your elbow—2077 (Т), 2148 (У)
You scratch my back, and I'll scratch yours—2077 (Т), 2148 (У)

SEA
It is hard to cross (to sail over) the sea in an egg-shell—2242 (Ч)
Sea cannot be scooped up in a tumbler (The)—1038 (Л)
When the sea is crossed, the saint is generally forgotten—1163 (М)
You cannot empty the sea with a nutshell (a spoon)—1038 (Л)

SEAMSTRESS
Bad seamstress uses a long thread (A)—463 (Д)

SEARCH
Search me—1518 (О)
You can (may) search me—1518 (О)

SEASON
Everything in its season—233 (В)
Everything is good in its season—247 (В), 503 (Д), 506 (Д)
There's a season for all things—214 (В), 247 (В), 279 (В), 284 (В), 1093 (Л), 1717 (П), 1771 (П)

SEAT
If you have a good seat, keep it—981 (Л), 1584 (О)

SECRET
It is no secret that is known to three—16 (Б)
It's an open secret—98 (Б)
Secret between more than two is no secret (A)—16 (Б)
Secrets are never long lived—243 (В)
Secret's a secret until it's told (A)—1825 (Р), 1895 (С), 2171 (Ф)
Secret shared is no secret (/A/)—16 (Б), 232 (В), 676 (З), 1529 (О), 1642 (П), 1825 (Р), 1895 (С), 2171 (Ф), 2291 (Ч)
There is nothing so secret but it comes to light—243 (В)
Two can keep a secret if one is dead—232 (В), 676 (З), 1529 (О), 1642 (П), 1825 (Р), 1895 (С), 2171 (Ф)

SECURITY
There's security in numbers—14 (А)

SEE
Eye that sees all things /else/ sees not itself (The)—1288 (Н)
Hunchback cannot see his hunch (A)—1288 (Н)
Hunchback does not see his hump, but sees his companion's (The)—1288 (Н)
Hunchback only sees the hump of his neighbor (The)—1288 (Н)
If we never see you again, it'll be too soon—1902 (С)
I have not seen you in a month of Sundays—1909 (С)
I haven't seen you for ages (in a month of Sundays)—1909 (С)
I'll believe it (that) when I see it—1062 (Л)
Let me see, as a blind man said—1922 (С)
Long time no see—1909 (С)
Never judge before you see—1062 (Л)
One cannot see through a brick wall—305 (В)
Seeing is believing—1062 (Л), 1286 (Н), 1289 (Н)
Some people can't see beyond the tip of their nose—2120 (У)
That remains to be seen—2351 (З)
We all see the world through different lenses—776 (К)
We'll wait and see—1678 (П), 1922 (С), 2280 (Ч)
We see a mote in other men's eyes when there's a beam in our own—298 (В)
We see a mote in our brother's eyes and don't see a (the) beam in our own—298 (В)
We see the failings of others but are blind to our own—298 (В)
We see the faults of others but not our own—298 (В)

We see the splinter in others' faults, but never the spike in our own—298 (В)
We shall see what we shall see—1678 (П), 2280 (Ч)
What we see depends mainly on what we look for—776 (К)
What we see we believe—1062 (Л), 1286 (Н), 1289 (Н)
What you don't see you won't get hung for—680 (З), 2237 (Н)
When we laugh, everyone sees; when we cry, no one sees—204 (В), 251 (В)

SEED
Everything has its seed—231 (В)
Good seed makes a good crop (A)—478 (Д), 1722 (П)
He that sows good seed, shall reap good corn—478 (Д)
Seeds of great things are often small (The)—1829 (Р)

SEEK
Fortune comes to him who seeks her—922 (К)
He that seeketh findeth—922 (К)
Seek, and you shall find—758 (И), 922 (К)

SELF
Self comes first—265 (В), 1868 (С)
Self is the best servant—1176 (Н)
Self loves itself best—265 (В), 1868 (С)
Self preservation is the first law of nature—1975 (С)

SELF-PRAISE
Self-praise is no praise (no recommendation)—1364 (Н), 1467 (Н)
Self-praise stinks—1467 (Н)

SERENE
It's all serene—1266 (Н)

SERPENT
He that hath been bitten by a serpent is afraid of a rope—1788 (П)
Serpents engender in still waters—294 (В)
Whom a serpent has bitten, a lizard alarms—1788 (П)

SERVANT
Good servant must have good wages (A)—791 (К), 794 (К), 1714 (П)

SEVEN
Same old seven and six (The)—427 (Д)

SHADOW
Beware lest you lose the substance by grasping the shadow—1383 (Н)
Catch not at the shadow and lose the substance—1383 (Н)
Every light has its shadow—54 (Б), 737 (И)

SHAKE
All that shakes falls not—1302 (Н), 1308 (Н), 1317 (Н)
What's shaking?—2290 (Ч)

SHALLOW
Shallowest persons are the most loquacious (The)—180 (В)
Shallow streams make most din (the most noise)—332 (Г)
Shallow waters make most din—332 (Г)

SHAME
Shame is worse than death—64 (Б), 1067 (Л)

SHARE
Thing is the bigger of being shared (A)—1814 (Р)

SHARP
People who are sharp cut their own fingers—940 (К), 1194 (Н)
That which is sharp is not long—722 (И), 1570 (О)

SHEARER
Bad shearer never had a good sickle (A)—1111 (М)

SHEEP
Bleating sheep loses her bit (A)—2364 (Я)
Every family has a black sheep—237 (В)
Every hand fleeces where the sheep goes naked—1627 (П)
Every sheep with its like—290 (В), 308 (В), 402 (Г), 674 (З), 675 (З), 1295 b (Н), 1852 (С), 1853 (С)

He that makes himself a sheep shall be eaten by the wolves—899 (К), 1944 (С)
He that maketh himself a sheep shall be eaten by the wolf 899 (К), 1944 (С)
If a sheep loops a dyke, all the rest will follow—976 (К)
If one sheep has left the fold, the rest will follow—976 (К)
If one sheep leaps over the ditch, all the rest will follow—975 (К)
Lazy sheep thinks its wool heavy (A)—465 (Д)
Let every sheep hang by its own shank—591 (Ж)
Make yourself a sheep and the wolves will eat you—1945 (С)
One black sheep will mar a whole flock—1536 (О)
One scabbed sheep infects the whole flock—1536 (О)
One scabbed sheep will mar a flock—1536 (О)
One sheep follows another—976 (К)
One sickly sheep infects the flock—1536 (О)
Sheep that bleats loses a mouthful (The)—2364 (Я)
There is a black sheep in every flock—237 (В)
There's a black sheep in every family—237 (В)
When one sheep leads the way, the rest follow—976 (К)

SHELL
He that will have the kernel must crack the shell—1400 (Н)
He who would eat the nut must first crack the shell—1400 (Н)

SHEPHERDS
Careless shepherds make many a feast for the wolf—1634 (П)
Wolves rend sheep when the shepherds fail—1634 (П)

SHIN
Never be breaking your shin on a stool that is not in your way—942 (К)

SHINE
Rain one day, shine the next—1725 (П), 1728 (П)

SHIP
Bad ship never casts anchor in port (A)—1811 (Р)
Big ships require deep waters—99 (Б), 1893 (С)
Every wind is ill to a broken ship—1811 (Р)
Great ship asks deep waters (A)—99 (Б), 1893 (С)
Great ship asks for deeper (deep) water (A)—99 (Б), 1893 (С)
Great ship requires deep waters (A)—99 (Б), 1893 (С)
To a crazy ship all winds are contrary—1811 (Р)

SHIPWRECK
Each man makes his own shipwreck—2248 (Ч)
He complains wrongly on the sea that twice suffers a shipwreck—1507 (О)
He who has suffered shipwreck fears sail upon the seas—1507 (О)
Let another's shipwreck be your beacon (sea-mark, sea work)—2315 (Ч)

SHIRT
Close sits my shirt, but closer my skin—265 (В), 1868 (С)
Near is my coat, but nearer is my shirt—1868 (С)
Shirt is nearer than the coat (The)—1868 (С)
You can't take the shirt off a naked man—375 (Г)

SHIVE
Men cut large shives of another's loaf—2324 (Ч)

SHOE
Better cut the shoe than pinch the foot—704 (И)
Don't throw away old shoes till you've got new ones—1319 (Н)
Don't throw away your old shoes before you get new ones—1319 (Н)
Every one knows best where his shoe pinches—2060 (Т)
Everyone knows where his shoe pinches—2060 (Т)
Every shoe fits not every foot—2297 (Ч)

He goes long barefoot that waits for dead men's shoes—1263 (Н)
He that waits for a dead man's shoes may long go barefoot—1263 (Н)
He that waits for dead men's shoes may go a long time barefoot—1263 (Н)
He who makes shoes goes barefoot—1855 (С), 2136 (У)
If the shoe fits, put it on (wear it)—673 (З), 1183 b (Н)
No one but the wearer knows where the shoe pinches—2060 (Т)
Old shoes wear best—2011 (С)
One cannot shoe a running horse—305 (В)
One shoe does not fit every foot—1089 (Л), 2297 (Ч)
One shoe will not fit all feet—2297 (Н)
Only he who wears the shoe knows where it pinches—2060 (Т)
Over shoes, over boots—323 (Г), 1884 (С)
That's where the shoe pinches—198 b (В)
There was never a shoe but had its mate—46 (Б), 2102 (У)
Wearer best knows where the shoe pinches (The)—2060 (Т)
You can't put the same shoe on every foot—143 (В), 1089 (Л), 2297 (Ч)

SHOEMAKER
Blacksmith's horse and the shoemaker's family always go unshod (The)—1855 (С)
None more bare than the shoemaker's wife and the smith's mare—1855 (С)
Shoemaker's child goes barefoot (The)—1855 (С)
Shoemaker should stick to his last (A)—1295 a (Н)
Shoemaker's son always goes barefoot (The)—1855 (С)
Shoemaker, stick to your last (shoes)—21 (Б), 62 (Б), 1295 a (Н), 1420 (Н)
Shoemaker's wife is the worst shod (The)—1855 (С)

SHOOT
Don't shoot till you see the whites of their eyes—1408 (Н)
He that's always shooting must sometimes hit—2044 (Т)
He that shoots oft at last will hit the mark—280 (В)
He who shoots may hit at last—55 (Б), 280 (В)

SHOP
Good shop needs (wants) no sign (A)—2195 (Х)

SHORE
Once on the shore, we pray no more—1163 (М)

SHOT
Every shot does not bring down a bird—262 (В), 1309 (Н)
Good shot (A)—1279 (Н)
There is plenty of shot in the locker—571 (Е)

SHOUT
Do not shout until you are out of the woods—1321 (Н), 1468 (Н), 1469 (Н), 2172 (Х)
Don't shout till you are out of the wood—1321 (Н), 1469 (Н), 2172 (Х)

SHOVEL
It's the shovel that laughs at the poker—358 (Г)

SHOWER
Heavy shower is soon over (A)—393 (Г), 722 (И), 1570 (О)

SHROUD
Dead man's shroud has no pockets (A)—2133 (У)
Richest man carries nothing away with him but his shroud (The)—2133 (У)
Shroud has no pockets (A)—1704 (П), 2133 (У)

SHRUB
High cedars fall when low shrubs remain—112 (Б)

SICK
Sickest is not the nearest to the grave (The)—66 (Б), 1915 (С)

SICKLE
Don't thrust your sickle into another's corn—1419 (Н)

SICKNESS
Sickness comes in haste and goes at leisure—90 (Б)
Study sickness while you are well—1555 (О)

SIDE
Every man has his weak side—235 (В), 737 (И)
There are two sides to every question (every story, everything)—2105 (У)

SIEVE
You cannot carry water in a sieve—1831 (Р), 1894 (С)
You cannot draw water with a sieve—1831 (Р), 1894 (С)
You can't measure water with a sieve—1831 (Р), 1894 (С)

SIGH
When we sing everybody hears us, when we sigh nobody hears us—204 (В)

SIGHT
Out of sight, out of mind—1816 (Р), 1871 (С)

SILENCE
No wisdom like silence—905 (К)
Silence gives (implies, is, means) consent—937 (К), 1154 (М)
Silence is a rare jewel—1933 (С)
Silence is golden—1899 (С), 1933 (С)
Silence is the best policy—905 (К), 1933 (С)
Silence is wisdom when speaking is folly—1501 (Н)
Speaking is silver; silence is golden—1899 (С), 1933 (С)
Speech is silver, but silence is gold—1899 (С), 1933 (С)
Speech is silvern but silence is golden—1899 (С), 1933 (С)
Speech is silver; silence is golden—1899 (С), 1933 (С)
Words is silver and silence is gold—1933 (С)

SILENT
Be silent, or say something better than silence—1501 (Н)
Be silent or speak something worth hearing—1501 (Н)
Beware of a silent dog and silent (still) water—58 (Б), 1273 (Н)
Speak fitly or be silent wisely—1501 (Н)

SILVER
All that shines is not silver—56 (Б)
No silver, no servant—1158 (М)
No silver without his dross—737 (И)

SIN
Every man has his besetting sin—236 (В), 1487 (Н)
Every sin brings its punishment with it—1602 (О)
Every sin carries its own punishment—1602 (О)
He sins as much who holds the bag as he who puts into it—1441 (Н)
Old sins cast (have) long shadows—1648 (П)
Sin confessed is half forgiven (A)—641 (З), 1661 (П)
Sins of fathers are visited on their children (The)—1618 (О)
Your sins will find you out—1602 (О)

SING
Sing before breakfast, and you'll cry before supper—1256 (Н), 1820 (Р)
Sing before breakfast, you'll cry before night (supper)—1256 (Н), 1820 (Р)
Who cannot sing, may whistle—947 (К), 1460 (Н)

SINGLE
If you want to stay single, look for a perfect woman—495 (Д)

SINK
Sink, swim, or die—727 (И)

SIT
He sits not sure that sits high—74 (Б)
It's as cheap sitting as standing—169 (В)

SIX
All at sixes and sevens—912 (К)
Everything is at sixes and sevens—912 (К)
It is six of one and half a dozen of the other—225 (В), 1461 (Н), 2215 (Х), 2285 (Ч)
It's six of one, half a dozen of the other—225 (В), 1461 (Н), 2034 (Т), 2049 (Т), 2215 (Х), 2285 (Ч)

SIZE
That's about the size of it—2035 (Т)

SKELETON
There is a skeleton in every house—773 (К), 1670 (П), 2104 (У)
There's a skeleton in everybody's closet (in every family /closet/)—773 (К), 1670 (П), 2104 (У)

SKILL
Few things are impossible to diligence and skill—277 (В), 431 (Д)
Skill and luck go together—1275 (Н)

SKILLET
Skillet can't call the pot black (The)—15 (А)

SKIN
If the lion's skin cannot, the fox's shall—310 (Г)
It's no skin off my back (butt, nose, tail)—1159 (М), 2372 (Я)
That's no skin off my teeth—1159 (М)
You cannot change your skin—1877 (С)

SKY
Every sky has its cloud—737 (И)
If the sky falls, we shall catch larks—453 (Д), 847 (К), 2351 (Э)
We shall catch larks if (when) the sky falls—2351 (Э)

SLANDER
Slander is sharper than the sword—669 (З)
Slander leaves a scar behind—837 (К)
Slander's sting is sharper than the sword—669 (З)
Slander that is raised is ill to fell—837 (К)

SLEEP
Good comes to some while they are sleeping—1967 (С)
Have a sleep on it—2158 (У)
He that sleeps catches no fish—1145 (М)
He who sleeps all the morning, may go a-begging all the day after—1145 (М)
He who sleeps catches no fish—1145 (М)
Interest runs on while you sleep—1967 (С)
Plow deep while sluggards sleep /, and you shall have corn to sell and to keep/—961 (К)
Sleep brings counsel—2158 (У)
Sleep on (over) it—2158 (У)
Sleep without supping, and wake without owing—1061 (Л)
While the fisher sleeps the net takes—1967 (С)

SLIGHT
Either by might or by slight—310 (В), 334 (Г)
'Tis slight, not strength, that gives the greatest lift—1024 (Л)

SLIP
Better /a/ slip with the foot than with the tongue—1063 (Л)
Better the foot slip than the tongue /trip/—1063 (Л)
Every slip is not a fall—1302 (Н)
None are so well shod but they may slip—1187 (Н)
Slip of the foot and you may soon recover, but a slip of the tongue you may never get over (A)—1063 (Л)
There is many a slip twixt /the/ cup and /the/ lip—1018 (Л), 1897 (С), 2351 (З)
There's many a slip between ('twixt) the cup and the lip—1018 (Л), 1897 (С), 2351 (Э)

SLOTH
Sloth is the key to poverty—1005 (Л)

Sloth is the mother of vice—35 (Б), 1006 (Л)

SLOW

Slow and steady wins the race—2053 (Т), 2054 (Т)

Slow at meat, slow at work—567 (Е), 820 (К)

Slow but certain wins the race—2053 (Т), 2054 (Т)

Slow but sure—1117 (М)

Slow but sure wins the race—2053 (Т), 2054 (Т)

Slow fire makes sweet malt (A)—2054 (Т)

Slow things are sure things—1117 (М)

Slow wind also brings the ship to harbor—1117 (М)

Wisely and slow /- they stumble that run fast/—1741 (П), 1979 (С)

SLOWLY

Slowly but surely—1117 (М)

SLUGGARD

Every day is holiday with sluggards—1003 (Л), 1035 (Л), 2075 (Т), 2113 (У)

Sluggard must be clad in rags (The)—1005 (Л)

Sluggard's convenient season never comes (The)—2091 (У)

Sluggards work best when the sun's in the west—2075 (Т), 2091 (У), 2113 (У)

SLUMBER

Sweet are the slumbers of the virtuous—2110 (У)

SMALL

Many small make (makes) a great—1686 (П), 1694 (П)

SMILE

Better the last smile than the first laughter—2198 (Х)

Smile and the world smiles with you /; weep and you weep alone/—204 (В)

Smile goes a long way (A)—986 (Л)

There are daggers behind men's smiles—360 (Г), 1170 (М), 1269 (Н)

SMOKE

Flame is not far from the smoke (The)—1432 (Н)

From smoke into smother—709 (И)

If you would enjoy the fire, you must put up with the smoke—1073 (Л)

Much smoke, little fire—1143 (М)

Smoke of a man's house is better than the fire of another's (The)—126 (В)

There is no smoke without fire—1432 (Н)

Where there is smoke, there is fire—1432 (Н)

SNAIL

Tramp on a snail, and she'll shoot out her horns—286 (В)

SNAFU

It's SNAFU—427 (Д), 435 (Д)

SNAKE

If it had been a snake, it would have bitten you—646 (З), 1355 (Н)

SNARE

He who lays a snare for another, himself falls into it—917 (К)

SNEEZE

If he had the 'flu, he wouldn't give you a sneeze—2147 (У)

SNOW

Just because there's snow on the roof, that doesn't mean the fire's out inside—1675 (П)

Snow year, a rich year (A)—1144 (М)

Fall of snow in May is worth a ton of hay (A)—9 (А)

Whether you boil snow or pound it, you can have but water of it—253 (В), 1581 (О)

SNOWY

Snowy winter, plentiful harvest—1144 (М)

SOLDIER

Every French soldier carries a marshal's baton in his knapsack—1656 (П)

Live soldier is better than a dead hero (A)—590 (Ж)

Many soldiers are brave at the table who are cowards in the field—1472 (Н)

SOME
Better some than none—1070 (Л)

SOMETHING
Better something than nothing /at all/—1070 (Л), 1974 (С)
Second-rate something is better than a first-rate nothing (A)—1070 (Л)
You get out of something only what you put in—2284 (Ч)

SONG
Let him that begins the song make an end—361 (Г), 652 (З)
No song, no supper—944 (К)

SOON
Soon enough is well enough—419 (Д), 1422 (Н)
Sooner begun, sooner done—1822 (Р)
Sooner, the better (The)—2259 (Ч)
Soon hot, soon cold—393 (Г)

SORE
Do not rip up old sores—970 (К)
Don't rip up old sores and cast up old scores—970 (К)
Never rip up old sores—970 (К)

SORROW
After joy comes sorrow—330 (Г)
After sunshine come showers; after pleasure comes sorrow—330 (Г)
All sorrows are less with bread—600 (Ж), 1683 (П)
Deeper the sorrow, the less the tongue hath it (The)—92 (Б)
Earth has no sorrow that heaven cannot heal—2040 (Т)
Fat sorrow is better than lean sorrow—600 (Ж), 1683 (П)
Hang sorrow—610 (З)
Joy and sorrow are next-door neighbors—1481 (Н), 2024 (С)
Let your joys be many and your sorrows be few!—1959 (С)
Light sorrows speak; great ones are dumb—92 (Б), 994 (Л)
Never lay sorrow to your heart—610 (З)
Of thy sorrow be not too sad, of thy joy be not too glad—1399 (Н)
Our sorrows are less if in our anguish we find a partner in distress—389 (Г)
Small sorrows speak; great ones are silent—92 (Б)
Sorrow and an evil (an ill) life make soon an old wife—391 (Г), 1323 (Н), 1397 (Н)
Sorrow is /always/ dry—92 (Б)
Sorrow never comes singly—22 (Б)
Sorrows remembered sweeten present joy—2306 (Ч)
Sorrow treads upon the heels of mirth—330 (Г), 2024 (С)
Sorrow will pay no debt—1157 (М), 1604 (О), 1920 b (С)
Time erases all sorrows—216 (В)
When sorrow is asleep, wake it not—1274 (Н)

SORT
It takes all sorts to make a world—143 (В)

SOUL
Penny soul never 'came (came to) twopence (A)—629 (З), 1339 (Н)

SOUR
He deserves not the sweet that will not taste of sour (the sour)—1291 (Н)
You must take the sour with the sweet—1299 (Н)

SOW
As you sow, so shall you reap—811 (К), 2303 (Ч)
He that sows thistles shall reap prickles—1598 (О), 2303 (Ч)
He who sows brambles reaps thorns—2303 (Ч)
He who sows thorns will never reap grapes—2303 (Ч)
Little knows the fat sow what the lean does mean (the lean one thinks)—2032 (С)
One man sows and another reaps—1114 (М)
Silent sow gets all the swill (The)—987 (Л)

Sow loves bran better than roses (The)—862 (К), 927 (К)
Sow may whistle, though it has an ill mouth for it (A)—113 (Б)
Still sow drinks all the slop (The)—987 (Л)
Still sow eats up all the draff (The)—987 (Л)
They that sow in tears shall reap in joy—2080 (Т), 2166 (У)
You must reap what you have sown—2303 (Ч)
You shall reap what you sow—825 (К), 2303 (Ч)

SPARE
Spare and have is better than spend and crave—637 (З)
Sparing is the first gaining—869 (К), 1856 (С), 2065 (Т)

SPARK
From a spark a conflagration—1096 (М), 1156 (М)
Of a small spark a great fire—1096 (М)
Little spark kindles a great fire (A)—1096 (М), 1156 (М)
Sparks become flame—1096 (М)

SPARROW
Better a sparrow in the hand than a vulture on the wing—1787 (П)
Sparrow in the hand is better than a pigeon in the roof (sky) (A)—1066 (Л), 1787 (П)
Sparrow in the hand is worth a pheasant that flies by (A)—1066 (Л), 1787 (П)
Two sparrows on one ear of corn make an ill agreement—420 (Д)

SPEAK
He cannot speak well that cannot hold his tongue—127 (В), 931 (К), 2366 (Я)
He is a wise man (wise) who speaks little—359 (Г), 936 (К)
He knows most who speaks least—359 (Г), 936 (К)
He who knows does not speak; he who speaks does not know—536 (Д), 936 (К)
Many speak much who cannot speak well—180 (В)
Speak fitly or be silent wisely—1501 (Н)
Speak kind words and you will hear kind answers—1197 (Н)
Speak not rather than speak ill—1058 (Л)
Speak of angels and you'll hear the rustling of their wings—1513 (О)
Speak of Satan and you'll see his horns—1513 (О)
Speak of the devil and he is sure to appear—1892 (С)
Speak of the devil /, and he'll appear/—1513 (О), 1892 (С)
Speak of the devil and in he walks—1892 (С)
There is a time to speak and a time to be silent—127 (В)

SPECTATOR
Spectator sees more (most) of the game (The)—1973 (С)

SPEECH
Fool is known by his speech (A)—1566 (О)
More have repented speech than silence—2364 (Я)
Speech is the index of the mind—681 (З), 1504 (О)
Speech is the picture of the mind—681 (З)

SPEND
He who spends more than he should shall not have to spend when he would—938 (К)
Soon got, soon spent—1779 (П)
Who spends more than he should, shall not have to spend when he would—938 (К)

SPICE
Spice is black but has sweet smack—870 (К), 891 (К)

SPIGOT
Save at the spigot and waste at the bung—629 (З)
We spare at the spigot and spill at the bung—629 (З)

SPINDLE
One by one spindles are made—730 (И)

SPIRIT
Sound spirit in a sound body (A)—148 (B)
Spirit is willing, but the flesh is weak (The)—552 (Д), 754 (И)

SPIT
Spit in a whore's face and she'll say it's raining—1225 (H)
Spit on a (the) stone, /and/ it will be wet at last—830 (K)
Who spits against the heaven (the wind), it falls in his face—1876 (C)
Who spits against the wind spits in his own face—1876 (C)

SPOIL
Don't spoil the ship for half a penny's worth of tar—629 (З), 1339 (H)
It is no use spoiling a ship for a halfpenny worth of tar—629 (З)
You must spoil before you spin well—1352 (H), 1639 (П)

SPOKE
Worst spoke in a cart breaks first (The)—336 (Г)

SPOON
Make a spoon or spoil a horn—726 (И), 727 (И)
You can't fill pails with a spoon—695 (И)

SPOT
There are spots /even/ in (on) the sun—737 (И)

SPRAT
Every sprat now-a-days calls itself a herring—257 (B)
Risk a sprat to catch a whale—1752 (П)
Set a sprat to catch a whale—1752 (П)
Throw out a sprat to catch a herring (a mackerel, a whale)—1752 (П)

SPRING
Muddy spring, muddy stream—1166 (M)
Muddy springs will have muddy streams—1166 (M)

SPUR
He who has love in his heart has spurs in his heels—318 (Г), 464 (Д)
Spur in the head is worth two in the feet (heel) (A)—318 (Г)

SQUARE
Don't square other men by your rule—1367 (H)

SQUEAK
Squeaking gate hangs the longest (A)—1915 (C)
Squeaking hinge lasts the longest (A)—1915 (C)
Squeaking wheel gets the oil (The)—460 (Д)
Wheel that does the squeaking is the one that gets the grease (The)—460 (Д)

SQUEAKY
Squeaky axe (gate) gets the oil (The)—460 (Д)

STAFF
If the staff is crooked, the shadow cannot be straight—818 (K), 1709 (П)
Never trust a broken staff—510 (Д)
Staff is quickly (soon) found to beat a dog with (A)—117 (Б)
Thirteen staves and never a hoop will never make a barrel—1948 (C)

STAKE
Ill stake stands long (longest) (The)—66 (Б), 1915 (C)
Ill stake stands the longest (An)—66 (Б), 1915 (C)
Loose stake stands long (longest) (The)—66 (Б), 1915 (C)
Nothing stake, nothing draw—1834 (P), 2180 (X)

STANDER-BY
Standers-by see more than the gamesters—1973 (C)

STAR
Aim for the star—1656 (П)
Hitch your wagon to a star—1656 (П)

If you can't be the sun, be a star—947 (К), 1460 (Н)
Stars are not seen by sunshine—784 (К)
Stars are not seen where the sun shines (The)—784 (К)

START
Don't start anything /what/ you can't finish—846 (К)
Getting started is half of the fight—656 (З)
Good start is half the race (A)—477 (Д)
If you start telling something, you have to finish—361 (Г)
Nobody starts at the top—627 (З)

STEADY
Steady does it—2054 (Т)

STEAL
He that steals an egg will steal a chicken (an ox)—935 (К)
He that will steal an egg, will steal an ox (a pound)—935 (К)
He that will steal an ounce will steal a pound—935 (К)
He that will steal a pin will steal a better thing—935 (К)
He who steals will always fail—1907 (С), 2221 (Х)
Nothing is stolen without hands—315 (Г)
Stolen apples are sweetest—640 (З)
Stolen cherries are the sweeter—640 (З)
Stolen fruit is always sweeter (is sweet)—640 (З), 1200 (Н)
Stolen kisses are sweet (sweetest, the best)—640 (З)
Stolen pleasures are sweetest—640 (З)
Stolen sweets are /always/ sweeter—640 (З)
Stolen waters are sweet—640 (З)

STEERSMAN
Gunner to the linstock, and the steersman to the helm (The)—62 (Б)

STEP
First step is /always/ the hardest (The)—1025 (Л), 2071 (Т)
First step is the only difficulty (The)—1025 (Л), 2071 (Т)
Hardest step is /that/ over the threshold (The)—278 (В), 1025 (Л)
It is the first step which is troublesome—1025 (Л)
It's the first step that costs—1025 (Л)
One step at a time—1980 (С)
Step after step the ladder is ascended—730 (И)
Step by step one goes a long way (far)—730 (И), 1107 (М), 2054 (Т)
Step by step the ladder is ascended—730 (И), 1107 (М)
Step in time saves nine (A)—2341 (Ш)

STEW
The same stew only the name is new—225 (В), 2049 (Т)

STICK
Any stick /will do/ to beat the dog—117 (Б)
Crooked stick throws a crooked shadow (A)—781 (К), 818 (К)
Crooked stick will cast (will have) a crooked shadow (A)—781 (К), 818 (К), 1709 (П)
Dress up a stick and it does not appear to be a stick—1234 (Н)
He who has a mind to beat a (his) dog will easily find a stick—117 (Б)
It's an easy thing to find a stick to beat a dog with—117 (Б)
It sticks out a mile—2374 (Я)
Little sticks kindle large fires—1156 (М)
One stick is easier broken than a bunch—139 (В)
Stick is quickly (soon) found to beat a dog with (A)—117 (Б)
Stick together or get stuck separately—139 (В), 517 (Д)
When you pick up a stick at one end, you also pick up the other end—1628 (П)
You can't make a crooked stick lay straight—892 (К)

STING
After your fling, watch for the sting—1075 (Л)

If you want to gather honey, you must bear the stings of bees—1073 (Л)
Sting is in the tail (The)—2352 (З)

STITCH
Dropped stitch is soon a hole (A)—2341 (Ш)
Stitch in time saves nine (A)—2341 (Ш)

STOMACH
Army marches (travels) on its stomach (An)—2155 (У)
Full stomach, contented heart—600 (Ж), 1683 (П)
Full stomachs make empty heads—2030 (С)
Lazy folks' stomachs don't get tired—1004 (Л)
Stomach carries the feet (The)—176 (В), 743 (И), 1208 (Н), 1327 (Н), 1359 (Н), 1379 (Н), 2029 (С), 2155 (У)
Way to a man's heart is through his stomach (The)—1800 (П)
When the stomach is full, the heart is glad—600 (Ж), 1745 (П)
You can win a man through his stomach—1800 (П)

STONE
Cast not the first stone—1798 (П)
Constant dripping (dropping) wears away a stone—830 (К)
Falling drops at last will wear the stone (The)—830 (К)
He that is without sin among you, let him cast the first stone—1798 (П)
He that is without sin among you, let him first cast a stone at her—1798 (П)
It's a steady stream that wears a stone—830 (К)
Let him that is without sin cast the first stone—1798 (П)
Little stone may upset a large cart (A)—1156 (М)
Man who flings a stone up a mountain may have it rolled back upon himself (The)—1876 (С)
Never take a stone to break an egg, when you can do it with the back of your knife—713 (И)
No man can flay a stone—375 (Г), 654 (З), 826 (К)
One stone alone cannot grind corn—1520 (О), 1524 (О), 1537 (О), 1544 (О), 1547 (О)
People living in glass houses should not throw stones—511 (Д)
People who live in glass houses shouldn't throw stones—511 (Д)
Rolling stone gathers no moss (A)—856 (К)
Spit on a (the) stone, /and/ it will be wet at last—830 (К)
Stone that lies not in your gate breaks not your toe (The)—1419 (Н)
Stone that may fit in a wall is never left by the way (A)—266 (В)

STOOL
Between two stools one falls (goes) to the ground—422 (Д), 1119 (М)
Between two stools we come to the ground—422 (Д), 1119 (М)

STOOP
It is no time to stoop when the head is off—1730 (П)

STORE
Store is no sore—637 (З)

STORM
Harder the storm, the sooner it's over (The)—393 (Г), 722 (И)
Sharper the storm, the sooner 'tis over (The)—393 (Г), 722 (И)

STORY
Cut the story—219 (В)
It's a different story—2354 (Э)
It's a good story that fills the belly—1968 a (С), 1968 b (С)
It's another story—2354 (Э)
Tell me the old, old story—1590 (О)
That's /quite/ a different (another) story—2354 (Э)

STRANGER
Save a stranger from the sea, and he'll turn your enemy—250 (В)

STRAW
Last straw breaks (will break) the camel's back (The)—1727 (П)
That's the last straw—2233 (Ч)

This is the last straw—2233 (Ч)
You cannot make bricks without straw—2367 (Я)

STREAM
Cross the stream where it is shallowest—1060 (Л)
He that is carried down the stream need not row—721 (И), 2199 (Х)
It's a steady stream that wears a stone—830 (К)
It's easy going with the stream—2199 (Х)
Large streams from little fountains flow—1829 (Р)
Little streams grow into mighty rivers—1829 (Р)
Little streams make big (great) rivers—1829 (Р)
Never cross the stream before you come to it—1402 (Н)
Shallow streams make most din (the most noise)—332 (Г)
Stream can never rise above the fountain (the spring-head) (The)—304 (В)
Stream cannot rise above its source (The)—304 (В)
Stream never rises higher than its source (A)—304 (В), 306 (В)

STREET
By the street of "by and by" one arrives at the house of never—1592 (О)
That's not my street—1159 (М)

STRENGTH
Strength is weak, but the desire is great (The)—754 (И)
There's strength in crowds (multitude, numbers)—14 (А)

STRING
I've got a bit of string with a hole in it—453 (Д)

STRIVE
It is ill striving against the stream—990 b (Л), 1647 b (П), 1786 b (П), 2082 (Т)
Strive not against the stream—990 b (Л), 1647 b (П), 1786 b (П), 2082 (Т)

STROKE
Different strokes for different folks—1182 (Н)
First stroke is half the battle (The)—1750 (П)
Little strokes fell big (great) oaks—558 (Д)
Oak is not felled at (with) one stroke (An)—636 (З), 730 (И), 1965 (О)
One stroke fells not an oak—636 (З), 730 (И), 1965 (С)
Small strokes cut down the oaks—558 (Д)
Small strokes fell big oaks—558 (Д)
With many strokes is an oak overthrown—558 (Д)

STRONG
The right is with the strongest—965 (К)

STUFF
Cut the funny stuff!—1278 (Н)
Stuff today and starve tomorrow—1818 (Р)

STUMBLE
Even a wise man stumbles—1187 (Н)
You will not stumble while on your knees—941 (К), 1384 (Н)

STUFFING
Stuffing holds out storm—1745 (П)

STYLE
Style is the man (The)—151 (В)

SUBLIME
Descent from the sublime to the ridiculous is quick (A)—1580 (О)
From the sublime to the ridiculous is only one step—1580 (О)
One step above the sublime makes the ridiculous—1580 (О)

SUBSTANCE
Beware lest you lose the substance by grasping the shadow—1383 (Н)
Catch not at the shadow and lose the substance—1383 (Н)

SUCCESS
Meet success like a gentleman and disaster like a man—1399 (Н)

Nothing succeeds like success—1538 (О)
Success breeds success—1538 (О)
Success has many friends—860 (К)
Success is befriended by many people—860 (К)
Success is never blamed—1657 (П)
Success is the child of audacity—1578 (О), 1937 (С)
Success makes a fool seem wise—573 (Е)
Success makes success as money makes money—1538 (О)

SUCKER
There's a sucker born every minute—525 (Д), 1211 (Н)

SUFFER
Man in suffering finds relief in rehearsing his ills (A)—1577 (О), 2111 (У)
Man only from himself can suffer wrong—2248 (Ч)

SUFFICIENT
Sufficient for (to, unto) the day /is the devil thereof/—1402 (Н)

SUGAR
Even sugar itself may spoil a good dish—467 (Д)
Teaspoon of sugar will catch more flies than a gallon of vinegar (A)—1118 (Л)

SUMMER
Bee works in the summer and eats honey all winter (The)—1015 (Л)
He who sings in summer will weep in winter—969 (К)
No summer but has its winter—54 (Б)
Winter discovers what summer conceals—1015 (Л), 2293 (Ч)
Winter eats what summer gets (lays up)—1015 (Л), 2293 (Ч)
Winter finds out what summer lays up—1015 (Л), 2293 (Ч)
You have to winter and summer with people to know them—2283 (Ч)

SUN
After a storm, the sun always shines—1724 (П)
After /black/ clouds, a clear sun—105 (Б)
After the rain, the sun—105 (Б), 1296 (Н), 1728 (П)
Behind the clouds the sun is shining—1728 (П)
No morning sun lasts a whole day—2196 (Х)
No sun without a shadow—737 (И)
Same sun that will melt butter will harden clay (The)—1628 (П)
Sun doesn't shine on both sides of the hedge at once (The)—1525 (О)
Sun is never the worse for shining on a dunghill (The)—399 (Г), 1773 (П)
Sun is not less bright for sitting on a dunghill (The)—399 (Г), 1773 (П)
Sun will always come up tomorrow (The)—1782 (Р)
Sun will shine down our street too—1772 (П)
Sun will shine on our side of the fence (The)—1772 (П)
Sun will shine through the darkest clouds (The)—1296 (Н)

SUNRISE
Sunrise never failed us yet (The)—1782 (П)

SUNSHINE
After clouds comes (there is) sunshine—105 (Б)
After rain comes sunshine—105 (Б), 311 (Г), 1296 (Н)
After rain, sunshine—105 (Б)
All sunshine makes a desert—2187 (Х)
Same sunshine that will melt butter will harden the clay (The)—1628 (П)

SUPPER
By suppers more have been killed than Galen ever cured—615 (З)
Eat few suppers and you'll need few medicines—615 (З)
Lightest suppers make long lives—615 (З)
Little suppers make long lives—615 (З)
Suppers kill more than the greatest doctors can cure—615 (З)

SURE
He sits not sure that sits high—74 (Б)

SURFEIT
Surfeit has killed more than hunger—327 (Г)

SURGEON
Call not a surgeon before you are wounded—1402 (Н)

SURPRISE
Surprises never cease—2314 (Ч)

SWALLOW
Man must not swallow more than he can digest (A)—1838 a (P)
One swallow does not make a spring (a summer)—1533 (O)
One swallow makes not a spring, nor a (one) woodcock a winter—1533 (O)

SWAP
Don't swap the witch for the devil—2215 (X)

SWEAT
It's no sweat off my back—1159 (M)
No sweat, no sweet—1632 (П), 2212 (X)
No sweet without /some/ sweat—1632 (П), 2212 (X)

SWEEP
Everybody ought to sweep before his own door—1247 (Н)
Sweep before (the path to) your own door—1128 (M)
Sweep in front of your own door first—1128 (M)
Sweep your own porch clean first—1128 (M)

SWEET
Bitter must come before the sweet (The)—34 (Б)
Every sweet has its bitter (sour)—1453 (Н)
No sweet without /some/ sweat—50 (Б)
One man's sweet is another man's sour—1182 (Н), 2307 (Ч)
Sweets to the sweet and sour to the sour—799 (К), 1679 (П)
What is sweet in the mouth is bitter in the stomach—1918 (С)

SWEETHEART
Nobody's sweetheart is ugly—1395 (Н), 1701 (П)

SWIM
He may well swim that is held up by the chin—721 (И), 2199 (X)
Sink or swim—727 (И)

SWINE
Still swine eat all the draff—987 (Л)

SWING
What we lose on the roundabouts we will make up on the swings—1219 (Н), 1389 (Н)

SWORD
All they that take the sword shall perish by (with) the sword—930 (К)
He who lives by the sword shall perish by the sword—930 (К)
One sword keeps another in the scabbard (sheath)—2213 (X)
They that live by the sword will die (perish) by the sword—930 (К)

SYMPATHY
Sympathy is akin to love—581 (Ж)

SYSTEM
All systems are go—429 (Д)

T

TAIL
Don't swallow the cow and worry with the tail—149 (В)
If you buy the cow, take the tail into the bargain—149 (В)
Let the tail follow the skin—149 (В)
Tail goes with the hide (The)—149 (В)

TAILOR
Let each tailor mend his own coat—591 (Ж)
Let every tailor stick to his goose—62 (Б)
Long thread, a lazy tailor (A)—463 (Д)

Nine tailors make the man—1517 (О)
Tailor makes the man (The)—1517 (О)
Tailor's sons wear patched pants (The)—2136 (У)
Tailor's wife is worse (the worst) clad (The)—1855 (С), 2136 (У)

TAKE
It takes one to know one—2334 (Ч)
Take no more on you than you're able to bear—60 (Б)
Take the evil with the good—1179 (Н)
Take the fat with the lean—1179 (Н)
Take us as you find us—1700 (П)
Take while taking is good—416 (Д)
You can't take it with you /when you die/—2133 (Х)
You have to take the bitter with the sweet (the fat with the lean, the good with the bad)—603 (Ж), 1179 (Н)
You must take the bad with the good (the fat with the lean, the sour with the sweet)—603 (Ж), 1179 (Н)
You must take the rough with the smooth—133 (В), 603 (Ж), 1179 (Н)

TALE
Don't tell tales out of school—1970 (С)
Put no faith in tale bearers—1303 (Н)
Varnished tale can't be round—712 (И)

TALK
All talk and no cider (no do)—1143 (М)
Big talking, but little saying—1139 (М), 1885 (С)
He that talks much lies much—931 (К)
He who talks much errs much—2366 (Я)
He who talks much makes many mistakes—2366 (Я)
He who talks much says many foolish things—931 (К), 2361 (Я)
I talk of chalk and you of cheese—2358 (Я)
I talk to you of cheese you talk to me of chalk—174 (В)
Less people think, the more they talk (The)—350 (Г)
Look, who is talking—15 (А)
Loose talk costs lives—91 (Б)
Much talk, little work—321 (Г), 932 (К), 1143 (М)
Now you're talking—2127 (У)
People who know little talk much; people who know much talk little—350 (Г), 536 (Д)
Talk about the devil and his imps will appear—1513 (О)
Talk does not cook rice—614 (З), 1216 (Н), 1968 а (С)
Talk is but talk—710 (И), 1596 (О)
Talk is but talk, but it's money that buys the house—710 (И), 1596 (О)
Talk is cheap—1216 (Н), 1596 (О)
Talk is cheap /, but it takes money to buy land (liquor, whiskey)/—710 (И)
Talk less; listen more—96 (Б)
Talk much and err much—2366 (Я)
Talk much, err much—2366 (Я)
Talk of the angel and you'll hear the fluttering of his wings—1513 (О)
Talk of the devil and you'll see his horns—1513 (О)
Talk of the devil and his imp appears—1513 (О)
Talk of the Dule and he'll put out his horns—1513 (О)
They talk most who have least to say—180 (В)
Wise men silent, fools talk—350 (Г)

TALKER
Big talker, little doer—321 (Г)
Greatest talkers are the least doers (The)—915 (К), 932 (К)
Great talkers are great liars—931 (К)
Great talkers are little doers—321 (Г), 608 (З), 932 (К), 1143 (М)
Great talkers, little doers—321 (Г), 608 (З), 932 (К)

TALKING
Much talking, much erring—2366 (Я)

Talking pays no toll—1270 (Н), 1960 (С)
Talking well will not make the pot boil—710 (И), 1216 (Н)

TAR
All tarred with the same brush—421 (Д)
One spoonful of tar spoils a barrel of honey—1037 (Л)
Tar of my country is better than the honey of others (The)—126 (В)

TASK
Always finish a task begun—652 (З)
If a task is once begun, never leave it till it's done—652 (Т), 1257 (Н)
Never leave a task until it is done—652 (З), 1257 (Н)
Some tasks require a strong back and a weak mind—1460 (Н)
Task well begun is half done (A)—656 (З)

TASTE
Each to his own taste—862 (К), 1182 (Н), 2087 (У)
Every man to his /own/ taste—929 (К), 1182 (Н), 2087 (У)
Tastes differ—927 (К), 1182 (Н)
There is no accounting for tastes—1512 (О)
There is no disputing about (concerning) tastes—1512 (О)
To him that lost his taste sweet is sour—2031 (С)

TEACH
Don't teach your grandmother to suck eggs—2368 (Я)
He teaches ill, who teaches all—613 (З)
Men learn while they teach—2167 (У)
Teaching others teaches yourself—2167 (У)
Teach your father to get children—2368 (Я)
We learn by (in) teaching—2167 (У)
What Johnnie will not teach himself, Johnnie will never learn—2167 (У)
While I teach, I learn—2167 (У)

TEACHER
Like teacher, like pupil—817 (К)

TEAM
One man does not make a team—12 (А)

TEAR
After laughter, tears—330 (Г)
Dainties of the great are tears of the poor (The)—879 (К)
It is easier to tear down than to build up—1040 (Л)
Laughter before sleep, tears when wakened—1820 (Р)
Never a rip without a tear—231 (В)
Nothing dries sooner than tears—216 (В), 2040 (Т)
Pleasures of the mighty are the tears of the poor (The)—879 (К)
Some swim in wealth but sink in tears—756 (И)
Tears and trouble are the lot of all—387 (Г)
Tears bring nobody back from the grave—1920 а (С)

TELL
Don't tell me—1826 (Р)
Never tell me—1826 (Р)
Tell an ox by his horns, but a man by his word—681 (З)
Tell it like it is—2179 (Х)
Tell it to Sweeney—1826 (Р), 1858 (С)
Tell it to the horse-marines (marines)—1826 (Р), 1858 (С)
Tell me another—1826 (Р), 1858 (С)
Tell me news!—1590 (О)
Tell me something I don't know—1590 (О)
Tell me something new—1590 (О)
Tell me the old, old story—1590 (О)
Tell me whom you live with, and I will tell you who you are—1896 (С), 1903 (С)
Tell me with whom you go, and I'll tell you what you are—1896 (С)
Tell me with whom you live, and I will tell you who you are—1903 (С)
Tell that for a tale—1590 (О), 1826 (Р)

Tell that to the marines /, the sailors won't believe it/—1826 (С), 1858 (С)
Tell us another—1826 (Р), 1858 (С)
You are telling me!—1590 (О)
You can't tell a book by its cover—168 (В)
You never can tell—18 (Б), 2265 а (Ч)

TEMPERANCE
Temperance is the best medicine (physic)—2122 (У)

THANK
Keep your thanks to feed your cat (chicken)—648 (З), 1976 (С)
Thanks is a poor pay (payment)—648 (З), 1976 (С)
Thanks is poor pay on which to keep a family—648 (З), 1976 (С)
Thanks killed the cat—648 (З), 1976 (С)
Thanks would starve a cat to death—648 (З), 1976 (С)
You can't put thanks into your pocket—648 (З), 1976 (С)

THERE
How is it up there?—557 (Д)
How's the weather up there?—557 (Д)
Is it cold up there?—557 (Д)
Not all there—2125 (У)

THICK
It's a bit (rather, too) thick—2350 (З)

THIEF
Accomplice is as bad as the thief (The)—197 (В)
All are not thieves that dogs bark at—1305 (Н)
All thieves come to some bad end—1907 (С)
End of the thief is the gallows (The)—122 (Б), 780 (К), 1042 (Л), 1659 (П), 1907 (С), 2037 (Т)
He is not a thief until he is caught—1390 (Н), 1443 (Н)
He who holds the ladder is as bad as the thief—197 (В), 1441 (Н)
It takes a thief to catch a thief—192 (В)
Little thieves are hanged, but great ones escape—2286 (Ч)
Old thief makes a good sheriff (An)—192 (В)
Once a thief, always a thief—643 (З), 1877 (С)
One thief robs another—193 (В)
One thief will not rob another—191 (В)
Opportunity makes a (the) thief—328 (Г), 1427 (Н), 1655 (П)
Receiver is as bad as the thief (The)—197 (В), 1441 (Н), 2112 (У)
Save a thief from the gallows, and he'll /be the first to/ cut your throat—250 (В), 300 (В), 631 (З), 1307 (Н), 2159 (У)
Set a thief to catch a thief—192 (В)
There is hono(u)r /even/ among thieves—191 (В), 196 (В), 671 (З), 1840 (Р)
Thief knows a thief, as a wolf knows a wolf (A)—1842 (Р)
Thief thinks that everyone else is a thief (The)—161 (В), 2100 (У)
We hang little thieves and take off out hats to great ones—6 (А), 2286 (Ч)
When thieves fall out, honest men come by their own (get their due)—418 (Д)

THIN
You can't be too rich or too thin—832 (К)

THING
Great things have a small beginning—2008 (С)
If it's not one thing, it's another—22 (Б)
Never too much of a good thing—832 (К)
Take things as they are—603 (Ж)
There are more things in heaven and earth than are dreamt of in our philosophy—2235 (Ч)
There are more things than are thought of in heaven and earth—2235 (Ч)
There are stranger things in reality than can be found in romances—1233 (Н), 2235 (Ч)

Thing easy to get is easy to lose (A)—993 (Л)
Things are going from bad to worse—2231 (Ч)
Things are not always as they seem—168 (В)
Things are not always the same—1716 (П), 1817 (Р)
Things couldn't be worse—427 (Д)
Things done cannot be undone—897 (К), 1872 (С)
Things turn out for the man who digs—317 (Г)
Things which hurt, instruct (The)—33 (Б)
When things are at their worst, they will mend—1725 (П)
You can never have too much of a good thing—832 (К)
You can't have too much of a good thing—832 (К)

THINK
First think, then speak—95 (Б), 1977 (С)
Think before you speak—1977 (С)
Think more and talk less—95 (Б)
Think—then act—1887 (С)
Think today and speak tomorrow—1977 (С)
Think twice before you act—1887 (С)
Think twice before you speak once—1977 (С)
Think twice; speak once—1977 (С)

THIRD
Third time is a charm (The)—86 (Б)
Third time is lucky—86 (Б)

THISTLE
Gather thistles, expect prickles—921 (К), 964 (К)
He that sows thistles shall reap prickles—1598 (О), 2303 (Ч)
Thistle is a fat salad to an ass's mouth (A)—927 (К), 2087 (У)

THONG
Men cut large thongs of other men's leather—2324 (Ч)

THORN
Always a thorn among roses—1452 (Н)
Every rose has its thorn—1452 (Н)
He that handles thorns shall prick the fingers—1477 (Н)
He that plants thorns must never expect to gather roses—2303 (Ч)
It early pricks that will be a thorn—707 (И)
No rose without thorns—1452 (Н)
Of a thorn springs not a fig (grape)—1608 (О)
Rose has its thorn, the peach its worm (The)—1452 (Н)
That which will become a thorn grows sharp early—707 (И)
Thorn is small, but he who has felt it doesn't forget it (A)—1098 b (М), 2375 (Я)

THOUGHT
It is the thought that counts—1334 (Н)
It's not the gift that counts, but the thought behind it—1334 (Н)
Second thoughts are best—1887 (С), 1977 (С)

THREAD
A bad seamstress uses a long thread—463 (Д)
Long thread, a lazy tailor (A)—463 (Д)
Thread follows the needle (The)—973 (К)
Thread is cut where the thread is thinnest (The)—2128 (У)
Where the needle goes, the thread follows—973 (К)

THREATEN
He threatens who is afraid—1325 (Н)
Those who threaten don't fight—1325 (Н), 1952 (С)
Threatened blow is seldom given (A)—1952 (С)

THREE
All good things come in threes—86 (Б)

THRICE
All things thrive at thrice—86 (Б)

THRIFT
Thrift is a great revenue—2065 (Т)

THRIVE
He that will (would) thrive must rise at five—252 (В), 645 (З), 961 (К), 1822 (Р)
Well thrives he whom God loves—2199 (Х)

THUNDER
It never thunders but it rains—1432 (Н)
When it thunders, the thief becomes honest—1163 (М)
When the thunder is very loud, there's very little rain—701 (И), 1140 (М), 1952 (С)

TICKLE
Tickle me, Bobby, and I'll tickle you—2077 (Т)

TIDE
Tide must be taken when it comes (The)—1032 (Л)
Tide never goes out so far but it comes in again (The)—1296 (Н)

TIGER
Tigers and deer do not stroll together—402 (Г), 675 (З), 1295 b (Н), 1852 (С), 2270 (Ч)

TIMBER
Cut your timber—201 (В)

TIME
All in good time—214 (В), 284 (В), 1717 (П), 1771 (П)
As times are, so are the customs—740 (И)
Best time is present time—1382 (Н)
Different times, different manners—740 (И)
Everything has its time—1093 (Л)
Everything in its time—233 (В), 279 (В)
Expense of time is the most costly of all expenses—1847 (С)
Grand instructor is time (The)—208 (В)
Greatest expense we can be at is that of our time (The)—445 (Д), 1847 (С)
Inch of time is an inch of gold (An)—209 (В)
Kill time and time will kill you—1784 (П), 1847 (С)
Life is short, and time is swift—207 (В)
Lost time is never found again—445 (Д), 1746 (П)
Now is the /best/ time—1382 (Н)
Other times, other customs (fashions, manners)—740 (И)
Take time by the forelock—1032 (Л)
Take time when time is, for time will away—1032 (Л)
There is a time and /a/ place for everything—234 (В)
There is a time for all things—233 (В), 696 (И)
There is a time to fish and a time to dry nets—233 (В)
There is a time to speak and a time to be silent—127 (В)
There is no better counsellor than time—208 (В)
There is no grief that time will not soften—211 (В)
There is no pain so great that time will not soften—211 (В)
There is no time like the present—1382 (Н)
There's always /a/ next time—106 (Б), 1639 (П)
Time alone will show—215 (В), 1678 (П)
Time alone will tell—215 (В), 1678 (П)
Time and tide stay for (tarry, wait for) no man—213 (В)
Time cures all griefs (ills)—211 (В), 216 (Т), 2040 (Т)
Time devours all things—1437 (Н)
Time dresses the greatest wounds—211 (В)
Time ends all things—1485 (Н), 2262 (Ч)
"Time enough" lost the ducks—583 (Ж)
Time erases all sorrows—211 (В), 216 (В), 2040 (Т)
Time flies like an arrow, and time lost never returns—1746 (П)
Time flies /like the wind/—207 (В)
Time has a wallet—209 (В)
Time has wings—207 (В)
Time heals all /wounds/—211 (В)
Time is a great healer—211 (В)

Time is a great teacher—208 (В)
Time is an herb that cures all diseases—211 (В)
Time is a true friend to sorrow—211 (В)
Time is money—209 (В)
Time is on our side—217 (В)
Time is running out—212 (В)
Time is short—212 (В)
Time is the best doctor (healer)—211 (В)
Time is the best teacher—208 (В)
Time is the father of truth—218 (В)
Time lost cannot be recalled—445 (Д)
Time marches on—207 (В)
Time presses—212 (В)
Times change, and men (we) change with them—740 (И)
Times change and people change /their ideas/—740 (И)
Time tames the strongest grief—211 (В)
Time waits for no man—213 (В)
Time wasted is time lost—445 (Д)
Time will show (tell)—215 (В), 1678 (П)
Who doesn't come at the right time must take what is left—952 (К), 956 (К), 1680 (П)
What greater crime than loss of time?—445 (Д), 1847 (С)
With time and art the leaf of the mulberry-tree becomes satin—2044 (Т)

TIT
Tit for tat—1550 (О)
Tit for tat's a fair play—1550 (О)

TOAD
Better be a big toad in a small puddle than a small toad in a big puddle—1046 (Л)

TODAY
One today is worth two tomorrows—1065 (Л), 1360 (Н), 1549 (О)

TOMORROW
Business tomorrow—432 (Д), 1196 (Н)
Enjoy the present moment and don't grieve for tomorrow—1402 (Н)
Every tomorrow supplies its loaf—83 (Б)
It will be here tomorrow—432 (Д), 1196 (Н)
Never leave for tomorrow what you can do today—1382 (Н)
Never leave till tomorrow what can be done today—1382 (Н)
Never put off until tomorrow what you can do today—1382 (Н)
There's always /a/ tomorrow—239 (В)
Tomorrow can look after (can take care of) itself—1402 (Н)
Tomorrow come never—2099 (У)
Tomorrow is a new day—432 (Д), 1196 (Н)
Tomorrow is another day—83 (Б), 239 (В)
Tomorrow may never come—2099 (У)
Tomorrow never comes—1592 (О), 2099 (У)
Why do today what you can do tomorrow—432 (Д)

TONGUE
Birds are entangled by their feet, and men by their tongues—2364 (Я)
Boneless tongue, so small and weak, can crush and kill (The)—1932 (С)
Don't cut off your head with your tongue—2362 (Я), 2364 (Я)
Don't let your tongue run away with your brains—1977 (С)
Drunken tongue tells what's on a sober mind (A)—2312 (Ч)
Empty head, like a bell, has a long tongue (An)—2098 (У), 2299 а (Ч)
Evil tongue may do much (An)—667 (З), 1932 (С)
False tongue will hardly speak the truth (A)—957 (К)
Foolish tongues talk by the dozen—180 (В), 2098 (У)
Fools cannot hold their tongues—180 (В), 2098 (У), 2361 (Я)
Fool's tongue is long enough to cut his /own/ throat (A)—2364 (Я)
Fool's tongue runs before his wit (A)—2098 (У)

TOWER
Highest towers begin (rise) from the ground (The)—1829 (Р)

TRACY
All the Tracys have always the wind in their faces—1172 (Н), 1253 (Н), 1658 (П)

TRADE
He that has a trade has a share everywhere—1396 (Н), 1830 (Р)
Jack of all trades is master of none—613 (З)
Learn a trade and earn a living—1396 (Н), 1830 (Р), 2141 (У)
Man of many trades begs his bread on Sunday (A)—613 (З)
Trade is the mother of money—1396 (Н), 1830 (Р), 2141 (У)
Useful trade is a mine of gold (A)—1396 (Н), 2141 (У)
Who has a trade has a share everywhere—1830 (Р)

TRAIL
To a friend's house the trail is never too long—318 (Г), 464 (Д)

TRAIN
There is always the next train coming—699 (И), 1136 (М), 1860 (С)

TRAVEL
He that travels much knows much—2322 (Ч)
Travel broadens the mind—2322 (Ч)

TREAD
He who treads softly goes far—2053 (Т)

TREE
As the tree is bent, so the tree is inclined—972 (К)
As the tree, so the fruit—810 (К), 953 (К), 1722 (П), 2357 (Я)
As the tree, so the wood—801 (К), 803 (К), 805 (К)
As the twig is bent, so grows the tree (so the tree is inclined)—461 (Д)
Bend the tree while it's young—357 (Г)
Big trees grow from little acorns—2008 (С)
Crooked tree throws a crooked shadow (A)—818 (К)
Crooked tree will never straighten its branches (A)—892 (К)
Good tree cannot bring forth evil fruit (A)—1615 (О)
Great tree has a great fall (A)—302 (В)
Great trees keep down little ones (little ones down)—94 (Б), 925 (К)
Like tree, like fruit—2357 (Я)
Old tree is hard to straighten (An)—1463 (Н)
Shake the tree when the fruit is ripe—233 (В)
Such as the tree is, so (such) is the fruit—807 (К)
Tree falls the way it leans (A)—972 (К)
Tree is no sooner down than everyone runs for his hatchet (The)—1627 (П)
Tree must be bent while it is young (A)—357 (Г), 1463 (Н)
Tree often transplanted bears no fruit (A)—856 (К)
Tree often transplanted neither grows nor thrives (A)—856 (К)
Trees often transplanted seldom prosper—856 (К)
When the tree is fallen everyone goes to it with his hatchet (runs to it with his axe)—1627 (П)
When the tree is thrown down any one who likes may gather the wood—1627 (П)
Whole tree or not a cherry on it (The)—725 (И)

TRIUMPH
Do not triumph before the victory—1321 (Н), 1468 (Н), 1821 (Р)
Don't sing your triumph before you have conquered—1468 (Н), 1821 (Р)
Don't whistle your triumph before you have conquered—1321 (Н)

TROOPER
Young trooper should have an old horse (A)—1232 (Н)

TROUBLE
All your future troubles be /but/ little ones!—1959 (С)
Do not trouble trouble until trouble troubles you—1274 (Н), 1354 (Н)
Don't borrow (look for) trouble—1354 (Н)
Stay out of trouble—1583 (О)
Laugh your troubles away—610 (З)
May all your troubles be little ones!—1959 (С)
Never meet trouble halfway—1402 (Н)
Never trouble yourself with trouble till trouble troubles you—1354 (Н)
Someone else's troubles don't make you wise—2317 (Ч)
Tears and trouble are the lot of all—387 (Г)
Trouble comes in bunches (in twos)—1778 (П)
Trouble never comes single (single-handed)—1753 (П), 1778 (П)
Troubles bring experience, and experience brings wisdom—33 (Б)
Troubles come in crowds—1753 (П), 1778 (П)
Trouble shared is /a/ trouble halved (/A/)—389 (Г)
Troubles never come alone (singly)—22 (Б), 1778 (П)

TROUSERS
You can't catch trout with dry trousers—50 (Б), 2282 (Ч)

TROUT
Live trout is better than a dead whale (A)—590 (Ж)

TRUE
If only it were true—123 (В)
It is too good to be true—123 (В)
May your words come true—123 (В)

TRUMPS
When in doubt, lead trumps—2180 (Х)

TRUST
First try and then trust—490 (Д), 1978 (С)
If you trust before you try, you may repent before you die—490 (Д), 1978 (С)
Put your trust in God, but keep your powder dry—1176 (Н)
Sudden trust brings sudden repentance—926 (К)
Test before trusting—490 (Д), 1978 (С)
Trust, but not too much—490 (Д), 1978 (С)
Trust is the mother of deceit—926 (К)
Try before you trust—490 (Д), 1978 (С)

TRUTH
All truth is not to be told at all times—1318 (Н)
Always tell the truth, but don't always be telling the truth—1318 (Н)
Better speak truth rudely, than lie correctly—1049 (Л)
Craft must have clothes, but truth loves to go naked—1764 (П)
Expression of truth is simplicity (The)—1764 (П)
Flattery begets friends, but the truth begets enmity—1761 (П), 1762 (П)
Follow not the truth too near the heels lest it dash out your teeth—1762 (П)
He who follows truth too closely will have dirt kicked in his face—1762 (П)
Home truths are hard to swallow—1756 (П)
It is truth that makes a man angry—1756 (П)
It pays to tell the truth—475 (Д)
Lie runs until it is overtaken by truth (A)—1760 (П)
No one wants to hear the truth—1756 (П), 1757 (П)
Nothing stings like the truth—1756 (П)
Out of the mouth of babes speaks the truth—2152 (У)
Out of the mouths of babes and sucklings come great truths—2152 (У)

Speak the truth and shame the devil—475 (Д), 2179 (Х)
Speak the truth bravely, cost as it may; hiding the wrong act is not the way—475 (Д), 2179 (Х)
Sting of a reproach is its truth (the truth of it) (The)—1756 (П)
Tell the truth all the time and you won't have to remember what you said—220 (В)
Tell the truth and shame the devil—475 (Д), 2179 (Х)
Time tries truth—218 (В)
Truth always pays (The)—475 (Д)
Truth and oil always come to the top (are always above)—1755 (П)
Truth and roses have thorns /about them/—1756 (П), 1757 (П)
Truth breeds hatred—1762 (П)
Truth comes out of the mouths of babes and sucklings—2152 (У)
Truth, crushed to earth, will rise again—1755 (П)
Truth fears nothing but concealment—1230 (Н), 1759 (П)
Truth fears no trial—1230 (Н)
Truth finds foes, where it makes none—1762 (П)
Truth has a good face, but bad clothes—1764 (П)
Truth has always a fast bottom—1763 (Р)
Truth has no need of figures (rhetoric)—1764 (П)
Truth hurts (The)—1756 (П), 1757 (П)
Truth is a naked lady—1764 (П)
Truth is at the bottom of a well (in a well)—1763 (П)
Truth is best—1049 (Л)
Truth is better than a lie—1049 (Л)
Truth is bitter—1756 (П)
Truth is mighty and will prevail—1755 (П)
Truth is often told in a joke (A)—157 (В)
Truth is stranger than fiction—1233 (Н), 2235 (Ч)
Truth is the daughter of time (time's daughter)—218 (В)
Truth keeps to the bottom of her well—1763 (П)
Truth lies at the bottom of a pit (a well)—1763 (П)
Truth may languish, but can never perish—1755 (П)
Truth needs no colo(u)rs—1764 (П)
Truth never perishes—1755 (П)
Truth pays best—1049 (Л)
Truths and roses have thorns about them—1756 (П), 1757 (П)
Truth seeks no corners—1230 (Н), 1759 (П)
Truth shall set you free (The)—2179 (Х)
Truth shows best being naked (The)—1764 (П)
Truth tastes bitter—1756 (П)
Truth will break (come) out—1755 (П), 1765 (П)
Truth will come to light (/The/)—1599 (О), 1755 (П), 1758 (П), 1765 (П)
Truth will out (/The/)—1599 (О), 1755 (П), 1758 (П), 1755 (П), 1765 (П)
Truth will prevail—1755 (П)

TRY

First try and then trust—490 (Д), 1978 (С)
If at first you don't succeed, try, try (, try) again—833 (К), 2044 (Т)
If you trust before you try, you may repent before you die—490 (Д), 1978 (С)
There is no harm in trying—1713 (П)
Try before you trust—490 (Д), 1978 (С)
You can never tell till you've tried—345 (Г)
You never know what you can do till you try—345 (Г)

TUB

Every tub must stand on its own bottom—267 (В)
Every tub smells of the wine it contains (holds)—2260 (Ч)
Let every tub stand on its own bottom—591 (Ж), 1975 (С)
Put out your tubs when it is raining—1032 (Л)
You don't have to eat a whole tub of butter to get the taste—1705 (П)

TUNE
He who calls the tune must pay the piper—1075 (Л)

TURN
Good turn goes a long way (A)—472 (Д)
One bad turn deserves another—1550 (О)
One good turn deserves another—622 (З), 1197 (Н), 2148 (У)
One never loses by doing a good turn—622 (З)
Ten good turns lie dead, and one ill deed report abroad does spread—471 (Д)

TURTLE
All thoughts of a turtle are of turtle, of a rabbit, rabbit—265 (В)

TWIG
As the twig is bent, so grows the tree (so the tree is inclined)—461 (Д)
Bend the twig while it is still green—357 (Г)
Best to bend while it is a twig—357 (Г), 1463 (Н)
Young twig is easier twisted than an old tree (A)—1463 (Н)

TWO
Two and two make four—2374 (Я)
Two are stronger than one—1532 (О)
Two in distress make (makes) sorrow less—389 (Г), 1209 (Н)
Two in distress make trouble less—389 (Г), 1209 (Н)
Two is a couple, three is a crowd—312 (Д)
Two is company and three is none—312 (Д)
Two is company; three is a crowd—312 (Д)
Two's company, three's trumpery—312 (Д)

TYPHOON
After a typhoon there are pears to gather up—1276 (Н)

U

UNDERDONE
Better underdone than overdone—1335 (Н)
Overdone is worse than underdone—1335 (Н)

UNDERTAKE
He who undertakes too much seldom succeeds—612 (З), 1886 (С)
Undertake no more than you can perform—1838 a (Р)
Who undertakes too much seldom succeeds—612 (З), 1886 (С)

UNEXPECTED
It's always the unexpected that happens—1478 (Н), 2239 (Ч)
Nothing is so certain as the unexpected—1478 (Н)

UNFORESEEN
It is the unforeseen that always happens—2239 (Ч)
Nothing is certain but the unforeseen—1224 (Н), 1478 (Н)

UNFORTUNATE
Unfortunate man would be drowned in a tea-cup (An)—845 (К), 857 (К), 1172 (Н), 1658 (П)

UNGRATEFUL
To do good to the ungrateful is like throwing water into the sea—1368 (Н)

UNION
In union there is strength—130 (В)
Union is strength—130 (В), 518 (Д), 519 (Д), 1532 (О), 1962 (С)

UNITE
Even weak men when united are powerful—130 (В)
United we stand, divided we fall—12 (А), 139 (В), 517 (Д)
Weak things united become strong—130 (В)

UNITY
In unity there is strength—519 (Д), 1532 (О)
Unity is strength—130 (В)

UNLOOKED
Many things happen unlooked for—1478 (Н), 2239 (Ч)

UNLUCKY
Unlucky man would be drowned in a tea-cup (An)—845 (К), 857 (К), 1172 (Н), 1658 (П)

UNSCATHED
Not one escapes unscathed—670 (З)

UNSEEN
Unseen, unrued—344 (Г)

UNSERVED
He who comes uncalled sits unserved—958 (К)

UNTAUGHT
Better untaught than ill taught (ill-taught)—1336 (Н)

UPS AND DOWNS
Life has its ups and downs—603 (Ж)
Our lives have ups and downs—206 (В)
We all have our ups and downs—206 (В), 603 (Ж), 1879 (С), 2056 (Т)

USE
Everything is of use to a housekeeper—266 (В)
It is nothing when you are used to it—841 (К), 2309 (Ч)
Once a use and ever a custom—841 (К)
Once a use, ever a custom—841 (К)
One can get used to everything—even hanging—841 (К)
Use is a second nature—1768 (П), 2076 (Т)

V

VACUUM
Nature abhors a vacuum—1775 (П), 1870 (С)
Vacuum is always filled (A)—1775 (П), 1870 (С)

VALLEY
He that stays in the valley shall (will) never get over the hill—1671 (П)

VALOUR
It's pot valour—1804 (П)

VARIETY
Variety is the spice of life—1129 (М)

VENTURE
Never venture all in one bottom—1217 (Н), 1414 (Н)
Nothing ventured, nothing gained—1671 (П), 1834 (Р)
Nothing venture, nothing gain (win)—1671 (П), 1834 (Р)
Venture not all in one boat—1414 (Н)

VESSEL
Full vessels give the least sound—536 (Д)
Old vessels must leak—2003 (С)
Too much in the vessel bursts the lid—2187 (Х)

VICAR
Not every man can be vicar of Bowden—1298 (Н)

VICE
Vice is often clothed in virtue's habit—355 (Г)
Vice knows she's ugly, so she puts on her mask—355 (Г)

VIEW
Everything is according to the color of the glass with which one views it—776 (К)

VIPER
No viper so little, but has its venom—1098 b (М), 2375 (Я)

VIRTUE
He that sows virtue, reaps fame—480 (Д)
Riches and virtue do not often keep each other company—1613 (О)
Virtue and riches seldom settle on the man—1613 (О)
Virtue is its own reward—473 (Д)

VIRTUOUS
Sweet are the slumbers of the virtuous—2110 (У)

VISIT
Don't wear your visit out—1715 (П)

Let's go before we wear out our visit—1715 (П)
Short visit is best (A)—1131 (M)
Short visits and seldom are best—1667 (П), 1827 (P), 1828 (P), 2186 (X), 2232 (Ч)
Short visits make long friends—1131 (M)
Visits should be short, like a winter's day—1131 (M)

VOICE
Voice of one man is the voice of none (The)—1520 (O)
Voice of the people is the voice of God (The)—346 (Г)

VOW
Vow made in the storm is forgotten in the calm (A)—1163 (M)
Vows made in storms are forgotten in the calms—1163 (M)

VOYAGE
When the voyage is over, the saint is forgotten—1163 (M)

W

WAGER
Fools for argument use wagers—1982 (C)
Wager is a fool's argument (A)—1982 (C)

WAGON
Hitch your wagon to a star—1656 (П)
Wagon must go wither the horses draw it (The)—973 (K)

WAIT
All good things come to those who wait—920 (K)
All things come to him who waits—920 (K)
Everything comes to him who knows how to wait—1188 (H)
Everything comes to him who waits—920 (K), 1188 (H)
Time brings everything to those who can wait—920 (K)
Wait and you will be rewarded—920 (K), 1188 (H)
Wait till we see how the cat jumps—215 (B)
We'll wait and see—215 (B), 1678 (П), 1922 (C)

WAKE
Don't wake a sleeping lion (wolf)—1274 (H)
Don't wake it up—1274 (H)
Wake up and smell the coffee—354 (Г), 1935 (C)
When sorrow is asleep, wake it not—1274 (H)

WALK
Man's walking is a succession of falls (A)—136 (B)
Walk your chalk—201 (B)

WALL
Wall between preserves love (A)—1990 (C)
Wall has ears and the plain has eyes (The)—1009 (Л), 1898 (C), 2153 (У)
Walls have ears—1009 (Л), 1898 (C)

WANT
Limit your wants by your wealth—1708 (П)
More one has, the more one wants (The)—2255 (Ч)
More you eat (get) the more you want (The)—7 (A), 2255 (Ч)
More you have, the more you want (The)—7 (A)
No woe to want—24 (Б)
Want makes strife—1495 (H), 1873 (C), 2223 (X)
Want makes strife between man and wife—1495 (H), 1873 (C), 2223 (X)
Want makes us acquainted with strange bedfellows—171 (B)
Want makes wit—378 (Г), 1781 (П)
When want comes in at the door, love flies out of the window—1873 (C), 2223 (X)

WAR
If you desire peace, be ever prepared (prepare) for war—2213 (X)
If you want (wish for) peace, be prepared for war—2213 (X)

Prepare for war in time of peace—2213 (Х)
War brings scars—181 (В)
War is /the/ death's feast—181 (В), 1479 (Н)

WARE
Good ware makes a good (quick) market—1255 (Н), 2194 (Х)
Good ware needs no chapman—2195 (Х)
Good ware will off (will sell itself)—2194 (Х)
Pleasing ware is half sold—1255 (Н), 2194 (Х)

WARM
He that is warm thinks all are so—81 (Б), 2015 (С), 2032 (С)

WASH
It will all come out (come right) in the wash—239 (В), 1782 (П)
That won't wash—2356 (З)

WASTE
Don't waste ten dollars looking for a dime—629 (З)
Save at the spigot and waste at the bung—629 (З)
Waste not, want not—2065 (Т)
Wilful waste makes woeful want—938 (К)
Willful waste makes wasteful want—938 (К)

WATCH
Careless watch invites the vigilant foe (A)—1634 (П)
Watched fire never burns (A)—967 (К)
Watched kettle never boils (A)—967 (К)
Watched pan (pot) is long in boiling (never boils) (A)—967 (К)
Watched rosebuds open slowly—967 (К)

WATER
Beware of a silent dog and silent (still) water—1273 (Н)
Cast not out /the/ foul water till you bring /in the / clean—1319 (Н)
Cast not out the foul water till you have clean—1319 (Н)
Dark are the waters in the clouds—2041 (Т)
Do not wade in unknown waters—1347 (Н)
Don't muddy the water, you may have to drink it—1386 (Н)
Don't throw away your dirty water until you get clean—1319 (Н)
Don't throw out your dirty water before you get in fresh—1319 (Н)
Don't throw water on a drowned rat—1001 (Л)
Every man drags water to his own mill—263 (В), 268 (В), 733 (И), 771 (К), 876 (К)
Every miller draws water to his own mill—263 (В), 268 (В), 733 (И), 771 (К), 876 (К)
It is too late to throw water on the cinder when the house is burned down—1730 (П), 1732 (П)
It's no safe wading in unknown water—1347 (Н)
Pour not water on a drowned mouse—1001 (Л)
Shallow brook warbles, while the still water is deep (The)—331 (Г), 2051 (Т)
Shallow waters make most din—332 (Г)
Smoothest waters are not always the safest (The)—294 (В)
Smooth waters run deep—331 (Г), 2051 (Т)
Spilled water cannot be gathered up—1747 (П), 1783 (П), 2308 а (Ч)
Stiller the water, the deeper it runs (The)—2051 (Т)
Still water breeds vermin—1218 (Н), 2014 (С)
Still water flows (runs) deep—2051 (Т)
Still waters have deep bottoms—294 (В), 2050 (Т)
Still waters run deep—331 (Г), 2051 (Т)
Too much water drowned the miller—2187 (Х)
Water afar won't quench a fire at hand—410 (Д)
Water finds its own level—1113 (М), 1842 (Р)

Water seeks its own level—1113 (М), 1842 (Р)
Waters that are deep don't babble—93 (Б), 2051 (Т)
Water that is past doesn't turn the wheel (The)—67 (Б)
We never know the value (the worth) of water till the well is dry—2227 (Ц)
We only know the worth of water when the well is dry—2227 (Ц)
You cannot get (wring) water from a flint—826 (К)
You can't draw water from a dry well—375 (Г), 654 (З), 826 (К)
You can't squeeze water from a stone—654 (З)
You never miss the water till the well runs dry—2227 (Ц), 2292 (Ч)
You seek cold water under cold ice—654 (З)

WAY
Farther (farthest) way about is the nearest way home (The)—1231 (Н)
God moves in a mysterious way /, his wonders to perform/—1351 (Н)
God moves in mysterious ways—1351 (Н)
Here lies your way—1902 (С)
Longest way about is the nearest way home (The)—1231 (Н)
Longest way around is the shortest way home (The)—1231 (Н)
Longest way round is the nearest (the shortest) way home (The)—1231 (Н)
Nearest way is commonly the foulest (The)—959 (К)
No way—2061 (Т), 2356 (Э)
That's the way it is—199 (В), 2035 (Т)
That's the way it goes—2035 (Т)
There are more ways than one to kill (to skin) a cat—1375 (Н)
There are more ways to kill a dog than by choking him (/to death/ on hot butter, than by hanging)—1375 (Н)
There are more ways to the wood than one—1375 (Н)
There is more than one way to cook a goose—1375 (Н)
There is no way out—975 (К), 2202 (Х)
There's more than one way to skin a cat without tearing her hide—1375 (Н)
Ways of God are inscrutable (The)—1351 (Н)
Willful ways make woeful want—938 (К)
You cannot have it both ways—1525 (О)

WE
We killed the bear—732 (И)

WEAK
Chain bursts at its weakest link (The)—336 (Г)
Every man has his weak side—235 (В), 737 (И)
Thread breaks where it is weakest (The)—336 (Г)
Weakest fruit drops earliest to the ground (The)—336 (Г)
Where it is weakest, the thread breaks—336 (Г)

WEAL
He is worth no weal that can bide no woe—1291 (Н)
No weal without woe—1453 (Н)

WEALTH
Ill-gotten wealth never thrives—2221 (Х)
Little wealth, little care (sorrow)—38 (Б), 1123 (М)
Somebody else's wealth is easy to dispose—2324 (Ч)
Wealth makes many friends—860 (К)
Wealth makes worship—573 (Е)

WEAR
Better wear out than rust out—1068 (Л)
/It is/ better to wear out than to rust out—1068 (Л)

WEATHER
After /black/ clouds, clear weather—105 (Б)
After rain comes fair weather—1728 (П)
After rain, fair weather—105 (Б)

Fair weather after foul—1891 (С)
How's the weather up there?—557 (Д)
In fair weather prepare for foul—394 (Г)

WEDDING
For one man that is missing there's no spoiling the wedding—1883 (С)
Hanging and wedding go by destiny—102 (Б)
You can't dance at two weddings with one pair of feet—1193 (Н)

WEED
Evil weed is soon grown—2217 (Х)
Ill weeds always grow apace (fast)—2217 (Х)
Ill weeds grow apace; folly runs a rapid race—2217 (Х)
One ill weed will mar a whole pot of porridge—1536 (О)
On fat land grow foulest weeds—79 (Б)
Weeds need (want) no sowing—539 (Д), 2217 (Х)

WEEP
He who weeps for everybody soon loses his eyesight—1226 (Н)
Laugh and the world laughs with you; cry and you cry alone (weep and you weep alone)—204 (В)
No weeping for shed milk—1920 a (С), 2302 (Ч)
Smile and the world smiles with you /; weep and you weep alone/—204 (В)

WEIGHT
Weight and measure take away strife—2025 (С)

WELCOME
Don't wear out your welcome—1131 (М), 1715 (П)
Such welcome, such farewell—824 (К)
Welcome to my humble abode—1133 (М)

WELL
Dig the well before it rains (before you get thirsty)—394 (Г)
Do well and have well—622 (З), 1197 (Н)
Do well, have well—622 (З), 1197 (Н)
Dry well pumps no water (A)—826 (К)
Leave well /enough/ alone—981 (Л), 1051 (Л), 1584 (О)
Let well /enough/ alone—981 (Л), 1051 (Л), 1584 (О)
Thatch your roof before rainy weather, dig your well before you are thirsty—398 (Г)
Well is that well does—1393 (Н), 1928 (С)
When the well is full, it will run over—286 (В), 1727 (П), 2047 (Т)
You can't draw water from a dry well—826 (К)

WHEEL
Bad wheel creaks the most (The)—1651 (П)
Weakest wheel creaks loudest (The)—1651 (П)
Wheels of the gods grind slowly (The)—1602 (О)
Worst wheel of the cart creaks most (The)—1651 (П)
Worst wheel of the cart (on the wagon) makes the most noise (The)—1651 (П)

WHELP
We may not expect a good whelp from an ill dog—1616 (О)

WHISKEY
When the whiskey is in, wit is out—156 (В), 960 (К)
Whiskey make rabbit hug lion—1804 (П)

WHISTLE
Don't whistle before you leap—1321 (Н), 1469 (Н), 2172 (Х)
Don't whistle till you are out of the wood—1321 (Н), 1469 (Н), 2172 (Х)

WHITE
Every white has its black /and every sweet its sour/—54 (Б), 1453 (Н)

WHY
Every why has a wherefore—47 (Б), 231 (В)

WICKED

No peace (rest) for the wicked—2108 (У)

Wicked flourish as the green bay tree (The)—2217 (X)

Wicked man is his own hell (A)—666 (З), 921 (K)

WIFE

All are good girls, but where do the bad wives come from?—223 (B)

All are good lasses, but whence come bad wives?—223 (B)

Choose not a wife by the eye only—1356 (H)

Good maid sometimes makes a bad wife (A)—223 (B)

Good wife and health are a man's best wealth (A)—468 (Д)

Good wife makes a good husband (A)—653 (З)

Good wives and good plantations are made by good husbands—2162 (У)

He that has a wife, has a strife—1434 (H)

He that has not got a wife is not yet a complete man—1160 (M)

He that takes a wife takes care—1434 (H)

He took it like a man, he blamed it on his wife—2134 (У)

Husband is the head of the house, but the wife is the neck—and the neck moves the head (The)—586 (Ж), 1161 (M)

Life isn't life without a wife—1160 (M)

Man is only half a man without a wife (A)—1160 (M)

Man's best fortune or his worst is his wife (A)—1521 (O)

Man's wife is his blessing or his bane (A)—1521 (O)

There is one good wife in the country, and every man thinks he has her—283 (B)

To him who has a good wife no evil can come which he cannot bear—1874 (C)

Two cats and a mouse, two wives in a house, two dogs and a bone never agree in one—420 (Д)

Two wives in a house never agree in one—179 (B), 425 (Д)

Where there is no wife there is no home—469 (Д)

Wife is the key of the house (The)—469 (Д), 2182 (X)

Wife make your own candle, spare penny to handle—469 (Д)

WILFUL

Wilful man must (will) have his way (A)—188 (B)

WILL

If one will not, another will /, so are all maidens wed/—260 (B)

If you will, you can—116 (Б)

It is easy to do what one's own self wills—116 (Б), 339 (Г)

To him that wills, ways are not wanting—339 (Г)

Where there's a will, there's a way—339 (Г)

Where the will is ready, the feet are light—318 (Г)

Will is his law—2181 (X)

Will is the cause of woe—1277 (H)

WILLFUL

Willful beast must have his own way (A)—188 (B)

WILLING

Nothing is impossible to a willing heart (mind)—116 (Б), 339 (Г)

Willing heart carries a weary pair of feet a long way (A)—318 (Г)

Willing mind makes a light foot (A)—318 (Г)

WILLINGLY

All things are easy, that are done willingly—339 (Г)

What we do willingly is easy—116 (Б)

WILLOW

Bend the willow while it's young—357 (Г)

WIN

One cannot win them all—1219 (H)

Win or lose—727 (И), 1019 (Л), 1020 (Л)

Win some, lose some—1389 (H)

WIND
Every wind blows not down the corn—262 (В), 1310 (Н)
Gone with the wind—757 (И)
He who sows the wind, reaps (shall reap) whirlwind—964 (К)
It is an ill wind that blows nobody any good—1456 (Н)
It's a bad wind that never changes—239 (В)
Little wind kindles a big flame (A)—1098 b (М), 1156 (М)
Never an ill wind blows but that it doesn't do someone some good—1456 (Н)
No wind can do him good who steers for no port—1811 (Р)
No wind is of service to him who is bound for nothing—1811 (Р)
Puff not against the wind—1786 b (П)
Slow wind also brings the ship to the harbor—1117 (М)
Sow the wind and reap the whirlwind—964 (К)
Wind cannot be caught in (with) a net (The)—141 (В), 160 (В), 1038 (Л), 1130 (М), 2339 (Ш)
You cannot catch the wind in the palm of your hand—141 (В), 160 (В), 688 (И), 1038 (Л), 1130 (М), 2242 (Ч), 2339 (Ч)

WINDMILL
What have I to do with Brawshaw's windmill?—1159 (М)

WINDOW
Windows of the heaven have opened (The) 1813 (Р)

WINE
Best wine comes out of an old vessel (The)—2009 (С)
Good wine needs no /ivy/ bush (/A/)—2195 (Х)
In wine there is truth—750 (И)
Sweet's the wine but sour's the payment—1806 (П)
When /the/ wine is in, wit is out—156 (В), 960 (К)
When wine sinks, words swim—2312 (Ч)
Wine /is/ in, truth /is/ out—750 (И), 2312 (Ч)
Wine is the discoverer of truth—750 (И), 2312 (Ч)
Wine wears no breeches—1805 (П)

WING
Don't try to fly without wings—49 (Б)
No flying without wings—42 (Б), 48 (Б)
You cannot fly with one wing—1544 (О)

WINNER
All the world loves a winner—860 (К)

WINNING
Light winnings make heavy purses—868 (К)

WINTER
No summer but has its winter—54 (Б)
Winter eats what summer gets (lays up)—1015 (Л), 2293 (Ч)
Winter finds out what summer lays up—1015 (Л), 2293 (Ч)
You have to winter and summer with people to know them—2283 (Ч)

WISDOM
From hearing comes wisdom—359 (Г)
Price of wisdom is above rubies (The)—78 (Б)
That's /good/ wisdom which is wisdom in the end—2198 (Х)
Trouble brings experience, and experience brings wisdom—33 (Б)
Under a ragged (threadbare) coat lies wisdom—742 (И)
Wisdom goes not always by years—100 (Б)
Wisdom is a pearl of great price—78 (Б)
Wisdom sometimes walks in clouted shoes—1488 (Н)
Without wisdom wealt is worthless—1428 (Н), 2096 (У)

WISE
After the danger everyone is wise—1749 (П)

Everybody is wise after the event—620 (З), 1749 (П)
Fool doth think he is wise, but the wise man knows himself to be a fool (The)—2129 (У)
Fool talks while a wise man thinks (A)—350 (Г)
Great men are not always wise—738 (И)
If things were to be done twice, all would be wise—620 (З)
It is better to sit with a wise man in prison than with a fool in paradise—1069 (Л)
It is easy to be wise after the event—620 (З)
No man is always wise—1187 (Н)
No man is wise at all times—738 (И)
Some men are wise and some are otherwise—2125 (У)
'Tis better to lose with a wise man than to win with a fool—1069 (Л)
We are all wise after the event—620 (З), 1983 (С)
Wind in a man's face makes him wise (The)—33 (Б)
Wise after the event—492 (Д), 1983 (С), 2175 (Х)
Wise man has long ears and a short tongue (The)—350 (Г)
Wise man keeps his own counsel (The)—536 (Д)
Wise man will learn (A)—2129 (У)
Wise men have their mouth in their heart, fools their heart in their mouth—350 (Г), 536 (Д)
Wise men silent, fools talk—350 (Г), 536 (Д)
Wise seek wisdom; the fool has found it (The)—2129 (У)
Wisest man may fall (The)—738 (И)

WISH
If you wish for too much, you will end up with nothing—1030 (Л), 1142 (М), 2081 (Т)
Wished for comes too late (The)—411 (Д), 1676 (П)
Wish is the father of (to) the thought (The)—2240 (Ч)
Wish not to taste what does not to you fall—1260 (Н)

WIT
Bought wit is best—1558 (О)
If you had all the wit of the world, fools would fell you—2125 (У)
Many wits are better than one—1531 (О), 2135 (У)
Ounce of wit that is bought is worth a pound that is taught (An)—1558 (О)
Want makes wit—1498 (Н)
Wit once bought is worth twice taught—1558 (О)

WITTY
Everyone is witty for his own purpose—255 (В), 531 (Д), 772 (К), 775 (К)

WOE
Every day has its night, every weal its /own/ woe—34 (Б)
One woe doth tread upon another's heels—22 (Б)
No woe to want—24 (Б)
Woes invite friends—1209 (Н)

WOLF
Don't set a wolf to watch the sheep—185 (В), 702 (И), 1284 (Н), 1792 (П)
Give never the wolf the wether to keep—702 (И), 1284 (Н)
He that lives with wolves will learn to howl—1904 (С)
He who kennels with wolves must howl—834 (К), 1866 (С)
If you cut down the woods, you'll catch the wolf—453 (Д), 847 (К)
Man is a wolf to /a/ man—2252 (Ч)
Never trust a wolf with the care of lambs—185 (В), 1792 (П)
Set not the wolf to keep the sheep—185 (В)
When the wolf comes in at the door, love creeps out of the window—1873 (С)
When you are with wolves, you must howl with them—834 (К), 1710 (П), 1866 (С)
Who keeps company with a wolf learns to howl—1904 (С)
Wolf can lose his teeth, but never his nature (The)—184 (В)

Wolf changes his coat (skin), but not his disposition (nature) (The)—184 (B), 672 (З)
Wolf finds a reason for taking the lamb (The)—965 (K)
Wolf never wars against wolf—183 (B)
Wolves may lose their teeth, but they never lose their nature—184 (B), 672 (З)
Wolves never prey upon wolves—183 (B), 1951 (C)

WOMAN
Behind every good man there is a good woman—653 (З)
Man is as old as he feels, and a woman as old as she looks (A)—589 (Ж)
Man is the head, but the woman turns it—586 (Ж)
Man without a woman is like a ship without a sail (A)—1160 (M)
Men build houses, women build homes—2182 (X)
Men get wealth and women keep it—2182 (X)
Men make houses, women make homes—2182 (X)
No house was ever big enough for two women—420 (Д)
Two women in the same house can never agree—179 (B), 420 (Д), 425 (Д)
Woman is no older than she looks /, and a man than he feels/ (A)—589 (Ж)

WONDER
No wonder lasts over three days—1489 (H)
Will wonders never cease? 2314 (Ч)
Wonder lasts but nine days (A)—1489 (H)
Wonders will never cease—2314 (Ч)

WOOD
Don't go through the woods and pick up a crooked stick—1695 (П)
If you cut down the woods, you'll catch the wolf—453 (Д), 847 (K)
It is a strange wood that never has a withered bough in it—237 (B)
Knock on wood—2278 (Ч)
Like wood, like arrows—805 (K)
Sometimes one can't see the wood for the trees—705 (И)
Touch wood—2278 (Ч)
Wood that grows warped can never be straightened—892 (K)
You can't see the wood for the trees—705 (И)

WOODSMAN
You can tell a woodsman by his chips—154 (B)

WOOL
Bad is the wool that cannot be dyed—2268 (Ч), 2269 (Ч)
Great cry but little wool—553 (Д)
It's ill wool that will take no dye—2269 (Ч)
No wool is so white that a dyer cannot blacken it—670 (З)
No wool is so white that the dye can't make it black—670 (З)
You go to a goat (an ass) for wool—375 (Г)

WORD
Belly is not filled with fair words (The)—614 (З), 1360 (H), 1968 a (C), 1968 b (C)
Big words seldom go with good deeds—934 (K)
Cool words scald not a tongue—1579 (O)
Fair words break no bones—1579 (O)
Fair words butter no cabbage—1505 (O), 1596 (O), 1744 (П), 1968 a (C), 2191 (X)
Fair words fill not the belly—1229 (H), 1505 (O), 1968 b (C), 2191 (X)
Fair words hurt not the mouth (the tongue)—1579 (O)
Fair words make the pot boil—484 (Д)
Fair words will not make the pot boil—1968 a (C)
Few words and many deeds—872 (K), 1122 (M)
Few words are best—2258 (Ч)
Few words, many deeds—1122 (M)
Fine words butter no parsnips—1505 (O), 1968 a (C)

Fine words dress ill deeds—360 (Г), 1170 (М), 1927 (С)
Fine words without deeds go not far—1216 (Н), 1503 (Н)
From word to deed is a great space—1605 (О)
Good word for a bad one is worth much and costs little (A)—985 (Л)
Good words and no deeds—1244 (Н), 2173 (Х), 2338 (Ш)
Good words are good cheap—985 (Л)
Good words cost nothing and are worth much (cost nought)—985 (Л)
Good words fill not the sack—1216 (Н), 1596 (О), 2191 (Х)
Good words without deeds are rushes and weeds—1596 (О)
Half a word is enough for a wise man—2126 (У), 2130 (У)
Hard words break no bones—103 (Б), 1929 (С), 1931 (С)
Hard words cut the heart (The)—667 (З), 1380 (Н), 1932 (С)
He who gives fair words feeds you with an empty spoon—1968 a (С)
Honest man's word is as good as his bond (An)—412 (Д)
In a multitude of words there wants not sin—2366 (Я)
Kind word goes a long way (A)—484 (Д)
Kind word is never lost (A)—484 (Д)
Kind word never hurt anyone (A)—1579 (О)
Kind words are worth much and they cost little—985 (Л)
Many words cut (hurt) more than swords—1380 (Н), 1575 (О), 1629 (П)
Many words, many buffets—2362 (Я)
Many words will not fill the bushel—1968 a (С), 2191 (Х)
Mere words will not fill the bushel—1968 a (С), 2191 (Х)
Saint's words and a cat's claws (A)—360 (Г)
Soft words break no bones—1579 (О)
Soft words win a hard heart—1692 (П)
Soft words win hard hearts—984 (Л), 1692 (П)
Speak kind words and you will hear kind answers—1197 (Н)
Spoken words are like flown birds: neither can be recalled—1930 (С), 2296 (Ч)
Sticks and stones may break my bones, but words can (will) never hurt (touch) me—103 (Б), 1929 (С), 2203 (Х)
Sweet words butter no parsnips—1596 (О)
Tart words make no friends: a spoonful of honey will catch more flies than a gallon of vinegar—983 (Л)
There is a big difference between word and deed—1540 (О)
Thousand words won't fill a bushel (A)—1968 a (С), 2191 (Х)
Time and words can never be recalled—303 (В), 865 (К), 1930 (С)
To one who understands, few words are needed—2126 (У), 2130 (У)
Weigh well your words before you give them breath—1977 (С)
When the word is out it belongs to another—1930 (С), 2296 (Ч)
Word before is worth two after (two behind) (A)—487 (Д), 503 (Д), 504 (Д), 506 (Д)
Word hurts more than a wound (A)—582 (Ж), 669 (З), 1380 (Н), 1575 (О), 1629 (П), 1802 (П), 1932 (С)
Word is enough to the wise (A)—2126 (У), 2130 (У)
Words and feathers the wind carries away—1596 (О)
Words are but wind—1596 (О)
Words bind men—412 (Д)
Words cut more than swords—669 (З), 1380 (Н), 1575 (О), 1629 (П), 1932 (С)
Words have wings and cannot be recalled—1930 (С)
Words hurt more than swords—669 (З), 1380 (Н), 1575 (О), 1629 (П), 1932 (С)
Words, like feathers, are carried away by the wind—1596 (О)
Words may pass, but blows fall heavy—103 (Б), 2203 (Х)

Words never filled a belly—1216 (H), 1968 a (C), 2191 (X)
Words once spoken you can never recall—303 (B), 865 (K), 1930 (C), 1969 (C)
Words pay no debts—710 (И), 1968 a (C)
Word spoken is an arrow let fly (A)—1930 (C), 2296 (Ч)
Word spoken is past recalling (A)—303 (B), 865 (K), 1969 (C), 2296 (Ч)
Word that is not spoken never does any mischief (A)—2258 (Ч)
Word to the wise (A)—2126 (У)
Word to the wise is sufficient (A)—2126 (У), 2130 (У)
Written word remains (The)—2298 (Ч)
You mark my words—644 (З)

WORK
All work and no play isn't much fun—1129 (M)
All work and no play makes Jack a dull boy—1129 (M), 2116 (У)
All work and no play makes Jack a dull boy; all work and no spree makes Jill a dull she—1129 (M)
All work and no play makes Johnny a dull boy—1129 (M), 2116 (У)
As is the workman, so is his work—431 (Д)
As the work, so the pay—791 (K), 794 (K), 1714 (П)
Hardest work is to do nothing (The)—1455 (H)
He has hard work /indeed/ who has nothing to do—1455 (H)
He who does not work, neither should he eat—944 (K)
He works best who knows his work—277 (B), 431 (Д)
He works hard who has nothing to do—1455 (H)
Lazy man works the hardest (A)—1455 (H)
Many hands make light (quick) work—13 (A)
Much talk, little work—553 (Д), 1244 (H), 2173 (X), 2338 (Ш)
No bees, no honey; no work, no money—329 (Г)
Nothing is gained without work—347 (Г)
No work, no recompense—944 (K)
One man works, and another reaps the benefits—529 (Д), 2200 (X)
Play while you play; work while you work—401 (Г), 696 (И)
That won't work—2356 (Э)
Those who will not work shall not eat—944 (K)
Work before play—436 (Д), 864 (K)
Work is afraid of a resolute man—277 (B), 431 (Д)
Work is done, time for fun—436 (Д), 864 (K)
Work is work, and play is play—401 (Г), 696 (И), 1635 (П)
Work makes life pleasant—337 (Г), 1839 (P)
Work praises the artist (the workman) (The)—154 (B)
Work shows the workman (The)—154 (B)
Work well begun is half ended—477 (Д)
Work while you work, and play while you play—433 (Д), 1635 (П)

WORKER
Bad worker finds faults with his tools (A)—566 (E), 1111 (M), 2063 (T)

WORKMAN
As is the workman, so is his (the) work—431 (Д), 788 (K), 793 (K), 795 (K), 802 (K), 819 (K), 1649 (П), 1702 (П)
Bad workman /always/ blames his tools (A)—1111 (M)
Bad workman quarrels with his tools (A)—566 (E), 1111 (M), 1654 (П), 2063 (T), 2139 (У)
Ill workman quarrels with his tools (An)—2063 (T)
It is working that makes a workman—1190 (H)
Workman is known by his work (A)—154 (B)
Workman is worth of his hire (A)—791 (K), 794 (K), 1714 (П)

WORLD
It's a small world—1137 (M)

YES
May be yes, may be no, may be rain, may be snow—1018 (Л)

YESTERDAY
No man can call again yesterday—67 (Б), 1127 (М)

YOU
And you too!—752 (И)

YOUNG
Have fun while you are young—1151 (М)
If the young knew, if the old could, there's nothing but would be done—561 (Е)
If the young man would and the old man could, there would be nothing undone—561 (Е)
Young will sow their wild oats (The)—1151 (М)
You're only young once—1151 (М)

YOUTH
Abundance of money ruins youth (/The/)—79 (Б)
Excesses of our youth are draughts upon our old age (The)—2346 (Щ)
Idle youth, a needy age (An)—2346 (Щ)
If youth but knew and age but could—561 (Е)
If youth but knew, if age but could—561 (Е)
Reckless youth makes rueful age—2346 (Щ)
What youth is used to, age remembers—2263 (Ч)
Youth is full of vitamins, age is full of germs—1152 (М)
Youth is nimble, age is lame—1152 (М)
Youth is wasted on the young—411 (Д), 1676 (П)
Youth comes but once in a lifetime—1151 (М)
Youth will be served—1151 (М)
Youth will have its course (its fling, its swing)—1151 (М)

Z

ZEAL
Zeal without knowledge is a fire without light (a runaway horse)—650 (З), 2146 (У)
Zeal without knowledge is /the/ sister of folly—650 (З)